# ISNM

INTERNATIONAL SERIES OF NUMERICAL MATHEMATICS
INTERNATIONALE SCHRIFTENREIHE ZUR NUMERISCHEN MATHEMATIK
SÉRIE INTERNATIONALE D'ANALYSE NUMÉRIQUE



VOL. 40

# Linear Spaces and Approximation

Proceedings of the Conference
held at the Oberwolfach Mathematical Research Institute, Black Forest,
August 20–27, 1977

Edited by
P. L. Butzer and B. Szőkefalvi-Nagy

# Lineare Räume und Approximation

Abhandlungen zur Tagung
im Mathematischen Forschungsinstitut Oberwolfach, Schwarzwald,
vom 20. bis 27. August 1977

Herausgegeben von
P. L. Butzer und B. Szőkefalvi-Nagy

1978
Birkhäuser Verlag Basel
und Stuttgart

CIP-Kurztitelaufnahme der Deutschen Bibliothek

**Linear spaces and approximation:** proceedings
of the conference held at the Oberwolfach Math.
Research Inst., Black Forest, August 20–27,
1977 – Lineare Räume und Approximation/ed.
by P. L. Butzer and B. Szökefalvi-Nagy. – 1.
Aufl. – Basel, Stuttgart: Birkhäuser, 1978. –
(International series of numerical mathematics; Vol. 40)
ISBN 3-7643-0979-2
NE: Butzer, Paul L. [Hrsg.]; Mathematisches
Forschungsinstitut ‹Oberwolfach›; PT



ISBN 3-7643-0979-2

# Preface

The publication of Oberwolfach conference books was initiated by Birkhäuser Publishers in 1964 with the proceedings of the conference 'On Approximation Theory', conducted by P.L. Butzer (Aachen) and J. Korevaar (Amsterdam). Since that auspicious beginning, others of the Oberwolfach proceedings have appeared in Birkhäuser's ISNM series. The present volume is the fifth* edited at Aachen in collaboration with an external institution. It once again addresses itself to the most recent results on approximation and operator theory, and includes 47 of the 48 lectures presented at Oberwolfach, as well as five articles subsequently submitted by V.A. Baskakov (Moscow), H. Esser (Aachen), G. Lumer (Mons), E.L. Stark (Aachen) and P.M. Tamrazov (Kiev). In addition, there is a section devoted to new and unsolved problems, based upon two special problem sessions augmented by later communications from the participants.

Corresponding to the nature of the conference, the aim of the organizers was to solicit both specialized and survey papers, ranging in the broad area of classical and functional analysis, from approximation and interpolation theory to Fourier and harmonic analysis, and to the theory of function spaces and operators. The papers were supplemented by lectures on fields represented for the first time in our series of Oberwolfach Conferences, so for example, complex function theory or probability and sampling theory. Many of the papers not only describe fundamental advances in their respective field but also emphasize basic interconnections between some or all of the various fields covered. It is hoped that some of them will inspire further research.

In accord with this conception, the volume is divided into nine chapters. Chapter I, on operator theory, is devoted to certain classes of operators such as kernel operators, biquasi-triangular operators, as well as to invariant operator ranges, matrices over $H^\infty$, and von Neumann's inequality. Chapter II, on functional analysis, contains papers on Banach graphs, non-archimedean function spaces, and best approximation in Hilbert spaces. Chapter III, on integral operators and inequalities, is concerned with finite convolutions and various fundamental inequalities in analysis such as those for fractional

* The earlier volumes are:
1. On Approximation Theory. Oberwolfach 1963. Eds.: P.L. Butzer and J. Korevaar. ISNM, vol. 5, Basel 1964 (second edition 1972), XVI + 261 pages.
2. Abstract Spaces and Approximation. Oberwolfach 1969. Eds.: P.L. Butzer and B. Sz.-Nagy. ISNM, vol. 10, Basel 1969, 423 pages.
3. Linear Operators and Approximation I. Oberwolfach 1971. Eds.: P.L. Butzer, J.P. Kahane and B. Sz.-Nagy. ISNM, vol. 20, Basel 1972, 506 pages.
4. Linear Operators and Approximation II. Oberwolfach 1974. Eds.: P.L. Butzer and B. Sz.-Nagy. ISNM, vol. 25, Basel 1974, 585 pages.

integrals, and the so-called 'basic inequality' of weak-type interpolation. Chapter IV includes abstract harmonic analysis: abstract dyadic analysis, Fourier series on compact Lie groups, and Fourier analysis: multipliers for the Mellin transform, Laguerre and Jacobi expansions. Chapter V treats various approximation processes, such as those of Korovkin, Meyer-König and Zeller, and Szász-Mirakjan, together with Müntz type results and Birkhoff interpolation, whereas Chapter VI provides several perspectives on best approximation and splines. Chapter VII is devoted to complex function theory aspects of approximation connected with harmonic and univalent functions, lacunary polynomials, and entire functions. Chapter VIII, on differential operators and equations, ranges from abstract boundary value problems to discretization problems associated with the Lax equivalence theorem. Finally, Chapter IX on probability theory and other applications, includes martingales, multiple orthogonal series and random fields, and the Shannon sampling theorem.

One paper is to be found at the end of the proceedings and not in the respective Chapter I as it reached the editors after the material had left for the publishers.

The editors' warm thanks are due to the participants and contributors, who helped to make the conference a success; to Franziska Fehér and Guido Weiss for compiling the new and unsolved problems; to Franziska Fehér and Josef Junggeburth, for their competent handling of the greater part of the general editorial work connected with this volume; to Ernst Görlich and Rolf J. Nessel for precious advice during the preparations of the conference; to the secretaries of Lehrstuhl A für Mathematik, Aachen, who not only retyped many of the papers but also handled many other tasks connected with the preparation of these proceedings; and last but not least to Carl Einsele of Birkhäuser Publishers for his continued personal interest in these conferences, and for his valuable cooperation in making these proceedings available to a world-wide public, in an always highly attractive form.

December 1977

P. L. Butzer, Aachen B. Sz.-Nagy, Szeged

Editors

# Contents

# Zur Tagung

Der vorliegende Band enthält das gesamte Vortragsprogramm der Tagung über ‹Lineare Räume und Approximation›, die vom 20. bis 27. August im Mathematischen Forschungsinstitut Oberwolfach stattfand. Diese Tagung, mit der die Reihe der alle zwei bis drei Jahre von Aachen und Szeged aus organisierten Konferenzen fortgesetzt wurde, war mit 64 Teilnehmern aus 17 Nationen - Australien, Brasilien, Bulgarien, Japan, Kanada, Polen, Ungarn, den USA sowie mehreren westeuropäischen Ländern - wie üblich international besetzt. Wieder gehörten zum Teilnehmerkreis auch viele Mathematiker, die zum ersten Male in Oberwolfach waren bzw. eine Tagung dieser Reihe besuchten, insbesondere auch jüngere Kollegen, die auf diese Weise die Gelegenheit erhielten, von vielen regen Diskussionen mit Experten zu profitieren. Die Tagungsleiter waren bemüht, eine breite Vielfalt von Themen anzubieten und auch Gebiete zu berücksichtigen, die beim letzten Mal nicht vertreten waren, wie etwa Funktionen- und Wahrscheinlichkeitstheorie.

Das grosse Interesse an dieser Tagung kam schon während der Vorbereitungszeit zum Ausdruck, so dass die Tagungsleiter zu ihrem Bedauern bei weitem nicht alle Teilnahmewünsche erfüllen konnten. Trotzdem konnten nicht alle Teilnehmer im Institut selbst untergebracht werden; 17 von ihnen mussten im Dorf wohnen.

Der erste Vortrag fand, wie es inzwischen zur Tradition geworden ist, bereits am Sonntag um 10 Uhr statt. Anreisetag war Samstag, während der letzte Vortrag am folgenden Samstagmittag endete. Auf diese Weise war es möglich, ein reichhaltiges wissenschaftliches Arbeitsprogramm zu verwirklichen, in dessen Mittelpunkt 48 Übersichts- und Spezialvorträge standen (der Programmablauf ist auf den Seiten 17–19 ausführlich wiedergegeben). Ergänzt wurden die Vorträge durch Ausflüge am Mittwochnachmittag, alternativ nach Baden-Baden, Freiburg, Freudenstadt, zum Schwimmen nach Bad Rippoldsau oder zu Wanderungen zum Glaswaldsee und zum Schliffkopf. Im Rahmen des traditionellen Weinabends hielt Russel Love einen farbigen Lichtbildervortrag über Australien, und John Todd gab eine lebendige Schilderung der Rettung des Oberwolfacher Instituts im Jahre 1945 durch ihn selbst und G.E.H. Reuter.

Die erfreulich kollegiale und gelöste Atmosphäre während der Tagung wurde von allen Anwesenden als sehr stimulierend empfunden. Nicht zuletzt trugen dazu auch die Freundlichkeit und Hilfsbereitschaft des gastgebenden Instituts bei, wofür sich die Tagungsleiter bei den Damen und Herren des Oberwolfacher Hauses, insbesondere dem Direktor des Forschungsinstituts, Herrn Professor Dr. M. Barner, und Herrn H.G. Förstendorf, herzlich bedanken möchten.

P. L. Butzer — B. Sz.-Nagy

Tagungsleiter

# List of participants

J.M. Anderson, Dept. of Mathematics, University College London, Gower Street, London WCIE 6 BT, Great Britain

M. Becker, Lehrstuhl A für Mathematik, RWTH Aachen, Templergraben 55, 5100 Aachen, Western Germany

C. Bennett, Dept. of Mathematics, McMaster University, 1280 Main Street West, Hamilton, Ontario, L8S 4K1, Canada

H. Berens, Mathematisches Institut der Universität Erlangen-Nürnberg, Bismarckstr. 1 1/2, 8520 Erlangen, Western Germany

P.L. Butzer, Lehrstuhl A für Mathematik, RWTH Aachen, Templergraben 55, 5100 Aachen, Western Germany

E.W. Cheney, Dept. of Mathematics, University of Texas, Austin, Tex. 78712, USA

Z. Ciesielski, Instytut Matematyczny, Polskiej Akademii Nauk, Oddzial W. Gdánsku, Ulica Abrahama 18, 81-825 Sopot, Poland

J.L.B. Cooper, Head, Dept. of Mathematics, Chelsea College, University of London, Manresa Road, London SW3 6LX, Great Britain

R. DeVore, Dept. of Mathematics and Computer Science, University of South Carolina, Columbia, S.C. 29208, USA

W. Dickmeis, Lehrstuhl A für Mathematik, RWTH Aachen, Templergraben 55, 5100 Aachen, Western Germany

M.J. Dixon, Mathematisch Instituut, Universiteit van Amsterdam, Roetersstraat 15, Amsterdam - 1004, Netherlands

B. Dreseler, Fachbereich Mathematik, Gesamthochschule Siegen, Hölderlinstr. 3, 5900 Siegen, Western Germany

P.L. Duren, Dept. of Mathematics, University of Michigan, Ann Arbor, Mich. 48109, USA

H. Esser, Institut für Geometrie und Praktische Mathematik, RWTH Aachen, Templergraben 55, 5100 Aachen, Western Germany

F. Fehér, Lehrstuhl A für Mathematik, RWTH Aachen, Templergraben 55, 5100 Aachen, Western Germany

W. Forst, Mathematisches Institut der Universität, Auf der Morgenstelle 10, 7400 Tübingen, Western Germany

C. Franchetti, Istituto Matematico, Università di Genova, Via L.B. Alberti 4, 16132 Genova, Italy

E. Görlich, Lehrstuhl A für Mathematik, RWTH Aachen, Templergraben 55, 5100 Aachen, Western Germany

G.W. Goes, Dept. of Mathematics, Illinois Institute of Technology, Chicago 60616, USA

M. v. GOLITSCHEK, Institut für Angewandte Mathematik und Statistik, Universität Würzburg, Am Hubland, 8700 Würzburg

M. DE GUZMÁN, Facultad de Matemáticas, Universidad Complutense de Madrid, Madrid 3, Spain

L. HAHN, Lehrstuhl A für Mathematik, RWTH Aachen, Templergraben 55, 5100 Aachen, Western Germany

W.K. HAYMAN, Dept. of Mathematics, Imperial College of Science and Technology, Queen's Gate, London SW 7 5HH, Great Britain

S. IGARI, Mathematical Institute, Tôhoku University, Sendai, Japan

H. KOMATSU, Faculty of Science, University of Tokyo, 7-3-1 Hongo, Bunkyo-ku, Tokyo, 113, Japan

J. KOREVAAR, Mathematisch Instituut, Universiteit van Amsterdam, Roetersstraat 15, Amsterdam 1004, Netherlands

G.G. LORENTZ, Dept. of Mathematics, University of Texas, Austin, Tex. 78712, USA

E.R. LOVE, Dept. of Mathematics, University of Melbourne, Parkville, Victoria 3052, Australia

G. LUMER, Faculté des Sciences, Université de l'Etat, Avenue Maistriau 15, 7000 Mons, Belgium

C. MARKETT, Lehrstuhl A für Mathematik, RWTH Aachen, Templergraben 55, 5100 Aachen, Western Germany

P.R. MASANI, Dept. of Mathematics, University of Pittsburgh, Pittsburgh, Pa. 15260, USA

W. MEYER-KÖNIG, Mathematisches Institut A, Universität Stuttgart, Pfaffenwaldring 57, 7000 Stuttgart 80, Western Germany

F. MÓRICZ, József Attila Tudományegyetem, Aradi vértanúk tere 1, Szeged, Hungary

M.W. MÜLLER, Lehrstuhl Mathematik VIII, Universität Dortmund, 4600 Dortmund 50, Western Germany

R.J. NESSEL, Lehrstuhl A für Mathematik, RWTH Aachen, Templergraben 55, 5100 Aachen, Western Germany

E.A. NORDGREN, Dept. of Mathematics, University of New Hampshire, Kingsbury Hall, Durham, N.H. 03824, USA

M. OKADA, Mathematical Institute, Tôhoku University, Sendai, Japan

C.W. ONNEWEER, Dept. of Mathematics and Statistics, University of New Mexico, Albuquerque, N.Mex. 87131, USA

P. PAPINI, Istituto Matematico, Universita di Bologna, Piazza di Porta S. Donato 5, 40127 Bologna, Italy

C.M. PEARCY, Dept. of Mathematics, 347 West Engineering Building, University of Michigan, Ann Arbor, Mich. 48109, USA

V.A. POPOV, Institute of Mathematics and Mechanics, Bulgarian Academy of Sciences, P.O. Box 373, 1000 Sofia, Bulgaria

J.B. PROLLA, Instituto dc Matcmática, Universidade Estadual de Campinas, Caixa Postal 1170, 13100 Campinas, SB, Brasilia

S.D. Riemenschneider, Dept. of Mathematics, University of Alberta, Edmonton, Canada

P.G. Rooney, Dept. of Mathematics, University of Toronto, Toronto, Ontario M5S 1A1, Canada

J.L. Rovnyak, Dept. of Mathematics, University of Virginia, Charlottesville, Va. 22903, USA

P.O. Runck, Mathematisches Institut der Hochschule Linz, Auhof, 4045 Linz, Österreich

F. Schipp, Eötvös Loránd Tudományegyetem, Numerikus és Gépi Matematikai Tanszék, Múzeum körút 6–8, 1088 Budapest, Hungary

A. Schönhage, Mathematisches Institut der Universität, Auf der Morgenstelle 10, 7400 Tübingen, Western Germany

Bl. Sendov, Institute of Mathematics and Mechanics, Bulgarian Academy of Science, P.O. Box 373, 1000 Sofia, Bulgaria

R.C. Sharpley, Dept. of Mathematics and Computer Science, University of South Carolina, Columbia, S.C. 29208, USA

A.L. Shields, Dept. of Mathematics, University of Michigan, Ann Arbor, Mich. 48109, USA

P.C. Sikkema, Afdeling der Algemene Wetenschappen, Onderafdeling der Wiskunde, Technische Hogeschool, Julianalaan 132, Delft 8, Netherlands

P. Sjölin, Dept. of Mathematics, University of Stockholm, Box 6701, 11385 Stockholm, Sweden

W. Splettstösser, Lehrstuhl A für Mathematik, RWTH Aachen, Templergraben 55, 5100 Aachen, Western Germany

E.L. Stark, Lehrstuhl A für Mathematik, RWTH Aachen, Templergraben 55, 5100 Aachen, Western Germany

R. Stens, Lehrstuhl A für Mathematik, RWTH Aachen, Templergraben 55, 5100 Aachen, Western Germany

J. Szabados, Magyar Tudományos Akadémia, Matematikai Kutato Intézete, Réaltanoda u. 13–15, 1088 Budapest V, Hungary

B. Sz.-Nagy, József Attila Tudományegyetem, Aradi vértanúk tere 1, Szeged, Hungary

O. Taussky-Todd, Dept. of Mathematics, California Institute of Technology, Pasadena, Calif. 91125, USA

J. Todd, Dept. of Mathematics, California Institute of Technology, Pasadena, Calif. 91125, USA

G.L. Weiss, Dept. of Mathematics, Washington University, St. Louis, Mo. 63130, USA

A.C. Zaanen, Mathematisch Instituut der Rijksuniversiteit te Leiden, Wassenaarseweg 80, Leiden, Netherlands

M. Zamansky, 1, rue du Val-de-Grâce, 75005 Paris, France

# Wissenschaftliches Programm der Tagung

**Sonntag, 21. August**
10.00 B. Sz.-Nagy, P. L. Butzer: Begrüssung
1. Frühsitzung, Vorsitz: A. C. Zaanen
10.15 G. G. Lorentz: Birkhoff'sche Quadratur
2. Frühsitzung, Vorsitz: P. L. Butzer
11.20 R. L. Stens: Weighted best approximation of continuous functions by algebraic polynomials
11.55 F. Fehér: Fractional Lipschitz spaces generated by rearrangement-invariant norms
Nachmittagssitzung, Vorsitz: B. Sz.-Nagy
16.00 A. L. Shields: Hyper-invariant subspaces and rank-one commutators of operators
17.00 R. DeVore: Approximation by algebraic polynomials in $L_p[-1,1]$
17.50 S. Igari: Remarks on Kronecker's approximation theorem and a unitary measure
Abendsitzung, Vorsitz: J. L. B. Cooper
19.45 J. Todd: Some applications of elliptic functions and integrals

**Montag, 22. August**
1. Frühsitzung, Vorsitz: G. Weiss
9.00 P. Sjölin: Lipschitz continuity of spherical means
9.45 J. L. B. Cooper: The exponential map in spaces with indefinite metric
2. Frühsitzung, Vorsitz: P. C. Sikkema
10.55 G. Goes: Multiplier representations of Lipschitz spaces and of spaces of functions of generalized bounded variation with applications
11.50 J. Szabados: On some problems and results in the theory of interpolation
1. Nachmittagssitzung, Vorsitz: E. A. Nordgren
16.00 C. M. Pearcy: Biquasitriangular operators and quasisimilarity
2. Nachmittagssitzung, Vorsitz: E. W. Cheney
17.00 V. A. Popov: Direct and converse theorems for onesided polynomial and spline approximation
17.45 M. Becker: Inverse results via smoothing
Abendsitzung, Vorsitz: G. G. Lorentz
19.45 M. Zamansky: Approximation et analyse harmonique

**Dienstag, 23. August**

1. Frühsitzung, Vorsitz: W. Meyer-König

9.00 P. G. ROONEY: Multipliers for the Mellin transformation

9.55 W.K. HAYMAN: Approximation von ebenen, harmonischen Funktionen durch solche mit Wachstumsbeschränkung

2. Frühsitzung, Vorsitz: A. L. Shields

11.10 E. A. NORDGREN: Invariant operator ranges

11.50 E. GÖRLICH: Norm estimates for Cesàro sums of Laguerre and Jacobi expansions

1. Nachmittagssitzung, Vorsitz: P. R. Masani

16.00 M. DE GUZMÁN: Real function methods in Fourier analysis

2. Nachmittagssitzung, Vorsitz: J. Korevaar

17.00 J. M. ANDERSON: Müntz-Szász theorems and lacunary entire functions

17.45 M. v. GOLITSCHEK: Jackson's theorem for polynomials and exponential sums with restricted coefficients

Abendsitzung, Vorsitz: J. Todd

19.45 A. C. ZAANEN: Kernel operators

20.45 1. Problem Session

**Mittwoch, 24. August**

1. Frühsitzung, Vorsitz: Z. Ciesielski

9.00 F. MÓRICZ: Maximal inequalities and convergence properties of multiple orthogonal series and random fields

9.50 F. SCHIPP: Fourierreihen und Martingale

2. Frühsitzung, Vorsitz: Bl. Sendov

11.00 C. W. ONNEWEER: Differentiation on a p-adic or p-series field

11.55 L. HAHN: Ein allgemeiner Grenzwertsatz in der Wahrscheinlichkeitstheorie mit Anwendungen

**Donnerstag, 25. August**

1. Frühsitzung, Vorsitz: M. de Guzmán

8.45 C. BENNETT: The Marcinkiewicz interpolation theorem

9.35 J. B. PROLLA: Nonarchimedean function spaces

2. Frühsitzung, Vorsitz: W.K. Hayman

10.30 J.L. ROVNYAK: Recent results and unsolved problems on finite convolution operators

11.20 BL. SENDOV: Convergence of sequences of monotonic operators in A-distance

12.00 W. SPLETTSTÖSSER: Some extensions of the sampling theorem

1. Nachmittagssitzung, Vorsitz: B. Sz.-Nagy

15.45 P. R. MASANI: Vector graphs and conditional Banach spaces

2. Nachmittagssitzung, Vorsitz: P. L. Duren

16.45 E. R. LOVE: Some inequalities for fractional integrals

17.45 B. Dreseler: Über das Verhalten der Lebesgue-Konstanten bei Fourier-Reihen auf kompakten Lie-Gruppen
Abendsitzung, Vorsitz: P. L. Butzer
19.45 G. Weiss: An extension of von Neumann's inequality to $L^p$ spaces
20.45 2. Problem Session

**Freitag, 26. August**
1. Frühsitzung, Vorsitz: R. J. Nessel
8.45 J. Korevaar: Approximation by lacunary polynomials
9.40 E. W. Cheney: Bivariate and multivariate interpolation with noncommutative projectors
2. Frühsitzung, Vorsitz: E. R. Love
10.20 Z. Ciesielski: Convergence of spline expansions
11.15 H. Berens: Beste Approximation in Hilberträumen
12.00 P. O. Runck: Erweiterung des Satzes von Markoff
1. Nachmittagssitzung, Vorsitz: J. B. Prolla
15.45 P. L. Duren: Extreme points of spaces of univalent functions
2. Nachmittagssitzung, Vorsitz: P. G. Rooney
16.40 P. C. Sikkema: Estimations involving a modulus of continuity for a generalization of Korovkin's operators
17.40 M. W. Müller: Die lokale $L_p$-Saturationsklasse des Verfahrens der integralen Meyer-König und Zeller Operatoren
Abendsitzung, Vorsitz: C. M. Pearcy
19.45 B. Sz.-Nagy: Matrices over $H^\infty$

**Samstag, 27. August**
1. Frühsitzung, Vorsitz: S. Igari
9.00 R. J. Nessel: Lax type theorems with orders
2. Frühsitzung, Vorsitz: E. Görlich
10.05 H. Komatsu: An analogue of the Cauchy-Kowalevsky theorem and boundary values of solutions of elliptic equations
11.00 R. C. Sharpley: The Marcinkiewicz theorem for Banach spaces

# I
# Operator Theory

# KERNEL OPERATORS

A.C. ZAANEN
Department of Mathematics
Leiden State University
Leiden (Netherlands)

This is a brief report on some recent results about kernel operators, the domain of which is an order ideal in a space of real measurable functions and the range of which is contained in an order ideal of the same type. A simple proof (due to A.R. Schep) is indicated of the theorem that any positive linear operator majorized by a kernel operator is itself a kernel operator. It follows easily that the kernel operators form a band in the Riesz space of all order bounded linear operators. Another important theorem is due to A.V. Buhvalov, stating a simple necessary and sufficient condition for an order bounded linear operator to be a kernel operator. One of the corollaries in Schep's approach is the theorem that any continuous linear operator from $L^1$ to $L^p$ ($1<p\leq\infty$) is a kernel operator (for the special case of Lebesgue measure in the real line due to N. Dunford, 1936); in Buhvalov's approach this corollary is proved first and the other abovementioned results are derived from it.

1. Introduction. It is our purpose to present a review of some recent work on kernel operators in the Soviet Union, Germany and the Netherlands. Kernel operators are also called integral operators because they can be written by means of integrals, but the name of integral operator is sometimes used in a different context as well. All results and some of the proofs in the following can be explained in purely measure theoretic terms, but for some other proofs and for a better understanding of the background it is desirable to be familiar with a few elementary facts about Riesz spaces (vector lattices).

We begin with some simple definitions. Let $M(Y,\nu)$ be the vector space of all real $\nu$-measurable functions on the $\sigma$-finite measure space $(Y,\Sigma,\nu)$ with the usual identification of $\nu$-almost equal functions. The notation $f\leq g$ for functions $f$ and $g$ in $M(Y,\nu)$ means that $f(y)\leq g(y)$ holds $\nu$-almost everywhere on $Y$; the function $|f|$ is defined by $|f|(y)=|f(y)|$ for all $y\in Y$. The non-empty subset $D$ of $M(Y,\nu)$ is called *solid* if it follows from $f\in M(Y,\nu)$, $g\in D$ and $|f|\leq|g|$ that $f\in D$. Any solid linear subspace of $M(Y,\nu)$ is called an *ideal* (*order ideal*) in $M(Y,\nu)$. Typical examples are the spaces $L^p(Y,\nu)$ for $0<p\leq\infty$. Of course, $M(Y,\nu)$ itself and $\{0\}$ are also ideals.

In the following the word "operator" will be used to denote any linear mapping from one vector space into another. Let $(Y,\Sigma,\nu)$ and $(X,\Lambda,\mu)$ be $\sigma$-finite measure spaces and let $L$ and $M$ be ideals in $M(Y,\nu)$ and $M(X,\mu)$ respectively. The operator $T:L\to M$ is called a *kernel operator* if there exists a $(\mu\times\nu)$-measurable real function $T(x,y)$ on $X\times Y$ such that

$$\int_Y |T(x,y)f(y)|\,d\nu(y)\in M \qquad \text{for all } f\in L,$$

$$(Tf)(x)=\int_Y T(x,y)f(y)\,d\nu(y) \qquad \text{for all } f\in L.$$

The function $T(x,y)$ is called the *kernel* of the operator $T$. Note immediately that the measurable function $T(x,y)$ is the kernel of a kernel operator if and only if $|T(x,y)|$ is so.

The first question that immediately arises is to investigate how the kernel operators are embedded in the vector space $\mathcal{L}(L,M)$ of all operators from $L$ into $M$. For an answer we first recall that the operator $T:L\to M$ is said to be *positive* if $T$ maps non-negative functions into non-negative functions and $T$ is called *order bounded* (or regular) if $T=T'-T''$ with $T'$ and $T''$ positive. The order bounded operators form a linear subspace $\mathcal{L}_b(L,M)$ of $\mathcal{L}(L,M)$, partially ordered by defining that $T_1\leq T_2$ means that $T_2-T_1$ is positive. Hence, denoting the null operator by $\theta$, we have $T_1\leq T_2$ if and only if $T_2-T_1\geq\theta$.

THEOREM 1.1. (i) The kernel operator $T$ is positive if and only if its kernel $T(x,y)$ is non-negative almost everywhere on $X\times Y$.

(ii) Every kernel operator is order bounded.

PROOF. (i) Routine.

(ii) If $T(x,y)$ is the kernel of $T$, then denote the operator with kernel $|T(x,y)|$ by $T_1$. It follows from $|T(x,y)|-T(x,y)\geq 0$ that $T_1-T$ is positive; call this operator $T_2$. Then $T=T_1-T_2$ with $T_1$ and $T_2$ positive, so $T$ is order bounded.

Note now that the kernel operators form a vector space $\mathcal{K}$, a subspace of $\mathcal{L}_b(L,M)$. The problem mentioned above is reduced, therefore, to the question how $\mathcal{K}$ is embedded in $\mathcal{L}_b$.

2. Schep's Theorem. The first theorem which we present is of fundamental importance for the structure of $\mathcal{K}$. The proof is due to A.R. Schep [8].

THEOREM 2.1. *If $\theta \leq S \leq T$ and T is a kernel operator, then S is a kernel operator. In other words, any positive operator majorized by a kernel operator is a kernel operator.*

PROOF. It is a technical matter to reduce the proof to the case that

$$\int_{X\times Y} T(x,y)\,d(\mu\times\nu)<\infty$$

and $e_Y \in L$, where $e_Y$ denotes the characteristic function of Y. Let $\Delta$ be the $\sigma$-algebra of all $(\mu\times\nu)$-measurable subsets of $X\times Y$ and let $\Gamma$ be the semiring of all sets $A\times B$ with A a $\mu$-measurable subset of X and B a $\nu$-measurable subset of Y. For any $P\in\Delta$ we define

$$\lambda(P)=\int_P T(x,y)\,d(\mu\times\nu).$$

The set function $\lambda$ is a measure on $\Delta$, absolutely continuous with respect to $\mu\times\nu$. Note that

$$\lambda(A\times B)=\int_A\left(\int_B T(x,y)\,d\nu\right)d\mu=\int_A Te_B\,d\mu.$$

Now define

$$\lambda_1(A\times B)=\int_A Se_B\,d\mu$$

for all $A\times B\in\Gamma$. It is not difficult to prove that $0\leq\lambda_1\leq\lambda$ on $\Gamma$ and $\lambda_1$ is $\sigma$-additive on $\Gamma$. It should be observed, however, that one has to be careful when proving first that $\lambda_1$ is finitely additive, because this is a typical "almost everywhere" argument and one has to see that the union of the exceptional sets of measure zero is still a set of measure zero. Having got the measure $\lambda_1$ on the semiring $\Gamma$, we apply Carathéodory's extension procedure to extend $\lambda_1$ to $\Delta$. Since the exterior measures satisfy $0\leq\lambda_1^*\leq\lambda^*$ for all subsets of $X\times Y$, we get $0\leq\lambda_1\leq\lambda$ on $\Delta$, so $\lambda_1$ is absolutely continuous with respect to $\mu\times\nu$. By the Radon-Nikodym theorem there exists a $(\mu\times\nu)$-measurable function $S(x,y)\geq 0$ such that

$$\lambda_1(P)=\int_P S(x,y)\,d(\mu\times\nu)$$

for all $P\in\Delta$, in particular

$$\lambda_1(A\times B)=\int_A\left(\int_B S(x,y)\,d\nu\right)d\mu.$$

Comparing this with the definition of $\lambda_1(A\times B)$, we get

$$(Se_B)(x)=\int_B S(x,y)\,d\nu=\int_Y S(x,y)e_B(y)\,d\nu$$

for all $\nu$-measurable subsets B of Y. It is a routine matter to derive now that for every $f \in L$ we have

$$(Sf)(x) = \int_Y S(x,y) f(y) d\nu.$$

3. The Kernel Operator Band. Before presenting further details about the structure of $\mathcal{K}$ we recall some facts on Riesz spaces (vector lattices). A Riesz space is a real vector space L, partially ordered such that $f \le g$ in L implies $f+h \le g+h$ for all $h \in L$ and $af \le ag$ for all real $a \ge 0$ and such that the partial ordering is a lattice ordering (i.e., any pair f, g in L has a least upper bound sup(f,g) and a greatest lower bound inf(f,g) with respect to the ordering). The spaces $M(Y,\nu)$ and $M(X,\mu)$ in the preceding sections, with the partial ordering pointwise almost everywhere, are typical examples. The ideals L and M in these spaces are Riesz spaces in their own right. Any Riesz space having the property that any subset bounded from above has a least upper bound is called a *Dedekind complete* space. The ideals L and M above are Dedekind complete. Of course one has to be careful again; if one has a collection of measurable functions, bounded from above, the least upper bound is in general not the pointwise supremum of the functions. For operators between Riesz spaces the definitions of a positive operator and an order bounded operator are exactly as already given in section 1. Let $\mathcal{L}_b(L,M)$ be the vector space of all order bounded operators from the Riesz space L into the Riesz space M, partially ordered by defining that $T_1 \le T_2$ means that $T_2 - T_1$ is positive. There is an important theorem, due to F. Riesz, H. Freudenthal and L.V. Kantorovitch, stating that if M is Dedekind complete, then $\mathcal{L}_b = \mathcal{L}_b(L,M)$ is not only a partially ordered vector space, but even a Dedekind complete Riesz space. For $T_1$ and $T_2$ in $\mathcal{L}_b$, the operator $T_3 = \sup(T_1, T_2)$ is given for any $0 \le f \in L$ by

$$T_3 f = \sup(T_1 f_1 + T_2 f_2 : f_1 \ge 0, f_2 \ge 0, f_1 + f_2 = f),$$

and a similar formula holds for $\inf(T_1, T_2)$.

Applied to the situation introduced in section 1, the problem is now, therefore , to find out how the subspace $\mathcal{K}$ of all kernel operators is embedded in the Dedekind complete Riesz space $\mathcal{L}_b(L,M)$.

We need a few more definitions. Given the element f in the Riesz space L, we write $f^+ = \sup(f,0)$, $f^- = \sup(-f,0)$ and $|f| = \sup(f,-f)$. It is easy to see that $f = f^+ - f^-$ and $|f| = f^+ + f^-$. The non-empty subset D of L is said to be *solid* if $f \in L$, $g \in D$ and $|f| \le |g|$ implies $f \in D$. Any solid linear subspace of L is called an *ideal* in L. Any ideal with the extra property that for any subset in the ideal possessing a least upper bound in L this least upper bound is in the ideal itself is called a *band*.

THEOREM 3.1. (i) *If* $\theta\leq S\leq T\in\mathcal{K}$, *then* $S\in\mathcal{K}$.

(ii) *If* $T_1,T_2\in\mathcal{K}$, *then* $T_3=\sup(T_1,T_2)\in\mathcal{K}$ *and* $T_3$ *has the pointwise maximum of* $T_1(x,y)$ *and* $T_2(x,y)$ *as kernel.*

(iii) *If* $T_0=\sup(T_\alpha:\alpha\in\{\alpha\})$ *holds in* $\mathcal{L}_b$, *where* $\{\alpha\}$ *denotes an index set, and if* $T_\alpha\in\mathcal{K}$ *for all* $\alpha$, *then* $T_0\in\mathcal{K}$.

*In other words,* $\mathcal{K}$ *is a band in* $\mathcal{L}_b$.

PROOF. Part (i) is the theorem in the preceding section. Part (ii) looks trivial, but is not trivial. The original proof by W.A.J. Luxemburg-A.C. Zaanen ([4], 1971), before Schep's proof of part (i) was available, was rather cumbersome. We indicate how to derive (ii) from (i). It may be assumed that $T_2=\theta$, since

$$\sup(T_1,T_2)=T_2+\sup(T_1-T_2,\theta).$$

We have to show, therefore, that the operator $T^+=\sup(T,\theta)$ is a kernel operator with kernel the pointwise maximum $T^+(x,y)$ of $T(x,y)$ and zero. The function $T^+(x,y)$ majorizes $T(x,y)$ as well as zero, so the kernel operator $T_0$ corresponding to $T^+(x,y)$ satisfies $T_0\geq T$ and $T_0\geq\theta$, which implies $T_0\geq\sup(T,\theta)=T^+\geq\theta$. It follows then from part (i) that $T^+\in\mathcal{K}$, and it is easy now to prove that the kernel of $T^+$ is $T^+(x,y)$. For the proof of (iii) we observe first that it may be assumed that the set of all $T_\alpha$ contains all finite suprema of its own elements (i.e., the set is directed upwards). By taking now from this set an appropriate increasing subsequence $T_n(n=1,2,\dots)$ and writing $T_0(x,y)=\lim T_n(x,y)$, it is not difficult to prove that the operator $T_0=\sup T_\alpha$ is a kernel operator with kernel $T_0(x,y)$.

The next question is whether it can happen that $\mathcal{K}$ contains only the null operator . The answer is affirmative. If $X=Y=\mathbb{R}$ with $\mu=\nu$ Lebesgue measure and $L=M=M(\mathbb{R},\mu)$, then the null operator is the only kernel operator. The same holds if $L=M=L^p(\mathbb{R},\mu)$ for $0<p<1$. In order to formulate a sufficient condition for $\mathcal{K}$ to contain non-trivial operators, we return to the domain L of the kernel operators. L is an ideal in the space $M(Y,\nu)$. The subset E of Y is called an L-null set if all $f\in L$ vanish almost everywhere on E. Such an L-null set is of no interest for L and for $\mathcal{L}_b(L,M)$ and may, therefore, just as well be removed from Y. It is not difficult to prove that there exists a maximal L-null set $E_{max}$, uniquely determined except for a set of measure zero. The set theoretic difference $Y_L=Y-E_{max}$ is called the *carrier* of the ideal L. It follows from the remark above that we may remove $E_{max}$ from Y. In other words, we may assume that the carrier of L is Y itself. Now let

$$L^{\wedge}=(g\in M(Y,\nu):\int_Y |fg|d\nu<\infty \text{ for all } f\in L).$$

Then $L^{\wedge}$ is an ideal in $M(Y,\nu)$. Let $g(y)\in L^{\wedge}$ and $h(x)\in M$. Then $T(x,y)=h(x)g(y)$ is the kernel of a kernel operator (from L into M), because for any $f\in L$ we have

$$\int_Y |T(x,y)f(y)|d\nu=|h(x)|\int_Y |f(y)g(y)|d\nu\in M.$$

Any finite real linear combination of operators of this simple type is called an *operator of finite rank*. If the carrier of the ideal $L^{\wedge}$ is of positive measure there are non-trivial operators of finite rank, and so there are non-trivial kernel operators. Evidently, the operators of finite rank form a linear subspace of $\mathcal{K}$, appropriately denoted by $L^{\wedge}\otimes M$, and so the band generated by $L^{\wedge}\otimes M$ (i.e., the smallest band in $\mathcal{L}_b$ containing $L^{\wedge}\otimes M$) is contained in the band $\mathcal{K}$.

THEOREM 3.2. <u>If the carrier of $L^{\wedge}$ is the set Y itself, then the band $\mathcal{K}$ of all kernel operators is exactly the band generated by the operators of finite rank.</u>

PROOF. It is sufficient to prove that if T is a kernel operator with kernel $T(x,y)\geq 0$, then there exists a sequence $(T_n(x,y):n=1,2,\ldots)$ such that $0\leq T_n(x,y)\uparrow T(x,y)$ pointwise and each $T_n$ is majorized by an operator of finite rank. Since Y is the carrier of $L^{\wedge}$, there exists a sequence $Y_n\uparrow Y$ such that $e_{Y_n}\in L^{\wedge}$ for all n. Similarly there exist sets $X_n\uparrow X_M$ (where $X_M$ is the carrier of M) such that $e_{X_n}\in M$ for all n. Then

$$T_n(x,y)=\min(T(x,y),ne_{X_n}(x)e_{Y_n}(y))$$

satisfies the required conditions.

A special case of the last theorem was proved by G. Ya. Lozanovskii ([3] 1966). In his case X=Y is the closed interval [0,1] with $\mu=\nu$ Lebesgue measure and L is a certain normed linear subspace of $M(Y,\nu)$, a so-called KB-space, such that $L^{\infty}(Y,\nu)\subset L\subset L^1(Y,\nu)$. Similarly for M. Lozanovskii's main theorem is that if T is an order bounded operator from L into M, then T is a kernel operator if and only if T is contained in the band generated by $L^*\otimes M$, where $L^*$ denotes the Banach dual of L. It can be proved that under the conditions mentioned L is in fact an ideal in $M(Y,\nu)$ and $L^*=L^\wedge$ (this last fact is not so easy to prove; one needs the theory of Banach function spaces). Anyhow, Lozanovskii's theorem is thus seen to be a special case of Theorem 3.2. His method of proof is very different from the method explained above. He considers first the case that $L=M=L^1[0,1]$ with Lebesgue measure. His proof for this case is then based on N. Dunford's theorem (1936) that every continuous operator from $L^1[0,1]$ into $L^p[0,1]$, for $1<p\leq\infty$, is a kernel operator. In the method explained above the order is reversed; Dunford's theorem will be a corollary of a general theorem due to A.V. Buhvalov, which will be stated in the next section. It is of some interest to observe also that until recently Dunford's theorem had only been extended to separable measures. The method of Buhvalov ([1], 1974) is somewhat similar to Lozanovskii's method. Dunford's theorem is first extended, also to non-separable measures (the proof makes use of Bochner integrals), and Theorem 3.2 is then derived from this extended Dunford's theorem. Finally, we mention that R.J. Nagel and U. Schlotterbeck ([5], 1972) have investigated a certain class of operators from L into M, where L and M are abstract Banach lattices satisfying certain conditions. The spaces L and M can be represented as spaces of continuous extended realvalued functions. It is shown that an order bounded operator T from L into M is contained in the band generated by $L^*\otimes M$ (where $L^*$ is the Banach dual of L) if and only if T corresponds to a kernel operator on these representation spaces. If L and M are $L^p$-spaces, the representations can be transferred back to the original spaces L and M, so T itself is now a kernel operator (see Ch. IV, Proposition 9.8 in the book by H.H. Schaefer [7]).

4. Buhvalov's Theorem. As in the preceding sections, let L and M be ideals in $M(Y,\nu)$ and $M(X,\mu)$, respectively. We assume that Y is the carrier of L as well as of $L^\wedge$. For a sequence of $\nu$-measurable funtions $(f_n:n=1,2,...)$ we write $f_n\to 0$ to denote that $f_n$ converges to zero pointwise almost everywhere on Y and we write $f_n\overset{*}{\to}0$ to denote that every subsequence of $(f_n:n=1,2,...)$ has a subsequence converging to zero almost everywhere on Y. Similarly for $\mu$-measurable functions on X. In 1975 A.V. Buhvalov published a short note [2], containing without proof the following theorem.

THEOREM 4.1. *The order bounded operator* T *(from* L *into* M) *is a kernel operator if and only if* $0 \leq f_n \leq f \in L$ *and* $f_n \overset{*}{\to} 0$ *implies* $Tf_n \to 0$.

PROOF. It is not difficult to see that every kernel operator has the stated property. The proof in the converse direction is reduced to showing that if $T_0$ is a positive operator with the stated property such that $\inf(T_0,T)=\theta$ for all positive kernel operators T, then $T_0=\theta$. The details of the proof are too technical to be reproduced here.

In 1953 H. Nakano published a paper on product spaces of semi-ordered vector spaces (again published in the book [6], 461-508), in which he proved (in Theorem 5.2) that a positive bilinear form is contained in the band generated by the finite rank bilinear forms if and only if it satisfies a certain condition analogous to the condition in the last theorem. It is not surprising, therefore, that Buhvalov's proof (in [1]) and Schep's proof (in [8]), independently, are analogous to each other and to some extent to Nakano's proof. It should be taken in account here that the text of Buhvalov's paper [1] became available to Schep after Schep's thesis [8] was finished.

We indicate finally how Dunford's (extended) theorem follows from Buhvalov's theorem. Actually, as shown by Schep, it is possible to derive from Buhvalov's theorem several general theorems about operators between Banach functions spaces; Dunford's theorem is a special case.

THEOREM 4.2 (i) *Any continuous operator from* $L^p(Y,\nu)$ *into* $L^\infty(X,\mu)$, *for* $1 \leq p < \infty$, *is a kernel operator.*

(ii) *Any continuous operator from* $L^1(Y,\nu)$ *into* $L^p(X,\mu)$, *for* $1 < p \leq \infty$, *is a kernel operator.*

PROOF. (i) Let $1 \leq p < \infty$, and let T be a continuous operator from $L^p(Y,\nu)$ into $L^\infty(X,\mu)$. For any $0 \leq f \in L^p$ and almost any $x \in X$ we have $|Tf(x)| \leq \|Tf\|_\infty \leq \|T\| \cdot \|f\|_p$, so the set $(Tg: 0 \leq g \leq f)$ is bounded in $L^\infty(X,\mu)$. It follows then from the Dedekind completeness of $L^\infty(X,\mu)$ that the function

$$T_1 f = \sup(Tg: 0 \leq g \leq f)$$

exists in $L^\infty$. The map $T_1$ is positive and additive on the set of non-negative functions in $L^p$; hence $T_1$ can be extended to a positive operator on $L^p$. Since $T_1 \geq T$, we get already that T is order bounded. It is sufficient, therefore, to prove that T is a kernel operator if T is continuous and positive. In this case, note that if $0 \leq f_n \leq f \in L^p$ and $f_n \overset{*}{\to} 0$, then $\|f_n\|_p \to 0$ (since $1 \leq p < \infty$), so on account of $0 \le Tf_n(x) \le \|T\| \cdot \|f_n\|_p$ we find that $Tf_n \to 0$. This shows, by Buhvalov's theorem, that T is a kernel operator.

(ii) Let $1<p\le\infty$, and let T be a continuous operator from $L^1(Y,\nu)$ into $L^p(X,\mu)$. Let $p^{-1}+q^{-1}=1$, so $q=1$ if $p=\infty$. The adjoint operator $T^*$ is a continuous operator from $(L^p)^*$ into $L^\infty(Y,\nu)$. For $p=\infty$, let $T^\sim$ be the restriction of $T^*$ to $L^1(X,\mu)$. For $1<p<\infty$ we have $(L^p)^*=L^q(X,\mu)$; in this case, let $T^\sim=T^*$. Hence, in both cases, $T^\sim$ is a continuous operator from $L^q(X,\mu)$ into $L^\infty(Y,\nu)$, with $1\le q<\infty$. Then $T^\sim$ is a kernel operator by part (i). Let T(y,x) be the kernel of $T^\sim$. It is not very difficult to prove now that T is a kernel operator with kernel T(x,y).

## REFERENCES


[1] Buhvalov, A.V., The integral representation of linear operators (Investigations on linear operators and the theory of functions, V), (Russian). **Zap. Naučn. Sem. Leningrad, Otdel. Math. Inst.** Steklov (LOMI) 47 (1974), 5-14.

[2] Buhvalov, A.V., Integral representability criterion for linear operators. Funktsional'nyi Analizi Ego Priloh. 9 (1975), 51.

[3] Lozanovskii, G.Ya., On almost integral operators in KB-spaces. Vestnik Leningrad. Gos. Univ. 7 (1966), 35-44.

[4] Luxemburg, W.A.J. - Zaanen, A.C., The linear modulus of an order bounded linear transformation. Proc. Netherl. Acad. Sci.74 (1971), 422-447 (Indag. Math. 33).

[5] Nagel, R.J. - Schlotterbeck, U., Integraldarstellung regulärer Operatoren auf Banachverbänden. Math. Z. 127 (1972), 293-300.

[6] Nakano, H., Semi-ordered Linear Spaces. Japan Soc. for the Promotion of Science, Tokyo 1955.

[7] Schaefer, H.H., Banach Lattices and Positive Operators. Springer Verlag, Berlin/Heidelberg/New York 1974.

[8] Schep, A.R., Kernel Operators. Thesis, Leiden State University 1977.

# INVARIANT OPERATOR RANGES

Eric A. Nordgren

Department of Mathematics

University of New Hampshire

Durham, New Hampshire

This report describes a portion of joint work with M. Radjabalipour, H. Radjavi and P. Rosenthal [8]. The set of Hilbert space operators that leave invariant a fixed dense operator range is given a matrical representation. Also it is shown that every operator on an infinite dimensional Hilbert space has an uncountable collection of infinite dimensional invariant operator ranges such that any two of them have only the vector 0 in common.

## 1. Introduction

By an *operator range* we mean a linear manifold in a Hilbert space H that is the range of a bounded operator on H. Operator ranges have been the subject of considerable study (see Fillmore and Williams [3] for an up-to-date account). Recent work of Foiaş [4] and of Douglas and Foiaş [2] has shown that not only are the operator ranges that are invariant under an operator important for describing its properties, but they are also somewhat more tractable than the invariant subspaces. See also [1], [5], [6], [7] and [9]. We are interested in the simplest cases of the following two questions, about which little is known at present: 1) what can be said about the operators that leave a given set of operator ranges invariant, and 2) what can be said about the operator ranges that are invariant under a given set of operators? We consider the case of each question in which the given set is a singleton.

## 2. Operators With a Given Invariant Operator Range

Let PH be a fixed dense but proper operator range, where P is a given operator on H. By examining the polar decomposition of P, we see there is no loss of generality in assuming P is positive. Since multiplying P by a scalar does not alter its range, we may also assume P is a contraction. The collection $\mathcal{A}(P)$ of all operators that take PH into itself is a subalgebra of the algebra $\mathcal{B}(H)$ of all operators which we are going to characterize.

By the spectral theorem, there is a spectral measure E on the unit interval such that $P = \int_0^1 \lambda dE(\lambda)$. For each $\lambda$ between 0 and 1 we obtain a direct sum decomposition $H = H_1 \oplus H_2 \oplus \ldots$ by taking $H_j$ to be the range of $E((\lambda^j, \lambda^{j-1}])$. Let $\mathcal{T}(P,\lambda)$ consist of all operators that are upper triangular with respect to this decomposition. Thus $T \in \mathcal{T}(P,\lambda)$ if and only if each of the subspaces $H_1$, $H_1 \oplus H_2$, $H_1 \oplus H_2 \oplus H_3$, ... is invariant under T. If $T \in \mathcal{T}(P,\lambda)$, then it can be shown that $P^{-1}TP$ is bounded. Writing $(P^{-1}\mathcal{T}(P,\lambda)P)^*$ for the collection of adjoints of operators $P^{-1}TP$ with T in $\mathcal{T}(P,\lambda)$, we can state our principal result as follows.

THEOREM 2.1. $\mathcal{A}(P) = \mathcal{T}(P,\lambda) + (P^{-1}\mathcal{T}(P,\lambda)P)^*$.

COROLLARY 2.1. *The algebra* $\mathcal{A}(P)$ *is neither uniformly dense nor uniformly closed in* $\mathcal{B}(H)$.

COROLLARY 2.2. *If* $0 < r < s$, *then* $\mathcal{A}(P^r) \supset \mathcal{A}(P^s)$. *In particular, for each* t *in* (0,1), *the range of* $P^t$ *is invariant under* $\mathcal{A}(P)$.

See [5] for an application of the theorem.

## 3. Operator Ranges Invariant Under a Given Operator

In [4] Foiaş proved a Burnside theorem for operator ranges.

THEOREM (Foiaş). *If the only operator ranges that are invariant under all operators in a strongly closed algebra of operators are* {0} *and* H, *then the algebra contains all operators.*

A consequence of this theorem is the existence of nontrivial operator ranges that are invariant for all operators commuting with a given non-scalar operator. The following striking result of Douglas and Foiaş [2] implies the existence of a large number of operator ranges invariant under a given operator.

THEOREM (Douglas and Foiaş). *Let* S *be a nonalgebraic operator. Every invariant operator range for* S *is invariant under a second operator* T *if and only if there is an entire function* u *such that* $T = u(S)$.

We give further indication of how large the lattice of invariant operator ranges for a given operator is in the next three theorems.

THEOREM 3.1. *The unilateral shift has an uncountable family of dense invariant operator ranges such that any two of them have only* 0 *in common*.

A result of Sz.-Nagy and Foiaş [10] that says every cyclic strict contraction has the unilateral shift as a quasi-affine transform allows this result to be carried over to all cyclic operators.

THEOREM 3.2. *Every cyclic operator on an infinite dimensional Hilbert space has an uncountable family of dense invariant operator ranges such that any two of them have only the vector* 0 *in common*.

By a theorem of Kaplansky, an arbitrary operator either has an infinite dimensional invariant subspace or else is algebraic. This leads to the following result.

THEOREM 3.3. *Every operator on an infinite dimensional Hilbert space has an uncountable collection of infinite dimensional invariant operator ranges such that any two of them have only the vector* 0 *in common*.

COROLLARY 3.1. *Let* M *be any infinite dimensional operator range invariant under an operator* T. *There exists an uncountable family of infinite dimensional operator ranges included in* M *and invariant under* T *such that any two of them intersect in* $\{0\}$.

REFERENCES

[1] Azoff, E.A., Invariant linear manifolds and the self-adjointness of operator algebras. to appear.

[2] Douglas, R.G. and Foiaş, C., Infinite dimensional versions of a theorem of Brickman and Fillmore. Indiana U. Math. J. 25 (1976), 315-320.

[3] Fillmore, P.A. and Williams, J.P., On operator ranges. Advances in Math. 7 (1971), 254-281.

[4] Foiaş, C., Invariant para-closed subspaces. Indiana U. Math. J. 21 (1972), 887-906.

[5] Jafarian, A.A. and Radjavi, M., Compact operator ranges and reductive algebras. to appear.

[6] Nordgren, E.A., Radjavi, H. and Rosenthal, P., Operator algebras leaving compact operator ranges invariant. Michigan Math. J. 23 (1976), 375-377.

[7] Nordgren, E.A., Radjabalipour, M., Radjavi, M., and Rosenthal, P., Algebras intertwining compact operators. Acta Sci. Math. 39 (1977), 115-119.

[8] Nordgren, E.A., Radjabalipour, M., Radjavi, H., and Rosenthal, P., On invariant operator ranges. to appear.

[9] Radjavi, H., On density of algebras with minimal invariant operator ranges. to appear.

[10] Sz. Nagy, B. and Foiaş, C., Vecteurs cyclique et quasi-affinites. Studia Math. 31 (1968), 35-42.

# DIAGONALIZATION OF MATRICES OVER $H^\infty$

B. Sz.-Nagy
Bolyai Institute
University of Szeged
Szeged

Interest in extending the classical equivalence theory for matrices over the algebra of complex polynomials to matrices over the disc algebra $H^\infty$ arose from the Jordan model theory of class $C_0$ operators on Hilbert space. This extension was accomplished by E.A. Nordgren with the help of the new concept of quasi-equivalence. We are going to present this theory in a new form, based upon a useful generalization of a lemma of M.J. Sherman on $H^\infty$ functions.

## 1. Introduction

Interest in canonical forms of matrices over the algebra $H^\infty$ of bounded analytic functions on the unit disc $|\lambda| < 1$ arose in particular from investigations on "Jordan models" of some classes of operators on Hilbert space.

Namely, it was known since 1969 [2] that every contraction operator T of class $C_0$ (see e.g. [1]) with finite defect index $N = \text{rank } (I-T^*T) = \text{rank } (I-TT^*)$ is quasi-similar to a unique operator of the form

$$S(m_1) + S(m_2) + \ldots + S(m_N),$$

where $m_1, m_2, \ldots, m_N$ are inner functions such that $m_i | m_{i-1}$ for $i = 2,3,\ldots,$ and, for every inner function m, the operator S(m) is defined on the subspace $\mathcal{H}(m) = H^2 - mH^2$ of the Hardy-Hilbert space $H^2$ for the disc by

$$S(m)u = P_{\mathcal{H}(m)}(\lambda u), \qquad u \in \mathcal{H}(m),$$

$P_{\mathcal{H}(m)}$ denoting orthogonal projection of $H^2$ onto $\mathcal{H}(m)$.

The problem naturally arose how this sequence $m_1, \ldots, m_N$ is directly connected with the "characteristic function" $\Theta_T(\lambda)$ of T, which in this case is an $N \times N$ matrix over $H^\infty$. It was conjectured in [2] that $m_1, \ldots, m_N$ can be obtained from the "determinant divisors" of $\Theta_T(\lambda)$, defined in analogy to the classical case of matrices over the algebra of polynomials, but the proof was only given for $m_1$, i.e. that $m_1$ is the quotient of det $\Theta_T$ by the "largest common inner divisor" of the determinants of the minors of order N-1 of $\Theta_T$.

The conjecture was soon fully proved by Moore and Nordgren [4] on the basis of a remarkable paper of Nordgren [3] in which the new concept of "quasi-equivalence" of finite rectangular matrices over $H^\infty$ was introduced and a "diagonalization" theorem for such matrices established.

This theory was recently extended in [6] to semi-infinite - and partly to infinite - matrices over $H^\infty$. This extension was made possible by the use of such non-linear and non-analytic tools as the Baire category theorem, and also of some other modifications of the arguments in [3].

In this paper we intend to indicate this modified method in the finite matrix case (where we need not refer to such topological tools).

## 2. A Basic Lemma

The difficulties with matrices over $H^\infty$ stem from the fact that the algebra $H^\infty$ does not possess some properties of the algebra of polynomials which are commonly used in classical matrix theory, namely the euclidian division. One important property however, which does hold for $H^\infty$, is the existence of a largest common inner divisor, denoted by

$$(1) \qquad \bigwedge_\alpha u_\alpha ,$$

for any family $\{u_\alpha\}$ of functions $u_\alpha \in H^\infty$, not all zero, and (1) is uniquely determined (if we disregard a constant factor of modulus 1, as we will). It is convenient to define (1) also if all $u_\alpha$ are 0, namely by 0. This property of the algebra $H^\infty$ follows from the canonical factorization of any non-zero $u \in H^\infty$ into an inner factor and an outer (i.e., "completely non-inner") factor, and from the "parametric" representation of an inner function $u = u(\lambda)$ as a product of a "Blaschke product"

$$(2)\qquad B(\lambda) = \prod_k b_{a_k}(\lambda), \quad \text{where} \quad |a_k| < 1, \quad \sum_k (1-|a_k|) < \infty,$$

and

$$b_a(\lambda) = \frac{\bar{a}}{|a|}\frac{a-\lambda}{1-\bar{a}\lambda} \quad \text{if } 0 < |a| < 1, \quad \text{and } b_a(\lambda) = \lambda \quad \text{if } a = 0,$$

and of a "singular" inner function

$$(3)\qquad S(\lambda) = \exp \int_0^{2\pi} \frac{e^{it}+\lambda}{e^{it}-\lambda}\, d\mu(t),$$

where $\mu$ is a finite, non-negative Borel measure on the unit circle C, singular with respect to the Lebesgue measure on C.

However, in contrast to the basic property of the algebra of polynomials, the largest common inner divisor is not always a linear combination of the $u_\alpha$, even for finite families $\{u_\alpha\}$. One can even find $u_1, u_2 \in H^\infty$ such that $x_1u_1 + x_2u_2$ will, for no choice of $x_1, x_2 \in H^\infty$, be equal to $u_1 \wedge u_2$ or at least to $h\cdot(u_1 \wedge u_2)$ with some outer function h.

In view of this "deficiency" of $H^\infty$, the following property may seem surprising.

LEMMA 1. _For any finite family_ $\{u_k\}$ $(k = 1,\dots,N)$ _of elements of_ $H^\infty$ _and for any given inner function_ $\omega$, _we have_

$$(4)\qquad \sum_{k=1}^{N} t^{k-1}u_k = h(t)\cdot\bigwedge_{k=1}^{N} u_k \quad \underline{\text{with}} \quad h(t)\wedge\omega = 1,$$

_for every value of the complex parameter_ t, _with the possible exception of a countable set of values._

In the case N = 2 this lemma is essentially due to M.J. Sherman [5], and it proved to be useful in several investigations. The proof below applies for any $N \geq 2$.

PROOF. The case when all $u_k$ are zero is trivial, so we can assume that $u = \bigwedge_1^N u_k$ is an inner function. Then $v_k = u_k/u \in H^\infty$ for $k = 1, \dots, N$, and we have $\bigwedge_1^N v_k = 1$. For any value of the complex parameter t, set

$$u(t) = u_1 + tu_2 + \dots + t^{N-1}u_N, \quad v(t) = v_1 + tv_2 + \dots + t^{N-1}v_N \;;$$

then

$$u(t) = v(t)u = v(t)\cdot\bigwedge_1^N u_k \quad . \tag{5}$$

Observe that, for any set $t_1, \dots, t_N$ of N different values of t, the linear span of $v(t_1), \dots, v(t_N)$, with complex coefficients, coincides with the linear span of $v_1, \dots, v_N$; indeed, this follows from the fact that the Vandermonde determinant $V(t_1,\dots,t_N) = \Pi_{i<k}(t_i - t_k)$ is non-zero. Hence we deduce that

$$\bigwedge_1^N v(t_k) = \bigwedge_1^N v_k \quad (= 1) \;,$$

and this also implies that

$$\bigwedge_1^N (v(t_k) \wedge \omega) = (\bigwedge_1^N v(t_k)) \wedge \omega = 1 \wedge \omega = 1.$$

Setting

$$\omega(t) = v(t) \wedge \omega \;, \tag{6}$$

we have a family $\{\omega(t)\}_{t\in\mathbb{C}}$ of inner divisors of $\omega$ such that

$$\bigwedge_1^N \omega(t_k) = 1 \qquad \text{for any N-tuple } \{t_1,\dots,t_N\} \tag{7}$$

of different values of t.

Now this implies that $\omega(t) = 1$ for every value of t, except at most countably many.

To prove this we can refer to a measure theoretic argument. By using the parametric representation $\omega = B\cdot S$ given by (2) and (3) we associate with $\omega$ the finite Borel measure $m_\omega(\sigma)$ on $\mathbb{C}$ by setting

$$m_\omega(\sigma) = \sum_{a_k\in\sigma} (1-|a_k|) + \mu_\omega(\sigma \cap C). \tag{8}$$

Since $\omega(t)$ is, for every t, an inner divisor of $\omega$, the corresponding measure $m_{\omega(t)}(\sigma)$ is majorized by $m_\omega(\sigma)$. Let $\sigma(t)$ be a (Borelian) support of the measure $m_{\omega(t)}$, determined up to a (Borelian) set of zero $m_\omega$-measure.

Fix a positive number p and consider a finite set $\{s_1,\ldots,s_n\}$ of (different) complex numbers (if any) such that

$$(9)\qquad m_\omega(\sigma(s_i)) \geqslant p \qquad (i = 1,\ldots,n).$$

Denote by $\sum_j$ $(j = 1,\ldots,n)$ the set of points of $\mathbb{C}$ which are covered by exactly j of the sets $\sigma(s_1),\ldots,\sigma(s_n)$. Then, clearly,

$$(10)\qquad \sum_{i=1}^{n} m_\omega(\sigma(s_i)) = m_\omega(\textstyle\sum_1) + 2m_\omega(\sum_2) + \ldots + n\, m_\omega(\sum_n).$$

Now, since for every N-tuple $\{t_1,\ldots,t_N\}$ we have (6), and hence $m_\omega(\cap_1^N \sigma(t_k)) = 0$, we have $m_\omega(\sum_j) = 0$ for $j \geqslant N$ in (10). Therefore, the sum (10) is less than or equal to $N\cdot m_\omega(\mathbb{C})$. On the other hand this sum is greater than or equal to np by (9). Thus,

$$n \leqslant N\cdot m_\omega(\mathbb{C})/p.$$

Letting p run over the sequence 1, 1/2, 1/3, ..., we conclude that the set of values t with $m_\omega(\sigma(t)) > 0$ is countable.

For any t not belonging to this countable set we have $m_\omega(\sigma(t)) = 0$, and therefore, $\omega(t) = 1$; in view of (5) and (6) this concludes the proof of Lemma 1, with $h(t) = v(t)$.

As the union of countably many countable sets is countable, Lemma 1 has as a corollary:

LEMMA 2. *Let* $[u_{ik}]$ $(i = 1,2,\ldots;\ k = 1,2,\ldots,N)$ *be a matrix over* $H^\infty$ *with a finite number* N *of columns and a countable (finite or infinite) number of rows, and let* $\omega$ *be a given inner function. Then we have, simultaneously for* $i = 1,2,\ldots,$

$$(11)\qquad \sum_{k=1}^{N} t^{k-1} u_{ik} = h_i(t)\cdot \bigwedge_{k=1}^{N} u_{ik} \quad \underline{\text{with}}\quad h_i(t)\wedge\omega = 1$$

_for every value of the complex parameter_ t, _with the possible exception of a countable set of values._

REMARKS. We could allow N and $\omega$ to vary from row to row, i.e. depend on i, but we do not need such a generalization. - An extension to the case $N = \infty$ was given in [6] (however, with coefficients 1, $t_1$, $t_2$, ... not just the powers of t), and it is in the proof of this generalization that the Baire category theorem was also used. For the study of finite matrices over $H^\infty$ the above Lemma 2 is sufficient.

## 3. Nordgren Diagonalization Theorem

We are now going to present the Nordgren diagonalization theory for finite matrices over $H^\infty$ as based on Lemma 2.

For $1 \leq m \leq n < \infty$, denote by $M(n,m)$ the set of $n \times m$ matrices over $H^\infty$. For any inner function $\omega$ denote by $N_\omega(k)$, $1 \leq k < \infty$, the set of matrices $\Phi \in M(k,k)$ which have a scalar multiple "prime" to $\omega$, i.e. for which there exists a matrix $\Phi^a \in M(k,k)$ such that

$$\Phi^a\Phi = \Phi\Phi^a = \varphi I_n \quad \text{with} \quad \varphi \in H^\infty, \quad \varphi \neq 0, \quad \varphi \wedge \omega = 1.$$

Two matrices from $M(n,m)$, say A and B, are called $\omega$-equivalent ($A \overset{\omega}{\sim} B$) if

$$\text{(12)} \qquad \Phi A = B\Psi \quad \text{for some} \quad \Phi \in N_\omega(n), \quad \Psi \in N_\infty(m).$$

If $A \overset{\omega}{\sim} B$ for every inner $\omega$, then A and B are called quasi-equivalent ($A \overset{q}{\sim} B$). They are equivalent in the usual sense ($A \sim B$) if $\Phi$, $\Psi$ can be chosen invertible, i.e. with the scalar multiple 1. Each of these relations is reflexive, symmetric, and transitive; in particular, (12) implies $A(\varphi\Psi^a) = (\Phi^a)B$, and both $\varphi\Psi^a$ and $\psi\Phi^a$ have the scalar multiple $\varphi\psi$, prime to $\omega$.

For $A \in M(n,m)$, let $n \geq m$, $\mathcal{D}_o(A) = 1$ and $\mathcal{D}_k(A) = \bigwedge_{D \in A_k} \det D$, where $A_k$ denotes the set of k order submatrices of A; $k = 1,\ldots,m$. Clearly, $\mathcal{D}_{k-1}(A) \mid \mathcal{D}_k(A)$ for $k = 1,\ldots,m$. If $A \overset{\omega}{\sim} B$, then (12) implies $\Phi A \Psi^a = \psi B$ and $\Phi^a B \Psi = \varphi A$, and hence we deduce

(13) $\mathcal{D}_k(A) \mid \varphi_k \mathcal{D}_k(B)$, $\mathcal{D}_k(B) \mid \psi_k \mathcal{D}_k(A)$, with $\varphi_k (= \psi^k)$ and $\psi_k = (\varphi^k)$ prime to $\omega$ .

It follows that, for a <u>k</u>, $\mathcal{D}_k(A)$, $\mathcal{D}_k(B)$ are either both zero, or none. If $A \overset{q}{\sim} B$ and if k is such that $\mathcal{D}_k(A)\cdot\mathcal{D}_k(B)$ is nonzero, i.e., inner, then choosing this product for $\omega$ we deduce from (13) that $\mathcal{D}_k(A) = \mathcal{D}_k(B)$. We conclude that if $A \overset{q}{\sim} B$, then $\mathcal{D}_k(A) = \mathcal{D}_k(B)$ for all k.

THEOREM (Nordgren). <u>Every matrix</u> $A = [a_{ik}] \in M(n,m)$ <u>is quasi-equivalent to the diagonal matrix</u>

$$E = \text{diag}_{n\times m}(E_1(A),\dots,E_m(A)), \text{ where } E_k(A) = \mathcal{D}_k(A) \mid \mathcal{D}_{k-1}(A);$$

$$E_k(A) = 0 \text{ if } \mathcal{D}_k(A) = 0.$$

PROOF. Given $A \in M(n,m)$, we fix an arbitrary inner function $\omega$ and set

$$\omega' = \omega \mathcal{D}_j(A), \tag{14}$$

j being the largest integer for which $\mathcal{D}_j(A) \neq 0$ $(0 \leqslant j \leqslant m)$.

Choose t according to Lemma 2 to fit $\omega'$ and all the rows of A. Denoting by $C_m(t)$ the $m\times m$ matrix whose first column is $[0,t,\dots,t^{m-1}]$ and all the other entries are zero, the first column of the matrix $A(I_m + C_m(t))$ will consist of the sequence

$$h_1\cdot\bigwedge_k a_{1k},\ h_2\cdot\bigwedge_k a_{2k},\dots,\ h_n\cdot\bigwedge_k a_{nk}, \text{ with } h_i \wedge \omega' = 1 \quad (i = 1,\dots,n). \tag{15}$$

Then choose s to fit $\omega'$ and the sequence (15). Denoting by $R_n(s)$ the $n\times n$ matrix whose first row is $[0,s,\dots,s^{n-1}]$ and all other entries are zero, the matrix

$$A' = [a'_{ik}] = (I_n + R_n(s))A(I_m + C_m(t))$$

will have the 1,1-entry

$$a'_{11} = h'\cdot\bigwedge_i (h_i \cdot \bigwedge_k a_{ik}), \text{ with } h' \wedge \omega = 1;$$

and hence,

$$a'_{11} = h\cdot\bigwedge_{i,k} a_{ik} = h\cdot\mathcal{D}_1(A), \quad \text{with} \quad h\wedge\omega = 1.$$

Indeed, for any $h_i$, $v_i \in H^\infty$ with $h_i \wedge \omega = 1$ and for $v = \bigwedge_i v_i$ we have $(\bigwedge_i h_i v_i)/v = {}_i\, h_i\, v_i/v$ and

$$(\bigwedge_i h_i \frac{v_i}{v})\wedge\omega' = \bigwedge_i ((h_i\frac{v_i}{v})\wedge\omega') = \bigwedge_i (\frac{v_i}{v}\wedge\omega') = (\bigwedge_i \frac{v_i}{v})\wedge\omega' = 1\wedge\omega' = 1,$$

[except for the - trivial - case $v = 0$]. Since $(I+R)^{-1} = I-R$, $(I+C)^{-1} = I-C$, we have $A\sim A'$, and therefore $\mathcal{D}_k(A) = \mathcal{D}_k(A')$ for every k.

Next we consider the matrix $A'' = [a''_{ik}]$ for which $a''_{11} = \mathcal{D}_1(A)$, $a''_{ik} = h\, a_{ik}$ if $i,k \geq 2$, and $a''_{ik} = a'_{ik}$ for the other entries. Then $A'' \overset{\omega'}{\sim} A'$ because

$$\mathrm{diag}_{n\times n}(h,1,\ldots,1)\cdot A'' = A'\ \mathrm{diag}_{m\times m}(1,h,\ldots,h),$$

and both diagonal matrices have the scalar multiple h, prime to $\omega'$.

Note that $a''_{11} = \mathcal{D}_1(A)\,|\,A''$; hence, in particular, $v_i = a''_{i1}/a''_{11}$ $(i = 2,\ldots,n)$ and $w_k = a''_{1k}/a''_{11}$ $(k = 2,\ldots,m)$ belong to $H^\infty$. Subtracting $v_i$ times the first row of $A''$ from the i-th row $(i = 2,\ldots,n)$ and $w_k$ times the first column from the k-th column $(k = 2,\ldots,m)$, we obtain a matrix $A'''$ equivalent to $A''$. Indeed, we have

$$A''' = (I_n - C_n[v])A''(I_m - R_m[w]),$$

where $C_n[v]$ is the nxn matrix whose first column is formed by the sequence $(0,v_2,\ldots,v_n)$ and all other entries are zero, and $R_m[v]$ is defined analogously, with the first row instead of the first column; both $I_n - C_n[v]$ and $I_m - R_m[w]$ are invertible in $H^\infty$.

Combining the above results we get that $A \overset{\omega'}{\sim} A'''$ and

$$A''' = \mathrm{diag}(\delta_1, A_1), \text{ where } \delta_1 = \mathcal{D}_1(A),\ A_1 \in M(n-1,m-1),\quad \delta_1 | A_1 \quad .$$

Repeating this procedure for $A_1$ in place of A, and so on, we eventually arrive at the result that

(16) $$A \overset{\omega'}{\sim} D = \mathrm{diag}_{n\times m}(\delta_1,\delta_2,\ldots,\delta_m),$$

the entries $\delta_k$ being inner functions or zero, and $\delta_{k-1}|\delta_k$ for $k = 1,\ldots,m$. Note that D may depend on the choice of $\omega$, and that $\mathcal{D}_k(D) = \delta_1\ldots\delta_k$ for $k = 1,\ldots,m$.

Relation (16) implies (cf.(13)) that

$$\text{(a)}\quad \mathcal{D}_k(A)\,|\,\varphi_k\mathcal{D}_k(D) \quad\text{and}\quad \text{(b)}\quad \mathcal{D}_k(D)\,|\,\psi_k\mathcal{D}_k(A) \qquad (k = 1,\ldots,m)$$

with $\varphi_k$, $\psi_k$ prime to $\omega'$, and hence to $\mathcal{D}_k(A)$ whenever $\mathcal{D}_k(A) \neq 0$, thus for $k = 1,\ldots,j$. In this case, (a) implies $\mathcal{D}_k(A)|\mathcal{D}_k(D)$; combining this with (b) we infer that

$$\text{(17)}\qquad \mathcal{D}_k(D) = \alpha_k\cdot\mathcal{D}_k(A) \quad\text{with}\quad \alpha_k|\psi_k \qquad (k = 1,\ldots,j).$$

It follows that

$$\text{(18)}\qquad \alpha_{k-1}\mathcal{D}_{k-1}(A)\,|\,\alpha_k\mathcal{D}_k(A) \qquad\text{for}\qquad k = 1,\ldots,j$$

(by setting $\mathcal{D}_o = 1$). Because $\alpha_{k-1}$ (being a divisor of $\psi_{k-1}$) is prime to $\omega'$ (and therefore, to $\mathcal{D}_k(A)$), we deduce from (18) that $\alpha_{k-1}|\alpha_k$, and $\alpha_k/\alpha_{k-1}$ is an inner function, for $k = 1,\ldots,j$.

Let us define the "invariant factors" $\mathcal{E}_k(A)$ by

$$\mathcal{E}_k(A) = \mathcal{D}_k(A)/\mathcal{D}_{k-1}(A) \quad\text{for } 1 \leqslant k \leqslant j,\text{ and}\quad \mathcal{E}_k(A) = 0 \quad\text{for } j < k \leqslant m.$$

We deduce from (17) that $\delta_k = (\alpha_k/\alpha_{k-1})\mathcal{E}_k(A)$ for $1 \leqslant k \leqslant j$. So we have

$$\text{(19)}\qquad (D=)\operatorname{diag}_{nxm}(\delta_1,\ldots,\delta_m) = \operatorname{diag}_{nxn}(\alpha_1,\alpha_2/\alpha_1,\ldots,\alpha_j/\alpha_{j-1}, 1,\ldots,1)E,$$

where

$$\text{(20)}\qquad E = \operatorname{diag}_{nxm}(\mathcal{E}_1(A),\mathcal{E}_2(A),\ldots,\mathcal{E}_m(A)).$$

The first matrix on the right of (19) has the scalar multiple $\alpha_j$, which is prime to $\omega'$. Combining (16), (19) we conclude that $A \overset{\omega'}{\sim} E$, and hence $A \overset{\omega}{\sim} E$. Now, E is, by its definition, independent of $\omega$, and this proves that A and E are quasi-equivalent. This concludes the proof of the theorem.

The last part of the above proof, concerning $D\overset{\omega'}{\sim}E$, is the same in [3]. The whole proof carries over to infinite matrices with a finite number of columns, except that in the first step, concerning $A'\sim A$, we have to apply the "infinite version" of Lemma 2, see [6].

## REFERENCES

[1] Sz.-Nagy, B. - Foiaş, C., Harmonic Analysis of Operators on Hilbert Space. North Holland - Akadémiai Kiadó (Amsterdam - Budapest, 1970), Chapter III; or

Sz.-Nagy, B., Hilbertraum-Operatoren der Klasse $C_o$, Abstract Spaces and Approximation. Proc. Conf. Oberwolfach 1968, Birkhäuser, Basel, ISNM 10 (1969), pp. 72 - 81.

[2] Sz.-Nagy, B. - Foiaş, C., Modèle de Jordan pour une classe d'opérateurs de l'espace de Hilbert. Acta Sci. Math., 31 (1970), 91 - 115.

[3] Nordgren, E.A., On quasi-equivalence of matrices over $H^\infty$. Acta Sci. Math. 34 (1973), 301 - 310.

[4] Moore III, B. - Nordgren, E.A., On quasi-equivalence and quasi-similarity. Acta Sci. Math. 34 (1973), 311 - 316.

[5] Sherman, M.J., Invariant subspaces containing all constant directions. J. Functional Anal., 8 (1971), 82 - 85.

[6] Sz.-Nagy, B., Diagonalization of matrices over $H^\infty$. Acta Sci. Math., 38 (1976), 223 - 238.

# BIQUASITRIANGULAR OPERATORS AND QUASISIMILARITY

Carl Pearcy
The University of Michigan
Ann Arbor, Michigan

and

Ciprian Foiaş and Dan Voiculescu
Mathematics Institute
Bucharest

The authors consider the question of whether the class $(BQT)_{qs}$ consisting of all those (bounded) operators on a fixed Hilbert space $\mathcal{H}$ that are quasisimilar to some biquasitriangular operator is equal to the algebra $\mathcal{L}(\mathcal{H})$ of all operators on the space. It is shown that $(BQT)_{qs}$ is at least norm-dense in $\mathcal{L}(\mathcal{H})$ .

Let $\mathcal{H}$ be a separable, infinite-dimensional, complex Hilbert space, and let $\mathcal{L}(\mathcal{H})$ denote the algebra of all bounded linear operators on $\mathcal{H}$ . Recall that two operators $T_1$ and $T_2$ in $\mathcal{L}(\mathcal{H})$ are quasisimilar if there exist operators $X$ and $Y$ in $\mathcal{L}(\mathcal{H})$ with trivial kernel and dense range such that $T_1X = XT_2$ and $YT_1 = T_2Y$ . The relation of quasisimilarity has been successfully used in the study of $C_0$-contractions [11], [12], and is also important because if $T_1$ and $T_2$ are quasisimilar operators, then $T_1$ has a nontrivial hyperinvariant subspace if and only if $T_2$ does [8].

We shall denote by (BQT) the class of all biquasitriangular operators in $\mathcal{L}(\mathcal{H})$ (cf. [7], [2], [5], and [10] for information about these operators) and by $(BQT)_{qs}$ the set of all operators $T$ in $\mathcal{L}(\mathcal{H})$ such that $T$ is quasisimilar to some biquasitriangular operator. In [6] it was shown that the set $(BQT)_{qs}$ properly contains (BQT), and this leads to the following interesting question.

PROBLEM 1.1. Is $(BQT)_{qs} = \mathcal{L}(\mathcal{H})$ ?

This question is important for several reasons. In the first place, if an affirmative answer could be found independent of the deep results of [2] (see also [5]), it would provide an alternate reduction of the hyperinvariant subspace problem to operators in the class (BQT) . Secondly, the equivalence relation of quasisimilarity is at present not sufficiently well understood, and an affirmative answer to the above question would provide the excitement needed to stimulate more interest in, and conjectures about, quasisimilarity of operators. On the other hand, a negative answer to this question would necessarily produce deeper insight into the relation of quasisimilarity and its invariants.

The purpose of this note is to make some progress toward the solution of this problem by showing that the set $(BQT)_{qs}$ is at least norm-dense in $\mathcal{L}(\mathcal{H})$. In fact, we shall prove the stronger result that every $T$ in $\mathcal{L}(\mathcal{H})$ is in the norm-closure of the unitary orbit of an operator in $(BQT)_{qs}$.

We begin by introducing some needed terminology and notation. The ideal of compact operators in $\mathcal{L}(\mathcal{H})$ will be denoted by $\mathcal{K} = \mathcal{K}(\mathcal{H})$ and the Calkin algebra by $\mathcal{L}(\mathcal{H})/\mathcal{K}$. If $T \in \mathcal{L}(\mathcal{H})$, the image of $T$ in $\mathcal{L}(\mathcal{H})/\mathcal{K}$ will be denoted by $\tilde{T}$. Furthermore, the <u>unitary orbit</u> of $T$ is the set

$$\mathcal{O}_u(T) = \{UTU^*: \ U \text{ is unitary in } \mathcal{L}(\mathcal{H})\},$$

and the norm-closure of $\mathcal{O}_u(T)$ will be denoted by $\mathcal{O}_u(T)^-$. The spectrum, essential spectrum, and left [right] essential spectrum of $T$ will be denoted, respectively, by $\sigma(T)$, $\sigma_e(T)$, and $\sigma_{le}(T)$ $[\sigma_{re}(T)]$. Finally, we remind the reader that the <u>Weyl spectrum</u> of $T$, denoted by $\omega(T)$, is the union of $\sigma_e(T)$ and the set of all complex numbers $\lambda$ such that $T - \lambda$ is a Fredholm operator of nonzero index.

THEOREM 1.2. Let $T$ be an arbitrary operator in $\mathcal{L}(\mathcal{H})$. Then there exist operators $R$ in $(BQT)$ and $T'$ in $\mathcal{O}_u(T)^-$ (equivalently, $T \in \mathcal{O}_u(T')^-$) such that $T'$ is quasisimilar to $R$ and such that $\sigma(R) = \sigma(T)$ and $\sigma_e(R) = \omega(T)$.

PROOF. Consider the set $G$ consisting of all those complex numbers $\lambda$ such that $T - \lambda$ is a semi-Fredholm operator with index different from $0$. (In other words, in the terminology of [10], $G$ consists of the union of all pseudoholes in $\sigma_e(T)$ together with the union of all holes in $\sigma_e(T)$ with nonzero index.) If $G$ is empty, then from [2] we know that $T \in (BQT)$, and the theorem is proved with $T' = R = T$. Thus we may suppose that $G$ is nonempty, and we set $\Gamma = \partial G$. One knows that $\Gamma$ is a compact subset of $\sigma_{le}(T)$ (cf. [10]), and we may choose a sequence $\{\lambda_j\}_{j=1}^{\infty}$ that is dense in $\Gamma$ and has the property that every isolated point of $\Gamma$ is repeated in this sequence infinitely often. It follows from one of the characterizations of $\sigma_{le}(T)$ (cf. [10]) that for every positive integer $j$, there exists a projection $P_j$ in $\mathcal{L}(\mathcal{H})$ of infinite rank and nullity such that $(T - \lambda_j)P_j \in \mathcal{K}$. Moreover it is easy to see that the sequence $\{P_j\}$ can be chosen to consists of mutually orthogonal projections (cf. [2], [5], or [10]). Let $\mathcal{A}$ be the $C^*$-subalgebra of $\mathcal{L}(\mathcal{H})/\mathcal{K}$ generated by $\tilde{T}$, $\tilde{I}$, and the sequence $\{\tilde{P}_j\}_{j=1}^{\infty}$, and let $\rho$ be a faithful *-representation of $\mathcal{A}$ on some separable Hilbert space. Then, since $(\rho(\tilde{T}) - \lambda_j)\rho(\tilde{P}_j) = 0$ for each $j$, it follows that $\rho(\tilde{T})$ can be written as a matrix

$$\rho(\tilde{T}) = \begin{pmatrix} N & B \\ 0 & A \end{pmatrix}$$

where $N$ is normal, $\sigma(N) = \sigma_e(N) = \Gamma$, and $\sigma(A) \subset \sigma_e(T)$. Using the results on closures of similarity orbits of normal operators from [9] (see also [4]), we may assert the existence of a normal operator $M$ satisfying $\sigma(M) = \sigma_e(M) = \overline{G}$ and a sequence $\{S_k\}_{k=1}^{\infty}$ of invertible operators such that $\|S_k^{-1}NS_k - M\| < 1/k$. If we define the sequence $\{W_k\}_{k=1}^{\infty}$ of invertible operators by

$$W_k = \begin{pmatrix} k\|S_k^{-1}\|S_k & 0 \\ 0 & I \end{pmatrix}$$

so that

$$W_k^{-1}\,\rho(\tilde{T})W_k = \begin{pmatrix} S_k^{-1}\,NS_k & (k\|S_k^{-1}\|)^{-1}S_k^{-1}\,B \\ 0 & A \end{pmatrix}$$

then, as is well known, the operators

$$T'' = T \oplus \rho(\tilde{T}) \oplus \rho(\tilde{T}) \oplus \cdots$$

and

$$T''' = T \oplus W_1^{-1}\,\rho(\tilde{T})W_1 \oplus W_2^{-1}\,\rho(\tilde{T})W_2 \oplus \cdots$$

are quasisimilar. Moreover, it follows from Theorem 1.3 of [13] that there exists an operator $T'$ in $\mathcal{O}_u(T)^-$ that is unitarily equivalent to $T''$, and we take $R$ to be any operator in $\mathcal{L}(\mathcal{H})$ that is unitarily equivalent to $T'''$. Thus $T'$ and $R$ are quasisimilar, and to complete the proof of the theorem it suffices to show that $T'''$ is biquasitriangular and that $\sigma_e(T''') = \sigma_e(T) \cup G$, $\sigma(T''') = \sigma(T)$. To establish the first assertion, we define for each positive integer $n$,

$$F_n = T \oplus \left(\sum_{k=1}^{n} \oplus W_k^{-1}\rho(\tilde{T})W_k\right) \oplus \begin{pmatrix} M & 0 \\ 0 & A \end{pmatrix} \oplus \begin{pmatrix} M & 0 \\ 0 & A \end{pmatrix} \oplus \cdots .$$

Clearly $\|T''' - F_n\| < (1/n)(1 + \|B\|)$, and since $M$ is normal and $\sigma_e(M) = \overline{G}$, it is easy to see that the essential spectrum of

$$Q_n = T \oplus \left(\sum_{k=1}^{n} \oplus W_k^{-1} \rho(\tilde{T})W_k\right) \oplus M \oplus M \oplus \cdots$$

possesses no pseudoholes or holes corresponding to nonzero integers. Thus by the main theorem of [2, IV], each $Q_n$ is biquasitriangular, and since $\sigma(A) \subset \sigma_e(T)$, each

$$F_n = Q_n \oplus A \oplus A \oplus \cdots$$

is biquasitriangular for the same reason. Thus $T'''$ is also biquasitriangular. Moreover, since for each $n$, $\sigma_e(F_n) = \sigma_e(T) \cup G = \omega(T)$, it follows from the upper semi-continuity of the essential spectrum that $\sigma_e(T''') \supset \omega(T)$. But on the other hand, if $\lambda \notin \sigma_e(T) \cup G$, then, since $\sigma(\rho(\tilde{T})) = \sigma_e(T)$, we know that for every positive integer $k$, $\lambda \notin \sigma(W_k^{-1}\rho(\tilde{T})W_k)$. Furthermore, it is obvious that $\lambda \notin (M \oplus A)$. Thus, from the equation

$$\lim_{k\to\infty} \|(W_k^{-1} \rho(\tilde{T})W_k - \lambda) - ((M \oplus A) - \lambda)\| = 0 ,$$

we conclude that

$$\lim_{k\to\infty} \| (W_k^{-1}\rho(\tilde{T})W_k - \lambda)^{-1} - ((M \oplus A) - \lambda)^{-1}\| = 0$$

from the continuity of the inverse mapping, and this last equation implies, in particular, that

$$\sup_k \| (W_k^{-1}\rho(\tilde{T})W_k - \lambda)^{-1}\| < +\infty .$$

Hence $\lambda \notin \sigma_e(T''')$, and thus $\sigma_e(T''') = \sigma_e(T) \cup G = \omega(T)$. Reasoning similarly, we conclude that $\sigma(T''') = \sigma(T)$, and thus the proof is complete.

COROLLARY 1.3. If $T$ is an arbitrary operator in $\mathcal{L}(\mathcal{H})$ and $\varepsilon > 0$ is given, then there exists an operator $T_0$ such that $\|T - T_0\| < \varepsilon$, $T - T_0 \in \mathcal{K}(\mathcal{H})$, and $T_0$ is quasisimilar to a biquasitriangular operator.

PROOF. It follows from [13] that if $T \in \mathcal{O}_u(T')^-$, then there exists a sequence $\{U_n\}$ of unitary operators such that $\|U_n^*T'U_n - T\| \to 0$ and such that $U_n^*T'U_n - T \in \mathcal{K}(\mathcal{H})$ for every $n$.

## REFERENCES


[1] C. Apostol, C. Foiaş, and C. Pearcy, Quasiaffine transforms of compact perturbations of normal operators. to appear.

[2] C. Apostol, C. Foiaş, and D. Voiculescu, Some results on non-quasitriangular operators II. Rev. Roum. Math. Pures et Appl. 18 (1973), 159-181; III ibidem, 18(1973), 309-324; IV ibidem, 18(1973), 487-514.

[3] C. Apostol, C. Pearcy, and N. Salinas, Spectra of compact perturbations of operators. Indiana Math. J., 26(1977), 345-350.

[4] C. Apostol and D. Voiculescu, The closure of the similarity orbit of a normal operator. to appear.

[5] R.G. Douglas and C. Pearcy, Invariant subspaces of non-quasitriangular operators. Proc. Conf. Operator Theory, Springer-Verlag, Lecture Notes in Mathematics No. 345, 13-57.

[6] C. Foiaş, C. Pearcy, and D. Voiculescu, The staircase representation of biquasitriangular operators. Mich. Math. J., 22(1975), 343-352.

[7] P. R. Halmos, Quasitriangular operators. Acta Sci. Math. (Szeged), 29(1968), 283-293.

[8] T. Hoover, Hyperinvariant subspaces for n-normal operators. Acta Sci. Math. (Szeged), 32(1971), 109-119.

[9] D. A. Herrero, Closure of similarity orbits of Hilbert space operators II: Normal operators. J. London Math. Soc. (2), 13(1976), 299-316.

[10] C. Pearcy, Some recent developments in operator theory. CBMS Regional Conference Series in Mathematics, to appear.

[11] B.Sz.-Nagy and C. Foiaş, Harmonic analysis of operators on Hilbert space. North-Holland-Akademiai Kiado, (Amsterdam-London-Budapest), 1970.

[12] B.Sz.-Nagy and C. Foiaş, Modèle de Jordan pour une classe d'opérateurs de l'espace de Hilbert. Acta Sci. Math., 31(1970), 91-115.

[13] D. Voiculescu, A noncommutative Weyl-von Neumann theorem Rev. Roum. Math. Pures et Appl., 21(1976), 97-113.

# APPLICATIONS OF TRANSFERENCE: THE $L^p$ VERSION OF von NEUMANN'S INEQUALITY AND THE LITTLEWOOD-PALEY-STEIN THEORY

R. R. Coifman and R. Rochberg and Guido Weiss[1]
Department of Mathematics
Washington University
St. Louis, Missouri

The following extension of von Neumann's inequality is discussed:

$$\|\sum_{0}^{N} a_k T^k\|_p \leq N_p\{a_k\} ,$$

where $T$ is a subpositive contraction on $L^p(X)$ and $N_p\{a_k\}$ is the $\ell^p$ operator norm of convolution with the sequence $\{a_k\}$ on $\mathbb{Z}$. This result is then used to study operators of the form $\int_0^\infty a(t)P_t dt$ where $P_t$ is a subpositive contraction semigroup on $L^p$. The use of Hilbert space valued kernels a enable us to obtain a new approach to some of Stein's Littlewood-Paley estimates.

The basic tools used are the method of transference and the result of Akcoglu that positive contractions on $L^p$ spaces have isometric dilations.

§1. von Neumann's Inequality. Suppose $(\mathfrak{M},\mu)$ is a measure space and $R$ a (linear) operator on $L^2(\mathfrak{M},\mu)$ with operator norm $\|R\|^{(2)} \leqq 1$ (that is, $R$ is a contraction). The von Neumann's inequality asserts that if $q(\lambda) = a_0 + a_1\lambda + \cdots + a_N\lambda^N$ is a polynomial then

$$\|q(R)\|^{(2)} \leqq \max_{|\lambda|\leqq 1} |q(\lambda)| \tag{1.1}$$

(see [9]). We would like to give an interpretation of this inequality that will enable us to formulate an extension of this result. Let us associate with $q$ the function $k$ defined on the integers $\mathbb{Z}$ by letting $k(j) = a_j$

---

(1) Research by R. R. Coifman and Guido Weiss partially supported by N.S.F. Grant #MCS75-02411 A02. Research by R. Rochberg was partially supported by N.S.F. Grant # MCS76-05789.

for $0 \leqq j \leqq N$ and $k(j) = 0$ otherwise. We can regard $k$ as an element of $\ell^1(\mathbb{Z})$. If $c = \{c_j\} \in \ell^2(\mathbb{Z})$ the convolution operator mapping $c$ onto the sequence $k * c$ whose $j^{th}$ term is

(1.2) $$(k * c)_j = \sum_{\ell=-\infty}^{\infty} k(\ell) c_{j-\ell} = \sum_{\ell=0}^{N} a_\ell c_{j-\ell}$$

is a bounded operator on $\ell^2(\mathbb{Z})$ with operator norm equal to $\max\{|q(e^{i\theta})| : -\pi \leqq \theta < \pi\} = \max\{|q(\lambda)| : |\lambda| \leqq 1\}$. Let $N_p(k)$ denote the norm of the convolution operator $c \to k * c$ acting on $\ell^p(\mathbb{Z})$, $1 \leqq p$. Inequality (1.1), then, can be restated in the form

(1.3) $$\|q(R)\|^{(2)} \leqq N_2(k) .$$

Now suppose $R$ is a contraction operator on $L^p(\mathfrak{M}, \mu)$ (i.e. its operator norm $\|R\|^{(p)}$ is not greater than 1). In view of what we just said it is natural to ask whether

(1.4) $$\|\sum_{\ell=0}^{N} a_\ell R^\ell\|^{(p)} = \|q(R)\|^{(p)} \leqq N_p(k)$$

for values of $p$ other than 2. When $p = 1$ it is easily seen that

$N_1(k) = \sum_{\ell=0}^{N} |a_\ell|$ and, thus, (1.4) is true. We do not know whether (1.4) holds for all contractions when $1 < p < 2$ or $2 < p$. We can, however, establish this extension of von Neumann's inequality if we assume that $R$ is a <u>subpositive contraction</u>. This notion is defined in terms of <u>positive</u> (or <u>positivity preserving</u>) operators (that is, operators that map non-negative functions into non-negative functions): $R$ is a subpositive contraction provided there exists a positive contraction $P$ such that $P + \Re e\{e^{i\theta} R\}$ are positivity preserving for all $\theta$. (If $R$ is an operator on $L^p(\mathfrak{M})$ we define $\bar{R}$ by letting $\bar{R}f = \overline{R\bar{f}}$ ; then the <u>real part of</u> $R$, $\Re e\{R\}$, is the operator $\frac{1}{2}(R + \bar{R})$). Note that $R$ must be a contraction and any positive contraction is automatically subpositive. If, say, $L^p(\mathfrak{M})$ is the n-dimensional space of all $x = (x_1, x_2, \ldots, x_n) \in \mathbb{C}^n$ with norm

$\|x\|_p = \left(\sum_{j=1}^{n} |x_j|^p\right)^{1/p}$ and $R$ is given by the $n \times n$ matrix $(R_{ij})$ then $R$ is a subpositive contraction if and only if $(|R_{ij}|)$ represents a contraction operator. We shall show the following result:

THEOREM (1.5). Let $R$ be a subpositive contraction on $L^p(\mathfrak{M})$ for some $p \geqq 1$; then

$$\| \sum_{j=0}^{N} a_j R^j f \|_{L^p(\mathfrak{M})} \leqq N_p(k) \|f\|_{L^p(\mathfrak{M})} .$$

In a monograph [5] that is scheduled to be published shortly one can find a brief discussion on how a technique called the "transference method" can be used in order to extend the von Neumann inequality to positive contraction operators acting on $L^p$ spaces. It has just come to our attention that a very similar extension was announced by V. V. Peller [6] at about the same time the subject of this monograph was being presented.(2) We learned from Peller that the question we posed above (see (1.4)) was raised by Macaev some 10 years ago. We would like to take this opportunity to develop our discussion of the von Neumann inequality further and to indicate the relation between our result and the result of Peller. Moreover, we shall show how the transference method can be extended and applied to obtain certain estimates involving Littlewood-Paley functions associated with certain diffusion semi-groups. This approach offers an alternative treatment (not involving the Calderòn-Zygmund theory for martingales) of the Littlewood-Paley theory that was developed by E. M. Stein [8].

§2. The transference method. In the monograph [5] cited above "transference" was associated with a general amenable group. Since we shall be dealing with a situation that involves only the group of integers we shall describe this method and its extensions only in this special case. The reader can verify that our arguments are valid for the more general situation.

Suppose $k$ is a function defined on $\mathbb{Z}$ having compact support; say $k(j) = 0$ if $|j| > m \geqq 0$. As before, we let $N_p(k)$ denote the operator

(2) This subject was presented by the last named author in a CBMS regional conference at the University of Nebraska in June 1976.

norm of the convolution operator induced by $k$ on $\ell^p(\mathbb{Z})$. Suppose $(\mathfrak{M},\mu)$ is a measure space and $R$ a linear operator on $L^p(\mathfrak{M},\mu)$ which is invertible and such that $R^j$, $j = 0,\pm 1,\pm 2,\dots$ have operator norms bounded by $c > 0$. Let

$$(Hf)(x) = \sum_{\ell=-\infty}^{\infty} k(\ell)(R^\ell f)(x) = \sum_{|\ell|\leq m} k(\ell)(R^\ell f)(x)$$

for $f \in L^p(\mathfrak{M},\mu)$. $H$ is obviously a bounded operator on $L^p(\mathfrak{M},\mu)$ and its operator norm is dominated by $c\|k\|_{\ell^1(\mathbb{Z})} = c\sum_{j=-m}^{m}|k(j)|$. The essential feature of the transference method is that the operator norm of $H$ is dominated by $c^2N_p(k)$ (it is easy to show, by examples, that the latter estimate is much better than the former). Let us establish this inequality:

$$\left(\int_{\mathfrak{M}} |(Hf)(x)|^p d\mu(x)\right)^{1/p} \leqq c^2N_p(k)\left(\int_{\mathfrak{M}} |f(x)|^p d\mu(x)\right)^{1/p}. \tag{2.1}$$

We assumed that $\|R^jf\|_{L^p(\mathfrak{M})} \leqq c\|f\|_{L^p(\mathfrak{M})}$. Applying this inequality to $R^{-j}f$ we obtain

$$\|f\|_{L^p(\mathfrak{M})} \leqq c\|R^{-j}f\|_{L^p(\mathfrak{M})} \tag{2.2}$$

for $j = 0,\pm 1,\pm 2,\dots$ . Thus,

$$\int_{\mathfrak{M}} |(Hf)(x)|^p d\mu(x) = \int_{\mathfrak{M}} \Big|\sum_{|\ell|\leqq m} k(\ell)(R^\ell f)(x)\Big|^p d\mu(x) \leqq$$

$$\int_{\mathfrak{M}} c^p\Big|R^{-j}\sum_{|\ell|\leqq m} k(\ell)(R^\ell f)(x)\Big|^p d\mu(x) \leqq$$

$$\frac{c^p}{2M+1}\int_{\mathfrak{M}} \sum_{j=-M}^{M} \Big|\sum_{|\ell|\leqq m} k(\ell)(R^{\ell-j}f)(x)\Big|^p d\mu(x).$$

If $\chi$ is the characteristic function of $\{n \in \mathbb{Z}: -m-M \leqq n \leqq m+M\}$ we have shown:

$$\|Hf\|^p_{L^p(\mathfrak{M})} \leqq \frac{c^p}{2M+1}\int_{\mathfrak{M}} d\mu(x) \sum_{j=-M}^{M} \Big| \sum_{|\ell|\leqq m} k(\ell)(R^{\ell-j}f)(x)\chi(\ell-j)\Big|^p .$$

But

$$\sum_{j=-\infty}^{\infty} \Big| \sum_{|\ell|\leqq m} k(\ell)(R^{\ell-j}f)(x)\chi(\ell-j)\Big|^p \leqq (N_p(k))^p \sum_{j=-\infty}^{\infty} |\chi(j)(R^j f)(x)|^p .$$

Consequently,

$$\|Hf\|^p_{L^p(\mathfrak{M})} \leqq \frac{(N_p(k)c)^p}{2M+1} \sum_{|j|\leqq m+M} \int_{\mathfrak{M}} |(R^j f)(x)|^p d\mu(x)$$

$$\leqq \frac{(N_p(k)c)^p}{2M+1} (2(m+M)+1)c^p \|f\|^p_{L^p(\mathfrak{M})} .$$

Letting $M \to \infty$ we obtain (2.1).(3)

Now let us return to von Neumann's inequaltiy. We are faced with a very similar situation: inequality (1.4) can be expressed in the form (2.1) with $k$ defined as in §1 (see (1.2)) and $c = 1$. Unfortunately we do not necessarily have inequality (2.2) for $j \geqq 1$. There is, however, a method that allows us to apply the argument used to establish (2.1) when $R$ is a subpositive contraction. Let us first, however, consider the case when $R$ is a positive contraction. Akcoglu and Sucheston [2] have obtained the following result for such operators:

THEOREM (2.3). *Let* $R : L^p(\mathfrak{M}) \to L^p(\mathfrak{M})$ *be a positive contraction. There exists another* $L^p$ *space,* $L^p(\mathfrak{N},\sigma)$, *and a positive invertible isometry* $U : L^p(\mathfrak{N},\sigma) \to L^p(\mathfrak{N},\sigma)$ *such that* $DR^n = PU^nD$ *for all* $n = 0,1,2,\ldots$, *where* $D : L^p(\mathfrak{M}) \to L^p(\mathfrak{N})$ *is a positive isometric imbedding of* $L^p(\mathfrak{M})$ *into* $L^p(\mathfrak{N})$ *and* $P : L^p(\mathfrak{N}) \to L^p(\mathfrak{N})$ *is a positive idempotent contraction.*

Thus, using this theorem we have:

$$\int_{\mathfrak{M}} \Big|\sum_{\ell=0}^{N} a_\ell R^\ell f\Big|^p d\mu = \int_{\mathfrak{N}} \Big|D\sum_{\ell=0}^{N} a_\ell R^\ell f\Big|^p d\sigma = \int_{\mathfrak{N}} \Big|P\sum_{\ell=0}^{N} a_\ell U^\ell Df\Big|^p d\sigma \leqq \int_{\mathfrak{N}} \Big|\sum_{\ell=0}^{N} a_\ell U^\ell Df\Big|^p d\sigma .$$

---

(3) The proof we just gave is modeled after a real-line argument of A. P. Calderòn (see [3]).

But now we can apply the transference method since (2.2) is satisfied by $U^j$ for all integers $j$ (with $c = 1$). Thus, the last expression is dominated by

$$[N_p(k)]^p \|Df\|^p_{L^p(\mathfrak{N})} = [N_p(k)]^p \|f\|^p_{L^p(\mathfrak{M})} .$$

We thus have obtained the extension of von Neumann's inequality for positive contractions. It turns out, however, that the Akcoglu-Sucheston result (i.e. theorem (2.3)) can be extended to subpositive contractions. We shall show why this is the case by explaining how the proof of theorem (2.3) can be changed to obtain the more general result. More precisely, we shall indicate what modifications are needed in a proof contained in an earlier paper by Akcoglu [1].

The first step is to reduce the problem to the case of a finite dimensional $L^p$-space $\ell^p$ which consists of vectors $s = (s_1, s_2, \dots, s_n) \in \mathbb{C}^n$ having norm $\|s\|_p = (\sum_i |s_i|^p m_i)^{1/p}$, where $m_1, m_2, \dots, m_n$ are fixed positive real numbers. The subpositive operator $R$ is then determined by a matrix $(R_{ij})$ which gives us the coordinates $(Rs)_j$ of $Rs$ by the equality $(Rs)_j = \sum_i R_{ij} s_i$. Let $T_{ij} = |R_{ij}|$ and define $\epsilon_{ij}$ by the equations

$$R_{ij} = \epsilon_{ij} T_{ij} .$$

It follows that $(T_{ij})$ is the matrix of a positive contraction operator $T$ and the argument presented by Akcoglu can be applied to it. In fact, we have set up the same notation used by him in the second section of his paper [1] (he also assumes $T_{ij} > 0$ and that the operator norm of $T$ equals 1; we shall also make these assumptions and will show later how they can be removed).

Akcoglu constructs a measure space $(Z, \mathfrak{F}, \mu)$ and an invertible transformation $\tau : Z \to Z$. The invertible isometry in question is then the composition of two operators: the change of variables $z \to \tau^{-1}(z)$ and the multiplication operator induced by the Jacobian of this transformation. More precisely, the space $Z$ is a union of $n$ rectangles $E_1, E_2, \dots, E_n$ in the plane of the form $E_j = I_j \times J_j$ where the $I_j$'s are disjoint intervals on the real line of length $m_j$ and the $J_j$'s are disjoint intervals on the real line of length 1. Each of these rectangles are then partitioned into subrectangles in two ways: $E_i = U_j R_{ij}$ and $E_j = U_i S_{ij}$ (these decompositions are obtained in terms of the numbers $T_{ij}$, $m_i$ and $m_j$). The transformation $\tau$ restricted to $R_{ij}$ maps onto $S_{ij}$, linearly in each variable; the multiplying factor we mentioned above is given by $\sum_{i,j}\left[\frac{\mu(R_{ij})}{\mu(S_{ij})}\right]^{1/p}\chi_{S_{ij}}$ (where $\chi_{S_{ij}}$ is the characteristic function of $S_{ij}$).

We claim that if we make the simple change of using the multiplying factor

$$\eta = \sum_{i,j}\left[\frac{\mu(R_{ij})}{\mu(S_{ij})}\right]^{1/p}\epsilon_{ij}\chi_{S_{ij}} ,$$

instead of the one used by Akcoglu then, the same argument he used shows that the operator

$$(Uf)(z) = \eta(z)f(\tau^{-1}z)$$

is an invertible isometry of $L^p(Z)$ for which we have

$$PU^nD = DR^n, \tag{2.4}$$

for $n = 0,1,2,\ldots,$ where $P$ is the conditional expectation operator mapping $f \in L^p(Z)$ into

$$Pf = \sum_{i=1}^{n} \chi_{E_i} \frac{1}{m_i}\int_{E_i} f d\mu$$

and $D: \ell^p \to L^p(Z)$ is defined by $Ds = \sum_{j=1}^{n} s_j \chi_{E_j}$ for $s = (s_1, s_2, \ldots, s_n) \in \ell^p$.

One can reduce our problem (obtaining von Neumann's inequality) to this finite dimensional case by making use of an approximation argument that can also be found in Akcoglu's paper (see lemma (3.1) in [1]). Alternatively, one can obtain the extension to subpositive contractions of the Akcoglu-Sucheston result (theorem (2.3)) from the finite dimensional case we just discussed by making use of their limit argument (see [2]).

When $p \neq 2$ this result gives us a characterization of subpositive contractions. An invertible isometry of $L^p$ is a composition of a transformation of the points of the underlying space and a multiplication by a fixed function (see the last result in Royden's book [7])(4); thus, the operator U is subpositive and equality (2.4) with n = 1, together with the positivity of P and D, implies that R must be subpositive.

We assumed that the operator norm $\|T\|^{(p)}$ of T was equal to 1. If $\|T\|^{(p)} < 1$, let $0 < c < 1$ be such that $\|c^{-1}T\|^{(p)} = 1$. Let us write

$$q(T) = \sum_{j=0}^{N} a_j c^j (c^{-1}T)^j = \int_{-\pi}^{\pi} P_c(\varphi) \sum_{j=0}^{N} a_j e^{-ij\varphi}(c^{-1}T)^j d\varphi,$$

where

$$P_c(\varphi) = \frac{1}{2\pi} \frac{1-c^2}{1-2c\cos\varphi + c^2}$$

is the Poisson kernel. If $b = \{\ldots, b_{-1}, b_0, b_1, \ldots\}$ is a doubly infinite sequence let $b_\varphi = \{e^{-ij\varphi}b_j\}$. A trivial calculation shows that $k_\varphi * b = [k * b_{-\varphi}]_\varphi$. It follows that $N_p(k_\varphi) \leqq N_p(k)$. Thus,

$$\|q(T)\|^{(p)} \leqq \int_{-\pi}^{\pi} P_c(\varphi) \Big\| \sum_{j=0}^{N} a_j e^{-ij\varphi}(c^{-1}T)^j \Big\|^{(p)} d\varphi$$

$$\leqq \int_{-\pi}^{\pi} P_c(\varphi) N_p(k_\varphi) d\varphi \leqq \int_{-\pi}^{\pi} P_c(\varphi) N_p(k) d\varphi$$

$$= N_p(k).$$

This shows that von Neumann's inequality holds for subpositive contractions having norm strictly less than 1.

We also assumed that $T_{ij} > 0$. But we can apply our argument to the operator whose matrix coefficients are $\tilde{T}_{ij} = cT_{ij} + \varepsilon$, for c close (but less than) to 1 and (small) $\varepsilon > 0$. Obtaining our estimate for the

---

(4) The underlying space there is [0,1]. It is not hard to extend this result to more general situations.

corresponding operator $\tilde{T}$ and then letting $c \to 1$ and $\epsilon \to 0$ we obtain our result.

We mentioned earlier that Peller also obtained this extension to $L^p$ of the von-Neumann inequality for a class of contraction operators. He considered contractions satisfying the property: if $f \cdot g = 0$ then $Rf \cdot Rg = 0$ (and certain limits of such contractions). He called these operators <u>disjoint contractions</u>. It is not hard to see that a disjoint contraction is subpositive. To see this choose a set $A$ of finite measure and let $\Phi(A)$ be the support of $R\chi_A$. For $x \in \Phi(A)$ let

$$\alpha_A(x) = \alpha_A(x)\chi_{\Phi(A)} = (R\chi_A)(x) .$$

We now observe that $\alpha_A(x)$ is independent of $A$. Suppose $B$ is another set of finite measure and $x \in \Phi(A) \cap \Phi(B)$. Since neither $(R\chi_A)(x)$ nor $(R\chi_B)(x)$ is 0 and

$$(R\chi_A)(x) - (R\chi_{A-A\cap B})(x) = (R\chi_{A\cap B})(x) = (R\chi_B)(x) - (R\chi_{B-A\cap B})(x)$$

we conclude $(R\chi_{A\cap B})(x) \neq 0$ (otherwise neither $(R\chi_{A-A\cap B})(x)$ nor $(R\chi_{B-A\cap B})(x)$ is 0, which cannot be because of disjointness). Thus,

$$\alpha_A(x) = (R\chi_A)(x) = (R\chi_{A\cap B})(x) = (R\chi_B)(x) = \alpha_B(x) .$$

Now suppose $f = \sum_{j=1}^{n} \lambda_j \chi_{A_j}$ is a simple function (with the $A_j$'s mutually disjoint). We then have

$$(Rf)(x) = \alpha(x) \sum_{j=1}^{n} \lambda_j \chi_{\Phi(A_j)} .$$

If we define $P$ on simple functions by letting

$$(Pf)(x) = |\alpha(x)| \sum_{j=1}^{n} \lambda_j \chi_{\Phi(A_j)}$$

then $\|Pf\|_p = \|Rf\|_p$. It follows that $P$ has a unique extension to $L^p(\mathfrak{M})$ that is a positive contraction and $P + \Re e\{e^{i\theta}R\}$ is positive for all $\theta$.

§3. The Littlewood-Paley-Stein theory. For $f \in L^p(\mathbb{R})$ the Littlewood-Paley g-function of $f$ is defined to be

(3.1)
$$g(f) = \left(\int_0^\infty \left(y \frac{\partial}{\partial y} P_y f\right)^2 \frac{dy}{y}\right)^{1/2} ,$$

where $P_y f$ is the Poisson integral of $f$

$$(P_y f)(x) = \frac{1}{\pi}\int_{-\infty}^{\infty} \frac{y}{y^2 + w^2} f(x-w)dw .$$

A basic inequality asserts that the operator mapping $f$ into $g(f)$ is a bounded operator on $L^p(\mathbb{R})$, $1 < p < \infty$:

(3.2)
$$\|g(f)\|_p \leqq A_p\|f\|_p .$$

As is well known, this inequality (as well as other properties of the g-function) can be used to study a wide class of convolution operators that are important in analysis. These and similar applications constitute what is known as the Littlewood-Paley theory. E. M. Stein has extended this theory to a very general setting. We shall give a brief description of his theory (see [8]) and show how the transference method can be used to obtain some of his results.

He considers a symmetric diffusion semi-group: a family $\{P_y\}$ of operators on a space $L^p(\mathfrak{M},\mu)$ indexed by the positive reals which, first of all, satisfies the semigroup axiom $P_{y_1+y_2} = P_{y_1}P_{y_2}$, each $P_y$ maps $L^2(\mathfrak{M},\mu)$ into itself and $\lim_{y\to 0}\|P_y f-f\|_2 = 0$. Moreover, each $P_y$ is a positive contraction on $L^p(\mathfrak{M},\mu)$. Stein also assumes that $P_y$ is self-adjoint on $L^2(\mathfrak{M},\mu)$ as well as satisfying another property; neither of these assumptions will be needed by us. For any $f \in L^p(\mathfrak{M},\mu)$ we can then, at least formally, define the g-function of $f, g(f)$, by formula (3.1).

Stein's program for establishing inequality (3.2) in this general context is the following: He considers a family of kernels

$$k_y^{\alpha}(t) = \frac{1}{\Gamma(\alpha)}\, y \frac{\partial}{\partial y}\left[\frac{1}{y}(1 - \frac{t}{y})_+^{\alpha-1}\right]\chi_+(t) ,$$

where $\chi_+$ is the characteristic function of the positive reals, $(1-s)_+$ denotes the positive part of the function (1-s) on $s > 0$ and $\alpha$ is a complex number. He then studies the operator

$$g_\alpha(f) = \left(\int_0^\infty |y \frac{\partial}{\partial y}(M_\alpha^y f)|^2 \frac{dy}{y}\right)^{1/2} ,$$

where

$$M_\alpha^y f = \frac{y^{-\alpha}}{\Gamma(\alpha)} \int_0^y (y-t)^{\alpha-1}(P_t f)dt .$$

When $\alpha = 0$ we obtain the g-function. In order to establish inequality (3.2) in this general setting Stein obtains inequalities

$$\|g_\alpha(f)\|_p \leqq A_{p,\alpha}\|f\|_p \qquad (1 < p < \infty) \tag{3.3}$$

for $p = 2$ and $\alpha = -1,-2,-3,\ldots$ (here the spectral theorem is used and, hence, the self-adjointness assumption for $P_y$ is used). In order to obtain estimates (3.3) for other values of $p$ (near 1 and for $\Re e\alpha > 1$) he develops the Calderòn-Zygmund singular integral theory for martingales. The desired inequality is then derived by applying the technique of interpolation of analytic families of linear operators. We refer the reader to Stein's book [8] for the details of this program.

Our purpose here is to show that the estimates for the cases $p > 1$ and $\Re e\, \alpha > 1$ can be obtained by transference. Moreover, we need only assume that $P_y$ is a subpositive contraction for each y. Thus, we offer an alternative to the martingale approach we described above that is applicable to a larger class of semigroups. If $L^2$ estimates could be obtained for some such semigroups (not necessarily self-adjoint) one would obtain results that are more general than those found in [8].

Toward this end we first observe that inequality (3.3) can be interpreted as an inequality expressing the boundedness of a linear operator involving functions whose values belong to the Hilbert space $H = L^2(\mathbb{R}^+, \frac{dy}{y})$; for $\varphi \in H$ the norm of $\varphi$ has the form

$$\|\varphi\| = \left(\int_0^\infty |\varphi(y)|^2 \frac{dy}{y}\right)^{1/2} .$$

More precisely, if $x \in \mathfrak{M}$

$$(g_\alpha f)(x) = \left(\int_0^\infty \left| \int_0^\infty k_y^\alpha(t)(P_t f)(x)dt\right|^2 \frac{dy}{y}\right)^{1/2} .$$

Thus, if $k^\alpha$ denotes the function on $\mathbb{R}$ with values that are functions of $y \in \mathbb{R}^+$ defined by $[k^\alpha(t)](y) = k_y^\alpha(t)$, for $t \in \mathbb{R}$, then

$$(g_\alpha f)(x) = \left\| \int_0^\infty k^\alpha(t)(P_t f)(x)dt\right\| .$$

Inequality (3.3), therefore, has the form

$$\text{(3.4)} \qquad \left(\int_{\mathfrak{M}} \left\| \int_0^\infty k^\alpha(t)(P_t f)(x)dt\right\|^p d\mu(x)\right)^{1/p} \leqq A_{p,\alpha}\|f\|_{L^p(\mathfrak{M},\mu)} .$$

The second observation is that the transference result we obtained for the non-negative integers is also valid for the non-negative reals:

THEOREM (3.5). Let $P_y$ be a continuous one-parameter semi-group of subpositive contractions on $L^p(\mathfrak{M},\mu)$. Then

$$\left\| \int_0^\infty k(y)P_y f \, dy\right\|_{L^p(\mathfrak{M})} \leqq N_p(k)\|f\|_{L^p(\mathfrak{M})} ,$$

where $k$ has compact support in $\mathbb{R}^+$ and is integrable.(5)

The derivation of this result from its discrete analog is given in [5] (see Corollary (4.17), where the operators $P_y$ are assumed to be positive; the same argument applies to subpositive contractions).

---

(5) Here $N_p(k)$ is the operator norm of the convolution operator with kernel $k$ acting on $L^p(\mathbb{R})$.

Inequality (3.4) has the form of the one in theorem (3.5). There is a difference, however, since in (3.4) the Hilbert space norm $\|\ \|$ is used since we are dealing with a vector valued kernel. In order to apply transference methods to this more general situation we can use the following result:

(3.6) <u>The Hilbert space valued convolution operator on</u> $L^p(\mathbb{R})$ <u>having kernel</u> $k^\alpha$ <u>is bounded.</u>

This follows from general results about Calderòn-Zygmund singular integrals (see pg. 149 of [ 4 ]) and the easily established relations

$$\int_{-\infty}^{\infty} |k_y^\alpha(x-t) - k_y^\alpha(x)|\,dx \leqq c_\alpha \left|\frac{t}{y}\right|^{\alpha-1}, \quad \int_{-\infty}^{\infty} k_y(t)\,dt = 0.$$

Next, suppose P is a bounded linear operator on $L^p(\mathfrak{M},\mu)$ and H is a Hilbert space. Let $L^p(\mathfrak{M},\mu;H) = L^p(\mathfrak{M};H)$ be the space of all H-valued measurable functions F such that

$$\|F\|_{L^p(\mathfrak{M};H)} = \left(\int_{\mathfrak{M}} \|F\|^p d\mu\right)^{1/p} < \infty .$$

(3.7) <u>There exists a unique linear operator</u> $P^\#$ <u>on</u> $L^p(\mathfrak{M},\mu;H)$ <u>having the same norm as</u> P <u>such that</u> $(P^\# F,v) = P(F,v)$ <u>for all</u> $v \in H$ <u>and</u> $F \in L^p(\mathfrak{M};H)$ (here $(w,v)$ denotes the inner product of H).

If $F \in L^p(\mathfrak{M};H)$ and $\{v_j\}$ is an orthonormal basis of H then $F(x) = \sum f_j(x)v_j$. $P^\#$ is defined by

$$P^\# F = \sum (Pf_j)v_j .$$

That the operator norm of $P^\#$ is the same as that of P is a result of Zygmund (see (2.10) on pgs. 224-5 of Vol. II of [10]). The uniqueness and the relation $(P^\# F,v) = P(F,v)$ are obvious.

Now, if $H = L^2(\mathbb{R}^+, \frac{dy}{y})$ it follows easily that

$$P_s^{\#}\int_0^\infty k^\alpha(t)(P_t f)(x)dt = \int_0^\infty k^\alpha(t)(P_s P_t f)(x)dt$$

(3.8)

$$= \int_0^\infty k^\alpha(t)(P_{s+t} f)(x)dt \ .$$

If $P_y$ is the restriction to $\mathbb{R}^+$ of a one parameter group of isometries, relation (3.8) and (3.7) give us an analog of inequality (2.2) and the rest of the transference argument goes through and we obtain (3.4). If we are dealing with only a semigroup of subpositive contraction operators we can then reduce the problem to the one involving a group of isometries by the methods described in §2 and in [5].

## REFERENCES

[1] Akcoglu, M. A., A pointwise ergodic theorem in $L_p$-spaces. Canad. J. Math., Vol XXVII, (1975), 1075-1082.

[2] Akcoglu, M. A. and Sucheston, L., Dilations of positive contractions on $L_p$-spaces. Canad. Math. Bulletin, (to appear).

[3] Calderòn, A.P., Ergodic theory and translation-invariant operators. Proc. Nat. Acad. Sci. U.S.A. 71 (1974), 3911-3912.

[4] Coifman, R. R. and Weiss, Guido, Analyse Harmonique Non-commutative sur Certains Espaces Homogenes. Lecture Notes in Math. Vol. 242, Springer-Verlag, Berlin and New York, 1971.

[5] Coifman, R. R. and Weiss, Guido, Transference Methods in Analysis CBMS regional conference series in mathematics, No. 31, Am. Math. Soc. (1977).

[6] Peller, V. V., An analog of J. von Neumann's inequality for the space $L_p$. Soviet Math. Dokl. 17 (1976), AMS transl. 1594-98.

[7] Royden, H. L., Real Analysis. MacMillan Co., 2nd Ed. New York (1968).

[8] Stein, E. M., Topics in Harmonic Analysis Related to the Littlewood-Paley Theory. Ann. of Math. Studies, 63, Princeton Univ. Press (1970), Princeton, N.J.

[9] Sz.-Nagy, B. and Foiaş, C., Harmonic Analysis of Operators on Hilbert Spaces. English transl., North-Holland, Amsterdam; American Elsevier, New York; Akadémiai Kiadó, Budapest, 1970 .

[10] Zygmund, A., Trigonometric Series. Vols. I, II, English transl., 2nd Ed., Cambridge Univ. Press, London and New York, 1968 .

# II
# Topics in Functional Analysis

# AN OUTLINE OF VECTOR GRAPHS AND CONDITIONAL BANACH SPACES

P. Masani
Department of Mathematics
University of Pittsburgh
Pittsburgh

Abstract. We show that in several analytic problems our concern is with a non-linear manifold $\mathfrak{M}$ of a vector space $\mathfrak{X}$, which is homogeneous and nearly additive in that for $x,y \in \mathfrak{M}$, we have $x+y$ in $\mathfrak{M}$ provided that x and y are in a relation c. We are thus led to the study of the graph $(\mathfrak{X},c)$. We outline the fundamentals of the theory of such graphs.

## 1. Introduction

In view of space limitations we shall present only the bare outlines of the subject of vector-graphs, our aim being to give the reader a glimpse of this new and almost unexplored territory. A more detailed study, including proofs, will be presented elsewhere.

We begin by giving four examples to motivate the concept of vector-graph.

1.1 EXAMPLE. Let $\mathfrak{X} \underset{d}{=} CL(\mathcal{H},\mathcal{H})$ be the Banach algebra of all continuous linear operators on $\mathcal{H}$ to $\mathcal{H}$, where $\mathcal{H}$ is any Hilbert space over the field $\mathbb{F}$.[1] An especially important subset of $\mathfrak{X}$ is the family

$$\mathfrak{N} \underset{d}{=} \{A: A \in \mathfrak{X} \ \& \ AA^* = A^*A\}$$

of normal operators. $\mathfrak{N}$ is closed under multiplication by scalars but not under addition, and is not therefore a linear manifold. Now let

$$c \underset{d}{=} \{(A;B) \ A,B \in \mathfrak{X} \ \& \ AB^* = B^*A\}.$$

It is easily seen that the relation c is symmetric and that [2]

---

[1] The symbol $\mathbb{F}$ will always refer to the fields $\mathbb{R}$ or $\mathbb{C}$.

[2] We shall often write "B c A" instead of "$(A;B) \in c$".

$$A, B \in \mathcal{N} \;\&\; A \, c \, B \Rightarrow A+B \in \mathcal{N}.$$

We may therefore say that $\mathcal{N}$ is conditionally-linear or c-linear. In fact, $\mathcal{N}$ is the set over which the relation c is reflexive: $A \in \mathcal{N} \Leftrightarrow A \, c \, A$. If our interest is in the set $\mathcal{N}$, then it is natural to consider the space $\mathcal{X}$ in conjunction with the relation c. But such a combination is a graph in the modern sense, cf. Berge [1: p.6]. Since $\mathcal{X}$ is a Banach space, it is natural to call $(\mathcal{X}, c)$ a vector graph or more specifically a Banach graph.

Hitherto only finite or denumerable graphs have been considered. Our graphs are of course of higher cardinality, and our interests are different from those of traditional graph theorists.

1.2 EXAMPLE.[3] Let $\forall f, g \in L_2^{loc}(\mathbb{R})$ and $\forall T \in \mathbb{R}_+$,

$$(f,g)_T = \frac{1}{2T} \int_{-T}^{T} f(t)\overline{g(t)}\,dt,$$

$$|f|_T \underset{d}{=} \sqrt{(f,f)_T}, \qquad \|f\| \underset{d}{=} \overline{\lim_{n\to\infty}}\, |f|_T.$$

Then as was shown by Marcinkiewicz [5] and Bohr & Folner [2] the space

$$\mathcal{X} \underset{d}{=} \{f\colon f \in L_2^{loc}(\mathbb{R}) \;\&\; \|f\| < \infty\}$$

is a Banach space over $\mathbb{F}$ under the norm $\|\cdot\|$, when functions $f, g \in \mathcal{X}$ such that $\|f-g\| = 0$ are identified. An especially important subclass of $\mathcal{X}$ is

$$\mathcal{P} \underset{d}{=} \{f\colon f \in \mathcal{X} \;\&\; \lim_{T\to\infty} (f,f)_T \text{ exists}\}.$$

$\mathcal{P}$ is the class of functions which according to Wiener [14] represent the optical disturbances at fixed points due to sunlight. For $f \in \mathcal{P}$ Wiener called $\|f\|^2$ the total mean-power of f.[4] The class $\mathcal{P}$ turned out to be just

---

[3] $L_2^{loc}(\mathbb{R})$ is the set of all Borel measurable functions f on $\mathbb{R}$ to $\mathbb{F}$ such that for all compact $C \subseteq \mathbb{R}$, $f.\chi_C \in L_2(\mathbb{R})$.

[4] For more on the physical side, see [6: §§1,4].

right for a generalized harmonic analysis in view of Wiener's Tauberian identity

$$\lim_{T\to\infty} \frac{1}{2T} \int_{-T}^{T} |f(t)|^2\, dt = \lim_{h\to 0+} \frac{1}{\pi h} \int_R \frac{\sin^2 ht}{t^2} |f(t)|^2\, dt.$$

cf. [15: (20.09) & (20.10)]. Obviously $\mathcal{P}$ is closed under multiplication by scalars, but it is known that $\exists f,g \in \mathcal{P} \ni f+g \notin \mathcal{P}$. Let, however,

$$\text{corr} \underset{d}{=} \{(f;g): f,g \in \mathcal{X} \ \&\ \lim_{T\to\infty} (f,g)_T \text{ exists}\}.$$

Then it is easy to see that $\mathcal{P}$ is corr-linear, i.e.

$$f,g \in \mathcal{P} \ \&\ f \text{ corr } g \Rightarrow f+g \in \mathcal{P}.$$

As in 1.1, $\mathcal{P}$ is the set on which the relation corr is reflexive. If our interest is in the class $\mathcal{P}$, then it is natural to consider the Banach space $\mathcal{X}$ in conjunction with the relation corr, i.e. to consider the Banach graph $(\mathcal{X}, \text{corr})$.

1.3 EXAMPLE. Let $\mathcal{O}\!\mathcal{L}$ be a $\sigma$-algebra over a set $\Lambda$, $\mathcal{H}$ be a Hilbert space over $\mathbb{F}$, and $\mathcal{X} \underset{d}{=} \text{BCA}(\mathcal{O}\!\mathcal{L}, \mathcal{H})$ be the set of all bounded countably additive measures on $\mathcal{O}\!\mathcal{L}$ to $\mathcal{H}$. It is well known that $\mathcal{X}$ is a Banach space over $\mathbb{F}$ under the semi-variation norm $|\cdot|_{sv}$, cf. [3: p.53,#7]. An especially important subset of $\mathcal{X}$ is

$$\mathcal{M} \underset{d}{=} \{\xi: \xi \in \mathcal{X} \ \&\ A,B \in \mathcal{O}\!\mathcal{L} \ \&\ A||B \Rightarrow \xi(A) \perp \xi(B)\}.$$

$\mathcal{M}$ comprises the <u>orthogonally scattered measures,</u> which are very useful because of their simple integration theory, and because they provide the foundation of harmonic analysis of $L_2$ functions over l.c.a. groups, cf. [7,8,9]. Again $\mathcal{M}$ is closed under multiplication by scalars, but not under addition. But let

$$b \underset{d}{=} \{(\xi;\eta): \xi,\eta \in \mathcal{X} \ \&\ A,B \in \mathcal{O}\!\mathcal{L} \ \&\ A||B \Rightarrow \xi(A) \perp \eta(B)\}.$$

$b$ is the relation of <u>biorthogonality</u>. $\mathcal{M}$ is the set over which $b$ is reflexive. It is easy to see that $\mathcal{M}$ is $b$-linear, i.e.

$$\xi,\eta \in \mathcal{M} \ \& \ \xi \, b \, \eta \Rightarrow \xi+\eta \in \mathcal{M}.$$

If our interest is in the space $\mathcal{M}$, then it is again natural to consider $\mathcal{X}$ along with $b$, i.e. to study the Banach graph $(\mathcal{X}, b)$.

1.4 EXAMPLE. Let $\mathcal{O}\!\mathcal{L}$ be a $\sigma$-algebra over a set $\Lambda$ and $\mathcal{H}$ be a Hilbert space over $\mathbb{F}$. Then the function space $\mathcal{X} \underset{d}{=} \mathcal{H}^{\Lambda}$ is a locally convex topological vector space over $\mathbb{F}$ under the topology of pointwise convergence. Let $\mathcal{B}_{\mathcal{H}} \underset{d}{=} \sigma\text{-alg}(\mathcal{K})$, where $\mathcal{K}$ is the family of all open balls of $\mathcal{H}$. Then an especially important subset of $\mathcal{X}$ is

$$\mathcal{M}(\mathcal{O}\!\mathcal{L},\mathcal{B}_{\mathcal{H}}) \underset{d}{=} \{f\colon f \in \mathcal{X}, \ \& \ \forall B \in \mathcal{B}_{\mathcal{H}}, \ f^{-1}(B) \in \mathcal{O}\!\mathcal{L}\},$$

i.e. the family of all <u>$\mathcal{O}\!\mathcal{L},\mathcal{B}_{\mathcal{H}}$ measurable functions</u>. Obviously $\mathcal{M}(\mathcal{O}\!\mathcal{L},\mathcal{B}_{\mathcal{H}})$ is closed under multiplication by scalars, but as was shown by Nedoma [13] if $\operatorname{card} \mathcal{H} > 2^{\aleph_0}$, then $\mathcal{M}(\mathcal{O}\!\mathcal{L},\mathcal{B}_{\mathcal{H}})$ is not closed under addition. Now define

$$c \underset{d}{=} \{(f\cdot g)\colon f,g \in \mathcal{X} \ \& \ (f(\cdot),g(\cdot))_{\mathcal{H}} \in \mathcal{M}(\mathcal{O}\!\mathcal{L},\mathrm{Bl}(\mathbb{F}))\},$$

where $\mathrm{Bl}(\mathbb{F})$ is the Borel algebra over $\mathbb{F}$, and $(\cdot,\cdot)_{\mathcal{H}}$ is the inner product for $\mathcal{H}$. Then it is easy to show that $\mathcal{M}(\mathcal{O}\!\mathcal{L},\mathcal{B}_{\mathcal{H}})$ is c-linear, i.e.

$$f,g \in \mathcal{M}(\mathcal{O}\!\mathcal{L},\mathcal{B}_{\mathcal{H}}) \ \& \ f\,c\,g \ \Rightarrow \ f+g \in \mathcal{M}(\mathcal{O}\!\mathcal{L},\mathcal{B}_{\mathcal{H}}),$$

cf. [10: §4] & [11]. The subset of $\mathcal{X}$ over which c is reflexive comprises precisely the functions f in $\mathcal{X}$ for which $|f(\cdot)|_{\mathcal{H}}$ is measurable. It is therefore natural in any measure-theoretic study of $\mathcal{H}^{\Lambda}$ to consider the graph $(\mathcal{H}^{\Lambda}, c)$. We might add for a separable $\mathcal{H}$, $c = \mathcal{X} \times \mathcal{X}$, and the graph becomes trivial.

In these four examples drawn from rather disparate areas of mathematical analysis the common ingredients are an overall vector space $\mathcal{X}$, a non-linear subspace $\mathcal{M}$ therein of special concern and importance, which is homogeneous and "nearly additive" in that for $f,g \in \mathcal{M}$ we have $f+g \in \mathcal{M}$ provided that f and g are in a certain relation c. This suggests the formulation of a general concept of <u>vector graph</u> $(\mathcal{X},c)$ and the concept of a conditionally-linear manifold $\mathcal{M}$ thereof (§2), as well as the formulation of the special but more interesting notions of topological vector graph, Banach graph, etc. (§3). §4 is devoted to graphs endowed with "conditional" sesquilinear functionals, and in §5 we give two existence theorems for vector graphs.

The following notation will be used:

1.5 NOTATION. (a) If $\mathcal{X}$ is a vector space and $A \subseteq \mathcal{X}$, then $\langle A \rangle$ will denote the linear manifold spanned by A. (b) If $\mathcal{X}$ is a topological vector space, and $A \subseteq \mathcal{X}$, $\mathfrak{S}(A)$ will denote the closed linear manifold spanned by A.

## 2. Vector graphs and Conditionally Linear Manifolds

In this section we shall define vector graphs and their conditionally linear manifolds, and narrate their fundamental properties.

2.1 DEF. $(\mathcal{X}, c)$ is called a vector graph over $\mathbb{F}$, iff, (i) $\mathcal{X}$ is a vector space over $\mathbb{F}$, (ii) $c \subseteq \mathcal{X} \times \mathcal{X}$ is a symmetric relation with $\mathcal{X}$ as its domain and range, (ii)

$$x_1, x_2, y \in \mathcal{X}, \quad x_1 \, c \, y \ \& \ x_2 \, c \, y \Rightarrow \forall a_1, a_2 \in \mathbb{F}, \ a_1 x_1 + a_2 x_2 \, c \, y.$$

The requirement of symmetry in 2.1(ii) seems to be essential for securing a fruitful theory, and is met by all the important examples known so far. The condition 2.1(iii) relates the relation c to the vector space operations, and is of course crucial. It follows from 2.1(iii) that c as a subset of the vector space $\mathcal{X} \times \mathcal{X}$ is homogeneous, i.e.

$$(x_1, y_1) \in c \Rightarrow \forall a \in \mathbb{F}, \ a(x\, y) \in c,$$

but it is not additive, i.e. in general

$$(x_1, y_1) \ \& \ (x_2, y_2) \in c \nRightarrow (x_1, y_1) + (x_2, y_2) \in c.$$

Thus c is not in general a linear manifold in the vector space $\mathcal{X} \times \mathcal{X}$. The following statement, essentially a paraphrase of Def. 2.1, exhibits the structure that the set c must have in order that $(\mathcal{X},c)$ may be a vector graph:

2.2 PROP. Let (i) $\mathcal{X}$ be a vector space over $\mathbb{F}$, and (ii) $c \subseteq \mathcal{X} \times \mathcal{X}$. Then the following conditions are equivalent:

(α) $(\mathcal{X},c)$ is a vector graph over $\mathbb{F}$,

(β) c is symmetric, and $\forall y \in \mathcal{X}$, the section $c^y \underset{d}{=} \{x : x \in \mathcal{X} \ \& \ (x;y) \in c\}$ is a linear manifold in $\mathcal{X}$.

This proposition suggests calling a relation c vector-graphical, iff. it satisfies the condition 2.2(β).

2.3 DEF. Let $(\mathcal{X},c)$ be a vector graph over $\mathbb{F}$ and $\emptyset \neq A,B \subseteq \mathcal{X}$. Then we write

(a) $A \, c \, B \underset{d}{\Leftrightarrow} \forall a \in A \ \& \ \forall b \in B, \ a \, c \, b$

(b) $A^c \underset{d}{=} c(A) \underset{d}{=} \{x : x \in \mathcal{X} \ \& \ \{x\} \, c \, A\}$;

$A^c$ is called the correlate of A;[5]

(c) A is self-correlated, iff. $A \, c \, A$

(d) A is maximal self-correlated, iff.

$$A \, c \, A \ \& \ A \subseteq B \subseteq \mathcal{X} \ \& \ B \, c \, B \Rightarrow B = A.$$

The relation c and the set $A^c$ behave rather like the relation $\perp$ and the set $A^\perp$ in Hilbert space theory, as the following triviality and lemma reveal.

2.4 TRIV. Let $(\mathcal{X},c)$ be a vector graph over $\mathbb{F}$ and $\emptyset \neq A,B \subseteq \mathcal{X}$. Then

(a) $A \, c \, B \Leftrightarrow A \times A \subseteq c$;

(b) $A_o \subseteq A \ \& \ B_o \subseteq B \ \& \ A \, c \, B \Rightarrow A_o \, c \, B_o$;

(c) $A \subseteq B \Rightarrow B^c \subseteq A^c \ \& \ A^{cc} \subseteq B^{cc}$;

(d) $A \subseteq B^c \Leftrightarrow A \, c \, B \Leftrightarrow B \subseteq A^c$;

(e) $0 \in \mathcal{X}^c$.

---

5 Notice that the section $c^y$ mentioned in 2.2(β) is just the correlated $\{y\}^c$ of the singleton $\{y\}$.

2.5 LMA. Let $(\mathfrak{X},c)$ be a vector graph over $\mathbb{F}$ and $\emptyset \neq A,B \subseteq \mathfrak{X}$ . Then

(a) $A \, c \, B \Leftrightarrow \langle A \rangle \, c \, \langle B \rangle$ (cf. 1.4)

(b) $A^c$ is a linear manifold in $\mathfrak{X}$

(c) $A^c = \langle A \rangle^c$

(d) $A \subseteq \langle A \rangle \subseteq A^{cc}$

(e) $A^{ccc} = A^c$

(f) $\exists B \subseteq \mathfrak{X} \ni A = B^c \Leftrightarrow A = A^{cc}$

(g) $(A \cup B)^c = A^c \cap B^c$.

2.5(f) asserts that a set is a correlate, iff. it is the correlate of its own correlate. From 2.5(a) we see that

$$(2.6) \quad \begin{cases} \forall i,j \in \{1,2\}: x_i, y_j \in \mathfrak{X} \ \& \ x_i \, c \, y_j \\ \qquad \Rightarrow \forall a_i, b_j \in \mathbb{F}, \ a_1x_1 + a_2x_2 \, c \, b_1y_1 + b_2y_2. \end{cases}$$

By 2.4(e), $\{0\} \subseteq \mathfrak{X}^c$. In general this inclusion cannot be strengthend to an equality; e.g. in Ex. 1.1, $I \in \mathfrak{X}^c$ and so $\{0\} \subset \mathfrak{X}^c$. But there are important graphs in which $\{0\} = \mathfrak{X}^c$, e.g. in Ex. 1.2. This will become clear in §4.

As the examples in §1 indicate, the relation c is not in general reflexive over $\mathfrak{X}$ , and the subset of $\mathfrak{X}$ over which it is reflexive is of considerable interest. This leads to the following definition:

2.7 DEF. For a vector graph $(\mathfrak{X},c)$ over $\mathbb{F}$ we define the set of all self-correlated vectors by $\mathfrak{X}_c \underset{d}{=} \{x: x \in \mathfrak{X} \ \& \ x \, c \, x\}$.

Self-correlated sets are related to the set $\mathfrak{X}_c$ as the next result reveals:

2.8 PROP. Let $(\mathfrak{X},c)$ be a vector graph over $\mathbb{F}$. Then

(a) for $\emptyset \neq \mathfrak{M} \subseteq \mathfrak{X}$, $\mathfrak{M} \, c \, \mathfrak{M} \Leftrightarrow \mathfrak{M} \subseteq \mathfrak{M}^c \cap \mathfrak{X}_c$

(b) $\mathfrak{M}$ is maxl. self-correlated $\Leftrightarrow \mathfrak{M} = \mathfrak{M}^c \cap \mathfrak{X}_c$

(c) $\mathfrak{M}$ is maxl. self-corr. $\Rightarrow \mathfrak{M}$ is a linear manifold $\subseteq \mathfrak{X}_c$

(d) $\mathfrak{M}$ & $\mathfrak{M}^c$ are self-correlated $\Leftrightarrow \mathfrak{M}^c = \mathfrak{M}^{cc}$

(e) $\mathfrak{M}$ & $\mathfrak{M}^c$ are maxl. self-correlated $\Leftrightarrow \mathfrak{M} = \mathfrak{M}^c$.

In general the set $\mathcal{X}_c$ is not self-correlated, i.e. $\mathcal{X}_c \not\subset \mathcal{X}_c$. This is so in Exs. 1.1 - 1.4. For instance in Ex. 1.1, $\mathcal{N} \not\subset \mathcal{N}$, since non-commuting normal operators exist.

We now introduce the concept of a homogeneous, nearly additive manifold the importance of which was alluded to in §1.

2.9 DEF. Let $(\mathcal{X},c)$ be a vector graph over $\mathbb{F}$. Then $\mathcal{M}$ is called a <u>conditionally-linear manifold</u>, more precisely, <u>c-linear manifold</u>, iff.

(i) $\emptyset \neq \mathcal{M} \subseteq \mathcal{X}$ & $\forall a \in \mathbb{F}$, $a\mathcal{M} \subseteq \mathcal{M}$,

(ii) $x,y \in \mathcal{M}$ & $x\,c\,y \Rightarrow x+y \in \mathcal{M}$.

A trivial but important consequence of this definition is the following result:

2.10 TRIV. <u>Let $(\mathcal{X},c)$ be a vector graph over $\mathbb{F}$. Then the set $\mathcal{X}_c$ is a c-linear manifold in $\mathcal{X}$.</u>

Another easy result is that all c-linear manifolds which are self-correlated are in fact linear submanifolds of $\mathcal{X}_c$:

2.11 TRIV. <u>Let</u> (i) $(\mathcal{X},c)$ <u>be a vector graph over $\mathbb{F}$</u>, (ii) $\mathcal{M}$ <u>be a c-linear manifold of $\mathcal{X}$</u>, (iii) $\mathcal{M}\,c\,\mathcal{M}$. <u>Then $\mathcal{M}$ is a linear manifold and $\mathcal{M} \subseteq \mathcal{X}_c$.</u>

From this we immediately conclude that

$$(2.12) \qquad \forall x,y \in \mathcal{X}, \quad x,y \in \mathcal{X}_c \;\&\; x\,c\,y \Rightarrow \langle x,y \rangle \subseteq \mathcal{X}_c.$$

The converse of (2.12) is by no means generally valid as the following simple example shows:

2.13 EXAMPLE. Let $\mathcal{X}$ be any vector space over $\mathbb{F}$ of dimension exceeding 2, and let

$$\partial = \{(x;y): x,y \in \mathcal{X} \;\&\; x,y \text{ are linearly dependent}\}.$$

$(\mathcal{X},\partial)$ is a vector graph over $\mathbb{F}$ for which $\mathcal{X}_\partial = \mathcal{X}$. Thus for any $x,y \in \mathcal{X}$, even linearly independent ones, $<x,y> \subseteq \mathcal{X}_\partial$, and so $<x,y> \subseteq \mathcal{X}_\partial \not\Rightarrow x \partial y$.

There are, however important vector graphs $(\mathcal{X}, c)$ for which we have

$$(*) \qquad \forall x,y \in \mathcal{X}, \quad <x,y> \subseteq \mathcal{X}_c \Rightarrow x\, c\, y.$$

This is the case, for instance, in Exs. 1.1, 1.3 when $\mathbb{F} = \mathbb{C}$. We have, respectively,

$$\forall a,b \in \mathbb{C}, \quad aA+bB \text{ is normal} \Rightarrow AB^* = B^*A$$
$$\forall a,b \in \mathbb{C}, \quad a\xi+b\eta \text{ is orthogonally scattered} \Rightarrow \xi\, \mathscr{b}\, \eta.$$

(*) also prevails in Exs. 1.2, 1.4 when $\mathbb{F} = \mathbb{C}$, but this is a little more involved.

It is also natural to ask when if ever the converse of 2.11 prevails, i.e. when

$$(\#) \qquad \mathcal{M} \text{ is a linear manifold } \& \mathcal{M} \subseteq \mathcal{X}_c \Rightarrow \mathcal{M}\, c\, \mathcal{M}.$$

It is not universally valid as the following example shows:

2.14 EXAMPLE. Let $\mathbb{F} = \mathbb{R}$ in Ex. 1.1, and $\mathcal{M}$ be the set of all hermitian operators in $\mathcal{X}$. Then since $\mathcal{M} \subset \mathcal{N} = \mathcal{X}_c$, we see on taking non-commuting $A,B \in \mathcal{M}$ that $<A,B> \subset \mathcal{M} \subset \mathcal{X}_c$, but $A \not c B$. Thus (*) fails as does (#).

But the statement (#) holds whenever (*) does, as the following proposition makes clear:

2.15 PROP. <u>Let</u> $(\mathcal{X}, c)$ <u>be a vector graph over</u> $\mathbb{F}$. <u>Then the conditions</u>:

(α) $\mathcal{M}$ <u>is a</u> c-<u>linear manifold</u> & $\mathcal{M}\, c\, \mathcal{M}$

(β) $\mathcal{M}$ <u>is a linear manifold</u> $\subseteq \mathcal{X}_c$

<u>are equivalent, iff. we have</u>

$$(\gamma) \qquad \forall x,y \in \mathcal{X}, \quad <x,y> \subseteq \mathcal{X}_c \Rightarrow x\, c\, y.$$

We conclude this section with a proposition which links the property of c being a linear manifold $\subseteq \mathcal{X} \times \mathcal{X}$ with that of $\mathcal{X}_c$ being self-correlated:

2.16 PROP. <u>Let</u> $(\mathcal{X}, c)$ <u>be a vector graph over</u> $\mathbb{F}$, <u>and consider the assertions</u>:

(α) c <u>is a linear manifold</u> $\subseteq \mathcal{X} \times \mathcal{X}$

(β) $\mathscr{X} c \mathscr{X}$, i.e. $c = \mathscr{X} \times \mathscr{X}$

(γ) $\mathscr{X}_c = \mathscr{X}$

(δ) $\mathscr{X}_c$ _is a linear manifold_ $\subseteq \mathscr{X}$

(ε) $\mathscr{X}_c$ _is self-correlated._

Then (α) ⇔ (β) ⇒ (γ) ⇒ (δ) ⇔ (ε).

It is easy to concoct examples to show that (γ) $\not\Rightarrow$ (β) and (δ) $\not\Rightarrow$ (γ). For instance, in Ex. 2.13, $\mathscr{X}_\partial = \mathscr{X}$ and so (γ) prevails; but (β) fails since $\exists x, y \in \mathscr{X} \ni x \not\partial y$. Next, consider the vector graph $(\mathcal{H}, \perp)$, where $\mathcal{H}$ is a Hilbert space over $\mathbf{F}$. Clearly

$$\mathcal{H}_\perp \underset{d}{=} \{x: x \in \mathcal{H} \ \&\ x \perp x\} = \{0\}$$

is a linear manifold of $\mathcal{H}$, i.e. (δ) holds. But obviously $\mathcal{H}_\perp = \{0\} \neq \mathcal{H}$, i.e. (γ) fails.

## 3. Topological Vector Graphs

In this section we shall deal with vector graphs $(\mathscr{X}, c)$ in which $\mathscr{X}$ is a convex topological vector space, in particular a Banach or Hilbert space. It now becomes necessary to relate the relation c to the topology τ of $\mathscr{X}$. This leads us to the following concepts:

3.1 DEF. (a) $(\mathscr{X}, \tau, c)$ is called a _topological vector graph_ over $\mathbb{F}$, iff:
(i) $\mathscr{X}$ is a locally convex Hausdorff vector space under the topology τ,
(ii) $(\mathscr{X}, c)$ is a vector graph over $\mathbb{F}$ (cf. 2.1),

(iii) $\left\{ \begin{array}{l} \forall \text{ nets } (x_\lambda)_{\lambda\in\Lambda}\ (y_\lambda)_{\lambda\in\Lambda} \text{ in } \mathscr{X}, \\ \qquad x_\lambda c y_\lambda \ \&\ x = \tau\lim_\lambda x_\lambda \ \&\ y = \tau\lim_\lambda y_\lambda \Rightarrow x c y. \end{array} \right.$

(b) $(\mathscr{X}, \tau, c)$ is called a _convergence vector graph_ over $\mathbb{F}$, iff. (a) (i), (ii) hold and

(iii)' $\left\{ \begin{array}{l} \forall \text{ sequences } (x_n)_1^\infty, (y_n)_1^\infty \text{ in } \mathscr{X}, \\ \qquad x_n c y_n \ \&\ x = \tau\lim_{n\to\infty} x_n \ \&\ y = \tau\lim_{n\to\infty} y_n \Rightarrow x c y. \end{array} \right.$

(c) $(\mathcal{X},|\cdot|,c)$ is called a Banach graph over $\mathbb{F}$, iff. $\mathcal{X}$ is a Banach space over $\mathbb{F}$ with norm $|\cdot|$, and with respect to the induced topology $\tau$, $(\mathcal{X},\tau,c)$ is a topological vector graph over $\mathbb{F}$.

(d) $(\mathcal{X},(\cdot,-),c)$ is called a Hilbert graph over $\mathbb{F}$, iff. $\mathcal{X}$ is a Hilbert space with inner product $(\cdot,-)$, and with respect to the induced topology $\tau$, $(\mathcal{X},\tau,c)$ is a topological vector graph over $\mathbb{F}$.

REMARKS. If the topology $\tau$ in 3.1(a) is first countable, we can of course replace (iii) by (iii)'. Since the Banach and Hilbert space topologies $\tau$ are metric and therefore first countable, this replacement is valid in 3.1 (c), (d). However, for non-first countable $\tau$ there are applications, e.g. in measure theory, in which only sequential convergence is germane and the hypotheses (iii) fails. For such purposes the relevant concept is that of convergence vector graph, 3.1(b). We will find that almost all the propositions concerning topological vector graphs remain valid for the wider category of convergence vector graphs if we replace "closure" by "sequential closure" throughout the enunciations.

The following is the analogue of Prop. 2.2 in the present setting:

3.2 PROP. Let (i) $(\mathcal{X},\tau)$ be a locally convex Hausdorff vector space over $\mathbb{F}$, and (ii) $c \subseteq \mathcal{X} \times \mathcal{X}$. Then

(a) the following conditions are equivalent:

(α) $(\mathcal{X},\tau,c)$ is a topological vector graph over $\mathbb{F}$,

(β) c satisfies 2.2(β), and c is a closed subset of $\mathcal{X} \times \mathcal{X}$ under the product topology;

(b) the following conditions are equivalent:

(γ) $(\mathcal{X},\tau,c)$ is a convergence vector graph over $\mathbb{F}$,

(δ) c satisfies 2.2(β), and c is a sequentially closed subset of $\mathcal{X} \times \mathcal{X}$ under the product topology.

The main improvement in the results of this section over those in §2 is that for $A \subseteq \mathcal{X}$, we can now assert for the closed subspace $\mathfrak{S}(A)$ what was formerly asserted merely for the linear manifold $\langle A \rangle$, and relevant spaces such as $A^c$ and $\mathcal{X}_c$ turn out to be closed. Thus the results of Triv. 2.4 and Lma. 2.5 strengthen as follows:

3.3 LMA. Let $(\mathcal{X},\tau,c)$ be a topological vector graph over $\mathbb{F}$, and $\emptyset \neq A,B \subseteq \mathcal{X}$ Then

(a) $A \subset B \Rightarrow \mathfrak{S}(A) \subset \mathfrak{S}(B)$;

(b) $A^c$ = a closed linear subspace of $\mathcal{X}$;

(c) $A^c = \{\mathfrak{S}(A)\}^c$;

(d) $A \subseteq \mathfrak{S}(A) \subseteq A^{cc}$;

(e) A is maxl. self-corr. $\Leftrightarrow$ $\mathcal{M}$ is a closed lin. subspace of $\mathcal{X}_c$.

3.3' LMA. Let $(\mathcal{X},\tau,c)$ be a convergence vector graph over $\mathbb{F}$ and $\emptyset \neq A,B \subseteq \mathcal{X}$. Then the results 3.3(a)-(e) hold, provided that we replace $\mathfrak{S}$ by seq $\mathfrak{S}$ and closure by sequential closure.

We now extend the notion of c-linear manifold (Def. 2.9) to that of a c-linear subspace:

3.4 DEF. Let $(\mathcal{X},\tau,c)$ be a topological vector graph over $\mathbb{F}$. Then

(a) $\mathcal{M}$ is called a c-linear (closed) subspace of $\mathcal{X}$, iff. $\mathcal{M}$ is a c-linear manifold and $\mathcal{M}$ is closed;

(b) $\mathcal{M}$ is called a c-linear sequentially closed subspace of $\mathcal{X}$, iff. $\mathcal{M}$ is a c-linear manifold and $\mathcal{M}$ is sequentially closed.

The results 2.10, 2.11 regarding $\mathcal{X}_c$ and self-correlated sets extend as follows:

3.5 TRIV. Let $(\mathcal{X},\tau,c)$ be a topological vector graph over $\mathbb{F}$. Then

(a) $\mathcal{X}_c$ is a c-linear subspace of $\mathcal{X}$;

(b) $\mathcal{M}$ is a c-linear subspace of $\mathcal{X}$ & $\mathcal{M} \subset \mathcal{M}$ $\Rightarrow$ $\mathcal{M}$ is a (closed) linear subspace of $\mathcal{X}_c$.

These results hold for convergence vector graphs $(\mathcal{X},\tau,c)$, provided that we replace "closed subspace" by "sequentially closed subspace".

## 4. Conditionally sesquilinear functionals

In certain applications the vector graphical relation $c \subseteq \mathcal{X} \times \mathcal{X}$ is the domain of a function from $\mathcal{X} \times \mathcal{X}$ to $\mathbb{F}$, which in a very definite sense is sesquilinear. Vector graphs endowed with such functionals have Hilbertian features, and posses a collection of genuine Hilbert subspaces. So far sesquilinearity has only been defined for functionals on $\mathcal{X} \times \mathcal{X}$. Our first task is to extend this concept to functionals whose domain is merely a vector graphical relation $c \subset \mathcal{X} \times \mathcal{X}$.

4.1 DEF. Let $(\mathcal{X}, c)$ be a vector graph over $\mathbb{F}$. Then

(a) a kernel $f(\cdot, -)$ is called a <u>c-sesquilinear functional</u>, iff.

(i) the domain of $f$ is $c \subseteq \mathcal{X} \times \mathcal{X}$

(ii)[6] $\forall x, y \in \mathcal{X}$ $\begin{cases} f(\cdot, y) \in L(\{y\}^c, \mathbb{F}) \\ f(x, \cdot) \in SL(\{x\}^c, \mathbb{F}); \end{cases}$

(b) a c-sesquilinear functional $f(\cdot, -)$ is called

<u>hermitian</u> $\Leftrightarrow \forall (x;y) \in c, \quad f(x,y) = \overline{f(x,y)}$,

<u>non-negative</u> $\Leftrightarrow \forall x \in \mathcal{X}_c, \quad f(x,x) \geqslant 0$,

<u>positive</u> $\Leftrightarrow \forall x \in \mathcal{X}_c \setminus \{0\}, f(x,x) > 0$.

4.2 DEF. Let $(\mathcal{X}, \|\cdot\|, c)$ be a normed vector graph over $\mathbb{F}$. Then a c-sesquilinear functional $f(\cdot, -)$ is called *<u>Lipschitzian</u>*, iff.

$$\|f\| \underset{d}{=} \sup \left\{ \frac{|f(x,y)|}{\|x\| \ \|y\|} : (0;0) \neq (x\,y) \in c \right\} < \infty.$$

c-sesquilinear functionals posses many of the attributes of ordinary sesquilinear functionals as the following proposition affirms:

4.3 PROP. <u>Let</u> (i) $(\mathcal{X}, c)$ <u>be a vector graph over</u> $\mathbb{F}$, (ii) $((\cdot, -))$ <u>be a c-sesquilinear functional</u>. <u>Then</u>

(a) $\forall x \in \mathbb{N}_+$, $\forall x_1, \ldots, x_r, y_1, \ldots, y_r \in \mathcal{X} \ni x_i \, c \, y_j$, & $\forall a_1, \ldots, a_r, b_1, \ldots, b_r \in \mathbb{F}$,

---

6 For vector spaces Y, Z over $\mathbb{F}$, $L(Y,Z)$ and $SL(Y,Z)$ denote the classes of linear and semi-linear operators from Y to Z, respectively.

$$((\sum_1^r a_i x_i, \sum_1^r b_j y_j)) = \sum_1^r \sum_1^r a_i \bar{b}_j ((x_i, y_j));$$

(b) $\forall x, y \in \mathcal{X}_c \ni x\,c\,y$,[7]

$$((x+y, x+y)) + ((x-y, x-y)) = 2((x,x)) + 2((y,y)),$$

&

$$((x,y)) = \frac{1}{4} \sum_{\omega \in 1^{1/4}} \omega((x+\omega y, x+\omega y));$$

(c) when $\mathbb{F} = \mathbb{C}$, we have

$$((\cdot,-)) \text{ is hermitian} \Rightarrow \forall x \in \mathcal{X}_c,\ ((x,x)) \in \mathbb{R}.$$

4.3 (b) states the parallelogram and polarization laws for c-sesquilinear functionals.

From the last proposition and Triv. 2.11 we obtain the following interesting corollary:

4.4 COR. Let (i), (ii) be as in Prop. 4.3, and (iii) $\emptyset \neq A \subseteq \mathcal{X}$, $A\,c\,A$, $\mathcal{M} \underset{d}{=} \mathfrak{S}(A)$ and $((\cdot,-))_{\mathcal{M}}$ be the restriction of $((\cdot,-))$ to $\mathcal{M} \times \mathcal{M}$. Then

(a) $((\cdot,-))_{\mathcal{M}}$ is a sesquilinear functional on $\mathcal{M} \times \mathcal{M}$;

(b) in case $((\cdot,-))$ is also hermitian and positive, $((\cdot,-))_{\mathcal{M}}$ is an inner product for $\mathcal{M}$, i.e. $\mathcal{M}$ is a pre-Hilbert subspace of $\mathcal{X}_c$.

It is useful to know some conditions under which the $\mathcal{M}$ of 4.4(b) is a Hilbert space. This is so, for instance, when $\mathcal{X}$ is a Banach space with a norm $\|\cdot\|$ such that the restriction of $((\cdot,-))$ to $\mathcal{X}_c$ tallies with $\|\cdot\|^2$. More fully, we have the following theorem:

4.5 THM. Let (i) $(\mathcal{X}, \|\cdot\|, c)$ be a Banach graph over $\mathbb{F}$, (ii) $((\cdot,-))$ be a c-sesquilinear non-negative, hermitian functional such that

$$\forall x \in \mathcal{X}_c, \quad ((x,x)) = \|x\|^2,$$

---

[7] Recall that by (2.12), $x+\omega y \in \mathcal{X}_c$, $\forall \omega \in \mathbb{F}$, in particular for any fourthroot $\omega$ of 1.

(iii) $\emptyset \neq A \subseteq \mathcal{X}$, $A \, c \, A$, $\mathcal{M} \underset{d}{=} \mathfrak{S}(A)$, and $((\cdot,-))_{\mathcal{M}}$ <u>be the restriction of</u> $((\cdot,-))$ to $\mathcal{M} \times \mathcal{M}$. <u>Then</u> $\mathcal{M}$ <u>is a Hilbert space over</u> $\mathbb{F}$ <u>with inner product</u> $((\cdot,-))_{\mathcal{M}}$, <u>and</u> $\mathcal{M} \subseteq \mathcal{X}_c$.

Thm. 4.5 permits us to extend to Banach graphs $(\mathcal{X}, \|\cdot\|, c)$ satisfying its premises, the fruitful theories of a stationary curve in Hilbert space and of a Hilbert-space valued orthogonally scattered measure, cf. [10:2.8] & [7:1.2]:

4.6 DEF. Let $(\mathcal{X}, \|\cdot\|, c)$ be a Banach graph over $\mathbb{F}$ and $((\cdot,-))$ be a c-sesqui-linear, hermitian, positive functional. (a) We call $x(\cdot)$ a <u>stationary curve in</u> $\mathcal{X}$, iff. $x(\cdot)$ is a function on $\mathbb{R}$ to $\mathcal{X}$ such that

$$\forall x,t,h \in \mathbb{R}, \quad x(s) \, c \, x(t) \ \& \ ((x(s+h), x(t+h))) = ((x(s), x(t))).$$

(b) The <u>covariance function</u> $\gamma_x(\cdot)$ of $x(\cdot)$ is defined by

$$\gamma_x(t) \underset{d}{=} ((x(t), x(0))), \ t \in \mathbb{R}.$$

(c) The <u>subspace of $x(\cdot)$</u> is defined by $\mathcal{M}_x \underset{d}{=} \mathfrak{S}\{x(t): t \in \mathbb{R}\}$.

4.7 DEF. Let $(\mathcal{X}, \|\cdot\|, c)$ be a Banach graph over $\mathbb{F}$ and $((\cdot,-))$ be as in the last definition. (a) We call $\xi(\cdot)$ a <u>$\mathcal{X}$-valued countably additive</u>, <u>orthogo-nally scattered</u> (c.a.o.s.) <u>measure on a ring $\mathcal{R}$ with control measure $\mu$</u>, iff. (i) $\mu$ is a c.a. measure on $\mathcal{R}$ to $\mathbb{R}_{0+}$, and (ii) $\xi(\cdot)$ is a function on $\mathcal{R}$ to $\mathcal{X}$ such that

$$\forall A,B \in \mathcal{R}, \ \xi(A) \, c \, \xi(B) \ \& \ ((\xi(A), \xi(B))) = \mu(A \cap B).$$

(b) The <u>subspace of $\xi(\cdot)$</u> is defined by $\mathcal{M}_\xi \underset{d}{=} \mathfrak{S}\{\xi(A): A \in \mathcal{R}\}$.

Let $x(\cdot)$ and $\xi(\cdot)$ be as in Defs. 4.6, 4.7. Then the ranges of $x(\cdot)$ and $\xi(\cdot)$ are self-correlated. Hence by Cor. 4.4(b), $\mathcal{M}_x$ and $\mathcal{M}_\xi$ are pre-Hilbert spaces contained in $\mathcal{X}_c$. Now suppose, that the graph $(\mathcal{X}, \|\cdot\|, c)$ satisfies the premises of Thm. 4.5. Then by Thm. 4.5, $\mathcal{M}_x$ and $\mathcal{M}_\xi$ are actually Hilbert subspaces of $\mathcal{X}_c$. In other words, $x(\cdot)$ is a genuine stationary curve in the Hilbert space $\mathcal{M}_x$, and $\xi(\cdot)$ is a genuine $\mathcal{M}_\xi$-valued c.a.o.s. measure. Thus, <u>the entire theory of Hilbert space-valued stationary curves and Hilbert space-valued c.a.o.s. measures carries over verbatim to Banach graphs</u> $(\mathcal{X}, \|\cdot\|, c)$ satisfying the premises of Thm. 4.5. This circumstance allows us to develop a generalized harmonic analysis (GHA) for such Banach graphs. Wiener's GHA [14] turns out to be a special instance of this.

## 5. Formation of Vector Graphs

We shall exhibit two ways in which a vector graph can be formed from familiar ingredients. Ex. 1.1 exemplifies the first method, and Ex. 1.2 exemplifies the second. We must first recall the notion of a sesquilinear, hermitian, non-negative operator taking values in an involutory linear algebra:

5.1 DEF. Let (i) $\mathcal{X}$ be a vector space over $\mathbb{F}$, (ii) $\mathbb{A}$ be an involutory (*) linear algebra over $\mathbb{F}$, (iii) $F(\cdot,-)$ be a function on $\mathcal{X} \times \mathcal{X}$ to $\mathbb{A}$.

(a) We say that $F(\cdot,\cdot)$ is *sesquilinear,* iff.

$$\forall\, y \in \mathcal{X}, \quad F(\cdot,y) \in L(\mathcal{X},\mathbb{A})$$
$$\forall\, x \in \mathcal{X}, \quad F(x,\cdot) \in SL(\mathcal{X},\mathbb{A}).$$

(b) We call $F(\cdot,\cdot)$ *hermitian,* iff.

$$\forall x,y \in \mathcal{X}, \quad F(y,x) = F(x,y)^*.$$

(c) We call $F(\cdot,\cdot)$ *non-negative,* iff.[8] $\forall x \in \mathcal{X}_c$, $F(x,x) \geqslant 0$.

5.2 PROP. Let (i), (ii) be as in Def. 5.1, (iii) $F(\cdot,-)$ be a sesquilinear hermitian operator on $\mathcal{X} \times \mathcal{X}$ to $\mathbb{A}$, (iv)

$$c \underset{d}{=} \{(x,y): x,y \in \mathcal{X} \;\&\; F(x,y) = 0\}.$$

Then (a) $(\mathcal{X},c)$ is a vector graph over $\mathbb{F}$; (b) when $\mathbb{F} = \mathbb{C}$,

$$\forall x,y \in \mathcal{X}, \quad \langle x,y\rangle \subseteq \mathcal{X}_c \Rightarrow x\,c\,y.$$

In case $\mathbb{A} = \mathbb{F}$, the requirement that $\mathbb{F} = \mathbb{C}$ in (b) is removable.

When $\mathcal{X}$ is a Banach space, $\mathbb{A}$ is a normed algebra and $F(\cdot,\cdot)$ is Lipschitzian, the graph $(\mathcal{X},c)$ of Lma. 5.2 becomes a Banach graph. More fully,

---

[8] For $a \in \mathbb{A}$, we write $a \geqslant 0 \underset{d}{\Leftrightarrow} \exists b \in \mathbb{A} \ni a \underset{d}{=} b^*b$.

5.3 PROP. Let (i) $(\mathcal{X},|\cdot|)$ be a Banach space over $\mathbb{F}$, (ii) IA be a normed involutory linear algebra over $\mathbb{F}$, (iii) $F(\cdot,\cdot)$ be a Lipschitzian, sesquilinear, hermitian operator on $\mathcal{X}\times\mathcal{X}$ to IA, (iv)

$$c \underset{d}{=} \{(x;y): x,y\in\mathcal{X} \ \&\ F(x,y) = 0\}.$$

Then (a) $(\mathcal{X},|\cdot|,c)$ is a Banach graph over $\mathbb{F}$; (b) when $\mathbb{F} = \mathbb{C}$,

$$\forall x,y\in\mathcal{X}, \quad \langle x,y\rangle \subseteq \mathcal{X}_c \ \Rightarrow\ x\,c\,y.$$

In case IA = $\mathbb{F}$, the requirement that $\mathbb{F} = \mathbb{C}$ in (b) is removable.

Consider Ex. 1.1. Letting $\forall A,B\in\mathcal{X}$, $F(A,B) =_d AB^* - B^*A$, we see that c is a Lipschitzian, sesquilinear, hermitian operator on $\mathcal{X}\times\mathcal{X}$ to IA $\underset{d}{=} \mathcal{X}$. Hence by Prop. 5.3, the vector graph in Ex. 1.1 is a Banach graph. Also (b) holds, but as noted in Ex. 2.14 the implication in (b) fails for $\mathbb{F} = \mathbb{R}$.

The graph of Ex. 1.2 suggested by Wiener's generalized harmonic analysis and other such graphs involve nets of sesquilinear, hermitian, non-negative functionals and their limits. The fundamental result stating the conditions on the net required for this purpose is as follows:

5.4 THM. Let (i) $(\mathcal{X},|\cdot|)$ be a Banach space over $\mathbb{F}$,

(ii) $\Lambda$ be a directed poset, and $\forall\lambda\in\Lambda$, $(\cdot,-)_\lambda$ be a sesquilinear, hermitian, non-negative functional on $\mathcal{X}\times\mathcal{X}$ to $\mathbb{F}$,

(iii) the functionals $(\cdot,-)_\lambda$ be related to the norm of $\mathcal{X}$ by

$$\forall x\in\mathcal{X}, \quad \|x\| \underset{d}{=} \sqrt{\overline{\lim_\lambda}\,(x,x)_\lambda} \leqslant |x|,$$

(iv) $$c \underset{d}{=} \{(x;y): x,y\in\mathcal{X} \ \&\ \lim_\lambda (x,y)_\lambda \text{ exists in } \mathbb{F}\},$$

(v) $$\forall (x;y)\in c, \quad ((x,y)) \underset{d}{=} \lim_\lambda (x,y)_\lambda .$$

Then

(a) $(\mathcal{X},|\cdot|,c)$ is a Banach graph over $\mathbb{F}$;

(b) $((\cdot,-))$ is a c-sesquilinear, hermitian, non-negative functional;

(c)[9] $$\forall x,y\in\mathcal{X} \ \&\ \forall\omega\in 1^{1/4},\ x+\omega y\in\mathcal{X}_c \ \Rightarrow\ x\,c\,y.$$

Taking $\Lambda = \mathbb{R}$ and taking $\forall T\in\mathbb{R}_+$, $(\cdot,-)_T$ as in Ex. 1.2, we see from

[9] For $\mathbb{F} = \mathbb{C}$, $1^{1/4} = \{1,-1,i,-i\}$; for $\mathbb{F} = \mathbb{R}$, $1^{1/4} = \{1,-1\}$.

Thm. 5.4 that in Ex. 1.2, $(\mathfrak{X}, \|\cdot\|, \text{corr})$ is a Banach graph over $\mathbb{F}$, $((\cdot,-))$ is a corr-sesquilinear functional, and that $\forall x,y \in \mathfrak{X}$ & $\forall \omega \in 1^{1/4}$, $x+\omega y \in \mathfrak{X}_{\text{corr}} \Rightarrow x \text{ corr } y$.

## REFERENCES

[ 1] Berge, C., The Theory of Graphs and Its Applications, Wiley, New York, 1962.

[ 2] Bohr, H. - Følner, E., On Some Types of Functional Spaces, Acta Math. 76 (1944), 31 - 155.

[ 3] Dinculeanu, N., Vector Measures, Pergamon Press, Oxford, 1967.

[ 4] Halmos, P.R., A Hilbert Space Problem Book, Van Nostrand, New York, 1967.

[ 5] Marcinkiewicz, J., Une Remarkque Sur Les Espaces de M. Besicovitch, C.R. Acad. Sci. Paris, 208 (1939), 157 - 159.

[ 6] Masani, P., Wiener's Contributions to Generalized Harmonic Analysis, Prediction Theory and Filter Theory, Bull. Amer. Math. Soc. 72 (1966), 73 - 125.

[ 7] Masani, P., Orthogonally Scattered Measures, Advances in Math. 2 (1968) 61 - 117.

[ 8] Masani. P., Explicit Form for the Fourier-Plancherel Transform Over Locally Compact Abelian Groups, in "Abstract Spaces and Approximation", edited by P.L. Butzer and B. Sz.-Nagy, Birkhäuser, Basel, 1969, 162 - 182.

[ 9] Masani. P., Quasi-isometric Measures and Their Applications, Bull. Amer. Math. Soc. 76 (1970), 427 - 528.

[10] Masani, P., On Helixes in Hilbert Space I, Theor. Probability & Appl. (USSR) 17 (1972), 3 - 20. (English Edition, Siam 17 (1972), 1 - 19.

[11] Masani, P., Measurability and Pettis Integration in Hilbert Spaces, in "Measure Theory" (Oberwolfach 1975) edited by A. Bellow and D. Kolzow, Springer Verlag, Berlin 1976, 69 - 106.

[12] Masani, P., Measurability and Pettis Integration in Hilbert Spaces, to appear in Crelles J.

[13] Nedoma, J., Note on Generalized Random Variables, Trans. of the First Prague Conference in Information Theory, Statistical Decision Functions, Random Processes (1956), 139 - 141.

[14] Wiener, N., Generalized Harmonic Analysis, Acta. Math. 55 (1930), 177 - 258.

[15] Wiener, N., The Fourier Integral and Certain of its Applications, Cambridge, 1933.

# THE EXPONENTIAL MAP FOR SYMMETRIC OPERATORS IN SPACES WITH AN INDEFINITE SCALAR PRODUCT

Jacob Lionel Bakst Cooper
Department of Mathematics
Chelsea College
University of London

The solutions of the Schrödinger equation $\frac{1}{i}\frac{d\psi}{dt} = A\psi$, $\psi(0) = \varphi$ are studied for symmetric operators A in a J-space for which the components of A linking positive and negative spaces are bounded. A solution exists for all t if the operator is fully selfadjoint, but not necessarily if it is selfadjoint. For fully maximal operators a solution exists either for all positive or all negative t; these define a semigroup of isometric operators and properties of these operators are studied.

Spaces with indefinite scalar products were first used in problems concerning differential equations, and later in applications to quantum field theory. The first to be studied were the Pontrjagin spaces, named after the originator of their theory [1]; these are spaces in which there is an upper bound to the dimension of the subspaces on which the scalar product is negative definite. Properties of hermitian and isometric operators in such spaces were studied more fully by Iohvidov and Kreĭn [2] and they and others have developed the theory of these spaces as well as of more general types of indefinite scalar products. Bognár [3] gives a full bibliography and definitions; an account of the applications to quantum theory can be found in [4]. The theory of bounded operators in general spaces and of unbounded operators in Pontrjagin spaces is now fairly well developed; but there is no rigorous theory of unbounded hermitian operators in spaces other than Pontrjagin spaces, and this is exactly the case considered for quantum field theory. In particular, as I pointed out in [5], the reason for the importance of the property of selfadjointness, as opposed to symmetry, in physics is that in Hilbert space it is only for selfadjoint operators that a solution of the Schrödinger equation valid for all time exists for arbitrary initial values; and the existence of such a solution is necessary if the operator is to represent a measurable physical observable, since only then the expectation values of the observable in a state can persist in order to be measured. The same argument must apply to indefinite scalar product spaces, and the purpose of this article is to discuss the existence of a solution of the Schrödinger equation for an operator A, that is, of the exponential map exp (itA), for a symmetric operator in such spaces which have a property we shall call crossboundedness. It turns out that, in contrast to the Hilbert space case, selfadjointness is not adequate for the existence of exp (itA); a further property, which we call full selfadjointness, is needed.

We consider a Kreĭn space K (see [3]), that is, one whose elements are those of a Hilbert space $H = H(K)$ whose scalar product we write $[x,y]$. That of K itself is defined by an operator $J = P_1 - P_2$ where $P_1$, $P_2$ are the orthogonal projectors of H onto complementary spaces $K_1$, $K_2$ and the scalar product in K is $(x,y) = [Jx, y]$. If $P_r x = x_r$, $r = 1,2$, we write $x = \{x_1, x_2\}$ and then $(x,y) = [x_1,y] - [x_2,y]$. $K_1$, $K_2$ are called maximal positive or negative spaces respectively; if either of $K_1$, $K_2$ is finite dimensional the space is a Pontrjagin space.

If A is a linear operator defined on a dense set D(A) of K, then the adjoint of A is defined by the equation $(Ax,y) = (x, A^*y)$ for all $x \in D(A)$, $D(A^*)$ consisting of all y for which such an $A^*y$ exists. If $A^{[*]}$ stands for the adjoint in the Hilbert space K(H) then $A^* = J A^{[*]} J$.

A is called symmetric if $A^* \supset A$, selfadjoint if $A = A^*$, and hermitian if, in addition, A is bounded. U is said to be unitary if $D(U) = R(U) = K$ and $UU^* = U^*U = I$; it is isometric if $D(U) = K$ and $(Ux, Uy) = (x,y)$ for all x,y, that is, $U^*U = I$.

For any A let $A^o{}_r$ stand for the restriction of A to $K_r$, and let $A^o{}_{rs} = P_r A^o{}_s$; and let $A^o$ be the direct sum of $A^o{}_1$ and $A^o{}_2$, that is, $\{x_1, x_2\} \in D(A^o)$ if and only if $x_r \in D(A^o{}_r)$, $r = 1,2$ and then $A^o x = Ax = A^o{}_1 x_1 + A^o{}_2 x_2$. We then write $A^+ = A^*{}_o$; we call $A^+$ the full adjoint of A. Since $A_o$ is a restriction of A, $A^+$ is an extension of $A^*$, and is clearly identical with $A^*$ if A is everywhere defined. If $A^+ = A$ we say that A is fully selfadjoint.

The definition of the exponential map for bounded functions raises no problems. We shall need the following result.

THEOREM 1. _Let_ A _be_ _a_ _hermitian_ _operator_, _let_ $A_{rs} = P_r A K_s$. _Then_ $A_{11}$ _and_ $A_{22}$ _are_ _hermitian_, _and_ $A^{[*]}_{12} = - A_{21}$. _The_ _equation_

$$\text{(1)} \qquad \frac{1}{i}\frac{d\psi}{dt} = A\psi, \quad \psi(o) = \varphi,$$

_has_ _a_ _unique_ _solution_ _for_ _any_ $\varphi$; _and_ _for_ _any_ _finite_ _positive_ T _there_ _is_ _a_ _constant_ M _depending_ _only_ _on_ T _and_ $\|A_{12}\|$ _such_ _that_ _if_ $|t| < T$ _then_

$$\|\psi(t)\| \leq M\|\varphi\|.$$

It is easy to see that if A is any bounded operator,

$$A = \begin{Vmatrix} A_{11} & A_{12} \\ A_{21} & A_{22} \end{Vmatrix}$$

then

$$A^{[*]} = \begin{Vmatrix} A^{[*]}_{11} & A^{[*]}_{21} \\ A^{[*]}_{21} & A^{[*]}_{22} \end{Vmatrix} \quad \text{and} \quad A^{[*]} = \begin{Vmatrix} A^{[*]}_{11} & -A^{[*]}_{21} \\ -A^{[*]}_{12} & A^{[*]}_{22} \end{Vmatrix}.$$

This proves the first statement.

The unique solution of (1) is obviously that given by the series

$$\psi(t) = \sum_{0}^{\infty} \frac{(itA)^n}{n!}\varphi \tag{2}$$

and it satisfies

$$\frac{d\psi_r}{dt} = iA_{rs}\,\psi_s(t),\ \psi_r(o) = \varphi,$$

so that

$$\frac{d}{dt}\|\psi\|_1^2 = i\,(A_{11}\,\psi_1 + A_{12}\,\psi_2,\ \psi_1) - i\,(\psi_1,\ A_{11}\,\psi_1 + A_{12}\,\psi_2)$$

$$= -\,2\mathrm{Im}\,(A_{12}\,\psi_2,\ \psi_1),$$

so that if $\|A_{12}\| = a$ then

$$\|\psi_1\|\,\frac{d\|\psi\|_1}{dt} \leq a\|\psi_2\|\,\|\psi_1\|,\quad \|\psi_1(o)\| = \|\varphi_1\|$$

and similarly

$$\|\psi_2\|\,\frac{d\|\psi\|_2}{dt} \leq a\|\psi_2\|\,\|\psi_1\|,\quad \|\psi_2(o)\| = \|\varphi_2\|.$$

Let $p_1(t)$, $p_2(t)$ be the solutions of the equations

$$\frac{dp_1}{dt} = a\,p_2,\quad \frac{dp_2}{dt} = a\,p_1,\ p_1(o) = \|\varphi_1\|,\ p_2(o) = \|\varphi_2\|,$$

that is, $p_1(t) = \|\varphi_1\| \cosh at + \frac{1}{a}\|\varphi_2\| \sinh at$

$$p_2(t) = \frac{1}{a}\|\varphi_1\|\ \sinh at + \|\varphi_2\|\ \cosh at$$

and let $u_r(t) = p_r(t) - \|\psi_r(t)\|$. Then $u_r(0) = 0$ and if $t > 0$ $u_r(t) \geq a^2\int_0^t (t - s)\,u_r(s)\,ds$. If $U(T) = \inf\{u_r(t): 0 \leq t \leq T\}$

then $U(t) \geq a\, U(T)\, \frac{1}{2}t^2$ in $(0,T)$ and so $U(T) > 0$ if $\frac{1}{2}aT^2 \leq 1$; then it is easy to show that $u_r(t)$ is everywhere nonnegative and so $|\psi_r(t)| \leq p_r(|t|)$, which proves the theorem.

We now use this to prove an existence theorem for an exponential map for a fairly general type of symmetric operator.

We call an operator A <u>crossbounded</u> if

(i) there are densely defined operators $A_{rs}: K_s \to K_r$ such that

$D(A_{rs}) = P_s\, D(A)$ for $r,s = 1,2$ and for $\{x_1, x_2\} \in D(A)$

$A\{x_1, x_2\} = \{A_{11}x_1 + A_{12}x_2,\ A_{21}x_1 + A_{22}x_2\}$.

(ii) the operators $A_{12}$ and $A_{21}$ are bounded and everywhere defined.

A crossbounded operator is symmetric if and only if $A_{12}^{[*]} = -A_{21}$ and $A_{11}$ and $A_{22}$ are symmetric, and selfadjoint if the latter operators are selfadjoint.

Let us write $\frac{df}{dt} = k$ if $\frac{d}{dt}(f(t),x) = (k(t),x)$ for all $x \in K$, that is, if the weak limit of $\frac{f(t+h) - f(t)}{h}$ as $h \to 0$ is $k(t)$. It is not hard to prove that

$$\frac{d}{dt}(f(t), g(t)) = (\frac{d}{dt} f(t), g(t)) + (f(t), \frac{d}{dt} g(t)).$$

If $U(t)$; $t \geq 0$ is a semigroup of isometric operators such that $U(t)\varphi$ is weakly differentiable for all $\varphi$, then since $\frac{d}{dt}(U(t)\varphi, U(t)\varphi) = 0$, $i\,\frac{d}{dt}U(t)_{t=0}$ is a symmetric operator. We are therefore led to consider what symmetric operators generate such semigroups.

We shall now prove:

THEOREM 2. <u>If A is a crossbounded symmetric operator, then for any</u> $\varphi \in D(A)$ <u>the equation</u>

$$\frac{1}{i}\frac{d\psi}{dt} = A^+\psi, \qquad \psi(0) = \varphi \tag{3}$$

<u>has a solution</u>.

Choose a complete orthonormal sequence $(e_n)$ such that each $e_n$ is in either $D(A_1^0)$ or $D(A_2^0)$, $e_1 = \varphi_1/\|\varphi_1\|$, $e_2 = \varphi_2/\|\varphi_2\|$ (if $\varphi_1$ and $\varphi_2$ are not zero), and the linear span of all the points $\{e_n, Ae_n\}$ in $K \times K$ is dense in $G(A_1^0)$ and in $G(A_2^0)$. Let $P(N)$ denote the projector onto the closed span of the $e_n$ with $n \leq N$, and let $A(N) = P(N)A\,P(N)$. Then $A(N)$ is a symmetric operator, and $\|A(N)_{12}\| \leq \|A_{12}\|$. According to Theorem 1 the equation

(4) $$\frac{1}{i}\frac{d\psi(N)}{dt} = A(N)\psi \;, \quad \psi(N)(0) = \varphi$$

has a unique solution; moreover, $\frac{d\psi(N)}{dt}$, $\frac{d^2\psi(N)}{dt^2}$ are the solutions of the same differential equation with $\varphi$ replaced by $iA(N)\varphi$ and $-A(N)^2\varphi$, respectively. It follows that there is for any finite $T > 0$ a constant $K(T)$ such that, for all $N$ and $|t| < T$

$$\|\psi(N)(t)\| \leq K(T)\|\varphi\| \;, \quad \left\|\frac{d\psi(N)}{dt}\right\| = \|A(N)\psi(N)\| \leq K(T)\|A\varphi\|$$

and for any $e_n$

$$\begin{aligned}\left|\left(\frac{d^2\psi(N)}{dt^2}, e_n\right)\right| &= |(A(N))^2\psi(N)e_n| \\ &= |(A(N)\psi(N), A(N)e_n)| \\ &\leq K(T)\|A\varphi\|\,\|Ae_n\|.\end{aligned}$$

Let $p(N)_n(t) = \frac{d}{dt}(\psi(N)(t), e_n)$. The set of functions $\{p(N)_n(t)\}$ for any fixed $n$ is uniformly bounded and equicontinuous and so relatively compact in the norm topology of $C(-T, T)$ for any finite positive $T$; denoting a copy of $C(-T, T)$ corresponding to $e_n$ by $C_n(T)$, the set of points $p(N)_n(t)$, $n=1,2\ldots$, for varying $N$ is relatively compact in the topological product of the $C_n(T)$ and hence has a limiting point $p_n(t)$ in that topology, which is the limit of some directed set of $p(N_\alpha)_n$. $p(N_\alpha)_n(t)$ converges uniformly to $p_n(t)$ for each $n$ along $N_\alpha$. For any finite set of indices $n$,

$$\begin{aligned}\sum_{n\in J}|p_n(t)|^2 &= \lim_\alpha \sum_{n\in J}|p(N_\alpha)_n(t)|^2 \\ &\leq \lim \left\|\frac{d\psi(N_\alpha)}{dt}\right\|^2 \\ &\leq K(T)^2\|A\varphi\|^2 .\end{aligned}$$

Hence $\xi(t) = \Sigma\, p_n(t)\, e_n$ is an element of $K$. Let $q_n(t) = \int_0^t p_n(u)\,du$ then similarly $\psi(t) = \varphi + \Sigma\, q_n(t)\, e_n$ is in $K$. Because of the boundedness of $\psi(N)(t)$ and $\frac{d\psi(N)}{dt}$ for varying $N$, $\psi(t)$ and $\xi(t)$ are the weak limits of

$\psi(N_\alpha)(t)$ and $d\psi(N_\alpha)/dt$, respectively. Moreover, for any $x \in K$

$$(\psi(t), x)) = (\varphi, x) + \int_0^t (\xi(u), x)\, du$$

because of the bounded convergence of the series for $\xi(u)$ and so $\frac{d\psi}{dt} = \xi(t)$. For any n

$$(5) \qquad (\xi(t), e_n) = \lim i\,(A(N_\alpha)\,\psi(N_\alpha)(t), e_n)$$

$$= \lim i\,(\psi(N_\alpha)(t),\; A(N_\alpha)\,e_n) = i\,(\psi(t), Ae_n)$$

because of the boundedness of the $\psi(N)$ and because $A(N)e_n$ tends boundedly to $Ae_n$ for each fixed n. The set $\{e_n\}$ has been chosen so that for each r the span of the points $\{e_n, Ae_n\}$ with $e_n \varepsilon K_r$ is dense in the graph of $A^o{}_r$; it follows from (5) that $(\xi(t), -i\psi(t))$ is orthogonal to the graph of $A^o{}_r$ and so that $\xi(t) = -iA^+\psi(t)$, that is, that $\frac{d\psi}{dt} = i\,A^+\psi\,(t)$. Since $\psi(0) = \varphi$ this proves the theorem.

An immediate corollary is the following:

THEOREM 3. Let A be a fully selfadjoint operator in a Kreĭn space. Then for any $\varphi \in D(A)$ the equation

$$(6) \qquad \frac{1}{i}\frac{d\psi}{dt} = A\psi, \quad \psi(0) = \varphi$$

has a unique solution for all t.

This result does not hold for operators A that are selfadjoint but not fully selfadjoint. This is shown by the following examples, which are typical and which also serve to illustrate the difference between fully and ordinarily selfadjoint operators.

Let $K_1 = K_2 = L_2\,(o, \infty)$, let $\partial\{f_1, f_2\} = \{f'_1, f'_2\}$, when $f'_1, f'_2 \varepsilon L_2$. Then

$$(\partial f, g) + (f, \partial g) = \int_0^\infty [f_1\overline{g'}_1 + f'_1\overline{g_1} - f_2\overline{g'}_2 - f'_2\overline{g_2}]\,dx$$

$$= \left[f_2(0)\,\overline{g_2(0)} - f_1(0)\,\overline{g_1(0)}\right].$$

If A is the restriction of $i\partial$ to the functions with $f_2(0) = f_1(0)$, A is selfadjoint; $A^o$ is the restriction of A to functions with

$f_1(0) = f_2(0) = 0$, and $A^+$ is $i\partial$ ; thus A is not fully selfadjoint. The equation $\frac{1}{i}\frac{d\psi}{dt} = A\psi$, $\psi(0) = \varphi$ has as formal solution $\psi(x,t) = \varphi(x - t)$. This is in D(A) only if $\varphi_1(-t) = \varphi_2(-t)$. Since $\varphi_r(t)$ can be chosen arbitrarily for $t < 0$ a solution of $\frac{1}{i}\frac{d\psi}{dt} = A\psi$, $\psi(0) = \varphi$ exists for all $t > 0$ but does not exist for all $t < 0$ unless $\varphi_1(t) = \varphi_2(t)$ for all t.

Let K be the set of elements $f = \{f_r\}_{r=1}^4$, $f_r \in L_2(0,\infty)$, $(f,g) = \sum_1^4 (-1)^r [f_r, g_r]$, and let $\partial$ take $f_r$ to $\{\alpha_r f_r'\}$, $\alpha_1 = \alpha_2 = 1$, $\alpha_3 = \alpha_4 = -1$. Then

$$(\partial f, g) + (f, \partial g) = \Sigma (-1)^r \alpha_r f_r(0) \overline{g_r(0)}.$$

The restriction of $i\partial$ to elements obeying $f_1(0) = f_2(0)$, $f_3(0) = f_4(0)$ is selfadjoint but the Schrödinger equation has no solution either for $t > 0$ or for $t < 0$ for except under special initial conditions.

For any symmetric A each of $A^o_{rr}$, $r = 1,2$, is symmetric, and by von Neumann's theory of symmetric operators ([6], [7]) $D(A^{o*}_{rr})$ is spanned by $D(A^o_{rr})$ with classes of elements $C^+_{rr}$ and $C^-_{rr}$ which are spanned by solutions of $A^o_{rr} x_r = \pm i x_r$. If for one r or the other both these classes are nonempty, then A can have a symmetric extension corresponding to a proper symmetric extension of $A^o$; if both $C^+_{11}$ and $C^+_{22}$ are nonempty, then we can find an extension of A which does not extend $A^o$. Thus if either both $C^+$ classes or both $C^-$ classes are empty, then if B is a symmetric extension of A, $B^o = A^o$. In this case we say that A is <u>bimaximal</u>.

Suppose for example that A is symmetric with both $C^+$ classes empty. Then the solution of (3) whose existence is proved in Theorem 2 satisfies, for all $t > 0$,

$$\|\psi_1(t)\|^2 \leq \lim \|\psi(N_\alpha)_1(t)\|^2$$

$$\leq \|\varphi_1\|^2 + 2 \lim \operatorname{Im} \int_0^t [\psi(N_\alpha)_1(u), A(N_\alpha)_{12}\psi(N_\alpha)_2(u)]\, du \qquad (7)$$

$$= \|\psi_1\|^2 + 2 \operatorname{Im} \int_0^t [\psi_1(u), A_{12}\, \psi_2(u)]\, du.$$

On the other hand any solution whatever of (3) satisfies

$$\|\psi_1(t)\|^2 = \|\psi_1\|^2 + 2\int_0^t \{\mathrm{Im}[\psi_1(u), A_{12}\,\psi_2(u)] - \mathrm{Im}\,[A^+_{11}\,\psi_1(u), \psi_1(u)]\}du.$$

Since the $C^+$ class is empty the second term in the last integral is always nonnegative; if it is nonzero anywhere the inequality (7) will not hold, and hence it is always zero. $\psi_1(u)$ must be in $D(A^o_{11})$ for otherwise $A^o_{11}$ would have a symmetric extension with $\psi_1(u)$ in its domain. Consequently the equation

$$\frac{1}{i}\frac{d\psi}{dt} = A^o\,\psi, \qquad \psi(0) = \varphi$$

has a solution for any $\varphi \in D(A^o)$ for all $t > 0$ when the $C^+$ classes are empty.

If $\varphi = 0$ then for any $t > 0$

$$\|\psi_1(t)\|^2 = 2\int_0^t \mathrm{Im}\;[\psi_1(u), A_{12}\,\psi_2(u)]\;du.$$

Let $M_r = \sup\,\{\|\psi_r(t)\|: 0 \le t \le T\}$. Then the last equation shows that $\|M_r\|^2 \le A_{12}\,M_1\,M_2\,T$ and so that $M_r \le 4\|A_{12}\|^2\,M_r T$, consequently $M_r \le 0$ if $4\|A_{12}\|^2 T \le 1$. This proves that the solution of (6) is unique over $(0, (4\|A_{12}\|)^{-1})$ and this can be extended to all $t > 0$.

A similar argument shows that the equation (3) has a unique solution for all $t > 0$, and by further examination of these solutions we arrive at the following theorem.

THEOREM 4. _If A is a symmetric operator with empty_ $C^+$ _classes, then the equation_ (6) _has a unique solution for all_ $t > 0$ _for all_ $\varphi \in D(A^o)$; _if this solution is_ $\psi(t)$ _then the map_ $\varphi \mapsto \psi(t)$ _extends by continuity to an isometry_ $U(t)$ _of_ K. _The equation_ (3) _has a unique solution for all_ $t < 0$; _if this solution is_ $\psi(t)$ _the map_ $\varphi \mapsto \psi(t)$ _extends by continuity to a continuous operator_ $V(t)$ _on_ K. _For any_ $t > 0$ $U^*(t) = V(-t)$, $V(-t)U(t) = I$, _and_ $U(t)\,V(-t) = E(t)$ _is the K-orthogonal projector onto the range of_ $U(t)$.

The space K decomposes into a subspace $E(\infty)$ K and its orthogonal complement, which are invariant for A and $A^+$. On the first of these the restriction of A is fully selfadjoint, and the restriction to the other part contains no fully selfadjoint component: this situation is of course similar to that of Hilbert space, but the description of the structure of the purely nonselfadjoint, or purely isometric, operators seems much more difficult in the case of indefinite metrics, as is, indeed, the structure of fully selfadjoint operators.

## REFERENCES


[1] Pontrjagin, L.S., Hermitian operators in spaces with indefinite metric. Izv. Akad. Nauk SSSR, Ser. Mat. 8 (1944), 243-280.

[2] Iohvidov, I.S. - Kreĭn, M.G., Spectral theory of operators in spaces with an indefinite metric. I. Trudy Moskov. Mat. Obsc. 5 (1956), 367-392 and 6 (1957), 486; II ibid. 8 (1959), 413-496, and 15 (1966), 452-454.

[3] Bognár Janos, Indefinite Product Spaces. Springer Verlag, Berlin, Heidelberg, New York, 1974.

[4] Cooper, J.L.B., The characterization of quantum-mechanical operators. Proc. Camb. Phil. Soc., 46 (1960), 614-619.

[5] Nagy, K.L., State Vector Spaces with Indefinite Metric in Quantum Field Theory. Noordhoff Groningen, and Akadémiai Kiadó Budapest, 1966.

[6] von Neumann, J., Allgemeine Eigenwerttheorie Hermitescher Funktionaloperatoren. Math. Ann. 102 (1929 - 1930), 49-131.

[7] Stone, M.H., Linear Transformations in Hilbert Spaces and their Applications to Analysis. Amer. Math. Soc. Colloquium Pub. Vol. 15, New York, 1932.

# NONARCHIMEDEAN FUNCTION SPACES

João B. Prolla
Instituto de Matemática
Universidade Estadual de Campinas
Campinas

Let E be a non-archimedean normed space over a non-archimedean valued field F. We establish a formula for the distance d(f,W) between a function $f \in C(X;E)$, where X is a compact Hausdorff space, and a vector subspace $W \subset C(X;E)$ which is a module over a subalgebra $A \subset C(X;F)$. As a corollary we obtain several approximation results and a non-archimedean analogue of Bishop's generalization of the Stone-Weierstrass Theorem.

## 1. Introduction

Throughout this paper X stands for a compact Hausdorff space, and F stands for a rank one valued field, i.e. a field with a real-valued valuation, denoted by $t \to |t|$. The letters $\mathbb{R}$ and $\mathbb{C}$ denote, respectively, the fields of the real and the complex numbers. The symbol C(X;F) denotes the algebra over F of all continuous F-valued functions on X. On C(X;F) we shall consider the topology of uniform convergence on X, given by the sup-norm

$$f \to \| f \| = \sup \{ | f(x) | ; x \in X\}.$$

A subset $A \subset C(X;F)$ is said to be separating over X, or to separate points, if for any pair of points x and y in X, with $x \neq y$, there is a function $a \in A$ such that $a(x) \neq a(y)$. If the valued field F is non-archimedean, then C(X;F) is separating over X if, and only if, the space X is 0-dimensional (see, for example, Théorème 1, §2, Chapitre II, Monna [10] or Theorem 2, Section 4.9, Narici, Beckenstein and Bachman [13]).

We shall denote by $X|A$ the equivalence relation defined on $X$ as follows: if $x, y \in X$, then $x \equiv y$ (modulo $X|A$) if, and only if, $a(x) = a(y)$ for all $a \in A$. Let $Y$ be the quotient topological space of $X$ modulo $X|A$ and let $\pi$ be the quotient map of $X$ onto $Y$; $\pi$ is continuous and for each $x \in X$, $y = \pi(x)$ is the equivalence class of $x$ modulo $X|A$. Hence, for each $a \in A$, there is a unique $b : Y \to F$ such that $a(x) = b(\pi(x))$, for all $x \in X$. We claim that $b \in C(Y;F)$. Indeed, for every open subset $G \subset F$, $a^{-1}(G)$ is open in $X$, and $a^{-1}(G) = \pi^{-1}(b^{-1}(G))$. By the definition of the quotient topology of $Y$, this means that $b^{-1}(G)$ is an open subset of $Y$. Let us define $B \subset C(Y;F)$ by setting $B = \{b \in C(Y;F); a = b \circ \pi, a \in A\}$. It follows that $B$ is a subalgebra (resp. a unitary subalgebra) of $C(Y;F)$, whenever $A$ is a subalgebra (resp. a unitary subalgebra) of $C(X;F)$. Notice the important fact that $B$ is separating over $Y$. This implies that $Y$ is a compact Hausdorff space, which is 0-dimensional, whenever the field $F$ is non-archimedean.

The following separating version of the Stone-Weierstrass theorem is well-known.

THEOREM 1.1. *Let $F$ be any valued field except $\mathbb{C}$. Let $A \subset C(X;F)$ be a unitary subalgebra which is separating over $X$. Then $A$ is uniformly dense in $C(X;F)$.*

For a proof, see Chernoff, Rasala and Waterhouse [3]. In fact they prove Theorem 1.1 in the more general case of arbitrary Krull valuations, i.e. not necessarily real-valued valuations. For a proof in the case of non - archimedean rank one valuations, see Theorem 2, Section 4.10 of Narici, Beckenstein, and Bachman [13].

The first author to prove a Stone-Weierstrass Theorem for non-archimedean valued fields was Dieudonné, who proved such a result in [4] for the field of p-adic numbers. Theorem 1.1 for the case of rank-one non-archimedean valuations is due to Kaplansky [7].

From Theorem 1.1 and the quotient construction described above, it is possible to derive a general version of the Stone-Weierstrass theorem, i.e. a description of the closure of a unitary subalgebra of $C(X;F)$.

THEOREM 1.2. *Let $F$ be any valued field except $\mathbb{C}$. Let $A \subset C(X;F)$ be a unitary subalgebra, and let $f \in C(X;F)$. Then $f$ belongs to the uniform closure of $A$ in $C(X;F)$ if, and only if, $f$ is constant on each equivalence class of $X$ modulo $X|A$.*

PROOF. Necessity is clear. Let $Y$, $\pi$ and $B$ as before. Let now $f \in C(X;F)$ be constant on each equivalence class of $X$ modulo $X|A$. There exists $g : Y \to F$ such that $f = g \circ \pi$. As in the proof that $B$ is contained in $C(Y;F)$ it is easy to see that $g$ belongs to $C(Y;F)$. By Theorem 1.1, $B$ is dense in $C(Y\ F)$. Therefore $g$ belongs to the closure of $B$ in $C(Y;F)$. Since the mapping $h \to h \circ \pi$ is an isometry of $C(Y;F)$ into $C(X;F)$, it follows that $f$ belongs to the closure of $A$ in $C(X;F)$.

The hypothesis that the algebra A be unitary can be very annoying, so let us remove it.

THEOREM 1.3. _Let F be any valued field except_ $\mathbb{C}$. _Let_ $A \subset C(X;F)$ _be a subalgebra, and let_ $f \in C(X;F)$. _Then f belongs to the uniform closure of A in_ $C(X;F)$ _if, and only if, the following conditions hold:_

(1) _given_ $x, y \in X$ _with_ $f(x) \neq f(y)$, _there exists_ $g \in A$ _such that_ $g(x) \neq g(y)$;

(2) _given_ $x \in X$ _with_ $f(x) \neq 0$, _there exists_ $g \in A$ _such that_ $g(x) \neq 0$.

PROOF. Necessity is clear. Let $f \in C(X;F)$ be a function satisfying conditions (1) and (2).

Case I. There exists a point $x \in X$ such that $g(x) = 0$ for all $g \in A$. By condition (2), we have $f(x) = 0$ too. Let $B \subset C(X;F)$ be the subalgebra generated by $A$ and the constants. The equivalence relations $X|A$ and $X|B$ are the same, and by condition (1), $f$ is constant on each equivalence class of $X$ modulo $X|A$. By Theorem 1.2, $f$ belongs to the closure of $B$ in $C(X;F)$. Let $\varepsilon > 0$ be given. There exists $g \in A$ and constant $\lambda \in F$ such that $| f(t) - g(t) - \lambda | < \varepsilon$, for all $t \in X$. Making $t = x$, we obtain $|\lambda| < \varepsilon$. If $F$ is non-archimedean, this implies that for all $t \in X$, $|f(t) - g(t)| < \varepsilon$. If $F$ is archimedean, then $|f(t) - g(t)| < 2\varepsilon$ for all $t \in X$. In any case, we see that $f$ belongs to the closure of $A$.

Case II. The algebra $A$ has no common zeros. By Proposition 2, [3], $A$ contains a function $h$ vanishing nowhere on $X$. Now $1/h$ belongs to $C(X;F)$ and it is constant on each equivalence class modulo $X|B$. By Theorem 1.2, $1/h$ belongs to the closure of $B$ in $C(X;F)$. On the other hand, $\bar{A}$ is a $\bar{B}$-modulo so $1 = h(1/h) \in \bar{A}$. Therefore, $\bar{A}$ is a unitary subalgebra. Since $A$ and $\bar{A}$ determine the same equivalence relations on $X$, by condition (1), $f$ is constant on each equivalence class modulo $X|\bar{A}$. By Theorem 1.2, f belongs to $\bar{A}$.

## 2. Stone-Weierstrass Theorem for Modules

Throughout this section E denotes a normed space over F, and we assume that $E \neq 0$. It follows that whenever E is non-archimedean, so is F. The space $C(X;E)$ of all continuous E-valued functions on X is endowed with the topology of uniform convergence on X, given by the sup-norm $f \to \|f\| = \sup\{\|f(x)\| ; x \in X\}$.

Let $A \subset C(X;F)$ be a subalgebra and let $W \subset C(X;E)$ be a vector subspace which is an A-module, i.e. $AW \subset W$. Our aim is to describe the closure of W in $C(X;E)$; or more generally, given a function $f \in C(X\ E)$ to find the **distance of** f from W, i.e. to find

$$d(f;W) = \inf\{\|f-g\| ; g \in W\}.$$

To solve this problem, we need a "partition of unity" result. To this end, we shall adapt the proof of Rudin [15], section 2.13, to the non-archimedean setting.

LEMMA 2.1. Let Y be a 0-dimensional compact Hausdorff space, and let $V_1, \ldots, V_n$ be a finite open covering of Y. Let F be a non-archimedean valued field. There exist functions $h_i \in C(Y;F)$, $i = 1,\ldots,n$, such that

(a) $h_i(y) = 0$ for all $y \notin V_i$, $i = 1, \ldots, n$;

(b) $\|h_i\| \leq 1$, $i = 1, \ldots, n$;

(c) $h_1 + \ldots + h_n = 1$ on Y.

PROOF. Each $y \in Y$ has a clopen (i.e., closed and open) neighborhood $W(y) \subset V_i$ for some i (depending on y). By compactness of Y there are points $y_1, \ldots, y_m$ such that $Y = W_1 \cup \ldots \cup W_m$, where we have set $W_j = W(y_j)$ for each $j = 1, \ldots, m$. If $1 \leq i \leq n$, let $H_i$ be the union of those $W_j$ which lie in $V_i$. Let $f_i \in C(Y;F)$ be the characteristic function of $H_i$, $i = 1, \ldots, n$. Define

$$h_1 = f_1$$
$$h_2 = (1 - f_1)f_2$$
$$\ldots\ldots\ldots\ldots$$
$$h_n = (1 - f_1)(1 - f_2)\ldots(1 - f_{n-1})f_n\ .$$

Then $H_i \subset V_i$ implies that $f_i(y) = 0$ for all $y \notin V_i$ and so $h_i(y) = 0$ for $y \notin V_i$ too, $i = 1,\ldots,n$. This proves (a). Clearly $\| h_i \| \leq 1$, $i = 1,\ldots,n$, since $h_i$ takes only the values 0 and 1, which proves (b). On the other hand $Y = H_1 \cup \ldots \cup H_n$ and

$$h_1 + \ldots + h_n = 1 - (1 - f_1)(1 - f_2) \ldots (1 - f_n) .$$

Hence, given $y \in Y$, at least one $f_i(y) = 1$ and therefore

$$h_1(y) + \ldots + h_n(y) = 1.$$

This proves (c).

THEOREM 2.2. _Let E be a non-archimedean normed space. Let $A \subset C(X;F)$ be a subalgebra and let $W \subset C(X;E)$ be a vector subspace which is an A-module. Let $f \in C(X;E)$. Then_

$$d(f;W) = \sup \{ d(f|S;\ W|S);\ S \in P_A \} ,$$

_where $P_A$ denotes the set of all equivalence classes $S \subset X$ modulo $X|A$._

Before proving Theorem 2.2, let us point out that it implies the following result.

THEOREM 2.3. _Let E, A, W and f be as in Theorem 2.2. Then f belongs to the uniform closure of W in C(X;E) if, and only if $f|S$ is in the uniform closure of $W|S$ in C(S;E) for each equivalence class $S \subset X$ modulo $X|A$._

The above Theorem 2.3 contains the non-archimedean analogue of Nachbin's Stone-Weierstrass Theorem for modules (Nachbin [11], §19), and 2.2 is the "strong" Stone-Weierstrass Theorem for modules (terminology of Buck [2] ).

Proof of Theorem 2.2. Let us put $d = d(f;W)$ and

$$c = \sup \{ d(f|S;\ W|S);\ S \in P_A \} .$$

Clearly, $c \leq d$. To prove the reverse inequality, let $\varepsilon > 0$. Without loss of generality we may assume that A is unitary. Indeed, the subalgebra A' of C(X;F) generated by A and the constants is unitary, and the equivalence relations $X|A$ and $X|A'$ are the same. Moreover, since W is a vector space, W is an A-module if, and only if, W is an A'-module.

Let Y be the quotient space of X modulo $X|A$, with quotient map $\pi$. For any $S \in P_A$, since $d(f|S; W|S) < c + \varepsilon$, there exists some function $w_S$ in the A-module W such that $\|w_S(t) - f(t)\| < c + \varepsilon$ for all $t \in S$. Let $K_S$ be the compact set $\{x \in X; \|w_S(x) - f(x)\| \geq c + \varepsilon\}$. Then $K_S$ disjoint from S. Hence, for each $y \in Y$, $y \notin \pi(K_S)$, if $S = \pi^{-1}(y)$. This implies that $\cap \{\pi(K_S); S = \pi^{-1}(y), y \in Y\}$ is empty. By the finite intersection property, there is a finite set $\{y_1, \ldots, y_n\} \subset Y$ such that $\pi(K_1) \cap \ldots \cap \pi(K_n) = \emptyset$, where $K_i = K_S$, for $S = \pi^{-1}(y_i)$, $i = 1,\ldots,n$. Let $V_i$ be the open subset given by the complement of $\pi(K_i)$, $i = 1,\ldots,n$. Y is a 0-dimensional compact Hausdorff space. Hence, by Lemma 2.1, there exist functions $h_i \in C(Y;F)$, $i = 1, \ldots, n$, such that

(a) $h_i(y) = 0$ for all $y \notin V_i$, $i = 1,\ldots,n$;

(b) $\|h_i\| \leq 1$, $i = 1, \ldots, n$;

(c) $h_1 + \ldots + h_n = 1$.

Put $g_i = h_i \circ \pi$, so that we have $g_i \in C(X;F)$, $i = 1, \ldots, n$, and each $g_i$ is constant on every equivalence class of X modulo $X|A$. By Theorem 1.2, $g_i$ belongs to the closure of A in the space $C(X;F)$, for each $i = 1,2,\ldots,n$. Notice that $g_i(x) = 0$ for all $x \in K_i$, $i = 1,\ldots,n$, since $h_i(y) = 0$ for all $y \in \pi(K_i)$, $i = 1,\ldots,n$. Moreover $\|g_i\| \leq 1$, $i = 1,\ldots,n$, and $g_1 + \ldots + g_n = 1$ on X. Let $g = \sum_{i=1}^{n} g_i w_i$ where $w_i = w_S$, with $S = \pi^{-1}(y_i)$, $i=1,\ldots,n$. Then $\|g(x) - f(x)\| < c+\varepsilon$, for all $x \in X$. Indeed, for any $x \in X$ we have

$$\|g(x) - f(x)\| = \|\sum_{i=1}^{n} g_i(x)(w_i(x) - f(x))\|$$

$$\leq \max_{1\leq i\leq n} |g_i(x)| \cdot \|w_i(x) - f(x)\| .$$

Now, for each $1 \leq i \leq n$, either $x \in K_i$ and then $g_i(x) = 0$; or else $x \notin K_i$ and then

$$|g_i(x)| \cdot \|w_i(x) - f(x)\| \leq \|w_i(x) - f(x)\| < c + \varepsilon .$$

Let $M = \max\{\|w_i\|; i = 1,\ldots,n\}$ and choose $\delta > 0$ such that $\delta M < c + \varepsilon$. For each $i = 1,\dots,n$, there is $a_i \in A$ such that $\|a_i - g_i\| < \delta$. Let us define $w = \sum_{i=1}^{n} a_i w_i$. Then $w \in W$ and for all $x \in X$,

$$\|w(x) - g(x)\| < c + \varepsilon .$$

Indeed, for any $x \in X$ we have

$$\|w(x) - g(x)\| = \|\sum_{i=1}^{n} (a_i(x) - g_i(x))w_i(x)\|$$

$$\leq \max_{1 \leq i \leq n} |a_i(x) - g_i(x)| \cdot \|w_i(x)\|$$

$$\leq \delta M < c + \varepsilon .$$

Finally, notice that $\| w(x) - f(x) \| = \|w(x) - g(x) + g(x) - f(x) \| \leq$ $\leq \max(\| w(x) - g(x)\| , \|g(x) - f(x)\|) < c + \varepsilon$, for all $x \in X$. Hence $d < c + \varepsilon$. Since $\varepsilon < 0$ was arbitrary, $d \leq c$.

THEOREM 2.4. Let $E$, $A$ and $W$ be as in Theorem 2.2. For each $f \in C(X;E)$, there exists an equivalence class $S \subset X$ modulo $X|A$ such that

$$d(f;W) = d(f|S; W|S).$$

PROOF. Let $Y$ and $\pi$ be as before. For each $g \in W$, the function

$$y \to \| f|\pi^{-1}(y) - g|\pi^{-1}(y)\|$$

is upper semicontinuous on $Y$, by Lemma 1, Machado and Prolla [9]. Hence

$$y \to \inf\{\| f|\pi^{-1}(y) - g|\pi^{-1}(y)\| ;\ g \in W\}$$

is upper semicontinuous on $Y$ too, and therefore attains its supremum on $Y$. By Theorem 2.2, this supremum is $d(f;W)$. Let then $y \in Y$ be the point where $d(f;W)$ is attained and let $S = \pi^{-1}(y)$. Then

$$d(f;W) = \inf\{\| f|S - g|S\| ,\ g \in W\} =$$

$$= d(f|S; W|S),$$

as desired.

COROLLARY 2.5. *Let* E, A *and* W *be as in Theorem 2.2. Assume that* A *is separating over* X. *Then* W *is dense in* C(X;E) *if and only if* $W(x) = \{g(x);\ g \in W\}$ *is dense in* E, *for each* $x \in X$. *More generally, for any* $f \in C(X;E)$, $f \in \bar{W}$ *if, and only if*, $f(x) \in \overline{W(x)}$ *in* E, *for each* $x \in X$.

Using the above corollary we can prove a result of Kaplansky on ideals in function algebras. Let E be a non-archimedean normed non-associative algebra with unit over a (necessarily) non-archimedean field F; that is, E is a not necessarily associative linear algebra with unit e over F equipped with a non-archimedean norm satisfying

(1) $\|uv\| \leq \|u\| \cdot \|v\|$ and

(2) $\|e\| = 1$.

Condition (1) implies that multiplication is jointly continuous. If X is any compact Hausdorff space, C(X;E) with pointwise operations and sup norm becomes a non-archimedean normed algebra with unit too (over the same field F). Now the problem arises of characterizing the closed right (resp. left) ideals $I \subset C(X;E)$. Suppose that for every $x \in X$ a closed right (resp. left) ideal $I_x \subset E$ is given, and let us define

$$I = \{f \in C(X;E);\ f(x) \in I_x \text{ for all } x \text{ in } X\}.$$

Manifestly, I is a closed right (resp. left) ideal in C(X;E). We shall prove that any closed right (resp. left) ideal in C(X;E) has the above form. Namely we have the following.

THEOREM 2.6. *Let* X *be a* 0-*dimensional compact Hausdorff space. Let* E *be a non-archimedean normed algebra with unit* e *over a (necessarily non-archimedean) valued field* F. *Let* $I \subset C(X;E)$ *be a closed right (resp. left) ideal. For each* $x \in X$, *let* $I_x$ *be the closure of* I(x) *in* E. *Then* $I_x$ *is a closed right (resp. left) ideal in* E, *and*

$$I = \{f \in C(X;E);\ f(x) \in I_x \text{ for all } x \text{ in } X\}.$$

PROOF. For every x in X, I(x) is clearly a right (resp. left) ideal in E.

Since the multiplication in E is jointly continuous, the closure $I_x$ of $I(x)$ is a right (resp. left) ideal in E. We claim that I is a C(X;F)-module. Indeed, let $f \in I$ and $g \in C(X;F)$ be given. Define $h \in C(X;E)$ to be $x \to g(x)e$, where e is the unit of E. If I is a right ideal, then for all $x \in X$.

$$g(x)f(x) = g(x)[f(x)e] = f(x)[g(x)e] = f(x)h(x).$$

Since $fh \in I$, gf belongs to I. (The case of a left ideal is treated similarly.) It remains to apply Corollary 2.5 to the separating algebra C(X;F) and the closed C(X;F)-module I.

COROLLARY 2.7. <u>Under the hypothesis of Theorem 2.6 assume that the algebra</u> E <u>is simple</u>. <u>Then any two-sided closed ideal consists of all functions vanishing on a closed subset of</u> X.

PROOF. We first recall that the unitary algebra E is said to be simple if it has no two-sided ideals other than 0 and E. Let $N \subset X$ be a closed subset of X. Clearly, the subset $Z(N) = \{f \in C(X;E);\ f(x) = 0 \text{ for all } x \text{ in } N\}$ is a closed two-sided ideal of C(X;E).

Conversely, if I is a closed two-sided ideal in C(X;E), let us define $N = \{x \in X;\ f(x) = 0 \text{ for all } f \in I\}$. Clearly, N is closed in X and $I \subset Z(N)$. Conversely, let $f \in Z(N)$, and assume by contradiction that $f \notin I$. By Theorem 2.6, there is some $x \in X$ such that $f(x) \notin I_x$. Since $I_x$ is a two-sided ideal, and E is simple, $I_x = \{0\}$. Therefore, $f(x) \neq 0$. Now $f \in Z(N)$, so $x \notin N$. However, $I_x = \{0\}$ implies $I(x) = 0$, and so $x \in N$. This contradiction shows that $f \in I$.

## 3. Some Applications

In this section E is a non-archimedean normed space over F, and we assume that $E \neq 0$. The vector subspace of C(X;E) consisting of all finite sums of functions of the form $x \to f(x)v$, where $f \in C(X;F)$ and $v \in E$, will be denoted by $C(X;F) \otimes E$. Clearly, $C(X;F) \otimes E$ is C(X;F)-module.

THEOREM 3.1. <u>Let</u> X <u>be a</u> <u>0-dimensional compact Hausdorff space</u>. <u>Then</u> $C(X;F) \otimes E$ <u>is uniformly dense in</u> C(X;E).

PROOF. Let $W = C(X;F) \otimes E$. Then $W$ is a $C(X;F)$-module, and $C(X;F)$ is separating over $X$. For each $x \in X$, $W(x) = E$. By corollary 2.5 $W$ is dense in $C(X;E)$.

If $X$ and $Y$ are two compact Hausdorff spaces, $C(X;F) \otimes C(Y;F)$ denotes the vector subspace of $C(X \times Y;F)$ consisting of all finite sums of functions of the form

$$(x,y) \to f(x)g(y)$$

where $f \in C(X;F)$ and $g \in C(Y;F)$. If both $X$ and $Y$ are 0-dimensional spaces, then $C(X;F) \otimes C(Y;F)$ is a separating unitary subalgebra of $C(X \times Y;F)$.

THEOREM 3.2. Let $X$ and $Y$ be two 0-dimensional compact Hausdorff spaces. Then $(C(X;F) \otimes C(Y;F)) \otimes E$ is uniformly dense in $C(X \times Y;E)$.

PROOF. Let $W = (C(X;F) \otimes C(Y;F) \otimes E$. $W$ is a $C(X;F) \otimes C(Y;F)$-module such that $W(x,y) = E$ for every pair $(x,y) \in X \times Y$. The result now follows from Corollary 2.5.

REMARK. When $E = F$, then the space $(C(X;F) \otimes C(Y;F)) \otimes E$ is just $C(X;F) \otimes C(Y;F)$ and one obtains Dieudonné's Theorem [4].

In [14] we studied polynomial algebras of functions with values in vector spaces over $\mathbb{R}$ or $\mathbb{C}$. To study the non-archimedean analogue let us adopt the following

DEFINITION 3.3. A vector subspace $W \subset C(X;E)$ is called a polynomial algebra if $A = \{u(f);\ u \in E',\ f \in W\}$ is a subalgebra of $C(X;F)$ such that $A \otimes E \subset W$.

Let us give an example of a polynomial algebra. Let

$$P_f(E;F) \subset C(E;F)$$

be the algebra over $F$ generated by the topological dual $E'$ of $E$. An element $p \in P_f(E;F)$ is called a continuous polynomial of finite type from $E$ into $F$, and is of the form

(1) $$p = \sum_{|\kappa| \leq m} a_\kappa u^\kappa$$

where $\kappa = (\kappa_1,\ldots,\kappa_n) \in \mathbb{N}^n$, $n \in \mathbb{N}^*$, $|\kappa| = \kappa_1 + \ldots + \kappa_n$, $m \in \mathbb{N}$, $a_\kappa \in F$, $u = (u_1,\ldots,u_n) \in (E')^n$, and we define

(2) $u^\kappa(t) = (u_1(t))^{\kappa_1} \ldots (u_n(t))^{\kappa_n}$

for all $t \in E$. Let us now consider two non-archimedean normed spaces $E_1$ and $E_2$ over the same non-archimedean valued field F. We define $P_f(E_1,E_2)$ as the vector subspace of $C(E_1;E_2)$ generated by the functions of the form $t \in E_1 \to p(t)v$ where $p \in P_f(E_1;F)$ and $v \in E_2$. Let now $A = \{u(p);\ u \in E_2',\ p \in P_f(E_1;E_2)\}$. Clearly, $A \subset P_f(E_1;F)$, and $A \otimes E_2 \subset P_f(E_1;E_2)$. Suppose $(E_2)' \neq 0$. Then $A = P_f(E_1;F)$ and $P_f(E_1;E_2)$ is a polynomial algebra. Also, if $X \subset E_1$ is any compact subset, then $W = P_f(E_1;E_2)|X$ is a polynomial algebra contained in $C(X;E_2)$. More generally, if $S \subset C(X;F)$ is any subset, let $A \subset C(X;F)$ be the subalgebra over F generated by S. If $E' \neq 0$, then $W = A \otimes E$ is a polynomial algebra. Indeed, in this case we have $A = \{u(f);\ u \in E',\ f \in W\}$. In particular, $C(X;E)$ is a polynomial algebra, when $E' \neq 0$ (e.g., when $E = F$).

When the field F is spherically complete, the Hahn-Banach Theorem is valid for any non-archimedean normed space E over F (see Ingleton [5]), and then E' is separating over E, and a fortiori, $E' \neq 0$.

Let us introduce the following notation. If $W \subset C(X;E)$ is an A-module, where $A \subset C(X;F)$, we denote by $L_A(W)$ the set of all $f \in C(X;E)$ such that the restriction $f|S$ is in the uniform closure of $W|S$ in $C(S;E)$, for each equivalence class $S \subset X$ modulo $X|A$. Thus, if $\bar{W}$ denotes the uniform closure of W in $C(X;E)$, the Theorem 2.3 may be stated as $f \in \bar{W} \iff f \in L_A(W)$.

THEOREM 3.4. *Let E be a non-archimedean normed space such that E' is separating over E, and let $W \subset C(X;E)$ be a polynomial algebra. Then, for every $f \in C(X;E)$ the following conditions are equivalent* :

(1) $f \in \bar{W}$;

(2) *given* $x, y \in X$ *and* $\varepsilon > 0$, *there is* $g \in W$ *such that* $\|f(x) - g(x)\| < \varepsilon$ *and* $\|f(y) - g(y)\| < \varepsilon$;

(3) (a) *given* $x, y \in X$, *with* $f(x) \neq f(y)$, *there is* $g \in W$ *such that* $g(x) \neq g(y)$; *and*

(b) *given* $x \in X$, *with* $f(x) \neq 0$ *there is* $g \in W$ *such that* $g(x) \neq 0$;

(4) $f \in L_A(A \otimes E)$, *where* $A = \{u(g);\ u \in E',\ g \in W\}$.

PROOF. (1) ⇒ (2). Obvious.

(2) ⇒ (3). Let $x, y \in X$ with $f(x) \neq f(y)$. Define $\varepsilon = \| f(x) - f(y)\| > 0$. By (2) there is $g \in W$ such that $\| f(x) - g(x)\| < \varepsilon$ and $\| f(y)-g(y)\| < \varepsilon$. If $g(x) = g(y)$, then $\varepsilon = \| f(x) - g(x) + g(y) - f(y)\| \leq \max(\| f(x) - g(x)\| , \| g(y) - f(y) \| ) < \varepsilon$, a contradiction. This proves (a). The proof of (b) is similar.

(3) ⇒ (4). Let $S \subset X$ be an equivalence class modulo $X|A$, and let $x,y \in S$. If $f(x) \neq f(y)$, by (a) there is $g \in W$ such that $g(x) \neq g(y)$. Since $E'$ is separating over $E$, there is $u \in E'$ such that $u(g(x)) \neq u(g(y))$. This is impossible, because $u(g) \in A$. Hence $f$ is constant over $S$. Let $t \in E$ be its constant value. If $t = 0$, then $0 \in A \otimes E$ agrees with $f$ over $S$. If $t \neq 0$, then, by (b) there is $g \in W$ such that $g(x) \neq 0$, where $x \in S$ is chosen arbitrarily. Let now $u \in E'$ be such that $u(g(x)) = 1$. Then the function $h = u(g) \otimes t$ belongs to $A \otimes E$ and agrees with $f$ over $S$. Therefore $f \in L_A(A \otimes E)$.

(4) ⇒ (1). By Theorem 2.3 applied to the A-module $A \otimes E \subset C(X;E)$, $f$ belongs to the uniform closure of $A \otimes E$ in $C(X;E)$. Since $A \otimes E \subset W$, the proof is complete.

COROLLARY 3.5. *Let $X$ be a 0-dimensional compact Hausdorff space, and let $E$ and $W$ be as in Theorem 3.4. The following statements are equivalent:*

(1) *$W$ is uniformly dense in $C(X;E)$;*

(2) *$W(x;y) = \{(g(x),g(y));\ g \in W\}$ is dense in $E \times E$, for every pair $x,y \in X$;*

(3) (a) *$W$ is separating over $X$; and*

(b) *$W$ is everywhere different from zero, i.e., given $x \in X$, there is $g \in W$ with $g(x) \neq 0$.*

(4) *Let $A = \{u(g);\ u \in E',\ g \in W\}$. Then $A$ is separating over $X$ and $W(x) = \{g(x);\ g \in W\} = E$ for every $x \in X$.*

PROOF. (1) ⇒ (2) ⇒ (3) are immediate from Theorem 3.4. (3) ⇒ (4) follows from the hypothesis that $E'$ is separating over $E$ and from $A \otimes E \subset W$.

Finally, (4) ⇒ (1) by Corollary 2.5 applied to the A-module $A \otimes E$, which is contained in $W$.

COROLLARY 3.6. (*Weierstrass Polynomial Approximation*) *Let $E_1$ and $E_2$ be two non-archimedean normed spaces over $F$ such that $E_i'$ is separating over $E_i$ $(i=1,2)$. For every compact subset $K \subset E_1$ the set $P_f(E_1;E_2)|K$ is uniformly dense in $C(K;E_2)$.*

PROOF. Let $W = P_f(E_1;E_2)|K$. Since $E_2'$ is separating over $E_2$, $W$ is a polynomial algebra contained in $C(K;E_2)$. Now $W$ contains the constants and it is separating over $K$, because $E_1'$ is separating over $E_1$. It remains to apply the preceding Corollary.

As another application of the general results proved above, let us give a non-archimedean analogue of Blatter's Stone-Weierstrass Theorems for finite-dimensional non-associative real algebras (see [1]).

Let $E$ be a finite-dimensional non-associative linear algebra over a complete non-archimedean non-trivially valued field $F$. Since every field provided with a topology induced by a non-trivial valuation is strictly minimal (see Nachbin [12]), there is a unique Hausdorff topology on $E$ that makes it a topological vector space over $F$, and moreover, under this topology, every linear transformation $T : E \to E$ is continuous. (See [12], Theorems 7 and 9.) We shall always consider $E$ endowed with its unique Hausdorff topology that makes it a topological vector space over $F$. This topology, called admissible in [12], can be defined as follows. If $\{e_1,\ldots,e_n\}$ is a basis of $E$ over $F$, then the non-archimedean sup-norm $\|v\| = \max\{|v_i|;\ 1 \leq i \leq n\}$, whenever $v = \sum_{i=1}^{n} v_i e_i$ is in $E$, defines the unique admissible topology of $E$.

If we define operations pointwise, $C(X;E)$ becomes a non-associative algebra over $F$ too, as well a bimodule over $E$: if $v \in E$ and $f \in C(X;E)$ then the mappings $x \to vf(x)$ and $x \to f(x)v$ belong to $C(X;E)$. A vector subspace $W \subset C(X;E)$ is called a submodule over $E$ if it is a bimodule over $E$, with the above operations. An algebra $E$ is called a zero-algebra if $uv = 0$ for all $u,v \in E$. The algebra $E$ is called simple if it is not a zero-algebra and has no subspaces invariant relative to the right and left multiplications, except $0$ and $E$. Let $M(E)$ be the subalgebra of $L(E)$ generated by the set of all right and left multiplications. $M(E)$ is called the multiplication algebra of $E$. If follows that a non-zero-algebra is simple if, and only if, $M(E)$ is an irreducible algebra of linear transformations. The centroid of $E$ is the set of all linear transformations $T \in L(E)$ which commute with all right and left multiplications. Clearly, all linear transformations of the form $\lambda I$ belong to the centroid of $E$, where $\lambda \in F$ and $I$ is the identity map of $E$. We say that $E$ is central if its centroid is just $\{\lambda I;\ \lambda \in F\}$.

THEOREM 3.7. _Let_ $F$ _be a complete and non-trivially valued non-archimedean field. Let_ $E$ _be a finite-dimensional central and simple non-associative algebra_ *over F. Let $W \subset C(X;E)$ be an F-subalgebra which is a submodule over E. Then, for every $f \in C(X;E)$, conditions (1) - (4) of Theorem 3.4 are equivalent.*

PROOF. The proof consists in showing that, under the above hypothesis on E, any F-subalgebra $W \subset C(X;E)$ which is a submodule over E is a polynomial algebra.

By Theorem 4, Chapter X, Jacobson [6], we have $M(E) = L(E)$. Hence the submodule W is invariant under composition with any linear transformation $T \in L(E)$. Let $A = \{u(f);\ u \in E',\ f \in W\}$. By Lemma 1.1 of [13], extended to the case of F, A is a vector subspace of $C(X;F)$ and $A \otimes E \subset W$. It remains to prove that A is closed under multiplication. Since E is not a zero-algebra, choose a pair $u_0$, $v_0$ in E such that $u_0 v_0 \neq 0$. Let $u \in E'$ be such that $u(u_0 v_0) = 1$. Let $v(f)$ and $w(g)$ be in A. The mappings $x \to v(f(x))u_0$ and $x \to w(g(x))v_0$ belong to W, since $A \otimes E \subset W$. By hypothesis, W is a subalgebra of $C(X;E)$. Therefore,

$$x \to [v(f(x))u_0] \cdot [w(g(x))v_0] = v(f(x))\, w(g(x))u_0 v_0$$

belongs to W. Call it h. Then $u(h) \in A$, and $u(h) = v(f)w(g)$, since $u(u_0 v_0)=1$. Thus W is polynomial algebra.

## 4. Bishop's Theorem

Let F be a non-archimedean valued field, and let K be a finite extension of F. If F is complete, then the rank one valuation $t \to |t| \in \mathbb{R}_+$ of F can be extended from F to K in a unique way as rank one valuation. If F is not complete, then its valuation can be extended to a rank one valuation of K in finitely many non-equivalent ways.

DEFINITION 4.1. *Let F be a non-archimedean valued field; let K be a finite algebraic extension of F, endowed with a rank one valuation extending that of F. Let $A \subset C(X;K)$ be a subalgebra. A subset $S \subset X$ is called A - antisymmetric (with respect to F) if, for every $a \in A$, $a|S$ being F-valued implies that $a|S$ is constant.*

DEFINITION 4.2. *Let $x, y \in X$. We write $x \equiv y$ if there is an A - antisymmetric set S which contains both x and y.*

The equivalence classes modulo the equivalence relation $x \equiv y$ are called maximal A-antisymmetric sets (with respect to F).

The following result is the non-archimedean analogue of Machado's version of Bishop's Theorem [8]. In it, F is a non-archimedean valued field; K is a finite algebraic extension of F, and K is valued by one extension to K of the valuation of F; X is a compact Hausdorff space and E is a non-archimedean normed space over K.

THEOREM 4.3. *Let $A \subset C(X;K)$ be a subalgebra; let $W \subset C(X;E)$ be a vector subspace which is an A-module. For each $f \in C(X;E)$, there is a maximal A-antisymmetric set (with respect to F) $S \subset X$ such that*

$$d(f;W) = d(f|S;\ W|S).$$

COROLLARY 4.4. *Let A and W be as in Theorem 4.3, and let $f \in C(X;E)$. Then f belongs to the closure of W in C(X;E) if, and only if, $f|S$ belongs to the closure of $W|S$ in C(S;E), for each maximal A-antisymmetric set (with respect to F) $S \subset X$.*

Proof of Theorem 4.3. Let $f \in C(X;E)$. Put $d = d(f;W)$. We can assume $d > 0$, the result being clear for $d = 0$, since $d(f|S;\ W|S) \leq d$ for any $S \subset X$. Let D be the set of all ordered pairs (P,S) such that

(i) P is a partition of X into non-empty pairwise disjoint and closed subsets of X;

(ii) $S \in P$ and $d = d(f|S;\ W|S)$.

The pair $(\{X\},X)$ belongs to D, so $D \neq \emptyset$. We partially order D by setting $(P,S) \leq (Q,T)$ if, and only if, the partition Q is finer than P, and $T \subset S$. The arguments in Machado's proof of Bishop's Theorem (see [8]) apply here, so that each chain in D has an upper bound. By Zorn's Lemma there is a maximal element $(Q,T) \in D$. We claim that T is A-antisymmetric (with respect to F). Indeed, let $A_T$ be the set $\{a \in A;\ a|T \text{ is F-valued}\}$. By contradiction admit that $B = A_T|T$ contains non-constant functions. Since $B \subset C(T;F)$, and $W|T$ is a B-module, by Theorem 2.4 we may find an equivalence class $V \subset T$ (modulo $T|B$) such that

$$d(f|T;\ W|T) = d(f|V;\ W|V).$$

Since $d = d(f|T; W|T)$, and $V$ is a proper subset of $T$, the partition $P$ of $X$ consisting of the elements of $Q$ distinct from $T$ and by the equivalence classes of $T$ modulo $T|B$ is strictly finer then $Q$, and therefore $(Q ; T) < (P , V)$, which contradicts the maximality of $(Q,T)$. The maximal A-antisymmetric set $S$, which contains $T$, is then such that $d = d(f|S; W|S)$.

## REFERENCES


[1] Blatter, J., Grothendieck spaces in approximation theory. Mem. Amer. Math. Soc. 120, 1972.

[2] Buck, R. C., Approximation properties of vector valued functions. Pacific J. Math. 53 (1974), 85 - 94.

[3] Chernoff, P.R. - Rasala, R. A., and Waterhouse, W.C., The Stone-Weierstrass theorem for valuable fields. Pacific J. Math. 27 (1968), 233 - 240.

[4] Dieudonné, J., Sur les fonctions continues p-adiques. Bull. Sci. Math. 68 (1944), 79 - 95.

[5] Ingleton, A. W., The Hahn-Banach theorem for non-Archimedean valued fields. Proc. Cambridge Philos. Soc. 48 (1952), 41 - 45.

[6] Jacobson, N., Lie Algebras. Interscience Tracts in Pure and Applied Mathematics, 10, Interscience Publishers, New York, 1962.

[7] Kaplansky, I., The Weierstrass theorem in fields with valuations. Proc. Amer. Math. Soc. 1 (1950), 356 - 357.

[8] Machado, S., On Bishop's generalization of the Weierstrass-Stone theorem. Indag. Math. 39 (1977), 218 - 224.

[9] Machado, S. and Prolla, J. B., An introduction to Nachbin spaces. Rend. Circ. Mat. Palermo, Serie II 21 (1972), 119 - 139.

[10] Monna, A. F., Analyse non-archimédienne. Ergebnisse der Mathematik und ihrer Grenzgebiete, Band 56, Springer-Verlag, Berlin 1970.

[11] Nachbin, L., Elements of Approximation Theory. D. Van Nostrand Co. Inc., 1967. Reprinted by R. Krieger Co., Inc., 1976.

[12] Nachbin, L., On strictly minimal topological division rings. Bull. Amer. Math. Soc. 55 (1949), 1128 - 1136.

[13] Narici, L., Beckenstein, E., and Bachman, G., Functional analysis and valuation theory. Pure and Applied Mathematics, vol. 5, Marcel Dekker, Inc., New York 1971.

[14] Prolla, J. B., and Machado, S., Weighted Grothendieck subspaces. Trans. Amer. Math. Soc. 186 (1973), 247 - 258.

[15] Rudin, W., Real and Complex analysis. McGraw-Hill Co., New York 1966.

# KODISSIPATIVE METRISCHE PROJEKTIONEN IN NORMIERTEN LINEAREN RÄUMEN

H. Berens
Mathematisches Institut
Universität Erlangen-Nürnberg
D-8520 Erlangen

U. Westphal
Fachbereich 3
Universität Osnabrück/Abt. Vechta
D-2848 Vechta

Let H be a real inner product space with inner product $<\cdot,\cdot>$. For any subset K of H the metric projection $P_K:H \to \mathcal{P}(K)$ is monotone, i.e., for any (x,k), $(x',k') \in P_K < k-k',x-x' > \geq 0$. This property is used to characterize closed convex sets in Hilbert space.
There is a natural extension of monotonicity of set-valued mappings in normed linear spaces. For a proximinal subset K in a normed linear space we can prove that $P_K$ is contractive iff K is solar and $P_K$ is monotone. Furthermore, an inner product space is characterized by the fact that for any K its projection $P_K$ is monotone.

## 1. Einleitung

Für eine abgeschlossene konvexe Teilmenge K eines reellen Hilbertraumes H sei $P_K:H \to K$ die metrische Projektion von H auf K, also der Operator, der durch die Ungleichung

$$\|x-P_K(x)\| < \|x-k\|, \text{ falls } k\in K \text{ und } k \neq P_K(x),$$

für jedes $x\in H$ definiert ist.

Es ist wohlbekannt, daß $P_K$ ein monotoner Operator auf H ist, d.h., daß

$$< P_K(x) - P_K(x'),x-x' > \geq 0$$

für jedes $x,x'\in H$ gilt.

Ist K eine beliebige Teilmenge von H, so ist die metrische Projektion i.a. ein mehrwertiger Operator, und obwohl elementar nachzuweisen, siehe Lemma 2.1, wird unseres Wissens nach nirgends in der Literatur erwähnt, daß auch dann $P_K$ monoton ist im Sinne der Erweiterung dieses Begriffs auf mehrwertige Operatoren. Es ist nun unser Anliegen, die Theorie der monotonen Operatoren und ihrer Verallgemeinerungen in normierten linearen Räumen, die sich in den letzten fünfzehn Jahren stark entwickelt hat, in der Approximationstheorie auf metrische Projektionsoperatoren anzuwenden und erste Ergebnisse darüber in dieser Arbeit vorzulegen.

In Abschnitt 2 zeigen wir, daß die metrischen Projektionen für abgeschlossene konvexe Mengen in Hilberträumen nicht nur monoton sondern sogar maximal monoton sind und sich genau durch diese Eigenschaft unter allen metrischen Projektionen auszeichnen. Wir erhalten dabei auch einen neuen Beweis und eine Verschärfung eines bekannten Ergebnisses von Asplund [2] über eine hinreichende Bedingung für die Konvexität einer Tschebyscheff-Menge.

Bei metrischen Projektionen in allgemeinen normierten linearen Räumen ist der Begriff "kodissipativ" eine adäquate Verallgemeinerung für "monoton". Wir zeigen im 3. Abschnitt, daß die Eigenschaft, daß $P_K$ für *jede* Teilmenge K des Raumes kodissipativ ist, für innere Produkträume charakteristisch ist.

Im 4. Abschnitt befassen wir uns mit einer speziellen Klasse von Teilmengen eines normierten linearen Raumes, nämlich den sog. Sonnen, die in der Theorie der besten Approximation eine wichtige Rolle spielen. Wir zeigen unter anderem, daß für Sonnen die Kodissipativität ihrer metrischen Projektion deren Kontraktivität nach sich zieht. Umgekehrt impliziert für proximinale Teilmengen K die Kontraktivität von $P_K$ die Sonneneigenschaft von K und die Kodissipativität von $P_K$.

## 2. Maximal monotone metrische Projektionen in Hilberträumen

Es sei H ein reeller innerer Produktraum mit dem Skalarprodukt $\langle\cdot,\cdot\rangle$ und der zugehörigen Norm $\|\cdot\|$. Unter einem mehrwertigen Operator A in H verstehen wir eine Abbildung von H in die Potenzmenge $\mathcal{P}(H)$ von H. Es ist $D(A) = \{x\in H; A(x) \neq \emptyset\}$ der Definitionsbereich und $R(A) = \bigcup\{A(x); x\in H\}$ der Wertebereich von A. Wir identifizieren A mit seinem Graphen in $H\times H$; d.h. $A = \{(x,y)\in H\times H; y\in A(x)\}$. Die Inverse $A^{-1}$ ist der Operator in H, dessen Graph durch $A^{-1} = \{(x,y)\in H\times H; (y,x)\in A\}$ gegeben ist.

A heißt *monoton*, falls für jedes $(x,y),(x',y')\in A$ gilt:

$$\langle y-y', x-x'\rangle \geq 0.$$

A heißt *maximal monoton*, wenn A in der Menge der monotonen mehrwertigen Operatoren bzgl. Inklusion in $H\times H$ maximal ist. Bzgl. Literatur über monotone Operatoren verweisen wir auf die Darstellung [4] von Brézis, die eine umfangreiche Bibliographie sowie zahlreiche Kommentare in einem Anhang enthält.

Für eine nichtleere Teilmenge K von H ist die *metrische Projektion* $P_K$ von H auf K durch

$$P_K(x) = \{k\in K; \|x-k\| = \inf_{k'\in K} \|x-k'\|\}$$

für jedes $x\in H$ definiert.

K heißt Existenzmenge (oder auch proximinal), falls $P_K(x) \neq \emptyset$ für jedes $x\in H$ ist, und K heißt Tschebyscheff-Menge, wenn $P_K(x)$ eine Einpunktmenge für jedes $x\in H$ ist.

LEMMA 2.1. *Für eine nichtleere Teilmenge K eines Prähilbertraumes H ist die metrische Projektion $P_K$ ein monotoner Operator.*

BEWEIS. Für $(x,k),(x',k')\in P_K$ gilt:

$$\|x-k\| \leq \|x-k'\| \text{ und } \|x'-k'\| \leq \|x'-k\|.$$

Benutzt man diese Ungleichungen zur Abschätzung der rechten Seite der folgenden Gleichung

$$2 < k-k', x-x' > = \|x'-k\|^2+\|x-k'\|^2-\|x-k\|^2-\|x'-k'\|^2,$$

so folgt die Behauptung. //

Ist nun K eine abgeschlossene konvexe Teilmenge eines Hilbertraumes, so ist bekanntlich K eine Tschebyscheff-Menge, also $P_K$ ein einwertiger Operator von ganz H auf K. Weiterhin ist $P_K$ ein Kontraktionsoperator, d.h. es gilt

$$\|P_K(x)-P_K(x')\| \leq \|x-x'\|$$

für alle $x,x'\in D(P_K) = H$. Bezüglich Literatur über metrische Projektionen auf abgeschlossenen konvexen Mengen verweisen wir auf die ausführliche Untersuchung[15] von Zarantonello.

Benutzt man nun zwei bekannte Ergebnisse über maximal monotone Operatoren, so ergibt sich der folgende Äquivalenzsatz:

SATZ 2.2. *Für eine nichtleere Teilmenge K eines Hilbertraumes H mit metrischer Projektion $P_K$ sind folgende Aussagen äquivalent:*

(1) K *ist abgeschlossen und konvex;*

(2) K *ist eine Tschebyscheff-Menge, und* $P_K$ *ist eine Kontraktion;*

(3) K *ist eine Tschebyscheff-Menge, und* $P_K$ *ist demi-stetig*, d.h. *stetig von* H, *versehen mit der Normtopologie, in* H, *versehen mit der schwachen Topologie;*

(4) K *ist eine Existenzmenge, und es existiert eine schwach hemi-stetige Selektion* $S_K$ *von* $P_K$, *d.h. für jedes* $x\in H$ *und jedes* $\xi\in H$ *gilt*

$$\lim_{t\to 0+} S_K((1-t)x+t\xi) = S_K(x)$$

<u>in der schwachen Topologie</u>;

(5) $P_K$ <u>ist maximal monoton</u>.

BEWEIS. Die Schritte (1) ⇒ (2) ⇒ (3) ⇒ (4) sind klar.

(4) ⇒ (5): Nach Brézis [4, Prop. 2.4] ist ein einwertiger, schwach hemistetiger monotoner Operator A mit D(A) = H (H ist vollständig) maximal monoton. Folglich ist $S_K = P_K$ maximal monoton.

(5) ⇒ (1): Sei $\overline{K}$ die Abschließung von K in der Normtopologie. Da trivialerweise $P_K \subset P_{\overline{K}}$ , folgt aus der maximalen Monotonie von $P_K$ die Abgeschlossenheit von K. Zum Beweis der Konvexität von K benutzen wir ein Ergebnis von Minty und Rockafellar, siehe [4, Thm. 2.2]: <u>Ist</u> A <u>maximal monoton in</u> H × H (H ist vollständig), <u>so ist</u> $\overline{D(A)}$ <u>konvex</u>. Da mit $P_K$ auch $P_K^{-1}$ maximal monoton ist und $\overline{D(P_K^{-1})} = \overline{K} = K$, ist demnach K konvex. //

Neben der Charakterisierung abgeschlossener konvexer Mengen mittels der maximalen Monotonie ihrer metrischen Projektionen berührt Satz 2.2 ein altbekanntes Problem aus der Theorie der besten Approximation in Hilberträumen, und zwar die Frage, ob es nicht-konvexe Tschebyscheff-Mengen gibt und wenn ja, unter welchen Zusatzbedingungen die Tschebyscheff-Eigenschaft Konvexität impliziert, siehe hierzu insbesondere die Ausführungen von Klee [9]. In diesem Zusammenhang hat Asplund [2] gezeigt: <u>Jede Tschebyscheff-Menge, deren metrische Projektion demi-stetig ist, ist abgeschlossen und konvex</u>. Dies ist die Implikation (3) ⇒ (1) von Satz 2.2. Satz 2.2 besagt darüberhinaus, daß die Demi-Stetigkeit durch die schwache Hemi-Stetigkeit ersetzt werden kann. Eine weitere Aussage in dieser Richtung ergibt sich aus der maximalen Monotonie von $P_K$: <u>Die Menge</u> $K \subset H$ <u>ist abgeschlossen und konvex, falls für jedes</u> $y \in H$ <u>ein</u> $(x,k) \in P_K$ <u>existiert mit</u> $y = x+k$. Hier wird keine Stetigkeitsforderung an $P_K$ gestellt, sondern die Surjektivität von $I+P_K$ verlangt, was zur maximalen Monotonie von $P_K$ äquivalent ist.

Asplund führt seinen Beweis mit Hilfe von Differenzierbarkeitseigenschaften konvexer Funktionen, insbesondere der folgenden stetigen konvexen Funktion

$$f(x) = \sup \{ \langle x,k \rangle - \frac{1}{2} \|k\|^2 ;\ k \in K \}$$
$$= \frac{1}{2} \|x\|^2 - \inf \{ \frac{1}{2} \|x-k\|^2 ;\ k \in K \},\ x \in H,$$

die durch die Beziehung

(2.1) $$P_K \subset \partial f$$

mit der metrischen Projektion $P_K$ verknüpft ist; dabei bedeutet $\partial f$ das Subdifferential von f. Es ist wohlbekannt, siehe z.B. [8, S. 19], daß das Subdifferential einer konvexen Funktion monoton ist. Die Beziehung (2.1) impliziert also die Monotonie von $P_K$ für jedes $K \subset H$. Asplund weist in seiner Arbeit jedoch nicht auf diese Eigenschaft hin, und er macht auch keinen Gebrauch davon im Beweis seiner Sätze.

## 3. Eine Charakterisierung innerer Produkträume

Wir haben gesehen, daß in einem inneren Produktraum H die metrische Projektion $P_K$ für jede Teilmenge $K \subset H$ ein monotoner Operator ist. Wir werden nun zeigen, daß diese Eigenschaft diese Räume unter allgemeinen normierten linearen Räumen auszeichnet. Zunächst einige Definitionen.

Sei X ein reeller normierter linearer Raum mit stetigem Dualen $X^*$. Die Norm auf X werde mit $\|\cdot\|$ bezeichnet und die durch die Dualität von X und $X^*$ bestimmte Bilinearform mit $\langle\cdot,\cdot\rangle$. Auf $X \times X$ sei ein "Skalarprodukt" wie folgt definiert: Für $x,y \in X$ sei

$$(3.1) \qquad \langle x,y \rangle_s = \lim_{t\to 0+} \frac{1}{2t} \{\|y+tx\|^2 - \|y\|^2\}$$

$$(3.2) \qquad = \sup \{\langle x,y^* \rangle; y^* \in F(y)\},$$

wobei $F : X \to \mathcal{P}(X^*)$ die sog. Dualitätsbildung von X ist, die für jedes $y \in X$ durch

$$F(y) = \{y^* \in X^*;\ \|y^*\| = \|y\|,\ \langle y,y^* \rangle = \|y\|\,\|y^*\|\}$$

gegeben ist. Im folgenden sind einige Eigenschaften dieses Skalarproduktes zusammengestellt. Für $x,y,z \in X$ gilt:

(1) $\langle \lambda y+x,y \rangle_s = \lambda\|y\|^2 + \langle x,y \rangle_s$ für jedes $\lambda \in \mathbb{R}$.

(2) $\langle \lambda x,\mu y \rangle_s = \lambda\mu \langle x,y \rangle_s$ für jedes $\lambda,\mu \in \mathbb{R}$ mit $\lambda\mu \geq 0$.

(3) $\langle x+y,z \rangle_s \leq \langle x,z \rangle_s + \langle y,z \rangle_s$.

(4) $|\langle x,y \rangle_s| \leq \|x\|\,\|y\|$.

(5) Ist X glatt, - d.h. besitzt die abgeschlossene Einheitskugel in X in jedem ihrer Randpunkte genau eine Stützhyperebene -, so gilt in (3) Gleichheit. Für jedes $z \in X$ ist $\langle \cdot,z \rangle_s$ folglich ein stetiges lineares Funktional.

Es sei nun A ein (mehrwertiger) Operator in X. Die Begriffsbildungen und Bezeichnungen im Zusammenhang mit mehrwertigen Operatoren gelten entsprechend zu denen, die im Falle eines inneren Produktraumes zu Beginn von Abschnitt 2 eingeführt wurden.

A heißt a k k r e t i v , falls für jedes Paar $(x,y),(x',y')\in A$ gilt:

$$< y-y',x-x' >_s \geq 0.$$

A ist genau dann akkretiv, wenn $(I+\lambda A)^{-1}$ für jedes $\lambda > 0$ eine Kontraktion ist; d.h. wenn für jedes $(x,y),(x',y')\in A$ und jedes $\lambda > 0$ gilt:

$$\|(x-x') + \lambda(y-y')\| \geq \|x-x'\|.$$

$A \subset X \times X$ heißt k o d i s s i p a t i v , falls $A^{-1}$ akkretiv ist, d.h. also, falls für jedes $(x,y),(x',y')\in A$ gilt:

$$< x-x',y-y' >_s \geq 0.$$

In inneren Produkträumen ist "monoton" gleichbedeutend mit "akkretiv" und "kodissipativ".

Nichtlineare akkretive Operatoren wurden Mitte der sechziger Jahre im Zusammenhang mit der Theorie der nichtlinearen Kontraktionshalbgruppen und der Theorie der nichtlinearen Evolutionsgleichungen in Banachräumen eingeführt. Es sind zwei Definitionen für "akkretiv" geläufig; die eine stammt von Browder, die andere, etwas umfassendere, von Kato. Die oben angegebene Definition stimmt mit der von Kato überein. Crandall und Liggett [6] haben die systematische Benutzung des Skalarproduktes $<\cdot,\cdot>_s$ in der Form (3.2) in die Behandlung akkretiver Operatoren aufgenommen, während Bénilan [3] die äquivalente Darstellung (3.1) einführte. Bzgl. weiterer Literatur siehe z.B. die Kommentare im Anhang von [4].

Bei unseren Ausführungen über die metrische Projektion erweist sich der Begriff der Kodissipativität als die geeignete Verallgemeinerung für die Monotonie. Der Hauptsatz dieses Abschnitts lautet:

SATZ 3.1. *Sei X ein reeller normierter linearer Raum. X ist ein innerer Produktraum genau dann, wenn für jede Teilmenge $K \subset X$ die metrische Projektion $P_K$ kodissipativ ist.*

Wir beweisen diesen Satz getrennt für Räume der Dimension $\geq 3$ und für 2-dimensionale Räume. In beiden Fällen benutzen wir dazu bekannte Resultate zur Charakterisierung von inneren Produkträumen. In Räumen der Dimension $\geq 3$ spielt dabei die Kontraktionseigenschaft der metrischen Projektion bzw. einer Selektion derselben eine entscheidende Rolle. Dies ist ein Ergebnis, das auf Kakutani in Verbindung mit der bekannten Charakterisierung von Jordan und v. Neumann zurückgeht. Wir benutzen hier einen Satz von Phelps, der implizit in

[12] enthalten ist; siehe auch Singer [13, Cor. 5.1]:

Sei X ein normierter linearer Raum, dessen Dimension mindestens 3 ist. X ist ein Prähilbertraum dann und nur dann, wenn für jeden eindimensionalen linearen Teilraum $K \subset X$ die metrische Projektion $P_K$ eine Kontraktion ist.

Daß die hinreichende Bedingung dieses Satzes erfüllt ist, wenn die metrische Projektion $P_K$ eines jeden eindimensionalen linearen Teilraumes K von X kodissipativ ist, ist als Sonderfall in Satz 4.1 von Abschnitt 4 enthalten. Damit wäre Satz 3.1 für Räume der Dimension $\geq 3$ bewiesen.

Für zweidimensionale Räume benutzen wir ein Ergebnis, das Mann [10] und Motzkin [11] gleichzeitig und unabhängig voneinander bewiesen haben. Es charakterisiert die inneren Produkträume mit Hilfe einer Approximationseigenschaft für zweipunktige Mengen:

Die Ebene $\mathbb{R}^2$ versehen mit einer Norm $\|\cdot\|$ ist genau dann ein innerer Produktraum, wenn für je zwei Elemente $k,k' \in \mathbb{R}^2$, $k \neq k'$, gilt, daß die Menge $P^{-1}_{\{k,k'\}}(k) = \{x \in \mathbb{R}^2; \|x-k\| \leq \|x-k'\|\}$ konvex ist.

Mann hat das Resultat allgemeiner für den $\mathbb{R}^n$ im Zusammenhang mit Untersuchungen über Wabenzellen bewiesen. Von Day [7] wurde es später auf normierte lineare Räume erweitert.

BEWEIS für dim X = 2: Im folgenden sei X der Raum $\mathbb{R}^2$ mit einer Norm $\|\cdot\|$, so daß für jedes $K \subset \mathbb{R}^2$ $P_K$ kodissipativ ist und folglich nach Satz 4.1 für jede konvexe Menge auch kontraktiv.

O.B.d.A. können wir annehmen, daß die Norm strikt konvex ist, denn sonst existiert eine Gerade G in $\mathbb{R}^2$, für die die metrische Projektion $P_G$ nicht eindeutig ist, was der Kontraktivität von $P_G$ widerspricht.

Wir nehmen an, die Norm sei nicht glatt. Dann existiert ein Punkt x auf der Einheitssphäre S, der mehr als eine Stützgerade besitzt. Sei $G_x$ die Gerade, die durch x und den Nullpunkt bestimmt wird, und seien $G'_x$ und $G''_x$ die Stützgeraden an S, die parallel zu $G_x$ verlaufen, mit den Berührungspunkten y' und y". Offenkundig liegen die beiden Punkte auf einer Geraden durch den Ursprung. Da die Sphäre S in x nicht glatt ist, existiert eine Stützgerade in x, deren Parallele G durch den Ursprung die Punkte y' und y" trennt.

Wir bezeichnen mit K den abgeschlossenen Halbraum mit Rand G, der den Punkt x nicht enthält. Wegen der strikten Konvexität ist K eine Tschebyscheff-Menge. Wir behaupten, daß $P_K$ nicht kontraktiv ist. In der Tat ist $P_K(x) = 0$. Nehmen wir an, daß y' im Komplement von K liegt, wir können dies o.B.d.A.tun, dann ist $P_K(x+y') = k$ der Schnittpunkt der Geraden $G'_x$ mit G. (K ist eine Sonne, siehe den folgenden Abschnitt, was unter anderem diese Aussage impliziert.) Nach Konstruktion ist jedoch k außerhalb von S, d.h.,

$$\|(x+y')-x\| = \|y'\| = 1 < \|k\| = \|P_K(x+y')-P_K(x)\|.$$

Wir nehmen an, die Norm sei glatt. In diesem Falle zeigen wir, daß für jede zweipunktige Menge $K \subset \mathbb{R}^2$ die Kodissipativität von $P_K$ die Konvexität von $P_K^{-1}(k), k \in K$, impliziert. Aus dem Resultat von Mann und Motzkin folgt die Hilbertraumstruktur von $\mathbb{R}^2$. //

Allgemeiner als oben angegeben gilt

LEMMA 3.2. Sei X ein glatter normierter linearer Raum, und seien $k,k' \in X$ mit $k \neq k'$. Ist die metrische Projektion $P_{\{k,k'\}}$ kodissipativ, dann gilt: $P^{-1}_{\{k,k'\}}(k)$ und $P^{-1}_{\{k,k'\}}(k')$ sind die von der Hyperebene $G = \{y \in X;\ \langle y,k-k'\rangle_s = \frac{1}{2}\|k-k'\|^2 + \langle k',k-k'\rangle_s\}$ bestimmten abgeschlossenen Halbräume.

BEWEIS. O.B.d.A. sei $k' = 0$. Wir setzen $P = P_{\{0,k\}}$, und $G = \{y \in X;\ \langle y,k\rangle_s = \frac{1}{2}\|k\|^2\}$ ist die Hyperebene, die die Kugeln um 0 und k mit Radius $\frac{1}{2}\|k\|$ trennt. Seien $E_0$ und $E_k$ die von G erzeugten abgeschlossenen Halbräume, also $E_0 = \{y \in X;\ \langle y,k\rangle_s \le \frac{1}{2}\|k\|^2\}$ und $E_k = \{y \in X;\ \langle y,k\rangle_s \ge \frac{1}{2}\|k\|^2\}$.

Wir zeigen: $P^{-1}(0) = E_0$ und $P^{-1}(k) = E_k$. Sei $x \in P^{-1}(0)$. Da P nach Voraussetzung kodissipativ ist, gilt für die Punkte $(\frac{1}{2}k,k)$ und $(x,0)$ die Ungleichung $\langle \frac{1}{2}k-x,k\rangle_s \ge 0$, d.h. $\langle x,k\rangle_s \le \frac{1}{2}\|k\|^2$, also ist $x \in E_0$. Entsprechend zeigt man: $P^{-1}(k) \subset E_k$. Ist $x \notin P^{-1}(0)$, so gilt $\|x-k\| < \|x\|$. Sei $x_t = tx$ und $\rho(t) = \|x_t\|-\|x_t-k\|$ für $t \in [0,1]$. Da $\rho(0) < 0$ und $\rho(1) > 0$, existiert ein $t_0 \in (0,1)$, so daß $\|x_{t_0}\| = \|x_{t_0}-k\|$ ist. D.h. $x_{t_0} \in P^{-1}(0) \cap P^{-1}(k) \subset G$. Damit ergibt sich: $\frac{1}{2}\|k\|^2 = \langle x_{t_0},k\rangle_s < \langle x,k\rangle_s$, d.h. $x \notin E_0$.

## 4. Sonnen mit kodissipativer metrischer Projektion

Der Begriff der Sonne wurde von Efimov und Stečkin eingeführt. Er ergibt sich in der Approximationstheorie in allgemeinen normierten Räumen auf natürliche Weise als eine Verallgemeinerung konvexer Mengen. In diesem Abschnitt geben wir einige Ergebnisse über Sonnen, deren metrische Projektion kodissipativ ist. Ein Charakterisierungsmerkmal wird dabei die Kontraktivität der metrischen Projektion sein.

Eine Teilmenge K eines linearen normierten Raumes X heißt S o n n e , falls für jedes $(x,k) \in P_K$ gilt:

$$(k+\lambda(x-k),k)\in P_K \text{ für jedes } \lambda \geq 0.$$

In vielen Untersuchungen über Sonnen und deren verschiedene Varianten, siehe z.B. den Übersichtsartikel von Vlasov [14], wird zur obigen Definition zusätzlich die Proximinalität von K gefordert.

Jede konvexe Menge ist eine Sonne. Eine teilweise Umkehrung dieses Sachverhaltes stammt von Phelps sowie Vlasov: Ist X glatt und $K \subset X$ eine proximinale Sonne, so ist K konvex. Brosowski [5] hat eine Sonne mit Hilfe des sogenannten verallgemeinerten Kolmogoroff-Kriteriums charakterisiert; für einen Beweis und für weitere Aussagen siehe auch Amir und Deutsch [1]:

$K \subset X$ _ist eine Sonne genau dann, wenn_ K _der folgenden Bedingung genügt: Für jedes_ $(x,k)\in P_K$ _und jedes_ $k'\in K$ gilt

$$< k-k',x-k >_s \geq 0.$$

SATZ 4.1. _Sei X ein reeller normierter linearer Raum und K eine nichtleere Teilmenge von X. Wir betrachten die folgenden Aussagen:_

(1) K _ist eine Sonne, und_ $P_K$ _ist kodissipativ;_

(2) $P_K^{-1}-I$ _ist akkretiv; d.h. für jedes_ $(x,k),(x',k')\in P_K$ _gilt_ $\|k-k'\|^2 \leq < x-x',k-k' >_s$;

(3) $P_K$ _ist eine Kontraktion._

_Dann gilt_: (1) $\Rightarrow$ (2) $\Leftrightarrow$ (3).

BEWEIS. Seien $(x,k),(x',k')\in P_K$. Aus der Sonneneigenschaft von K ergibt sich $(x_\lambda,k),(x'_\lambda,k')\in P_K$ für jedes $\lambda \geq 0$, wobei $x_\lambda = k+\lambda(x-k)$ ist, entsprechend für $x'_\lambda$, und weiter aus der Kodissipativität von $P_K$

$$0 \leq < x_\lambda-x'_\lambda,k-k' >_s = (1-\lambda)\|k-k'\|^2 + \lambda < x-x',k-k' >_s$$

für jedes $\lambda \geq 0$. Dividiert man diese Ungleichung durch $\lambda$ und läßt $\lambda \to \infty$ streben, so ergibt sich daraus

$$\|k-k'\|^2 \leq < x-x',k-k' >_s ,$$

womit (2) bewiesen ist. Diese Ungleichung und die Abschätzung

$$|< x-x',k-k' >_s| \leq \|x-x'\| \, \|k-k'\|$$

implizieren die Kontraktivität von $P_K$, also (3). Da $(x,k)\in P_K$ $(x_\lambda,k)\in P_K$, $0 \leq \lambda \leq 1$, nach sich zieht, folgt aus (3) für die Paare $(x,k),(x',k')\in P_K$ und $0 \leq \lambda \leq 1$

$$\|k-k'\| \leq \|x_\lambda-x'_\lambda\| = \|k-k' + \lambda\{(x-k) - (x'-k')\}\|,$$

was nach (3.1)

$$< (x-k) - (x'-k'), k-k' >_s \geq 0$$

und damit (2) impliziert. //

Es ist eine offene Frage, ob die Aussagen (1) und (2) des Satzes äquivalent sind. Wir können dies unter zusätzlichen Voraussetzungen an den Raum X und/oder die Menge K beweisen. So gilt die Äquivalenz in inneren Produkträumen, hier ist die Forderung der Kodissipativität von $P_K$ in (1) redundant. Weiter können wir die Äquivalenz für proximinale Teilmengen K beweisen. Dies sind die Aussagen der folgenden Sätze. Zu ihren Beweisen benötigen wir das folgende Lemma. Es ist, zumindest für Banachräume, in einem allgemeineren Ergebnis von Brosowski [5] enthalten. Wir geben hier für den Spezialfall einen elementaren Beweis, der auch in nicht vollständigen normierten linearen Räumen gültig ist.

LEMMA 4.2. *Es sei K eine proximinale Menge in einem linearen normierten Raum X.*
*Dann gilt: Ist $P_K$ eine Kontraktion, so ist K eine Sonne.*

BEWEIS. Angenommen K ist keine Sonne, dann existieren ein $(x,k) \in P_K$ und ein $\lambda > 1$, so daß $(y,k) \notin P_K$, wobei $y = k + \lambda(x-k)$. Da K jedoch Existenzmenge ist, gibt es ein $k' \in K, k' \neq k$, so daß $(y,k') \in P_K$ und damit auch $(y_t,k') \in P_K$ für $0 \leq t \leq 1$ und $y_t = k' + t(y-k')$. Nach Voraussetzung ist $P_K$ kontraktiv, und folglich gilt für jedes $t \in [0,1]$:

$$\|k'-k\| \leq \|y_t - x\|.$$

Im Falle $t = 1/\lambda$ lautet diese Ungleichung

$$\|k'-k\| \leq (1-1/\lambda)\|k'-k\|.$$

Dies ist ein Widerspruch, da $\lambda > 1$. //

Kombinieren wir Satz 4.1 und Lemma 4.2, so ergibt sich

SATZ 4.3. *Sei K eine proximinale Teilmenge eines normierten linearen Raumes X. Dann sind die Aussagen (1) und (3) von Satz 4.1 äquivalent.*

Ist insbesondere X ein innerer Produktraum, dann gilt sogar

SATZ 4.4. *Für eine Teilmenge K eines Prähilbertraumes H sind folgende Aussagen äquivalent:*

(1) *K ist eine Sonne.*

(2) *$P_K^{-1} - I$ ist monoton.*

(3) *$P_K$ ist eine Kontraktion.*

*Ist H vollständig, dann ist $P_{\overline{co}K}$ eine maximale monotone Fortsetzung von $P_K$*

auf H, wobei $\overline{co}K$ die abgeschlossene konvexe Hülle von K ist.

Satz 4.3 erweitert die Äquivalenz (1) ⇔ (2) von Satz 2.2 auf normierte lineare Räume. Wie einfache Beispiele im $\mathbb{R}^2$ zeigen, existieren nichtkonvexe, proximinale Sonnen mit kodissipativer metrischer Projektion. Wir können also nicht generell die Solarität der Menge K durch Konvexität ersetzen. Ist jedoch die Norm des Raumes X glatt oder strikt konvex (Phelps [12]), dann muß die Sonne K notwendig konvex sein.

Satz 4.4 erweitert die Äquivalenz (1) ⇔ (2) von Satz 2.2 in dem Sinne, daß in inneren Produkträumen auf die Proximinalität der Menge K verzichtet werden kann, wenn wir die Konvexität der Menge zur Sonneneigenschaft abschwächen.

## LITERATUR


[1] Amir, D. - Deutsch, F., Suns, moons and quasi-polyhedra. J. Approximation Theory 6 (1972), 176-201.

[2] Asplund, E., Chebyshev sets in Hilbert space. Trans. Amer. Math. Soc. 144 (1969), 236-240.

[3] Bénilan, Ph., Equations d'évolution dans un espace de Banach quelconque et applications. Thèse. Orsay, 1972.

[4] Brézis, H., Opérateurs Maximaux Monotones. Mathematics Studies Vol. 5, North-Holland Publishing Company, Amsterdam/London 1973.

[5] Brosowski, B., Fixpunktsätze in der Approximationstheorie. Mathematica II (34) (1969), 195-220.

[6] Crandall, M. - Liggett, T., Generation of semi-groups of nonlinear transformations on general Banach spaces. Amer. J. Math. 93 (1971), 265-298.

[7] Day, M. M., Some characterizations of inner-product spaces. Trans Amer. Math. Soc. 62 (1947), 320-337.

[8] Holmes, R. B., A course of Optimization and Best Approximation. Lecture Notes in Mathematics Vol. 257, Springer-Verlag, Berlin/Heidelberg/New York 1972.

[9] Klee, V., Remarks on nearest points in normed linear spaces. Proceedings of the Colloquium on Convexity, Copenhagen 1965. Universität von Ko-

penhagen 1967. 168-176.

[10] Mann, H., Untersuchung über Wabenzellen bei allgemeiner Minkowskischer Metrik. Monatsh. Math. Phys. 42 (1935), 417-424.

[11] Motzkin, Th., Sur quelques propriétés caractéristiques des ensembles bornés non convexes. Rend. Reale Acad. Lincei, Classe Sci. Fis., Mat. e Nat. 21 (1935), 773-779.

[12] Phelps, R. R., Convex sets and nearest points. Proc. Amer. Math. Soc. 8 (1957), 790-797.

[13] Singer, I., Best Approximation in Normed Linear Spaces by Elements of Linear Subspaces. Grundl. math. Wiss. Bd. 171. Springer-Verlag, Berlin/Heidelberg/New York 1970.

[14] Vlasov, L. P., Approximative properties of sets in normed linear spaces. Uspehi Mat. Nauk 28 (1973), No. 6 (174), 3-66 = Russian Math. Surveys 28 (1973) No. 6, 1-66.

[15] Zarantonello, E. H., Projections on convex sets in Hilbert space and spectral theory. In Contributions to Nonlinear Functional Analysis, ed. E. H. Zarantonello. Academic Press, New York/London 1971. 237-424.

NACHTRAG. Klaus Bartke, Universität Erlangen-Nürnberg, hat eine nichtproximinale Menge in $\mathbb{R}^2$ konstruiert, deren metrische Projektion bezüglich der gegebenen Norm kontraktiv ist, die jedoch keine Sonne ist.

# III
# Integral Operators and Inequalities

# RECENT RESULTS AND UNSOLVED PROBLEMS ON FINITE CONVOLUTION OPERATORS

Richard Frankfurt and James Rovnyak[1)]

Department of Mathematics
University of Kentucky
Lexington, Kentucky

Department of Mathematics
University of Virginia
Charlottesville, Virginia

Finite convolution operators are studied by means of a complex Fourier transform technique. Questions concerning unicellularity and similarity are related to asymptotic properties of bounded analytic functions in a half-plane. The purpose of the paper is to survey recent work, and to call attention to open problems. The theory is illustrated by a list of examples.

1. Introduction. The term *Volterra operator* has come to mean any completely continuous operator on a Hilbert space which has the origin as the only point in its spectrum. An interesting and extensive theory of Volterra operators has been constructed centering around the concepts of characteristic operator function and triangular representation. The theory includes structural results generalizing the Jordan canonical form, as well as applications in analysis and connections with classical function theory. Treatments of the theory are given in the books of Brodskiǐ [3] and Gohberg and Kreǐn [15].

We are concerned with a particular class of Volterra operators, which for the most part falls beyond the scope of the general theory, but for which analogous results seem possible because of connections with complex function theory. Namely, we study the class of *finite convolution operators*, that is, operators on $L^2(0,1)$ having the form

$$T:f(x) \to \int_0^x k(x-t)f(t)\,dt, \tag{1}$$

where $k(x)$ is a fixed function in $L^1(0,1)$. The fractional integration operators

$$J^\alpha:f(x) \to \Gamma(\alpha)^{-1}\int_0^x (x-t)^{\alpha-1}f(t)\,dt, \quad \mathrm{Re}\,\alpha > 0, \tag{2}$$

are particular instances of special interest. Finite convolution operators are special cases of Volterra integral operators

$$T:f(x) \to \int_0^x k(x,t)f(t)\,dt, \tag{3}$$

1) Research supported by NSF Grants MCS 76-06297 and MCS 75-04594.

which are also Volterra operators under mild restrictions on kernels. Operators of the form (1) - (3) are very familiar in analysis and as examples of operators on Hilbert space. Much that is known about finite convolution operators is obtained by methods that apply more generally to operators of the form (3). Our methods do not apply to operators of the form (3), but they are easily extended to operators of the form (1) in which the right side is replaced by convolution with respect to a complex Borel measure on [0,1]. Such operators are bounded but generally not Volterra operators.

The main problems that we consider are to give criteria for the unicellularity and similarity of operators of the form (1): Recall that operators S and T on a Hilbert space are called *similar* if there exists an operator X possessing a bounded, everywhere defined inverse such that $S = X^{-1}TX$. An operator T on a Hilbert space is called *unicellular* (by analogy with a single cell in the Jordan form of a matrix) if given any two closed invariant subspaces M and N of T, either $M \subseteq N$ or $N \subseteq M$. It is easy to see that an operator of the form (1) is unicellular if and only if every closed invariant subspace has the form $M_a = \chi_{(a,1)}L^2(0,1)$, $0 \leq a \leq 1$, where $\chi$ indicates a characteristic function. For general invariant subspace concepts see Radjavi and Rosenthal [29] and Sz.-Nagy and Foiaş [39].

The operator $J^{\alpha}$ is unicellular when $\operatorname{Re} \alpha > 0$; see [15, p. 397]. For the case $J = J^1$, unicellularity was discovered independently by Brodskiĭ [1], Donoghue [5], Kalisch [17] (where the result is stated for $J^n$, n any positive integer), Levin (unpublished; see [15, p. 38]), and Sahnovič [30], at least! In this special case, the result is equivalent to the Titchmarsh convolution theorem [2, 19, 20]; see also [3, p. 113] and [15, p. 39]. It is also closely connected with Beurling's invariant subspace theorem [29 (p. 68), 36]. Kalisch [20] views the unicellularity problem for finite convolution operators as one of generalizing the Titchmarsh convolution theorem. He asks if the operator (1) is unicellular whenever there exists no interval (0,a) with $0 < a < 1$ in which $k(t) = 0$ a.e. Work of Ginsberg and Newman [14] implies that the answer is negative; see [10, p. 371]. Kalisch [20] also notes that if $k \in L^2(0,1)$, then the operator (1) is unicellular if and only if the linear span of $k$, $k*k$, $k*k*k, \cdots$ is dense in $L^2(0,1)$, where $k*f = Tf$ for any $f \in L^2(0,1)$. This does not seem to be a practical way to prove unicellularity except in some special cases, but when unicellularity can be proved by other means, an interesting approximation theorem follows. The earliest unicellularity theorems of a general nature were obtained by stronger similarity theorems.

If an operator is similar to a known unicellular operator, then it is surely unicellular. A sufficient condition for the operator (1) to be similar to $J^n$ for some positive integer n is that $k(t) = t^{n-1}g(t)/(n-1)!$, where $g \in C^{n+1}[0,1]$ and $g(0) = 1$. See Kalisch [17] and Sahnovič [33]; the Sahnovič version of the theorem is actually slightly stronger. A generalization of this result to fractional powers of J is given by the authors [10, p.368]. A generalization to the case of vector-valued functions and matrix kernels is given by Sahnovič [34]. In addition to the papers of Kalisch and Sahnovič, see also [4, 11, 22, 23, 26, 27].

Our approach [8, 9, 10] uses complex analytic methods and is based on the classical Laplace transform method for treating integral equations involving convolutions. By a *symbol* for the operator (1) we mean any holomorphic function A(z) defined in a half-plane $y > \eta$, where $\eta$ is a real number, having the form

$$A(z) = \int_0^1 e^{itz} k(t)\, dt + e^{iz} G(z), \tag{4}$$

where G(z) is bounded and holomorphic for $y > \eta$. The fundamental problem is to describe structural properties of finite convolution operators (1), not in terms of their kernels, but in terms of their symbols (4). One of the difficulties of the theory is that the asymptotic properties of bounded analytic functions defined in a half-plane are not very well understood. We hope that our study will lead to insights in this area of function theory.

The main results of the theory are outlined in Section 2; Section 3 is devoted to examples and Section 4 to open problems. Our list of references contains only works that are more or less directly relevant to our purposes. We make no attempt to reflect the enormous literature on operators of the form (1) - (3) and their appearance in other areas of analysis.

## 2. A Survey of Recent Results.

Assertions that we state without reference are taken from [10]. For each p = 1, 2, ∞, let $\Pi^p$ denote the class of all functions F(z) which are analytic in some half-plane $y > \eta$, where $\eta$ is a real number depending on F(z), such that $F(z+i\eta)$ belongs to the Hardy class $H^p$ as a function of z in the upper half-plane $y > 0$. Throughout the paper we identify any two analytic functions which are defined on half-planes $y > \eta_1$ and

$y > \eta_2$ if they coincide on the intersection of the half-planes. We define algebraic operations pointwise so that $\Pi^1$ and $\Pi^2$ become linear spaces and $\Pi^\infty$ becomes a commutative algebra. We do not give the spaces $\Pi^p$ any metric or topological structures. However, it is a theorem that the mapping $F + e^{iz}H^p \to F + e^{iz}\Pi^p$ is a one-to-one mapping of $H^p/e^{iz}H^p$ onto $\Pi^p/e^{iz}\Pi^p$ which preserves all algebraic structure, and we use this mapping to endow $\Pi^p/e^{iz}\Pi^p$ with the corresponding metric and topological structures of $H^p/e^{iz}H^p$. Thus $\Pi^1/e^{iz}\Pi^1$ is a Banach space, $\Pi^2/e^{iz}\Pi^2$ is a Hilbert space, and $\Pi^\infty/e^{iz}\Pi^\infty$ is a commutative Banach algebra. There is a natural isometric isomorphism

$$\Pi^\infty/e^{iz}\Pi^\infty \approx (\Pi^1/e^{iz}\Pi^1)^*$$

given as follows: A coset $A + e^{iz}\Pi^\infty$ in $\Pi^\infty/e^{iz}\Pi^\infty$ induces the functional

$$L(A+e^{iz}\Pi^\infty): F + e^{iz}\Pi^1 \to \int A(\zeta)F(\zeta)\, e^{-i\zeta} d\zeta$$

where integration is along any horizontal line in the domains of both $A(z)$ and $F(z)$. In particular, $\Pi^\infty/e^{iz}\Pi^\infty$ carries a weak* topology. A coset $A + e^{iz}\Pi^\infty$ is called a *weak* generator* of $\Pi^\infty/e^{iz}\Pi^\infty$ if the linear span of $1 + e^{iz}\Pi^\infty$, $A + e^{iz}\Pi^\infty$, $A^2 + e^{iz}\Pi^\infty, \cdots$ is dense in $\Pi^\infty/e^{iz}\Pi^\infty$ in the weak* topology.

There is an isometric isomorphism $f \to F + e^{iz}\Pi^2$ from $L^2(0,1)$ onto $\Pi^2/e^{iz}\Pi^2$ determined by

$$F(z) = (2\pi)^{-\frac{1}{2}} \int_0^1 e^{itz} f(t)\, dt.$$

Under this isomorphism, the operator (1) appears on $\Pi^2/e^{iz}\Pi^2$ in the form

$$T(A+e^{iz}\Pi^\infty): F + e^{iz}\Pi^2 \to AF + e^{iz}\Pi^2, \tag{5}$$

where $A(z)$ is any symbol (4) for the operator (1). More generally, we define an operator (5) for any coset $A + e^{iz}\Pi^\infty$ in $\Pi^\infty/e^{iz}\Pi^\infty$, and we call any representative in the coset a *symbol* for the operator. The study of finite convolution operators is thus conveniently subsumed in the study of operators of the form (5).

There is a simple description of the spectrum of an operator of the form (5) due to Foiaş and Mlak [7] and Fuhrman [12].

THEOREM 1. <u>Let $A \in \Pi^\infty$. A complex number $\lambda$ is in the spectrum of</u> $T(A+e^{iz}\Pi^\infty)$ <u>if and only if there exists a sequence $(z_n)_1^\infty$ such that</u> $\operatorname{Im} z_n \to \infty$ <u>and</u> $A(z_n) \to \lambda$.

Using a theorem of Sarason [38] it can be shown that for any $A \in \Pi^{\infty}$, the operator $T(A+e^{iz}\Pi^{\infty})$ is compact if and only if there is a representative $C(z)$ in the coset $A + e^{iz}\Pi^{\infty}$ such that $C(z) \to 0$ as $z \to \infty$ in some half-plane $y > \eta$. This fact, coupled with Theorem 2, gives one way (of many ways) to show that if $A(z)$ is a symbol for an operator (1) with kernel $k(t) \in L^1(0,1)$, then $T(A+e^{iz}\Pi^{\infty})$ is a Volterra operator.

Fundamental to our investigation is a theorem of Sarason [38], which we state in a form suitable to our purposes.

THEOREM 2. *A bounded operator* $T$ *on* $\Pi^2/e^{iz}\Pi^2$ *has the form* (5) *if and only if it commutes with the operator* $S$ *obtained from* (5) *by taking* $A(z) = (z-i)/(z+i)$. *The mapping* $A + e^{iz}\Pi^{\infty} \to T(A+e^{iz}\Pi^{\infty})$ *which takes cosets in* $\Pi^{\infty}/e^{iz}\Pi^{\infty}$ *to operators on* $\Pi^2/e^{iz}\Pi^2$ *is an isometric Banach algebra isomorphism from* $\Pi^{\infty}/e^{iz}\Pi^{\infty}$ *to the set of operators of the form* (5) *in the operator norm, and it is a homeomorphism from* $\Pi^{\infty}/e^{iz}\Pi^{\infty}$ *with its weak* topology to the set of operators* (5) *taken with the weak operator topology.*

The unicellularity problem is reformulated in the following result. The result is an analogue of a criterion, due to Kisilevskiǐ [24], for the unicellularity of a simple dissipative Volterra operator having trace class imaginary component.

THEOREM 3. *For any* $A \in \Pi^{\infty}$, *the operator* $T(A+e^{iz}\Pi^{\infty})$ *is unicellular if and only if* $A + e^{iz}\Pi^{\infty}$ *is a weak* generator of* $\Pi^{\infty}/e^{iz}\Pi^{\infty}$.

It follows from our description of $\Pi^{\infty}/e^{iz}\Pi^{\infty}$ as a dual space and general Banach space principles that for any $A \in \Pi^{\infty}$, $A + e^{iz}\Pi^{\infty}$ is a weak* generator of $\Pi^{\infty}/e^{iz}\Pi^{\infty}$ if and only if from the assumptions that $F \in \Pi^1$ and

$$\int A(\zeta)^n F(\zeta) e^{-i\zeta} d\zeta = 0, \qquad n = 0, 1, 2, \cdots ,$$

it follows that $F \in e^{iz}\Pi^1$.

The weak* generators of $H^{\infty}$ have been completely characterized by Sarason [37]. Weak* generators of $H^{\infty}$ induce weak* generators of $\Pi^{\infty}/e^{iz}\Pi^{\infty}$. Using this we obtain simple sufficient conditions for unicellularity.

THEOREM 4. *For* $T(A+e^{iz}\Pi^{\infty})$ *to be unicellular, it is sufficient that* $A(z)$ *be univalent in some half-plane* $y > \eta$, *and that* $A(z)$ *approach a limit as* $z \to \infty$ *in this half-plane.*

Stronger results can easily be stated using Sarason's work [37]. For example, for $T(A+e^{iz}\Pi^\infty)$ to be unicellular, it is sufficient that $A(z)$ be univalent on some half-plane $y > \eta$, and that it maps this half-plane onto a Carathéodory domain. Foiaş and Williams [7] use a very similar result, which they prove using the functional calculus for contraction operators [39, Chapt. III]. See Examples 17 and 18 in Section 3.

There is a method for constructing new weak* generators from old ones. Let $\Omega$ denote the class of functions $\theta(z)$ which are analytic in some half-plane $y > \eta$ such that an inequality $\operatorname{Im}\theta(z) > y - c$ holds in the half-plane for some real constant c. The idea of the definition is that for any preassigned half-plane $y > \lambda$, we may artificially restrict the domain of $\theta(z)$ to a half-plane $y > \eta$ where $\eta$ is chosen so large that the range of $\theta(z)$ is contained in the half-plane $y > \lambda$. Therefore, for any $A \in \Pi^\infty$ and any $\theta \in \Omega$, the composite function $A \circ \theta$ defined by $(A\circ\theta)(z) = A(\theta(z))$ exists as a function in $\Pi^\infty$.

THEOREM 5. *Let $\theta \in \Omega$. The following conditions are equivalent:*

(i) *For any weak* generator $A + e^{iz}\Pi^\infty$ of $\Pi^\infty/e^{iz}\Pi^\infty$, $A \circ \theta + e^{iz}\Pi^\infty$ is a weak* generator of $\Pi^\infty/e^{iz}\Pi^\infty$.*

(ii) *There exists a $C \in \Pi^\infty$ such that $C \circ \theta + e^{iz}\Pi^\infty$ is a weak* generator of $\Pi^\infty/e^{iz}\Pi^\infty$.*

(iii) *The coset $1/\theta + e^{iz}\Pi^\infty$ is a weak* generator of $\Pi^\infty/e^{iz}\Pi^\infty$.*

COROLLARY. *Assume $\theta \in \Omega$ and $\theta$ is univalent. Then if $A + e^{iz}\Pi^\infty$ is any weak* generator of $\Pi^\infty/e^{iz}\Pi^\infty$, $A \circ \theta + e^{iz}\Pi^\infty$ is a weak* generator of $\Pi^\infty/e^{iz}\Pi^\infty$.*

See [9]. Actually, the class $\Omega$ was originally introduced for a different purpose, namely to construct operators on $\Pi^2/e^{iz}\Pi^2$ that intertwine operators of the form (5). It is known that for any $\theta \in \Omega$

$$X_\theta : F + e^{iz}\Pi^2 \to \frac{\theta(z) + i}{z + i} F(\theta(z)) + e^{iz}\Pi^2 \tag{6}$$

defines a bounded operator on $\Pi^2/e^{iz}\Pi^2$. For any $A, C \in \Pi^\infty$ and $\theta \in \Omega$, we have

$$X_\theta\, T(C+e^{iz}\Pi^\infty) = T(A+e^{iz}\Pi^\infty)\, X_\theta$$

if and only if $C \circ \theta - A \in e^{iz}\Pi^\infty$. If $\phi, \psi \in \Omega$, then $\phi \circ \psi \in \Omega$ and $X_{\phi\circ\psi} = X_\psi X_\phi$. This fact is used to give conditions for an operator of the form (6) to be invertible.

THEOREM 6. *Let $\theta(z) = z + \chi(z)$, where $\chi(z)$ is analytic in some half-plane $y > \eta$ and there satisfies:*

(i) *$\operatorname{Im}\chi(z)$ is bounded,*

(ii) $\chi(z)/z \to 0$ as $z \to \infty$, and

(iii) $|\chi'(z)| \leq \rho$, where $0 < \rho < 1$. Then $\theta$ is univalent for $y > \eta$, $\theta$ and $\theta^{-1}$ belong to $\Omega$, and $X_\theta$ is invertible with inverse $X_\theta^{-1} = X_{\theta^{-1}}$.

The hypotheses in Theorem 6 are automatically satisfied if $\chi \in \Pi^\infty$. In this case the theorem is proved in [10]. The stronger version of the theorem is stated in [8].

COROLLARY. *Let $A, C \in \Pi^\infty$. For $T(A+e^{iz}\Pi^\infty)$ and $T(C+e^{iz}\Pi^\infty)$ to be similar, it is sufficient that there exists a function $\theta(z) = z + \chi(z)$ such that $\chi(z)$ satisfies the conditions in Theorem 6 and $A(z) = C(\theta(z))$ in some half-plane $y > \eta$.*

Symbols $C(z)$ arising in examples often satisfy the following conditions: (a) $C'(z)/C(z)$ is analytic and nonvanishing in some half-plane $y > \eta$, (b) $C(z) \to 0$ and $C'(z)/C(z) \to 0$ as $z \to \infty$ in the half-plane, and (c) $C(iy) > 0$ for $y > \eta$. For ease of reference, we shall refer to such functions as *functions of regular growth*. This class includes all functions of the form

$$C(z) = L(-iz)/(-iz)^\alpha , \tag{7}$$

where $0 < \alpha < \infty$ and $L(z)$ is an analytic function defined in a half-plane $x > \eta$ and *slowly varying* at infinity, that is, $zL'(z)/L(z) \to 0$ as $z \to \infty$ in the half-plane and $L(x) > 0$ for $x > \eta$; e.g., $L(z) = \log z$.

If $C(z)$ is any function of regular growth, we choose $\arg C(z)$ continuously so as to vanish for $z = iy$. We then define

$$h^+(\theta;C) = \limsup_{r\to\infty} |\arg C(i\delta+ire^{i\theta})| ,$$

$$h^-(\theta;C) = \liminf_{r\to\infty} |\arg C(i\delta+ire^{i\theta})|$$

for $0 \leq \theta \leq \pi/2$. These functions are independent of the choice of $\delta$, which may be any sufficiently large number. They are called the *upper* and *lower asymptotic argument functions* of $C(z)$. In case they coincide, the common function $h(\theta;C)$ is called simply the *asymptotic argument function* of $C(z)$. If $C(z)$ has the form (7), then $h(\theta;C) = \alpha\theta$ in $[0,\pi/2]$. If $C(z) = \exp(-(-iz)^\alpha)$, $0 < \alpha < 1$, then $h(0;C) = 0$ and $h(\theta;C) = +\infty$ for $0 < \theta \leq \pi/2$. If $C(z) = 1/\log(-iz)$, then $h(\theta;C) = 0$ for $0 < \theta \leq \pi/2$.

Roughly speaking, the asymptotic argument functions measure the asymptotic properties of the range of a function $C(z)$ of regular growth. This can best be seen by relating their behavior to the geometric properties of the lifting $\hat{C}(z)$ of $C(z)$ to the universal covering space of the punctured plane. The universal covering space can be regarded as the half-plane $\{(r,\theta): 0 < r < \infty, -\infty < \theta < \infty\}$, in which case we may take $\hat{C}(z) = (|C(z)|, \arg C(z))$. It is desirable to be able to relate the range of $\hat{C}(z)$ to rectangles of the form $R = \{(r,\theta): 0 < r \leq \rho, |\theta| \leq \beta\pi\}$ where $\rho, \beta > 0$. This can be done by imposing simple conditions on the asymptotic argument functions. For example, if

$$h^{-}(\pi/2;C) > 0, \tag{8}$$

then the range of $\hat{C}(z)$ contains such a rectangle. If

$$h^{+}(\pi/2;C) < \infty, \tag{9}$$

then the range of $\hat{C}(z)$ restricted to an appropriate half-plane will be contained in such a rectangle. The conditions (9) and (10) together have the effect of trapping the range of $\hat{C}(z)$ asymptotically between two such rectangles. This phenomenon is believed to be intimately connected with the unicellularity problem. For example, it is known [9] that condition (8), coupled with the assumption $|\arg C(z)| < \pi$, which is stronger than (9), implies that $C + e^{iz}\Pi^{\infty}$ is a weak* generator of $\Pi^{\infty}/e^{iz}\Pi^{\infty}$.

A similarity theory has been constructed for operators whose symbols are functions of regular growth. In its initial form [10], the theory was restricted to symbols of the form (7). The generalization is made in [8]. The following result is fundamental to the method. It is contained in [8]. Although it is not explicitly stated there.

THEOREM 7. *Let* $C(z)$ *be a function of regular growth satisfying* (8). *If* $A(z) = C(z)[1+P(z)]$ *where* $P(z) \to 0$ *as* $z \to \infty$ *in some half-plane* $y > \eta$, *then there exists an analytic function* $\theta(z)$ *such that the relation* $A(z) = C(\theta(z))$ *is meaningful and valid in some half-plane* $y > \delta$.

This result, by itself, is of little use, since nothing is said about the properties of $\theta(z)$. Additional hypotheses are needed to be able to draw conclusions about $\theta(z)$. These hypotheses are conveniently stated in terms of a growth scale which was constructed in [8], and which we now present in slightly more general form.

By an *asymptotic test function* we mean any complex valued function $\sigma(z)$ defined in a half-plane $y > \eta$, not necessarily continuous even, such that $\operatorname{Im} \sigma(z) \to \infty$ as $y \to \infty$, and at the same time $\sigma(z) \to \infty$ as $z \to \infty$.

We identify two such functions if one is a restriction of the other. Given a function $C(z)$ of regular growth, an asymptotic test function $\sigma(z)$, and any other function $A \in \Pi^{\infty}$, we say that $A(z)$ is $\sigma$-*majorized* relative to $C(z)$ if there exist numbers $\alpha$ and $\beta$ with $0 < \alpha, \beta < 1$ such that the relations

$$\alpha|C(w)| \leq |C(z)| \leq \alpha^{-1}|C(w)| \tag{10}$$

imply

$$\beta|A(\sigma(z))| \leq |A(w)|$$

whenever $z$ and $w$ lie in some half-plane $y > \eta$. For fixed $A$ and $C$, the class of all asymptotic test functions $\sigma(z)$ satisfying this condition is denoted by MAJ $(A;C)$. Similarly, if (10) implies that

$$|A(w)| \leq \beta^{-1}|A(\sigma(z))|,$$

we say that $A(z)$ is $\sigma$-*minorized* relative to $C(z)$. For fixed $A$ and $C$, the class of asymptotic test functions $\sigma(z)$ satisfying this condition is denoted MIN $(A;C)$. It can be shown that the classes MAJ $(A;C)$ and MIN $(A;C)$ are always nonvoid. In the special case $A = C'/C$ this is done in [8, Th. 4], and the general case is handled similarly. These classes contain exceedingly delicate information regarding the relative asymptotic behavior of the functions $A(z)$ and $C(z)$.

THEOREM 8. *Let* $C(z)$ *be a function of regular growth satisfying* (8). *Suppose that*

$$A(z) = C(z)[1+P(z)],$$

*where* $P(z) = \mathcal{O}(C'(\sigma(z))/C(\sigma(z)))$ *as* $z \to \infty$ *in a half-plane* $y > \eta$ *for some* $\sigma \in$ MAJ $(C'/C;C)$. *Then* $T(A+e^{iz}\Pi^{\infty})$ *and* $T(C+e^{iz}\Pi^{\infty})$ *are similar*.

The key to the successful application of this result is to find particularly tractable functions in the class MAJ $(C'/C;C)$. While this is often possible in certain restricted classes of functions it is not generally obvious how to do it.

## 3. Examples

| Operator | Kernel $k(t)$<br>Symbol $A(z)$ | Remarks and references |
|---|---|---|
| Ex. 1<br>$J^{\alpha}$<br>($\operatorname{Re} \alpha>0$) | $k(t) = t^{\alpha-1}/\Gamma(\alpha)$<br>$A(z) = (i/z)^{\alpha}$ | Unicellularity: references are given in the introduction. Similarity: [15 (p. 401), 18]. Resolvents: see [16, p. 667] and the references cited there. Estimates on norms and s-numbers: [15 (p. 400), 18, 22]. Special functional calculus: [10, p.356]; see also e.g. [39, Chapt. IV]. Commutant: [36, 38]; see Th. 1. |
| Ex. 2<br>$J^{i\beta}$<br>($\beta$ real, $\beta \neq 0$) | This operator is not given by convolution with any $L^1$ kernel.<br>$A(z) = (i/z)^{i\beta}$ | Existence and group properties: [16 p. 665), 21, 25]. The spectrum is an annulus: $1/\rho \leq \lvert\lambda\rvert \leq \rho$, $\rho = \exp(\frac{1}{2}\pi\lvert\beta\rvert)$. This is easily proved using Th. 1, filling a gap in [16, p. 669]. In the special case $\beta = 1$, the operator implements a similarity between M (multiplication by x in $L^2(0,1)$) and M + iJ. See [32] and the Kalisch review of this article for a reference to a generalization. |
| Ex. 3 | $k(t) = t^{\alpha-1}g(t)/\Gamma(\alpha)$<br>$A(z) = \cdots$<br>($0 < \alpha < \infty$, $g \in C^{n+1}[0,1]$ where n is the least integer $\geq \alpha$, $g(0) = 1$) | The operator is similar to $J^{\alpha}$. See [10, 17, 33]. A commonly occurring special case is where the operator is a function of J of the form $J^{\alpha}\phi(J)$, where $\phi(z) = 1 + a_1 z + a_2 z^2 + \cdots$ in a neighborhood of the origin. In this case $k(t) = t^{\alpha-1}[1/\Gamma(\alpha) + a_1 t/\Gamma(\alpha+1) + a_2 t^2/\Gamma(\alpha+2) + \cdots]$ and $A(z) = (i/z)^{\alpha}\phi(i/z)$. |

| Operator | Kernel k(t)<br>Symbol A(z) | Remarks and references |
|---|---|---|
| Ex. 4 | $k(t) = t^{\frac{1}{2}(\alpha-1)} J_{\alpha-1}(2c^{\frac{1}{2}}t^{\frac{1}{2}})$<br>$A(z) = c^{\frac{1}{2}(\alpha-1)}(i/z)^{\alpha}e^{-ic/z}$<br>$(0 < \alpha < \infty,\ 0 < c < \infty)$ | This is a special case of Ex. 3. A large number of such examples can be easily constructed. |
| Ex. 5<br>$N_\rho$<br>$(-\infty<\rho<\infty)$ | $k(t) = \pi^{-\frac{1}{2}}t^{\rho}e^{-1/t}$<br>$A(z) = 2\pi^{-\frac{1}{2}}(-iz)^{-\frac{1}{2}(\rho+1)}\times$<br>$\times K_{\rho+1}(2(-iz)^{\frac{1}{2}})$ | In the case $\rho = -3/2$, the symbol is $A(z) = \exp(-2(-iz)^{\frac{1}{2}})$. In this case the operator is the first and still the simplest known example of a non-unicellular operator whose kernel is not 0 a.e. in an interval (0,a). See [10, 14]. The operators $N_\rho$ are studied in [8]. It is unknown if they are all nonunicellular. |
| Ex. 6 | $k(t) = (2\pi)^{-\frac{1}{2}}t^{-1}e^{-1/(2t)}\times$<br>$\times W_{\frac{1}{2},\nu}(1/t)$<br>$A(z) = 2\pi^{-1}(-iz)^{\frac{1}{2}}\times$<br>$\times K_{\nu+\frac{1}{2}}((-iz)^{\frac{1}{2}})K_{\nu-\frac{1}{2}}((-iz)^{\frac{1}{2}})$<br>$(-\infty<\nu<\infty)$ | This operator is similar to $N_{-3/2}$ and hence it is nonunicellular. See [8]. |
| Ex. 7 | $k(t) = \cdots$<br>$A(z) = L(-iz)/(-iz)^{\alpha}$<br>($L(z)$ slowly varying,<br>$0 < \alpha < \infty$) | This is a common form. Slowly varying functions are defined above. Such operators are known to be unicellular if $0 < \alpha < 2$ and are conjectured to be unicellular in general. See [10, p. 362] where a similarity theory for operators with symbols of this form is also given. Specific examples are given in Ex. 8, 9, 11, below. |

| Operator | Kernel k(t)<br>Symbol A(z) | Remarks and references |
|---|---|---|
| Ex. 8<br>$L_\alpha = \frac{\partial}{\partial\alpha} J^\alpha$<br>$(0<\alpha<\infty)$ | $k(t) = \Gamma(\alpha)^{-1} t^{\alpha-1}[\log t -$<br>$- \Gamma'(\alpha)/\Gamma(\alpha)]$<br>$A(z) = -(i/z)^\alpha \log(-iz)$ | This operator appears prominently in the operational calculus of Volterra and Pérès [41]; see also [40]. It is unicellular for $0 < \alpha < 2$ (at least). |
| Ex. 9<br>$M_\alpha$<br>$(0<\alpha<\infty)$ | $k(t) = \int_\alpha^\infty \Gamma(s)^{-1} t^{s-1} ds$<br>$A(z) = (i/z)^\alpha / \log(-iz)$ | The operator is unicellular for $0 < \alpha < 2$ (at least); see [10]. |
| Ex. 10<br>$M_0$ | $k(t) = \int_0^\infty \Gamma(s)^{-1} t^{s-1} ds$<br>$A(z) = 1/\log(-iz)$ | The operator is unicellular by Th. 4. The symbol in this example is not of the form in Ex. 7. It is a function of regular growth with asymptotic argument function identically zero. |
| Ex. 11 | $k(t) = -\Gamma(0,t)$<br>$= -\int_t^\infty s^{-1} e^{-s} ds$<br>$A(z) = -(i/z)\log(-iz+1)$ | The operator is similar to $L_1$. See [10]. |
| Ex. 12<br>$J(I+J^\gamma)$<br>$(0<\gamma<\infty)$ | $k(t) = \cdots$<br>$A(z) = \frac{i}{z}(1+(i/z)^\gamma)$ | The operator is similar to J if $\gamma \geq 1$ and not similar to J if $\gamma < 1$; see [18]. Th. 4 can be used to show that the operator is unicellular even for $\gamma < 1$. Some variations on this example are discussed in [23, 26]. A more delicate example is given in [22]. |

| Operator | Kernel k(t)<br>Symbol A(z) | Remarks and references |
|---|---|---|
| Ex. 13<br>$J^{\alpha}(I+\delta J^{\beta})^{\gamma}$<br>($0<\alpha<\infty$,<br>$0<\beta<1$,<br>$\delta,\gamma$ real) | $k(t) = \cdots$<br>$A(z) = (\frac{i}{z})^{\alpha}[1 + \delta(\frac{i}{z})^{\beta}]^{\gamma}$ | These two examples from [9] illustrate the Corollary to Th. 5. In both cases the operators are unicellular for $\delta\gamma < 0$ (at least). |
| Ex. 14<br>$J^{\alpha}(I+\delta M_{\beta})^{\gamma}$<br>($0<\alpha<\infty$,<br>$0<\beta<1$,<br>$\delta,\gamma$ real) | $k(t) = \cdots$<br>$A(z) = (\frac{i}{z})^{\alpha}[1 + \delta(\frac{i}{z})^{\beta}/\log(-iz)]^{\gamma}$ | |
| Ex. 15<br>$J(I-iL_1)$ | $k(t) = \cdots$<br>$A(z) = \frac{i}{z}[1-z^{-1}\log(-iz)]$ | These two examples show the delicate nature of the similarity problem: $J(I-iL_1)$ is similar to $J$ (see [8]), but $J(I-L_1)$ is not similar to $J$ (see [22]). We note that $J(I-L_1)$ is unicellular by Ex. 7. |
| Ex. 16<br>$J(I-L_1)$ | $k(t) = \cdots$<br>$A(z) = \frac{i}{z}[1+\frac{i}{z}\log(-iz)]$ | |

Operators of the form $T(A+e^{iz}\Pi^{\infty})$, $A \in \Pi^{\infty}$, are used by Foiaş and Williams [7] to construct counterexamples in operator theory. We cite two of their examples:

Ex. 17. There exists an unicellular operator whose spectrum contains more than one point.

Ex. 18. There exists a Volterra operator $T$ such that $T$ is not similar to $T(I-T)^{-1}$.

Such operators cannot be constructed on finite dimensional spaces. In both cases, the examples given in [7] can be realized as operators of the form $T(A+e^{iz}\Pi^{\infty})$ where $A(z)$ is chosen as the Riemann mapping function from a half-plane to some suitable simply connected domain.

4. Open Problems. We include some specialized questions, such as examples that fall beyond the scope of known results, as well as deeper structural problems. We begin with the former and conclude with the latter.

a) Can $||J^\alpha||$ be written in closed form? If not, can one at least find a simple function $P(\alpha)$ such that $||J^\alpha||/P(\alpha) \to 1$ as $\alpha \to \infty$? More generally, how do the singular numbers of $J^\alpha$ behave as $\alpha \to \infty$?

b) What are the structural properties of $J^{i\beta}$ ($\beta$ real, $\beta \neq 0$); e.g., is it similar to some more tractable operator? What are the invariant subspaces of $J^{i\beta}$? See Example 2.

c) Let $k_1(t)$, $k_2(t) \in L^1(0,1)$ and assume that $k_1(t) = k_2(t)$ a.e. in an interval $(0,a)$, and that for any b with $0 < b \leq a$, $k_1(t)$ does not vanish a.e. on $(0,b)$. Are the operators defined by (1) with these two kernels similar? Is one unicellular iff the other is? For a partial result see Kalisch [17, Th. 31]. The answer to the first question is blatantly negative if the last hypothesis about $k_1(t)$ is dropped, a trivial counterexample being provided by any two nilpotent operators of the form (1) having different indices of nilpotence. With this in mind, suppose that $A_1, A_2 \in \Pi^\infty$ and $T(A_1 + e^{iz}\Pi^\infty)$ is similar to $T(A_2 + e^{iz}\Pi^\infty)$. Then if $C_k(z) = e^{iaz}A_k(z)$, $k = 1,2$ and $0 \leq a \leq 1$, is $T(C_1 + e^{iz}\Pi^\infty)$ similar to $T(C_2 + e^{iz}\Pi^\infty)$?

d) It is known that the coset $A + e^{iz}\Pi^\infty$, where $A(z) = \exp(-a(-iz)^\alpha)$, $0 < a < \infty$, $0 < \alpha < 1$, fails to be a weak* generator when $\alpha = \frac{1}{2}$ (see Example 5). Is this true for any or all other values of $\alpha$?

e) Are the operators of Examples 13 and 14 unicellular when $\gamma\delta > 0$? See also the conjecture of Example 7.

The next three questions suggest ways in which known unicellularity criteria might be generalized. The questions are closely related. An affirmative answer to any one of them would yield a powerful new result.

$f_1$) Can the univalence hypothesis of Theorem 4 be replaced by some notion of p-valence?

$f_2$) The first author has conjectured that $T(C + e^{iz}\Pi^\infty)$ is unicellular if $C(z)$ is a function of regular growth satisfying (8) and (9). (If true, this implies the conjecture of Example 7). To prove this, it would suffice to show that if $C(z)$ is a function of regular growth such that $T(C + e^{iz}\Pi^\infty)$ is unicellular, then $T(C^n + e^{iz}\Pi^\infty)$ is unicellular for all $n = 1,2,3,\cdots$. It is also natural to ask if conditions (8) and (9) are necessary for unicellularity. However, Example 10 shows that the answer is negative.

$f_3$) Examples indicate that operators $T(A+e^{iz}\Pi^\infty)$ which satisfy the condition

(11) $$\liminf_{y\to\infty} |y^\alpha A(iy)| > 0$$

for some $0 < \alpha < \infty$ tend to be unicellular, while the condition fails for the few known examples of nonunicellular operators. Is this a coincidence, or can condition (11) be used to give criteria for unicellularity and nonunicellularity? Symbols such as those in Example 7 satisfy (11). Some other functions satisfying (11) are symbols of finite convolution operators whose kernels $k(t)$ are $C^\infty$ on $[0,1]$ with $k^{(n)}(0) \neq 0$ for some $n > 0$. Do there exist unicellular operators having $C^\infty$ kernels $k(t)$ on $[0,1]$ such that $k^{(n)}(0) = 0$ for all $n \geq 0$?

The next three problems are of a more technical nature.

g) The operator $T(A+e^{iz}\Pi^\infty)$ depends only on the coset $A + e^{iz}\Pi^\infty$ and not on the choice of representative. However, some results, such as Theorem 4 and constructions involving functions of regular growth, evidently depend on special choices of the representative functions. Simpler and more general results might be obtained if they can be recast in a coset-invariant form.

h) The similarity result of Theorem 8 is proved by appealing to the Corollary to Theorem 6. However, the hypotheses of Theorem 8 imply that the function $\theta(z)$ obtained will satisfy the strong condition $\theta(z) - z \in \Pi^\infty$, whereas it is known that the conclusion of the Corollary is valid under more general conditions on $\theta(z)$. Is it possible to relax the hypotheses of Theorem 8 in such a way as to exploit the full strength of the Corollary?

i) The conclusions of Theorem 5 are generally enforced by appealing to its more restrictive Corollary. Are there ever instances in which the function $\theta(z)$ of Theorem 5 need not be univalent? Moreover, is the converse of Theorem 5 valid? That is, if $\theta \in \Omega$ and $A \circ \theta + e^{iz}\Pi^\infty$ is a weak* generator, is $A + e^{iz}\Pi^\infty$ a weak* generator?

We conclude this section by mentioning two possible avenues by which the theory might be extended.

j) A few results are known in the direction of a vector generalization of the theory. Fuhrman [12, Th. 2.9] has extended Theorem 1. Muhly [28] gives conditions for compactness in the vector case. The lifting theorem of Sz.-Nagy and Foiaş [39, p. 258] may be used to generalize Theorem 2.

Sahnovič [34] has generalized the result of Example 3 to the case of operators with matrix kernels acting on vector valued-functions. While much of our apparatus extends routinely to the vector case, at the present time there is no general similarity theory that includes the Sahnovič theorem as there is in the scalar case.

k) Portions of the theory can also be extended to tensor products of operators. Let $I^n$ denote the n-fold Cartesian product of [0,1] in $R^n$. We say that a subset D of $I^n$ has <u>rectangular type at the origin</u> if for each $(a_1,\ldots,a_n)\in D$, $(x_1,\ldots,x_n)\in D$ whenever $0 \leq x_k \leq a_k$ for all k = 1,...n. Let $J_k$, k = 1,...,n, denote integration with respect to $x_k$ on $L^2(I^n)$. Kalisch [20] has shown that a subspace $M$ of $L^2(I^n)$ is invariant under each $J_k$, k = 1, ...,n, if $M$ consists of all functions in $L^2(I^n)$ which vanish a.e. on some fixed set D of rectangular type at the origin. The first author has recently proved the following generalization: Let $T_1,\ldots.T_n$ be arbitrary unicellular operators on $L^2(0,1)$ belonging to the commutant of J. Let $\tilde{T}_k$, k = 1,...,n, be the operator on $L^2(I^n)$ which maps any product $f_1(x_1)\ldots f_k(x_k)\ldots f_n(x_n)$ to $f_1(x_1)\ldots T_k f_k(x_k)\ldots f_n(x_n)$. Then the lattice of common invariant subspaces of $\tilde{T}_1,\ldots,\tilde{T}_n$ is exactly the same as the lattice of common invariant subspaces of $J_1,\ldots,J_n$ described above.

REFERENCES

[1] M.S. Brodskiĭ, On a problem of I.M. Gel'fand. Uspehi Mat. Nauk 12 (1957), no. 2 (74), 129-132. (Russian) MR 20 #1229.

[2] M.S. Brodskiĭ, On the unicellularity of the integration operator and a theorem of Titchmarsh. Uspehi Mat. Nauk 20 (1965), no. 5 (125), 189-192. (Russian) MR 32 #8055.

[3] M.S. Brodskiĭ, Triangular and Jordan Representations of Linear Operators. Moscow, 1969. Transl. Math., Monographs, Vol. 32, Amer. Math. Soc., Providence, R.I., 1970.

[4] V.W. Daniel, Invariant subspaces of convolution operators. Dissertation, University of Virginia, 1970.

[5] W.F. Donoghue, Jr., The lattice of invariant subspaces of a completely continuous quasi-nilpotent transformation. Pacific J. Math. 7 (1957), 1031-1036. MR 19 # 1066.

[6] C. Foiaş and W. Mlak, The extended spectrum of completely non-unitary contractions and the spectral mapping theorem. Studia Math. 26 (1966), 239-245. MR 34 #610.

[7] C. Foiaş and J.F. Williams, Some remarks on the Volterra operator. Proc. Amer. Math. Soc. 31 (1972), 177-184. MR 45 #4194.

[8] R. Frankfurt, Spectral analysis of finite convolution operators. Trans. Amer. Math. Soc. 214 (1975), 279-301.

[9] R. Frankfurt, On the unicellularity of finite convolution operators. Indiana Univ. Math. J. 26 (1977), 223-232.

[10] R. Frankfurt and J. Rovnyak, Finite convolution operators. J. Math. Anal. Appl. 49 (1975), 347-374. MR 51 #3947.

[11] J.M. Freeman, Volterra operators similar to $J: f(x) \to \int_0^x f(y)\,dy$. Trans. Amer. Math. Soc. 116 (1965), 181-192. MR 33 #592.

[12] P.A. Fuhrman, On the corona theorem and its application to spectral problems in Hilbert space. Trans. Amer. Math. Soc. 132 (1968), 55-56. MR 36 #5751.

[13] P.A. Fuhrman, A functional calculus in Hilbert space based on operator valued analytic functions. Israel J. Math. 6 (1968), 267-278. MR 38 #5029.

[14] J.I. Ginsberg and D.J. Newman, Generators of certain radical algebras. J. Approximation Theory 3 (1970), 229-235. MR 41# 9014.

[15] I.C. Gohberg and M.G. Kreĭn, Theory and Applications of Volterra Operators in Hilbert Space. Moscow, 1967. Transl. Math. Monographs, Vol. 24, Amer. Math. Soc., Providence, R.I., 1970. MR 36 #2007.

[16] E. Hille and R.S. Phillips, Functional Analysis and Semi-Groups. Amer. Math. Soc. Coll. Publ., Vol XXXI, Providence, 1957.

[17] G.K. Kalisch, On similarity, reducing manifolds, and unitary equivalence of certain Volterra operators. Ann. of Math. 66 (1957), 481-494. MR 19 # 970.

[18] G.K. Kalisch, On similarity invariants of certain operators in $L_p$. Pacific J. Math. 11 (1961), 247-252. MR 22 # 11261.

[19] G.K. Kalisch, A functional analytic proof of Titchmarsh's convolution theorem. J. Math. Anal. Appl. 5 (1962), 176-183. MR 25 #4307.

[20] G.K. Kalisch, Théorème de Titchmarsh sur la convolution et opérateurs de Volterra. Séminaire d'Analyse, dirigé par P. Lelong, 1962/63, no. 5, 6 pp. Secretariat mathematique, Paris, 1963. MR 31 #6123.

[21] G.K. Kalisch, On fractional integrals of pure imaginary order in $L_p$. Proc. Amer. Math. Soc. 18 (1967), 136-139. MR 35 #7145.

[22] I.I. Kal'muševskiĭ, On the linear equivalence of Volterra operators. Uspehi Mat. Nauk 20 (1965), no. 6 (126), 93-97. MR 32 #8161; errata, MR 46, p. 2168.

[23] I.I. Kal'muševskiĭ, On a certain class of mutually non-equivalent Volterra operators. (Russian) Ukrain. Mat. Ž. 18 (1966), no. 3, 116-119. MR 33 #1678.

[24] G.E. Kisilevskiĭ, Invariant subspaces of dissipative Volterra operators with nuclear imaginary components. Izv. Akad. Nauk SSSR Ser. Mat. 32 (1968), 3-23. Math. USSR-Izv. 2 (1968), 1-20. MR 36 #4375.

[25] H. Kober, On a theorem of Schur and on fractional integrals of purely imaginary order. Trans. Amer. Math. Soc. 50 (1941), 160-174. MR 3, 39.

[26] M.M. Malamud, Sufficient conditions for the linear equivalence of Volterra operators. Teor. Funkciĭ Funkcional. Anal. i Priložen. Vyp. 23 (1975), 59-69, 170 (Russian). MR 53 #3799.

[27] M.M. Malamud and E.R. Cekanovskiĭ, Tests for the linear equivalence of Volterra operators in the $L^p$ scale. Uspehi Mat. Nauk 30 (1975), no. 5 (185), 217-218 (Russian). MR 33 # 3800.

[28] P.S. Muhly, Compact operators in the commutant of a contraction. J. Functional Analysis 8 (1971), 197-224. MR 47 # 4035.

[29] H. Radjavi and P. Rosenthal, Invariant Subspaces. Springer-Verlag, New York, 1973.

[30] L.A. Sahnovič, Spectral analysis of Volterra operators and inverse problems. Dokl. Akad. Nauk SSSR 115, no. 4 (1957), 666-669. (Russian) MR 19 # 866.

[31] L.A. Sahnovič, On reduction of Volterra operators to the simplest form and on inverse problems. Izv. Akad. Nauk SSSR Ser. Mat. 21 (1957), 235-262. MR 19 # 970.

[32] L.A. Sahnovič, Reduction of a non-selfadjoint operator with continuous spectrum to diagonal form. Uspehi Mat. Nauk 13 (1958), no. 4 (42), 193-196. (Russian) MR 20 # 7222.

[33] L.A. Sahnovič, Spectral analysis of operators of the form $Kf = \int_0^x f(t)k(x-t)dt$. Izv. Akad. Nauk SSSR 22 (1958), 299-308. MR 20 # 5409.

[34] L.A. Sahnovič, Spectral analysis of Volterra operators prescribed in the vector-function space $L^2_m(0,\ell)$, Ukrain. Mat. Ž. 16 (1964), 259-268. Amer. Math. Soc. Transl. (2) 61 (1967), 85-95. MR 29 # 2680.

[35] L.A. Sahnovič, Dissipative Volterra operators. Mat. Sb. 76 (118) (1968), 323-343. Math. USSR Sb. 5 (1968), 311-331. MR 37 # 3389.

[36] D. Sarason, A remark on the Volterra operator. J. Math. Anal. Appl. 12 (1965), 244-246. MR 33 # 580.

[37] D. Sarason, Weak-star generators of $H^\infty$. Pacific J. Math. 17 (1966), 519-528. MR 35 # 2151.

[38] D. Sarason, Generalized interpolation in $H^\infty$. Trans. Amer. Math. Soc. 127 (1967), 179-203. MR 34 # 8193.

[39] B. Sz.-Nagy and C. Foiaş, Harmonic Analysis of Operators on Hilbert Space. North Holland, New York, 1970.

[40] V. Volterra, Theory of Functionals. Dover, New York, 1959.

[41] V. Volterra and J. Pérès, Leçons sur la Composition et les Fonctions Permutables. Gauthier-Villars, Paris, 1924.

# WEAK-TYPE INEQUALITIES IN ANALYSIS

Colin Bennett
Department of Mathematics
McMaster University
Hamilton

and

Robert C. Sharpley
Department of Mathematics
University of South Carolina
Columbia

The purpose of this article is to survey some recent extensions of the Marcinkiewicz interpolation theorem due to C. Bennett - K. Rudnick and R.A. DeVore - S.D. Riemenschneider - R.C. Sharpley. These results are based on the observation that existing definitions of weak-type operators are somewhat inadequate and that a more natural definition is obtained by considering those operators that are dominated by the Calderón operator $S_\sigma$. Since the corresponding interpolation theorems can be lifted into a general Banach space context, this approach has important applications not only in harmonic analysis but in other areas such as approximation theory as well.

## 1. The Marcinkiewicz interpolation theorem

Denote by $f^*$ the decreasing rearrangement on the interval $(0,\infty)$ of a measurable function f defined on some measure space $(X,\mu)$. For $0 < p,q \le \infty$, the Lorentz space $L^{pq}$ consists of all (classes of) measurable f on X for which the quasinorm

$$(1.1) \qquad ||f||_{p,q} = \begin{cases} \left(\int_0^\infty [t^{1/p} f^*(t)]^q \, dt/t\right)^{1/q}, & 0 < q < \infty, \\ \sup_{t>0} t^{1/p} f^*(t), & q = \infty, \end{cases}$$

is finite. The spaces $L^{pq}$ increase with q; in particular

$$(1.2) \qquad L^{p1} \subseteq L^{pp} = L^p \subseteq L^{p\infty}, \qquad 1 \le p \le \infty.$$

A.P. Calderón's formulation [3] of the Marcinkiewicz interpolation theorem in terms of Lorentz spaces is as follows.

THEOREM 1.1. *Suppose*

$$(1.3) \qquad 0 < p_1 < p_2 \le \infty; \qquad 0 < q_1,q_2 \le \infty, \qquad q_1 \ne q_2.$$

*Let T be a quasilinear operator of weak types* $(p_1,q_1)$ *and* $(p_2,q_2)$. *Suppose*

$0 < \theta < 1$ and let

$$\frac{1}{p} = \frac{1-\theta}{p_1} + \frac{\theta}{p_2}, \qquad \frac{1}{q} = \frac{1-\theta}{q_1} + \frac{\theta}{q_2}.$$

Then T is a bounded linear operator from $L^{pa}$ into $L^{qa}$, i.e.,

(1.4) $$T : L^{pa} \to L^{qa},$$

whenever $0 < a \leq \infty$.

Here, an operator is of weak type $(p,q)$ if it is bounded from $L^{p1}$ into $L^{q\infty}$. The case $p = \infty$ is excluded however because, as is clear from (1.1), the space $L^{\infty 1}$ contains only the zero-function. It is customary in this case to substitute $L^{\infty}$ for $L^{\infty 1}$ in the above definition; in particular, an operator is of weak type $(\infty,\infty)$ if and only if it is bounded from $L^{\infty}$ into itself. This makeshift definition is satisfactory for some purposes (the Hardy-Littlewood maximal operator is then of weak type $(\infty,\infty)$) but is unsuitable for others (the Hilbert transform fails to be of weak type $(\infty,\infty)$).

In the next section we shall remedy this defect by modifying the definition of "weak type". As it turns out, most of the necessary machinery is already available: it has only to be assembled in a slightly different way.

## 2. The Calderón operator

With parameters as in (1.3), let $\nu$ be the slope of the line segment $\sigma$, say, joining the points $(1/p_i, 1/q_i)$, $i = 1,2$, in the plane.

The integral operator $S_\sigma$, defined by

(2.1) $$(S_\sigma g)(t) = t^{-1/q_1} \int_0^{t^\nu} s^{1/p_1} g(s)ds/s + t^{-1/q_2} \int_{t^\nu}^{\infty} s^{1/p_2} g(s)ds/s, \qquad t > 0,$$

was introduced by A.P. Calderón [3] in connection with the following fundamental result for weak-type operators.

THEOREM 2.1 (A.P. Calderón). *Suppose, in addition to* (1.3), *that* $p_2 < \infty$. *Then a quasilinear operator* T *is of weak types* $(p_1,q_1)$ *and* $(p_2,q_2)$ *if and only if, for all* f *and some constant* c *independent of* f,

(2.2) $$(Tf)^*(t) \leq c\, S_\sigma(f^*)(t), \qquad 0 < t < \infty.$$

The theorem characterizes the weak-type operators as those that are dominated by $S_\sigma$. It fails when $p_2 = \infty$ precisely because of the unnatural definition of "weak type $(p_2,q_2)$" in this case. Observe however that $S_\sigma$ is perfectly well-defined when $p_2 = \infty$, and hence it makes sense to use (2.2) as a definition of "weak type", now for all values of the parameters.

DEFINITION 2.2 [1,2]. Suppose $p_i, q_i$, $i = 1,2$, satisfy (1.3). A quasilinear operator T is said to be of weak type $(p_1,q_1; p_2,q_2)$ if (2.2) holds.

Interpolation theorems follow rather easily with this definition. Thus, Calderón's proof of Theorem 1.1 proceeds by applying the $L^{qa}$-norm to both sides of (2.2); the classical Hardy inequalities then reduce the right-hand side to the $L^{pa}$-norm of f, hence establishing (1.4).

Our objective was to establish a definition of "weak type" that would apply to such operators as the Hilbert transform H. The desired result is that H be of weak type $(1,1; \infty,\infty)$:

$$(Hf)^*(t) \le c\left(t^{-1}\int_0^t f^*(s)ds + \int_t^\infty f^*(s)ds/s\right), \qquad 0 < t < \infty. \tag{2.3}$$

This inequality can be derived fairly easily from a closely-related inequality due to R. O'Neil - G. Weiss [8]. Similarly, the maximal Hilbert transform and certain Calderón-Zygmund singular integrals are also of weak type $(1,1; \infty,\infty)$; complete details are given in [2].

## 3. Lorentz-Zygmund spaces

Besides the $L^{pq}$ spaces, the Zygmund spaces $L^p(\log L)^\alpha$ also play an essential role in classical harmonic analysis. It is therefore desirable that both classes be incorporated into the interpolation scheme.

For $0 < p < \infty$, $-\infty < \alpha < \infty$, the Zygmund space $L^p(\log L)^\alpha$ consists of those f on the unit circle $\Gamma$ for which

$$\int_0^{2\pi}\left\{|f(e^{i\theta})|\ \log^\alpha(2 + |f(e^{i\theta})|)\right\}^p d\theta < \infty. \tag{3.1}$$

The Orlicz norms with which these spaces are usually endowed are of a quite different character to the Lorentz $L^{pq}$ norms. However, it can be shown that (3.1) holds if and only if

$$\left(\int_0^1\left\{f^*(t)(1-\log t)^\alpha\right\}^p dt\right)^{1/p} < \infty, \tag{3.2}$$

and this quantity is a Lorentz-type norm on $L^p(\log L)^\alpha$, equivalent to the Orlicz norm. Now it is easy to incorporate the Lorentz spaces and the Zygmund spaces in a larger class of spaces.

DEFINITION 3.1 [2]. Suppose $0 < p,q \le \infty$ and $-\infty < \alpha < \infty$. The Lorentz-Zygmund space $L^{pq}(\log L)^{\alpha}$ on $(X,\mu)$ consists of those (classes of) measurable functions f on X for which the quasinorm

$$||f||_{p,q;\alpha} = \begin{cases} \left(\int_0^{\infty}\left\{t^{1/p}(1 + |\log t|)^{\alpha}f^*(t)\right\}^q dt/t\right)^{1/q}, & 0 < q < \infty, \\ \sup_{t>0} t^{1/p}(1 + |\log t|)^{\alpha}f^*(t), & q = \infty, \end{cases}$$

is finite.

The spaces $L^{pq}(\log L)^{0}$ are immediately recognizable as the Lorentz spaces $L^{pq}$. On the unit circle, the spaces $L^{pp}(\log L)^{\alpha}$ are the Zygmund spaces $L^{p}(\log L)^{\alpha}$. Furthermore, the Zygmund spaces of functions whose $1/\alpha$-th powers are "exponentially integrable" occur as the Lorentz-Zygmund spaces $L^{\infty\infty}(\log L)^{-\alpha}$, and the O'Neil spaces $K^{p}(\log^{+} K)^{\alpha p}$ arise as the spaces $L^{p1}(\log L)^{\alpha}$. Several other types of spaces occurring in classical harmonic analysis can also be regarded as Lorentz-Zygmund spaces (cf. [2]).

## 4. Two interpolation theorems

Now we can present the interpolation theorems established by C. Bennett - K. Rudnick [2]. They describe the action of operators of weak type $(p_1,q_1; p_2,q_2)$ on the Lorentz-Zygmund spaces $L^{pa}(\log L)^{\alpha}$.

THEOREM 4.1. Suppose $0 < p_1 < p_2 \le \infty$ and $0 < q_1,q_2 \le \infty$, with $q_1 \neq q_2$. Let T be a quasilinear operator of weak type $(p_1,q_1; p_2,q_2)$. Suppose $0 < \theta < 1$ and let

$$\frac{1}{p} = \frac{1-\theta}{p_1} + \frac{\theta}{p_2}, \quad \frac{1}{q} = \frac{1-\theta}{q_1} + \frac{\theta}{q_2}.$$

Then

$$T : L^{pa}(\log L)^{\alpha} \to L^{qa}(\log L)^{\alpha}$$

whenever $0 < a \le \infty$ and $-\infty < \alpha < \infty$.

This result is a direct extension of Calderón's theorem (Theorem 1.1). The next result corresponds to the limiting cases $\theta = 0$ and $\theta = 1$ of Theorem 4.1. The principal feature is that the "index" $\alpha + 1/a$ of $L^{pa}(\log L)^{\alpha}$ always decreases by a factor of one. We state the theorem only in the form valid for finite measure spaces; the general statement can be found in [2, Theorem C].

THEOREM 4.2. *Suppose* $0 < p_1 < p_2 \le \infty$ *and* $0 < q_1 < q_2 \le \infty$. *Let* T *be a quasi-linear operator of weak type* $(p_1,q_1;\ p_2,q_2)$. *Suppose* $1 \le a \le b \le \infty$ *and* $-\infty < \alpha,\beta < \infty$. *Then*

(a) $$T : L^{p_1 a}(\log L)^{\alpha+1} \to L^{q_1 b}(\log L)^{\beta}$$

*whenever* $\alpha + 1/a = \beta + 1/b > 0$;

(b) $$T : L^{p_2 a}(\log L)^{\alpha+1} \to L^{q_2 b}(\log L)^{\beta}$$

*whenever* $\alpha + 1/a = \beta + 1/b < 0$.

These interpolation theorems contain (and in many cases extend) a wide variety of estimates from classical harmonic analysis, involving such operators as the Fourier transform, the Hardy-Littlewood maximal operator, the fractional integrals, and the Hilbert transform (cf. [2] for details). As an illustration we consider the classical estimates for the Weyl fractional-integral operators $I_\lambda$ $(0 < \lambda < 1)$ on the unit circle (cf. [2, 12; Chapter XII]).

(a) (Hardy-Littlewood) $I_\lambda : L^p \to L^q$, $1 < p < q < \infty$, $1/p - 1/q = \lambda$;

(b) (Zygmund) $I_\lambda : L(\log L)^{1-\lambda} \to L^{(1-\lambda)^{-1}}$;

(c) (O'Neil) $I_\lambda : L(\log L)^{\alpha} \to K^{(1-\lambda)^{-1}}(\log^+ K)^{(1-\lambda)^{-1}(\alpha-1)}$, $\alpha \ge 1$;

(d) (O'Neil) $I_\lambda : L(\log L)^{\alpha} \to L^{(1-\lambda)^{-1},1/\alpha}$, $0 < \alpha < 1$;

(e) (Zygmund) If $||f||_{\lambda^{-1}} \le 1$, there are constants $\gamma$ and C independent of f such that $\int_{-\pi}^{\pi} \exp\left\{\gamma |I_\lambda f|^{\frac{1}{1-\lambda}}\right\} \le C < \infty$.

These diverse estimates can be neatly reformulated in terms of Lorentz-Zygmund spaces as follows:

(a') $I_\lambda : L^{p,p}(\log L)^0 \to L^{q,q}(\log L)^0$, $1 < p < q < \infty$, $1/p - 1/q = \lambda$;

(b') $I_\lambda : L^{1,1}(\log L)^{1-\lambda} \to L^{(1-\lambda)^{-1},(1-\lambda)^{-1}}(\log L)^0$;

(c') $I_\lambda : L^{1,1}(\log L)^{\alpha} \to L^{(1-\lambda)^{-1},1}(\log L)^{\alpha-1}$, $\alpha \ge 1$;

(d') $I_\lambda : L^{1,1}(\log L)^{\alpha} \to L^{(1-\lambda)^{-1},\ \alpha^{-1}}(\log L)^0$, $0 < \alpha < 1$;

(e') $I_\lambda : L^{\lambda^{-1},\lambda^{-1}}(\log L)^0 \to L^{\infty,\infty}(\log L)^{\lambda-1}$.

Since $I_\lambda$ is of weak type $(1,(1-\lambda)^{-1};\ \lambda^{-1},\infty)$ it is a simple matter to check that (a') follows immediately from Theorem 4.1, (b'), (c') and (d') from the first part of Theorem 4.2, and (e') from the second part of Theorem 4.2.

## 5. Multilinear interpolation

Observe that the Calderón operator in (2.1) can be written as a kernel operator

$$(S_\sigma g)(t) = \int_0^\infty g(s)\, \Psi_\sigma(s,t)\, ds/s, \tag{5.1}$$

with kernel $\Psi_\sigma(s,t) = \min\left\{s^{1/p_i}\, t^{-1/q_i} : i = 1,2, \quad 0 < s,t < \infty\right\}$. R.C. Sharpley [9] has shown that a natural generalization of this operator can be used to control multilinear interpolation. Such theorems are needed to deal with, for example, convolution operators [6] and tensor product operators [7].

Convolution operators C satisfy three initial estimates

$$C : \begin{cases} L^1 \times L^1 \to L^1 \\ L^1 \times L^\infty \to L^\infty \\ L^\infty \times L^\infty \to L^\infty \end{cases} \tag{5.2}$$

and, similarly, tensor product operators T satisfy two initial estimates

$$T : \begin{cases} L^1 \times L^1 \to L^1 \\ L^\infty \times L^\infty \to L^\infty \end{cases} \tag{5.3}$$

Thus, Sharpley [9] considers bilinear (or multilinear) operators satisfying m weak-type estimates, of the form

$$T(\chi_E,\chi_F)^{**}(t) \le c\, \frac{\mu(E)^{1/p_i}\, \mu(F)^{1/q_i}}{t^{1/u_i}}, \qquad i = 1,2,\dots,m \tag{5.4}$$

(where $h^{**}(t) = t^{-1}\int_0^t h^*(s)ds$). Operators of this kind are said to satisfy the $\sigma((p_1,q_1;\ u_1),\dots,(p_m,q_m;\ u_m))$ weak-type conditions. This leads easily to the inequality

$$T(\chi_E,\chi_F)^{**}(t) \le c\ \mathfrak{L}_\sigma(\mu(E),\mu(F);t)$$
$$\le \int_0^\infty \int_0^\infty \chi_E^*(r)\ \chi_F^*(s)\ \mathfrak{L}_\sigma(r,s;t)\ \frac{dr}{r}\frac{ds}{s},$$

since the kernel

$$\mathfrak{L}_\sigma(r,s;t) = \min\left\{r^{1/p_i}\ s^{1/q_i}\ t^{-1/u_i} : i = 1,2,\ldots,m\right\}$$

is concave in r and s, and decreasing in t. Passing to simple functions, we obtain the $\sigma$-weak-type inequality (cf. Definition 2.2)

$$T(f,g)^{**}(t) \le c\int_0^\infty \int_0^\infty f^*(r)\ g^*(s)\ \mathfrak{L}_\sigma(r,s;t)\ \frac{dr}{r}\frac{ds}{s} \tag{5.5}$$
$$\equiv c\ S_\sigma(f^*,g^*)(t).$$

As before, interpolation theorems are established by applying appropriate norms to both sides of (5.5). As corollaries, they yield the following results for convolution operators, which are of weak type $\sigma((1,1,1),(1,\infty,\infty);(\infty,\infty,\infty))$, and tensor product operators, which are of weak type $\sigma((1,1,1);(\infty,\infty;\infty))$ (cf. (5.2) and (5.3)), acting on Lorentz-Zygmund spaces.

THEOREM 5.1 [9]. *Let C be a convolution operator. Then*

$$C : L^{pa}(\log L)^\alpha \times L^{qb}(\log L)^\beta \to L^{uc}(\log L)^\gamma \tag{5.6}$$

*where*

$$1/p + 1/q = 1/u + 1, \qquad 1/a + 1/b \ge 1/c, \qquad \alpha + \beta \ge \gamma.$$

In fact, by considering estimates which are essentially inverse to (5.5), it is possible to obtain best-possible results for convolution (cf. [10]).

THEOREM 5.2 [9]. *Let T be a tensor product operator. Then*

$$T : L^{pa}(\log L)^\alpha \times L^{pb}(\log L)^\beta \to L^{pc}(\log L)^\gamma$$

*where*

$$1/a + 1/b \ge 1/c + 1, \qquad \gamma \le \min(\alpha,\beta).$$

These theorems contain as special cases many of the results established by O'Neil [6,7]. Finally, we remark that the $S_\sigma$-operator associated with the tensor products maps $L^1 \times L^1$ into $L^{1,\infty}$ and $L^2 \times L^2$ into $L^{2,\infty}$ but does not carry $L^p \times L^p$ into $L^p$ (cf. [11]). This confirms a conjecture of J. Peetre to the effect that the Marcinkiewicz theorem does not extend to bilinear operators in this manner.

## 6. The conjugate-function operator

Let H be the conjugate-function operator (i.e., the Hilbert transform for the unit circle). There is the following inequality for H in terms of the modulus of continuity $\omega(f,t)$ (cf. [12, Chapter III, p.121]):

$$t^{-1}\omega(Hf,t) \le c\left\{t^{-1}\int_0^t s^{-1}\omega(f,s)ds + \int_t^\infty s^{-1}\omega(f,s)ds/s\right\}. \tag{6.1}$$

Clearly, if the quantities $t^{-1}\omega(h,t)$ are replaced by decreasing rearrangements $h^*$, then the fundamental inequality (2.3) results. This observation was made by R.A. DeVore - S.D. Riemenschneider - R.C. Sharpley [4], and it suggested to them that Marcinkiewicz-type theorems might play a role far outside of the familiar Banach function space setting. This prompted their development of a weak-type interpolation theory in a general Banach space context. As we shall see below and in section 8, it has a number of interesting applications.

Notice that once a "weak-type" inequality such as (6.1) (or (2.3)) is established, then, by applying Lorentz-Zygmund norms to each side, we obtain interpolation theorems that are entirely analogous to Theorems 4.1 and 4.2.

Thus, in the present case we obtain the estimates

$$H : B_\infty^{\theta,a;\alpha} \to B_\infty^{\theta,a;\alpha}, \qquad 0 < \theta < 1, \qquad a > 0, \qquad -\infty < \alpha < \infty, \tag{6.2}$$

where the norm in $B_p^{\theta,a;\alpha}$ is given in terms of the $L^p$-modulus of continuity by

$$||f||_{B_p^{\theta,a;\alpha}} = ||\frac{\omega(f,.)_p}{(.)}||_{q,a;\alpha}, \qquad q = (1-\theta)^{-1}. \tag{6.3}$$

These spaces reduce to the Besov spaces when $\alpha = 0$, and to the Lipschitz spaces when we further require $a = p = \infty$. Thus (6.2) contains, for instance, the familiar result on the boundedness of H on Lip($\theta$), for $0 < \theta < 1$. Similarly, in the limiting cases $\theta = 0$ and $\theta = 1$ (corresponding to Theorem 4.2) we obtain as easy corollaries the following well-known classical estimates:

$$\omega(f,t) = O(t) \quad \Rightarrow \quad \omega(Hf,t) = O(t|\log t|);$$

$$\omega(f,t) = O(|\log t|^{-(\alpha+1)}) \Rightarrow \omega(Hf,t) = O(|\log t|^{-\alpha}), \quad \alpha > 0.$$

For further details, and extensions to higher order moduli, see [4].

## 7. The general theory

The crucial link between the inequalities (2.3) and (6.1), and the means by which we can pass to a more general setting, is of course the Peetre K-functional K(f,t) (cf. [4]). Thus, for the pair $(L^1,L^\infty)$ the K-functional is given by $K(f,t;\ L^1,L^\infty) = \int_0^t f^*(s)ds$ (so its derivative k(f,t) coincides with $f^*(t)$), and for the pair (C,Lip 1) it is given (up to equivalence) by $K(f,t;\ C^1,\text{Lip } 1) \approx \omega(f,t)$.

It is therefore natural to consider inequalities of the form

$$t^{-1}K(Tf,t;\ Y_1,Y_2) \leq c\ S_\sigma((.)^{-1}K(f,(.);\ X_1,X_2)(t), \qquad t > 0, \tag{7.1}$$

for appropriate segments σ. An operator T satisfying (7.1) is said to be of generalized weak-type σ with respect to the compatible couples $(X_1,X_2)$ and $(Y_1,Y_2)$ of Banach spaces (cf. [4]).

In many instances only a part of the Calderón operator is needed. Thus, if $S_{\sigma,1}(g)$ and $S_{\sigma,2}(g)$ denote respectively the first and second integrals in (2.1), we extend the definition of $S_\sigma$ to mean

$$S_\sigma = \begin{cases} S_{\sigma,1} & \text{if } \sigma = \sigma(p_1,q_1;\ p_2,q_2]; \\ S_{\sigma,2} & \text{if } \sigma = \sigma[p_1,q_1;\ p_2,q_2); \\ S_{\sigma,1} + S_{\sigma,2} & \text{if } \sigma = \sigma(p_1,q_1;\ p_2,q_2), \end{cases}$$

where the closed bracket indicates that the corresponding endpoint is included in the segment σ.

With this notation, the inequality (6.1) asserts that H is of generalized weak type $\sigma(1,1;\ \infty,\infty)$ for the pair C and Lip 1. Similarly, if the functional $t^{-1}K(f,t)$ is replaced by k(f,t), the inequality (2.3) shows that H is of generalized weak type $\sigma(1,1;\ \infty,\infty)$ for the pair $L^1$ and $L^\infty$.

Notice that it is the presence of the $S_\sigma$ operator in (7.1) which enables us to establish interpolation theorems exactly analogous to Theorems 4.1 and 4.2. This process can be carried out regardless of the particular choice of functional (such as $t^{-1}K(f;t)$ or k(f,t), as above, or the "degree of approximation functional" $t^{-1}E(f,t)$, as in the next section). Different types of functionals do, of course, yield different types of spaces appearing in those interpolation theorems, and so the choice is made to suit the particular application in mind. This freedom of choice provides the theory with great flexibility.

## 8. Applications

Marchaud's inequality [5] for the circle

$$\frac{\omega_r(f,t)_p}{t^r} \leq c \int_t^\infty \frac{\omega_{r+k}(f,s)_p}{s^r}\frac{ds}{s} \tag{8.1}$$

can be rewritten to show that the identity operator is of generalized weak type $\sigma[1,1;\ (r+k)/k,\infty)$ with respect to $(L^p, W_p^{r+k})$ and $(L^p, W_p^r)$, where

$\omega_r(f,t^{1/r})_p \sim K(f,t;L^p,W_p^r)$ and $W_p^r$ is the Sobolev space of $L^p$-functions whose r-th order distributional derivatives are in $L^p$. The basic inequality (8.1) is the converse of the trivial estimate

$$\omega_{r+k}(f,s)_p \leq c\ \omega_r(f,s)_p. \tag{8.2}$$

Consider, for simplicity, the case $r = k = 1$. Using (8.1) and (8.2), we find that when $0 \leq \theta < 1$ it is possible to replace $\omega(f,t)_p$ in (6.3) by the second order modulus $\omega_2(f,t)_p$ to get an equivalent norm. In the extreme case $\theta = 1$, $\alpha = -1$ and $a = \infty$ there is the anticipated loss of logarithm:

$$\omega_2(f,t)_p = O(t) \Rightarrow \omega(f,t)_p = O(t|\log t|).$$

Inequalities similar to (8.1) and (8.2) hold for moduli of smoothness for domains in $R^n$ satisfying a cone condition, or for equibounded $C_o$-semigroups of operators (cf. [4, §5]). The reduction theorems for Besov spaces follow from the inequality

$$\omega_{r+k}(f,t)_p \leq c\ t^k \sup_{|\beta|=k} \omega_r(D^\beta f,t)_p$$

and the weak-type inequality for differentiation

$$\omega_r(D^\beta f,t)_p \leq c \int_0^t \frac{\omega_{r+k}(f,s)_p}{s^k}\frac{ds}{s},$$

where $\beta$ is a multi-index of length k. For more details and the reduction theorems in terms of semigroup generators see [4, §5].

Jackson's direct approximation theorem on the circle [5] gives

$$E(f,1/t)_p \leq c\omega(f,t)_p, \qquad 0 < t \leq 1,$$

where $E(f,s)_p$ is the error of approximation in $L^p$ by trigonometric polynomials of degree at most [s]. Bernstein's inverse theorem [5] can be interpreted as the weak-type inequality

$$t^{-1}\omega(f,t)_p \leq c\ S_\sigma(E(f,.)_p)(t),$$

where $\sigma = \sigma(1,\infty;\ \infty,1]$. Consequently, we obtain the standard results

$$\omega(f,t)_p = O(t^\theta) \Rightarrow E(f,1/t) = O(t^\theta), \qquad 0 \le \theta < 1.$$

The loss of logarithm at $\theta = 1$ occurs as before [4, §8].

Next, we consider embeddings of Besov spaces. If $\Omega$ is a bounded domain satisfying a cone property, or all of $R^n$, there is an estimate of the form

$$\omega_r(f,t)_q \le c \int_0^t \omega_r(f,s)_p\ s^{-\theta}\ ds/s, \tag{8.3}$$

where $r \ge n$, $1 \le p \le q \le \infty$, and $\theta = n/p - n/q$. Hence the identity operator is of generalized weak type $\sigma(r/(r-\theta),1;\ \infty,r/\theta]$ for the pairs $(L^p,W_p^r)$ and $(L^q,W_q^r)$. Interpolation gives the embeddings

$$B_p^{\lambda+\theta,a;\alpha} \subset B_q^{\lambda,a;\alpha}, \qquad \lambda > 0,$$

and

$$B_p^{\theta,1} \subset L^q,$$

with similar results involving the additional log term at the endpoints.

In order to estimate growth in terms of smoothness, the inequality

$$f^{**}(t) \le c \int_{t^{1/n}}^{\infty} \omega_n(f,s)_p\ s^{-n/p}\ ds/s, \qquad 1 < p < \infty, \tag{8.4}$$

is established in [4, §6]. This asserts that the identity operator is of generalized weak type $\sigma[1,p;\ p',\infty)$ with respect to $(L^p,W_p^n)$ and $(L^1,L^\infty)$. By interpolation we obtain the embeddings

$$B_p^{\theta,a;\alpha} \subset L^{q,a;\alpha}, \qquad B_p^{n/p,1} \subset L^\infty,$$

where $p < q$ and $\theta = n/p - n/q$, etc.

As a final application we mention absolute convergence of Fourier transforms $\hat{f}$ on $R^n$. In [4, §8] it is shown that

$$(\hat{f})^{**}(t) \le ct^{-1} \int_{t^{-1/n}}^{\infty} \omega_r(f,s)_p\ s^{-n/p}\ ds/s,$$

i.e., the Fourier transform is of generalized weak type $\sigma[1,p';\ pr/(pr-n),1)$ for the pairs $(L^p,W_p^r)$ and $(L^1,L^\infty)$. Interpolation gives

$$(B_p^{\theta,a;\alpha})^\wedge \subset L^{q,a;\alpha}; \qquad (B_p^{n/p,1})^\wedge \subset L^1, \text{ etc.}$$

Weak-type methods also play an important role in the development of abstract interpolation itself. Indeed, the equivalence, reiteration, and multilinear theorems of the Peetre J-and K-methods can be written as weak-type inequalities (cf. [4, §§4,9]).

REFERENCES

[1] Bennett, C., Banach function spaces and interpolation methods. II. Interpolation of weak-type operators. Linear Operators and Approximation II, Butzer, P.L.-Nagy, Sz., Eds., (ISNM 25) Birkhäuser Verlag, Basel-Stuttgart, 1974, 129-139.

[2] Bennett, C. - Rudnick, K., On Lorentz-Zygmund spaces. Dissertationes Math. (to appear).

[3] Calderón, A.P., Spaces between $L^1$ and $L^\infty$ and the theorem of Marcinkiewicz. Studia Math. 26 (1966), 273-299.

[4] DeVore, R.A. - Riemenschneider, S.D. - Sharpley, R.C., Weak interpolation in Banach spaces. (to appear).

[5] Lorentz, G.G., Approximation of Functions. Holt, Rinehart and Winston, New York, 1966.

[6] O'Neil, R., Convolution operators and L(p,q) spaces. Duke Math. J. 30 (1963), 129-142.

[7] O'Neil, R., Integral transforms and tensor products on Orlicz spaces and L(p,q) spaces. J. Analyse Math. 21 (1968), 1-276.

[8] O'Neil, R. - Weiss, G., The Hilbert transform and rearrangement of functions. Studia Math. 23 (1963), 189-198.

[9] Sharpley, R.C., Multilinear weak type interpolation of m n-tuples with applications. Studia Math. 60 (1977), 179-194.

[10] Sharpley, R.C., Counterexamples for classical operators on Lorentz-Zygmund spaces. (to appear).

[11] Sharpley, R.C., On the failure of the Marcinkiewicz theorem for bilinear maps. (to appear).

[12] Zygmund, A., Trigonometric Series, Vols. I and II, Cambridge Univ. Press, Cambridge, 1968.

# FRACTIONAL LIPSCHITZ SPACES GENERATED BY REARRANGEMENT-INVARIANT NORMS

Franziska Fehér
Lehrstuhl A für Mathematik
Rheinisch-Westfälische Technische Hochschule
Aachen

The generalized Lipschitz space generated via fractional powers of differences of semigroup operators on a Banach space X is defined with respect to rearrangement-invariant norms. The Boyd indices of the norm are used as an instrument to yield a reprensentation of this Lipschitz space as an interpolation space. In this frame theorems of interpolation of Riesz-Thorin-type, of reduction and duality are established. The case of optimal approximation as well as particular norms such as the Lebesgue-, Lorentz-, and Orlicz norm are subsumed.

## 1. Definition and Elementary Properties

Let X denote a Banach space, [X] the algebra of bounded endomorphisms of X, and $\mathcal{T} = \{T(t);\ t \geq 0\}$ an equibounded semigroup of class $(C_0)$ on [X] with infinitesimal generator A. In analogy to a well known formula for the r-th difference (r=1,2,...), U. Westphal [19] (1974) defined for any $\gamma>0$

$$(1.1)\qquad [I-T(t)]^{\gamma}f := \sum_{j=0}^{\infty} \binom{j-\gamma-1}{j} T(jt)f \qquad (f \in X),$$

and the fractional power of A by

$$(1.2)\qquad (-A)^{\gamma}f := \text{s-}\lim_{t\to 0+} t^{-\gamma}[I-T(t)]^{\gamma}f$$

whenever the limit exists. The domain of $(-A)^{\gamma}$, denoted by $D[(-A)^{\gamma}]$, is a Banach space with respect to the norm $\|f\|_X + \|(-A)^{\gamma}f\|_X$. The above definition can be shown to coincide with those given by A.V. Balakrishnan [1] (1960) and H. Komatsu [14] (1967). Starting from (1.1), U. Westphal established the representation formula

$$(1.3)\qquad t^{-\gamma}[I-T(t)]^{\gamma}f = \int_0^{\infty} p_{\gamma}(u/t)T(u)(-A)^{\gamma}\,du/t$$

for $f \in D[(-A)^{\gamma}]$. Here $p_{\gamma}$ denotes the $L_1(0,\infty)$-function

$$(1.4)\qquad p_\gamma(u) = \frac{1}{\Gamma(\gamma)} \sum_{0\leq j\leq u} \binom{j-\gamma-1}{j}(u-j)^{\gamma-1} \qquad (u>0),$$

which in case $\gamma=r$ reduces to the B-spline (see [10]) of degree $r-1$ with respect to the knots $0,1,2,\ldots,r$, namely

$$(1.5)\qquad M_r(u;0,1,\ldots,r) = \frac{1}{(r-1)!} \sum_{j=0}^{r} (-1)^{r-j}\binom{r}{j}(u-j)_+^{r-1}.$$

Moreover, some basic notations from the theory of function norms are needed: Let $M$ (resp. $P$) denote the set of all realvalued (resp. nonnegative) Lebesgue measurable functions on $(0,\infty)$, and $\rho$ a rearrangement-invariant (r.i.) norm on $P$, i.e. a mapping $\rho: P \to [0,\infty]$ such that

i) a) $\rho(f) = 0 \Leftrightarrow f = 0$ a.e.;
b) $\rho(\lambda f) = \lambda\rho(f)$ $(\lambda>0)$; c) $\rho(f+g) \leq \rho(f) + \rho(g)$;

ii) $f \leq g$ a.e. $\Rightarrow$ $\rho(f) \leq \rho(g)$;

iii) $\rho(f^*) = \rho(f)$, with $f^*$ denoting the nonincreasing rearrangement of $f$;

iv) $\rho(\chi_{(0,t)}) < \infty$ and there exists a number $A_t>0$, depending only on $t>0$, such that $\int_0^t f(s)\,ds \leq A_t\rho(f)$;

v) $f_n \nearrow f$ a.e. $\Rightarrow$ $\rho(f_n) \nearrow \rho(f)$ (Fatou property).

Then the r.i. space $L^\rho$ is defined as the set of all $f \in M$ such that $\|f\|_\rho :=$ $\rho(|f|)$ is finite, functions which agree almost everywhere being identified. With respect to the norm $\|\cdot\|_\rho$ the space $L^\rho$ is an intermediate Banach space of $L_1$ and $L_\infty$, i.e. $L_1 \cap L_\infty \subset L^\rho \subset L_1 + L_\infty$.

The indicator function $h(s) := \|E_s\|_{[L^\rho]}$ of the space $L^\rho$ is defined as the operator norm on $L^\rho$ of the dilation operator $E_s$, with $(E_s f)(t) := f(st)$, $s>0$, and the upper, resp. lower, index of the r.i. norm $\rho$ as

$$(1.6)\qquad \alpha := \inf_{0<s<1} -\frac{\log h(s)}{\log s}, \qquad \beta := \sup_{s>1} -\frac{\log h(s)}{\log s};$$

(see D.W. Boyd [5]). The importance of these indices may be deduced from the fact that in case of Lebesgue norms $\rho = \|\cdot\|_p$, $1\leq p<\infty$, one has $\alpha=\beta=1/p$.

With the above definitions in mind, we give

DEFINITION 1.1. <u>For any</u> $a>0$ <u>and</u> $0<a\leq\gamma$ <u>the generalized Lipschitz space of exponent</u> $\gamma$ <u>and order</u> $a$ <u>with respect to</u> $\rho$ <u>is defined by</u>

$$X_{a,\gamma,\rho;T} := \{f \in X;\ t^{-a}\|[I-T(t)]^{\gamma} f\|_X \in L^{\rho}\}.$$

REMARK. By a change of variable $s \to \log s$ the modified Lebesgue norm $\|f\|_q^* := \{\int_0^\infty (f(s))^q ds/s\}^{1/q}$, $1 \leqslant q < \infty$, becomes a r.i. norm. Hence the spaces $X_{a,r,q}$ of J.L. Lions [15] (1959), J.L. Lions - J. Peetre [17] (1964) (for $a<r$, $q<\infty$), as well as the case of optimal approximation and the Favard class $X_{r,r,\infty}$ of P.L. Butzer [6] (1956/57) (for $r=1$) and of H. Berens [3] (1965) (for $r = 1,2,\ldots$), and also the fractional case of U. Westphal [19] (1974) are included in the above definition. In the particular case of the semigroup of left translations, see also [8].

The following theorem is readily established:

THEOREM 1.1. a) <u>The generalized Lipschitz space</u> $X_{a,\gamma,\rho;T}$ <u>is a Banach space with respect to the norm</u>

$$\|f\|_{a,\gamma,\rho;T} := \|f\|_X + \rho(t^{-a}\|[I-T(t)]^{\gamma} f\|_X).$$

b) <u>If</u> $t^{-a}\min(1,t^{\gamma}) \in L^{\rho}$, <u>then</u> $D[(-A)^{\gamma}] \subset X_{a,\gamma,\rho;T} \subset X$.

c) <u>If the upper index</u> $\alpha$ <u>is less than</u> a, <u>i.e.</u> $\alpha<a$, <u>then</u> $t^{-a}\min(1,t^{\gamma}) \in L^{\rho}$.

d) <u>If</u> $\alpha<a\leqslant b\leqslant\gamma$, <u>then</u> $X_{b,\gamma,\rho;T} \subset X_{a,\gamma,\rho;T}$.

Note that $t^{-\gamma}\min(1,t^{\gamma}) \in L_\infty$, hence the Favard class is an intermediate space of X and $D[(-A)^{\gamma}]$ in the sense of b).

The first statement of Thm. 1.1 is proved by standard arguments using Fatou's property, see [7, p. 161]. Concerning b), one has by (1.3) since $\int_0^\infty p_\gamma(v)dv = 1$ that

$$\|[I-T(t)]^{\gamma} f\|_X \leqslant t^{\gamma} M \|(-A)^{\gamma} f\|_X \int_0^\infty p_\gamma(u/t)du/t = t^{\gamma} M \|(-A)^{\gamma} f\|_X,$$

where M is an upper bound of $\|T(t)\|$, $t>0$. On the other hand, $\|[I-T(t)]^{\gamma} f\|_X \leqslant (1+M)^{\gamma}\|f\|_X$. Hence $t^{-a}\|[I-T(t)]^{\gamma} f\|_X \leqslant (1+M)^{\gamma} t^{-a}\min(1,t^{\gamma})(\|f\|_X + \|(-A)^{\gamma} f\|_X)$. Part c) follows by [12, Satz 1.1a], since - under the same notations -

$$t^{-a}\min(1,t^{\gamma}) = \gamma P_a(t^{\gamma-a}\chi_{(0,1)}(t))$$

and $t^{\gamma-a}\chi_{(0,1)}(t) \in L^{\rho}$ because $a\leqslant\gamma$. Assertion d) is verified by observing that $t^{-a}$ can be estimated by $t^{-a} \leqslant t^{-b}\chi_{(0,1)}(t) + t^{-a}\chi_{[1,\infty)}(t) \leqslant t^{-b} + t^{-a}\min(1,t^{\gamma})$.

## 2. The Lipschitz Spaces as Interpolation Spaces

For the following recall that if $X_1, X_2$ are two Banach spaces continuously embedded into a linear Hausdorff space $\mathcal{X}$, then the K-functional $K(t,f) \equiv K(t,f;X_1,X_2)$ for $f \in X_1+X_2$ is given by

$$K(t,f) := \inf\{\|f_1\|_{X_1} + t\|f_2\|_{X_2}; f=f_1+f_2,\ f_1 \in X_1,\ f_2 \in X_2\} \qquad (t>0).$$

DEFINITION 2.1. *Let* $\rho$ *be a r.i. norm and* $\theta \in \mathbb{R}$. *Then*

$$(X_1,X_2)_{\theta,\rho;K} := \{f \in X_1+X_2;\ t^{-\theta}K(t,f) \in L^\rho\}.$$

The following theorem, to be found in [12] for $\theta \in \mathbb{R}$ and in [2] for $\theta=1$, is proved analogously to Thm. 1.1.

THEOREM 2.1. a) *The space* $(X_1,X_2)_{\theta,\rho;K}$ *is a Banach space with respect to the norm*

$$\|f\|_{\theta,\rho;K} := \rho(t^{-\theta}K(t,f)).$$

b) *If* $t^{-\theta}\min(1,t) \in L^\rho$, *then* $X_1 \cap X_2 \subset (X_1,X_2)_{\theta,\rho;K} \subset X_1+X_2$.

c) *If* $\alpha<\theta\leqslant 1$, *then* $t^{-\theta}\min(1,t) \in L^\rho$.

d) *If* $\alpha<\theta_1\leqslant\theta_2\leqslant 1$, *then* $(X_1,X_2)_{\theta_2,\rho;K} \subset (X_1,X_2)_{\theta_1,\rho;K}$.

The question now is whether the particular case of these spaces for $X_1=X$ and $X_2=D[(-A)^\gamma]$ can be interpreted as a generalized Lipschitz space in the sense of Def. 1.1, i.e. generated by a rearrangement-invariant norm (compare [7] for the case of $\|\cdot\|_q^*$-norm). For this purpose we need some auxiliary lemmas.

LEMMA 2.2. *Let* $0<c<1$ *and* $\rho$ *be a r.i. norm with upper index* $\alpha<c$. *If* $\rho_c$ *and* $\rho_c^*$ *are defined by* $\rho_c(f(t)) := \rho(f^*(t^c))$ *and* $\rho_c^*(f(t)) := \rho(f^{**}(t^c))$, *then*

$$\rho_c(f) \leqslant \rho_c^*(f) \leqslant c A_c \rho_c(f) \tag{2.1}$$

*where* $A_c = \int_0^1 s^{c-1}h(s)ds$ *and* $f^{**}(t) = t^{-1}\int_0^t f^*(s)ds$.

PROOF. Since $f^*(t) \leqslant f^{**}(t)$, $t>0$, the left-hand inequality of (2.1) is obvious. Moreover, by a simple substitution one has

$$f^{**}(t^c) = c\,t^{-c}\int_0^t s^{c-1} f^*(s^c)\,ds.$$

Applying now a generalized version of Hardy's inequality (see P.L. Butzer - F. Fehér [9]), possible since $\alpha<c$, then

$$\rho_c^*(f) = c\rho(t^{-c}\int_0^t s^{c-1} f^*(s^c)\,ds) \leqslant c\,A_c\rho(f^*(s^c)) = c\,A_c\rho_c(f).$$

LEMMA 2.3. <u>Let</u> $c>0$ <u>and</u> $\rho$ <u>be a r.i. norm with indices</u> $\alpha,\beta$.

a) <u>If</u> $c\geqslant 1$, <u>then</u> $\rho_c$ <u>is a r.i. norm with indicator function</u> $h_c(s)=h(s^{1/c})$ <u>and indices</u> $\alpha_c = \alpha/c$ <u>and</u> $\beta_c = \beta/c$.

b) <u>If</u> $c<1$ <u>and</u> $\alpha<c$, <u>then</u> $\rho_c$ <u>is a r.i. quasinorm with the triangular inequality</u>

$$\rho_c(f+g) \leqslant c\,A_c(\rho_c(f)+\rho_c(g)),$$

<u>and</u> $\rho_c^*$ <u>is a r.i. norm which is equivalent to</u> $\rho_c$.

PROOF. First let us consider the case $c\geqslant 1$. The properties i),...,v) for $\rho_c$ are easily verified with the exception of ic) and iv). Concerning ic), it follows from $(f+g)^{**} \leqslant f^{**} + g^{**}$ and the definition of $f^{**}$ that for any $s>0$

$$\int_0^s (f+g)^*(u)\,du \leqslant \int_0^s (f^*(u)+g^*(u))\,du.$$

Since $c\geqslant 1$ and $u^{-1+1/c}$ is monotonely nonincreasing,

$$\int_0^s u^{-1+1/c}(f+g)^*(u)\,du \leqslant \int_0^s u^{-1+1/c}(f^*(u)+g^*(u))\,du,$$

see e.g. [18]. A change of variable $u=t^c$ yields

$$\int_0^{s^{1/c}} (f+g)^*(t^c)\,dt \leqslant \int_0^{s^{1/c}} (f^*(t^c)+g^*(t^c))\,dt \qquad (s>0),$$

and therefore

$$\rho((f+g)^*(t^c)) \leqslant \rho(f^*(t^c)+g^*(t^c)) \leqslant \rho(f^*(t^c))+\rho(g^*(t^c)).$$

Concerning iv), using the same substitution and again $c\geqslant 1$, one has

$$\int_0^s f(u)\,du \leqslant \int_0^s f^*(u)\,du = c\int_0^{s^{1/c}} f^*(t^c)\,t^{c-1}\,dt$$
$$\leqslant c\,s^{1-1/c}\int_0^{s^{1/c}} f^*(t^c)\,dt \leqslant c\,s^{1-1/c}\,\mathrm{const.}\,\rho_c(f).$$

For the indicator function one has for any $s>0$ (comp. [2])

$$\rho_c(E_s f) = \rho(f^*(st^c)) = \rho(E_{s^{1/c}}(f^*(t^c))) \leq h(s^{1/c})\rho_c(f);$$

hence $h_c(s) \leq h(s^{1/c})$. The converse inequality follows by interchanging $\rho_c$ and $\rho$.

If $c<1$, apply La. 2.2 to obtain the quasi-triangular inequality

$$\rho_c(f+g) \leq \rho_c^*(f+g) \leq \rho_c^*(f)+\rho_c^*(g) \leq c\,A_c(\rho_c(f)+\rho_c(g)),$$

iv) for $\rho_c^*$ being obvious. Moreover, if $c<1$, for any $s>0$

$$\int_0^s f(u)du \leq \int_0^s f^*(u)du = c\,s\int_0^1 u^{c-1} f^*(s\,u^c)\,du.$$

Now let $g^*(u) := f^*(s\,u^c)$, and choose p so that $\alpha<1/p<c<1$; then it is well known (see [5]) that $L^\rho \subset L^{p1}+L_\infty$, where $L^{p1}$ denotes the Lorentz space. Hence it follows that

$$\int_0^s f(u)du \leq c\,s\int_0^1 u^{c-1} g^*(u)du \leq c\,s\int_0^1 u^{-1+1/p} g^*(u)du$$

$$\leq c\,s\,\|g\|_{L^{p1}+L_\infty} \leq s\text{ const.}\,\rho(g) \leq s\text{ const.}\,h(s^{1/c})\rho_c(f),$$

which establishes iv).

REMARK. Lemma 2.3 seems to be of interest by itself since it enables one to sharpen most of the results of [12], making them applicable to norms with indices $\alpha=\beta=0$, e.g. the $\|\cdot\|_\infty$-norm. In particular, the following sharper version of the theorem of stability can be proved, which will enable us to incorporate the Favard class $X_{\gamma,\gamma,\|\cdot\|_\infty;T}$ even in the intricate fractional case $\gamma<1$, see Cor. 2.8 and Sec. 3.

PROPOSITION 2.4. _Let_ $0\leq\theta_1<\theta_2\leq 1$, $0<\theta'\leq 1$, $\theta := (1-\theta')\theta_1+\theta'\theta_2$, _and_ $X_{\theta_i}$ _for_ $i=1,2$ _be intermediate Banach spaces of class_ $\mathcal{H}(\theta_i;X_1,X_2)$ _of the Banach spaces_ $X_1,X_2$. _If the r.i. norm_ $\hat\rho$ _is defined by_ $\hat\rho(f) := \rho(f^*(t^{1/(\theta_2-\theta_1)}))$ _and has indices_ $\theta-1<\beta_{\hat\rho}\leq\alpha_{\hat\rho}<\theta$, _then_

$$(X_{\theta_1},X_{\theta_2})_{\theta',\rho;K} = (X_1,X_2)_{\theta,\hat\rho;K}.$$

For the definition of the class $\mathcal{H}(\theta_i;X_1,X_2)$ comp. e.g. [4]. The proof follows along the same lines as in [12], now using La. 2.3.

The third lemma needed is due to U. Westphal [19].

LEMMA 2.5. <u>For any</u> $\gamma>0$ <u>there exist</u> $c_1,c_2,c_3>0$ <u>such that</u>

$$c_1\|[I-T(t)]^\gamma\|_X \leqslant K(t^\gamma,f;X,D[(-A)^\gamma]) \leqslant \int_0^\infty |p_\gamma(u)|\,\|[I-T(tu)]^\gamma f\|_X\,du$$

$$+\; c_2\min(1,t^\gamma)\|f\|_X + c_3\sum_{j=1}^\infty \left|\binom{j-\gamma-1}{j}\right| j^{-\gamma}\|[I-T(tj)]^\gamma f\|_X .$$

The desired representation theorem of generalized Lipschitz spaces now reads as follows.

THEOREM 2.6. <u>Let</u> $0<a\leqslant\gamma$, $\theta=a/\gamma$, <u>and</u> $\rho$ <u>be a r.i. norm with indices</u> $\alpha,\beta$.

a) <u>If</u> $\alpha<a$, <u>then</u>

$$X_{a,\gamma,\rho;T} = \begin{cases} (X,D[(-A)^\gamma])_{\theta,\rho_\gamma;K} & (\gamma\geqslant 1) \\ (X,D[(-A)^\gamma])_{\theta,\rho^*_\gamma;K} & (\gamma<1). \end{cases}$$

b) <u>If</u> $\alpha<\min(\theta,1/\gamma)$, <u>then</u>

$$(X,D[(-A)^\gamma])_{\theta,\rho;K} = \begin{cases} X_{a,\gamma,\rho^*_{1/\gamma};K} & (\gamma>1) \\ X_{a,\gamma,\rho_{1/\gamma};K} & (\gamma\leqslant 1). \end{cases}$$

PROOF. In case $\gamma\geqslant 1$ we apply La. 2.3a) and b) with $c=\gamma$ and $c=1/\gamma$, resp., as well as the left-hand inequality of La. 2.4 to deduce

$$c_1\rho(t^{-a}\|[I-T(t)]^\gamma f\|_X) \leqslant \rho(t^{-a}K(t^\gamma,f)) = \rho_\gamma(t^{-\theta}K(t,f))$$

and (noting that $\alpha<1/\gamma$)

$$c_1\rho^*_{1/\gamma}(t^{-a}\|[I-T(t)]^\gamma f\|_X) \leqslant \rho^*_{1/\gamma}(t^{-a}K(t^\gamma,f)) \leqslant \text{const.}\,\rho(t^{-\theta}K(t,f)),$$

respectively. Hence

$$(X,D[(-A)^\gamma])_{\theta,\rho_\gamma;K} \subset X_{a,\gamma,\rho;T}$$

and

$$(X,D[(-A)^\gamma])_{\theta,\rho;K} \subset X_{a,\gamma,\rho^*_{1/\gamma};T},$$

respectively. If $\gamma\leqslant 1$ one obtains similarly

$$(X,D[(-A)^\gamma])_{\theta,\rho^*_\gamma;K} \subset X_{a,\gamma,\rho;T}$$

and

$$(X,D[(-A)^\gamma])_{\theta,\rho;K} \subset X_{a,\gamma,\rho_{1/\gamma};T}$$

by applying La. 2.3b) with $c=\gamma$ and a) with $c=1/\gamma$ as well as La. 2.5. The converse inclusions are verified in a similar manner using La. 2.3 and the second inequality of La. 2.5.

REMARK. In case of integral $\gamma=r$, Thm. 2.6 can be proved by means of the B-splines $M_r$ (see (1.5)) instead of the function $p_\gamma$, and the generalized Hardy-inequality for r.i. norms (see [9]); for the $L_q^*$-case, $\gamma=r$, compare R. DeVore [11].

If one introduces the generalized modulus of continuity of exponent $\gamma>0$ by

$$(2.2) \qquad \omega_\gamma(t,f;T) = \sup_{|h|\leq t} \|[I-T(h)]^\gamma f\|_X \qquad (t>0,\ \gamma>0),$$

then there holds the following corollary

COROLLARY 2.7. _If_ $\alpha<a\leq\gamma$, _then the following norms are equivalent on_ $X_{a,\gamma,\rho;T}$:

(i) $\|f\|_X + \rho(t^{-a}\|[I-T(t)]^\gamma f\|_X)$;

(ii) $\rho(t^{-a}K(t^\gamma,f;X,D[(-A)^\gamma]))$;

(iii) $\|f\|_X + \rho(t^{-a}\omega_\gamma(t,f;T))$.

Whereas inequality "(i)≤(iii)" is obvious, "(ii)≤const.(i)" follows by Thm. 2.6. For the proof of "(iii)≤const.(ii)" recall (comp. proof of Thm. 1.1) that for any representation $f=f_1+f_2$ with $f_2\in D[(-A)^\gamma]$

$$\|[I-T(h)]^\gamma f\|_X \leq (M+1)^\gamma(\|f_1\|_X + h^\gamma\|f_2\|_{D[(-A)]^\gamma}),$$

and therefore

$$\omega_\gamma(t,f;T) \leq (M+1)^\gamma(\|f_1\|_X + t^\gamma\|f_2\|)_{D[(-A)^\gamma]}.$$

Taking the infimum of all representations of f yields

$$(2.3) \qquad \omega_\gamma(t,f;T) \leq (M+1)^\gamma K(t^\gamma,f;X,D[(-A)^\gamma]).$$

On the other hand, $\min(1,t^\gamma)\|f\|_X \leq K(t^\gamma,f)$; hence

$$(2.4) \qquad \|f\|_X \leq \{1/\rho(t^{-a}\min(1,t^\gamma))\}\rho(t^{-a}K(t^\gamma,f)).$$

As a first consequence of Thm. 2.6 we now can reduce the fractional case under suitable indexconditions to the integral case.

COROLLARY 2.8. _Let_ $r=1,2,\ldots$ _and_ $0<a\leq\gamma<r$. _If_ $\rho$ _is a r.i. norm with upper index_ $\alpha<a$, _then_ $X_{a,\gamma,\rho;T} = X_{a,r,\rho;T}$.

PROOF. Applying Thm. 2.6 to the spaces $X_{a,\gamma,\rho;\mathcal{T}}$ and $X_{a,r,\rho;\mathcal{T}}$, we see it just remains to show that

$$(2.5)\qquad (X,D[(-A)^{\gamma}])_{\frac{a}{\gamma},\rho_{\gamma};K} = (X,D(A^{r}))_{\frac{a}{r},\rho_{r};K} \qquad (\gamma\geqslant 1),$$

$$(2.6)\qquad (X,D[(-A)^{\gamma}])_{\frac{a}{\gamma},\rho^{*}_{\gamma};K} = (X,D(A^{r}))_{\frac{a}{r},\rho^{*}_{r};K} \qquad (\gamma<1).$$

In [4] H. Berens proved that the domain $D[(-A)^{\gamma}]$ is of class $\mathcal{H}(\gamma/r, X, D(A^{r}))$. Hence (2.5) and (2.6) easily follow from Prop. 2.4 (thm. of stability) by chosing $\theta_1=0$, $\theta_2=\gamma/r$, $\theta'=a/\gamma$, $\theta=a/r$, as well as $X_1=X$, $X_2=D(A^{r})$, $X_{\theta_1}=X$, $X_{\theta_2}=D[(-A)^{\gamma}]$, $\rho=\rho_{\gamma}$ ($\rho=\rho^{*}_{\gamma}$ resp.). Let us remark that $\hat{\rho}_{\gamma}=(\rho_{\gamma})_{r/\gamma}=\rho_{r}$.

## 3. Main Theorems on Generalized Lipschitz Spaces; Applications

In this section we briefly collect a number of theorems on Lipschitz spaces which, on account of Thm. 2.6 can now be obtained from the general theory of intermediate spaces generated by the K-interpolation method, see [12]. In view of Cor. 2.8 it suffices to consider the integral case, i.e. $\gamma=r=1,2,\ldots$ .

THEOREM 3.1 (Interpolation). Let $\mathcal{T}$ and $\mathcal{S}$ denote two equibounded semigroups of class $(C_o)$ on $[X]$ and $[Y]$, resp., with infinitesimal generators A and B, resp. Assume $0<a\leqslant r$ and $\rho$ a r.i. norm with $\alpha<a$. Then the spaces $X_{a,r,\rho;\mathcal{T}}$ and $Y_{a,r,\rho;\mathcal{S}}$ are interpolation spaces of $(X,D(A^{r}))$ and $(Y,D(B^{r}))$, i.e., if $T\in[X,Y]$ is such that the restriction of T to $D(A^{r})$ maps $D(A^{r})$ continuously into $D(B^{r})$, then T maps $X_{a,r,\rho;\mathcal{T}}$ continuously into $Y_{a,r,\rho;\mathcal{S}}$. Moreover,

$$\|T\|_{[X_{a,r,\rho;\mathcal{T}},Y_{a,r,\rho;\mathcal{S}}]} \leqslant c\,h((M_2/M_1)^{1/r})\|T\|_{[X,Y]}^{1-\frac{a}{r}}\|T\|_{[D(A^{r}),D(B^{r})]}^{\frac{a}{r}},$$

with $c>0$ and $M_1=\|T\|_{[X,Y]}$, $M_2=\|T\|_{[D(A^{r}),D(B^{r})]}$, respectively.

This theorem immediately follows from the interpolation theorem of [12] and Thm. 2.5.

Let us recall (comp. e.g. J.L. Lions [16]) that in case of reflexive Banach spaces X, the class $\mathcal{T}^{+}=\{T(t)^{+};\ t\geqslant 0\}$, with $T(t)^{+}$ denoting the adjoint operator of T(t), forms a semigroup of class $(C_o)$ on the dual space $D(A^r)^*$ of $D(A^r)$ with infinitesimal generator $B=A^+$, provided $T=\{T(t);\ t\geq 0\}$ is a semigroup on [X] with generator A. Further, let $\rho'$ denote the associate r.i. norm of $\rho$, i.e.

$$\rho'(f) = \sup\{\int_0^\infty f^*(t)g^*(t)dt;\ g\in L_\rho,\ \|g\|_\rho\leq 1\}.$$

Then the duality theorem for Lipschitz spaces reads (comp. [13])

THEOREM 3.2 (Duality). <u>As above let</u> $0<a\leq r$, $\theta=a/r$ <u>and</u> $\rho$ <u>be an absolutely continuous r.i. norm with index condition</u> $a-r<\beta\leq\alpha<a$. <u>Let</u> $D(A^r)$ <u>be a dense subspace of</u> X. <u>Then the dual of</u> $X_{a,r,\rho;T}$ <u>is</u>

$$X^*_{a,r,\rho;T} = (D(A^r)^*, D[(A^+)^r])_{2-\theta,\rho'_r;K}.$$

REMARK. If $a<r$, then $a-r<0\leq\beta$, i.e. the index condition $a-r<\beta$ is automatically true; hence it is needed only in the case of optimal approximation with $a=r$.

The third main theorem on Lipschitz spaces can similarly be deduced from Prop. 2.4.

THEOREM 3.3 (Reduction). <u>Assume that</u> $r=1,2,\ldots;\ k=0,1,\ldots,r-1;\ a=k+b<r$ <u>and</u> $0<b\leq 1$.

a) <u>If</u> $b<1$ <u>and</u> $\rho$ <u>is a r.i. norm with index condition</u> $\alpha<b$, <u>then</u>

$$f\in X_{a,r,\rho;T} \text{ iff } f\in D(A^k) \text{ and } A^k f\in X_{b,1,\rho;T}.$$

b) <u>If</u> $b=1$ <u>and</u> $\rho$ <u>is a r.i. norm with index condition</u> $\alpha<1/2$, <u>then</u>

$$f\in X_{a,r,\rho;T} \text{ iff } f\in D(A^k) \text{ and } A^k f\in X_{1,2,\rho;T}.$$

PROOF. Since $D(A^k)\in\mathcal{H}(k/r;X,D(A^r))$ for any k (comp. [7, p. 195]), we can again apply Prop. 2.4, this time to $X_1=X$, $X_2=D(A^r)$, $X_{\theta_1}=D(A^k)$, $X_{\theta_2}=D(A^{k+1})$ with $\theta_1=k/r$, $\theta_2=(k+1)/r$, $\theta=a/r$, $\theta'=a-k=b$ and $\hat{\rho}=\rho_r$, as well as Thm. 2.6. This gives

$$(3.1)\quad X_{a,r,\rho;T} = (X,D(A^r))_{a/r,\rho_r;K} = (D(A^k),D(A^{k+1}))_{b,\rho;K}$$

if $b-1<\beta\leq\alpha<b$. Analogously one has with $r=1$, $k=0$, $b=a$,

(3.2) $$X_{b,1,\rho;T} = (X,D(A))_{b,\rho;K}$$

if $b-1<\beta\leqslant\alpha<b$.

In case $0<b<1$ consider the operator $T_k := (I-A)^k$ which is an isomorphism between $D(A^k)$ and $X$ as well as between $D(A^{k+1})$ and $D(A)$. Therefore by Thm. 3.1. it is also an isomorphism between the interpolation spaces $(D(A^k), D(A^{k+1}))_{b,\rho;K}$ and $(X,D(A))_{b,\rho;K}$; the representation formulas (3.1), (3.2) therefore yield part a). Note that $b-1<\beta$ holds automatically if $b<1$.

If $b=1$ apply Prop. 2.4 to $X_1=X$, $X_2=D(A^r)$, $X_{\theta_1}=D(A^k)$, $X_{\theta_2}=D(A^{k+2})$ with $\theta_1=k/r$, $\theta_2=(k+2)/r$, $\theta=a/r\equiv(k+1)/r$, $\theta'=1/2$, as well as Thm. 2.6 to obtain

(3.3) $$X_{a,r,\rho;T} = (X,D(A^r))_{\frac{k+1}{r},\rho_r;K} = (D(A^k),D(A^{k+2}))_{\frac{1}{2},\rho;K}$$

if $\alpha<1/2$; analogously with $r=2$, $k=0$, $a=b=1$,

(3.4) $$X_{1,2,\rho;T} = (X,D(A^2))_{\frac{1}{2},\rho;K}$$

if $\alpha<1/2$. Since $T_k$ is also an isomorphism between $D(A^k)$ and $X$, as well as between $D(A^{k+2})$ and $D(A^2)$, it is also an isomorphism between $(D(A^k), D(A^{k+2}))_{1/2,\rho;K}$ and $(X,D(A^2))_{1/2,\rho;K}$, which proves b).

EXAMPLE. If $\rho$ is in particular equal to the generalized Lorentz norm $\|\cdot\|_{\Lambda(\phi,p)}$, i.e.

$$\rho(f) = \left(\int_0^\infty \phi(t)f^*(t)^p dt\right)^{1/p} \qquad (1\leqslant p<\infty)$$

and $\Phi(t) = \int_0^t \phi(s)ds$, then the index condition (in case $b<1$) can be interpreted by the condition that there exists a $\delta_1\in(0,pb)$ and a $\delta_2>0$ such that

(3.5) $$\sup_{t>0}\frac{\Phi(t)}{\Phi(st)} = \begin{cases} O(s^{-\delta_1}) & (s\to 0+) \\ O(s^{-\delta_2}) & (s\to\infty). \end{cases}$$

Thm. 3.3 then states that under the assumption (3.5) one has $f\in \mathrm{Lip}(a,r;\|\cdot\|_{\Lambda(\phi,p)})$ iff $f,f',\dots,f^{(k-1)}$ are locally absolutely continuous, $f^{(k)}\in L_p$ and

$$\left\{\int_0^\infty \phi(t)[t^{-b}\|[I-T(t)]f^{(k)}\|_{L_p}]^{*p}dt\right\}^{1/p} < \infty.$$

Here $X=L_p$ and $T$ is the semigroup of left translations.

Analogously the above theorems can also be formulated for other semigroups such as those given by the Abel-Poisson integral or the singular integral of Weierstraß. On the other hand, the norm $\rho$ may be any r.i. norm such as the usual Lebesgue norm, the Lorentz norm or Orlicz norm.

Acknowledgements

The author would like to thank Professors Colin Bennett (Hamilton,Ontario) for helpful suggestions in connection with La.2.3, Hubert Berens (Erlangen) with Cor. 2.7, Paul L. Butzer for suggesting the incorpation of the Favard space, as well as Dr. Gerhard Wilmes for his critical reading of the manuscript.

## REFERENCES

[ 1] Balakrishnan, V.A., Fractional powers of closed operators and the semigroups generated by them. Pacific J. Math. 10 (1960), 419-437.

[ 2] Bennett, C., Banach function spaces and interpolation methods I. The abstract theory. J. Functional Analysis 17 (1974), 409-440.

[ 3] Berens, H., Equivalent representations for the infinitesimal generator of higher orders in semi-group theory. Nederl. Akad. Wetensch. Indag. Math. 27 (1965), 497-512.

[ 4] Berens, H., Interpolationsmethoden zur Behandlung von Approximationsprozessen auf Banachräumen. Lecture Notes in Mathematics 64, Springer-Verlag, Berlin-Heidelberg-New York, 1968.

[ 5] Boyd, D.W., Indices of function spaces and their relationship to interpolation. Canad. J. Math. 21 (1969), 1245-1254.

[ 6] Butzer, P.L., Über den Grad der Approximation des Identitätsoperators durch Halbgruppen von linearen Operatoren und Anwendungen auf die Theorie der singulären Integrale. Math. Ann. 133 (1957), 410-425.

[ 7] Butzer, P.L. - Berens, H., Semi-Groups of Operators and Approximation. Springer Verlag, Berlin-Heidelberg-New York, 1967.

[ 8] Butzer, P.L. - Dyckhoff, H. - Görlich, E. - Stens, R.L., Best trigonometric approximation, fractional order derivatives and Lipschitz classes. Canad. J. Math. 29 (1977), 781-793.

[ 9] Butzer, P.L. - Fehér, F., Generalized Hardy and Hardy-Littlewood in-

equalities in rearrangement-invariant spaces. Comment. Math. Prace Mat. 21 (1978), W. Orlicz anniversary volume (in print).

[10] Curry, H.B. - Schoenberg, I.J., On Pólya frequency functions IV: The fundamental spline functions and their limits. J. Analyse Math. 17 (1966), 71-107.

[11] DeVore, R., Degree of approximation. in: Approximation Theory II. eds.: G.G. Lorentz - Ck. Chui - L.L. Schumaker, Academic Press, New York, 1976, pp. 117-161.

[12] Fehér, F., Interpolation und Indexbedingungen auf rearrangement-invarianten Banachräumen. I. Grundlagen und die K-Methode. J. Functional Analysis 25 (1977), 147-161. II. Die J-Methode und ihr Zusammenhang mit der K-Methode. J. Functional Analysis (in print).

[13] Fehér, F., The K- and J-interpolation methods for rearrangement-invariant Banach spaces and their duality. Proceedings of the Colloquium on Fourieranalysis and Approximation. Budapest August 15-21. 1976 (in print).

[14] Komatsu, H., Fractional powers of operators. II. Interpolation spaces. Pacific J. Math. 21 (1967), 89-111.

[15] Lions, J.L., Théorèmes de traces et d'interpolation I. Ann. Scuola Norm. Sup. Pisa (3) 13 (1959), 389-403.

[16] Lions, J.L., Sur les espaces d'interpolation; dualité. Math. Scand. 9 (1961), 147-177.

[17] Lions, J.L. - Peetre, J., Sur une classe d'espaces d'interpolation. Inst. Hautes Etudes Sci. Publ. Math. 19 (1964), 5-68.

[18] Luxemburg, W.A.J., Rearrangement-invariant Banach function spaces. Queen's Papers, Queen's University Canada 10 (1967), 83-144.

[19] Westphal, U., An approach to fractional powers of operators via fractional differences. Proc. London Math. Soc. (3) 29 (1974), 557-576.

# SOME INEQUALITIES FOR FRACTIONAL INTEGRALS

Eric Russell Love
Department of Mathematics
University of Melbourne
Melbourne

In 1958 T.M. Flett, building on work of Hardy, Littlewood and others, gave an inequality relating an $L^p$-norm of a function with an $L^q$-norm of a fractional integral of it. Two generalizations of this inequality are given, with the fractional integral operator replaced by a more general integral operator. Additional proofs, one arising out of a comment made at the Conference, are also given; these show relationships with some known inequalities.

## 1. Introduction

1.1 Descriptive Remarks. The inequalities discussed are concerned with bounds for integral operators K in Lebesgue spaces $L^p$ on $(0,\infty)$. Our main result, Theorem 2.1, generalizes both Flett's Inequality and the Schur-Hardy Inequality; these are stated below. Theorem 3.2 establishes the same inequality as Theorem 2.1, but under different conditions. §4 was added after the Conference. It contains other ways of proving the same inequality; one of them arose from a comment made at the lecture.

We use the notation

$$Kf(x) = \int_0^\infty K(x, y)f(y)\,dy, \qquad \|f\|_p = \left(\int_0^\infty |f(t)|^p\,dt\right)^{1/p},$$

the functions f being in general complex valued, except in §3.

The inequalities had their beginnings in the work of Hardy and Littlewood; for detailed references see Flett [4]. The basic one for the present line of development is the following, a generalization of Hardy's Inequality.

1.2 Schur-Hardy Inequality (1928). *If* $p \geq 1$, $f \in L^p$, $K(x, y)$ *is non-negative, measurable and homogeneous of degree* $-1$, *and*

$$A = \int_0^\infty K(1, t)t^{-1/p}\,dt < \infty,$$

*then* $Kf \in L^p$ *and*

$$\|Kf\|_p \leq A\|f\|_p.$$

This appears in Hardy, Littlewood and Pólya [2] as Theorem 319(c), with a rather indirect proof which proceeds via a proof of a generalized Hilbert's Inequality. See also Schur [1], pages 23 and 24, to whom the first equation of the proof below is due.

ANOTHER PROOF. We may suppose f to be non-negative. For $x > 0$,

$$Kf(x) = \int_0^\infty K(x, xt) f(xt)\, x\, dt = \int_0^\infty K(1, t) f(xt)\, dt.$$

Taking norms with respect to x, Minkowski's Inequality gives

$$\|Kf\|_p \le \int_0^\infty \|K(1, t) f(xt)\|_p\, dt = \int_0^\infty K(1, t) t^{-1/p} \|f\|_p\, dt = A\|f\|_p.$$

REMARKS. If $0 < p \le 1$ instead, we obtain $\|Kf\|_p \ge A\|f\|_p$.

If $p > 1$ we have, by Hölder's Inequality,

$$|(Kf, \bar{g})| \le \|Kf\|_p \|\bar{g}\|_{p'} \le A\|f\|_p \|g\|_{p'}.$$

This is the Generalized Hilbert's Inequality given by Hardy, Littlewood and Pólya [2] as Theorem 319(a), after interchanging f and g, and p and p'.

<u>1.3 Flett's Inequality</u> (1958). <u>If</u> $q \ge p > 1$, $\alpha > p^{-1} - q^{-1}$, $\gamma > -1$, $x^{-\gamma-1/p} f(x) \in L^p$ <u>and</u>

$$M_\alpha f(x) = \frac{1}{x^\alpha} \int_0^x \frac{(x-t)^{\alpha-1}}{\Gamma(\alpha)} f(t)\, dt,$$

<u>then</u> $x^{-\gamma-1/q} M_\alpha f(x) \in L^q$ <u>and there is</u> $B = B(\not f)$ <u>such that</u>

$$\|x^{-\gamma-1/q} M_\alpha f(x)\|_q \le B\|x^{-\gamma-1/p} f(x)\|_p.$$

[The notation $B(\not f)$ means that B is independent of f.]

This is part of Theorem 2 of Flett [4]. The other part of that theorem is concerned with a case $\alpha = p^{-1} - q^{-1}$; Flett's proof of it makes use of the difficult Theorem 383 of Hardy, Littlewood and Pólya [2]. We do not prove either part here; but the one stated above is a special case of Theorem 2.1 below, as we show in the subsequent Corollary 2.2.

Flett's proof of 1.3, given in §2.2 of [4], is based on the three-factor version of Hölder's Inequality. The constant B that he obtains is a product of powers of beta functions; whereas ours, in Corollary 2.2, involves only a single beta function.

## 2. First Generalization of Flett's Inequality

THEOREM 2.1. *If* $q \ge p \ge 1$, $r^{-1} = 1 - (p^{-1} - q^{-1})$, $K(x, y)$ *is non-negative, measurable and homogeneous of degree* $-r^{-1}$,

$$C = \|K(1, t)\, t^{-1/q}\|_r < \infty$$

*and* $f \in L^p$, *then* $Kf \in L^q$ *and*

$$\|Kf\|_q \le C\|f\|_p.$$

PROOF. The case $q = p$ is the Schur-Hardy Inequality 1.2. So we may suppose that $q > p \ge 1$, and as before that f is non-negative. Then

$$0 \le 1 - p^{-1} = r^{-1} - q^{-1} < r^{-1} < 1,$$

so that r has a conjugate index r' and

$$r'^{-1} = 1 - r^{-1} = p^{-1} - q^{-1}. \tag{1}$$

Hölder's Inequality with indices r and r' gives, supposing $x > 0$,

$$\begin{aligned} Kf(x) &= \int_0^\infty K(x, y) f(y)^{\frac{p}{q}} f(y)^{1-\frac{p}{q}}\, dy \\ &\le \left(\int_0^\infty K(x, y)^r f(y)^{\frac{pr}{q}}\, dy\right)^{\frac{1}{r}} \left(\int_0^\infty f(y)^{\left(1-\frac{p}{q}\right)r'} dy\right)^{\frac{1}{r'}} \\ &= \left(\int_0^\infty H(x, y) g(y)\, dy\right)^{\frac{1}{r}} \left(\int_0^\infty f(y)^p\, dy\right)^{\frac{1}{r'}} \\ &= Hg(x)^{\frac{1}{r}} \|f\|_p^{\frac{p}{r'}}. \end{aligned} \tag{2}$$

Here H and g are newly defined: $H(x, y) = K(x, y)^r$ is homogeneous of degree $-1$, and $g(y) = f(y)^{pr/q} \in L^{q/r}$.

By hypothesis $r^{-1} \ge q^{-1}$, so that $q/r \ge 1$. The Schur-Hardy Inequality 1.2 thus gives

$$\|Hg\|_{q/r} \le C^r \|g\|_{q/r} = C^r \|f\|_p^{rp/q} \tag{3}$$

with

$$C^r = \int_0^\infty H(1, t) t^{-r/q}\, dt = \int_0^\infty K(1, t)^r t^{-r/q}\, dt = \|K(1, t) t^{-1/q}\|_r^r,$$

so that C is as defined in the statement.

From (2), (3) and (1) we now have

$$\|Kf\|_q \le \|Hg\|_{q/r}^{1/r} \|f\|_p^{p/r'} \le C\|f\|_p^{(p/q)+(p/r')} = C\|f\|_p.$$

COROLLARY 2.2. *Flett's Inequality 1.3 follows by taking*

$$(4)\qquad \begin{cases} K(x, y) = x^{-\alpha-\gamma-1/q}(x - y)^{\alpha-1}y^{\gamma+1/p}/\Gamma(\alpha) & \text{for } 0 < y < x, \\ K(x, y) = 0 & \text{otherwise,} \end{cases}$$

*and replacing* $f(y)$ *by* $y^{-\gamma-1/p} f(y)$. *These give 1.3 with*

$$B = \Gamma(\alpha)^{-1}B\{(\alpha - (p^{-1} - q^{-1}))r,\ (\gamma + 1)r\}^{1/r},$$

*where B on the right denotes the beta function.*

## 3. Second Generalization of Flett's Inequality

*3.1 Descriptive Remarks.* This generalization assumes stricter conditions than Theorem 2.1; they permit a constant D which is sometimes finite when C is infinite. Further this generalization is confined to real-valued functions.

First we require the following form of Chebyshev's Inequality.

LEMMA 3.1. *If* $f$ *is increasing,* $g$ *is decreasing,* $h$ *is measurable but not null, and all are non-negative, in* $(a, b)$, *then*

$$\int_a^b f(t)\, g(t) h(t)\, dt \le \int_a^b f(t) h(t)\, dt \int_a^b g(t) h(t)\, dt \Big/ \int_a^b h(t)\, dt,$$

*provided that the three integrals on the right are finite.*

PROOF. As in [2], Theorem 43.

THEOREM 3.2. *If* $\quad q \ge p > 1, \quad r^{-1} = 1 - (p^{-1} - q^{-1}),$
$K(x, y)$ *is non-negative and homogeneous of degree* $-r^{-1}$, *and* $f \in L^p$ (*almost exactly as in Theorem* 2.1); *and if further*

$K(1, t)$ *is increasing in* $(0, 1)$, *integrable on it, and zero in* $(1,\infty)$,

$\mu \ge 1 - p^{-1}$ *and* $t^{1-\mu}f(t)$ *is decreasing in* $(0,\infty)$,

*then* $Kf \in L^q$ *and there is* $D = D(\not f)$ *such that*

$$\|Kf\|_q \le D\|f\|_p.$$

PROOF. First we show that $f$ is non-negative. If it were otherwise, the monotony of $t^{1-\mu}f(t)$ would imply the existence of positive $\lambda$ such that $t^{1-\mu}f(t) < -\lambda$ for all sufficiently large $t$. Consequently $|f(t)| > \lambda t^{\mu-1}$ for such $t$, and so $t^{\mu-1} \in L^p(1, \infty)$. It would follow that $(\mu - 1)p < -1$, and so

$\mu < 1 - p^{-1}$, contradicting hypothesis.

By hypothesis we also have that $p^{-1} < 1$ and so $\mu > 0$.

Suppose now that $x > 0$. Lemma 3.1 with a, b, f(t), g(t), h(t) replaced by 0, x, K(x, t), $t^{1-\mu}f(t)$, $t^{\mu-1}$ respectively, gives

$$\int_0^x K(x, t) f(t)\, dt \le \int_0^x K(x, t) t^{\mu-1}\, dt \int_0^x f(t)\, dt \Big/ \int_0^x t^{\mu-1}\, dt .$$

Thus
$$Kf(x) \le \frac{\mu}{x^\mu} \int_0^1 K(x, xs)\, x^\mu s^{\mu-1}\, ds \int_0^x f(t)\, dt$$
$$= \mu x^{-1/r} \int_0^1 K(1, s) s^{\mu-1}\, ds \int_0^x f(t)\, dt$$
$$= \int_0^\infty H(x, t) f(t)\, dt = Hf(x), \tag{5}$$

where $H(x, y) = kx^{-1/r}$ for $0 < y < x$, $H(x, y) = 0$ otherwise,

and
$$k = \mu \int_0^1 K(1, s)\, s^{\mu-1}\, ds;$$

this k is finite because $s^{\mu-1}$ is integrable on $(0, \frac{1}{2})$ and $K(1, s)$ is bounded, while in $(\frac{1}{2}, 1)$ these roles are interchanged.

Since $H(x, y)$ is homogeneous of degree $-r^{-1}$, Theorem 2.1 gives, using (5),

$$\|Kf\|_q \le \|Hf\|_q \le D\|f\|_p$$

with

$$D = \|H(1, t)t^{-1/q}\|_r = k\left(1 - \frac{r}{q}\right)^{-1/r} = \left(\frac{p'}{r}\right)^{1/r} \int_0^1 K(1, t)\mu t^{\mu-1}\, dt. \tag{6}$$

COROLLARY 3.3. <u>Fractional integral case</u>. <u>If</u> $q \ge p > 1$, $0 < \alpha \le 1$, $\gamma \ge -p^{-1}$, $\mu \ge 1 - p^{-1}$, $x^{-\gamma-1/p}f(x) \in L^p$ <u>and</u> $x^{1-\mu-\gamma-1/p}f(x)$ <u>is decreasing, then</u>

$$\|x^{-\gamma-1/q}M_\alpha f(x)\|_q \le E\|x^{-\gamma-1/p}f(x)\|_p,$$

<u>where</u> $M_\alpha f$ <u>is defined as for Flett's Inequality</u> 1.3,

$$E = \left(\frac{p'}{r}\right)^{1/r} \frac{\mu\Gamma(\mu + \gamma + 1/p)}{\Gamma(\alpha + \mu + \gamma + 1/p)} \quad \text{and} \quad r^{-1} = 1 - (p^{-1} - q^{-1}).$$

PROOF. We specialize Theorem 3.2, again taking K as in (4) and replacing f(x) by $x^{-\gamma-1/p}f(x)$; in particular

$$K(1, t) = \Gamma(\alpha)^{-1}(1 - t)^{\alpha-1}t^{\gamma+1/p} \quad \text{in } 0 < t < 1.$$

This is increasing and integrable since $0 < \alpha \le 1$ and $\gamma + p^{-1} \ge 0$.

The other requirements of Theorem 3.2 are all obviously met, and we obtain the stated inequality. For E we have, by (6),

$$E = \left(\frac{p'}{r}\right)^{1/r} \frac{\mu}{\Gamma(\alpha)} \int_0^1 (1 - t)^{\alpha-1} t^{\gamma+(1/p)+\mu-1}\, dt,$$

and this has the stated value.

REMARK. The case $\alpha = p^{-1} - q^{-1}$ overlaps one case of Flett's Theorem 2 [4: §2.1 and §2.4].

## 4. Additional Proofs

4.1 Via Convolutions. After hearing the lecture, Prof. P.G. Rooney suggested that Theorem 2.1 might be derivable from Young's Inequality by means of exponential substitutions. This turns out to be correct in the main, as is shown below. Two extreme cases are not covered by it, and the Schur-Hardy Inequality is one of these.

The proof rests on the following consequence of Young's Inequality, which is given in [2] as Theorem 280.

*Convolution Inequality. If* $\lambda > 0$, $\mu > 0$, $\lambda + \mu < 1$, $F \in L^{1/(1-\lambda)}$, $G \in L^{1/(1-\mu)}$

*and*
$$H(s) = \int_{-\infty}^{\infty} F(t)G(s - t)\, dt,$$

*then*
$$\|H\|^*_{1/(1-\lambda-\mu)} \leq \|F\|^*_{1/(1-\lambda)} \|G\|^*_{1/(1-\mu)},$$

*where the asterisked norms are defined on* $(-\infty, \infty)$.

SECOND PROOF of Theorem 2.1. For this method we need to omit the case q = p again; it is the Schur-Hardy Inequality, as already remarked. We also need to omit the case p = 1. So we are given that

$$q > p > 1, \qquad r^{-1} = 1 - (p^{-1} - q^{-1}),$$

$K(x, y)$ is non-negative, measurable and homogeneous of degree $-r^{-1}$, $K(1, t)\, t^{-1/q} \in L^r$ and $f \in L^p$.

Define
$$\lambda = 1 - p^{-1}, \qquad \mu = p^{-1} - q^{-1} = 1 - r^{-1},$$
$$F(t) = e^{(1-\lambda)t} f(e^t), \qquad G(t) = e^{-\lambda t} K(1, e^{-t});$$

and let H be the convolution of F and G as above. Then $\lambda$ and $\mu$ fulfil the three requirements of the convolution inequality.

Noting that $K(x, y)$ is homogeneous of degree $\mu - 1$, we have

$$H(s) = e^{(1-\lambda-\mu)s} \int_{-\infty}^{\infty} K(e^s, e^t) f(e^t) e^t \, dt = e^{(1-\lambda-\mu)s} Kf(e^s);$$

$$\|H\|^*_{1/(1-\lambda-\mu)} = \left(\int_{-\infty}^{\infty} |Kf(e^s)|^{1/(1-\lambda-\mu)} e^s \, ds\right)^{1-\lambda-\mu} = \|Kf\|_q;$$

$$\|F\|^*_{1/(1-\lambda)} = \left(\int_{-\infty}^{\infty} |f(e^t)|^{1/(1-\lambda)} e^t \, dt\right)^{1-\lambda} = \|f\|_p;$$

$$\|G\|^*_{1/(1-\mu)} = \left(\int_{-\infty}^{\infty} K(1, e^{-t})^{\frac{1}{1-\mu}} e^{\frac{1-\lambda-\mu}{1-\mu}t} e^{-t} \, dt\right)^{1-\mu} = \|K(1, s) s^{-1/q}\|_r.$$

Thus the convolution inequality becomes

$$\|Kf\|_q \le \|K(1, t) t^{-1/q}\|_r \|f\|_p,$$

and the result follows.

<u>4.2 Via Bilinear Forms</u>. Theorem 2.1 can also be deduced from an inequality of Bonsall [3: Theorem 2]; I am indebted to Prof. A. Erdélyi for telling me of this paper. After interchanging $f$ and $g$, and replacing $p$ by $q'$ and $q$ by $p$ (with apologies for the resulting inelegance), it takes the form

<u>Bonsall's Inequality</u>. <u>If</u> $p > 1$, $q > 1$,

$$\frac{1}{p} + \frac{1}{q'} \ge 1, \qquad \lambda = \frac{1}{p'} + \frac{1}{q},$$

$H(x, y)$ <u>is non-negative, measurable and homogeneous of degree</u> $-1$, <u>and</u>

$$C = \left(\int_0^{\infty} H(1, t) t^{-1/\lambda q} \, dt\right)^{\lambda} < \infty,$$

<u>then</u>

$$\left|\int_0^{\infty} \int_0^{\infty} H(x, y)^{\lambda} f(y) g(x) \, dx \, dy\right| \le C \|f\|_p \|g\|_{q'}.$$

THIRD PROOF of Theorem 2.1. Taking $\lambda = 1/r$ and $H(x, y) = K(x, y)^r$, Bonsall's Inequality becomes

$$|(Kf, \bar{g})| \le C \|f\|_p \|g\|_{q'}$$

for every $g \in L^{q'}$. By the converse of Hölder's Inequality, Theorem 191 of [2], it follows that

$$\|Kf\|_q \le C \|f\|_p,$$

with C the same constant as before.

This argument is reversible, using the direct Hölder Inequality, so that Bonsall's Inequality is actually equivalent to Theorem 2.1.

## REFERENCES

[1] Schur, J., Bemerkungen zur Theorie der beschränkten Bilinearformen mit unendlich vielen Veränderlichen. J. Reine Angew. Math. 140 (1911), 1-28.

[2] Hardy, G.H., Littlewood, J.E., and Polya, G., Inequalities. Cambridge (1934).

[3] Bonsall, F.F., Inequalities with non-conjugate parameters. Quart. J. Math. Oxford Ser. (2) 2 (1951), 135-150.

[4] Flett, T.M., A note on some inequalities. Proc. Glasgow Math. Assoc. 4 (1958), 7-15.

# IV
# Harmonic Analysis

# DIFFERENTIATION ON A p-ADIC OR p-SERIES FIELD

C. W. Onneweer
Department of Mathematics
University of New Mexico
Albuquerque, NM 87131

In this paper we give a definition for differentiation of complex-valued functions defined on a field $\mathbb{K}$ of p-adic or p-series numbers, both in the pointwise and in the strong sense. We show that the characters of $\mathbb{K}$ are eigenvectors of the differentiation operator and that the strong differentiation operator on $L_1(\mathbb{K})$ is a closed operator. Finally we present saturation and non-optimal approximation results for the operators which define the strong $L_1(\mathbb{K})$ derivative.

## 1. Introduction and Notation

In 1969 J. E. Gibbs introduced the concept of differentiability for $\mathbb{C}$-valued functions defined on the dyadic group $\Delta$, where $\Delta = \{x; x = (x_i)_0^\infty$, $x_i \in \{0,1\}$ for each $i \geq 0\}$, with addition in $\Delta$ being defined coordinatewise modulo 2. In [3] Butzer and Wagner somewhat modified Gibbs' definition and arrived at the following.

DEFINITION BW. *For* $f : \Delta \to \mathbb{C}$, $x \in \Delta$ *and* $n \geq 1$, *let*

$$d_n f(x) = \sum_{j=0}^{n-1} 2^{j-1} (f(x) - f(x+e_j)),$$

*where* $e_j \in \Delta$ *is given by* $(e_j)_i = \delta_{ji}$. *If* $\lim_{n\to\infty} d_n f(x)$ *exists then this limit is called the pointwise (dyadic) derivative of* $f$ *at* $x$, *denoted by* $f^{[1]}(x)$.

In [3] Butzer and Wagner showed that the Walsh-Paley functions $(\psi_m)_{m=0}^\infty$ are pointwise differentiable at every $x \in \Delta$ and $\psi_m^{[1]}(x) = m\,\psi_m(x)$. In addition they showed that with the definition of differentiability as given here we obtain a theory which in many respects is similar to the classical theory of differentiability for functions defined on the circle group, although there are also important differences between the two theories, see also [4] or [6]. In this paper we will extend the ideas of Gibbs, Butzer and Wagner by defining differentiability for functions $f : \mathbb{K} \to \mathbb{C}$, where $\mathbb{K}$ is either a p-series field $\mathbb{K}_p$ or a p-adic field $\mathbb{Q}_p$.

Thus $\mathbb{K} = \{x ; x = (x_i)_{-\infty}^{\infty}, 0 \leq x_i < p$ for each $i \in \mathbb{Z}$ and $x_i = 0$ for $i < r$ for some $r \in \mathbb{Z}\}$. Addition and multiplication in $\mathbb{K}$ are defined by identifying $x \in \mathbb{K}$ with either the formal Laurent series in one variable over the finite field $\mathbb{Z}_p$, $x = \sum_{i=-\infty}^{\infty} x_i X^i$ (if $\mathbb{K} = \mathbb{K}_p$), or else with the formal infinite series $x = \sum_{i=-\infty}^{\infty} x_i p^i$ (if $\mathbb{K} = \mathbb{Q}_p$), and adding or multiplying such series in the usual way, see [5] or [8] for details. The topology on $\mathbb{K}$ can be described by means of the non-archimedian norm $\|\cdot\|$, where $\|x\| = p^{-r}$ if $x_r \neq 0$ and $x_i = 0$ for $i < r$, and $\|0\| = 0$. If for $\ell \in \mathbb{Z}$ we set $G_\ell = \{x \in \mathbb{K} ; \|x\| \leq p^{-\ell}\}$ then the $G_\ell$ are subgroups of $\mathbb{K}^+$, $\mathbb{K}$ considered as additive group, and the $G_\ell$ form a basis for the neighborhoods of $0 \in \mathbb{K}$. We shall denote the elements $z \in \mathbb{K}$ for which $z_i = 0$ for $i \geq \ell$ by $z_{q,\ell}$. Next, let $dx$ or $m$ denote Haar measure on $\mathbb{K}^+$, normalized so that $m(G_0) = 1$. Then $m(G_\ell) = p^{-\ell}$ for each $\ell \in \mathbb{Z}$.

The dual group $\hat{\mathbb{K}}$ of $\mathbb{K}^+$ can be described as follows. For $x \in \mathbb{K}$ we define $\chi(x)$ by

$$\chi(x) = \begin{cases} \exp(2\pi i\, x_{-1} p^{-1}), & \text{if } \mathbb{K} = \mathbb{K}_p, \\ \exp(2\pi i \sum_{i=-\infty}^{-1} x_i p^i), & \text{if } \mathbb{K} = \mathbb{Q}_p. \end{cases}$$

It can be shown, see [8], that the elements of $\hat{\mathbb{K}}$ are all of the form $\chi_y(x) = \chi(yx)$ for some $y \in \mathbb{K}$. Thus, if $y = (y_i)_{-\infty}^{\infty}$, with $y_s \neq 0$ and $y_i = 0$ for $i < s$, then

$$\text{(1)} \qquad \chi_y(x) = \begin{cases} \exp(2\pi i \sum_{j=-\infty}^{-s-1} x_j y_{-1-j} p^{-1}), & \text{if } \mathbb{K} = \mathbb{K}_p, \\ \exp(2\pi i \sum_{j=-\infty}^{-s-1} x_j \sum_{i=s}^{-j-1} y_i p^{i+j}), & \text{if } \mathbb{K} = \mathbb{Q}_p. \end{cases}$$

From this representation of $\chi_y(x)$ we see that $\chi_y(x)$ is constant on the cosets of $G_{-s}$ in $\mathbb{K}$ but not on the cosets of $G_{-s-1}$; thus $\chi_y(x)$ is constant on sets of measure equal to $p^s = \|y\|^{-1}$.

## 2. Differentiation on $\mathbb{K}$

DEFINITION 1. *For* $f : \mathbb{K} \to \mathbb{C}$ , $x \in \mathbb{K}$ *and* $m \in \mathbb{N}$ , *let*

$$D_m f(x) = \sum_{\ell=-m}^{m-1} P(\ell,m) \sum_{(\ell,m)} (f(x) - f(x + z_{q,m})) ,$$

*where* $P(\ell,m) = p^{-m+1}(p+1)^{-1}(p^{2\ell+1} + p^{-2m})$ *and where* $\sum_{(\ell,m)}$ *denotes summation over all* $z_{q,m} \in G_\ell \setminus G_{\ell+1}$ .

(a) *If* $\lim_{m\to\infty} D_m f(x)$ *exists, we call the limit the pointwise derivative of* $f$ *at* $x$ , *denoted by* $f^{(1)}(x)$ .

(b) *If* $f \in X(\mathbb{K})$ *and if there exists a* $g \in X(\mathbb{K})$ *such that* $\lim_{m\to\infty} \|D_m f - g\|_{X(\mathbb{K})} = 0$ , *then we call* $g$ *the strong derivative of* $f$ *in* $X(\mathbb{K})$ , *denoted by* $D_X^{(1)} f$ . *Here* $X(\mathbb{K}) = L_r(\mathbb{K})$ , $1 \le r < \infty$ , *or* $X(\mathbb{K}) = C(\mathbb{K})$.

Higher order derivatives can be defined recursively.

REMARK. In [7] J. Pál gives a definition of differentiation for $\mathbb{C}$-valued functions defined on $[0,\infty)$ considered as the dyadic (= 2-series) field, extending the definition of Butzer and Wagner as given in [3] . The theory of Pál differs from the theory presented in this paper. Among other things, the eigenvalues corresponding to the eigenvectors of the differentiation operator are different.

THEOREM 1. (a) *For each* $x,y \in \mathbb{K}$ , $\chi_y(x)$ *is pointwise differentiable and* $\chi_y^{(1)}(x) = \|y\| \chi_y(x)$ . (b) *For each* $y \in \mathbb{K}$ , $\chi_y$ *is strongly differentiable in* $C(\mathbb{K})$ *and* $D_C^{(1)} \chi_y = \|y\| \chi_y$ .

PROOF. (a) The theorem clearly holds if $y = 0$ , because $\chi_0(x) = 1$ for all $x \in \mathbb{K}$ . Assume $y = (y_i)_{-\infty}^{\infty}$ , with $y_s \neq 0$ for some $s \in \mathbb{Z}$ and $y_i = 0$ for $i < s$ . For fixed $m \in \mathbb{N}$ such that $m \ge -s$ and $x \in \mathbb{K}$ we have

$$\begin{aligned} D_m \chi_y(x) &= \chi_y(x) \sum_{\ell=-m}^{m-1} P(\ell,m) \sum_{(\ell,m)} (1 - \chi_y(z_{q,m})) \\ &= \chi_y(x)\, D_m \chi_y(0) . \end{aligned}$$

Thus, in order to determine $D_m \chi_y(x)$ we must evaluate the sums $\sum_{(\ell,m)} (1 - \chi_y(z_{q,m}))$ for $-m \le \ell < m$ . First we observe that if $z_{q,m} = (z_i)_{-\infty}^{\infty}$ , then, according to (1) ,

$$(2) \quad \chi_y(z_{q,m}) = \begin{cases} \exp(2\pi i z_{-s-1} y_s p^{-1}) \exp(2\pi i \sum_{j=-\infty}^{-s-2} z_j y_{-1-j} p^{-1}), & \text{if } \mathbb{K} = \mathbb{K}_p , \\ \exp(2\pi i z_{-s-1} y_s p^{-1}) \exp(2\pi i \sum_{j=-\infty}^{-s-2} z_j \sum_{i=s}^{-j-1} y_i p^{i+j}), & \text{if } \mathbb{K} = \mathbb{Q}_p . \end{cases}$$

Now we distinguish three cases.

(i) $\ell > -s-1$ . If $z_{q,m} \in G_\ell \setminus G_{\ell+1}$ , then $z_i = 0$ for $i < \ell$ , hence certainly for $i \leq -s-1$ . Thus, $\chi_y(z_{q,m}) = 1$ and therefore, $\Sigma_{(\ell,m)}(1 - \chi_y(z_{q,m})) = 0$ .

(ii) $\ell = -s-1$ . If $z_{q,m} \in G_\ell \setminus G_{\ell+1}$ , then $z_i = 0$ for $i < -s-1$ . Thus, according to (2), $\chi_y(z_{q,m}) = \exp(2\pi i\, z_{-1-s} y_s p^{-1})$ . Divide the elements $z_{q,m}$ in $G_\ell \setminus G_{\ell+1}$ into sets $S$ of $p-1$ elements, all of which have the same coordinates $z_i$ for $i \neq \ell$ , whereas $z_\ell$ assumes the values $1,2,\ldots,$ $p-1$ . Since $y_s \neq 0$ we have

$$\sum_{z_{q,m} \in S} (1 - \chi_y(z_{q,m})) = \sum_{k=1}^{p-1} (1 - \exp(2\pi i\, y_s k\, p^{-1})) = p .$$

Since $G_\ell \setminus G_{\ell+1}$ contains $p^{m-\ell-1}$ such sets $S$ we have

$$\Sigma_{(m,\ell)}(1 - \chi_y(z_{q,m})) = p^{m-\ell} = p^{m+s+1} .$$

(iii) $\ell < -s-1$ and $\ell \leq m-1$ . In this case we divide the elements $z_{q,m}$ in $G_\ell \setminus G_{\ell+1}$ into sets $S$ of $p$ elements, all of which have the same coordinates $z_i$ for $i \neq -s-1$ , whereas $z_{-s-1}$ assumes the values $0,1,\ldots,p-1$ . Then it follows from (2) that

$$\sum_{z_{q,m} \in S} (1 - \chi_y(z_{q,m})) = p - C_S \sum_{k=0}^{m-1} \exp(2\pi i\, y_s k\, p^{-1}) = p ,$$

where $C_S$ is a constant depending on $S$ and on $\mathbb{K}$ . Since in this case there are $(p-1)p^{m-\ell-2}$ different sets $S$ in $G_\ell \setminus G_{\ell+1}$ we see that

$$\Sigma_{(m,\ell)}(1 - \chi_y(z_{q,m})) = (p - 1)p^{m-\ell-1} .$$

Consequently, we have

$$D_m \chi_y(x) = \chi_y(x)\left( \Sigma_{\ell=-m}^{-s-2} P(\ell,m)(p-1)p^{m-\ell-1} + P(-s-1,m)p^{m+s+1}\right) .$$

A simple computation shows that $D_m \chi_y(x) = p^{-s}\chi_y(x) = \|y\|\chi_y(x)$ , which concludes the proof of (a) . Obviously, the same argument can be used to prove (b) .

From here on we shall only consider strong differentiability in $L_1(\mathbb{K})$ . Extending the following results to $L_r(\mathbb{K})$ , $1 \leq r \leq 2$ , is fairly straightforward, but will not be considered here. To simplify the notation we shall write $D^{(1)}$ instead of $D_{L_1}^{(1)}$ .

LEMMA 1. If $f \in L_1(\mathbb{K})$, then for each $m \in \mathbb{N}$ we have

$$(3) \qquad (D_m f)^\wedge(y) = \begin{cases} \|y\|\hat{f}(y), & \text{if } y \in G_{-m}, \\ Q(m)\hat{f}(y), & \text{if } y \notin G_{-m}, \end{cases}$$

where $Q(m) = p^{-m+1}(p+1)^{-1}(p^{2m} - p^{-2m})$.

PROOF. We first observe that if $f \in L_1(\mathbb{K})$, $y \in \mathbb{K}$ and $m \in \mathbb{N}$, then

$$(D_m f)^\wedge(y) = \hat{f}(y) \sum_{\ell=-m}^{m-1} P(\ell,m) \sum_{(\ell,m)} (1 - \chi_y(z_{q,m}))$$
$$= \hat{f}(y)\, D_m \chi_y(0) .$$

If $y \in G_{-m}$, then $\|y\| = p^{-s} \leq p^m$ for some $s \in \mathbb{Z}$. Thus $m \geq -s$ and in the proof of Theorem 1 it was shown that in this case $D_m\chi_y(0) = \|y\|$. If $y \notin G_{-m}$ and $\|y\| = p^{-s}$ for some $s \in \mathbb{Z}$, then $m < -s$. Hence, for $\ell \in \mathbb{Z}$ such that $-m \leq \ell < m-1$ we have $\ell < -s-1$. In part (iii) of the proof of Theorem 1 it was shown that in this case $\sum_{(\ell,m)}(1 - \chi_y(z_{q,m})) = (p-1)p^{m-\ell-1}$. Then a simple computation shows that $D_m\chi_y(0) = Q(m)$, which completes the proof of Lemma 1.

COROLLARY 1. If $f$, $D^{(1)}f \in L_1(\mathbb{K})$, then for all $y \in \mathbb{K}$ we have $(D^{(1)}f)^\wedge(y) = \|y\|\, \hat{f}(y)$.

PROOF. This result follows immediately from Lemma 1 and the fact that for all $y \in \mathbb{K}$ we have $|(D_m f)^\wedge(y) - (D^{(1)}f)^\wedge(y)| \leq \|D_m f - D^{(1)}f\|_1$.

In Theorem 2 we shall prove that the converse of Corollary 1 is also true. However, we first prove the following lemma in which $I(A)$ denotes the characteristic function of a set $A \subset \mathbb{K}$.

LEMMA 2. For each $k \in \mathbb{Z}$ there exists a function $V_k \in L_1(\mathbb{K})$ such that $(V_k)^\wedge(y) = \|y\|^{-1} I(\mathbb{K}\setminus G_k)(y)$ for all $y \in \mathbb{K}$. Moreover, the sequences $\{\|p^{-k}V_k\|_1\}_{-\infty}^{\infty}$ and $\{\|D_k V_k\|_1\}_{-\infty}^{\infty}$ are both bounded.

PROOF. For each $\ell \in \mathbb{Z}$ with $\ell < k$ define the function $V_{k,\ell}$ by

$$V_{k,\ell}(x) = \int_{G_\ell \setminus G_k} \|y\|^{-1} \chi_y(x)dy .$$

For $n < m$ we have

$$\|V_{k,n} - V_{k,m}\|_1 = \| \int_{G_n \setminus G_m} \|y\|^{-1}\chi_y(\cdot)dy\|_1$$

$$= \Big\| \sum_{j=n}^{m-1} \int_{G_j \setminus G_{j+1}} \|y\|^{-1} \chi_y(\cdot) dy \Big\|_1$$

$$\leq \sum_{j=n}^{m-1} p^j \int_{\mathbb{K}} \Big| \int_{G_j \setminus G_{j+1}} \chi_y(x) dy \Big| dx$$

$$= \sum_{j=n}^{m-1} p^j \sum_{\ell=-\infty}^{\infty} \int_{\|x\|=p^\ell} \Big| \int_{\|y\|=p^{-j}} \chi_y(x) dy \Big| dx .$$

Now we use the fact, see [8, p. 20], that if $\|x\| = p^r$ for some $r \in \mathbb{Z}$, then for each $s \in \mathbb{Z}$ we have

$$\int_{\|y\| = p^s} \chi_x(y) dy = \begin{cases} p^s(1 - p^{-1}) , & \text{if } s < -r + 1 , \\ - p^{-r} , & \text{if } s = -r + 1 , \\ 0 , & \text{if } s > -r + 1 . \end{cases}$$

Thus, for fixed $j$ with $n \leq j \leq m - 1$ we have

$$\sum_{\ell=-\infty}^{\infty} \int_{\|x\|=p^\ell} \Big| \int_{\|y\|=p^{-j}} \chi_y(x) dy \Big| dx$$

$$= \sum_{\ell=-\infty}^{j} p^{-j}(1-p^{-1}) m(\{x; \|x\|=p^\ell\}) + p^{-(j+1)} m(\{x; \|x\|=p^{j+1}\})$$

$$= p^{-j}(1-p^{-1}) \sum_{\ell=-\infty}^{j} (p^\ell - p^{\ell-1}) + p^{-j-1}(p^{j+1} - p^j) = 2(1-p^{-1}) .$$

Consequently, $\|V_{k,n} - V_{k,m}\|_1 \leq \sum_{j=n}^{m-1} 2p^j(1-p^{-1})$ , which converges to zero as $m \to -\infty$ . Thus $\{V_{k,\ell}\}_{\ell=-\infty}^{k-1}$ is a Cauchy sequence in $L_1(\mathbb{K})$ converging to a function in $L_1(\mathbb{K})$ which we call $V_k$ , and we have $(V_k)^\wedge(y)$ $= \lim_{\ell \to -\infty} (V_{k,\ell})^\wedge(y) = \lim_{\ell \to -\infty} \|y\|^{-1} I(G_\ell \setminus G_k)(y) = \|y\|^{-1} I(\mathbb{K} \setminus G_k)(y)$ . Also, by the same argument as was used in estimating $\|V_{k,n} - V_{k,m}\|_1$ we obtain for all $n < k$ , $\|V_{k,n}\|_1 \leq \sum_{j=n}^{k-1} 2p^j(1-p^{-1}) \leq 2p^{k-1}$ . Therefore, $\|V_k\|_1 \leq C\, p^k$ for all $k \in \mathbb{Z}$ . In order to prove the boundedness of the sequence $\{\|D_k V_k\|_1\}$ we first observe that in [8, p. 23] it is shown that if the functions $\Delta_k$ $(k \in \mathbb{Z})$ are defined by $\Delta_k(x) = p^k\, I(G_k)(x)$ , then $\|\Delta_k\|_1 = 1$ and $(\Delta_k)^\wedge(y) = I(G_{-k})(y)$ for all $y \in \mathbb{K}$ . Moreover, for each $f \in L_1(\mathbb{K})$ we have $\lim_{m \to \infty} \|\Delta_m * f - f\|_1 = 0$ . Thus, it follows immediately from (3) that

$$(D_m V_m - \Delta_m + \Delta_{-m})^\wedge(y) = \begin{cases} 0, & \text{if } y \in G_{-m}, \\ (D_m V_m)^\wedge(y), & \text{if } y \notin G_{-m}. \end{cases}$$

Hence the Uniqueness Theorem for Fourier transforms implies that

$$D_m V_m - \Delta_m + \Delta_{-m} = Q(m) V_{-m} .$$

Therefore,

$$\|D_m V_m\|_1 \leq \|\Delta_m\|_1 + \|\Delta_{-m}\|_1 + Q(m)\|V_{-m}\|_1 = O(1) .$$

This completes the proof of Lemma 2 .

Using the same notation as in [1, pages 226 and 381] we define two spaces of functions on $\mathbb{K}$ .

DEFINITION 2. (a) $V(L_1, \|y\|) = \{f \in L_1(\mathbb{K});\ \|y\|\hat{f}(y) = \hat{\mu}(y)$ <u>for all</u> $y \in \mathbb{K}$ <u>and some measure</u> $\mu \in M(\mathbb{K})\}$.

(b) $W(L_1, \|y\|) = \{f \in L_1(\mathbb{K});\ \|y\|\hat{f}(y) = \hat{g}(y)$ <u>for all</u> $y \in \mathbb{K}$ <u>and some function</u> $g \in L_1(\mathbb{K})\}$.

THEOREM 2. <u>Let</u> $f \in L_1(\mathbb{K})$. <u>Then</u> $f \in \mathcal{D}(D^{(1)})$ , <u>the domain of the operator</u> $D^{(1)}$, <u>if and only if</u> $f \in W(L_1, \|y\|)$.

PROOF. If $f \in \mathcal{D}(D^{(1)})$, then $D^{(1)}f \in L_1(\mathbb{K})$ and the conclusion is derived in Corollary 1 . Assume $f \in W(L_1, \|y\|)$ and let $g \in L_1(\mathbb{K})$ satisfy $\hat{g}(y) = \|y\|\hat{f}(y)$ for all $y \in \mathbb{K}$ . Then Lemma 1 implies that for each $m \in \mathbb{N}$ we have

$$(D_m f)^\wedge(y) = \begin{cases} \hat{g}(y), & \text{if } y \in G_{-m}, \\ Q(m)(V_{-m})^\wedge(y)\hat{g}(y), & \text{if } y \notin G_{-m}. \end{cases}$$

Thus,

$$D_m f = g * \Delta_m + Q(m) V_{-m} * g .$$

Also, since $V_{-m} * \Delta_m = 0$ in $L_1(\mathbb{K})$ we find

$$D_m f - g = \Delta_m * g - g + Q(m) V_{-m} * (g - \Delta_m * g) .$$

Hence,

$$\|D_m f - g\|_1 \leq (1 + Q(m)\|V_{-m}\|_1)\|\Delta_m * g - g\|_1 .$$

Since, according to Lemma 2, the sequence $\{p^m\|V_{-m}\|_1\}$ is bounded and $\|\Delta_m * g - g\|_1 \to 0$ as $m \to \infty$ , we may conclude that $\|D_m f - g\|_1 \to 0$ as

$m \to \infty$ , that is, $D^{(1)}f$ exists and $D^{(1)}f = g$ .

COROLLARY 2. The operator $D^{(1)}$ is a closed operator on $\mathcal{D}(D^{(1)})$ .

PROOF. Let $f_n (n \geq 1)$, $f$, $g$ be functions in $L_1(\mathbb{K})$ such that (i) $D^{(1)}f_n$ exists for each $n \geq 1$ , (ii) $\lim_{n\to\infty}\|f_n - f\|_1 = 0$ and (iii) $\lim_{n\to\infty}\|D^{(1)}f_n - g\|_1 = 0$ . It follows from (ii) that $\hat{f}(y) = \lim_{n\to\infty}(f_n)^\wedge(y)$ for all $y \in \mathbb{K}$ and it follows from (iii) and Corollary 1 that $\hat{g}(y) = \lim_{n\to\infty}(D^{(1)}f_n)^\wedge(y) = \lim_{n\to\infty}\|y\|\hat{f}_n(y) = \|y\|\hat{f}(y)$ for all $y \in \mathbb{K}$ . Therefore, Theorem 2 implies that $f \in \mathcal{D}(D^{(1)})$ with $D^{(1)}f = g$ , which means that $D^{(1)}$ is a closed operator.

Observe that since $D^{(1)}$ is a closed operator, $\mathcal{D}(D^{(1)})$ is a Banach space with respect to the norm $\|\cdot\|_D$ , where $\|f\|_D = \|f\|_1 + \|D^{(1)}f\|_1$ for $f \in \mathcal{D}(D^{(1)})$ .

## 3. Saturation and Non-optimal Approximation Results

In this section we prove a saturation theorem for the operators $D_m$ on $L_1(\mathbb{K})$ . Furthermore, we prove a Bernstein and a Jackson-type inequality from which we can deduce some non-optimal approximation results.

THEOREM 3. Let $f \in L_1(\mathbb{K})$. (a) $\|D_m f\|_1 = o(1)$ if and only if $f = C$ in $L_1(\mathbb{K})$ . (b) The following conditions are equivalent: (a) $\|D_m f\|_1 = O(1)$ , (b) $f \in V(L_1, \|y\|)$ , (c) $f \in \widetilde{W(L_1,\|y\|)}^{L_1} = \widetilde{\mathcal{D}(D^{(1)})}^{L_1}$ , where $\widetilde{\mathcal{D}(D^{(1)})}^{L_1}$ denotes the completion of $\mathcal{D}(D^{(1)})$ relative to $L_1(\mathbb{K})$, see [1, Section 10.4] .

PROOF. (a) If $\|D_m f\|_1 = o(1)$ , then $f \in \mathcal{D}(D^{(1)})$ and $D^{(1)}f = 0$ . Corollary 1 implies that $\hat{f}(y) = 0$ for all $y \neq 0$ . Therefore $f = \hat{f}(0)$ . The converse is trivial.

(b) Assume $f \in V(L_1, \|y\|)$ with corresponding $\mu \in M(\mathbb{K})$. The Uniqueness Theorem shows that for $m \in \mathbb{N}$ we have

$$D_m f = D_m V_m * \mu + \Delta_{-m} * \mu \quad .$$

Therefore, according to Lemma 2 , we have

$$\|D_m f\|_1 \leq (\|D_m V_m\|_1 + \|\Delta_{-m}\|_1)\|\mu\|_M = O(1) \ .$$

Next, assume $\|D_m f\|_1 = O(1)$ . Then for each $m,n \in \mathbb{N}$ we have $\|\Delta_m * D_n f\|_1 = O(1)$ . Since $(\Delta_m)^\wedge = p^m \Delta_{-m}$ , it follows from a standard computation, see [1, Proposition (5.1.15)] , that for each $x \in \mathbb{K}$

$$(\Delta_m * D_n f)(x) = \int_{\mathbb{K}} p^m \Delta_{-m}(t)(D_n f)^\wedge(t)\chi_x(t)dt.$$

Applying the Dominated Convergence Theorem and Lemma 1 we see that for each $m \in \mathbb{N}$ and $x \in \mathbb{K}$ we have

$$\lim_{n \to \infty} (\Delta_m * D_n f)(x) = \int_{\mathbb{K}} p^m \Delta_{-m}(t)\|t\|\hat{f}(t)\chi_x(t)dt = \Phi_m(x) .$$

Then it follows from Fatou's Lemma that

$$\|\Phi_m\|_1 \leq \liminf_{n \to \infty} \left\| \int_{\mathbb{K}} p^m \Delta_{-m}(t)(D_n f)\hat{}(t)\chi_{(\cdot)}(t)dt \right\|_1$$

$$= \liminf_{n \to \infty} \|\Delta_m * D_n f\|_1 = O(1) .$$

Also, we observe that $\Phi_m(x)$ is the Fourier transform of the function $(\Delta_m)\hat{}(t)\|t\|\hat{f}(-t)$ in $L_1(\mathbb{K})$. Next, consider the measures $\mu_m(x) = \Phi_m(x)dx$. Then $\|\mu_m\|_M = \|\Phi_m\|_1 = O(1)$. Thus there exists a subsequence $\{m_j\}$ and a measure $\mu \in M(\mathbb{K})$ which is the weak* limit of the sequence $\{\mu_{m_j}\}$. Next, if $T$ denotes the set of all finite linear combinations of translates of the functions $\Delta_m$ $(m \in \mathbb{Z})$ then it is shown in [8, Chapter II] that $T$ is dense in $C_0(\mathbb{K})$ and that the Fourier transform maps $T$ onto itself. Thus if $g \in T$ then there exists a $G \in T$ such that $g = \hat{G}$ and we have

$$\int_{\mathbb{K}} \|t\|\hat{f}(-t)g(t)dt = \lim_{j\to\infty} \int_{G_{-m_j}} \|t\|\hat{f}(-t)g(t)dt$$

$$= \lim_{j\to\infty} \int_{\mathbb{K}} (\Delta_{m_j})\hat{}(t)\|t\|\hat{f}(t)g(t)dt$$

$$= \lim_{j\to\infty} \int_{\mathbb{K}} \Phi_{m_j}(t)G(t)dt$$

$$= \int_{\mathbb{K}} G(t)d\mu(t)$$

$$= \int_{\mathbb{K}} \hat{g}(t)d\mu(t) = \int_{\mathbb{K}} g(t)\hat{\mu}(-t)dt .$$

Consequently, $\|t\|\hat{f}(-t) = \hat{\mu}(-t)$ for all $t \in \mathbb{K}$, which means that $f \in V(L_1, \|y\|)$.

To prove the equivalence of (b) and (c) we argue as follows. First assume that $f \in V(L_1, \|y\|)$ and let $\mu \in M(\mathbb{K})$ satisfy $\hat{\mu}(y) = \|y\|\hat{f}(y)$ for all $y \in \mathbb{K}$. For $n \in \mathbb{N}$ let $f_n = \Delta_n * f$. It follows from Lemma 1 that for $m \geq n$ we have $(D_m f_n)\hat{}(y) = \|y\|\hat{f}(y)I(G_{-n})(y)$. Consequently, $\lim_{m\to\infty} D_m f_n$ exists in $L_1(\mathbb{K})$ and $(D^{(1)} f_n)\hat{}(y) = \|y\|\hat{f}(y)I(G_{-n})(y)$ for all $y \in \mathbb{K}$. Thus $D^{(1)} f_n = \Delta_n * \mu$. Therefore,

$$\|f_n\|_D = \|f_n\|_1 + \|D^{(1)} f_n\|_1$$
$$\leq \|\Delta_n\|_1 \|f\|_1 + \|\Delta_n\|_1 \|\mu\|_M = O(1) .$$

Also, $\lim_{n\to\infty} \|f_n - f\|_1 = 0$ . Hence $f \in \widetilde{\mathcal{D}(D^{(1)})}^{L_1}$ . Next, assume $f \in \widetilde{\mathcal{D}(D^{(1)})}^{L_1}$ . Thus, there exist sequences $\{f_n\}_1^\infty$ and $\{g_n\}_1^\infty$ in $L_1(\mathbb{K})$ such that (i) $(g_n)^\wedge(y) = \|y\| (f_n)^\wedge(y)$ for all $y \in \mathbb{K}$ and $n \in \mathbb{N}$ , (ii) $\{\|f_n\|_1 + \|g_n\|_1\}_1^\infty$ is bounded and (iii) $\lim_{n\to\infty} \|f_n - f\|_1 = 0$ . For $m,n \in \mathbb{N}$ consider the functions $\Delta_m * g_n$ . The same argument that was used for the functions $\Delta_m * D_n f$ in proving the equivalence of (a) and (b) can be used here to show that there exists a measure $\mu \in M(\mathbb{K})$ such that $\hat{\mu}(y) = \|y\| \hat{f}(y)$ for all $y \in \mathbb{K}$ , that is, $f \in V(L_1, \|y\|)$ . This completes the proof of the saturation theorem for the operators $D_m$ on $L_1(\mathbb{K})$ .

In the remainder of this paper we shall outline the proof of a non-optimal approximation result for the operators $D_m$ . In [2, Section 4] it is shown that if $\{V_n\}_0^\infty$ is a sequence of bounded and commutative linear transformations of a Banach space $X$ such that $\lim_{n\to\infty} \|(V_n - I)f\|_X = 0$ for all $f \in X$ , and if there exists a Banach space $Y \subset X$ and positive constants $C$, $D$, $\rho$ such that for all $n \in \mathbb{N}$ we have $\|(V_n - I)g\|_X \leq C\, n^{-\rho} \|g\|_Y$ for all $g \in Y$, and $V_n f \in Y$ with $\|V_n f\|_Y \leq D n^{\rho} \|f\|_X$ for all $f \in X$ , then a non-optimal approximation result holds for the $\{V_n\}$ , see [2, Section 4] for details. We shall show that the operators $D_m$ on $L_1(\mathbb{K})$ determine operators $V_n$ with the properties just mentioned. We first prove a Jackson-type inequality.

LEMMA 3. <u>There exists a</u> $C > 0$ <u>such that for all</u> $f \in \mathcal{D}(D^{(1)})$ <u>and</u> $m \in \mathbb{N}$ <u>we have</u> $\|D_m f\|_1 \leq C \|f\|_D$ .

PROOF. In the proof of Theorem 2 we showed that

$$D_m f = \Delta_m * D^{(1)} f + Q(m)\, V_{-m} * D^{(1)} f .$$

Thus it follows from Lemma 2 that

$$\|D_m f\|_1 \leq (\|\Delta_m\|_1 + Q(m) \|V_{-m}\|_1) \|D^{(1)} f\|_1$$
$$\leq C \|D^{(1)} f\|_1 \leq C \|f\|_D .$$

Next we prove a Bernstein-type inequality.

LEMMA 4. *There exists a* $D > 0$ *such that for all* $f \in L_1(\mathbb{K})$ *and all* $k \in \mathbb{N}$ *we have* $\Delta_k * f \in \mathcal{D}(D^{(1)})$ *and*

$$\|\Delta_k * f\|_D \leq C\, p^k \|\Delta_k * f\|_1 . \tag{4}$$

PROOF. In the proof of Theorem 3 we showed that $\Delta_k * f \in \mathcal{D}(D^{(1)})$ and that for $m \geq k$, $D_m(\Delta_k * f) = D^{(1)}(\Delta_k * f)$. Since $(\Delta_k * f)(x) = (\Delta_k * f)(x + z_{q,m})$ for $z_{q,m} \in G_k$, we have

$$D_m(\Delta_k * f)(x) = \sum_{\ell=-m}^{k-1} P(\ell,m) \sum_{(\ell,m)}((\Delta_k * f)(x) - (\Delta_k * f)(x + z_{q,m})).$$

Therefore,

$$\|D_m(\Delta_k * f)\|_1 \leq \sum_{\ell=-m}^{k-1} P(\ell,m)\, 2\, p^{m-\ell}(1 - p^{-1})\|\Delta_k * f\|_1$$
$$\leq C\, p^k \|\Delta_k * f\|_1 ,$$

as follows from a simple computation. From this we immediately obtain (4).

Next, we observe that for each $f \in L_1(\mathbb{K})$ and $m \in \mathbb{N}$, $\|D_m f\|_1 \leq \sum_{\ell=-m}^{m-1} P(\ell,m)\, 2\, p^{m-\ell}(1 - p^{-1})\|f\|_1 \leq C\, p^m \|f\|_1$. Furthermore, Lemma 2 and the Uniqueness Theorem imply that $D_m$ and $D_n$ commute for $m,n \in \mathbb{N}$. Finally we show that $\lim_{m\to\infty}\|p^{-m}D_m f\|_1 = 0$ for $f \in L_1(\mathbb{K})$. Namely, given $\epsilon > 0$ there exists a $k_0 \in \mathbb{N}$ such that for $k \geq k_0$ and $z \in G_k$ we have $\|f - f_z\|_1 < \epsilon$. Thus,

$$\|D_m f\|_1 \leq \sum_{\ell=-m}^{k_0-1} P(\ell,m) \sum_{(\ell,m)} 2\|f\|_1 + \sum_{\ell=k_0}^{m-1} P(\ell,m) \sum_{(\ell,m)}\epsilon$$
$$\leq C_1 p^{k_0} \|f\|_1 + C_2\, p^m \epsilon .$$

Hence, $\lim_{m\to\infty}\|p^{-m}D_m f\|_1 = 0$.

In conclusion, if we set $V_n = I - (Q(m))^{-1}D_m$ for $p^m \leq n < p^{m+1}$, and $Y = \mathcal{D}(D^{(1)})$, we can show easily that the operators $V_n$ satisfy all the conditions mentioned before with $\rho = 1$. Thus we may apply Theorem 4.1 of [2] to obtain, among others, the following result.

THEOREM 4. *For* $0 < \theta < 1$, $1 \leq q \leq \infty$ *and* $f \in L_1(\mathbb{K})$ *we have* $\|f\|_1 + (\sum_{m=1}^{\infty} p^{m\theta}(\|p^{-m}D_m f\|_1)^q)^{1/q} < \infty$ *if and only if* $f \in (L_1(\mathbb{K}), \mathcal{D}(D^{(1)}))_{\theta,q,\mathbb{K}}$, *with the usual modification for* $q = \infty$.

## REFERENCES

[1] Butzer, P.L. - Nessel, R.J., Fourier Analysis and Approximation, Volume I. Academic Press, New York 1971.

[2] Butzer, P.L. - Scherer, K., On the fundamental approximation theorems of D. Jackson, S.N. Bernstein and theorems of M. Zamansky and S.B. Stečkin. Aequat. Math. 3 (1969), 170-185.

[3] Butzer, P.L. - Wagner, H.J., Walsh-Fourier series and the concept of a derivative. Applicable Anal. 3 (1973), 29-46.

[4] Butzer, P.L. - Wagner, H.J., On dyadic analysis based on the pointwise dyadic derivative. Anal. Math. 1(1975), 171-196.

[5] Hewitt, E. - Ross, K.A., Abstract Harmonic Analysis, Volume I. Springer-Verlag, Berlin 1963.

[6] Onneweer, C.W., Fractional differentiation on the group of integers of a p-adic or p-series field. Anal. Math., to appear.

[7] Pál, J., On the concept of a derivative among functions defined on the dyadic field. SIAM J. Math. Anal. 8(1977), 375-391.

[8] Taibleson, M.H., Fourier analysis on local fields. Mathematical Notes, Princeton University Press, Princeton 1975.

# REMARKS ON THE KRONECKER'S APPROXIMATION THEOREM AND A UNITARY MEASURE

Satoru Igari
Mathematical Institute
Tôhoku University
Sendai

We give a variant of the Kronecker's approximation theorem which has an application to a theorem on the unitary measures.

## 1. The Kronecker's approximation theorem

A well-known approximation theorem of Kronecker is as follows

THEOREM. *Let* $\theta_1, \theta_2, \ldots, \theta_m$ *be any real numbers such that* $\theta_1, \theta_2, \ldots, \theta_m, 1$ *are rationally independent and let* $\alpha_1, \alpha_2, \ldots, \alpha_m$ *be any real numbers. Then for every positive number* $\varepsilon$ *there exist integers* $p_1, p_2, \ldots, p_m, p$ *such that*

$$|p\theta_j - \alpha_j - p_j| < \varepsilon \qquad ( j=1,2,\ldots,m ).$$

In this paper we shall give the folloing variant of the above theorem.

THEOREM 2. *Let* $\theta_1, \theta_2, \ldots, \theta_m$ *be any real numbers as before and let* $\phi_1, \phi_2, \ldots, \phi_m$ *be any real valued almost periodic functions. Then for every positive number* $\varepsilon$ *there exist integers* $p_1, p_2, \ldots, p_m, p$ *such that*

$$|p\theta_j - \phi_j(p) - p_j| < \varepsilon \qquad ( j=1,2,\ldots,m ).$$

We shall prove this theorem in a locally compact abelian group setting and give an application to a theorem on unitary measures.

Let $G$ be a locally compact abelian group and $\hat{G}$ be the dual to $G$ with the unit $e$. A set $\{ \gamma_1, \gamma_2, \ldots, \gamma_m \}$ in $\hat{G}$ is said to be independent if for any integers $n_1, n_2, \ldots, n_m$

$$\gamma_1^{n_1} \gamma_2^{n_2} \cdots \gamma_m^{n_m} = e \quad \text{implies} \quad \gamma_1^{n_1} = \gamma_2^{n_2} = \ldots = \gamma_m^{n_m} = e.$$

THEOREM 1. _Let_ $G$ _be a locally compact abelian group and_ $\{ \gamma_1, \gamma_2, \ldots, \gamma_m \}$ _be an independent set of_ $\hat{G}$. _If_ $\phi_1, \phi_2, \ldots, \phi_m$ _are real-valued almost periodic functions on_ $G$ _and_ $\varepsilon$ _is a positive number, then there is an element_ $g$ _of_ $G$ _such that_

$$|\gamma_j(g) - \exp i\phi_j(g)| < \varepsilon \quad ( j=1,2,\ldots,m ).$$

PROOF. Since an almost periodic function is a uniform limit of finite linear combinations of characters, we may suppose

$$\phi_j(g) = \sum_{k=-K}^{K} a_{jk} \tau_{jk}(g) \quad ( j=1,2,\ldots,m )$$

where $\tau_{jk} \in \hat{G}$ and $a_{jk}$ are complex numbers such that $a_{jk} = \overline{a_{j\,-k}}$ and $\tau_{jk} = \overline{\tau_{j\,-k}}$. Let $\Gamma_0$ be a maximal independent subset of $\{ \gamma_j, \tau_{jk} : j=1,2,\ldots,m,\ k=0,1,2,\ldots,K \}$ containing $\{ \gamma_j : j=1,2,\ldots,m \}$. Thus for every $\tau_{jk}$ there are integers $p = p_{jk} \neq 0$, $q = q_{jk\ell}$ and $r = r_{jk\ell n}$ such that

$$\tau_{jk}^{p} = \prod \gamma_\ell^{q} \prod \tau_{\ell n}^{r}$$

where the first product runs over $\ell=1,2,\ldots,m$ and the second over $\tau_{\ell n} \in \Gamma_0$.

Put $P = \prod_{j,k} p_{j,k}$ and $Q_{jk\ell} = Pq_{jk\ell}/p_{jk}$. For real numbers $\alpha_1, \alpha_2, \ldots, \alpha_m$ define

$$\Phi_j(\alpha_1, \alpha_2, \ldots, \alpha_m) = \sum_{k=-K}^{K} a_{jk} \exp 2\pi i[\, Q_{jk1}\alpha_1 + Q_{jk2}\alpha_2 + \ldots + Q_{jkm}\alpha_m \,]$$

$( j=1,2,\ldots,m )$. $\Phi_j$ are real valued trigonometric polynomials.

In fact, if there exists $g$ in $G$ such that

(1) $$\tau_{jk}(g) = 1 \qquad \text{for} \quad \tau_{jk} \in \Gamma_o$$

and

(2) $$\gamma_j(g) = \exp 2\pi i \alpha_j \quad \text{for} \quad j=1,2,\dots m,$$

then

$$\begin{aligned} \phi_j(g^P) &= \sum_{k=-K}^{K} a_{jk}\, \tau_{jk}^P(g) \\ &= \sum_{k=-K}^{K} a_{jk} \left( \gamma_1^{Q_{jk1}}(g)\, \gamma_2^{Q_{jk2}}(g) \dots \gamma_m^{Q_{jkm}}(g) \right) \\ &= \Phi_j(\alpha_1, \alpha_2, \dots, \alpha_m). \end{aligned}$$

Thus $\Phi_j(\alpha_1,\alpha_2,\dots,\alpha_m)$ is real. On the other hand, by the Kronecker's approximation theorem ( cf. W.Rudin [ 2 ; p.98 ]) the equations (1) and (2) hold approximately for a $g$ in $G$. Thus $\Phi_j$ are real valued bounded continuous functions.

Fix real numbers $\alpha_1,\alpha_2,\dots,\alpha_m$ such that

$$2\pi P\alpha_j = \Phi_j(\alpha_1,\alpha_2,\dots,\alpha_m) \qquad ( j=1,2,\dots,m ) .$$

Then for a $g$ in $G$ which satisfies approximately (1) and (2) we have

$$|\gamma_j(g^P) - \exp i\phi_j(g^P)| < \varepsilon \qquad ( j=1,2,\dots,m ) .$$

## 2. Application

THEOREM 3. Let $g$ be an element of a locally compact abelian group $G$ which is of infinite order, $\delta_g$ be the Dirac measure concentrated on $\{ g \}$ and $\nu$ be a hermitian discrete measure on $G$. Then the spectrum of $\delta_g *$ $\exp i\nu$ coincides with the unit circle.

In particular $\delta_g \neq \exp \mu$ for any Borel measure $\mu$ on $G$.

The last statement is given by L.Corwin [1].

PROOF. The Fourier Transform of $\delta_g * \exp i\nu$ is $\overline{\gamma(g)} \exp i\hat{\nu}(\gamma)$. For any real number $\alpha$ $\hat{\nu}(\gamma) - 2\pi\alpha$ is a real valued almost periodic function on $\hat{G}$. Thus by Theorem 1 there exists $\gamma$ in $\hat{G}$ such that the equation $\gamma(g) = \exp i[\hat{\nu}(\gamma) - 2\pi\alpha]$ holds approximately.

For the second part, remark that $i\mu$ may be supposed to be a discrete hermitian measure and if $\delta_g = \exp \mu$, then the spectrum of $\delta_g * \exp(-\mu)$ consists of the single point 1.

## REFERENCES

[1] Corwin, L., Unitary measures on LCA groups. Trans. Amer. Math. Soc. 196 (1974), 425-430.

[2] Rudin, W., Fourier Analysis on Groups. Interscience Publishers, New York 1962.

# LEBESGUE CONSTANTS FOR CERTAIN PARTIAL SUMS OF FOURIER SERIES ON COMPACT LIE GROUPS

Bernd Dreseler
Fachbereich 6 - Mathematatik
Gesamthochschule Siegen
Siegen

The main purpose of this paper is to prove a transference result for estimates of $L_1$ norms of central trigonometric polynomials on compact connected Lie groups. As a consequence of this result estimates of Lebesgue constants for certain partial sums of Fourier series on G will follow which allow the extension of the classical Dini-Lipschitz theorem on uniform convergence to this context. Another consequence is an inequality which is basic for the proof of $L_p$ multiplier theorems on G.

## 1. Introduction

Let G be a compact connected Lie group and let $G^\wedge$ be the dual space of equivalence classes of irreducible finite dimensional representations of G. The formal Fourier series of a function f in $L_1(G)$ has the form

$$(1.1) \qquad f \sim \sum_{\lambda\in G^\wedge} d_\lambda \chi_\lambda * f$$

where $\chi_\lambda$ is the character and $d_\lambda = \chi_\lambda(e)$ is the dimension of the corresponding $\lambda\in G^\wedge$. A function $\phi: G^\wedge \to \mathbb{C}$ is said to be a (central) $L_p$ Fourier multiplier on G if

$$(1.2) \qquad \|\phi\|_{m_p(G)} = \sup_{0\neq f\in L_p} \|\check{\phi}*f\|_{L_p(G)} / \|f\|_{L_p(G)} < \infty.$$

Here $\check{\phi}$ denotes the inverse Fourier transform of $\phi$, i.e.

$$(1.3) \qquad \check{\phi}(g) \sim \sum_{\lambda\in G^\wedge} d_\lambda \phi(\lambda)\chi_\lambda(g) \quad (g\in G).$$

For supp$\phi$ finite $\check{\phi}$ is a central trigonometric polynomial on G and we call the number $\|\phi\|_{m_1(G)}$ Lebesgue constant for $\phi$ on G.

Previous results on $L_p$ multipliers on G have been obtained for instance in [1], [2], [3], [4], [11], and [13]. In [5] we proved an estimate for Lebesgue constants for spherical partial sums of Fourier series on G. The main result of this paper is a transference result (Lemma 3.2) for estimates of general Lebesgue constants $\|\phi\|_{m_1(G)}$. On the one hand this leads to a more elementary proof and a generalization of our result in [5] and on the other hand Lemma 2.2 of Vretare [13], which is basic for the proof of various sharp $L_p$ multiplier theorems on G, is a direct consequence of our Lemma 3.2. The idea of the proof is an application of the classical Bernstein inequality for trigonometric polynomials on the one dimensional torus group $\mathbf{T}$.

## 2. Preliminaries on Compact Lie Groups

Let G be a compact semisimple simply connected Lie group of dimension n and T a maximal torus in G. Let $\underline{g}$ and $\underline{t}$ be their Lie algebras and $\underline{g}_c$ and $\underline{t}_c$ the respective complexifications. Let $\Delta$ be the set of roots of $(\underline{g}_c,\underline{t}_c)$, P be a system of positive roots in $\Delta$, W be the corresponding Weyl group, and $S = \{\alpha_1,\ldots,\alpha_l\}$ the corresponding system of simple roots. Then the dimension of $\underline{t}$ is equal to l and l is called the rank of G. We fix once for all a positive definite inner product (X,Y) on $\underline{g}$ which is invariant under the adjoint representation Ad of G. Put $|X|=(X,X)^{1/2}$. A pure imaginary valued linear form $\lambda$ on $\underline{t}$ is identified with an element $H_\lambda$ in $\underline{t}$ which satisfies $\lambda(H)=i(H_\lambda,H)$ for all H in $\underline{t}$. We put $\lambda(H)=i(\lambda,H)$ and $(\lambda,\mu)=(H_\lambda,H_\mu)$. The exponential function exp on $\underline{g}$ is a homomorphism of $\underline{t}$ onto T. Let $T^\wedge$ be the character group of T. If $\xi\in T^\wedge$, $\xi\circ\exp$ is a character of $\underline{t}$. Thus there is a $\lambda\in\underline{t}_c^*$, which takes pure imaginary values on $\underline{t}$, such that $\xi\circ\exp=e^\lambda$. $\lambda$ is uniquely determined by $\xi$. Let L(G) be the set of all $\lambda\in\underline{t}_c^*$ with the property $e^\lambda=\xi\circ\exp$ for some $\xi\in T^\wedge$. Since G is simply connected, L(G) is precisely the set of all integral linear forms on $\underline{t}$ and if $\Gamma_T$ is the kernel of exp we have $L(G) = \{\lambda\in i\underline{t}^*: \lambda(H)\in 2\pi i\mathbf{Z} \text{ for all } H\in\Gamma_T\}$ where $i\underline{t}^*$ is the set of all pure imaginary valued linear forms on $\underline{t}$. Define $H_i = (2/\alpha_i(H_{\alpha_i}))H_{\alpha_i}$, i=1,...,l. The lattice $\Gamma_T$ is generated by $2\pi i H_i$, i=1,...,l, over the non negative integers $\mathbf{N}$ [14]. Let $\Lambda(G)$ be the set of all dominant integral linear forms on $\underline{t}_c$, i.e. the set of all $\lambda\in L(G)$ for which $\lambda(H_i)\in\mathbf{N}$. For any $\lambda\in\Lambda(G)$ let $\pi_\lambda$ be an element in the equivalence class of irreducible finite dimensional representations with highest weight $\lambda$. The map $\lambda\to\pi_\lambda$ is a bijection between $\Lambda(G)$ and the set $G^\wedge$. The fundamental weights $(\pi_i)_{1\leq i\leq l}$ are defined by $\pi_i(H_j) = \delta_{ij}$, $j=1,\dots,l$. Thus $\lambda$ belongs to $\Lambda(G)$ if and only if $\lambda = \sum_{1\leq i\leq l} m_i \pi_i$ with $m_i \in \mathbb{N}$. Using the fundamental weights as a basis, we may identify $i\underline{t}^*$ with $\mathbb{R}^l$ and $G^\wedge = \Lambda(G)$ with the semilattice $\mathbb{N}^l$. Using $(iH_j)_{1\leq j\leq l}$ as a basis we may identify $\underline{t}$ with $\mathbb{R}^l$ and $\Gamma_T$ with the lattice $2\pi\mathbb{Z}^l$ in $\mathbb{R}^l$. For $\lambda \in L(G)$ and $H \in \underline{t}$ we have $\lambda(H) = i\sum_{1\leq j\leq l} m_j h_j$ with $\lambda = \sum m_j \pi_j$ and $H = \sum h_j (iH_j)$. Define $\rho = 1/2\sum_{\alpha\in P}\alpha$,

$$D(H) = \prod_{\alpha\in P}\left[e^{\alpha(H)/2} - e^{-\alpha(H)/2}\right],$$

and $\pi(H) = \prod_{\alpha\in P}\alpha(H)$ $(H\in\underline{t}_c)$. Then we have the following formula of Weyl:

$$(2.1) \qquad \chi_\lambda(\exp H) = D(H)^{-1}\sum_{s\in W}\det s \; e^{s(\lambda+\rho)(H)}$$

$(H\in\underline{t},\ \pi(H) \neq 0)$ from which the dimension formula

$$(2.2) \qquad d_\lambda = \prod_{\alpha\in P}\frac{(\lambda+\rho,\alpha)}{(\rho,\alpha)}$$

may be deduced. Finally, let Q be the fundamental parallelepiped $\{H\in\underline{t}: |\alpha(H)| < 2\pi \text{ for all } \alpha\in\Delta\}$ in $\underline{t}$. Then for all central functions f in $L_1(G)$ holds

$$(2.3) \qquad \int_G f(g)dg = \frac{1}{|W|}\int_Q f(\exp(H))\ |D(H)|^2 dH$$

where dH is a Lebesgue measure on $\underline{t}$ and $|W|$ the order of the Weyl group W.

## 3. A Transference Result

Let $\phi:\mathbb{R}^l \to \mathbb{C}$ be of compact support and Weyl group invariant. Our aim is to prove an estimate of type

$$(3.1) \qquad \|\phi(\cdot+\rho)\|_{m_1(G)} \leq C_{\mathrm{supp}\phi}\|\phi\|_{m_1(\mathbb{T}^l)}$$

where $C_{\mathrm{supp}\phi}$ only depends on $\mathrm{supp}\phi$ and G. As a first step we have

LEMMA 3.1. Let $\phi:\mathbb{R}^l \to \mathbb{C}$ be of compact support and Weyl group invariant. Then

$$(3.2)\qquad \|\phi(\cdot+\rho)\|_{m_1(G)} \leq C\int_Q |\sum_{\tau\in L(G)}\phi(\tau)\, \Pi_{\alpha\in P}(\tau,\alpha)e^{\tau(H)}|\,dH$$

with a constant C which only depends on G.

In view of the fact that $\|\phi(\cdot+\rho)\|_{m_1(G)} = \|\check{\phi}(\cdot+\rho)\|_{L_1(G)}$ the proof follows by a rather easy computation involving the formulas (2.1), (2.2) and (2.3) and the fact that for all $\tau\in L(G)$ with $\pi(\tau)\neq o$ there exists a unique $\lambda\in\Lambda(G)$ and a unique $s\in W$ such that $\tau = s(\lambda+\rho)$ (cf. [1;Chapter 2], [15;Chapter 3] for analogous proofs).

We shall now establish our tranference result for Lebesgue constants on G.

LEMMA 3.2. Let $\phi:\mathbb{R}^l \to \mathbb{C}$ be Weyl group invariant, and let $\phi$ have compact support contained in the ball $\{h\in \mathbb{R}^l:\ |h|\leq R\}$, $R>o$. Then

$$(3.3)\qquad \|\phi(\cdot+\rho)\|_{m_1(G)} \leq CR^m\|\phi\|_{m_1(\mathbf{T}^l)}$$

where the constant C only depends on G and $m = (n-1)/2$.

PROOF. Let $Q_1 = \{h\in \mathbb{R}^l:\ -\pi<h_i\leq\pi,\ i=1,\dots,l\}$ be the fundamental cube in $\mathbb{R}^l$ with center $0\in\mathbb{R}^l$. For $\alpha\in P$ let $\tilde{\alpha}\in\mathbb{R}^l$ be defined by $H_\alpha = \sum_{1\leq j\leq l}\tilde{\alpha}_j(iH_j)$ and denote by $(\cdot|\cdot)$ the usual scalar product on $\mathbb{R}^l$. Then we have

$$(3.4)\qquad \sum_{\tau\in L(G)}\phi(\tau)\Pi_{\alpha\in P}(\tau,\alpha)e^{\tau(H)} = \sum_{m\in\mathbf{Z}^l}\phi(m)\Pi_{\alpha\in P}i(m|\tilde{\alpha})e^{i(m|h)}$$

where $\tau = \sum_{1\leq j\leq l}m_j\pi_j$ and $H = \sum_{1\leq j\leq l}h_j(iH_j)$. If $\frac{\partial}{\partial\tilde{\alpha}}$ is the derivative in the direction of $\tilde{\alpha}$ on $\mathbb{R}^l$ the differential operator $\partial(\pi) = \Pi_{\alpha\in P}\frac{\partial}{\partial\tilde{\alpha}}$ is a linear differential operator of order m with constant coefficients. By (3.2) and (3.4) we get

$$(3.5)\qquad \|\phi(\cdot+\rho)\|_{m_1(G)} \leq C_1\int_{Q_1}\left|\partial(\pi)\left(\sum_{m\in\mathbf{Z}^l}\phi(m)e^{i(m|h)}\right)\right|dh.$$

For $N\in\mathbb{N}^l$ let $\Pi_N$ be the space of all trigonometric polynomials on $\mathbb{T}^l$ of degree $\le N$. $\Pi_N$ is generated by the characters $e^{i(m|h)}$ of $\mathbb{T}^l$ with $|m_j|\le N_j$, $1\le j\le l$. For $l=1$ the classical Bernstein inequality states that

$$\|(d/dx)^r f\|_{L_1(\mathbb{T})} \le N^r \|f\|_{L_1(\mathbb{T})} \qquad (f\in\Pi_N,\ r\in\mathbb{N}). \tag{3.6}$$

For $l\ge 1$ every polynomial $f$ in $\Pi_N$ is a polynomial of degree $\le N_j$ in the variable $h_j$. Hence we have the $l$-dimensional analogue of (3.6)

$$\|D^k f\|_{L_1(T^l)} \le \left(\Pi_{1\le j\le l} N_j^{k_j}\right) \|f\|_{L_1(\mathbb{T}^l)} \qquad (f\in\Pi_N) \tag{3.7}$$

where

$$D^k f = \frac{\partial^{|k|_1} f}{\partial h_1^{k_1} \cdots \partial h_l^{k_l}} \qquad (k\in\mathbb{N}^l) \tag{3.8}$$

with $|k|_1=\sum_{1\le j\le l} k_j$. Now we prove that (3.3) follows from (3.5) and the $l$-dimensional Bernstein inequality (3.7). The trigonometric polynomial $\sum_{m\in Z^l}\phi(m)e^{i(m|h)}$ belongs to $\Pi_N$ with $N=([R],\dots,[R])$. Since $\partial(\pi)$ is a linear combination of differential operators of type (3.8) with $|k|_1\le m$ we get

$$\int_{Q_l} \left|\partial(\pi)\left(\sum_{m\in\mathbb{Z}^l}\phi(m)e^{i(m\,h)}\right)\right| dh \le CR^m \|\phi\|_{m_1(\mathbb{T}^l)}.$$

This proves our assertion.

## 4. Applications of the Transference Result

We are going to give two main applications for our Lemma 3.2. It is well known how to deduce theorems on uniform convergence of partial sums of Fourier series on G from Jackson theorems combined with non trivial estimates of the corresponding Lebesgue constants (cf.[5]). Our first application is a transference result for certain Lebesgue constants on G. Let $\mathbb{K}$ be the set of all compact Weyl group invariant subsets K of $\mathbb{R}^l$ with $0\in\mathring{K}$ and $aK\subset K$ for $0\le a\le 1$ and denote the characteristic function of a set $K\in\mathbb{K}$ by $1_K$. We call the numbers

$$(4.1) \qquad L_R^K(G) = \| 1_K(\frac{\cdot+\rho}{R}) \|_{m_1(G)} \qquad (R > o)$$

the K Lebesgue constants on G.

THEOREM 4.1. *If* $K \in \mathbb{K}$, *then there exists a constant* C *independant of* R *such that*

$$(4.2) \qquad L_R^K(G) \leq CR^m \| 1_K(\frac{\cdot}{R}) \|_{m_1(\mathbf{T}^1)}.$$

PROOF. There exists a constant C' independent of R such that

$$\{h \in \mathbb{R}^1 : h \in RK\} \subset \{h \in \mathbb{R}^1 : |h| \leq C'R\}.$$

Hence (4.2) follows from (3.3).

We assign to $K \in \mathbb{K}$ the upper surface measure in the sense of Minkowski [6] of the boundary $\partial K$ of K which is defined by $\mu(\partial K) = \overline{\lim_{\varepsilon \to o}} \frac{dh(\partial K_\varepsilon)}{2\varepsilon}$ where $\partial K_\varepsilon$ is the union of all balls of radius $\varepsilon$ with centers in $\partial K$ (the $\varepsilon$-hull of $\partial K$). Then we have

COROLLARY 4.2. *Let* $\dim G = n$ *and* $\operatorname{rank} G = 1 \geq 2$. *Assume that* $K \in \mathbb{K}$ *has the property* $\mu(\partial K) < \infty$. *Then*

$$(4.3) \qquad L_R^K(G) = O(R^{(n-1)/2}) \quad (R \to \infty).$$

The proof follows from Theorem 4.1 and the estimate

$$L_R^K(\mathbf{T}^1) = \| 1_K(\frac{\cdot}{R}) \|_{m_1(\mathbf{T}^1)} = O(R^{(1-1)/2}) \qquad (R \to \infty)$$

of Yudin [16]. All compact and convex subsets K in $\mathbb{R}^1$ have the property $\mu(\partial K) < \infty$. For $K = \{h \in \mathbb{R}^1 : |h| \leq 1\}$ we proved (4.3) by a less elementary method in [5].

Define the difference operator $\Delta^\nu = \Delta_1^{\nu_1} \cdots \Delta_1^{\nu_1}$, $\nu = (\nu_1, \ldots, \nu_1) \in \mathbb{N}^1$, for functions $g : \mathbf{Z}^1 \to \mathbb{C}$ where $\Delta_j g(m) = g(m+e_j) - g(m)$ and $e_j$ is the jth unit vector in $\mathbf{Z}^1$. We introduce the spaces $1_p$ and $h_p^L$ corresponding to the norms

$$\| g \|_{1_p} = \left( \sum_{m \in \mathbf{Z}^1} |g(m)|^p \right)^{1/p},$$

$$\| g \|_{h_p^L} = \max_{|\nu|=L} \| \Delta^\nu g \|_{1_p}$$

and put

$$b_p^{s,q} = (1_p, h_p^L)_{s/L,q} \qquad (L > 0).$$

Concerning the interpolation spaces $( \cdot , \cdot )_{\theta, q}$ see [10].

THEOREM 4.3. *Let* $\phi$ *be as in Lemma* 3.2. *Then*

$$\| \phi(\cdot + \rho) \|_{m_1(G)} \leq CR^m \| \phi \|_{b_2^{n/2,1}} .$$

The proof follows from Lemma 3.2 and the estimate $\| \phi \|_{m_1(\mathbf{T}^1)} \leq C \| \phi \|_{b_2^{n/2,1}}$ on the standard torus $\mathbf{T}^1$ [9].

Theorem 4.3 has been proved by Vretare in [13] with different methods. The three multiplier theorems listed in [13] are consequences of Theorem 4.3 combined with estimates of the $b_2^{n/2,1}$ norm in [9].

## 5. A Divergence Result

According to the theorem of Banach-Steinhaus the convergence or divergence behaviour of the K partial sums of the Fourier series $\check{\phi}_R * f$ in $L_p(G)$, $1 \leq p < \infty$, where $\phi_R(\lambda) = 1_K(\frac{\lambda}{R})$, $\lambda \in G^\wedge$, depends on the boundedness or unboundedness of the norms $\| \phi_R \|_{m_p(G)}$.

THEOREM 5.1. *Let* $K \in \mathbb{K}$ *be Weyl group invariant and assume that the boundary* $\partial K$ *of* $K$ *in* $t$ *has Lebesgue measure zero. Then*

(5.1) $$\sup_{R > 0} \| \phi_R \|_{m_p(G)} = \infty$$

*for* $p \neq 2$.

PROOF. Suppose $\sup_{R>o} \| \phi_R \|_{m_p(G)} < \infty$. Since $dH(\partial K) = 0$ the function $1_K : \underline{t} \to \mathbb{R}$ is dH a.e. continuous. Define $K^G = \{X \in \underline{g}: X = \mathrm{Ad}gH,\ g \in G,\ H \in \underline{t}\}$. Using the passage theorem of Clerc [1;Theorem 9] gives that $1_{K^G} : \underline{g} \to \mathbb{R}$ is a $L_p$ multiplier on $\underline{g}$. The torus T operates on $\underline{g}$ via Ad by orthogonal transformations and $\underline{g}$ splits as a T-space in the form $\underline{g} = \underline{t} \oplus \sum_{1 \leq j \leq m} V_j$ where T acts on $\underline{t}$ trivially, $\dim V_j = 2$ $(1 \leq j \leq m)$, and T acts on $V_j$ as SO(2). Hence the assumption $K \in \mathbb{K}$ implies that the orthogonal projection $D_j = pr_{V_j} K^G$ is a non trivial disc in $V_j$ with center $0 \in V_j$. According to the restriction theorem of Jodeit [8] the characteristic function $1_{D_j} : V_j \to \mathbb{R}$ is a $L_p$ multiplier on $V_j$. In view of the negative $L_p$ multiplier result of Fefferman [7] for the unit disc this implies $p = 2$.

REMARK. Theorem 5.1 has been proved by Clerc [1] for spherical partial sums and by Stanton and Tomas [12] for polyhedral partial sums. Theorem 5.1 is the only result in this paper which does not extend to arbitrary compact connected Lie groups G, because this theorem is false in the abelian case $G = \mathbf{T}^1$.

## REFERENCES


[1] Clerc, J.L., Sommes de Riesz et multiplicateurs sur un groupe de Lie compact. Ann. Inst. Fourier, Grenoble 24 (1974), 149-172.

[2] Coifman, R.R. – Weiss, G., Central multiplier theorems for compact Lie groups. Bull. Amer. Math. Soc. 80 (1974), 124-126.

[3] Dreseler, B., Zu Entwicklungen nach sphärischen Funktionen gehörende Approximationsverfahren auf kompakten symmetrischen Mannigfaltigkeiten. Habilitationsschrift. Gesamthochschule Siegen 1976.

[4] Dreseler, B., On summation processes of Fourier expansions for spherical functions. In: Proceedings of the Conference at Oberwolfach April 25 – May 1, 1976. Lecture Notes in Math. 571 (1976), 65-84.

[ 5] Dreseler, B., Lebesgue constants for spherical partial sums of Fourier series on compact Lie groups. In: Proceedings of the Colloquium on Fourier Analysis and Approximation Theory, Budapest 1976 (to appear).

[ 6] Federer, H., Geometric measure theory. Springer Verlag. Berlin/Heidelberg/New York 1969.

[ 7] Fefferman, C., The multiplier problem for the ball. Ann. of Math. 94 (1971), 330-336.

[ 8] Jodeit, M., A note on Fourier multipliers. Proc. Amer. Math. Soc. 27 (1971), 423-424.

[ 9] Löfström, J.L., Besov spaces in theory of approximation. Ann. Mat. Pura Appl. 85 (1970), 93-184.

[10] Peetre, J., Applications de la théorie des espaces d'interpolation dans l'Analyse Harmonique. Ricerche Mat. 15 (1966), 3-36.

[11] Stanton, R.J., Mean convergence of Fourier series on compact Lie groups. Trans. Amer. Math. Soc. 218 (1976), 61-87.

[12] Stanton, R.J. Tomas, P.A., Convergence of Fourier series on compact Lie groups. Bull. Amer. Math. Soc. 82 (1976), 61-62.

[13] Vretare, L., On $L_p$ Fourier multipliers on compact Lie groups. Math. Scand. 35 (1974), 49-55.

[14] Wallach, N.R., Harmonic analysis on homogeneous spaces. Marcel Dekker, INC. New York 1973.

[15] Warner, G., Harmonic analysis on semi-simple Lie groups I. Springer Verlag. Berlin/Heidelberg/New York 1972.

[16] Yudin, V.A., Behaviour of Lebesgue constants. Math. Notes 17 (1975), 233-235.

# REAL FUNCTION METHODS IN FOURIER ANALYSIS

Miguel de Guzmán
Facultad de Matemáticas
Universidad Complutense de Madrid
Madrid

A short survey of some of the real variable methods recently developed in Fourier analysis for the study of the maximal operator associated to a sequence of operators.

## 1. Introduction

There is quite a number of important problems in Fourier analysis and in other areas in which a sequence (or generalized sequence) of operators arise in a natural way.

i) If $f \in L^1([0, 2\pi))$, $f$ periodic of period $2\pi$, the partial sums

$$S_k f(x) = \sum_{j=-k}^{k} c_j \, e^{ijx} \quad , \quad c_j = \frac{1}{\sqrt{2\pi}} \int_0^{2\pi} f(y) e^{-ijy} dy$$

of its Fourier series can be interpreted as the application of the operators $S_k$ to the function $f$.

ii) In an analogous way, the Cesaro sums

$$\sigma_k f(x) = \frac{S_0 f(x) + \ldots + S_k f(x)}{k+1}$$

can be interpreted as the application of the operators $\sigma_k$ to $f$.

iii) The Abel sums of the Fourier series of $f$ are

$$A_r f(x) = \sum_{j=-\infty}^{\infty} r^j c_j e^{ijx} \quad , \quad 0 < r < 1.$$

iv) If $f \in L^1(\mathbb{R}^n)$, $B(z,r) = \{x \in \mathbb{R}^n : |x-z| \leq r\}$ and $\phi_r(x) = \chi_{B(0,r)} / |B(0,r)|$, where $\chi_A$ means the characteristic function of the set $A$ and $|A|$ its Lebesgue measure, then

$$\Phi_r(x) = f * \phi_r(x) = \frac{1}{|B(0,r)|} \int_{y \in B(0,r)} f(x-y)dy$$

is the mean value of $f$ over $B(\dot{x}, r)$, considered in the theory of differentiation of integrals.

v) In a more general way, if $k \in L^1(\mathbb{R}^n)$, $\int k(y)dy = 1$, $k_\varepsilon(x) = \varepsilon^{-n}k(\frac{x}{\varepsilon})$ for $\varepsilon > 0$, then

$$K_\varepsilon f(x) = k_\varepsilon * f(x)$$

are the operators considered in the study of the approximations of the identity.

vi) If $f \in L^1(\mathbb{R}^n)$ and

$$h_\varepsilon(x) = \begin{cases} \frac{1}{x} & \text{if } |x| \geq \varepsilon > 0 \\ 0 & \text{if } |x| < \varepsilon \end{cases}$$

then

$$H_\varepsilon f(x) = h_\varepsilon * f(x) = \int_{|y|\geq\varepsilon} \frac{f(x-y)}{y} dy$$

is the truncated (at $\varepsilon$) Hilbert transform.

vii) If $k$ is a complex valued function defined on $\mathbb{R}^n - \{0\}$ such that

a) $k(\lambda x) = \lambda^{-n}k(x)$ for $\lambda > 0$, $x \in \mathbb{R}^n - \{0\}$,

b) $\int_{\bar{x}\in\Sigma} |k(\bar{x})| d\bar{x} < \infty$, $\int_\Sigma k(\bar{x})d\bar{x} = 0$, where $\Sigma = \{\bar{x} \in \mathbb{R}^n : |\bar{x}| = 1\}$,

c) $k_\varepsilon(x) = \begin{cases} k(x) & , \text{ if } |x| \geq \varepsilon > 0 \\ 0 & , \text{ if } |x| < \varepsilon \end{cases}$

then, for $f \in L(\mathbb{R}^n)$, $K_\varepsilon f(x) = k_\varepsilon * f(x)$ defines the truncated (at $\varepsilon$) Calderón-Zygmund transform of the function $f$ considered in the theory of singular integral operators.

One can place all these operators in the following general setting:

(a) We consider $(\Omega, \mathfrak{F}, \mu)$, a measure space that will be in some cases of finite measure and in some others $\sigma$-finite.

(b) We denote by $\mathfrak{M}$ the set of real (or complex) valued measurable functions from $\Omega$ to $\mathbb{R}$ (or to $\mathbb{C}$).

(c) With $X$ we denote a Banach space of measurable functions from $\Omega$ to $\mathbb{R}$ (or to $\mathbb{C}$).

(d) The sequence $\{T_k\}$ will be an ordinary sequence of operators from $X$ to $\mathfrak{M}$. In many cases there will be no problem in assuming $k$ to be a continuous parameter.

(e) Each $T_k$ will be assumed to be linear and, in some cases, just to satisfy the following condition: for $f_1, f_2 \in X$, $\lambda_1, \lambda_2 \in \mathbb{R}$, we have

$$|T_k(\lambda_1 f_1 + \lambda_2 f_2)| \leq |\lambda_1| \; |T_k f_1(x)| + |\lambda_2| \; |T_k f_2(x)|$$

(f) With $T^*$ we denote the maximal operator associated to the sequence $\{T_k\}$, i.e. for $f \in X$ and $x \in \Omega$,

$$T^*f(x) = \sup_k |T_k f(x)|$$

(g) With $T$ we design the limit operator when it exists in some sense.

The most natural question in this situation is the following:

<u>To find out whether</u>, <u>or under which non trivial additional conditions</u> <u>on</u> $f$ <u>or on the operators</u> $T_k$, <u>the corresponding sequence</u> $T_k f(x)$ <u>converges for every</u> $x$ <u>or for almost every</u> $x$ <u>of</u> $\Omega$, <u>and what are the properties of the limit function</u> $Tf(x)$.

It is not difficult to show that this problem is deeply connected with the properties of the maximal operator $T^*$.

In the following we shall state without proof, some results that show how the behaviour of $T^*$ governs that of the sequence $\{T_k\}$.

## 2. Finiteness a.e. of the maximal operator and pointwise convergence

The first result is a very general theorem according to which, if one has the finiteness a.e. of $T^*f(x)$ for every $f \in X$, it is sufficient to establish the a.e. convergence of the sequence $\{T_k g\}$ for a set of nice functions $g \in X$ in order to have it for the whole of $X$.

THEOREM 2.1. *Let* $(\Omega, \mathcal{F}, \mu)$ *be a measure space,* $\mathcal{M}(\Omega)$ *the set of real (or complex) valued measurable functions. Let* $X$ *be a complete normed subspace of* $\mathcal{M}$. *Let* $\{T_k\}$ *be a sequence of linear operators, continuous in measure, from* $X$ *to* $\mathcal{M}$ *and* $T^*$ *its maximal operator.*

*Then, if for each* $f \in X$, $T^*f(x) < \infty$ *at a.e.* $x \in \Omega$, *the set* $E$ *of functions* $f \in X$ *such that* $\{T_k f(x)\}$ *converges at a.e.* $x \in \Omega$ *is closed in* $X$.

Also interesting is the fact that the continuity in measure of $T^*$ implies already that the set of functions $f \in X$ such that $\{T_k f(x)\}$ converges at a.e. $x \in \Omega$ is closed in $X$. It does not require that $X$ be a Banach space.

THEOREM 2.2. *Let* $(\Omega, \mathcal{F}, \mu)$ *be a measure space. Let* $\mathcal{M}$ *be the set of real (or complex) valued measurable functions defined on* $\Omega$. *Let* $X$ *be a normed subspace of* $\mathcal{M}$. *Let* $\{T_k\}$ *be a sequence of linear operators from* $X$ *to* $\mathcal{M}$ *and* $T^*$ *its maximal operator. Assume that* $T^*$ *is continuous in measure from* $X$ *to* $\mathcal{M}$. *Then the set* $E \subset X$ *of functions of* $X$ *such that* $\{T_k f\}$ *converges a.e. is closed in* $X$.

## 3. Finiteness a.e. and the type of the maximal operator

In order to obtain some knowledge about the type of the limit operator $T$, when it exists, it is of interest to know that in many cases one can determine, starting from the finiteness of $T^*$, the type of $T^*$ by looking at the particular structure of the operators $T_k$. This is the philosophy of the following three results. The first one, which contains the main idea of the others is due to A.P. Calderón (Cf. [10] p.165). The other results are due to Stein [6] and to Sawyer [5]. All three are based on some commutativity property of the operators $T_k$ with certain transformations acting on $\Omega$, in the sense specified below.

THEOREM 3.1. *For* $f$ *periodic of period* $2\pi$ *and in* $L^2([0, 2\pi))$ *let*

$$S_N f(x) = \sum_{-N}^{N} c_k e^{ikx}$$

be the N-th partial sum of its Fourier series. Let S* be the corresponding maximal operator, i.e.

$$S^*f(x) = \sup_N |S_N f(x)|.$$

Then $S_N f(x)$ converges a.e. as $N \to \infty$ if and only if S* is of weak type (2,2).

The following version of Stein's theorem is due to Sawyer [5]. The more or less common setting for the two next theorems is the following:

(a) $(\Omega, \mathfrak{F}, \mu)$ will be a measure space with $\mu(\Omega) = 1$.

(b) $\{T_k\}$ is a sequence of linear operators frome some $L^p(\Omega)$ to $\mathfrak{M}(\Omega)$, that are continuous in measure.

(c) We assume that there is a family of mappings $(\xi_\alpha)_{\alpha \in I}$ from $\Omega$ to $\Omega$ that are measure preserving.

(d) We also assume that $(\xi_\alpha)_{\alpha \in I}$ is a mixing family of mappings in the following sense: If $A, B \in \mathfrak{F}$ and $\rho > 1$, then there exists $\xi_\alpha$ such that $\mu(A \cap \xi_\alpha^{-1}(B)) \leq \rho\mu(A)\mu(B)$.

(e) We assume that $\{T_k\}$ and $(\xi_\alpha)_{\alpha \in I}$ commute in the following sense: If $f \in L^p(\Omega)$ and $\xi_\alpha f(x) \equiv f(\xi_\alpha x)$, then $T_k \xi_\alpha = \xi_\alpha T_k$.

Stein's theorem is as follows:

THEOREM 3.2. Let $(\Omega, \mathfrak{F}, \mu)$ be a measure space with $\mu(\Omega) = 1$. Let $T_k$ be a sequence of linear operators from some $L^p(\Omega)$, $1 \leq p \leq 2$, to $(\Omega)$. Let $(\xi_\alpha)_{\alpha \in I}$ be a measure preserving family of mappings from $\Omega$ to $\Omega$, that mix the measurable sets of $\Omega$. Assume that $\{T_k\}$ commute with $(\xi_\alpha)_{\alpha \in I}$. Then the two following conditions are equivalent:

(a) For each $f \in L^p(\Omega)$, $T^*f(x) < \infty$, a.e.

(b) $T^*$ is of weak type $(p, p)$.

The theorem of Sawyer removes some restrictions in Stein's theorem at the price of considering only positive operators.

THEOREM 3.3. Let $(\Omega, \mathfrak{F}, \mu)$ be a measure space with $\mu(\Omega) = 1$. Let $\{T_k\}$ be a sequence of linear positive operators from some $L^p(\Omega)$, $1 \leq p < \infty$, to $\mathfrak{M}(\Omega)$. Assume that the operators $\{T_k\}$ commute with a family $(\xi_\alpha)_{\alpha \in I}$ of measure preserving mappings from $\Omega$ to $\Omega$, that mix the measurable sets of $\Omega$. Then the two following conditions are equivalent

(a) $T^*$ is of weak type $(p, p)$.

(b) For each $f \in L^p(\Omega)$, $T^*f(x) < \infty$, a.e.

## 4. General techniques for the study of the maximal operator

The philosophy of the above results has been the following: If $T^*$ is a.e. finite and if the structure of $T_k$ is such and such, then $T_k f$ converges a.e. But, how can one find out whether $T^*$ is a.e. finite? We now turn out attention to some techniques that can be employed to find and answer to this question.

The first observation is that in many cases we can restrict our consideration to a dense subspace.

THEOREM 4.1. Let $(\Omega, \mathfrak{F}, \mu)$ be a measure space, $\mathfrak{M}(\Omega)$ the set of measurable real (or complex) valued functions, $X$ a normed space of functions in $\mathfrak{M}(\Omega)$ and $S$ a dense subspace of $X$. Let $\{T_k\}_{k=1}$ be a sequence of sublinear operators from $X$ to $\mathfrak{M}(\Omega)$ that are continuous in measure. Let $T^*$ be their maximal operator.

Then, if $T^*$ is of weak type $(p, p)$ over $S$ for some $p$, $1 \leq p < \infty$, it is of weak type $(p, p)$ (over $X$). If $T^*$ is of type $(p, p)$ over $S$ for some $p$, $1 \leq p < \infty$, it is of type $(p, p)$ (over $X$).

Here, and in the following, we say that $T^*$ is of weak type $(p, q)$, $1 \leq p \leq \infty$, $1 \leq q < \infty$, when for each $\lambda > 0$ and $f \in L^p(\Omega)$, we have

$$\mu\{x: T^*f(x) > \lambda\} \leq (c \frac{\|f\|_p}{\lambda})^q$$

with $c > 0$ independent of $f$ and $\lambda$. We also say that $T^*$ is of type $(p, q)$, $1 \leq p \leq \infty$, $1 \leq q \leq \infty$, when $\|T^*f\|_q \leq c \|f\|_p$ with $c$ in independent of $f$.

Particularly useful for dealing with the maximal operator $T^*$ are certain covering theorems of which we just offer an example essentially due to Besicovitch [1].

THEOREM 4.2. Let $A$ be a bounded set in $\mathbb{R}^n$. For each $x \in A$ a closed cubic interval $Q(x)$ centered at $x$ is given. Then one can choose, from among the given intervals $(Q(x))_{x \in A}$, a sequence $\{Q_k\}$ (possibly finite) such that:

i) The set $A$ is covered by the sequence, i.e. $A \subset \cup Q_k$.

ii) No point of $\mathbb{R}^n$ is in more than $\Theta_n$ (a number that only depends on $n$) cubes of the sequence $\{Q_k\}$, i.e. for every $z \in \mathbb{R}^n$

$$\sum \chi_{Q_k}(z) \leq \Theta_n \quad .$$

iii) The sequence $\{Q_k\}$ can be distributed in $\xi_n$ (a number that depends only on $n$) families of disjoint cubes.

Certain de-composition lemmas are also extremely useful when dealing with maximal operators. The classic one here is the following, due to Calderón and Zygmund [2].

THEOREM 4.3. Let $f$ be a function in $L^1(\mathbb{R}^n)$, $f \geq 0$, $\lambda > 0$. Then there exists a countable disjoint family (possibly empty) of half-open cubic intervals $\{Q_k\}_{k\geq 1}$ such that for each $k$

$$\lambda < \frac{1}{|Q_k|} \int_{Q_k} f \leq 2^n \lambda$$

and $f(x) \leq \lambda$ at almost each $x \notin \cup Q_k$.

Weak type inequalities present sometimes certain undesirable aspects, which make them difficult to handle. One can replace them by strong type inequalities according to the following result.

THEOREM 4.4. *Let* T *be a sublinear operator from* $\mathfrak{M}(\Omega)$ *to* $\mathfrak{M}(\Omega)$. *Assume that* T *is of weak type* (p, s), $1 \leq p$, $s < \infty$ *with constant* c. *Then, if* $0 < \sigma < s$ *and* A *is any measurable subset of* $\Omega$ *with finite measure, we have, for each* $f \in \mathfrak{M}(\Omega)$, *the following inequality,*

$$\int_A |Tf(x)|^\sigma \, d\mu(x) \leq c^\sigma \frac{s}{s-\sigma} |A|^{1-\sigma/s} \|f\|_p^\sigma$$

*Conversely, if* T *satisfies this inequality for some* $\sigma$, $0 < \sigma < s$, *and for each* $f \in L^p(\Omega)$ *and each* $A \subset \Omega$ *with* $\mu(A) < \infty$, *then* T *is of weak type* (p, s).

## 5. Interpolation, extrapolation, linearization

The common feature in the techniques of interpolation and extrapolation is the following. Assume that we know that an operator T behaves well on some spaces of a certain family of function spaces. Can one say anything about its behaviour on the intermediate spaces of that family (interpolation) or on the extreme cases of that family (extrapolation)?

Certain methods of functional analysis apply only when the operators in question are linear. The maximal operator T* is not linear and therefore in many cases one utilizes a technique consisting in majorizing it by another one that is so. This is the linearization technique.

Among the wellknown theorems on interpolation are the Riesz-Thorin and the Marcinkiewicz theorems. Here we state a result of Stein and Weiss [7]. Then, in order to show how the linearization technique can work, we extend it to the nonlinear maximal operators.

That T is of restricted weak type (p, q) in these theorems means that T is of weak type (p, q) when restricted to characteristic functions of measurable sets.

THEOREM 5.1. *Let* $T$ *be a linear operator from* $\mathfrak{M}(\Omega)$ *to* $\mathfrak{M}(\Omega)$, *of restricted weak types* $(p_0, q_0)$ *and* $(p_1, q_1)$ *with* $1 \le p_0 \le q_0 < \infty$, $1 \le p_1 \le q_1 < < \infty$, $q_0 \neq q_1$. *Let* $0 < s < 1$ *and* $\frac{1}{p_s} = \frac{1}{p_0}(1-s) + \frac{1}{p_1} s$, $\frac{1}{q_s} = \frac{1}{q_0}(1-s) + \frac{1}{q_1} s$. *Then* $T$ *is of strong type* $(p_s, q_s)$

THEOREM 5.2. *Let* $\{T_k\}_{k=1}^{\infty}$ *be a sequence of linear operators from* $\mathfrak{M}(\Omega)$ *to* $\mathfrak{M}(\Omega)$. *Let* $T^*$ *be their maximal operator. Assume that* $T^*$ *is of restricted weak types* $(p_0, q_0)$ *and* $(p_1, q_1)$, *with* $1 \le p_0 \le q_0 < \infty$, $1 \le p_1 \le q_1 < \infty$, $q_0 \neq q_1$. *Then* $T^*$ *is of strong type* $(p_s, q_s)$ *with* $0 < s < 1$, $\frac{1}{p_s} = \frac{1}{p_0}(1-s) + \frac{1}{p_1} s$, $\frac{1}{q_s} = \frac{1}{q_0}(1-s) + \frac{1}{q_1} s$.

PROOF. Let $\psi : \Omega \to \mathbb{N}$ be any arbitrary measurable function. For $g \in \mathfrak{M}(\Omega)$ and $x \in \Omega$ we define $T_\psi g(x) = T_{\psi(x)} g(x)$. The operator $T$ so defined is obviously linear from $\mathfrak{M}(\Omega)$ to $\mathfrak{M}(\Omega)$. We clearly have, for each $x \in \Omega$ and $g \in \mathfrak{M}(\Omega)$,

$$|T_\psi g(x)| \le T^* g(x)$$

and so $T_\psi$ is majorized by $T^*$. Hence $T_\psi$ is of restricted weak types $(p_0, q_0)$, $(p_1, q_1)$ with the same constants as $T^*$, i.e. with constants independent of $\psi$. Hence, by Theorem 1.5., $T_\psi$ is of strong type $(p_s, q_s)$ with constant independent of $\psi$.

Let now $f \in L^{p_s}$. We choose $\phi : \Omega \to \mathbb{N}$ measurable such that $T^* f(x) \le 2\, |T_\phi f(x)|$ for each $x \in \Omega$. (To do this define $\phi(x)$ on the set $\{x \in \Omega : 2^{k+1} \ge T^* f(x) > 2^k\}$ as the first $j$ such that $|T_j f(x)| > 2^k$). Thus we have

$$\| T^* f \|_{q_s} \le 2\, \| T_\phi f \|_{q_s} \le c\, \| f \|_{p_s}$$

with $c$ independent of $f$. So $T^*$ is of strong type $(p_s, q_s)$.

The extrapolation technique will be exemplified with the following result due to Yano [8].

THEOREM 5.3. *Let* $T$ *be a sublinear operator from* $\mathcal{M}(\Omega)$ *to* $\mathcal{M}(\Omega)$. *Assume that* $T$ *is of restricted type* $(p, p)$, $1 < p < 2$, *with constant* $c(p)$ *that satisfies the following inequality*: $c(p) \leq c/(p-1)^s$ *for some* $s > 0$.

*Then* $T$ *satisfies the following condition*: *For any measurable subset* $X$ *of* $\Omega$ *with* $\mu(X) < \infty$ *and for any* $f \in L(1 + \log^+ L)^s$ *we have*

$$\int_X |Tf| \leq c_1(1+ (X)) + c_2\int_X |f| \, (1+\log^+|f|)^s$$

*with* $c_1$, $c_2$ *independent of* $X$ *and* $f$.

## 6. Especial techniques for convolution operators

Many of the operators of interest in Fourier Analysis are operators of convolution type. In particular all operators which appear in the Introduction as motivation for this whole work are of such type.

We consider a sequence or generalized sequence of functions $\{k_j\} \subset \subset L^1(\Omega)$ (kernels) where $\Omega$ will be here either the n-dimensional torus $\mathbb{T}^n$ or $\mathbb{R}^n$ ($\Omega$ could be as well a locally compact group) and for a function $f \in L^p(\Omega)$, $1 \leq p < \infty$, we define

$$K_j f(x) = k_j * f(x) .$$

We ask about the convergence of $K_j f$ in $L^p$ or pointwise. In order to treat the convergence in $L^p$ we are led to consider $\|K_j f\|_p$, as explained in the Introduction, and to study the pointwise convergence we are led to investigate the behaviour of $K^*$ defined by

$$K^*f(x) = \sup_j |k_j * f(x)|.$$

It is therefore quite interesting to know that the problem can be reduced to the study of the action of the operators $K_j$ or $K^*$ over finite sums of Dirac deltas concentrated at different points of $\Omega$ (for the weak or strong type (1, 1)) and over linear combinations of Dirac deltas (for the weak or strong type $(p, p)$, $1 < p < \infty$). This reduction permits the discretization of the operators in question, which greatly simplifies their study, as we shall show later. The results in these two sections appear here for the first time.

THEOREM 6.1. *Let* $\{k_j\}_{j=1}^{\infty} \subset L^1(\Omega)$ *be an ordinary sequence of functions* $\{K_j\}_{j=1}^{\infty}$ *the sequence of convolution operators associated to it and* $K^*$ *the corresponding maximal operator.*

*Then* $K^*$ *is of weak type* (1, 1) *if and only if* $K^*$ *is of weak type* (1, 1) *over finite sums of Dirac deltas.*

*In other words (forgetting about Dirac deltas)* $K^*$ *is of weak type* (1, 1) *if and only if there exists* $c > 0$ *such that, for each finite set of different points* $a_1, a_2, \ldots, a_H \in \Omega$ *and for each* $\lambda > 0$, *we have*

$$|\{x \in \Omega: \sup_j |\sum_{h=1}^{H} k_j(x-a_h)| > \lambda\}| \leq c \frac{H}{\lambda} .$$

For $p > 1$ one has the following result.

THEOREM 6.2. *Let* $\{k_j\}_{j=1}^{\infty} \subset L^1(\Omega)$ *and* $K_j f(x) = k_j * f(x)$ *for* $f \in L^p(\Omega)$, $1 < p < \infty$. *Let* $K^*f(x) = \sup_j |K_j f(x)|$. *Assume that* $K^*$ *is of weak type* (p, p) *over linear combinations of Dirac deltas, in the following sense: There exists* $c > 0$ *such that for each*

$$f = \sum_{h=1}^{H} c_h \delta_h$$

*and each* $\lambda > 0$.

$$|\{x: K^*f(x) > \lambda\}| = |\{x: \sup_j |\sum_{h=1}^{H} c_h k_j(x-a_h)| > \lambda\}| \leq c \frac{\sum_1^H |c_h|^p}{\lambda^p} .$$

*Then* $K^*$ *is of weak type* (p, p) .

In order to show the power of the method we shall present here a very simple proof of the fact that the maximal Hilbert transform is of weak type (1, 1).

LEMMA 6.3. *Let* $a_j \in \mathbb{R}$, $j = 1,2,3,\ldots, N$ *and* $\lambda > 0$. *Let* $f = \sum_{j=1}^{N} \delta_j$ *where* $\delta_j$ *is the Dirac delta concentrated* at $a_j$. *Then*

$$|\{x: |Hf(x)| > \lambda\}| = |\{x: |\sum_{j=1}^{N} \frac{1}{x-a_j}| > \lambda\}| = \frac{2N}{\lambda}$$

PROOF. By looking at the graph of the function $y = \sum_{j=1}^{N} \frac{1}{x-a_j}$

it is quite clear that $|\{x: \sum_{j=1}^{N} \frac{1}{x-a_j} > \lambda\}| = \sum_{j=1}^{N} (y_i - a_j)$ where $y_j$, $j = 1,2,\ldots, N$, are the roots of the equation

$$\sum_{j=1}^{N} \frac{1}{x-a_j} = \lambda, \quad \text{i.e. of} \quad \lambda \prod_{j=1}^{N} (x - a_j) = \\ = \sum_{j=1}^{N} \prod_{\substack{j\neq k \\ k=1}}^{N} (x-a_k)$$

From here we easily obtain $\sum_{j=1}^{N} y_j = \frac{N}{\lambda} + \sum_{j=1}^{N} a_j$. Hence $\sum_{j=1}^{N} (y_j - a_j) = = \frac{N}{\lambda}$. Thus we get

$$|\{x: |\sum_{j=1}^{N} \frac{1}{x-a_j}| > \lambda\}| = |\{\sum_{1}^{N} \frac{1}{s-a_j} > \lambda\}| + |\{\sum_{1}^{N} \frac{1}{x-a_j} < -\lambda\}| = \\ = \frac{2N}{\lambda},$$

since the second term can be handled as the first one.

The above lemma is due to Loomis [4].

THEOREM 6.4. <u>The maximal Hilbert operator</u> $H^*$ <u>is of weak type</u> (1, 1).

PROOF. According to Theorem 6.1. it is sufficient to prove that $H^*$ is of weak type (1, 1) over finite sums of Dirac deltas. Let $a_j \in \mathbb{R}$, $j=1,2,..N$, $\lambda > 0$, and $f = \sum_{j=1}^{N} \delta_j$, where $\delta_j$ is the Dirac delta concentrated at $a_j$. We have to prove that

$$|\{x: H^*f(x) > \lambda\}| = |\{x: \sup_{\varepsilon>0} |\sum_{j=1}^{N} h\,(x-a_j)| > \lambda\}| \leq c\,\frac{N}{\lambda}$$

with $c$ independent of $f$ and $\lambda$.

We take an arbitrary compact set $K$ contained in $\{x: H^*f(x) > \lambda\} - \{a_1, a_2, \ldots, a_N\}$. If $x \in K$, there exists $\varepsilon(x) > 0$ such that $|H_{\varepsilon(x)} f(x)| > \lambda$. We take a finite number of disjoint intervals $I_j = [x_j - \varepsilon(x_j), x_j + \varepsilon(x_j)]$, such that $|K| \leq 2\,|\bigcup_{1}^{M} I_j|$. For each $j=1,2,..,M$, let $f_j = f\chi_{I_j}$ and $f = f_j + \tilde{f}_j$. We easily see that

$$H_{\varepsilon(x_j)} f(x_j) = Hf(x_j) - Hf_j(x_j) = H\tilde{f}_j(x_j)$$

and so $|H\tilde{f}_j(x_j)| > \lambda$. Now the function $H\tilde{f}_j(\cdot)$ is decreasing over $I_j$, since $H\tilde{f}_j(\cdot)$ has no singularity over $I_j$. Thus $|H\tilde{f}_j(y)| > \lambda$ for each $y$ in $[x_j, x_j + \varepsilon(x_j)]$ or for each $y$ in $[x_j - \varepsilon(x_j), x_j]$.

We can write

$$|K| \leq 2 \left|\bigcup_1^M I_j\right| \leq 4 \left|\bigcup_1^M (\tfrac{1}{2} I_j)\right| \leq 4 \left|\bigcup_1^M \{|H\tilde{f}_j| > \lambda\}\right|$$

We shall try to estimate the last set. We have

$$H\tilde{f}_j = Hf - Hf_j$$

and so

$$\{|H\tilde{f}_j| > \lambda\} \subset \{|Hf| > \tfrac{\lambda}{2}\} \cup \{|Hf_j| > \tfrac{\lambda}{2}\} .$$

Hence

$$\bigcup_1^M \{|H\tilde{f}_j| > \lambda\} \subset \{|Hf| > \tfrac{\lambda}{2}\} \cup (\sum_{j=1}^M \{|Hf_j| > \tfrac{\lambda}{2}\}) .$$

Therefore we can set, using Lemma 6.3.,

$$|K| \leq 4(\frac{4}{\lambda} \|f\|_1 + \frac{4}{\lambda} \sum_1^M \|f_j\|_1) = \frac{32}{\lambda} \|f\|_1 .$$

Since $|K|$ is arbitrarily close to $|\{H^*f > \lambda\}|$ we get our theorem.

## 7. Approximation kernels

Many approximation problems take the following form. To find out whether or under which conditions on $k \in L^1(\mathbb{R}^n)$, $\int k = 1$, the convolution integral $k_\varepsilon * f$, where $k_\varepsilon(x) = \varepsilon^{-n} k(x/\varepsilon)$, $\varepsilon > 0$, and $f \in L^p(\mathbb{R}^n)$, converges to $f$. It is rather easy to prove that $k * f \to f$ in the $L^p$-norm as $\varepsilon \to 0$. A more delicate problem consists in obtaining the pointwise convergence. Calderón and Zygmund [2] have given a rather general result.

THEOREM 7.1. *Let* $k \in L^1(\mathbb{R}^n)$, $k \geq 0$, $k_\varepsilon(x) = \varepsilon^{-n}k(x/\varepsilon)$. *Assume* $k$ *radial* $(k(x) = k(y)$, if $|x| = |y|)$ *and nonincreasing along rays* (*i.e.* $k(x) \geq k(y)$, *if* $|x| \leq |y|)$. *For* $f \in L^p(\mathbb{R}^n)$, $1 \leq p \leq \infty$, *let*

$$K^*f(x) = \sup_{\varepsilon>0} |k_\varepsilon * f(x)|$$

*Then* $K^*$ *is of type* $(\infty, \infty)$, *of weak type* $(1, 1)$ *and therefore of strong type* $(p, p)$, $1 < p < \infty$. *Hence if* $\int k = 1$, *for* $f \in L^p(\mathbb{R}^n)$, $1 \leq p < \infty$, $k_\varepsilon * f(x) \to f(x)$, *a.e.* $x \in \mathbb{R}^n$.

When the approximation kernel $k$ is not radial and its radial majorization is not in $L^1(\mathbb{R}^n)$, one can still get some general pointwise convergence results with suitable conditions on $k$. One of the results in this direction belongs to R. Coifman.

THEOREM 7.2. *Let* $k \in L^1(\mathbb{R}^n)$, $k \geq 0$, *be such that for each* $\bar{x}$ *with* $|\bar{x}| = 1$, *the function of* $r \geq 0$, $k(r\bar{x})r^{-\alpha}$ *is nonincreasing in* $r$ *with some* $\alpha$ *independent of* $\bar{x}$. *Then the maximal operator* $K^*$ *defined through*

$$K^*f(x) = \sup_{\varepsilon>0} |k_\varepsilon * f(x)|, \quad \textit{where} \quad k_\varepsilon(x) = \varepsilon^{-n}(\frac{x}{\varepsilon})$$

*is of strong type* $(p, p)$, $1 < p \leq \infty$. *Hence if* $\int k = 1$, $k_\varepsilon * f(x) \to f(x)$ *at almost every* $x \in \mathbb{R}^n$ *for each* $f \in L^p(\mathbb{R}^n)$ $1 < p < \infty$.

Another generalization of the theorem of Calderón and Zygmund has been obtained by Felipe Zo [9].

THEOREM 7.3. *Let* $(k_\alpha)_{\alpha \in I}$ *be a family of functions in* $L^1(\mathbb{R}^n)$ *such that*

i) *There exists* $c_1 > 0$ *such that* $\int |k_\alpha(x)| dx \leq c_1 < \infty$ *for each* $\alpha$.

ii) *If* $\phi(x, y) = \sup_\alpha |k_\alpha(x-y) - k_\alpha(x)|$, *then* $\int_{|x| \geq 4|y|} \phi(x,y)dx \leq c_2 < \infty$, *with* $c_2$ *independent of* $y \in \mathbb{R}^n$.

*Then, if* $K^*f(x) = \sup_{\alpha \in I} |k_\alpha * f(x)|$, $K^*$ *is of weak type* $(1, 1)$ *and of strong type* $(1, 1)$ *for* $1 < p < \infty$.

There are many other recent real function methods that will be more systematically treated in a forthcoming work [3] by the author. Perhaps the ones we have examined here give already an idea of the wealth of the techniques created in the last decades in this field.

## REFERENCES


[1] Besicovitch, A.S., A general form of the covering principle and relative differentiation of additive functions, Proc. Cambridge Philos. Soc. 41 (1945), 103-110.

[2] Calderón, A.P. and Zygmund, A., On the existence of certain singular integrals, Acta Math. 88 (1952), 85-139.

[3] de Guzmán, M., Real Function Methods in Fourier Analysis (book in preparation).

[4] Loomis, L.H., A note on the Hilbert transform, Bull. Amer. Math. Soc. 52 (1946), 1082-1086.

[5] Sawyer, S., Maximal inequalities of weak type, Ann. Math. 84 (1966), 157-173.

[6] Stein, E.M., On limits of sequences of operators, Ann. Math. 74 (1961), 140-170.

[7] Stein, E.M. and Weiss, G., An extension of a theorem of Marcinkiewicz and some of its applications, J. Math. Mech. 8 (1959), 263-284.

[8] Yano, S., An extrapolation theorem, J. Math. Soc. Japan 3 (1951), 296-305.

[9] Zo, F., A note on approximation of the identity, Studia Math. 55 (1976), 111-122.

[10] Zygmund, A., Trigonometric series, vol.II, Cambridge University Press, Cambridge 1959.

# LIPSCHITZ CONTINUITY OF SPHERICAL MEANS

Per Sjölin
Department of Mathematics
Stockholm University
Stockholm

The purpose of this paper is to give a new proof of a theorem of J. Peyrière concerning the regularity of spherical means of functions in $L^p_{loc}(R^n)$.

For $f \in L^1_{loc}(R^n)$ we set

$$F_x(t) = \int_{S^{n-1}} f(x - ty)d\sigma(y) , \qquad (x \in R^n, t > 0)$$

where $\sigma$ denotes the surface measure on $S^{n-1}$. It follows from Fubini's theorem that for every $x \in R^n$ $F_x(t)$ is well-defined for almost all t. We let the space $\Lambda_\alpha(R)$, $\alpha > 0$, be defined as in E.M. Stein [2], i.e. a function $g \in L^\infty(R)$ belongs to $\Lambda_\alpha(R)$ if its Poisson integral u(t,y), $t \in R$, $y > 0$, satisfies

$$\|g\|_{\Lambda_\alpha} = \|g\|_\infty + \sup_{t,y} y^{k-\alpha} \left|\frac{\partial^k u}{\partial y^k}(t,y)\right| < \infty ,$$

where k is the smallest integer greater than $\alpha$. We also say that a function g defined and measurable on $(0,\infty)$ belongs to $\Lambda^{loc}_\alpha((0,\infty))$ if $\phi g \in \Lambda_\alpha(R)$ for every $C^\infty$ function $\phi$ with support in the interval $(0,\infty)$. J. Peyrière has proved the following theorem (see J. Peyrière and P. Sjölin [1]).

THEOREM. <u>Assume</u> $n \geqslant 3$, $n/(n-1) < p \leqslant 2$ <u>and</u> $f \in L^p_{loc}(R^n)$. <u>If</u> $\alpha < n(1-1/p) - 1$ <u>then</u> $F_x \in \Lambda^{loc}_\alpha((0,\infty))$ <u>for almost every</u> $x \in R^n$.

The purpose of this paper is to give an alternative proof of this theorem by use of an identity in E.M. Stein [3].

We define the Fourier transform $\hat{f}$ of a function $f \in \mathcal{S}(R^n)$ by setting

$$\hat{f}(\xi) = \int_{R^n} e^{-2\pi i\xi\cdot x} f(x)dx \qquad (\xi \in R^n).$$

We also define distributions $m_\alpha \in \mathcal{S}'(R^n)$, $\alpha > 1/2 - n/2$, by setting

$$\hat{m}_\alpha(\xi) = \pi^{-\alpha+1}|\xi|^{-n/2-\alpha+1} J_{n/2+\alpha-1}(2\pi|\xi|) ,$$

where $J_a$ denotes the Bessel function of order a. Then let the operators $M_t^\alpha$, $t > 0$, be defined by

$$(M_t^\alpha f)\hat{}(\xi) = \hat{m}_\alpha(t\xi)\, \hat{f}(\xi) \qquad (\xi \in R^n, f \in \mathcal{S}(R^n)).$$

Then $F_x(t) = c\, M_t^0 f(x)$ for some constant c and

$$(1) \qquad F_x(t) = c_{\alpha'} \int_0^1 M_{st}^{\alpha'} f(x)\, (1-s^2)^{-\alpha'-1} s^{n+2\alpha'-1} ds \qquad (x \in R^n, t > 0),$$

for $f \in \mathcal{S}(R^n)$ and $\alpha' < 0$, where $c_{\alpha'}$ is a constant depending on $\alpha'$ (see [3]).

We shall now prove the theorem by use of the identity (1) with $\alpha' = -\alpha$. We assume that n, p and $\alpha$ satisfy the conditions in the theorem and set $\alpha_p = n(1 - 1/p) - 1$ so that $\alpha < \alpha_p$. Fix a $C^\infty$ function $\phi$ with support in the interval $[a,b]$, where $0 < a < b < \infty$, and let $f \in \mathcal{S}(R^n)$. Since $-\alpha > -\alpha_p$ it follows from Theorem 2 in [3] that

$$(2) \qquad \int_{R^n} (\sup_{t>0} |M_t^{-\alpha} f(x)|)^p dx \leq C_{p,\alpha} \int_{R^n} |f(x)|^p dx.$$

We may assume that $\alpha$ is not an integer and let $\ell$ denote the integral part of $\alpha$. Fixing x we set $g(t) = M_t^{-\alpha} f(x)$. We shall prove that

$$(3) \qquad \sum_{j=0}^{\ell} \sup_{a\leq t\leq b} |F_x^{(j)}(t)| + \sup_{a\leq s<t\leq b} \frac{|F_x^{(\ell)}(s) - F_x^{(\ell)}(t)|}{|s-t|^{\alpha-\ell}} \leq C\|g\|_\infty ,$$

where the constant C may depend on $\alpha$, a and b.

It follows from a change of variable in (1) that

$$F_x(t) = C\, t^{2-n} \int_0^t g(u)(t^2-u^2)^{\alpha-1} u^{n-2\alpha-1} du \; .$$

We denote the above integral by H(t). It is then clear that it is sufficient to prove (3) with $F_x$ replaced by H. Differentiating H we see that to prove (3) it is sufficient to prove that the functions

$$H_j(t) = \int_0^t g(u)(t^2-u^2)^{\alpha-j-1} u^{n-2\alpha-1} du$$

satisfy

(4) $$\sup_{a \leqslant t \leqslant b} |H_j(t)| \leqslant C \|g\|_\infty \qquad (j = 0,1,\ldots,\ell),$$

and

(5) $$|H_\ell(s) - H_\ell(t)| \leqslant C \|g\|_\infty |s-t|^{\alpha-\ell} \qquad (s,t \in [a,b]).$$

We have

$$\alpha - j - 1 \geqslant \alpha - \ell - 1 > -1 \; , \qquad (j = 0,1,\ldots,\ell),$$

and since $\alpha < \alpha_p$

$$n - 2\alpha - 1 > n - 2\alpha_p - 1 = n(2/p-1) + 1 \geqslant 1$$

and (4) is a consequence of these inequalities.

To prove (5) we set $\gamma = n - 2\alpha - 1$ and assume $a \leqslant t < t+\varepsilon \leqslant b$. We have

$$H_\ell(t+\varepsilon) - H_\ell(t) =$$

$$= \int_0^t g(u) u^\gamma [((t+\varepsilon)^2 - u^2)^{\alpha-\ell-1} - (t^2-u^2)^{\alpha-\ell-1}] du + \int_t^{t+\varepsilon} g(u) u^\gamma ((t+\varepsilon)^2 - u^2)^{\alpha-\ell-1} du =$$

$$= A + B \; .$$

We split the integral A in integrals over the intervals $[0,t-\varepsilon]$ and $[t-\varepsilon,t]$, which we denote by $A_1$ and $A_2$ (we may assume $\varepsilon < a$). Invoking the mean value theorem we obtain

$$\begin{aligned}|A_1| &\leq C\|g\|_\infty \varepsilon \int_0^{t-\varepsilon} (t-u)^{\alpha-\ell-2}du \\ &\leq C\|g\|_\infty \varepsilon\, \varepsilon^{\alpha-\ell-1} \\ &= C\|g\|_\infty \varepsilon^{\alpha-\ell} .\end{aligned}$$

We also have

$$\begin{aligned}|A_2| &\leq C\|g\|_\infty \int_{t-\varepsilon}^{t} (t-u)^{\alpha-\ell-1}du \\ &= C\|g\|_\infty \int_0^{\varepsilon} v^{\alpha-\ell-1}dv = \\ &= C\|g\|_\infty \varepsilon^{\alpha-\ell} .\end{aligned}$$

Finally

$$\begin{aligned}|B| &\leq C\|g\|_\infty \int_{t}^{t+\varepsilon} (t+\varepsilon-u)^{\alpha-\ell-1}du \\ &= C\|g\|_\infty \int_0^{\varepsilon} v^{\alpha-\ell-1}dv \\ &= C\|g\|_\infty \varepsilon^{\alpha-\ell} .\end{aligned}$$

Combining the above estimates we obtain (5) and hence (3) is proved. It is obvious that (3) holds also with $F_x$ replaced by $\phi F_x$ and it then follows from Proposition 9 on p. 147 in [2] that

$$\|\phi F_x\|_{\Lambda_\alpha} \leq C\|g\|_\infty .$$

Using (2) we conclude that

(6) $$\int_{R^n} \|\phi F_x\|^p_{\Lambda_\alpha} dx \leqslant C \int_{R^n} |f(x)|^p dx$$

for $f \in \mathcal{S}(R^n)$.

It now follows from an approximation argument that (6) holds for every $f \in L^p(R^n)$. We first prove (6) for step functions and then for general f.

First assume that (6) holds for step functions and let $f \in L^p(R^n)$. We may assume that f is non-negative and let $(f_m)_1^\infty$ denote a non-decreasing sequence of step functions tending to f almost everywhere. We let $u_x$ and $u_{x,m}$ denote the Poisson integrals of $\phi F_x$ and the corresponding functions $\phi F_{x,m}$. It then follows that for almost every x $F_{x,m} \to F_x$ almost everywhere and $\|\phi F_{x,m} - \phi F_x\|_1 \to 0$ as m tends to infinity (see [1], pp. 13-14). Letting k denote the smallest integer greater than $\alpha$ we conclude that

$$\lim_{m\to\infty} \frac{\partial^k u_{x,m}}{\partial y^k}(t,y) = \frac{\partial^k u_x}{\partial y^k}(t,y), \qquad ((t,y) \in R\times(0,\infty)).$$

Hence

$$\|\phi F_x\|_{\Lambda_\alpha} = \|\phi F_x\|_\infty + \sup_{t,y} y^{k-\alpha} \left|\frac{\partial^k u_x}{\partial y^k}(t,y)\right| =$$

$$= \|\lim_{m\to\infty} \phi F_{x,m}\|_\infty + \sup_{t,y} \lim_{m\to\infty} y^{k-\alpha} \left|\frac{\partial^k u_{x,m}}{\partial y^k}(t,y)\right| \leqslant$$

$$\leqslant \underline{\lim}_{m\to\infty} \|\phi F_{x,m}\|_\infty + \underline{\lim}_{m\to\infty} \sup_{t,y} y^{k-\alpha} \left|\frac{\partial^k u_{x,m}}{\partial y^k}(t,y)\right| \leqslant \underline{\lim}_{m\to\infty} \|\phi F_{x,m}\|_{\Lambda_\alpha}$$

and an application of Fatou's lemma yields (6).

The estimate (6) for step functions can be obtained in a similar way by approximation with functions in $\mathcal{S}(R^n)$.

Using (6) we can now conclude the proof of the theorem.

Let $f \in L^p_{loc}(R^n)$ and let $\phi$ be as above. It is sufficient to prove that for every ball B in $R^n$ $\phi F_x \in \Lambda_\alpha$ for almost every x in B. But this follows from the inequality (6) since $\phi F_x$, $x \in B$, depends only on the values of f in a compact set. The proof of the theorem is complete.

## REFERENCES

[1] Peyrière, J., - Sjölin, P., Regularity of sperical means. To appear in Ark. Mat.

[2] Stein, E.M., Singular Integrals and Differentiability Properties of Functions. Princeton University Press 1970.

[3] Stein, E.M., Maximal functions: Spherical means. Proc. Nat. Acad. Sci. U.S.A. 73(1976), 2174 - 2175.

# MULTIPLIER REPRESENTATIONS OF SEQUENCE SPACES WITH APPLICATIONS TO LIPSCHITZ SPACES AND SPACES OF FUNCTIONS OF GENERALIZED BOUNDED VARIATION

Günther Goes
Department of Mathematics
Illinois Institute of Technology
Chicago

For a wide class of Banach spaces of complex sequences, multiplier representations are given. If $Lip(E,\alpha)$ is a Banach space of sequences of Fourier coefficients of distributions in a Lipschitz space of order $\alpha$ and $V_E$ is a Banach space of sequences of Fourier coefficients of distributions of generalized bounded variation, then these representations lead to extensions to $Lip(E.\alpha)$ and $V_E$ of theorems of Privalov (on the conjugate invariance of $Lip\alpha$ $(0<\alpha<1)$), of Bernstein(on the absolute convergence of Fourier series of $f\varepsilon\ Lip(L_{2\pi},\alpha),(\alpha>\frac{1}{2})$) and of Zygmund (on the absolute convergence of Fourier series of $f\varepsilon\ BV_{2\pi}\cap Lip\alpha,(\alpha>0)$).

## 1. Introduction

The main purpose of this paper is to show how theorems from one Banach space can be transferred to another Banach space with the help of some multiplier representation involving a certain "universal space". To be concret, let us consider the following two theorems of Hardy and Littlewood [12];[11], II (see also Duren [2] p. 74-75 and p.78-79):

Let f be a function analytic in $|z|<1$. Then

(i) f is continuous on $|z|\le 1$ and $f(e^{it})\varepsilon\Lambda_\alpha(0<\alpha\le 1)$ if and only if

$$M_\infty(r,f') = \max_{0\le t<2\pi}|f'(re^{it})| = O((1-r)^{\alpha-1}) \quad (r\to 1-)$$

(ii) $f\varepsilon\ H^p$ and $f(e^{it})\varepsilon\ \Lambda^p_\alpha$ $(1\le p<\infty,\ 0<\alpha\le 1)$ if and only if

$$M_p(r,f') = \{\frac{1}{2\pi}\int_0^{2\pi} |f'(re^{it})|^p\, dt\}^{1/p} = O((1-r)^{\alpha-1}).$$

Hardy and Littlewood, as well as Duren give separate proofs for both statements. We shall see that (ii) follows immediately from (i), if one uses our multiplier representation theorem 3.5, yet an analogous statement is true for the Lipschitz spaces Lip$(E,\alpha)$, if E belongs to a large class of Banach spaces of sequences of Fourier coefficients of distributions on $T = R/(2\pi Z)$ (see our statement 4.6).

Another example from Hardy and Littlewood ([11],II) ([2], p.80) is the following;

(iii) Suppose $0<p \leq \infty$, $\beta>0$ and f is analytic in $|z|<1$.
Then
$M_p(r,f) = O((1-r)^{-\beta})$ if and only if $M_p(r,f') = O((1-r)^{-1-\beta})$.

Again the question arises if an analogous statement is true for more general spaces. The answer is yes (see our statement 4.6).

We use the theory of sequence spaces and consider instead of distributions on T the associated spaces of sequences of Fourier coefficients. For the special case of Lipschitz spaces our representation theorem 3.8,4. was given already in [9]. It turns out, that the general case is not more complicated, yet more transparent.

## 2. Definitions and Notations

2.1 FK-spaces, BK-spaces, Sections of a Sequence. Let $\Omega$ be the space of complex sequences $x = (x_k)_{k=-\infty}^{\infty}$ with $x_0 = 0$. This last condition is imposed for purely technical reasons. Occasionally we shall consider also the space $\omega$ of complex sequences $x = (x_k)_{k=1}^{\infty}$.

A Fréchet space $E \subset \Omega$ is called an FK-space ([18],[17],[10]), if the coordinate functionals $x \to x_k$ $(k\varepsilon Z)$ are continuous on E, An FK-space which is also a Banach space is called a BK-space.

For each $k\varepsilon Z$ let $\delta^k = (\delta_n^k)$, where $\delta_n^k = 1$ if $k=n$ and $\delta_n^k = 0$ if $k \neq n$. Let $s^n = \sum_{k=-n}^{n} \delta^k$ $(n\varepsilon Z^+)$. Then for any $x\varepsilon\Omega$, $s^n x = \sum_{k=-n}^{n} x_k\delta^k$ is called the n-th section of x and if $\sigma^n = \sum_{k=-n}^{n} (1-\frac{|k|}{n+1})\, \delta^k$, then $\sigma^n x = \sum_{k=-n}^{n} (1-\frac{|k|}{n+1})\, x_k\delta^k$ **is called** the n-th Cesàro-section (of order one) of x.

Let E be an FK-space. An element x is said to have bounded sections in E or AB (see [19]) in E, if $\{s^n x\}$ is a bounded set in E. Correspondingly:

$x$ is said to have bounded Cesàro-sections in $E$ or $\sigma B$ in $E$, if $\{\sigma^n x\}$ is a bounded set in $E$. Let $E_{AB} = \{x \in \Omega : x$ has $AB$ in $E\}$ and $E_{\sigma B} = \{x \in \Omega : x$ has $\sigma B$ in $E\}$.

If $\{p_j\}$ is a set of seminorms defining the topology of $E$, then $E_{AB}$ and $E_{\sigma B}$ are FK-spaces under the seminorms $q_j$ and $r_j$ respectively, where $q_j(x) = \sup_n p_j(s^n x)$ and $r_j(x) = \sup_n p_j(\sigma^n x)$.

2.2 Spaces of Multipliers. Let $A, B \subset \Omega$. Then

$$(A \to B) = \{x \in \Omega: xy = (x_k y_k) \in B \text{ for all } y \in A\}$$

is the set of multipliers from $A$ to $B$.

Let $\Phi = \{x \in \Omega: x_k \neq 0$ for at most finitely many $k$'s$\}$. If $E$ is a BK-space containing $\Phi$ or at least separating points of $Z \setminus \{0\}$ (i.e. for every $k \in Z \setminus \{0\}$ there exists a $y \in E$ such that $y_k \neq 0$) and if $F$ is an FK-space under the seminorms $\{p_j\}$, then $(E \to F)$ is an FK-space under the seminorms $\rho_j$, where

$$\rho_j(x) = \sup_{\|y\|_E \leq 1} p_j(xy) .$$

Let

$$bs = \{x \in \Omega: \sup_n \left| \sum_{k=-n}^{n} x_k \right| < \infty \},$$

$$\sigma b = \{x \in \Omega: \sup_n \left| \sum_{k=-n}^{n} \left(1 - \frac{|k|}{n+1}\right) x_k \right| < \infty\}.$$

The spaces $(A \to bs)$ and $(A \to \sigma b)$ are denoted $A^\gamma$ and $A^{\sigma b}$ respectively.

2.3 Almost FK- and almost BK-spaces. $E \subset \Omega$ is called an almost FK-space, if there exists an FK-space $F$, such that $E = F + \Phi$. If $F$ is a BK-space, then $E$ is called an almost BK-space.

EXAMPLE. $(bs)^\gamma = bv_e + \Phi$, where

$$bv_e = \{x \in \Omega: x_k = x_{-k} \text{ and } \sum_{k=-n}^{n} |x_k - x_{k+1}| = \|x\| < \infty\}$$

is a BK-space. Evidently $E = F + \Phi$ implies $E^\gamma = F^\gamma$ and $E^{\sigma b} = F^{\sigma b}$.

2.4 Translation Invariant FK-spaces. For $t \in T = R/(2\pi Z)$ let $e(t)$ denote the sequence $x \in \Omega$, where $x_k = e^{ikt}$. An FK-space $E \subset \Omega$ is called translation invariant, if $x \in E$ implies $x \cdot e(t) = (x_k e^{ikt}) \in E$ for every $t \in T$ and $p_j(x) = p_j(x \cdot e(t))$

for every continuous seminorm $p_j$ on E and for every $t\varepsilon T$.

<u>2.5 The Universal Space</u> $A_E^Y$. Let E be an FK-space, S an index set and $Y = (y^s)_{s\varepsilon S}$ a family of elements $y^s \varepsilon \Omega$, which separates points of $Z\setminus\{0\}$. Then

$$A_E^Y = \{x\varepsilon\Omega:\ \{y^s x\}_{s\varepsilon S} \text{ is a bounded set in } E\}.$$

<u>2.6 Examples of Spaces</u> $A_E^Y$. Let E be any FK-space with defining seminorms $p_j$ $(j=1,2,\ldots)$. In the following we list first the family Y and describe then the space $A_E^Y$.

(i) $Y = \{s^n\}_{n=1}^{\infty}$ ; $A_E^Y = E_{AB}$.

(ii) $Y = \{\sigma^n\}_{n=1}^{\infty}$ ; $A_E^Y = E_{\sigma B}$,

(iii) $Y = \{y^s\}_{0\leq s<1}$ where $y_k^s = s^{|k|}$; $A_E^Y = \{x\varepsilon\Omega: \{\sum_{k=-\infty}^{\infty} s^{|k|} x_k \delta^k\}_{0\leq s<1}$ is a bounded set in E}, i.e. the Abel means of x are bounded in E.

(iv) $Y = \{e(s)\}_{s\varepsilon T}$ ; $A_E^Y$ is the greatest translation invariant subspace of $E_{\sigma b}$ with seminorms $\rho_j$, where $\rho_j(x) = \sup_{s\varepsilon T} p_j(e(s)x)$.

(v) $Y = \{(e(s) - e(0)) \log s\}_{s>0}$; $A_E^Y = \Lambda_{\log}^E$ is the space of sequences which satisfy a Dini-Lipschitz condition in E.

(vi) $Y = \{(e(s)-e(0))s^{-\alpha}\}_{s>0}$ , $0 < \alpha \leq 1$; $A_E^Y \equiv \mathrm{Lip}(E,\alpha) \equiv \Lambda_{\infty\alpha}^E$. If E is an FK-space of tempered sequences ([3],p.46), then Lip(E,$\alpha$) is the space of sequences of Fourier coefficients of distributions on T which fulfill a Lipschitz condition of order $\alpha$ in the topology of a Fréchet-space $\check{E}$ associated with E. In particular if $E = \hat{L}^{\infty}$ is the space of sequences of Fourier coefficients of $f\varepsilon L_{2\pi}^{\infty}$ , then $A_E^Y \equiv \mathrm{Lip}\ \alpha \equiv \Lambda_\alpha$ is the space of sequences of Fourier coefficients of functions in the classical Lipschitz space of order $\alpha$.

(vii) $Y = \{(e(s)-2e(0)+e(-s))s^{-1}\}_{s>0}$ ;$A_E^Y \equiv \mathrm{Lip}^*(E,1)\equiv\Lambda_*^E$ .

If E is again an FK-space of tempered sequences, then Lip* (E,1) is the space of sequences of Fourier coefficients of distributions on T which belong to the Zygmund space in E.

(viii) $Y = \{y^s\}_{s\varepsilon S}$ where $y^s = \sum_{j=1}^{N(s)} [e(-b_j^{(s)})-e(-a_j^{(s)})]$; $\{[a_j^{(s)},b_j^{(s)}]\}_{s\varepsilon S}$

is the family of all systems of finitely many, say $N(s)$, disjoint intervals in the interval $[0,2\pi)$: $A_E^Y = V_E$. If E is an FK-space of tempered sequences, then $V_E$ is the space of sequences of Fourier coefficients of distributions on T which are of generalized bounded variation in the associated Fréchet space $\check{E}$ of distributions on T. For example if $E = \hat{L}^p$ $(1 \leq p \leq \infty)$ is the space of sequences of Fourier-coefficients of functions $f \in L^p_{2\pi}$, then $V_E = \hat{V}_p$ is the space of sequences of Fourier coefficients of $f \in V_p$, a space which was considered for p=1 by Verblunsky [16] and for $1 \leq p < \infty$ by Kaczmarz [14]. Actually $\hat{V}_p = \{x \in \Omega : |k\, x_k| = O(1)\ (|k| \to \infty)\}$ for $1 \leq p \leq 2$, [7]. More explicitely:

$$V_p = \{f \in L^p_{2\pi}:\ \sup_{s \in S} \int_0^{2\pi} \Big| \sum_{j=1}^{N(s)} [f(t-b_j^{(s)}) - f(t-a_j^{(s)})]\Big|^p dt < \infty\} \text{ for } 1 \leq p < \infty \text{ and}$$

$V_\infty = BV_{2\pi}$.

## 3. Multiplier Representations of the Spaces $A_E^Y$

PROPOSITION 3.1 *Let $E \subset \Omega$ be an FK-space with $\{p_j\}$ as defining set of seminorms. Then for given Y according to 2.5 the space $A_E^Y$ is an FK-space under the seminorms $q_j$, where*

$$(1) \qquad q_j(x) = \sup_{y \in Y} p_j(yx).$$

*Furthermore* $A_E^Y = (A_E^Y)_{\sigma B}$ if $E = E_{\sigma B}$ *and* $A_E^Y = (A_E^Y)_{AB}$ *if* $E = E_{AB}$.

PROOF. $A_E^Y$ is a linear space and (1) defines a seminorm. Furthermore $q_j(x)=0$ for every j implies $xy = 0$ for all $y \in Y$ and thus $x = 0$, since Y separates points of $Z \setminus \{0\}$. $A_E$ is complete: Let $\{x^n\}$ be a Cauchy sequence in $A_E^Y$. Then $\{x^n y\}$ is a Cauchy sequence in E for each $y \in Y$. By the completeness of E there exists $z=z(y) \in E$. By the coordinatewise convergence in E and since Y separates points of $Z \setminus \{0\}$ there exists $x \in \Omega$ such that $x^n y \to xy = z(y)\ (n \to \infty)$ in E for every $y \in Y$ and $p_j(xy) \leq p_j(xy - x^n y) + p_j(x^n y)$ for every j and every $y \in Y$ implies $x \in A_E^Y$. Evidently $x^n \to x \in A_E^Y$. The remaining facts can be proved as in [9], 4.1.

EXAMPLES 3.2. The spaces $\hat{L}^p$ $(1 \leq p \leq \infty)$ are BK-spaces under the norms of the generating functions in $L^p_{2\pi}$ and $\hat{L}^p = (\hat{L}^p)_{\sigma B}$ if $1 < p \leq \infty$, [21]. Thus for $1 < p \leq \infty$ the spaces $\mathrm{Lip}(\hat{L}^p, \alpha)$ $(0 < \alpha \leq 1)$ and $\hat{V}_p$ are examples of spaces of type $A_E^Y = (A_E^Y)_{\sigma B}$.

THEOREM 3.3 *Let* G *be an almost BK-space*, $G = F + \Phi$, *where* F *is a BK-space separating points of* $Z\setminus\{0\}$. *Let* E *be an FK-space containing* $\Phi$ *and let* Y *be given according to* 2.5. *Then*

$$(G\to A_E^Y) = A^Y_{(G\to E)}. \tag{2}$$

PROOF. The condition $\Phi\subset E$ implies $\Phi\subset A_E^Y$ and $(\Phi\to E) = (\Phi\to A_E^Y) = \Omega$. Thus $(G\to A_E^Y) = (F\to A_E^Y)$ and $(G\to E) = (F\to E)$. By 2.2 and 3.1 both spaces in the equation (2) are FK-spaces. If $\{p_j\}$ is a defining set of seminorms for E then by 2.2 and 3.1

$$x\varepsilon(F\to A_E^Y) \leftrightarrow \sup_{||v||_F\le 1}\ \sup_{y\varepsilon Y} p_j(vyx)<\infty \quad \text{for every } p_j$$

$$\leftrightarrow \sup_{y\varepsilon Y}\ \sup_{||v||_F\le 1} p_j(vyx)<\infty \quad \text{for every } p_j \quad \leftrightarrow x\,\varepsilon\, A^Y_{(F\to E)}. \ //$$

REMARKS 3.4. The spaces $\sigma b$ and bs are FK-spaces containing $\Phi$ under the seminorms $p_j$ and $q_j$ respectively, where

$$p_0(x) = \sup_n \left|\sum_{k=-n}^{n} \left(1-\frac{|k|}{n+1}\right) x_k\right|, \quad p_j(x) = |x_j| \text{ for } j\varepsilon Z\setminus\{0\} \text{ and}$$

$$q_0(x) = \sup_n \left|\sum_{k=-n}^{n} x_k\right|, \quad q_j(x) = |x_j| \text{ for } j\ \varepsilon\ Z\setminus\{0\}.$$

Furthermore $\sigma b = (\sigma b)_{\sigma B}$ and $bs = (bs)_{AB}$ (see 2.1).The last equation is obvious. The second last equation can be proven as for sequences in $\omega$ ([1];p. 193).

For the proof of the next statement we use the fact that for FK-spaces E containing $\Phi$, $E = E_{AB}$ if and only if $E = (E^\gamma)^\gamma$ and $E = E_{\sigma B}$ if and only if $E = (E^{\sigma b})^{\sigma b}$ (]8]; p. 493, 1.7).

THEOREM 3.5 (i) *If* $\Phi\subset E = E_{AB}$ *is an FK-space and* $E^\gamma$ *an almost BK-space*, $E^\gamma = F + \Phi$, *where* F *is a BK-space separating points of* $Z\setminus\{0\}$, *then for given* Y *according to* 2.5

$$A_E^Y = (E^\gamma\to A_{bs}^Y) = ((A_{bs}^Y)^\gamma\to E). \tag{3}$$

*If* $A_{bs}^Y\subset bs$, *then* $A_E^Y\subset E$.

(ii) *If* $\Phi \subset E = E_{\sigma B}$ *is an FK-space and* $E^{\sigma b}$ *an almost BK-space*, $E^{\sigma b} = F + \Phi$, *where* F *is a BK-space separating points of* $Z\setminus\{0\}$, *then for given*

Y according to 2.5

(4) $$A_E^Y = (E^{\sigma b} \to A_{\sigma b}^Y) = ((A_{\sigma b}^Y)^{\sigma b} \to E).$$

If $A_{\sigma b}^Y \subset \sigma b$, then $A_E^Y \subset E$.

PROOF. (i) Replacing in the last theorem G by $E^\gamma$ and E by bs we obtain by 3.4

$$(E^\gamma \to A_{bs}^Y) = A_{(E^\gamma \to bs)}^Y = A_E^Y.$$

The last equation in (3) follows from 3.1 and 3.4 according to which $E = (E^\gamma)^\gamma$ and $A_{bs}^Y = (A_{bs}^Y)_{AB} = ((A_{bs}^Y)^\gamma)^\gamma$. Thus (see also [6] p. 140, Satz 12)

$$(E^\gamma \to A_{bs}^Y) \subset ((A_{bs}^Y)^\gamma \to (E^\gamma)^\gamma) \subset (E^\gamma \to A_{bs}^Y).$$

Finally: $A_{bs}^Y \subset bs$ implies $A_E^Y = (E^\gamma \to A_{bs}^Y) \subset (E^\gamma \to bs) = E$.

(ii) This can be proved correspondingly replacing now in 3.3 G by $E^{\sigma b}$ and E by $\sigma b$.

NOTATION 3.6. IF $A \subset \Omega$, then $\int^1 A = \{x \in \Omega: (ik\, x_k) \in A\}$ and $\int^{-1} A = \{x \in \Omega: ((ik)^{-1} x_k)_{k \neq 0} \in A\}$.

COROLLARY 3.7 (i) If E fulfills the conditions of 3.5 (i) then $V_E = (E^\gamma \to \widehat{BV}) = (E^\gamma \to \int^1 (\hat{L}^\infty)^\gamma) = (\int^{-1} \hat{L}^\infty \to E)$ or equivalently $\int^{-1} V_E = (E^\gamma \to \hat{M}) = (E^\gamma \to (\hat{L}^\infty)^\gamma) = (\hat{L}^\infty \to E)$. Here

$$(\hat{L}^\infty)^\gamma = \hat{L}_{AB} = \{x \in \Omega: \sup_n \int_0^{2\pi} \left| \sum_{k=-n}^{n} x_k e^{ikt} \right| dt < \infty\}$$ and

$\hat{M}$ is the space of sequences of Fourier-Stieltjes coefficients.

(ii) If E fulfills the conditions of 3.5 (ii) then $V_E = (E^{\sigma b} \to \widehat{BV}) = (\int^{-1} (\hat{L}^\infty \to E)$ or equivalently $\int^{-1} V_E = (E^{\sigma b} \to \hat{M}) = (\hat{L}^\infty \to E)$.

PROOF. (i) By (3) $V_E = (E^\gamma \to V_{bs})$. Now $V_{bs} = (V_{\sigma b})_{AB}$ since $(\sigma b)_{AB} = ((\sigma b)^{\sigma b})^\gamma = bs$ by 3.4 and [8], p. 492, 1.4 and 1.5 and by the theorem of Hardy-Bohr [15]. Furthermore $V_{\sigma b} = V_{\hat{L}^\infty}$ by the definition of $V_E$. But $V_{\hat{L}^\infty} = \widehat{BV}$. Hence $V_{bs} = (\widehat{BV})_{AB} = \int^1 (\hat{L}^\infty)^\gamma$ together with $E^\gamma = (E^\gamma)_{AB}$ by [8] p.495, 1.16 implies that

$$V_E = (E^\gamma \to \int^1 (\hat{L}^\infty)^\gamma) = (E^\gamma \to (\widehat{BV})_{AB}) = (E^\gamma \to \widehat{BV}) = ((\int^1 (\widehat{L^\infty})^\gamma)^\gamma \to (E^\gamma)^\gamma)$$

$$\subset (\int^1 \hat{L}^\infty \to E) \subset (E^\gamma \to \int^1 (\hat{L}^\infty)^\gamma).$$

This proves (i). (ii) can be derived similarly.

REMARKS 3.8. 1. E fulfills the conditions in theorem 3.5 (i) and (ii) if E is a translation invariant BK-space containing $\Phi$ and $E = E_{AB}$ or $E = E_{\sigma B}$ respectively, because in these cases $E^{\gamma} = (E \to \hat{M}^{\gamma})$ and $E^{\sigma b} = (E \to \hat{L}^{\infty})$ respectively ([9], 3.1).

2. The case $E = \hat{L}^p$ $(1<p<\infty)$ of 3.7 (ii), was proven by Kaczmarz [14].

3. If one considers in 3.7 (ii) sequences in $\omega$ (instead in $\Omega$). then one obtains:

$$(5)\qquad \int^{-1} V_{(\hat{L}_c^{\infty} + \hat{L}_s^{\infty})_{\infty}} = \int^{-1} V_{\widehat{BMO}} = (\hat{H}^1 \to \hat{H}^1), \text{ where}$$

$$\hat{H}^1 = \{x \in \omega: \sum_{k=1} x_k e^{ikt} \sim h(t),\ h \in L^1_{2\pi}\},$$

$$\hat{L}_c^{\infty} = \{x \in \omega: \sum_{k=1}^{\infty} x_k \cos kt \sim f(t),\ f \in L^{\infty}_{2\pi}\},$$

$$\hat{L}_s^{\infty} = \{x \in \omega: \sum_{k=1}^{\infty} x_k \sin kt \sim g(t),\ g \in L^{\infty}_{2\pi}\}.$$

$\widehat{BMO}$ is the space of sequences of Fourier coefficients of functions of bounded mean oscillation [13], which can be identified with the conjugate space of $\hat{H}^1$ [4],[5]. But the conjugate space of $\hat{H}^1$ can also be identified with $\hat{L}_c^{\infty} + \hat{L}_s^{\infty} = (\hat{H}^1)^{\sigma b} = (\hat{L}_c^1 \cap \hat{L}_s^1)^{\sigma b}$ [8], 2.3. This justifies equation one in (5). Now $\hat{L}_c^{\infty} + \hat{L}_s^{\infty}$ is a BK-space under the norm $||x|| = \inf_{x=a+b} ||a||_{\hat{L}_c^{\infty}} + ||b||_{\hat{L}_s^{\infty}}$, $a \in \hat{L}_c^{\infty}$, $b \in \hat{L}_s^{\infty}$ and $\hat{L}_c^{\infty} + \hat{L}_s^{\infty} = (\hat{L}_c^{\infty} + \hat{L}_s^{\infty})_{\sigma B}$. Since $(\hat{L}_c^{\infty} + \hat{L}_s^{\infty})^{\sigma b} = \hat{H}^1$, (5) follows from 3.7 (ii).

4. If in 3.5 the space E is in addition translation invariant, then 3.5 (i) remains valid if one replaces bs by $\hat{M}^{\gamma} = (\hat{L}^{\infty})_{AB}$ and 3.5 (ii) remains valid if one replaces $\sigma b$ by $\hat{L}^{\infty}$.

If E is such a translation invariant space and $0 < \alpha \leq 1$, then $\mathrm{Lip}(E,\alpha) = (E^{\gamma} \to \mathrm{Lip}(\hat{M}^{\gamma},\alpha)) = ((\mathrm{Lip}(\hat{M}^{\gamma},\alpha)^{\gamma} \to E) = (E^{\gamma} \to \mathrm{Lip}\,\alpha)$ if $E = E_{AB}$, and $\mathrm{Lip}(E,\alpha) = (E^{\sigma b} \to \mathrm{Lip}\,\alpha) = ((\mathrm{Lip}\,\alpha)^{\sigma b} \to E)$ if $E = E_{\sigma b}$. These equations were proved already in [9]. Corresponding equations are true for the Zygmund spaces $\mathrm{Lip}^*(E,1)$.

## 4. Extensions of theorems of Privalov, Bernstein, Zygmund, Hardy and Littlewood

THEOREM 4.1 (Extended theorem of Privalov and Zygmund).
*If $E = E_{\sigma B}$ is a translation invariant FK-space and $E^{\sigma b}$ is an almost BK-space, $E^{\sigma b} = F + \Phi$, where F is a BK-space separating points of $Z\setminus\{0\}$ then for $0<\alpha<1$ the spaces $\mathrm{Lip}(E,\alpha)$ and $\mathrm{Lip}^*(E,1)$ are conjugate invariant. i.e.*

$Lip(E,\alpha) = \widetilde{Lip}(E,\alpha) \equiv \{x\varepsilon\Omega: (-i \text{ sign } k\ x_k)\varepsilon Lip(E,\alpha)\}$ and $Lip^*(E,1)=\widetilde{Lip}^*(E,1)$.

PROOF. By Privalov [21],Vol.I, p.121: $Lip\alpha = \widetilde{Lip}\ \alpha$. From this the extension to $Lip(E,\alpha)$ follows with the second multiplier representation in 3.8, 4. Similarly Zygmund's equation ([20]; [21]Vol.I, p.121), $Lip^*(\hat{L}^\infty,1)=\widetilde{Lip}^*(\hat{L}^\infty, 1)$ can be extended to $Lip^*(E,1)$.

THEOREM 4.2 (Extended theorem of Bernstein). Let E be as in 4.1 and $\alpha > \frac{1}{2}$, then

(5) $Lip((\hat{L}^2 \to E),\alpha) \subset (1^\infty \to E)$, where $1^\infty = \{x\varepsilon\Omega: \sup_k |x_k| \equiv ||x||_\infty < \infty\}$.

PROOF. By Bernstein [21], Vol. I,p. 241: $Lip(\hat{L}^2, \alpha > \frac{1}{2}) \subset 1^1 \equiv \{x\varepsilon\Omega: \sum_k |x_k| < \infty\}$.
Since $(E^{\sigma b} \to \hat{L}^2) = ((\hat{L}^2)^{\sigma b} \to (E^{\sigma b})^{\sigma b}) = (\hat{L}^2 \to E)$ and $(E^{\sigma b} \to 1^1) = (1^\infty \to E)$ we obtain by 3.3 $(E^{\sigma b} \to Lip(\hat{L}^2, \alpha > \frac{1}{2})) = Lip((E^{\sigma b} \to \hat{L}^2), \alpha > \frac{1}{2})$
$= Lip((\hat{L}^2 \to E), \alpha > \frac{1}{2}) \subset (1^\infty \to E)$.

EXAMPLE 4.3 If $E = \hat{L}^2$ then (5) becomes $Lip(1^\infty, \alpha > \frac{1}{2}) \subset \hat{L}^2$. However more can be said: By [9], 6.8 we have $Lip(1^\infty, \alpha) = \{x\varepsilon\Omega: \sup_k |k^{(1+\alpha)} x_k| < \infty\}$ for any $0<\alpha<1$. This together with the foregoing inclusion shows once more that Bernstein's theorem cannot be valid for $\alpha = \frac{1}{2}$.

THEOREM 4.4 (Extended theorem of Zygmund). Let E be as in 4.1 and $\alpha > 0$, then

(6) $Lip(E,\alpha) \cap V_E \subset (1^\infty \to E)$.

PROOF. By Zygmund [21], Vol. I, p. 241, for any $\alpha>0$: $Lip\alpha \cap \hat{BV} \subset 1^1$. Thus by 3.8, 4. and 3.7 (ii) we obtain

$$(E^{\sigma b} \to Lip\alpha \cap \hat{BV}) = (E^{\sigma b} \to Lip\alpha) \cap (E^{\sigma b} \to \hat{BV}) = Lip(E,\alpha) \cap V_E \subset (E^{\sigma b} \to 1^1) = (1^\infty \to E).$$

REMARK 4.5. For many spaces E we have $V_E \subset (1^\infty \to E)$ and thus 4.4 gives nothing new for these spaces. It is therefore of interest to note, that besides the space $E = \hat{L}^\infty$, which was considered by Zygmund, also the space $E = (\hat{L}_{AB})^\gamma = ((\hat{L}^\infty)^\gamma)^\gamma$ has the property that $V_E \not\subset (1^\infty \to E)$. In fact, for this space we have by 3.7 (i) $(k^{-1}) \varepsilon V_E = (L_{AB} \to \int^1 (\hat{L}^\infty)^\gamma) = (\hat{L}_{AB} \to \int^1 \hat{L}_{AB}) \not\subset (1^\infty \to (\hat{L}_{AB})^\gamma) = (\hat{L}_{AB} \to 1^1)$ since $(1/\log|k|)_{|k|\geq 2}\ \varepsilon \hat{L}_{AB}$.

The following theorem is concerned with sequences in $\omega$. This necessitates a few obvious changes in our definitions. For example the sequences $e(t)$ which occur in the definition of a translation invariant space, have to be restricted to the positive integers; correspondingly the sequences $y^s$ in the family Y of the definition of $A_E^Y$, etc.

THEOREM 4.6 (Extensions of theorems of Hardy and Littlewood). Let $E = E_{\sigma B} \subset \omega$ be a translation invariant BK-space, $-\infty < \alpha < \infty$ and

$$HL(E,\alpha) = \{A_E^Y : Y = \{y^s\}_{0\le s<1},\ y^s = (ik\, s^k (1-s)^{1-\alpha})_{k=1}^{\infty}\}.$$ Then

(i) $HL(E,\alpha) = Lip^+(E,\alpha) = \{x\varepsilon\omega : \sup_{s>0} ||x\cdot(e(s)-e(0))s^{-\alpha}||_E < \infty\}$ if $0<\alpha\le 1$.

(ii) $HL(E,\ 1+\alpha) = \int^1 HL(E,\alpha)$ if $\alpha < 0$.

PROOF. (i) By Hardy and Littlewood ([11], II, p. 426, Th. 40; our introduction (i)): $HL(\hat{H}^\infty,\alpha) = Lip^+(\hat{H}^\infty,\alpha)$ where $\hat{H}^\infty = \hat{L}_c^\infty \cap \hat{L}_s^\infty$ (see 3.8, 2.). Hence by 3.8, 4. with obvious changes due to the fact that we are dealing here with sequences in $\omega$, it follows that $HL(E,\alpha) = (E^{\sigma b} \to HL(\hat{H}^\infty,\alpha)) = (E^{\sigma b} \to Lip^+(\hat{H}^\infty,\alpha)) = Lip^+(E,\alpha)$.

(ii) By Hardy and Littlewood ([11], II, p. 425, Th. 39; our introduction (iii)): $HL(\hat{H}^\infty, 1+\alpha) = \int^1 HL(H^\infty,\alpha)$ if $\alpha < 0$. The extension follows with 3.8.4.

REMARK 4.7. It should be clear by now, how in other situations extensions of existing theorems are possible. For example, the classical Dini-Lipschitz theorem [21], Vol. I, p. 63, on the uniform convergence of Fourier series of functions whose modulus of continuity $\omega(\delta)$ fulfills $\omega(\delta)\log\delta \to 0(\delta\to 0+)$, leads to the conclusion that for all spaces E satisfying the conditions of 4.1 we have (see 2.6 (v)),

$$\Lambda_{\log}^E \subset E_{AB}.$$

Statements on fractional integration and differentiation such as in [11] and in [21] vol. II, pp. 136, 138 can easily be extended to spaces E satisfying the conditions of 4.1.

REFERENCES

[1] Buntinas, M., Convergent and bounded Cesàro sections in FK-spaces. Math. Z. 121 (1971), 191-200.

[2] Duren, P.L., Theory of $H^p$-spaces. Academic Press, New York 1970.

[3] Edwards, R. E., Fourier Series. Vol. II, Holt, Rinehart and Winston, New York 1967.

[4] Fefferman, C., Characterization of bounded mean oscillation. Bull. Amer. Math. Soc. 77 (1971), 587-588.

[5] Fefferman, C. – E.M.Stein, $H^p$-spaces of several variables. Acta Math. 129 (1972), 137-193.

[6] Goes, G., Charakterisierung von Fourierkoeffizienten mit einem Summierbarkeitsfaktorentheorem und Multiplikatoren. Studia Math. 19 (1960), 133-148.

[7] ________, Über einige Multiplikatorenklassen. Math Z. 80 (1963), 324-327.

[8] ________, Summen von FK-Räumen, Funktionale Abschnittskonvergenz und Umkehrsätze. Tôhoku Math. J. 26 (1974), 487-504.
[9] ________, Multipliers between Lipschitz spaces and Zygmund spaces. Comment.Math. (In print)
[10] Goffman, C.-G.Pedrick, A First Course in Functional Analysis. Prentice-Hall, Englewood Cliffs, 1965.
[11] Hardy, G.H. – J.E. Littlewood, Some properties of fractional integrals I, Math. Z. 27 (1928). 565-606. II, Math. Z. 34 (1932), 403-439.
[12] ________, A Convergence criterion for Fourier series. Math. Z. 28 (1928). 612-634.
[13] John, F. – L. Nirenberg, On functions of bounded mean oscillation. Comm. Pure Appl. Math. 14 (1961), 415-426.
[14] Kaczmarz, S., On some classes of Fourier series. J. London Math. Soc. 8 (1933), 39-46.
[15] Lorentz, G. G. – K. Zeller, Abschnittslimitierbarkeit und der Satz von Hardy-Bohr. Arch. Math. 15 (1964) 208-213.
[16] Verblunsky, S., On some classes of Fourier series. Proc. London Math. Soc., 33 (1932), 287-327.
[17] Wilansky, A., Functional Analysis. Blaisdell, New York 1964.
[18] Zeller, K., Allgemeine Eigenschaften von Limitierungsverfahren. Math. Z. 53 (1950-51), 463-487.
[19] ________, Abschnittskonvergenz in FK-Räumen. Math. Z. 55(1951), 55-70.
[20] Zygmund, A., Smooth functions. Duke Math. J. 12 (1945), 47-76.
[21] ________, Trigonometric series. 2nd rev. ed. Vols. I,II, Cambridge Univ. Press New York 1959.

# MULTIPLIERS FOR THE MELLIN TRANSFORMATION

P.G. Rooney
Department of Mathematics
University of Toronto
Toronto, Canada

Abstract. A technique is developed for converting multiplier theorems for Fourier transformation into multiplier theorems for the Mellin transformation. Applications to Hankel transformations are made.

For functions $f$, measurable on $(0,\infty)$, and $1 \leq p < \infty$, $\mu$ real, define

$$\|f\|_{\mu,p} = \left\{ \int_0^\infty x^{\mu-1} |f(x)|^p \, dx \right\}^{1/p} ,$$

and denote by $L_{\mu,p}$ the collection of functions for which $\|f\|_{\mu,p} < \infty$. Denote by $C_0$ the collection of continuous functions compactly supported in $(0,\infty)$. It can be shown that $C_0$ is dense in $L_{\mu,p}$; indeed one can show that if $f \in L_{\mu_i,p_i}$, $i = 1, 2$, and $\varepsilon > 0$, then $g$ exists in $C_0$ such that $\|f - g\|_{\mu_i,p_i} < \varepsilon$, $i = 1, 2$; see [1, Lemma 23].

Let $C_{\mu,p}$ be defined by $(C_{\mu,p}f)(x) = e^{\mu x/p} f(e^x)$. It is easy to see that $C_{\mu,p}$ maps $L_{\mu,p}$ isometrically onto $L_p(-\infty,\infty)$. For $1 \leq p \leq 2$, we define the Mellin transformation $M$ on $L_{\mu,p}$ by $(Mf)\left(\frac{\mu}{p} + it\right) = (C_{\mu,p}f)^\wedge(t)$.

We say $m \in A$ if (i) there are extended real numbers $\alpha$, $\beta$, depending on $m$, with $\alpha < \beta$ so that $m(s)$ is holomorphic in the strip $\alpha < \operatorname{Re} s < \beta$; (ii) in every closed substrip, $\sigma_1 \leq \operatorname{Re} s \leq \sigma_2$, where $\alpha < \sigma_1 \leq \sigma_2 < \beta$, $m(s)$ is bounded; (iii) for $\alpha < \sigma < \beta$, $|m'(\sigma+it)| = O(|t|^{-1})$ as $|t| \to \infty$. It will be recognized that by the Mihlin multiplier theorem [3; Chapter IV, Theorem 3], for each $\sigma$, $\alpha < \sigma < \beta$, $m(\sigma+it)$ is an $L_p(-\infty,\infty)$ multiplier for $1 < p < \infty$. Let $T_\sigma$ be the bounded transformation on $L_p(-\infty,\infty)$ generated by $m(\sigma+it)$ and for

$\alpha < \mu/p < \beta$ let $H_{m,\mu,p} = C^{-1}_{\mu,p} T_{\mu/p} C_{\mu,p}$. Then clearly $H_{m,\mu,p}$ is bounded on $L_{\mu,p}$ for $1 < p < \infty$ if $\alpha < \mu/p < \beta$, and if $1 < p \le 2$ and $f \in L_{\mu,p}$,

$$(MH_{m,\mu,p}f)(s) = m(s)(Mf)(s) , \quad \text{Re } s = \mu/p .$$

Further, $H_{m,\mu,p}$ is really independent of $\mu$ and $p$ for $\alpha < \mu/p < \beta$; that is if $f \in L_{\mu_1,p_1} \cap L_{\mu_2,p_2}$, where $\alpha < \mu_i/p_i < \beta$, $H_{m,\mu_1,p_1}f = H_{m,\mu_2,p_2}f$. It is sufficient to prove this for $f \in C_0$, since as mentioned, we can approximate $f$ simultaneously in $L_{\mu_1,p_1}$ and $L_{\mu_2,p_2}$ by functions in $C_0$. Hence suppose $f \in C_0$ and let $F(s) = \int_0^\infty t^{s-1}f(t)dt$. $F$ is clearly entire and using the Riemann-Lebesgue lemma it is easy to prove that $F(\sigma + it) \to 0$ as $t \to \pm\infty$.

By using standard inversion theorems for the Fourier transformation, it is easy to show that there is a sequence $\{S_k\}$ of positive real numbers, with $\lim_{k\to\infty} S_k = \infty$, so that for almost all $x > 0$

$$(H_{m,\mu_j,p_j}f)(x) = \lim_{k\to\infty} \frac{1}{2\pi i} \int_{\mu_j/p_j - iS_k}^{\mu_j/p_j + iS_k} x^{-s}m(s)F(s)ds , \quad j = 1,2 .$$

But if $\gamma_k$ denotes the rectangle with vertices $\mu_j/p_j \pm iS_k$, $j = 1,2$, $\int_{\gamma_k} x^{-s}m(s)F(s)ds = 0$. Also since $F(\sigma + it) \to 0$ as $t \to \pm\infty$, and $m$, is bounded, the integrals along the top and bottom of $\gamma_k$ tend to zero as $k \to \infty$, and thus $H_{m,\mu_1,p_1}f = H_{m,\mu_2,p_2}f$ a.e. (for full details see [2]). Thus $H_{m,\mu,p}$ is independent of $\mu$ and $p$ for $\alpha < \mu/p < \beta$, $1 < p < \infty$, and we can denote it by $H_m$. Thus we have proved the following theorem.

THEOREM. <u>For</u> $1 < p < \infty$, $\alpha < \mu/p < \beta$, $H_m$ <u>is a bounded operator on</u> $L_{\mu,p}$ <u>to itself</u>. <u>If</u> $1 < p \le 2$, $\alpha < \mu/p < \beta$, <u>and</u> $f \in L_{\mu,p}$,

$$(MH_mf)(s) = m(s)(Mf)(s) , \quad \text{Re } s = \mu/p .$$

Certain generalizations are possible. By trivial changes of variables it is possible to obtain similar results for operators $T$ such that

$$(MTf)(s) = m(s)(Mf)(\lambda \pm s) .$$

Also, if we define $H_{m,\lambda,\mu,\nu,p}$ by $H_{m,\lambda,\mu,\nu,p} = C_{\nu,p}^{-1} T_{\lambda/p} C_{\mu,p}$, it is possible to prove by the same technique that if $f \in L_{\mu_1,p_1} \cap L_{\mu_2,p_2}$, $i = 1,2$, then $H_{m,\lambda_1,\mu_1,\nu_1,p_1} f = H_{m,\lambda_2,\mu_2,\nu_2,p_2} f$ a.e. if $\frac{\lambda_1}{p_1} - \frac{\lambda_2}{p_2} = \frac{\mu_1}{p_1} - \frac{\mu_2}{p_2} = \frac{\nu_1}{p_1} - \frac{\nu_2}{p_2}$, and $\alpha < \lambda_i/p_i < \beta$.

As an example of the use of this theorem, let us consider the operator $F_c H_\lambda$, where $H_\lambda$ is the Hankel transformation, that is, if $f \in C_0$

$$(H_\lambda f)(x) = \int_0^\infty (xt)^{\frac{1}{2}} J_\lambda(xt) f(t)\,dt ,$$

$J_\lambda$ being the Bessel function of order $\lambda$, and $F_c$ is the Fourier cosine transformation, that is, $F_c = H_{-\frac{1}{2}}$. It is well known that if $\lambda > -1$, $H_\lambda$ is bounded on $L_{1,2}$ — see [4, Chap. 7] — and using known results, if $f \in L_{1,2}$, and $\lambda > -1$

$$(MF_c H_\lambda f)(s) = m(s)(Mf)(s) , \quad \mathrm{Re}\, s = \tfrac{1}{2} ,$$

where $m(s) = \left[\Gamma\left(\frac{1}{2}(1-s)\right)\Gamma\left(\frac{1}{2}(\lambda + \frac{1}{2} + s)\right)\right] \Big/ \left[\Gamma(\frac{1}{2}s)\Gamma\left(\frac{1}{2}(\lambda + \frac{3}{2} - s)\right)\right]$, and thus on $L_{1,2}$, $F_c H_\lambda$ can be identified with $H_m$. But $\alpha(m) = -(\lambda + \frac{1}{2})$, and $\beta(m) = 1$. Hence for $-(\lambda + \frac{1}{2}) < \mu/p < 1$, $1 < p < \infty$, $H_m$ is bounded on $L_{\mu,p}$, and thus $F_c H_\lambda$ can be extended as a bounded operator on $L_{\mu,p}$ for $1 < p < \infty$, $-(\lambda + \frac{1}{2}) < \mu/p < 1$. This result, combined with known results about the boundedness of $F_c$ can be used to extend $H_\lambda$ — see [1; §7].

## REFERENCES

[1] Rooney, P.G., On the ranges of certain fractional integrals. Canad.J. Math. 24 (1972), 1198-1216.

[2] Rooney, P.G., A technique for studying the boundedness and extendability of certain types of operators . Canad.J.Math.25(1973), 1090-1102.

[3] Stein, E.M., Singular Integrals and Differentiability Properties of Functions. Princeton 1970.

[4] Titchmarsh, E.C., Fourier Integrals. Oxford 1948.

# ON A RELATION BETWEEN THE NORMS OF CESARO MEANS OF JACOBI EXPANSIONS

E. Görlich and C. Markett*)
Lehrstuhl A für Mathematik
Rheinisch-Westfälische Technische Hochschule
Aachen

## 1. Introduction

As remarked in [6], there is an analogue for Jacobi expansions of a relation between the rates of divergence of Cesàro means of different orders for Laguerre expansions [6,(1.9)]. The purpose of this note is to prove this remark (see Corollary below) and to determine the rate of divergence in those cases where the norms increase like some power of n (see Thm.). Our interest in this mainly lies in the fact that such a relation, being (nearly) independent of the parameters of the space and of the expansion, may be a particular instance of a relation between Cesàro means of some more general class of orthogonal expansions, rather than in the proof which, except for one additional step, consists in known arguments.

For $\alpha \geqslant \beta \geqslant -1/2$, $\alpha > -1/2$, $x \in [-1,1]$ let

$$(1.1) \qquad P_k^{(\alpha,\beta)}(x) = \sum_{j=0}^{k} \binom{\alpha+k}{j}\binom{\beta+k}{k-j}\left(\frac{x-1}{2}\right)^{k-j}\left(\frac{x+1}{2}\right)^{j}$$

denote the Jacobi polynomials, orthogonal in $L_w^p = L_{w^{\alpha,\beta}}^p[-1,1]$, where

$$\|f\|_p = \{\int_{-1}^{1} |f(x)|^p w^{\alpha,\beta}(x)dx\}^{1/p}, \qquad w(x) = w^{\alpha,\beta}(x) = (1-x)^{\alpha}(1+x)^{\beta};$$

$$\|f\|_\infty = \operatorname*{ess\,sup}_{x\in[-1,1]} |f(x)|.$$

*) This author was supported by a DFG grant (Ne 171/3) which is gratefully acknowledged.

Setting

(1.2) $$h_k^{(\alpha,\beta)} = \{\int_{-1}^{1} (P_k^{(\alpha,\beta)}(x))^2 w^{\alpha,\beta}(x)dx\}^{-1} =$$

$$= \frac{(2k+\alpha+\beta+1)\Gamma(k+\alpha+\beta+1)k!}{2^{\alpha+\beta+1}\Gamma(k+\alpha+1)\Gamma(k+\beta+1)}, \qquad (k \in \mathbb{P}),$$

where $\mathbb{P} = \{0,1,\ldots\}$, the k-th Fourier coefficient of $f \in L_w^p$ is

$$f^\wedge(k) = \int_{-1}^{1} f(x)\, P_k^{(\alpha,\beta)}(x) w^{\alpha,\beta}(x)dx,$$

and the n-th Cesàro mean of order $\delta \geqslant 0$ is given by

(1.3) $$(C,\delta)_n^{(\alpha,\beta)}(f;x) = (A_n^\delta)^{-1} \sum_{k=o}^{n} A_{n-k}^\delta h_k^{(\alpha,\beta)} f^\wedge(k) P_k^{(\alpha,\beta)}(x) ,$$

where

$$A_n^\delta = \binom{n+\delta}{n} = \frac{\Gamma(n+\delta+1)}{\Gamma(n+1)\Gamma(\delta+1)} .$$

Writing $\|(C,\delta)_n^{(\alpha,\beta)}\|_{[p]}$ for the norm of $(C,\delta)_n^{(\alpha,\beta)}$ as an operator from $L_w^p$ into itself, our main result is the following.

THEOREM. *Let* $\alpha \geqslant \beta \geqslant -1/2$, $\alpha > -1/2$, *and* $\delta \geqslant 0$. *Then*

$$\|(C,\delta)_n^{(\alpha,\beta)}\|_{[p]} \leqslant \begin{cases} B(n)n^{(2\alpha+2)/p-(2\alpha+3)/2-\delta} & ; \quad p \in I_1(\delta), \\ A & ; \quad p \in I_2(\delta), \\ B(n)n^{(2\alpha+1)/2-(2\alpha+2)/p-\delta} & ; \quad p \in I_3(\delta), \end{cases}$$

*for each* $n \in \mathbb{P}$, *where*

$$I_1(\delta) = [1,\frac{4\alpha+4}{2\alpha+3+2\delta}],\ I_2(\delta) = (\frac{4\alpha+4}{2\alpha+3+2\delta},\frac{4\alpha+4}{2\alpha+1-2\delta}),\ I_3(\delta) = [\frac{4\alpha+4}{2\alpha+1-2\delta},\infty],$$

A *is a constant independent of* n, *and* $B(n) = B(n,p,\delta,\alpha,\beta) = \mathcal{O}(n^\tau)$ *as* $n \to \infty$ *for any* $\tau > 0$. *Moreover, there is a constant* A *such that*

$$\| (C,\delta)_n^{(\alpha,\beta)} \|_{[p]} \geqslant A \begin{cases} n^{(2\alpha+2)/p-(2\alpha+3)/2-\delta} & ; \quad p \in I_1 \\ 1 & ; \quad p \in I_2 \\ n^{(2\alpha+1)/2-(2\alpha+2)/p-\delta} & ; \quad p \in I_3 \end{cases} .$$

With the notation $g(n) \sim h(n)$ for $g(n) = O(h(n))$ and $h(n) = O(g(n))$ as $n \to \infty$, this implies

COROLLARY. *If* $\alpha \geqslant \beta \geqslant -1/2$, $\alpha > -1/2$, $\delta > \gamma \geqslant 0$, *and* $p \in I_1(\delta) \cup I_3(\delta)$, *one has*

$$\| (C,\delta)_n^{(\alpha,\beta)} \|_{[p]} \sim B(n) n^{\gamma-\delta} \| (C,\gamma)_n^{(\alpha,\beta)} \|_{[p]}$$

*where* $B(n)$ *and* $1/B(n)$ *are* $o(n^\tau)$ *as* $n \to \infty$ *for each* $\tau > 0$.

Compare also [6] for a discussion of certain remarks by Lorch [8] and Askey [1] on general properties of Cesàro means.

The assertion of the theorem for $p \in I_2(\delta)$ is well-known; it is due to Pollard [13] in case $\delta = 0$ (who also proved the divergence in the interior of $I_1(\delta)$, $I_3(\delta)$; more general weight functions were treated by Muckenhoupt [9]), to Askey-Hirschman [3;p.172] in case $\delta \geqslant 0$, $\alpha = \beta$, and for general $\alpha$, $\beta$ the uniform boundedness was settled by the results of Askey-Wainger [4] on convolution structure (cf. also Gasper [5]). In case $p = (4\alpha+4)(2\alpha+3+2\delta)^{-1}$ or $p = (4\alpha+4)(2\alpha+1-2\delta)^{-1}$, where the lower estimate of the theorem is not sharp, better results were established by Askey-Hirschman [3,p.173] (for $\alpha = \beta$, $\delta \geqslant 0$), the divergence for $\delta = 0$ being due to Newman-Rudin [11].

Concerning the rate of increase of the norms in $I_1(\delta)$ and $I_3(\delta)$, the result for $p = 1$, $\delta = 0$ was established by Lorch [8]. Also for general $p \in I_1(\delta) \cup I_2(\delta)$ and $\delta = 0$ the lower estimate is known in view of a lower estimate for the Lagrange interpolation operator $L_n^{(\alpha,\beta)}$ at the Jacobi knots on $I_3(\delta)$, given by Askey [2;p.77,(15)]. Indeed, since the operator norms of the $L_n^{(\alpha,\beta)}$ are majorized by those of $(C,0)_n^{(\alpha,\beta)}$ (cf.also Nevai [10;p.181]), this already implies $\| (C,0)_n^{(\alpha,\beta)} \|_{[p]} \geqslant C\, n^{(2\alpha+1)/2-(2\alpha+2)/p}$ for $p \in I_3(\delta)$ and, by duality, the corresponding result on $I_1(\delta)$.

The only lower estimate which applies for $\delta > 0$ known so far (apart from Szegö's [14] important estimates of the kernel of $(C,\delta)_n^{(\alpha,\beta)}$ at the points $x = \pm 1$, which will of course be used in the sequel) seems to be the one by Kal'nei [7]. He established an analogue of Sidon's inequality in case $-1/2 < \alpha = \beta < 1/2$, $p = \infty$, thus a lower estimate for the norms of general polynomial summation processes of ultrasperical series, which implies our lower estimate for $\delta \geq 0$ and the $\alpha,\beta,p$ admitted. But his proof does not carry over to the general Jacobi case. He also announced upper estimates for the norms of summation of Legendre series, one of which [7;Thm.3] giving the exact rate of increase for $\| (C,\delta)_n^{(0,0)} \|_{[\infty]}$.

## 2. Auxiliary Results

The proof of the above Theorem essentially consists in revisiting Szegö's formulas [14;Sec.9.4 and 9.41], which leads to Lemma 2 below, the rest being standard arguments using convolution, duality and interpolation. For convenience we collect some of the preliminaries here.

LEMMA 1. (Askey-Wainger [4], Gasper [5]). *Let* $\alpha \geq \beta \geq -1/2$, $\alpha > -1/2$. *There is a function* $K(x,y,z)$, $x,y,z \in [-1,1]$, *such that, for each* $f \in L_w^1$, $n \in \mathbb{P}$,

$$(2.1) \qquad (C,\delta)_n^{(\alpha,\beta)}(f;x) = (f * \sigma_n^{(\delta)})(x),$$

*where the convolution* $f * \sigma_n^{(\delta)}$ *is defined by*

$$(2.2) \qquad (f * \sigma_n^{(\delta)})(x) = \int_{-1}^{1} \int_{-1}^{1} f(y)\sigma_n^{(\delta)}(z)K(x,y,z)w^{\alpha,\beta}(y)w^{\alpha,\beta}(z)\,dy\,dz$$

*and the kernel* $\sigma_n^{(\delta)}$ *is given by*

$$(2.3) \qquad \sigma_n^{(\delta)}(x) = (A_n^{\delta})^{-1} \sum_{k=o}^{n} A_{n-k}^{\delta} h_k^{(\alpha,\beta)} P_k^{(\alpha,\beta)}(1) P_k^{(\alpha,\beta)}(x).$$

*Moreover,* $K(x,y,z) \geq 0$ *for all* $x,y,z \in (-1,1)$,

$$(2.4) \qquad \int_{-1}^{1} K(x,y,z)w^{\alpha,\beta}(x)\,dx = 1 \qquad \forall\, y,z \in (-1,1),$$

and

(2.5) $$\|(C,\delta)_n^{(\alpha,\beta)}\|_{[1]} = \|(C,\delta)_n^{(\alpha,\beta)}\|_{[\infty]} = \|\sigma_n^{(\delta)}\|_{L_w^1}.$$

Further the following relations are needed.

(2.6) $$A_n^\delta \sim n^\delta \qquad (\delta \geq 0, n\to\infty),$$

(2.7) $$\|P_n^{(\alpha+\delta+j+1,\beta)}(x)\|_{L_w^1} \sim n^{-1/2} \qquad (\delta+j < \alpha+1/2; n\to\infty),$$

(2.8) $$\|P_n^{(\alpha+\delta+j+1,\beta)}(x)\|_{L_w^1} \sim n^{-1/2}\log n \qquad (\delta+j = \alpha+1/2; n\to\infty),$$

(see [14;(7.34.1)]).

For each polynomial $r_n(x)$ of degree $\leq n$ and $\alpha,\beta > -1$, $1 \leq p \leq q \leq \infty$

(2.9) $$\|r_n\|_{L_w^q} \leq C\, n^{(2\gamma+1)(1/p-1/q)}\|r_n\|_{L_w^p} \qquad (n \in \mathbb{P}),$$

where $\gamma = 1/2 + \max(\alpha,\beta)$; see Nessel - Wilmes [12], where this is obtained as a particular case of a general inequality of Jackson-Nikolskii type for regular orthonormal systems. For $q = \infty$, (2.9) was also given in [2;p.76].

LEMMA.2. Let $\alpha \geq \beta \geq -1/2$, $\alpha > -1/2$. Then, as $n\to\infty$,

$$\|\sigma_n^{(\delta)}\|_{L_w^1} \sim c \begin{cases} n^{\alpha+1/2-\delta} & ; \quad 0 \leq \delta < \alpha+1/2 \\ \log n & ; \quad \delta = \alpha+1/2, \\ 1 & ; \quad \delta > \alpha+1/2. \end{cases}$$

PROOF. The assertions for $\delta = \alpha + 1/2$ and $\delta > \alpha + 1/2$ follow by [14;9.41]. For the proof of the first assertion we follow the same lines, starting with [14,(9.41.12)]

(2.10) $$P_n^{(\alpha+\delta+1,\beta)}(x) = b_n(\alpha,\beta,\delta)\sum_{\rho=0}^{\infty} a_{n,\rho}(\alpha,\beta,\delta)A_n^{\delta+\rho}\sigma_n^{(\delta+\rho)}(x)$$

for $\delta \geqslant 0$, where

$$b_n(\alpha,\beta,\delta) = 2^{\alpha+\beta+1}\,\Gamma(\alpha+1)\frac{\Gamma(n+\beta+1)\Gamma(2n+\alpha+\beta+2\delta+3)}{\Gamma(n+\alpha+\beta+\delta+2)\Gamma(2n+\alpha+\beta+\delta+3)},$$

$$a_{n,\rho}(\alpha,\beta,\delta) = \begin{cases} 1 \;; & \rho = 0 \\ (-1)^{\rho}\binom{\delta+\rho}{\rho}\dfrac{\delta(\delta-1)\,\ldots\,(\delta-\rho+1)}{(2n+\alpha+\beta+\delta+3)\,\ldots\,(2n+\alpha+\beta+\delta+\rho+2)} \;; & \rho \in \mathbb{N}. \end{cases}$$

In view of (2.6), one has

$$b_n(\alpha,\beta,\delta) \sim n^{-\alpha-1} \qquad (n\to\infty). \tag{2.11}$$

Obviously

$$a_{n,\rho}(\alpha,\beta,\delta) = 0 \qquad (\delta \in \mathbb{P}, \rho > \delta)$$

and, otherwise,

$$|a_{n,\rho}(\alpha,\beta,\delta)| \sim n^{-\rho} \qquad (n\to\infty). \tag{2.12}$$

Given $\alpha > -1/2$, $0 \leqslant \delta < \alpha + 1/2$, there exists $j_o \in \mathbb{P}$ such that

$$\alpha - 1/2 < \delta + j_o \leqslant \alpha + 1/2. \tag{2.13}$$

Consider first the case when $\alpha-1/2 < \delta+j_o < \alpha+1/2$. Replacing in (2.10) $\delta$ by $\delta+j$, multiplying by a number $c_j$ to be determined later, and summing up over j, we have

$$\sum_{j=o}^{j_o} \frac{c_j P_n^{(\alpha+\delta+j+1,\beta)}(x)}{b_n(\alpha,\beta,\delta+j)} = \sum_{j=o}^{j_o} c_j \sum_{\rho=o}^{\infty} a_{n,\rho}(\alpha,\beta,\delta+j) A_n^{\delta+j+\rho}\sigma_n^{(\delta+j+\rho)}(x)$$

$$= \sum_{j=o}^{j_o} c_j \sum_{k=j}^{\infty} a_{n,k-j}(\alpha,\beta,\delta+j) A_n^{\delta+k}\sigma_n^{(\delta+k)}(x) = \Sigma_1 + \Sigma_2,$$

say, where

$$\Sigma_1 = \sum_{j=o}^{j_o} c_j \sum_{k=j}^{j_o} a_{n,k-j}(\alpha,\beta,\delta+j) A_n^{\delta+k} \sigma_n^{(\delta+k)}(x) \ ,$$

$$\Sigma_2 = \sum_{j=o}^{j_o} c_j \sum_{k=j_o+1}^{\infty} a_{n,k-j}(\alpha,\beta,\delta+j) A_n^{\delta+k} \sigma_n^{(\delta+k)}(x) \ .$$

Now the $c_j$ can be chosen in such a way that

$$\Sigma_1 = A_n^{\delta} \sigma_n^{(\delta)}(x). \tag{2.14}$$

Indeed, since

$$\Sigma_1 = \sum_{k=o}^{j_o} \{ \sum_{j=o}^{k} c_j a_{n,k-j}(\alpha,\beta,\delta+j) \} A_n^{\delta+k} \sigma_n^{(\delta+k)}(x),$$

and $a_{n,0}(\alpha,\beta,\delta) = 1$, (2.14) will be satisfied if $c_o = 1$ and the $c_1,\dots,c_{j_o}$ are chosen such that they solve the system

$$\sum_{j=o}^{k} c_j a_{n,k-j}(\alpha,\beta,\delta+j) = 0 \qquad (1 \leqslant k \leqslant j_o). \tag{2.15}$$

Clearly such numbers $c_j$ exist, and, using (2.12) and induction, one obtains that their dependence on n is

$$|c_j| = |c_j(n)| = \mathcal{O}(n^{-j}) \qquad (0 \leqslant j \leqslant j_o;\ n \to \infty). \tag{2.16}$$

Hence we have

$$A_n^{\delta}\, \sigma_n^{(\delta)}(x) = \sum_{j=o}^{j_o} \frac{c_j P_n^{(\alpha+\delta+j+1,\beta)}(x)}{b_n(\alpha,\beta,\delta+j)} - \Sigma_2 \ , \tag{2.17}$$

where

$$\Sigma_2 = \sum_{j=o}^{j_o} c_j \sum_{\rho=j_o+1-j}^{\infty} a_{n,\rho}(\alpha,\beta,\delta+j) A_n^{\delta+j+\rho}\, \sigma_n^{(\delta+j+\rho)}(x) \quad ,$$

and in view of (2.11), (2.16), (2.7), and the fact that $\delta+j_o < \alpha+1/2$, it follows that

$$(2.18)\qquad A_n^{\delta}\,\|\sigma_n^{(\delta)}\|_{L_w^1} = \mathcal{O}(n^{\alpha+1/2}) + \mathcal{O}(\Sigma_3) \qquad (n\to\infty),$$

where, in view of the last entry in Lemma 2

$$\Sigma_3 = \sum_{j=0}^{j_o} |c_j| \sum_{\rho=j_o+1-j}^{\infty} |a_{n,\rho}(\alpha,\beta,\delta+j)|\,A_n^{\delta+j+\rho} .$$

From [14;(9.41.16)] one deduces the existence of an absolute constant M such that for $0\leqslant j\leqslant j_o$ and n sufficiently large

$$(2.19)\qquad \sum_{\rho=j_o+1-j}^{\infty} |a_{n,\rho}(\alpha,\beta,\delta+j)|\,A_n^{\delta+j+\rho} \leqslant M\, n^{\delta+j} ,$$

whence, with (2.16)

$$\Sigma_3 = \mathcal{O}\Big(\sum_{j=0}^{j_o} n^{-j+\delta+j}\Big) = \mathcal{O}(n^{\delta}) = \mathcal{O}(n^{\alpha+1/2}) \qquad (n\to\infty),$$

since $\delta<\alpha+1/2$ by hypothesis. By (2.18) and (2.6) we finally have

$$\|\sigma_n^{(\delta)}\|_{L_w^1} = \mathcal{O}(n^{\alpha+1/2-\delta}) \qquad (n\to\infty),$$

and in view of (2.5) this gives the asserted estimate from above.

In case $\delta+j_o=\alpha+1/2$, $j_o>0$, the reasoning is the same, except for the fact that, when passing from (2.17) to (2.18), the term for $j=j_o$ in the first sum of (2.17) has to be treated separately. In view of (2.8), (2.16), (2.11) this term behaves like

$$\frac{c_{j_o}}{b_n(\alpha,\beta,\delta+j_o)}\,\|P_n^{(\alpha+\delta+j_o+1,\beta)}\| = \mathcal{O}(n^{\delta}\log n) \qquad (n\to\infty)$$

and, since $j_o>0$, we have $\delta<\alpha+1/2$, whence (2.18) again holds, and the upper estimate follows as before.

Concerning the estimate from below, the term for $j=0$ in the first sum of (2.17) is essential. E.g. in case $\alpha-1/2<\delta+j_0<\alpha+1/2$ we have, using (2.17), (2.11), (2.16), (2.7), the last entry of Lemma 2, and (2.19),

$$A_n^\delta \| \sigma_n^{(\delta)} \|_{L_w^1} \geq \frac{\| P_n^{(\alpha+\delta+1,\beta)} \|_{L_w^1}}{b_n(\alpha,\beta,\delta)}$$

$$- \sum_{j=1}^{j_0} \frac{|c_j| \, \| P_n^{(\alpha+\delta+j+1,\beta)} \|_{L_w^1}}{b_n(\alpha,\beta,\delta+j)} - \| \Sigma_2 \|_{L_w^1}$$

$$\geq C\, n^{\alpha+1/2} - C \sum_{j=1}^{j_0} n^{\alpha+1/2-j} - C\, n^\delta \geq C\, n^{\alpha+1/2}$$

for some positive constant C and n sufficiently large. Similarly the lower estimate for $\delta+j_0=\alpha+1/2$, $j_0>0$ follows.

3. Proof of the Theorem.

Only the cases $p\in I_1(\delta)$, $p\in I_3(\delta)$ have to be considered. If $p\in(1,\frac{4\alpha+4}{2\alpha+3+2\delta}]$, thus $\delta<\alpha+1/2$, an application of the Riesz-Thorin theorem to

$$\text{(3.1)} \qquad \| (C,\delta)_n^{(\alpha,\beta)} \|_{[1/q_1]} = \mathcal{O}(1) \qquad (n\to\infty),$$

where $q_1 = (2\alpha+3+2\delta-\varepsilon)/(4\alpha+4)$, $\varepsilon>0$, and

$$\text{(3.2)} \qquad \| (C,\delta)_n^{(\alpha,\beta)} \|_{[1]} = \mathcal{O}(n^{\alpha+1/2-\delta}) \qquad (n\to\infty),$$

which hold in view of the case $I_2(\delta)$ of the theorem and Lemma 2, respectively, gives

$$\| (C,\delta)_n^{(\alpha,\beta)} \|_{[p]} = \mathcal{O}(n^{(2\alpha+2)/p-(2\alpha+3)/2-\delta+R(\varepsilon)}) \qquad (n\to\infty)$$

for $1 < p < 1/q_1$, where $R(\varepsilon) = 2\varepsilon(\alpha+1)(1-1/p)(2\alpha+1-2\delta+\varepsilon)^{-1}$ tends to zero for $\varepsilon \to 0+$. This establishes the upper estimate in $I_1(\delta)$, and the corresponding estimate in $I_3(\delta)$ follows by duality.

For the proof of the lower estimate, let $p \in (\frac{4\alpha+4}{2\alpha+1-2\delta}, \infty)$, $\delta < \alpha+1/2$. Following [ 2 ;p.76], an application of (2.9) with $q = \infty$ to $(C,\delta)^{(\alpha,\beta)} f$ gives

$$\| (C,\delta)_n^{(\alpha,\beta)} f \|_{L_w^\infty} \leq C\, n^{(2\alpha+2)/p} \| (C,\delta)_n^{(\alpha,\beta)} f \|_{L_w^p} . \tag{3.3}$$

Choosing $\varepsilon > 0$ and $f_{n,\varepsilon}(x) \in L_w^\infty$ such that $\| f_{n,\varepsilon} \|_{L_w^\infty} = 1$ and

$$\| (C,\delta)_n^{(\alpha,\beta)} f_{n,\varepsilon} \|_{L_w^\infty} \geq \| (C,\delta)_n^{(\alpha,\beta)} \|_{[\infty]} - \varepsilon ,$$

one has $\| f_{n,\varepsilon} \|_{L_w^p} \leq C \| f_{n,\varepsilon} \|_{L_w^\infty}$ for each $n \in P$ and

$$\| (C,\delta)_n^{(\alpha,\beta)} \|_{[p]} \geq C \| (C,\delta)_n^{(\alpha,\beta)} f_{n,\varepsilon} \|_{L_w^p} \geq C \| (C,\delta)_n^{(\alpha,\beta)} f_{n,\varepsilon} \|_{L_w^\infty} n^{-(2\alpha+2)/p}$$

$$\geq C \{ \| (C,\delta)_n^{(\alpha,\beta)} \|_{[\infty]} - \varepsilon \} n^{-(2\alpha+2)/p}$$

$$\geq C\, n^{(2\alpha+1)/2 - (2\alpha+2)/p - \delta} ,$$

by Lemma 2 and (2.5). The corresponding estimate for $p \in (1, \frac{4\alpha+4}{2\alpha+3+2\delta})$ again follows by duality.

## REFERENCES


[1] Askey, R., Norm inequalities for some orthogonal series. Bull. Amer. Math. Soc. 72(1966), 808 - 823.

[2] Askey, R., Mean convergence of orthogonal series and Lagrange interpolation. Acta Math. Acad. Sci. Hungar. 23(1972), 71 - 85.

[3] Askey, R. - Hirschman, I.I., Mean summability for ultrasperical polynomials. Math. Scand. 12(1963), 167 - 177.

[4] Askey, R. - Wainger, S., A convolution structure for Jacobi series. Amer. J. Math. 91(1969), 463 - 485.

[5] Gasper, G., Banach algebras for Jacobi series and positivity of a kernel. Ann. of Math. (2) 95(1972), 261 - 280.

[6] Görlich, E. - Markett, C., Mean Cesàro summability and operator norms for Laguerre expansions. (to appear).

[7] Kalnei, S.G., Uniform boundedness in the L-metric of polynomials with respect to the Jacobi polynomials. Soviet Math. Dokl. 16(1975), 714 - 718.

[8] Lorch, L., The Lebesgue constants for Jacobi series I. Proc. Amer. Math. Soc. 10(1959), 756 - 761.

[9] Muckenhoupt, B., Mean convergence of Jacobi series. Proc. Amer. Math. Soc. 23(1969), 306 - 310.

[10] Nevai, G.P., Lagrange interpolation at zeros of orthogonal polynomials. In: Approximation Theory II (Ed. by G.G. Lorentz, C.K. Chui, L.L. Schumaker) Proceedings Symp. on Approx. Theory, Austin, Texas, 1976. Academic Press, New York 1976, pp. 163 - 201.

[11] Newman, J. - Rudin, W., Mean convergence of orthogonal series. Proc. Amer. Math. Soc. 3(1952), 219 - 222.

[12] Nessel, R.J. - Wilmes, G., On Nikolskii-type inequalities for orthogonal expansions. In: Approximation Theory II (Ed. by G.G. Lorentz, C.K. Chui, L.L. Schumaker) Proceedings Symp. on Approx. Theory, Austin, Texas, 1976. Academic Press, New York 1976, pp. 479 - 484.

[13] Pollard, H., The mean convergence of orthogonal series II, III. Trans. Amer. Math. Soc. 63(1948), 355 - 367, Duke Math. J. 16(1949), 189 - 191.

[14] Szegö, G., Orthogonal Polynomials. AMS Coll. Publ., Providence, Rh. I., 1967.

# V
# Approximation Processes and Interpolation

# APPROXIMATION ET ANALYSE HARMONIQUE

Marc ZAMANSKY
Institut Henri Poincaré
PARIS

Abstract. The parts I and II give the main results of two texts (Bull. Sci. Math., 2e série, 101, 1977, p. 3-70 et p. 149-188).

The first text concerns the approximation for the Fourier expansions (normed spaces with orthogonal operators). The results are founded on three general and very simple theorems A, B, C. We give specially three theorems for the equivalence between approximation processes.

The second text illustrates the first : we expose in fifteen pages (with new results) all what concerns the approximation of periodic functions.

In this abstract, the third part, which is a schema, explains how it is possible to extend the previous results in the case where the measures are not discrete.

I. Théorèmes généraux. Approximation dans un espace normé muni d'opérateurs orthogonaux.

II. Approximation des fonctions périodiques.

III. Cas de mesures non discrètes. Convolution. Explication d'un paradoxe.

Dans les parties I et II de ce document, on trouvera les principaux résultats parmi ceux qui sont exposés dans deux mémoires qui paraîtront dans le Bulletin des Sciences mathématiques (2e série, tome 101, 1977, p. 3-70, 149-188). Ces mémoires contiennent des notes, commentaires et remarques, et le second une brève bibliographie historique.

La troisième partie, nouvelle, est le schéma de l'extension de la théorie précédente au cas de mesures non discrètes, et explique pourquoi (ce qui est paradoxal) la transformée de Fourier ne joue à peu près aucun rôle quand on considère les fonctions périodiques.

## INTRODUCTION

Bref historique. On connaît le rôle joué, depuis le début du siècle, par l'approximation des fonctions périodiques, qui a mis en évidence des phénomènes et problèmes importants, dépassant naturellement le cadre initial.

Après les premiers travaux de défrichement (FEJÉR, LEBESGUE, BERNSTEIN, de LA VALLÉE-POUSSIN), JACKSON (1911) évalue les approximations polynômiales connaissant des propriétés différentielles des fonctions, BERNSTEIN (1912) étudie principalement le problème inverse et de LA VALLÉE-POUSSIN (1919) procède à une première synthèse. FAVARD (1937), puis ACHIESER et KREIN, construisent les meilleurs procédés.

Le foisonnement des procédés qui avaient été introduits, mène Sz. NAGY (1948) à établir l'approximation des fonctions continues périodiques qui, elles ou leurs dérivées, satisfont à une condition de Lipschitz, par des polynômes construits à partir d'une série de Fourier au moyen d'une fonction sommatoire $[\varphi]$, définie sur $[0, 1]$, c'est-à-dire qui, à une série $\sum u_k$, associe la suite $\sum_{0\leqslant k\leqslant n} \varphi(k/n)\, u_k$.

A partir de 1948, je donne les premières réponses (sous plusieurs formes) au problème de la saturation des procédés (CESARO, JACKSON- de LA VALLÉE POUSSIN, fonctions sommatoires).

Tous ces résultats sont établis pour la topologie de la convergence uniforme. Divers auteurs les étendent aux espaces $L^p$, et étudient encore des procédés particuliers. En règle générale, on traite séparément les problèmes de convergence, d'approximation proprement dite, de saturation, on n'établit de propriétés différentielles d'une fonction connaissant l'approximation que si cette approximation est $O(1/n^{\alpha})$, $\alpha>0$. Il est visible cependant que beaucoup de résultats se "ressemblent", ce que commençait de mettre en évidence, au moins dans un sens, le mémoire de Sz. NAGY.

En 1967-1969, H. S. SHAPIRO publie un essai sur l'approximation (pour la topologie de la convergence uniforme) d'une fonction numérique $f$ de variable réelle au moyen de convolées $\nu_x * f$ où $(\nu_x)$ est une famille de mesures (finies) sur $R$, qui s'écrivent sous la forme $\nu_x(\theta) = \chi(x\theta)$. On y réserve une place importante à la saturation, on démontre des résultats classiques, mais aussi apparaît le problème de la comparaison (et de l'équivalence) entre procédés. L'instrument principal est la transformation de Fourier, et on cherche des critères de divisibilité de transformées (Cf. Théorèmes de Wiener).

En 1974, BUTZER, NESSEL et TREBELS montrent que s'il s'agit de développements orthogonaux dans un espace de Banach, relativement à une famille totale d'opérateurs $u_i$ tels que $\|T_n\| = O(1)$ où $T_n$ est la première moyenne arithmétique des $S_k = u_0 + \dots + u_k$, alors les procédés obtenus par les fonctions sommatoires $[1 - t^p]$, $p > 0$, $0 \leqslant t \leqslant 1$ (moyennes typiques) et $[\exp(- t^p)[$, $t \geqslant 0$, avec un paramètre entier, sont équivalents.

Le problème de la comparaison et de l'équivalence des procédés. Lorsqu'on part des séries de Fourier classiques et de procédés simples, deux voies se présentent : celle d'un espace normé muni d'opérateurs orthogonaux, idempotents, et celle de la convolution. Comme on le verra, c'est la première voie qu'il faut choisir, une fois encore.

Quant à la comparaison et l'équivalence des procédés, des résultats particuliers (auxquels il faudrait joindre nombre de théorèmes taubériens), ne donnent guère d'indications.

En 1954, j'écrivais dans le fascicule 128 du Mémorial des sciences mathématiques ("La sommation des séries divergentes") que, probablement, les procédés définis par des fonctions sommatoires dont on précisait le comportement en $t = 0$ et $t = 1$, étaient équivalents aux procédés $[(1 - t^p)^q]$, $p > 0$, $q > 0$ au moins pour des approximations $O(1/n^\alpha)$.

On peut présenter la question ainsi.

Soit $\mathcal{E}$ un espace normé dont un élément quelconque est noté $f$, soit $E = \mathcal{L}(\mathcal{E})$ l'espace des opérateurs (linéaires, continus) sur $\mathcal{E}$ et soient $(T_x)$, $(U_x)$ deux familles d'éléments de $E$ ; on cherche, quand $x \longrightarrow +\infty$, à quelles conditions on a

$$\|T_x(f) - f\| = O(1)\ \|U_x(f) - f\|$$

ou

$$\|U_x(f) - f\| = O(1)\ \|T_x(f) - f\|$$

ou (cas de l'équivalence) les deux inégalités à la fois.

Si $\mathcal{E}$ est muni d'opérateurs orthogonaux $u_i \in E$, à $f$ on associe $\sum u_k(f)$ et un procédé est un élément du sous-espace de $E$ engendré par les $u_k$ (éventuellement de l'adhérence de ce sous-espace si $\mathcal{E}$, donc $E$, est un espace de Banach). De là viendra la représentation d'un procédé par une famille $(\varphi_x)$ de fonctions numériques. On trouvera des critères de comparaison (théorèmes A, B) en ne considérant que des séries dans un normé. Mais on fera appel à $E$ et l'orthogonalité des $u_i$ quand il s'agira de critères d'équivalence.

Les idées et les méthodes. J'introduis le concept de c l a s s e s d' a p p r o x i m a t i o n s . Une telle classe est une inéquation fonctionnelle portant sur les approximations $\rho$ et qui exige peu d'hypothèses (Exemple : $\{\sigma(0)\}$ est l'ensemble des $\rho$ tels que $\sigma_n(0, \rho) = (1/n) \sum_0^n \rho_k = O(\rho_n)$ et contient les $\rho\uparrow$, les $\rho_n = n^\alpha(\log n)^\beta$ pour $0 < -\alpha < 1$, $\beta$ quelconque, ou $\alpha = 0$, $\beta < 0$ ). Cela évite d'écrire explicitement $\rho$ en fonction de $n$.

J'introduis les notions de p r o c é d é s - é t a l o n s (ici les moyennes typiques) et celles de c l a s s e s d e p r o c é d é s définis par "ressemblance" avec les procédés-étalons, cependant assez générales.

Ainsi, quand on cherchera à établir des théorèmes de comparaison ou d'équivalence entre procédés, on les exprimera le plus souvent avec des quantités fonctions de $\rho$ qui introduisent naturellement des classes d'approximations.

Quant à ces théorèmes de comparaison, l'idée naturelle consiste à comparer un procédé d'une classe au procédé-étalon qui lui donne naissance et deux procédés-étalons entre eux.

On aboutit alors aux théorèmes généraux.

Les théorèmes généraux

T h é o r è m e A (Séries dans un espace normé). On compare un procédé d'une classe au procédé-étalon.

T h é o r è m e B (Séries dans un espace de Banach). En général, l'approximation fournie par un procédé-étalon est déterminée (asymptotiquement) quand on connaît celle fournie par la différence de deux procédés-étalons.

T h é o r è m e C (Ce théorème, d'une autre nature, donnera en particulier les propriétés différentielles à partir de l'approximation).

Pour $\mathcal{P} = \cup \mathcal{P}_n$, $\mathcal{P}_n \subset \mathcal{P}_{n+1}$ sous-espaces d'un normé $E$, $D$ est une application linéaire de $\mathcal{P}$ dans un normé $\mathcal{E}$, continue sur les $\mathcal{P}_n$ ; connaissant une majoration des normes des restrictions de $D$ aux $\mathcal{P}_n$ et l'approximation de $f \in E$ par des $P_n \in \mathcal{P}_n$, on établit le comportement (quantitatif) des $DP_n$.

Approximation dans un espace normé muni d'une famille d'opérateurs orthogonaux $(u_i)$. Les $u_i$ sont continus, $u_i u_j = u_j u_i = 0$ si $i \neq j$, $u_i u_i = u_i$, et on suppose (h y p o t h è s e N) que les normes des opérateurs définis par la première moyenne arithmétique des $\sum_0^n u_i$ (ou par un procédé-étalon quelconque) sont bornées dans leur ensemble. On obtient alors, entre autres résultats, trois théorèmes d'équivalence entre un procédé d'une classe et le procédé-étalon. Le premier théorème est un théorème d'équivalence "absolu" (il ne fait pas intervenir de classes d'approximations) ; le troisième est lié à une classe d'approximations mais englobe les aspects de l'approximation "d e l a c o n v e r g e n c e à l a s a t u r a t i o n i n c l u s i v e m e n t" ; le deuxième est plus restrictif (mais englobe la saturation). Quant au problème de la saturation, il est résolu essentiellement par le théorème B, dans un espace de Banach.

Pour des raisons historiques, je donne à la fin de la partie consacrée aux fonctions périodiques, de nombreux exemples d'équivalence entre procédés.

Approximation des fonctions périodiques. Cette question se réduit à quelques pages. Les propriétés principales (on en trouvera de nouvelles) sont le plus souvent des conséquences immédiates des théorèmes précédents. Les démonstrations ne demandent que peu de calculs, la transformation de Fourier ne joue à peu près aucun rôle, voire aucun, la topologie est celle de $L^p$ ou $\mathcal{C}$ sans qu'il soit besoin de préciser davantage (encore qu'il soit évident qu'on peut, de même, considérer des aspects plus particuliers ou "plus fins", par exemple d'approximation locale).

La troisième partie. La première partie se transpose facilement quand on ne se borne plus à des mesures discrètes. Je me suis contenté de présenter un schéma (car il n'est besoin que de c a l q u e r hypothèses et méthodes de la première partie), en introduisant autant que possible des notations qui mènent évidemment à une vue plus générale. Du même coup est expliqué ce paradoxe, à savoir le rôle à peu près inexistant de la transformation de Fourier quand il s'agit de fonctions périodiques.

# I. THÉORÈMES GÉNÉRAUX. APPROXIMATION DANS UN ESPACE NORMÉ MUNI D'OPÉRATEURS ORTHOGONAUX

## 1. Approximations et classes d'approximations

1.1. Une *approximation* est une fonction $\rho$ à valeurs positives, d'une variable $x \in \mathfrak{J}$, ensemble non borné de $R_+$ $(x \geqslant x_0 > 0)$. Le cas qui sera le plus souvent considéré ici est celui où les $x$ sont les valeurs d'une suite croissante à l'infini, en particulier $x = n$ entier. Si, dans des conditions à préciser, à $\rho$ on fait correspondre une approximation $r = F(\rho)$, on appellera *classe d'approximations* l'ensemble des $\rho$ tels que $F(\rho) = O(1)\rho$ quand la variable $\longrightarrow +\infty$ ; elle sera notée $\{F\}$.

Dans la suite interviendront les fonctions $F$, définies pour des suites $(\rho_n)$ par

$$\Lambda_n(\lambda , \delta , \rho) = (1/n) \textstyle\sum_{\lambda n \leqslant k \leqslant \delta n} \rho_k , \quad 0 < \lambda < \delta < +\infty ;$$

$$\Lambda'_n(\lambda , \rho) = \rho_{\lambda n} , \quad 0 < \lambda < +\infty \quad ( \rho \text{ défini sur } R_+ ) ;$$

$$\sigma_n(a , \rho) = (1/|A_n|) \textstyle\sum_{0 \leqslant k \leqslant n} |a_k| \rho_k , \quad A_n = a_0 + \ldots + a_n \neq 0 , \forall n ;$$

$$\tau_n(a , \rho) = \textstyle\sum_{k \geqslant n} (|a_k|/|A_{k-1}|)\rho_k ;$$

$$\sigma_n(\Phi , \rho) = (1/n) \textstyle\sum_{1 \leqslant k \leqslant n} \Phi(k/n)\rho_k , \quad \Phi(t) > 0 \text{ pour } t > 0 ;$$

$$\tau_n(\Phi , \rho) = (1/n) \textstyle\sum_{k \geqslant n} \Phi(k/n)\rho_k \quad (< +\infty) .$$

Si $\Phi(t) = t^{\alpha}$ pour $0 < t \leqslant 1$, $\alpha > -1$, on écrit $\sigma_n(\alpha , \rho)$.
Si $\Phi(t) = t^{-\beta-1}$ quand $t \longrightarrow +\infty$, on écrit $\tau_n(\beta , \rho)$. Pour $\beta = 0$, on écrit aussi $\tau_n(0 , \rho) = \tau_n(\rho) = \sum_{k \geqslant n} \rho_k/k$.

Les expressions précédentes sont définies si on remplace $n$ par $x$. (On peut considérer les expressions analogues définies par des intégrales pour une mesure donnée.)

Les *classes d'approximations* correspondantes sont notées : $\{\Lambda(\lambda , \delta)\}$, $\{\Lambda'(\lambda)\}$, $\{\sigma(a)\}$, $\{\tau(a)\}$, $\{\sigma(\Phi)\}$, $\{\tau(\Phi)\}$, $\{\sigma(\alpha)\}$, $\{\tau(\beta)\}$, $\{\tau(0)\}$ ou $\{\tau\}$.

1.2. De nombreuses propriétés se démontrent facilement. Par exemple :

$$\rho\downarrow \Longrightarrow \rho \leqslant \sigma(a , \rho) , \text{ donc } \rho \in \{\sigma(a)\} \Longrightarrow \rho \sim \sigma(a , \rho) ;$$

$a_0 > 0$ , $a_n \geqslant 0$ , $\rho \in \{\sigma(a)\}$ , $\sum (a_k/A_k) = +\infty \Rightarrow \sum a_k \rho_k = +\infty$ ;

$a_0 > 0$ , $a_n \geqslant 0$ , $\rho\downarrow \Rightarrow \sigma(a , \rho)\downarrow$ ;

$\sigma(\alpha , \rho) \in \{\Lambda'(\lambda)\}$ si $0 < \lambda \leqslant 1$ ;

$\sigma(\alpha , \rho) \in \{\Lambda(\lambda , 1)\}$ ;

$\alpha' \geqslant \alpha \ (> -1) \Rightarrow \sigma(\alpha',\rho) = O(1)\ \sigma(\alpha,\rho)$ , donc $\{\sigma(\alpha)\} \subset \{\sigma(\alpha')\}$ ;

$\alpha > -1$ , $\alpha + \beta > -1 \Rightarrow \sigma(\alpha,\tau(\beta,\rho)) = O(1)(\sigma(\alpha,\rho) + \tau(\beta,\rho))$

et $\tau(\beta,\sigma(\alpha,\rho)) = O(1)(\sigma(\alpha,\rho) + \tau(\beta,\rho))$

qu'on peut écrire

$\sigma(\alpha) \circ \tau(\beta)$ et $\tau(\beta) \circ \sigma(\alpha) = O(1)(\sigma(\alpha) + \tau(\beta))$ ;

etc.

Voici des propriétés moins évidentes :

Si $\rho_n\downarrow$ , $\{\Lambda(\lambda , 1)\} = \{\Lambda'(\lambda)\}$ ;

Si $\varepsilon_n > 0$ , $\varepsilon_n \longrightarrow 0$ , on peut trouver $\rho_n \downarrow 0$ , $\rho_n \geqslant \varepsilon_n$ tel que $\rho \in \{\sigma(\alpha)\}$ pour tout $\alpha > -1$ ;

Si $\rho\downarrow$ et $\alpha > -1$ , $\rho \in \{\sigma(\alpha)\} \Leftrightarrow \rho_n = O(1)(\mu^{\alpha+1}/\log \mu)\rho_{\mu n}$ , où $\mu \geqslant 2$ et $O(1)$ est uniformément borné en $n$ et $\mu$ ;

Si $r\downarrow$ , $\rho\downarrow$ et $0 < r \leqslant \rho = O(1)\ \sigma(\alpha , r)$ , on a $r \in \{\sigma(\alpha)\} \Leftrightarrow \rho \in \{\sigma(\alpha)\}$, et si $r \in \{\sigma(\alpha)\}$ (ou $\rho \in \{\sigma(\alpha)\}$ ), on a $r \sim \rho$ .

## 2. Procédés, procédés-étalons, classes de procédés

2.1. Soit E un espace normé réel ou complexe, $\sum u_k$ une série dans E désignée par $u$ . Tout **procédé** (linéaire) d'**approximation** est défini par la donnée des $c(x , k)$ où $x \in \mathfrak{J}$ , $x \geqslant x_0 > 0$ et $k = 0 , 1 , 2 , \ldots$ On considère $\sum_k c(x , k)\ u_k$ .

On pose $t = k/x$ , et on désigne par $\varphi_x$ la fonction définie par $\varphi_x(t) = c(x , k)$ . Tout procédé est donc défini par une famille de fonctions $(\varphi_x)_{x\in\mathfrak{J}}$ , et on écrit $T((\varphi_x) , u) = \sum_k \varphi_x(k/x)\ u_k$ . On note ce procédé $(\varphi_x)$ ou $[\varphi_x[$ ou $(\varphi_x(t))$ ou $[\varphi_x(t)[$ . On désigne par $[\varphi_x]$ ou $[\varphi_x(t)]$ la restriction de $\varphi_x$ à $0 \leqslant t \leqslant 1$ .

Les procédés $[\varphi_x]$ sont des cas particuliers des procédés $[\varphi_x[$ , mais cette distinction est justifiée par les aspects usuels des problèmes d'approximation.

Lorsque le procédé est défini par u n e fonction $\varphi$ (i.e. $c(x,k)=\varphi(k/x)$), $\varphi$ est appelée f o n c t i o n s o m m a t o i r e (en particulier, de nombreux procédés sont donnés par $[\varphi]$ ). Mais il ne faut pas dissocier $\varphi$ de $\mathfrak{J}$ .

Par exemple, $c(n\ ,\ k) = \exp(-\ k^p/n)$ , où $p > 0$ , est défini par $[\exp(-t^p)[$ avec, pour $\mathfrak{J}$ , l'ensemble des $n^{1/p}$ . Pour ne pas l'oublier, on écrira $(\varphi(t))_{\mathfrak{J}}$ ou, si cela est plus commode, $(\varphi(t))_n$ , $(\varphi(t))_{n^{1/p}}$ , ... .

2.2. Si $\sum_k \varphi_x(k/x)\ u_k$ converge dans E et si $\lim_{x\to+\infty} \sum_k \varphi_x(k/x)u_k = s \in E$, soit $\rho_{\varphi_x} = \|T((\varphi_x)\ ,\ u) - s\|$ . Comparer deux procédés $(\varphi_x)$ , $(\gamma_x)$ c'est chercher une relation entre $\rho_{\varphi_x}$ et $\rho_{\gamma_x}$ pour une série u ou une classe de séries, en particulier chercher si $\rho_{\varphi_x} = O(1)\ \rho_{\gamma_x}$ ou $\rho_{\gamma_x} = O(1)\ \rho_{\varphi_x}$ . Si $\rho_{\varphi_x} \sim \rho_{\gamma_x}$ , on dira que les procédés sont é q u i v a l e n t s .

2.3. On prend pour procédés de référence, les procédés $[(1 - t^p)_n]$ , $p > 0$ , que nous appelons p r o c é d é s - é t a l o n s .

Pour une série u dans E et un $s \in E$ , on pose

$$\|T([(1 - t^p)_n]\ ,\ u) - s\| = \rho_n^{(p)} \quad \text{ou} \quad O(1)\ \rho_n^{(p)}\ .$$

2.4. <u>Les classes</u> $\{p\}$ <u>de procédés</u> (hypothèses simplifiées). Pour une fonction f réelle de $t > 0$ ou $t \geqslant 0$ , on pose

$$\Delta^1 f(t) = f(t + (1/x)) - f(t)\ ,\quad \Delta^{n+1} f(t) = \Delta^n(\Delta^1 f(t)) \quad \text{pour} \quad x \in \mathfrak{J}\ .$$

Soit $\Phi$ une fonction réelle $> 0$ de $t > 0$ , telle que

$$\Phi(t \pm (1/x)) - \Phi(t) = O(1)\ \Phi(t) \quad \text{pour} \quad t \quad \text{et} \quad x \longrightarrow +\infty\ .$$

On dira qu'un procédé $(\varphi_x)$ appartient à la c l a s s e $\{p\}$ , si les hypothèses suivantes sont satisfaites :

$(H_{0,\eta})$ Au voisinage de $t = 0$ $(0 \leqslant t \leqslant \eta\ ,\ \eta > 0)$ ,

$$\varphi_x(t) = \varphi_x(0) - t^p(a_x + \psi_x(t)) \quad \text{où} \quad p > 0\ ,$$

$a_x$ est constant par rapport à t , $\psi_x(0) = 0$ et, pour $t > 0$ ,

$|\psi_x(t)| \leqslant t\Phi(t)$ , $|x\Delta^1\psi_x(t)| \leqslant \Phi(t)$ ,

$$|x^2\ \Delta^2\ \psi_x(t)| \leqslant \Phi(t)/t \quad \text{uniformément en } x\ ;$$

$(H_{\eta,\delta})$ Sur tout compact $[\eta\ ,\ \delta]$ de $]0\ ,\ +\infty[$ ,

$$x\Delta^1\varphi_x(t) = O(1) \quad \text{uniformément en} \quad x \quad \text{et} \quad t \in [\eta\ ,\ \delta]\ ,$$

$$x^2 \Delta^2 \varphi_x(t) = O(1) \text{ uniformément en } x \text{ et } t ,$$

cette dernière condition pouvant n'être satisfaite que dans le complémentaire d'un ensemble fini de valeurs de $t$ ;

$(H_{\delta,\infty})$ Pour $\delta$ assez grand, sur $[\delta , +\infty[$ , $|\varphi_x(t)|$ , $|x\Delta^1\varphi_x(t)|$ , $|x^2 \Delta^2 \varphi_x(t)|$ sont majorés par $\Phi(t)$ uniformément en $x$ .

La fonction $\Phi$ est dite *majorante associée* à $(\varphi_x)$ .

S'il s'agit de $[\varphi_x]$ , on suppose usuellement $\varphi_x(1) = 0$ , mais $\varphi_x(1)=O(1/x)$ suffit. On peut même, dans certains cas, adopter une hypothèse plus faible.

## 3. Les théorèmes généraux

3.1. Le théorème A (Comparaison d'un procédé $(\varphi_x)$ de la classe $\{p\}$ et du procédé-étalon de cette classe). **Soit $X$ la partie entière de $x$ et** $S_n = u_0 + \ldots + u_n$ .

S'il s'agit de $[\varphi_x[$ , on suppose $E$ complet et $\tau_x(t\Phi(t) , \rho^{(p)}) < +\infty$ pour tout $x$ (c'est-à-dire $\sum_k k\Phi(k/x)\, \rho_k^{(p)} < +\infty$ ).

On a, pour $s \in E$ ,

$$T([\varphi_x],u) - \varphi_x(0)\, s = \varphi_x(X/x)(S_X-s) + O(1)\Big(\sum_i \rho^{(p)}_{t_i x} + \Lambda_X(\eta,1,\rho^{(p)}) + \rho_X^{(p)} + \sigma_x(t^p\, \Phi(t) , \rho^{(p)})\Big) ,$$

$$T([\varphi_x[,u) - \varphi_x(0)\, s = O(1)\Big(\sum_i \rho^{(p)}_{t_i x} + \Lambda_x(\eta,\delta,\rho^{(p)}) + \sigma_x(t^p\, \Phi(t),\rho^{(p)}) + \tau_x(t^p\, \Phi(t),\rho^{(p)})\Big) ,$$

où les entiers $t_i\, x$ sont en nombre fini.

### 3.1.1. Conséquences.

1° Pour toute série dans $E$ normé, les procédés-étalons de $\{p\}$ et $\{q\}$ , $p \neq q$ , sont équivalents pour les approximations $\rho \in \{\sigma(\inf(p,q) - 1)\}$ .

2° Propriété (N). On suppose que pour un procédé-étalon,

$$\|T([(1 - t^q)_n] , u)\| = O(1) .$$

Soit $(\varphi_x) \in \{p\}$ . S'il s'agit de $[\varphi_x]$ , on suppose que $|\varphi_x(X/x)|\,\|S_X\|=O(1)$ et $\sigma_x(t^p\, \Phi(t) , 1) = O(1)$ . S'il s'agit de $[\varphi_x[$, on suppose $\sigma_x(t^p\Phi(t),1)=O(1)$ et $\tau_x(t\Phi(t) , 1) = O(1)$ . Alors, pour tout $p > 0$ et tout $(\varphi_x) \in \{p\}$ , on a

$$\|T(\varphi_x , u)\| = O(1) .$$

(Cas particulier : $\varphi_x(1) = O(1/x)$ , $\Phi(t) = O(1)\, t^{\varepsilon-1}$ avec $p + \varepsilon > 0$ si $t \longrightarrow 0$ , $\Phi(t) = O(1)$ sur tout compact de $]0\,, +\infty[$ , $\Phi(t) = t^{-\beta-2}$ avec $\beta > 0$ si $t \longrightarrow +\infty$ ).

3.2. Le théorème B (Comparaison de deux procédés-étalons).

LEMME. Soit $A_n = a_0 + \ldots + a_n \neq 0$ pour tout $n \geqslant n_0$ ( $n_0$ fixé). Dans E normé, on a

$$s \in E \text{ et } \|S_n - s\| \leqslant \rho_n \Rightarrow \|\textstyle\sum_1^n A_{k-1}\, u_k\| \leqslant |A_n|(\rho_n + \sigma_n(a,\rho)) .$$

Dans E complet, on a

$$\textstyle\sum_k |a_k/A_{k-1}|\,\rho_k < +\infty \text{ et } \|\sum_1^n A_{k-1}\, u_k\| \leqslant |A_n|\,\rho_n$$

$$\Rightarrow \exists\, s \in E \text{ et } \|S_n - s\| \leqslant \rho_n + \tau_{n+1}(a,\rho) .$$

THÉORÈME B. Soit E un espace de Banach, $\sum \rho_k/k < +\infty$ , $p > 0$ , $q > 0$ , $p \neq q$ . On a

$$T([(t^p-t^q)_n],u) = T([(1-t^q)_n],u) - T([(1-t^p)_n],u) = O(1)\rho_n$$

$$\Rightarrow \exists\, s \in E \text{ et } T([(1-t^r)_n],u) - s = O(1)(\rho_n + \tau_{n+1}(0,\rho)) \text{ pour } r=p \text{ ou } q.$$

COROLLAIRE. Dans un espace de Banach E , pour les approximations

$$\rho \in \{\sigma(q-1)\} \cap \{\tau(0)\} ,$$

on a

$$T([(1-t^p)_n],u) - s = O(\rho_n) \Leftrightarrow T([(t^p-t^q)_n],u) = O(\rho_n) .$$

3.3. Le théorème C. Pour une fonction d réelle $> 0$ de l'entier $n \geqslant 1$ et pour un entier $a \geqslant 2$ , on pose $\delta(n) = \sum_1^{n+1} d(a^k)$ et, pour $x \in R$ , $x \geqslant 1$ , on prolonge $\delta$ en fonction continûment dérivable strictement croissante.

Soit E normé, $\mathcal{P}_n$ une famille de sous-espaces tels que $\mathcal{P}_n \subset \mathcal{P}_{n+1}$ . Soit $\mathcal{P} = \bigcup \mathcal{P}_n$ , et D une application linéaire de $\mathcal{P}$ dans un normé $\mathcal{E}$ , continue sur tout $\mathcal{P}_n$ . Soit d une fonction réelle $> 0$ de n telle que

$$\|D\|_{\mathcal{L}(\mathcal{P}_n;\mathcal{E})} \leqslant d(n) .$$

On suppose que, pour un $f \in E$ et une suite $(P_n)$ telle que $P_n \in \mathcal{P}_n$ pour tout n , on a $\|P_n - f\|_E \leqslant \rho(n)$ , où $\rho$ est continue, positive, décroissante. Alors, on a, avec a entier $\geqslant 2$ , $a^2 \leqslant n_0 < n$ ,

$$\|DP_n - DP_{n_0}\|_{\mathcal{E}} \leqslant 6 \int_{n_0/a^2}^{n} \rho(\theta)\, d\delta(\log\theta/\log a) .$$

N.-B. On peut établir une inégalité encore un peu plus précise.

Cas particuliers. Si $d(x) = x^m$ , $m \geqslant 0$ , $x \geqslant 1$ , on a

$$\|P_n - f\|_E \leqslant \rho(n) \Rightarrow \|D(P_n)-D(P_{n_0})\|_{\mathcal{E}} = O(1) \int_{n_0/a^2}^{n} \rho(\theta)\ \theta^{m-1}\ d\theta$$

$$\text{et} \quad \|DP_n\|_{\mathcal{E}} = O(1)\ n^m\ \sigma_n(m-1,\rho)\ .$$

Si de plus $\mathcal{E}$ est complet et $\int^{+\infty} \rho(\theta)\ \theta^{m-1}\ d\theta < +\infty$ , $DP_n$ converge dans $\mathcal{E}$ et, si on note $Df$ la limite, on a

$$\|DP_n - Df\| = O(1) \sum_{k\geqslant n/4} k^{m-1}\ \rho_k\ .$$

Applications. Cas où $E$ est un espace de fonctions, $\mathcal{P}_n$ sous-espace de polynômes de degré $\leqslant n$ , $D$ un opérateur de dérivation. Cas où les $P_n$ sont des fonctions qui sont, "par morceaux", des polynômes se raccordant, eux et leurs dérivées jusqu'à un certain ordre. Cas de la convolution, $K_x * f$ (en particulier quand $K_x(\theta) = xg(x\theta)$ ), moyennant des hypothèses sur les dérivées des $K_x$ par rapport à $\theta$ .

## 4. Approximation dans un espace normé muni d'une famille d'opérateurs orthogonaux (Développements de Fourier généraux)

Soit $\mathcal{E}$ normé, $(u_i)$ une famille dénombrable d'opérateurs (linéaires) continus dans $\mathcal{E}$ tels que $u_i\, u_j = u_j\, u_i = 0$ si $i \neq j$ , $u_i\, u_i = u_i$ pour tout $i$ .

4.1. On dira qu'une famille d'opérateurs continus dans $\mathcal{E}$ possède la p r o p r i é t é (N), si l'ensemble des normes de ces opérateurs est borné.

Si $\|T([(1 - t)_n])\| = O(1)$ , alors, dans les conditions de (3.1.1., 2°), pour tout $p > 0$ et pour tout $(\varphi_x) \in \{p\}$ , on a $\|T(\varphi_x)\| = O(1)$ .

4.2. Quand $\|T([(1 - t)_n])\| = O(1)$ , on désigne l'espace précédent par $(\mathcal{E}\ , u_i\ , N)$ .

4.3. Théorèmes d'équivalence entre procédés dans un espace $(\mathcal{E}\ , u_i\ , N)$

4.3.1. Hypothèses communes aux premier et deuxième théorèmes. On suppose $(\varphi_x) \in \{p\}$ , $p > 0$ , $x \in \mathfrak{J}$ , la fonction majorante associée $\Phi$ est $\Phi(t) = O(1)$ sur tout compact de $]0\ , +\infty[$ , $\Phi(t) = t^{-\beta-2}$ avec $\beta > 0$

quand $t \longrightarrow +\infty$ ; au voisinage de $t = 0$ ,

$\varphi_x(t) = 1 - t^p(a_x + t^{\varepsilon}(b_x + \chi_x(t)))$ ,

où $t = k/x$ , $\varepsilon > 0$ , $\lim_{x\to\infty} \inf|a_x| > 0$ ,

et où $\chi_x$ satisfait aux hypothèses $(H_{o,\eta})$ de 2.4 avec une fonction majorante associée $\Phi_1(t) = t^{\varepsilon'-1}$ , $\varepsilon + \varepsilon' > 0$ (ce qui entraîne $\Phi(t) = t^{\varepsilon-1} + t^{\varepsilon+\varepsilon'-1}$).

Enfin, s'il s'agit de $(\varphi_x)$ , $\varphi_x(1) = O(1/x)$ , et s'il s'agit de $(\varphi_x($ , $\mathcal{E}$ est complet.

THÉORÈME 1. Si $1 - \varphi_x(t) > 0$ pour $t > 0$ et $\inf_{x, t \geq \eta > 0} |1 - \varphi_x(t)| > 0$ , **les procédés** $(\varphi_x)$ **et** $((1 - t^p)_x)$ **sont équivalents.**

(La preuve repose sur la propriété N essentiellement.)

THÉORÈME 2. On suppose $\mathcal{E}$ **complet,** $(u_i)$ **totale.** Si J **contient une suite** $(x_m)$ **telle que** $x_m \uparrow +\infty$ , $x_{m+1} - x_m = O(1)$ , **il existe** $m_n$ **et** $\lambda_n$ **pour** $n \geq n_0$ , **tels que** $1 \leq \mu_1 \leq \lambda_n \leq \mu_2 < +\infty$ **et** $x_{m_n} = n\lambda_n$ , **et le procédé** $(\varphi_{n\lambda_n})$ **est équivalent à** $((1 - t^p)_n)$ **pour les approximations** $\rho$ , **telles que** $\rho_n \longrightarrow 0$ , $\rho_{\lambda n} = O(1)\rho_n$ **pour** $1 \leq \lambda \leq \mu < +\infty$ ( $\mu$ **fixe) et appartenant à la classe** $\{\sigma(p + \varepsilon - 1 + \inf(0 , \varepsilon'))\} \cap \{\tau(0)\}$ .

(La démonstration utilise A, B, N.)

N.-B. La condition $\rho_{\lambda n} = O(1)\, \rho_n$ est nécessaire. Il est, d'autre part, inutile de la mentionner si $\rho\downarrow$ ou si $\mathfrak{J}$ est la suite des entiers et si $1 - \varphi_n(t) \neq 0$ , $0 \leq t \leq 1$ .

4.3.2. <u>Le troisième théorème</u>

LEMME (<u>Théorème A'</u>). Soit $\mathcal{P}_n$ le sous-espace de $(\mathcal{E} , u_i , N)$ engendré par les $f_k \neq 0$ tels que $u_k(f_k) = f_k$ pour $k = 0 , 1 , \ldots , n$ ("polynômes" de degré n ).

On a

$$\rho > 0 , \ \rho\downarrow , \ P_n \in \mathcal{P}_n , \ P_n - f = O(\rho_n) \Longrightarrow T(((1 - t^p)_n) , f) - f = O(1)\, \sigma_n(p - 1 , \rho) .$$

(La démonstration utilise N et C .)

THÉORÈME 3. Si $(\varphi_n) \in \{p\}$ , $\varphi_n(0) = 1$ , $\varphi_n(1) = O(1/n)$ , $\lim \inf_{n\infty} |a_n| > 0$, et si la fonction majorante associée est $\Phi(t) = O(1)\ t^{\varepsilon-1}$ avec $p + \varepsilon > 0$, $(\varphi_n)$ est équivalent à $((1 - t^p)_n)$ pour les approximations décroissantes $\rho \in \{\sigma(p + \varepsilon - 1)\}$.

(La démonstration utilise A et C .)

Remarques

1° On peut donner des énoncés plus généraux en ne supposant pas $\beta > 0$, et en conservant $\Phi$ et $\Phi_1$.

2° Les théorèmes les "plus simples" sont le premier et le troisième. Si $\rho\downarrow$, le deuxième n'a pas d'intérêt pour les procédés $(\varphi_x)$. En pratique, le deuxième intéresse les procédés $(\varphi_x($, quand les hypothèses du premier ne sont pas satisfaites.

3° On peut énoncer le troisième théorème pour un ensemble $\mathfrak{J}$.

4° On peut démontrer un théorème d'équivalence entre $(\varphi_x)$ et $((1)_x)$ (par exemple pour $(\varphi_n)$, $\lim_{n\infty} \inf|\varphi_n(1)| > 0$, etc.).

4.4. Propriétés des approximations fournies par les procédés-étalons. Les $\rho_n^{(p)}(f) = \rho_n^{(p)} = \|T(((1 - t^p)_n), f) - f\| = \|T_n^{(p)}(f) - f\|$ possèdent des propriétés simples :

$$q > p \Rightarrow \rho_n^{(q)} = O(1)\ \rho_n^{(p)}\ ;\quad \rho_x^{(p)} \sim \rho_X^{(p)}\ ;$$

$$\rho_{\lambda x}^{(p)} = O(1)\ \rho_x^{(p)} \quad \text{pour} \quad 0 < \lambda_0 \leqslant \lambda \leqslant \mu_0 < +\infty\ ;\quad \rho_x^{(p)} = O(1)\ \sigma_x(\alpha, \rho^{(p)})\ ;\ \text{etc.}$$

4.5. Saturation. Une fois définie la saturation et données des conditions suffisantes pour qu'un procédé se sature (ou ne se sature pas), le théorème B donne une condition nécessaire et suffisante définissant la classe de saturation d'un procédé-étalon, donc celle d'un procédé d'une classe $\{p\}$, car s'il y a saturation, les théorèmes d'équivalence valent pour l'approximation de saturation. On notera que les premier et troisième théorèmes vont "de la convergence à la saturation inclusivement".

N.-B. Pour des raisons historiques, les exemples illustrant les théorèmes d'équivalence sont exposés dans la partie II.

## II. APPROXIMATION DES FONCTIONS PÉRIODIQUES

1. Modules de continuité. Soit $E$ un espace normé, réel ou complexe, $E_1$ un sous-espace de $E$, $\mathcal{L}(E)$ l'espace des opérateurs linéaires continus sur $E$. On considère les $\delta_h \in \mathcal{L}(E)$, où $h$ appartient à une boule ouverte (de centre $0$, de rayon $r > 0$) d'un espace normé $A$. On suppose :

1° $\delta_0 = I$ (identité) ;
2° $\delta_h \delta_{h'} = \delta_{h+h'}$ quels que soient $h$, $h'$ (et $\|h + h'\| < r$) ;
3° $\|\delta_h\| \leqslant a$ pour tout $h$ où $a =$ constante $\geqslant 1$ indépendante de $h$ ;
4° pour tout $f \in E_1$, $\lim_{h\to 0} \|(\delta_h - \delta_0)f\| = 0$.

On appelle m o d u l e d e c o n t i n u i t é (d'ordre entier $m \geqslant 1$) de $f$, relativement à $E_1$, la fonction réelle positive $\omega_m(f)$ définie pour $0 \leqslant t < r/m$ par $\omega_m(f, t) = \sup_{\|h\| \leqslant t} \|(\delta_h - \delta_0)^m\| f$.

1.1. Les propriétés des $\omega_m(f)$ sont les propriétés classiques des modules de continuité. On notera que si on définit $\omega_m$ par les différences itérées à partir de $\Delta^1 \delta_h = \delta_h - \delta_0$ et $\Omega_m$ par les différences symétriques à partir de $\delta_h - \delta_{-h'}$, on a $\omega_m \leqslant a\Omega_m \leqslant a^2 \omega_m$.

1.2. Pour les fonctions réelles de variable réelle, la définition adoptée de $\omega_m$ permet de trouver rapidement les propriétés de $\omega_m$ quand on fait intervenir les propriétés différentielles de $f$. En particulier, on obtient, comme conséquence, l'inégalité suivante (connue sous une autre forme) :

$$\|f^{(m)}\| \leqslant 2\sqrt{6}\, \|f^{(m-1)}\|^{\frac{1}{2}} \|f^{(m+1)}\|^{\frac{1}{2}} .$$

De cette inégalité, on déduira aisément celle de Bernstein, non seulement pour les polynômes périodiques, mais pour d'autres polynômes orthogonaux (LEGENDRE, LAGUERRE, HERMITE, ...).

On dira que $f$ satisfait à une condition Lip $\alpha$ (resp. lip $\alpha$) avec $0 < \alpha \leqslant 1$ (resp. $0 \leqslant \alpha < 1$), relativement à la topologie de $E$, si $\omega_1(f, t) = O(1)\, t^\alpha$ quand $t \to 0$ (resp. $\omega_1(f, t) = o(1)\, t^\alpha$).

N.-B. Si $f = \int g$ est absolument continue, on convient d'écrire abusivement $f' = g$.

2. Les espaces $(E, u_i, N)$ des fonctions périodiques. La norme est indifféremment celle de $\mathcal{C}$ ou $L^p$. La série de Fourier $u(f)$ de $f$ est $\sum u_k(f)$ ou $\sum u_k.f$. On écrit $T(\varphi_x, f)$ au lieu de $T(\varphi_x, u(f))$.

2.1. La propriété (N) est vérifiée.

2.2. On note $\varpi(f, (1/n))$ ou $\varpi(1/n)$ la meilleure approximation de $f$ par des polynômes périodiques $P_n$ de degré $\leq n$.

2.3. Inégalité de Bernstein. En utilisant (1.2) et le fait que

$$\|T([(1 - t^2)_n])\| = O(1),$$

on a $\|P_n'\| \leq \gamma n \|P_n\|$, $\gamma$ = constante absolue.

2.4. Théorème C pour les modules de continuité.

$$P_n - f = O(1)\, \omega_m(f, (1/n)) \Rightarrow P_n^{(m)} = O(1)\, n^m\, \omega_m(f, (1/n)).$$

(C'est une application immédiate de la propriété $\omega_m \in \{\sigma(\alpha)\}$ pour tout $\alpha > m - 1$.)

3. Approximation des fonctions périodiques. On suppose que les approximations sont décroissantes (cette hypothèse correspond aux cas "usuels" et est, de plus, justifiée par I, 4.4).

Les démonstrations des propriétés principales, qui vont être exposées, sont souvent brèves, plus souvent encore très brèves. Sauf 3.1.1, elles utilisent les théorèmes A, B, C, A'. Le théorème $\overline{A}$' concerne les fonctions conjuguées.

3.1. Des propriétés différentielles vers l'approximation

3.1.1. Pour tout entier $m \geq 1$, il existe une suite $(P_n)$ de polynômes de degré $n$, tels que $P_n - f = O(1)\, \omega_m(f, (1/n))$.

La démonstration utilise des combinaisons linéaires de procédés $[(1-t^2)_n^m]$ ; elle n'exige que de considérer la transformée de Fourier de $(1 - t^2)^m$ et l'inverse. Mais on trouvera en III, 2.3 ci-dessous, une démonstration plus simple qui repose sur le premier théorème d'équivalence.

Si on suppose $\omega_m(f) \in \{\tau(0)\}$ (c'est-à-dire
$$\sum_{k\geqslant n} \omega_m(f\ ,\ (1/k))/k = O(1)\ \omega_m(f\ ,\ (1/n))\ ),$$
le théorème B donne aussitôt le résultat s a n s aucun calcul d'intégrale. Dans ce dernier cas, on peut aussi obtenir les résultats concernant l'approximation de la fonction conjuguée $\overline{f}$.

3.1.3. Approximation par des procédés-étalons. Pour $p > 0$ , $m$ entier $\geqslant 1$ , on a :

$$p \leqslant m\ ,\quad T(\{(1 - t^p)_n\}\ ,\ f) - f = O(1)\ \sigma_n(p - 1\ ,\ \omega_m(f))\ ;$$

$$p > m\ ,\quad T(\{(1 - t^p)_n\}\ ,\ f) - f = O(1)\ \omega_m(f\ ,\ (1/n))\ ;$$

$$p = 2m\ ,\quad T(\{(1 - t^{2m})_n\}\ ,\ f) - f = O(1)\ \omega_{2m}(f\ ,\ (1/n))\ .$$

(Les deux premières propriétés ne font que traduire le théorème A' ; la dernière est une conséquence des théorèmes A' et C .)

3.1.4. Meilleures approximations et modules de continuité.
$$\omega_m \in \{\sigma(m - 1)\} \Leftrightarrow \varpi \in \{\sigma(m - 1)\}\ ,$$
et l'une de ces propriétés entraîne $\omega_m \sim \varpi$ (ce n'est que la dernière propriété indiquée en I, 1.2).

3.2. De l'approximation vers les propriétés différentielles

3.2.1. Pour tout entier $m \geqslant 1$ , si $P_n - f = O(\rho_n)$ , $\rho > 0$ , $\rho\downarrow$ , on a $\omega_m(f) = O(1)\ \sigma(m - 1\ ,\ \rho)$ (c'est une application immédiate du théorème C).

3.2.2. $\omega_m(f) = O(1)\ \sigma(m - 1\ ,\ \omega_{m'}(f))$ , $m$ , $m'$ entiers $\geqslant 1$ (sans intérêt si $m' \leqslant m$ ).

3.2.3. Si pour $\nu \geqslant 1$ (non nécessairement entier), $\sum k^{\nu-1}\ \rho_k < +\infty$ et $P_n - f = O(\rho_n)$ , on a, pour tout entier $m \leqslant \nu$ , $f^{(m)}$ existe, $f^{(m)} \in E$ et $P^{(m)}_{n+1} - f^{(m)} = O(1)\ n^m(\rho_n + \tau_n(-\ m\ ,\ \rho))$ .
(C'est une conséquence du théorème C.)

3.2.4. On appelle a p p r o x i m a t i o n p o l y n o m i a l e , et on la note $\rho_n(f)$ , une approximation de $f$ par des polynômes $P_n$ de degré $n$ , c'est-à-dire $P_n - f = O(1)\ \rho_n(f)$ . On a :

1° m entier $\geq 1$ , $\exists f^{(m)}$ , $f^{(m)} \in E \Rightarrow \rho_n(f) = O(1)\, n^{-m}\, \sigma_n(\alpha-1, \rho(f^{(m)}))$ pour tout $\alpha \geq 1$ .

2° $\sum k^{m-1}\, \rho_k(k) < +\infty \Rightarrow \exists f^{(m)}$ , $f^{(m)} \in E$ et

$$\rho_{n+1}(f^{(m)}) = O(1)\, n^m\, (\rho_n(f) + \tau_n(-m , \rho(f))) .$$

(Cela résulte de manière évidente de 3.2.1 et 3.2.3.)

3.2.5. Approximations appartenant à des classes $\{\sigma\}$ ou $\{\tau\}$ . Toutes les propriétés classiques sont contenues dans celle-ci qui est une conséquence évidente de 3.2.1 :

$$\rho\downarrow , \quad \rho \in \{\sigma(\alpha - 1)\} , \quad \alpha > 0 \text{ et } P_n - f = O(1)\, \rho_n$$
$$\Longrightarrow \begin{cases} \omega_m(f , (1/n)) = O(1)\, \rho_n & \text{pour tout entier } m \geq \alpha , \\ \omega_m(f , (1/n)) = O(1)\, \sigma_n(m-1 , \rho) & \text{pour tout } m < \alpha . \end{cases}$$

D'où : les seules approximations polynomiales décroissantes appartenant à une classe $\{\sigma(\alpha)\}$ sont les $\omega_m$ .

3.3. Approximation des fonctions **conjuguées**. Toutes les propriétés (anciennes ou nouvelles) résultent principalement du théorème suivant dont la preuve utilise les théorèmes B et C :

THÉORÈME $\overline{A}$'. Si $\rho\downarrow$ et $\sum \rho_k/k < +\infty$ , on a, pour tout $p > 0$ ,

$$P_n - f = O(1)\rho_n \Rightarrow \overline{f} \in E \text{ et } T([(1-t^p)_n],\overline{f}) - \overline{f} = O(1)(\sigma_n(p-1,\rho) + \tau_n(\rho)) .$$

On obtient aussitôt les relations entre $\rho(f)$ et $\rho(\overline{f})$ , $\omega_m(f)$ et $\omega_m(\overline{f})$, l'approximation de $\overline{f}$ par les procédés-étalons, etc.

4. Approximation par des procédés des classes $\{p\}$

4.1. Saturation. Voir I, 4.5

4.2. Développement de l'approximation. Soit $(\varphi_n)$ , m entier $\geq 1$ , tel qu'au voisinage de $t = 0$ ,

$$\varphi_n(t) = 1 + \sum_{k=1}^m a_{n,k}\, t^k + t^m\, \psi_{n,m}(t) ,$$

$\psi_{n,m}$ possédant une fonction majorante associée pour laquelle $\varepsilon > 0$ (Cf. I, 2 et I, 4). Si $f^{(m)} \in \mathrm{Lip}\,\alpha$ $(0 < \alpha \leq 1)$ , on a :

$$T(\varphi_n,f) = f - a_{n,1}\frac{f'}{n} - a_{n,2}\frac{f''}{n^2} + a_{n,3}\frac{f^{(3)}}{n^3} + a_{n,4}\frac{f^{(4)}}{n^4} + \ldots + O(1/n^{m+\alpha}) .$$

On peut donner un résultat analogue en considérant les $\omega_\nu(f^{(m)})$ .

5. Les principaux résultats connus, cas particuliers des théorèmes précédents

On trouvera des indications dans les notes et commentaires des mémoires à paraître, et une brève bibliographie historique jusqu'en 1976.

Voici les principaux exemples concernant des procédés souvent employés et qui sont équivalents à un procédé-étalon (Cf. N.-B. en I, 4.5). Il suffit d'utiliser le premier théorème d'équivalence. La vérification des conditions de validité est en général immédiate.

- Les procédés $[(1-t)^p_n]$ , les procédés de CESARO (C , p) , sont équivalents à $[(1-t)_n]$ qui est la p r e m i è r e m o y e n n e a r i t h m é t i q u e , dit procédé de FEJÉR.

- Les procédés de RIESZ, BOCHNER-RIESZ $[(1-t^p)^q_n]$, $p>0$ , $q>0$, sont équivalents à $[(1-t^p)_n]$ .

- Le procédé de ROGOSINSKI $[(\cos(\pi(t/2)))_n]$ est équivalent à $[(1-t^2)_n]$ (les procédés $[(\cos(\lambda_n\,\pi(t/2)))_n]$ s'étudient aisément).

- Les meilleurs procédés de FAVARD et ACHIESER-KREIN sont équivalents à $[(1-t^{2m})_n]$ si $p = 2m$ , à $[(1-t^{2m+2})_n]$ si $p = 2m+1$ .

- Les procédés de JACKSON, de JACKSON - de LA VALLÉE-POUSSIN (définis par des convolées de f avec un noyau positif pair) sont équivalents à $[(1-t^2)_n]$.

- Un procédé de FEJÉR, défini par

$$[\varphi_n(t)] = (1-t)\cos t\pi + (1/n)(\mathrm{cotg}(\pi/n))\sin t\pi$$

est équivalent à $[(1-t^2)_n]$ .

- Le procédé $[\varphi(t)] = \int_0^{1-t} \lambda(\theta)\,\lambda(\theta+t)\,d\theta$ , avec $\lambda$ , $\lambda'$ , $\lambda''$ continus et $\int_0^1 \lambda^2(\theta)\,d\theta \neq 0$ , est équivalent à $[(1-t)_n]$ si $\lambda^2(0)+\lambda^2(1)\neq 0$, à $[(1-t^2)_n]$ si $\lambda(0)=\lambda(1)=0$ .

- Les procédés de PICARD $[(\varphi(t))_n[$ , où $\varphi(t) = (1+t^p)^{-q}$ , $p>0$ , $q>0$ , $t\geqslant 0$ , sont équivalents à $[(1-t^p)_n]$ si $pq>2$ . Si $pq\leqslant 2$, on établit l'équivalence mais pour des classes d'approximations ou pour des sous-espaces de E .

- Les procédés généralisés de RIEMANN, LEBESGUE, $[((\sin t)/t)_n^p[$ sont équivalents à $[(1-t^2)_n]$ si $p > 2$ (Si $p \leqslant 2$, cf. procédés de PICARD).

- Les procédés du type GAUSS-WEIERSTRASS $[(\exp(-t^p))_n[$ (dit souvent de CAUCHY si $p = 1$) sont équivalents à $[(1-t^p)_n]$.

- Le procédé d'ABEL (noyau de Poisson) $[\varphi_n(t)[ = (1-(1/n))^{nt}$ est équivalent à $[(1-t)_n]$.

- Les procédés généralisés $[(1-(1/n))^{k^p}[$, $[\exp(-k^p/n)[$ sont équivalents à $[(1-t^p)_{n^{1/p}}]$.

- Le procédé de LA VALLÉE-POUSSIN, défini par $C(n,k) = (n!)^2/(n-k)!(n+k)!$, est équivalent à $[(1-t^2)_{\sqrt{n}}]$.

## III. CAS DE MESURES NON DISCRÈTES. CONVOLUTION. EXPLICATION D'UN PARADOXE

Les idées et les méthodes ont été testées sur des séries (ou des suites) et sur des espaces que j'ai notés $(E, u_i, N)$. Elles se transposent facilement lorsqu'on ne considère plus des mesures discrètes. C'est pourquoi je me borne à un schéma qui concerne les points les plus importants.

### 1. Cas de mesures non discrètes

1.1. On considère sur $R$ des mesures définies par des fonctions continues dont les dérivées premières sont absolument continues par rapport à la mesure de Lebesgue (on peut même supposer cette hypothèse satisfaite par "morceaux"). Soit $\theta \longrightarrow S_\theta$ une fonction $S$, continue pour $\theta \geqslant 0$, à valeurs dans un espace de Banach $E$ (l'hypothèse que $E$ est complet n'est pas nécessaire dans tous les cas).

Sous des hypothèses faciles à préciser (Cf. I), une famille $(\nu_x)$ de mesures finies où $x \geqslant x_0 > 0$, $x \longrightarrow +\infty$, définit un procédé, noté $(\nu_x)$ ou $[\nu_x[$ ou $(\varphi_x)$ si on pose $\nu_x(\theta) = \varphi_x(\theta/x)$, et on considère

$$T(\nu_x, S) = -\int_0^{+\infty} S_\theta \, d\nu_x(\theta) .$$

Si $\nu_x(\theta) = 0$ quand $\theta > x$, on écrit $[\nu_x]$ et

$$T([\nu_x), S) = -\int_0^x S_\theta \, d\nu_x(\theta) .$$

On définit un procédé-étalon $(\mu)$ en prenant $[\nu_x(\theta)]=1-\frac{\mu(\theta)}{\mu(x)}$ avec $\mu(0) = 0$ et $\mu > 0$, $\mu' \neq 0$ si $\theta > 0$.

1.2. Voici comment se présente le théorème A et comment s'introduisent classes de procédés et classes d'approximations.

De $T(\mu(x), S) = \frac{1}{\mu(X)} \int_0^x S_\theta \, d\mu(\theta)$, il vient $S \, d\mu = d(\mu T(\mu, S))$, donc

$$T(\nu_x, S) = -\int S \, d\nu_x = -\int \frac{d\nu_x}{d\mu} \, d(\mu T(\mu, S))$$

et, en intégrant par parties, on obtient :

pour $[\nu_x[$, $T(\nu_x, S) = \int_0^{+\infty} T(\mu, S) \, \mu \, d(\frac{d\nu_x}{d\mu})$ ;

pour $[\nu_x)$, $T([\nu_x), S) = \int_0^x T(\mu, S) \, \mu \, d(\frac{d\nu_x}{d\mu}) - \mu(x) \, T(\mu(x), S)(\frac{d\nu_x(\theta)}{d\mu(\theta)})_{\theta=x}$.

De là, avec $\nu_x(0) = 1$, pour un $s \in E$,

$$T(\nu_x, S) - s = \int_0^{+\infty} (T(\mu, S) - s) \, \mu \, d(\frac{d\nu_x}{d\mu})$$

ou

$$T([\nu_x), S) - s = \int_0^x (T(\mu, S) - s) \, \mu \, d(\frac{d\nu_x}{d\mu}) - \mu(x)(T(\mu(x), S) - s)(\frac{d\nu_x(\theta)}{d\mu(\theta)})_{\theta=x} .$$

Si on écrit $\|T(\mu(x), S) - s\| = \rho_x$ ou $O(1) \, \rho_x$, on obtient une majoration de $\|T(\nu_x, S) - s\|$ en fonction de $\rho$ et, naturellement, de $\mu$ et $\nu_x$. On simplifie le problème en supposant que $\nu_x$ a certaines propriétés par rapport à $\mu$.

Par exemple, avec $\mu(\theta) = \theta^p$, $p > 0$ et si, en particulier, au voisinage de $\theta = 0$,

$$\nu_x(\theta) = \varphi_x(\frac{\theta}{x}) = 1 - \frac{\mu(\theta)}{\mu(x)} (a_x + \psi_x(\frac{\theta}{x}))$$

où, pour les dérivées de $\xi \longrightarrow \psi_x(\xi)$, on a

$$\psi_x'(\xi) = O(1) \, \xi^{\varepsilon-1} , \quad \psi'' = O(1) \, \xi^{\varepsilon-2} \quad \text{avec} \quad \varepsilon > 0 ,$$

uniformément, on définit une classe de procédés notée $\{p\}$. Alors, la majoration de $\|T(\nu_x, S) - s\|$ fait intervenir, entre autres, des quantités $\sigma_x(p + \varepsilon - 1, \rho)$, ce qui mène à définir la classe d'approximations $\{\sigma(\alpha)\}$, $\alpha > -1$.

De ce qui précède résulte aussi que

$$\|T(\mu(x))\| = O(1) \ \text{(hypothèse N)} \Longrightarrow \|T(\nu_x)\| = O(1) \ \text{(propriété N)}.$$

1.3. Le théorème B (ici : (I, 3.2) ; dans le premier mémoire : (3.4)), qui permet de trouver les classes de saturation, et intervient dans la démonstration du deuxième théorème d'équivalence quand il s'agit des espaces $(E, u_i, N)$, vient d'un lemme (ici : (I, 3.2) ; dans le premier mémoire : (3.3)). Ce lemme s'énoncera avec des hypothèses convenables (on supposera $\theta \longrightarrow S_\theta$ par exemple continûment dérivable) sous les formes suivantes :

dans un espace normé $E$,

$$S_x - s = O(1)\ \rho_x \Rightarrow \int_0^x \mu\ dS = O(1)\ \mu(x)\ (\rho_x + \sigma_x(d\mu\ ,\ \rho))\ ;$$

dans un espace de Banach,

$$\int \rho \frac{|d\mu|}{\mu} < +\infty \quad \text{et} \quad \int_0^x \mu\ dS = O(1)\ \mu(x)\ \rho_x$$
$$\Rightarrow \exists\ s \in E \quad \text{et} \quad S_x - s = O(1)\ (\rho_x + \int_x^{+\infty} \rho \frac{|d\mu|}{\mu})\ .$$

On obtient ensuite le théorème B en suivant la démonstration établie pour des séries. On arrive à

$$\int_0^x \nu_x(\theta)\ d(T(\mu(\theta)\ ,\ S)) = \int_0^x S_\theta\ d\chi_x(\theta)\ ,$$

où $\chi_x(t) = \mu(t) \int_{\theta=t}^{\theta=x} \nu_x(\theta)\ d(\frac{1}{\mu(\theta)})$, et on choisit convenablement $\nu_x$ ou $\chi_x$. Puis on applique le résultat précédent à $\int_0^x \nu_x(\theta)\ d(T(\mu(\theta)\ ,\ S))$. Par exemple avec $\mu(\theta) = \theta^p$ et $\nu_x(\theta) = \theta^q/x^q$, on obtient le théorème B de I.

1.4. La forme générale du théorème C n'a pas besoin de commentaire.

1.5. On considère ensuite un espace de Banach $\mathcal{E}$, et une famille d'opérateurs continus $S_x \in E = \mathcal{L}(\mathcal{E})$, tels que, pour tout $f \in \mathcal{E}$, $x \longrightarrow S_x(f)$ est continu en $x$. Pour $f \in \mathcal{E}$, on écrit

$$T(\nu_x\ ,\ f) = -\int S_\theta(f)\ d\nu_x(\theta) = -\int S_\theta(f)\ d\varphi_x(\theta/x)\ .$$

Sous cette forme, on peut appliquer les théorèmes A et B, introduire une hypothèse N et, moyennant des conditions supplémentaires sur une dérivée de $\nu_x$ ou $\varphi_x$, utiliser le théorème C.

1.6. Supposons de plus que $S_\theta$ et $\int$ commutent et que $S_\theta\ S_{\theta'} = S_{\inf(\theta,\theta')}$ (condition d' o r t h o g o n a l i t é ). En transposant les hypothèses adoptées dans I, on obtient (Cf. 4.3.1 dans le premier mémoire) pour deux procédés $(\varphi_x)$, $(\gamma_x)$ :

$$T(\varphi_x)\ T(\gamma_x) = T(\varphi_x\ \gamma_x)\ .$$

(Noter que l'hypothèse N n'intervient pas encore, et que les hypothèses sur $\varphi_x$ , $\gamma_x$ sont plus faibles que dans le théorème A.)

Pour obtenir le premier théorème de comparaison, puis d'équivalence entre procédés, on considère le procédé $(\Gamma_x)$ défini par $(1 - \varphi_x)\Gamma_x = \gamma_x - \varphi_x$ , $1 - \varphi_x(t) \neq 0$ si $t > 0$ . Si on suppose (ou si on démontre) que $(\Gamma_x)$ possède la propriété N, on en déduit un théorème de comparaison, puis, en échangeant $\gamma_x$ et $\varphi_x$ , un théorème d'équivalence.

On notera encore que ce premier théorème ne fait pas appel à la notion de procédé-étalon au sens de 1.1 ci-dessus.

Les deux autres théorèmes d'équivalence font intervenir des procédés-étalons et des classes d'approximations (en général, on ne peut se passer de celles-ci) et supposent qu'un procédé-étalon (ici $\mu(\theta) = \theta$ ) possède la propriété N.

L'espace $\mathcal{E}$ est alors naturellement noté $(\mathcal{E}\ ,\ S_x\ ,\ N)$ .

Pour un espace particulier, il faudra choisir la famille des $S_x$ et vérifier leurs propriétés.

## 2. Convolution

Voici quelques remarques sur l'emploi de la convolution dans l'approximation des fonctions numériques.

2.1. Si on désigne par $\delta$ la translation (à gauche ou à droite), la convolée de $f$ avec une mesure $\nu_x$ s'écrit $\nu_x * f = \int \delta_{-\theta}(f)\ d\nu_x(\theta)$ et, avec des hypothèses convenables, on aura

$$\nu_x * f - f = \int (\delta_{-\theta} - \delta_0)(f)\ d\nu_x(\theta) = \int (\delta_{-\theta/x} - \delta_0)(f)\ d\nu_x(\tfrac{\theta}{x})\ .$$

Sous cette forme, on peut employer les résultats précédents (de 1.1 à 1.5) où $S$ est remplacé par $\delta$ .

L'introduction d'un module de continuité est évidente. Inversement, on obtient des propriétés différentielles en fonction de l'approximation grâce au théorème C, moyennant des hypothèses sur $\nu_x$ et en écrivant

$$\omega(f\ ,\ 1/x) \leqslant \omega(f - \nu_x * f\ ,\ 1/x) + \omega(\nu_x * f\ ,\ 1/x)\ .$$

2.2. Un cas particulier est celui où $\nu_x(\theta) = \chi(x\theta)$ . Cette forme des $\nu_x$ mène plus facilement aux résultats, et simplifie l'énoncé des hypothèses (par exemple, pour le théorème C, on supposera la dérivée de $\chi$ absolument continue). De plus, on peut introduire des modules de continuité $\omega_m$ pour un entier $m \geqslant 1$ (en changeant $x$ en $2x$ , $4x$ , ... et en procédant aux combinaisons linéaires convenables).

2.3. J'en viens au cas des fonctions périodiques qui est exposé dans II. Il s'agit essentiellement d'établir les théorèmes qu'on appelle parfois directs et inverses, c'est-à-dire (on se borne aux polynômes) construire des polynômes $P_n$ de degré $n$ tels que $P_n - f = O(1)\ \omega_m(f\ ,\ 1/n)$ , et trouver la réciproque.

Pour ce qui est de la réciproque, (II, 3.2.1) donne un résultat général. Dans l'autre sens, on dispose des théorèmes d'équivalence entre procédés, en particulier du premier (I, 4.3). Si on fait appel à la convolution, on prendra par exemple $\chi(\theta)$ tel que $\chi'(\theta) = a \exp(-\theta^2)$ où $a^{-1} = \int \exp(-\theta^2)\,d\theta$ et avec $\nu_x(\theta) = \chi(x\theta)$ , on a

$$\nu_x * f = \int \delta_{-\theta/x}(f)\ \chi'(\theta)\ d\theta\ ,$$

puis,

$$\nu_x * f - f = \frac{1}{2}\int (\delta_{\theta/x} - \delta_{-\theta/x})^2(f)\ \chi'(\theta)\ d\theta\ .$$

En changeant $x$ en $2x$ , $4x$ , ... (Cf. 2.2 ci-dessus), on met en évidence $\omega_m(f)$ pour $m = 2\ ,\ 4\ ,\ \ldots$ Mais le procédé défini par $\chi$ est donné, à partir de la série de Fourier de $f$ , par la fonction sommatoire

$$[\varphi(t)[\ = a \int \exp(it\theta)\ \exp(-\theta^2)\ d\theta\ .$$

On voit tout de suite que $[\varphi[$ appartient à la classe $\{2\}$ , que les autres procédés appartiennent aux classes $\{4\}$ , $\{6\}$ , ... et satisfont aux conditions du premier théorème d'équivalence. Ils sont donc équivalents aux procédés polynomiaux définis par les fonctions sommatoires $[(1 - t^2)_x]$ , $[(1 - t^4)_x]$ , ... .

## 3. Explication d'un paradoxe, et conclusion

On constate donc (2.3 ci-dessus) que s'il s'agit des fonctions périodiques, la transformation de Fourier $\mathfrak{F}$ ne joue aucun rôle.

On ne peut, en effet, considérer que $\mathfrak{F}$ intervient parce qu'on écrit une intégrale telle que $\int \exp(it\theta)\exp(-\theta^2)\,d\theta$ !

Cela est d'autant plus paradoxal que deux essais (voir introduction) ont fait jouer un rôle important à la transformation de Fourier.

Or, dans les cas "usuels", si on pose d'une part

$$\Omega_\theta(\xi) = \exp(i\theta\xi)\ ,\quad S_x(f) = \int_{|\theta|\leqslant x} \mathfrak{F} f(\theta)\,\Omega_\theta\,d\theta\ ,$$

d'autre part

$$d\nu_x(\theta) = x\,\mathfrak{F}\,\varphi_x(x\theta)\,d\theta\ ,$$

on a

$$\text{(i)}\quad T(\varphi_x\,,\,f) = -\int_{\theta\geqslant 0} S_\theta(f)\,d\varphi_x(\tfrac{\theta}{x})$$

$$\text{(ii)}\quad = \int_R \mathfrak{F} f(\theta)\,\Omega_\theta\,\varphi_x(\tfrac{\theta}{x})\,d\theta$$

$$\text{(iii)}\quad = \nu_x * f\ .$$

Dans le premier essai que je viens de citer, on part en fait de (ii) qu'on transforme en (iii), et on en tire l'approximation de $f$ par des polynômes définis par une fonction sommatoire $(\varphi)$.

Dans le second, on utilise systématiquement la convolution, ce qui pratiquement consiste à n'employer que la forme (iii).

La méthode que j'ai exposée fait jouer le rôle principal à la forme (i), c'est-à-dire aux espaces que j'ai notés $(\mathcal{E}\,,\,S_x)$ , puis $(\mathcal{E}\,,\,S_x\,,\,N)$ . Quand il s'agit de fonctions numériques, la transformation de Fourier intervient essentiellement pour montrer que $S_\theta\,S_{\theta'} = S_{\inf(\theta,\theta')}$ . Une fois établis des critères d'équivalence entre procédés (en particulier le premier), on fait appel à (iii), en choisissant commodément $\nu_x$ pour obtenir les théorèmes "directs", le théorème C fournissant aussitôt les théorèmes "inverses".

Mais lorsqu'on considère les fonctions périodiques, la propriété (N) est bien connue et la condition $S_n\,S_{n'} = S_{\inf(n,n')}$ ne fait qu'exprimer l'orthogonalité des $u_i$ .

Cela explique le paradoxe. Mais le lecteur aura compris que ce n'était pas la question la plus importante.

# ESTIMATIONS INVOLVING A MODULUS OF CONTINUITY FOR A GENERALIZATION OF KOROVKIN'S OPERATORS

P.C. Sikkema
Department of Mathematics
University of Technology
Delft, Netherlands

## 1. Introduction

In 1959 Korovkin [4] studied operators $K_n : C[a,b] \to C(a,b)$ of the form

$$K_n(f;x) = \frac{1}{I_n} \int_a^b f(t)\beta^n(t-x)dt \qquad (n = 1,2,\ldots),$$

where $\beta(t) \in C[-\gamma,\gamma]$, $(0 < b - a \le \gamma)$, $\beta(0) = 1$, $0 \le \beta(t) < 1$ $(0 < |t| \le \gamma)$ and $I_n = \int_{-\gamma}^{\gamma} \beta^n(t)dt$. He proved that if $x \in (a,b)$ then $K_n(f;x) \to f(x)$ $(n \to \infty)$ and uniformly on every interval $I_\xi : [a+\xi, b-\xi]$ $(0 < \xi < (b-a)2^{-1})$. In general this approximation does not take place at $x = a$ and at $x = b$. Concerning the speed with which the approximation on $(a,b)$ takes place Bojanic and Shisha [1] published in 1973 an investigation involving the modulus of continuity $\omega(\delta)$ of $f$ on $[a,b]$. However, they imposed on $\beta$ rather severe restrictions, viz. $\beta$ should not only satisfy Korovkin's conditions but it should also be even on $[-\gamma,\gamma]$ and monotonically decreasing on $[0,\gamma]$. In addition they assumed that there exist two constants $\alpha > 0$, $c > 0$ such that

$$\lim_{t \downarrow 0} \frac{1-\beta(t)}{t^\alpha} = c \; .$$

Then they proved that for all sufficiently large n

$$(1) \qquad ||K_n(f;x) - f(x)||_{I_\xi} \le L(\beta)\omega(n^{-\frac{1}{\alpha}}) + M(\beta)||f||\{\xi n^{\frac{1}{\alpha}}\}^{-2} \; ,$$

where $L(\beta)$ and $M(\beta)$ are positive quantities not depending on $n,\xi$.

In this connection we mention a 1976 paper by Grinshpun [3] where for a sequence of operators closely related to those of Korovkin, results are derived of a character similar to those of Bojanic and Shisha, though not so sharp.

In the present paper we generalize the above operators. In this generalization the interval of integration is $[-\infty,\infty]$ and $\beta(t)$, defined on R, satisfies much less stringent conditions. By extending in case of the operators of Korovkin $\beta(t)$ and $f(t)$ to the whole of R by setting $\beta(t) = 0$ $(|t| > \gamma)$, $f(t) = f(a)$ $(t < a)$, $f(t) = f(b)$ $(t > b)$ these operators become a special case of the operators considered in this paper and the modulus of continuity of f is unchanged by this extension. Essentially the operators of Grinshpun are also special cases of those considered here.

In section 1. some definitions are given; in section 2. an approximation theorem is derived. Section 3. is devoted to an estimation of the difference between f and its $\rho$-th image; this estimation contains the modulus of continuity of f on R and it is shown that it cannot be improved. Thus a class of best constants is arrived at. Unlike (1) our estimation has as its right-hand side only an expression containing the modulus of continuity, not an extra term. In section 4. an asymptotic value of best constants is derived, while in section 5. an application is treated and some well-known operators are mentioned as special cases of those studied here.

For the operators studied in this paper theorems of Voronovskaya type are derived in [7], [8].

## 2. Definitions

We consider operators $U_\rho$ defined on a class F of functions f, defined by

$$U_\rho(f;x) = \frac{1}{I_\rho} \int_{-\infty}^{\infty} f(x - t)\beta^\rho(t)dt. \tag{2}$$

In (2) $\beta(t)$ belongs to the class G, consisting of all real-valued functions defined on the whole of the real axis R, which possess the following four properties:

1. $\beta(t) \geq 0$ on R,
2. $\beta(t)$ is continuous in a neighbourhood of $t = 0$ (which may depend on $\beta$) and $\beta(0) = 1$,
3. for all $\delta > 0$ is $\sup_{|t|\geq\delta} \beta(t) < 1$,
4. there exists a $\rho_0 > 0$, $\rho_0 = \rho_0(\beta)$ such that $|t|\beta^{\rho_0}(t) \in L^1$.

F denotes the class of all real-valued functions f(t), defined and continuous on R and which possess on R a modulus of continuity $\omega(\delta)$ $(\delta > 0)$.

In (1)

$$I_\rho = \int_{-\infty}^{\infty} \beta^\rho(t)dt \qquad (\rho \geq \rho_0). \tag{3}$$

If $f \in F$ then $f(t) = O(|t|)(|t| \to \infty)$ and this means that the integral

$$\int_{-\infty}^{\infty} f(x - t)\beta^\rho(t)dt$$

for each $x \in R$ exists for all $\rho \geq \rho_0$. Hence in (2) we shall always assume that $\rho \geq \rho_0$.

According to property 3. there exists to each $\delta > 0$ a number r with $0 < r < 1$ such that

$$\sup_{|t|\geq\delta} \beta(t) \leq 1 - r.$$

This number r, corresponding to $\delta$ will be denoted by $r_\delta$.

By $||\cdot||$ and $||\cdot||_1$ are understood the uniform norm on R and the $L^1$-norm on R, respectively.

REMARK. From the fact that $\beta \in G$ it follows from (3) and an argument used in the proof of assertion 1 of Theorem I (section 3.) that the "kernel" $\{\frac{1}{I_\rho} \beta^\rho(t)\}$ $(\rho \geq \rho_0)$ is an approximate identity in the sense of Butzer-Nessel [2, p. 120-121].

## 3. An approximation theorem

THEOREM I. *If* $\beta \in G$ *and* $f \in F$ *then*

a) *for each fixed* $x \in R$

(4) $$U_\rho(f;x) - f(x) \to 0 \qquad (\rho \to \infty)$$

*and* (4) *holds uniformly in* x *on every closed bounded interval of* R;

b) *if* f *is moreover bounded and uniformly continuous on* R:

(5) $$||U_\rho(f;x) - f(x)|| \to 0 \qquad (\rho \to \infty);$$

c) *if* $\beta$ *moreover possesses property* 5. (see section 5.) *then* (5) *also holds*.

PROOF. a) Since f is continuous at x there exists to each $\varepsilon > 0$ an $\eta_x > 0$ such that

$$|f(x - t) - f(x)| < \frac{\varepsilon}{2} \qquad (|t| \le \eta_x).$$

Further, as f possesses a modulus of continuity there exist two constants $A_x > 0$ and $B_x > 0$ such that

$$|f(x - t) - f(x)| \le A_x + B_x|t| \qquad (t \in R).$$

Hence, writing for $\rho \ge \rho_0$

$$U_\rho(f;x) - f(x) = \frac{1}{I_\rho}\{\int_{|t|\le\eta_x} + \int_{|t|\ge\eta_x}\}(f(x - t) - f(x))\beta^\rho(t)dt,$$

it follows that

(6) $$|U_\rho(f;x) - f(x)| < \frac{\varepsilon}{2} + \frac{A_x}{I_\rho}\int_{|t|\ge\eta_x}\beta^\rho(t)dt + \frac{B_x}{I_\rho}\int_{|t|\ge\eta_x}|t|\beta^\rho(t)dt.$$

From property 3. of $\beta$ follows the existence of a number $r_{\eta_x}$ $(0 < r_{\eta_x} < 1)$ such that

$$\sup_{|t|\geq\eta_x} \beta(t) \leq 1 - r_{\eta_x}$$

and by property 2. there exists a number $\theta_x > 0$ such that

$$\beta(t) \geq 1 - \tfrac{1}{2}r_{\eta_x} \qquad (|t| \leq \theta_x).$$

Consequently, the right-hand side of (6) is not greater than

$$\frac{A_x(1 - r_{\eta_x})^{\rho-\rho_0}||\beta^{\rho_0}||}{2\theta_x(1 - \frac{1}{2}r_{\eta_x})^{\rho}} + \frac{B_x(1 - r_{\eta_x})^{\rho-\rho_0}||\,|t|\beta^{\rho_0}||_1}{2\theta_x(1 - \frac{1}{2}r_{\eta_x})^{\rho}} = S_\rho .$$

Obviously

$$S_\rho < \frac{\varepsilon}{2}$$

for all sufficiently large $\rho$, say $\rho \geq \rho_x \geq \rho_0$. Then it follows that

$$|U_\rho(f;x) - f(x)| < \varepsilon \qquad (\rho \geq \rho_x).$$

Because of the arbitrariness of $\varepsilon > 0$ this proves the first part of assertion a).

If D is an arbitrary closed bounded interval of R, f is uniformly continuous on D and this means that in the above proof the numbers $\eta_x$, $A_x$, $B_x$, $r_{\eta_x}$, $\theta_x$ and $\rho_x$ can be chosen such that they are independent of $x \in D$, which proves the second part of assertion a).

b) Since f is bounded there exists a constant $M > 0$ such that for all $x,t \in R$

$$|f(x - t) - f(x)| \leq M$$

and as f is uniformly continuous on R there exists to each $\varepsilon > 0$ an $\eta > 0$, not depending on x such that

$$|f(x - t) - f(x)| < \frac{\varepsilon}{2} \qquad (|t| \leq \eta).$$

Consequently, for all $\rho \geq \rho_0$

$$|U_\rho(f;x) - f(x)| < \frac{\varepsilon}{2} + \frac{M}{I_\rho} \int_{|t|\geq\eta} \beta^\rho(t)dt$$

and thus

$$|U_\rho(f;x) - f(x)| < \varepsilon$$

for all sufficiently large $\rho$, say $\rho \geq \rho_1$, where $\rho_1$ can be chosen independent of $x \in R$. Hence assertion b) is proved.

c) This assertion follows from theorem V and the fact that from theorem IV it is evident that

$$A_\rho(\rho^{-\frac{1}{\alpha}})$$

remains bounded as $\rho \to \infty$, while

$$\omega(\rho^{-\frac{1}{\alpha}}) \to 0$$

as $\rho \to \infty$.

## 4. Best estimation of $|U_\rho(f;x) - f(x)|$ by means of $\omega(\delta)$

The following theorem holds:

THEOREM II. *If* $\beta \in G$, $f \in F$ *and if* $\omega(\delta)$ $(\delta > 0)$ *denotes the modulus of continuity of* f *then for each* $x \in R$, *each* $\delta > 0$ *and each* $\rho \geq \rho_0$

(7) $$|U_\rho(f;x) - f(x)| \leq A_\rho(\delta)\omega(\delta),$$

with

$$A_\rho(\delta) = 1 + \frac{1}{I_\rho} \int_{|t|\geq\delta} [|t|\delta^{-1}]\beta^\rho(t)dt. \tag{8}$$

REMARK. [a] with $a \in R$ means as usual the integral number satisfying $[a] \leq a < [a] + 1$.

PROOF OF THEOREM II. Using the modulus of continuity $\omega(\delta)$ $(\delta > 0)$ of f, we have for all $x \in R$ and all $\rho \geq \rho_0$

$$\begin{aligned} |U_\rho(f;x) - f(x)| &\leq \frac{1}{I_\rho} \int_{-\infty}^{\infty} |f(x - t) - f(x)|\beta^\rho(t)dt \\ &\leq \frac{1}{I_\rho} \int_{-\infty}^{\infty} \omega(|t|)\beta^\rho(t)dt \\ &\leq \frac{\omega(\delta)}{I_\rho} \int_{-\infty}^{\infty} \{1 + [|t|\delta^{-1}]\beta^\rho(t)\}dt \\ &= \{1 + \frac{1}{I_\rho} \int_{-\infty}^{\infty} [|t|\delta^{-1}]\beta^\rho(t)dt\}\omega(\delta), \end{aligned}$$

which proves the theorem.

The next theorem shows that $A_\rho(\delta)$ as given by (8) is best possible in (7) if f runs through F.

THEOREM III. <u>For each</u> $x \in R$, <u>each</u> $\delta > 0$ <u>and each</u> $\rho \geq \rho_0$

$$\sup_{f\in F} |U_\rho(f;x) - f(x)| = A_\rho(\delta)\omega(\delta). \tag{9}$$

PROOF. Taking for x an arbitrary but fixed point of R, for $0 < \sigma < \delta$ a function $g_\sigma(t)$ is constructed on R, possessing the following five properties:

1. $g_\sigma(x) = 0$,
2. $g_\sigma(x + t) = g_\sigma(x - t)$ for all $t > 0$,
3. $g_\sigma(x + t) = k + 1$ if $k\delta + \sigma \leq t \leq (k + 1)\delta$ $(k=0,1,\ldots)$,
4. $g_\sigma(x + t)$ is linear if $k\delta < t < k\delta + \sigma$ $(k=0,1,\ldots)$,
5. $g_\sigma(t)$ is continuous on R.

Obviously, the modulus of continuity $\omega_{g_\sigma}(\delta)$ of $g_\sigma(t)$ exists and $\omega_{g_\sigma}(\delta) = 1$ for all $\delta > 0$. Hence $g_\sigma \in F$. Then, for all $\rho \geq \rho_0$

$$U_\rho(g_\sigma;x) - g_\sigma(x) = U_\rho(g_\sigma;x)$$

(10) $$= \frac{1}{I_\rho}\{\int_{-\infty}^{\infty} \beta^\rho(t)dt + \sum_{k=1}^{\infty} k \int_{k\delta\le|t|\le(k+1)\delta} \beta^\rho(t)dt\} - H(g_\sigma)$$

$$= A_\rho(\delta) - H(g_\sigma),$$

where $A_\rho(\delta)$ is given by (8) and

$$H(g_\sigma) = \sum_{k=0}^{\infty} \int_{k\delta}^{k\delta+\sigma} (1 - \frac{t-k\delta}{\sigma})\{\beta^\rho(t) + \beta^\rho(-t)\}dt .$$

From this it follows that

(11) $$0 \le H(g_\sigma) \le \sum_{k=0}^{\infty} \int_{k\delta}^{k\delta+\sigma} \{\beta^\rho(t) + \beta^\rho(-t)\}dt.$$

Since $\int_{-\infty}^{\infty} \beta^\rho(t)dt$ converges there exists to each $\varepsilon > 0$ a positive integer T such that $\int_{|t|\ge T\delta} \beta^\rho(t)dt < \frac{\varepsilon}{2}$ . Then it is obvious that

(12) $$\sum_{k=T}^{\infty} \int_{k\delta}^{k\delta+\sigma} \{\beta^\rho(t) + \beta^\rho(-t)\}dt < \frac{\varepsilon}{2} .$$

Further,

(13) $$\sum_{k=0}^{T-1} \int_{k\delta}^{k\delta+\sigma} \{\beta^\rho(t) + \beta^\rho(-t)\}dt < 2T\sigma.$$

It follows from (11), (12) and (13) that

$$0 \le H(g_\sigma) < \frac{\varepsilon}{2} + 2T\sigma$$

which means that for all $\sigma$ satisfying $0 < \sigma < \frac{\varepsilon}{4T}$ we have $0 < H(g_\sigma) < \varepsilon$. Hence $\lim_{\sigma\downarrow 0} H(g_\sigma) = 0$ and from (10) the theorem follows.

## 5. Asymptotic behaviour of $A_\rho(\delta)$ if $\delta = \delta(\rho)$ is properly chosen

As to the question whether (5) may hold for all $f \in F$, $\delta$ is made dependent of $\rho$, $\delta = \delta(\rho)$, in such a way that if $\rho \to \infty$, $\delta(\rho) \to 0$ and at the same time $A_\rho(\delta(\rho))$ remains bounded. To that end it is assumed that in addition to the properties 1.-4. $\beta(t)$ possesses property 5.:

$$5. \quad \begin{cases} \beta(t) = 1 - ct^{\alpha} + \phi(t) \text{ if } t > 0,\ \alpha > 0,\ c > 0,\ \phi(t) = o(t^{\alpha}) \ (t \downarrow 0) \\ \beta(t) = 1 - c'|t|^{\alpha'} + \psi(t) \text{ if } t < 0,\ \alpha' > 0,\ c' > 0,\ \psi(t) = o(|t|^{\alpha'}) \\ \qquad (t \uparrow 0). \end{cases}$$

THEOREM IV. <u>If</u> $\beta \in G$ <u>and if</u> $\beta$ <u>possesses property</u> 5. <u>with</u> $\alpha > \alpha'$, <u>if</u> $f \in F$, <u>then for</u> $A_\rho(\delta)$ <u>as defined in</u> (8) <u>the relation</u>

$$(14) \qquad \lim_{\rho\to\infty} A_\rho(\rho^{-\frac{1}{\alpha}}) = 1 + \frac{1}{\Gamma(\frac{1}{\alpha})} \int_c^{\infty} [(uc^{-1})^{\frac{1}{\alpha}}] u^{\frac{1}{\alpha}-1} e^{-u} du$$

<u>holds</u>.

ADDENDUM. (i) <u>If in theorem IV not</u> $\alpha > \alpha'$ <u>but</u> $\alpha' > \alpha$, <u>then in</u> (14) $\alpha$ <u>and</u> c <u>have to be replaced by</u> $\alpha'$ <u>and</u> $c'$ <u>respectively</u>.
(ii) <u>If in theorem IV not</u> $\alpha > \alpha'$ <u>but</u> $\alpha = \alpha'$, <u>then</u> (14) <u>takes the form</u>

$$(15) \qquad \lim_{\rho\to\infty} A_\rho(\rho^{-\frac{1}{\alpha}}) = 1 + p\{ c^{-\frac{1}{\alpha}} \int_c^{\infty} [(uc^{-1})^{\frac{1}{\alpha}}] u^{\frac{1}{\alpha}-1} e^{-u} du + \\ + (c')^{-\frac{1}{\alpha}} \int_{c'}^{\infty} [(uc'^{-1})^{\frac{1}{\alpha}}] u^{\frac{1}{\alpha}-1} e^{-u} du\}$$

<u>where</u>

$$p = \{\Gamma(\tfrac{1}{\alpha})\{c^{-\frac{1}{\alpha}} + (c')^{-\frac{1}{\alpha}}\}\}^{-1} .$$

REMARK. If $\alpha = \alpha'$ and $c = c'$ then (15) reduces to (14).

Before establishing theorem IV we prove the following lemma.

LEMMA. <u>If</u> $\gamma > -1$, $c \geq 0$, $\lambda > 0$, $\mu > 0$ <u>then</u>

$$\lim_{\lambda\to\mu} \int_c^{\infty} \{[\lambda u] - [\mu u]\} u^{\gamma} e^{-u} du = 0.$$

PROOF. Obviously, it may be assumed that $\lambda \geq \mu$. Then we have with $d > c$

$$(16)\qquad 0 \le \int_c^\infty \{[\lambda u] - [\mu u]\}u^\gamma e^{-u}du = \Big(\int_c^d + \int_d^\infty\Big)\{[\lambda u] - [\mu u]\}u^\gamma e^{-u}du .$$

To each $\varepsilon > 0$ it is possible to choose d so large, say $d = d_1$, that for all $\lambda$ with $\mu \le \lambda \le 2\mu$

$$(17)\qquad \int_{d_1}^\infty \{[\lambda u] - [\mu u]\}u^\gamma e^{-u}du < \lambda \int_{d_1}^\infty u^{\gamma+1}e^{-u}du < \frac{\varepsilon}{2} .$$

Moreover, there exists a $\nu$ $(\mu < \nu \le 2\mu)$ such that for all $\lambda$ with $\mu \le \lambda \le \nu$

$$(18)\qquad \int_c^{d_1} \{[\lambda u] - [\mu u]\}u^\gamma e^{-u}du < \frac{\varepsilon}{2} .$$

From (16) with $d = d_1$, (17) and (18) it then follows that for all $\lambda$ with $\mu \le \lambda \le \nu$

$$0 \le \int_c^\infty \{[\lambda u] - [\mu u]\}u^\gamma e^{-u}du < \varepsilon ,$$

which proves the lemma.

PROOF OF THEOREM IV. From (8) it follows with $\delta = \rho^{-\frac{1}{\alpha}}$, $\rho \ge \rho_0$,

$$A_\rho(\rho^{-\frac{1}{\alpha}}) = 1 + \frac{1}{I_\rho} \int_{|t|\ge\rho^{-\frac{1}{\alpha}}} [|t|\rho^{\frac{1}{\alpha}}]\beta^\rho(t)dt$$

$$(19)\qquad = 1 + \frac{1}{I_\rho}\Big\{ \int_{\rho^{-\frac{1}{\alpha}}}^\infty [t\rho^{\frac{1}{\alpha}}]\beta^\rho(t)dt + \int_{\rho^{-\frac{1}{\alpha}}}^\infty [t\rho^{\frac{1}{\alpha}}]\beta^\rho(-t)dt\Big\} .$$

Firstly, we investigate

$$(20)\qquad \int_{\rho^{-\frac{1}{2}}}^\infty [t\rho^{\frac{1}{\alpha}}]\beta^\rho(t)dt.$$

By properties 1., 2. and 5. of $\beta(t)$ there exists to each $\varepsilon$ $(0 < \varepsilon \le \frac{1}{2}c)$ an $\eta > 0$ such that

$$(21)\qquad \left.\begin{array}{c} \beta(t) > 0 \\ -(c+\varepsilon)t^\alpha \le \log\beta(t) \le -(c-\varepsilon)t^\alpha \end{array}\right\} 0 \le t \le \eta .$$

Then for all sufficiently large fixed $\rho$, say $\rho \geq \rho_1 \geq \rho_0$ it is possible to choose $m \in N$ such that

$$m\rho^{-\frac{1}{\alpha}} \leq \eta < (m+1)\rho^{-\frac{1}{\alpha}} .$$

We now write (20) as

$$(22) \qquad \int_{\rho^{-\frac{1}{\alpha}}}^{\infty} [t\rho^{\frac{1}{\alpha}}]\beta^{\rho}(t)dt = \sum_{k=1}^{m-1} k \int_{k\rho^{-\frac{1}{\alpha}}}^{(k+1)\rho^{-\frac{1}{\alpha}}} \beta^{\rho}(t)dt + m \int_{m\rho^{-\frac{1}{\alpha}}}^{\eta} \beta^{\rho}(t)dt + \int_{\eta}^{\infty} [t\rho^{\frac{1}{\alpha}}]\beta^{\rho}(t)dt$$

With respect to the integral in the first term in the right-hand side it follows from (21) that

$$\int_{k\rho^{-\frac{1}{\alpha}}}^{(k+1)\rho^{-\frac{1}{\alpha}}} e^{-\rho(c+\varepsilon)t^{\alpha}}dt \leq \int_{k\rho^{-\frac{1}{\alpha}}}^{(k+1)\rho^{-\frac{1}{\alpha}}} \beta^{\rho}(t)dt \leq \int_{k\rho^{-\frac{1}{\alpha}}}^{(k+1)\rho^{-\frac{1}{\alpha}}} e^{-\rho(c-\varepsilon)t^{\alpha}}dt$$

and by substitution of $\rho(c+\varepsilon)t^{\alpha} = u$, $\rho(c-\varepsilon)t^{\alpha} = u$ resp.,

$$\frac{1}{\alpha(c+\varepsilon)^{\frac{1}{\alpha}}\rho^{\frac{1}{\alpha}}} \int_{(c+\varepsilon)k^{\alpha}}^{(c+\varepsilon)(k+1)^{\alpha}} u^{\frac{1}{\alpha}-1} e^{-u}du \leq \int_{k\rho^{-\frac{1}{\alpha}}}^{(k+1)\rho^{-\frac{1}{\alpha}}} \beta^{\rho}(t)dt \leq \frac{1}{\alpha(c-\varepsilon)^{\frac{1}{\alpha}}\rho^{\frac{1}{\alpha}}} \int_{(c-\varepsilon)k^{\alpha}}^{(c-\varepsilon)(k+1)^{\alpha}} u^{\frac{1}{\alpha}-1} e^{-u}du.$$

Hence,

$$(23) \qquad \sum_{k=1}^{m-1} \frac{k}{\alpha(c+\varepsilon)^{\frac{1}{\alpha}}\rho^{\frac{1}{\alpha}}} \int_{(c+\varepsilon)k^{\alpha}}^{(c+\varepsilon)(k+1)^{\alpha}} u^{\frac{1}{\alpha}-1} e^{-u}du \leq \int_{\rho^{-\frac{1}{\alpha}}}^{m\rho^{-\frac{1}{\alpha}}} [t\rho^{\frac{1}{\alpha}}]\beta^{\rho}(t)dt \leq \sum_{k=1}^{m-1} \frac{k}{\alpha(c-\varepsilon)^{\frac{1}{\alpha}}\rho^{\frac{1}{\alpha}}} \int_{(c-\varepsilon)k^{\alpha}}^{(c-\varepsilon)(k+1)^{\alpha}} u^{\frac{1}{\alpha}-1} e^{-u}du .$$

Further,

$$(24)\qquad \int_{m\rho^{-\frac{1}{\alpha}}}^{\eta} [t\rho^{\frac{1}{\alpha}}]\beta^{\rho}(t)dt \le (m+1)\rho^{-\frac{1}{\alpha}} \sup_{|t|\ge m\rho^{-\frac{1}{\alpha}}} \beta^{\rho}(t)$$

$$\le (m+1)\rho^{-\frac{1}{\alpha}}(1-r_{\tau})^{\rho} = o(\rho^{-\frac{1}{\alpha}}) \qquad (\rho \to \infty),$$

where $\tau = \eta - \rho^{-\frac{1}{\alpha}}$, and

$$(25)\qquad \int_{\eta}^{\infty} [t\rho^{\frac{1}{\alpha}}]\beta^{\rho}(t)dt \le \rho^{\frac{1}{\alpha}} \int_{\eta}^{\infty} t\beta^{\rho_0}(t)\cdot\beta^{\rho-\rho_0}(t)dt$$

$$\le \rho^{\frac{1}{\alpha}} \|\, |t|\beta^{\rho_0} \|_1 (1-r_{\eta})^{\rho-\rho_0} = o(\rho^{-\frac{1}{\alpha}}) \quad (\rho \to \infty).$$

When $\varepsilon$ and hence also $\eta$ are kept fixed, $m \to \infty$ if $\rho \to \infty$. It then follows from (22)-(25) that

$$\frac{1}{\alpha(c+\varepsilon)^{\frac{1}{\alpha}}} \sum_{k=1}^{\infty} k \int_{(c+\varepsilon)k^{\alpha}}^{(c+\varepsilon)(k+1)^{\alpha}} u^{\frac{1}{\alpha}-1} e^{-u}du \le \liminf_{\rho\to\infty} \rho^{\frac{1}{\alpha}} \int_{\rho^{-\frac{1}{\alpha}}}^{\infty} [t\rho^{\frac{1}{\alpha}}]\beta^{\rho}(t)dt$$

$$\le \limsup_{\rho\to\infty} \rho^{\frac{1}{\alpha}} \int_{\rho^{-\frac{1}{\alpha}}}^{\infty} [t\rho^{\frac{1}{\alpha}}]\beta^{\rho}(t)dt$$

$$\le \frac{1}{(c-\varepsilon)^{\frac{1}{\alpha}}} \sum_{k=1}^{\infty} k \int_{(c-\varepsilon)k^{\alpha}}^{(c-\varepsilon)(k+1)^{\alpha}} u^{\frac{1}{\alpha}-1} e^{-u}du,$$

which we write as

$$(26)\qquad \frac{1}{\alpha(c+\varepsilon)^{\frac{1}{\alpha}}} \int_{c+\varepsilon}^{\infty} [(\frac{u}{c+\varepsilon})^{\frac{1}{\alpha}}]u^{\frac{1}{\alpha}-1} e^{-u}du \le \liminf_{\rho\to\infty} \rho^{\frac{1}{\alpha}} \int_{\rho^{-\frac{1}{\alpha}}}^{\infty} [t\rho^{\frac{1}{\alpha}}]\beta^{\rho}(t)dt$$

$$\le \limsup_{\rho\to\infty} \rho^{\frac{1}{\alpha}} \int_{\rho^{-\frac{1}{\alpha}}}^{\infty} [t\rho^{\frac{1}{\alpha}}]\beta^{\rho}(t)dt$$

$$\le \frac{1}{\alpha(c-\varepsilon)^{\frac{1}{\alpha}}} \int_{c-\varepsilon}^{\infty} [(\frac{u}{c-\varepsilon})^{\frac{1}{\alpha}}]u^{\frac{1}{\alpha}-1} e^{-u}du.$$

However, neither the lim inf nor the lim sup depend on $\varepsilon$. Therefore, because of the arbitrariness of $\varepsilon$ in the interval $0 < \varepsilon \le \frac{1}{2}c$ it follows from (25) and application of the lemma that

$$\text{(27)}\qquad \lim_{\rho\to\infty} \rho^{\frac{1}{\alpha}} \int_{\rho^{-\frac{1}{\alpha}}}^{\infty} [t\rho^{\frac{1}{\alpha}}]\beta^{\rho}(t)dt = \frac{1}{\alpha c^{\frac{1}{\alpha}}} \int_{c}^{\infty} [(uc^{-1})^{\frac{1}{\alpha}}]u^{\frac{1}{\alpha}-1} e^{-u}du .$$

Secondly, we write

$$\text{(28)}\qquad \int_0^{\infty} \beta^{\rho}(t)dt = \left(\int_0^{\eta} + \int_{\eta}^{\infty}\right)\beta^{\rho}(t)dt .$$

Because of (21)

$$\text{(29)}\qquad \frac{1}{\alpha(c+\varepsilon)^{\frac{1}{\alpha}}\rho^{\frac{1}{\alpha}}} \int_0^{\rho(c+\varepsilon)\eta^{\alpha}} u^{\frac{1}{\alpha}-1} e^{-u}du \le \int_0^{\eta} \beta^{\rho}(t)dt \le \frac{1}{\alpha(c-\varepsilon)^{\frac{1}{\alpha}}\rho^{\frac{1}{\alpha}}} \int_0^{\rho(c-\varepsilon)\eta^{\alpha}} u^{\frac{1}{\alpha}-1} e^{-u}du .$$

Further

$$\text{(30)}\qquad \int_{\eta}^{\infty} \beta^{\rho}(t)dt = o(\rho^{-\frac{1}{\alpha}}) \qquad (\rho \to \infty) .$$

From (28)-(30) it follows with an argument used above, that

$$\text{(31)}\qquad \lim_{\rho\to\infty} \rho^{\frac{1}{\alpha}} \int_0^{\infty} \beta^{\rho}(t)dt = \frac{\Gamma(\frac{1}{\alpha})}{\alpha c^{\frac{1}{\alpha}}} .$$

If, as is assumed in the theorem, $\alpha > \alpha'$, it can be proved along the above lines, that

$$\text{(32)}\qquad \int_{\rho^{\frac{1}{\alpha}}}^{\infty} [t\rho^{\frac{1}{\alpha}}]\beta^{\rho}(-t)dt = o(\rho^{-\frac{1}{\alpha}}) \text{ and } \int_0^{\infty} \beta^{\rho}(-t)dt = o(\rho^{-\frac{1}{\alpha}}) \qquad (\rho \to \infty) .$$

Hence, using (19), (27), (31) and (32) the theorem follows.

The proof of the assertions of the Addendum can easily be derived from the arguments used in the proof of theorem IV.

THEOREM V. _If_ $\beta \in G$ _and_ $\beta$ _possesses property_ 5. _with_ $\alpha \ge \alpha'$ _and if_ $f \in F$, _then_

$$\text{(33)}\qquad ||U_{\rho}(f;x) - f(x)|| \le A_{\rho}(\rho^{-\frac{1}{\alpha}})\omega(\rho^{-\frac{1}{\alpha}}) .$$

PROOF. (33) follows from theorems III and IV together with the latter's Addendum.

## 6. Application

Of the many well-known operators which are special cases of the operators $U_\rho$ studied in this paper we only mention those of Picard [2] where $\beta(t) = e^{-|t|}$, Weierstrass [10] where $\beta(t) = e^{-t^2}$, Mamedov [6] where $\beta(t) = 1 - |t|^{2k}$ $(|t| \leq 1, k \in N)$, $\beta(t) \equiv 0$ $(|t| > 1)$, Landau [5] which are a special case of those of Mamedov, viz. $k = 1$, De la Vallée-Poussin [9] where $\beta(t) = \cos \frac{\pi t}{2}$ $(|t| \leq 1)$, $\beta(t) \equiv 0$ $(|t| > 1)$.

As an application of the above results we consider the Picard operators $U_\rho$, defined on F by

$$U_\rho(f;x) = \tfrac{1}{2}\rho \int_{-\infty}^{\infty} f(x-t)e^{-\rho|t|}dt .$$

Thus $\beta = e^{-|t|} \in G$ and $\beta$ possesses property 5. with $\alpha = \alpha' = c = c' = 1$. Further $\rho_0 > 0$. Theorem II gives for $x \in R$, $\delta > 0$, $\rho > 0$

$$A_\rho(\delta) = 1 + \tfrac{1}{2}\rho \int_{|t|\geq\delta} [|t|\delta^{-1}]e^{-\rho|t|}dt = 1 + \rho \int_{\delta}^{\infty} [t\delta^{-1}]e^{-\rho t}dt$$

$$= 1 + \rho \sum_{k=1}^{\infty} k \int_{k\delta}^{(k+1)\delta} e^{-\rho t}dt = \frac{e^{\rho\delta}}{e^{\rho\delta}-1} .$$

According to theorem III for each $x \in R$, each $\delta > 0$ and each $\rho > 0$

$$\sup_{f\in F} \left| \tfrac{1}{2}\rho \int_{-\infty}^{\infty} f(x-t)e^{-\rho|t|}dt - f(x)\right| = \frac{e^{\rho\delta}}{e^{\rho\delta}-1}\,\omega(\delta)$$

and with $\delta = \rho^{-1}$

$$\sup_{f\in F} \left| \tfrac{1}{2}\rho \int_{-\infty}^{\infty} f(x-t)e^{-\rho|t|}dt - f(x)\right| = \frac{e}{e-1}\,\omega(\rho^{-1}), \tag{34}$$

which is in accordance with theorem V since

$$1 + \int_{1}^{\infty} [u]e^{-u}du = \frac{e}{e-1} .$$

As a consequence of (34) we have for all $f \in F$

$$\left|\left|\tfrac{1}{2}\rho \int_{-\infty}^{\infty} f(x-t)e^{-\rho|t|}dt - f(x)\right|\right| \to 0 \qquad (\rho \to \infty).$$

REFERENCES


[ 1] Bojanic, R. - Shisha, O., On the precision of uniform approximation of continuous functions by certain linear positive operators of convolution type. J.Approximation Theory 8 (1973), 101 - 113.

[ 2] Butzer, P.L. - Nessel, R.J., Fourier Analysis and Approximation. Vol. I, One-Dimensional Theory. Birkhäuser Verlag, Basel and Stuttgart, 1971.

[ 3] Grinshpun, Z.S., On an estimation of the approximation of continuous functions by a class of linear positive operators. Izv. Akad. Nauk Kazah. SSR Ser.Fiz.-Mat. (1976), 29 - 34. (In russian).

[ 4] Korovkin, P.P., Linear Operators and Approximation Theory. Hindustan Publ. 1960 (Orig. Russ. ed. Moscow 1959).

[ 5] Landau, E., Über die Approximation einer stetigen Funktion durch eine ganze rationale Funktion. Rend.Circ.Mat. Palermo 25 (1908),337 - 345.

[ 6] Mamedov, R.G., The approximation of functions by generalised linear Landau operators (in russian). Dokl. Akad. Nauk. SSSR 139 (1961) 28-30. English translation in: Soviet Math. Dokl. 2 (1961),861-864.

[ 7] Sikkema, P.C. - R.K.S. Rathore, Convolutions with powers of bell-shaped functions. Report Dept. of Math., Univ. of Technology, Delft, 1976, 22p. .

[ 8] Sikkema, P.C., Approximation formulae of Voronovskaya-type for certain convolution operators (to appear).

[ 9] Vallée-Poussin, C. de la, Note sur l'approximation par un polynôme d'une fonction dont la dérivée est à variation bornée. Bull. Soc. Math. Belg. 3 (1908),403-410.

[10] Weierstrass, K., Über die analytische Darstellbarkeit sogenannter willkürlicher Funktionen einer reellen Veränderlichen. Sitzungsber. Akad. Berlin (1885),633-639.

# DIE LOKALE $L_p$ - SATURATIONSKLASSE DES VERFAHRENS DER INTEGRALEN MEYER - KÖNIG UND ZELLER OPERATOREN

Manfred W. Müller und Volker Maier
Lehrstuhl Mathematik VIII
Universität Dortmund
Dortmund

For the linear approximation method $(\hat{M}_n)$ of so - called integrated Meyer - König and Zeller operators [4] on the spaces $L_p(I)$, $1 \leq p < \infty$, $I = [0,1]$, a local $O(n^{-1})$-saturation theorem will be proved, stating roughly speaking that

$$\| f - \hat{M}_n f \|_p [a,b] = O(n^{-1}) \Leftrightarrow x(1-x)^2 f'(x) \neq C$$

$$(C \in \mathbb{R}, x \in [a,b], 0 < a < b < 1).$$

$$\| f - \hat{M}_n f \|_p [a,b] = o(n^{-1}) \Leftrightarrow x(1-x)^2 f'(x) = C$$

The inverse parts of these statements are proved by studying convergence properties of a suitable sequence of bilinear functionals. An explicite representation of f is obtained then as a solution of an integral equation.

## 1. Vorbemerkungen

Der in [4] eingeführte n-te i n t e g r a l e Meyer-König und Zeller Operator $\hat{M}_n$, $n \in \mathbb{N}$, ordnet einer auf dem Intervall $I = [0,1]$ definierten reellwertigen Lebesgue-integrierbaren Funktion f die für $0 \leq x < 1$ konvergente Funktionenreihe

$$\hat{M}_n f(x) := \sum_{k=0}^{\infty} \hat{m}_{nk}(x) \int_{I_k} f(t)dt \tag{1.1}$$

zu. Hierbei ist

$$I_k := [\frac{k}{k+n}, \frac{k+1}{k+n+1}] \quad (k \in \mathbb{N}_0) \quad \text{und}$$

$$\hat{m}_{nk}(x) := (n+1) \binom{k+n+1}{k} (1-x)^n x^k .$$

$\hat{M}_n f$ läßt sich als singuläres Integral vom Typ

(1.2) $$\hat{M}_n f(x) = \int_I H_n(x,t) f(t) dt$$

schreiben mit dem positiven Kern

$$H_n(x,t) = \sum_{k=o}^{\infty} \hat{m}_{nk}(x) \, \underline{1}_{I_k}(t) ,$$

wobei $\underline{1}_{I_K}$ die charakteristische Funktion des Intervalls $I_k$ bezüglich $I$ ist.

Der Zusammenhang zwischen $\hat{M}_n$ und dem (nichtintegralen) n-ten Operator $M_n$ von Meyer-König und Zeller, der für $g \varepsilon C(I)$ definiert ist durch

$$M_n g(x) := \sum_{k=o}^{\infty} m_{nk}(x) g\left(\frac{k}{k+n}\right), \quad m_{nk}(x) := \binom{k+n}{k} (1-x)^{n+1} x^k ,$$

ist gegeben durch

(1.3) $$\hat{M}_n f = DM_n F,$$

wobei $D$ der Operator der ersten Ableitung und $F$ das unbestimmte Integral von $f$ (also eine absolut stetige Funktion) ist.

Die einzelnen Operatoren $\hat{M}_n$ sind linear, positiv und identitätserhaltend. Die Folge $(\hat{M}_n)_{n \varepsilon \mathbb{N}}$ erzeugt ein lineares Approximationsverfahren auf dem Raum $(L_p(I,\mathbb{R}), \|\cdot\|_p)$, $1 \leq p < \infty$ kurz: $L_p(I)$, d.h. es gilt $\lim_{n\to\infty} \| f-\hat{M}_n f \|_p = o$ für alle $f \varepsilon L_p(I)$ (vgl. [4], Theorem 1). Die Approximationsgüte des Verfahrens im Raum $L_p(I)$ läßt sich abschätzen in der Form

$$\| f-\hat{M}_n f \|_p = O\left(\omega_{1,p}\left(f, \frac{1}{\sqrt{n}}\right)\right) \quad (n \to \infty),$$

wobei das Landau-Symbol $O$ (hier und im folgenden) unabhängig von $n$ ist und mit $\omega_{1,p}(f,\cdot)$ der integrale Stetigkeitsmodul erster Ordnung bezüglich der $L_p$-Norm bezeichnet wird (vgl. [4], Theorem 3). Diese Ordnung ist $O(n^{-\frac{\alpha}{2}})$, falls $f$ einer Lipschitz-Klasse $Lip(\alpha,L_p)$, $o < \alpha \leq 1$, angehört. Für $f \varepsilon L_p^1(I) := \{f \varepsilon L_p(I) \mid f \varepsilon AC(I), f' \varepsilon L_p(I)\} \subset Lip(\alpha,L_p)$, $1 \leq p < \infty$, gilt $\| f-\hat{M}_n f \|_p = O(n^{-\frac{1}{2}})$ $(n \to \infty)$ (vgl. [4], Theorem 2). (Mit $AC(I)$ wird der lineare Raum der auf $I$ definierten reellwertigen absolut stetigen Funktionen bezeichnet).

Wir zeigen in Abschnitt 2 u. a., daß für geeignete Teilräume von $L_p^1(I)$, $p > 1$, sogar die Approximationsordnung $O(n^{-1})$ erreicht wird, und zwar sowohl global (d.h. auf $[o,1]$) als auch lokal (d.h. auf Intervallen $[a,b] \subset (o,1)$). In Abschnitt 3 weisen wir dann nach, daß diese Ordnung lokal die Saturationsordnung des Verfahrens $(\hat{M}_n)_{n\in\mathbb{N}}$ ist. Die zugehörige lokale Saturationsklasse wird explizit angegeben. Im wesentlichen stellt sich hierbei heraus (vgl. Satz 3.1), daß

$$\| f-\hat{M}_n f \|_p \, [a,b] = O(\tfrac{1}{n}) \quad (n \to \infty)$$

(wobei $\| \cdot \|_p \, [a,b]$ anzeigt, daß die $L_p$-Norm über das Intervall $[a,b]$ genommen wird) äquivalent ist mit $x(1-x)^2 f'(x) \neq c$, $c \in \mathbb{R}$, $x \in [a,b]$. Die Beweistechnik beruht weitgehend auf der bekannten Parabelmethode.

Für das Verfahren der Kantorovič-Operatoren erhielten Z. Ditzian und C.P. May [1] vergleichbare Resultate.

## 2. Ein direkter Satz

Das Hauptergebnis dieser Nummer besagt, daß Funktionen aus $L_p^2\,[a,b] := \{f \in L_p(I) \mid f' \in AC[a,b],\ f'' \in L_p[a,b],\ o < a < b < 1\}$, $p > 1$ durch das Verfahren $(\hat{M}_n)_{n\in\mathbb{N}}$ bezüglich der $L_p$-Norm auf Teilintervallen $[a_1,b_1] \subset (a,b)$ mindestens mit der Ordnung $O(n^{-1})$ approximiert werden. Der Beweis stützt sich auf die beiden folgenden Lemmata.

LEMMA 2.1. <u>Zu jedem</u> $m \in \mathbb{N}$ <u>gibt es eine von</u> $n$ <u>und</u> $x$ <u>unabhängige positive Konstante</u> $A_m$ <u>derart, daß gilt</u>

$$\hat{M}_n(\cdot-x)^{2m}(x) \leq \frac{A_m}{n^m}, \quad x\in[o,1),\ n \geq 2. \tag{2.1}$$

Beweis. Für den n-ten nichtintegralen Operator $M_n$ gilt zunächst (vgl. [2], Nr. 1 und 2)

$$M_n(\cdot-x)^{2m} \leq \frac{k_m}{n^m},\quad x\in[o,1),\ n\in\mathbb{N},\ m\in\mathbb{N}, \tag{2.2}$$

mit einer von $n$ und $x$ unabhängigen positiven Konstanten $k_m$. Weiter ist nach (1.2)

$$\hat{M}_n(\cdot-x)^{2m}(x) = \sum_{k=o}^{\infty} m_{nk}(x) \int_{I_k} (t-x)^{2m}dt,\ x\varepsilon[o,1),$$

und $|t-x|$ läßt sich für $t\varepsilon I_k$ nach oben abschätzen durch

$$|t-x| \leq \begin{cases} \frac{2n}{(k+n-1)(k+n)} \leq \frac{4}{n},\ n \geq 2,\ x\varepsilon[\frac{k-1}{k+n-1},\ \frac{k+2}{k+n+2}]\ . \\ 2|\frac{k}{k+n-1} - x| + \frac{4}{n},\ n \geq 2,\ x\varepsilon[o,1)\setminus[\frac{k-1}{k+n-1},\ \frac{k+2}{k+n+2}]\ . \end{cases}$$

Wegen $\hat{m}_{nk}(x) \int_{I_k} dt = m_{n-1,k}(x)$ und (2.2) gilt somit für $n \geq 2$

$$\hat{M}_n(\cdot-x)^{2m}(x) \leq 2\frac{4^{2m}}{n^{2m}} \sum_{k=o}^{\infty} \hat{m}_{nk}(x) \int_{I_k} dt + 2^{2m} \sum_{k=o}^{\infty} \hat{m}_{nk}(x) \int_{I_k} dt\ (\frac{k}{k+n-1} - x)^{2m}$$

$$= 2\frac{4^{2m}}{n^{2m}} + 2^{2m} M_{n-1}(\cdot-x)^{2m}(x)$$

$$\leq \frac{1}{n^m}(\frac{4^{2m+1}}{n^m} + 2^{3m}k_m) \leq \frac{A_m}{n^m}$$

mit $A_m = (4 + k_m)2^{3m}$ .

Bemerkung. Durch direktes Ausrechnen folgt zusätzlich zu (2.1) noch

$$\text{(2.3)} \qquad \hat{M}_n(\cdot-x)(x) \leq \frac{A}{n},\ x\varepsilon[o,1),\ n\varepsilon\mathbb{N}$$

mit einer von $n$ und $x$ unabhängigen positiven Konstanten $A$ .

LEMMA 2.2 Für beliebiges $g\varepsilon L_p(I)$, $p > 1$ und $[a_1,b_1]\subset(a,b)$ gilt

$$\text{(2.4)} \quad \|\hat{M}_n g - \hat{M}_n 1_{[a,b]}g\|_p\,[a_1 b_1] \leq \frac{B_p}{n^r} \|g\|_p,\ n\varepsilon\mathbb{N},$$

wo $B_p$ eine von $g$ und $n$ unabhängige positive Konstante und $r\varepsilon\mathbb{N}$ beliebig ist.

Bemerkung. Lemma 2.2 bringt eine Lokalisationseigenschaft des Verfahrens $(\hat{M}_n)_{n\varepsilon\mathbb{N}}$ zum Ausdruck. Setzt man nämlich die zu approximierende Funktion $g$ außerhalb einer Umgebung von $[a_1,b_1]$, deren Komplement bezüglich I einen positiven Abstand von $[a_1,b_1]$ hat, gleich Null, so unterscheiden sich aufgrund von (2.4) für hinreichend großes $n$ und im Sinne der $L_p$-Norm auf $[a_1,b_1]$ die $\hat{M}_n$-Bilder der Funktion $g$ und der abgeänderten Funktion beliebig wenig voneinander.

Definieren wir zu $I \sim [a,b]$ die charakteristische Funktion $\lambda_{[a,b]}$ durch

$$\lambda_{[a,b]}(t) := 1 - \underline{1}_{[a,b]}(t), \quad t \varepsilon I,$$

so geht (2.4) über in

$$\text{(2.5)} \qquad \| M_n \lambda_{[a,b]} g \|_{p\,[a_1,b_1]} \leq \frac{B_p}{n^r} \| g \|_p, \quad n \varepsilon \mathbb{N}, \ r \varepsilon \mathbb{N}.$$

Beweis von Lemma 2.2. Sei $x \varepsilon [a_1,b_1]$ beliebig und fest gewählt. Da nach Voraussetzung $\delta := \min (a_1 - a, b - b_1) > 0$ ist, gilt

$$\text{(2.6)} \qquad \lambda_{[a,b]}(t) \leq \frac{1}{\delta^{2m}} (t-x)^{2m}, \quad t \varepsilon I$$

mit einem zunächst noch beliebigen $m \varepsilon \mathbb{N}$.

Aus (1.2) folgt aufgrund der Hölderschen Ungleichung mit $p^{-1} + q^{-1} = 1$, $p > 1$, für festes $n \geq 2$

$$|\hat{M}_n \lambda_{[a,b]} g(x)|^p = | \int_I H_n(x,t) \lambda_{[a,b]}(t) g(t) dt |^p$$

$$\text{(2.7)} \qquad \leq (\int_I H_n(x,t) |g(t)|^p dt) (\int_I H_n(x,t) \lambda_{[a,b]}(t) dt)^{\frac{p}{q}}.$$

Wegen (2.6) und Lemma 2.1 ist

$$\text{(2.8)} \qquad \int_I H_n(x,t) \lambda_{[a,b]}(t) dt \leq \frac{1}{\delta^{2m}} \int_I H_n(x,t)(t-x)^{2m} dt \leq \frac{A_m}{\delta^{2m} n^m}.$$

Für festes $m \geq r [\frac{q}{p}] + 1$ folgt somit aus (2.7) unter Beachtung des Satzes von Fubini

$$\| \hat{M}_n \lambda_{[a,b]} g \|_{p\,[a_1,b_1]} \leq \left(\frac{A_m}{\delta^{2m}}\right)^{\frac{p}{q}} \cdot \frac{1}{n^r} \left( \int_{a_1}^{b_1} \int_0^1 H_n(x,t) |g(t)|^p dt \, dx \right)^{\frac{1}{p}}$$

$$=: \frac{B_p}{n^r} \left( \int_0^1 |g(t)|^p \int_{a_1}^{b_1} H_n(x,t) dx \, dt \right)^{\frac{1}{p}} \leq \frac{B_p}{n^r} \| g \|_p.$$

Nach diesen Vorbereitungen kommen wir nun zu

SATZ 2.3. <u>Für</u> $f\in L_p^2[a,b]$, $p>1$ <u>und</u> $[a_1,b_1]\subset(a,b)$ <u>gilt</u>

$$\| f-\hat{M}_n f\|_{p}\,[a_1,b_1] = O(\tfrac{1}{n}) \quad (n\to\infty).$$

Beweis. Aufgrund von (1.2) und der identitätserhaltenden Eigenschaft der Operatoren $\hat{M}_n$ gilt für festes $x\in[a_1,b_1]$ und $n\in\mathbb{N}$ zunächst

$$\begin{aligned}\hat{M}_n f(x) - f(x) &= \int_I H_n(x,t)(f(t)-f(x))dt\\ &= \int_a^b H_n(x,t)(f(t)-f(x))dt + M_n(\lambda_{[a,b]}f)(x) -\\ &\qquad - f(x)\hat{M}_n\lambda_{[a,b]}(x)\,. \qquad (2.9)\end{aligned}$$

Wegen

$$\begin{aligned}f(t)-f(x) &= (t-x)f'(\xi) = (t-x)f'(x) + (t-x)[f'(\xi)-f'(x)]\\ &= (t-x)f'(x) + (t-x)\int_x^\xi f''(u)du\end{aligned}$$

für $x$ und $t$ aus $[a,b]$ und $\xi=\xi(t)$ zwischen $x$ und $t$ folgt weiter

$$\begin{aligned}\int_a^b H_n(x,t)(f(t)-f(x))dt &= f'(x)[\int_I H_n(x,t)(t-x)dt - \int_I \lambda_{[a,b]}(t)H_n(x,t)\cdot\\ &\qquad\cdot(t-x)dt]\\ &+ \int_a^b H_n(x,t)(t-x)(\int_x^\xi f''(u)du)dt\end{aligned}$$

und hieraus mit (2.3), (2.8) für $m=1$ und Lemma 2.1

$$\begin{aligned}|\int_a^b H_n(x,t)(f(t)-f(x))dt| &\le (A+\frac{2A_1}{\delta^2})\frac{1}{n}|f'(x)| + \int_a^b H_n(x,t)|t-x|\,|\int_x^t|f''(u)|du|dt\\ &\le (A+\frac{2A_1}{\delta^2})\frac{1}{n}|f'(x)| + \Theta_{f''}(x)\,\hat{M}_n(\cdot-x)^2(x)\\ &\le \frac{C}{n}(|f'(x)| + \Theta_{f''}(x)), \qquad (2.10)\end{aligned}$$

wo $C := \max(A+\frac{2A_1}{\delta^2}, A_1)$ und

$$\Theta_{f''}(x) := \sup_{\substack{a\le t\le b \\ t\ne x}} \frac{1}{t-x} \int_x^t |f''(u)|\,du, \quad x\varepsilon[a,b]$$

die Hardy-Littlewoodsche Majorante von $f''$ auf $[a,b]$ ist.

$f''\varepsilon L_p[a,b]$ impliziert für $p > 1$ nach einem Satz von Hardy und Littlewood (vgl. [5, Theorem 13.15]) $\Theta_{f''}\varepsilon L_p[a,b]$ mit

$$(2.11) \qquad \int_a^b \Theta_{f''}^p(x)\,dx \leqq 2\left(\frac{p}{p-1}\right)^p \int_a^b |f''(x)|^p dx.$$

Insgesamt ist somit

$$|\hat{M}_n f(x) - f(x)| \leqq \frac{C}{n}(|f'(x)| + \Theta_{f''}(x)) + |\hat{M}_n(\lambda_{[a,b]}f)(x)| +$$

$$+ |f(x)|\, \hat{M}_n\lambda_{[a,b]}(x)\ ,$$

woraus für $p > 1$ mit Hilfe der Minkowskischen Ungleichung, (2.11), (2.6) und (2.8) für $m = 1$ folgt

$$\| f-\hat{M}_n f\|_p [a_1,b_1] \leqq \frac{C}{n} (\| f'\|_p [a,b] + \sqrt[p]{2}\ \frac{p}{p-1}\ \| f''\|_p [a,b]) +$$

$$+ \frac{B_p}{n} \| f\|_p + \frac{A_1}{\delta^2 n} \| f\|_p\ ,$$

womit der Satz bewiesen ist.

Bemerkung. Für $f\varepsilon L_p^2(I)$, $p > 1$ vereinfacht sich der Beweis beträcht - lich, und man erhält auch hier die Approximationsordnung $\| f-\hat{M}_n f\|_p = O(\frac{1}{n})$ $(n \to \infty)$.

## 3. Der lokale $O(n^{-1})$ - Saturationssatz

Der folgende Satz beinhaltet die lokale Umkehrung zu Satz 2.3 und zeigt ferner, daß die Elemente der Klasse

$$S_p := \{f\varepsilon L_p(I),\ p > 1 \mid f'\varepsilon AC[a,b] \text{ und } x(1-x)^2 f'(x) = c + \int_a^x h(u)du,$$

$$x\varepsilon[a,b],\ c\varepsilon\mathbb{R}\ ,\ h\varepsilon L_p[a,b]\}$$

durch das Verfahren $(\hat{M}_n)_{n\in\mathbb{N}}$ lokal genau von der Ordnung $O(n^{-1})$ approximiert werden. Der Fall $p = 1$ und globale Aussagen bleiben offen.

SATZ 3.1. <u>Für</u> $f\in L_p(I)$, $p > 1$ <u>und</u> $o < a < a_1 < b_1 < b < 1$ <u>gelten folgende Aussagen:</u>

(i) $\|f-\hat{M}_n f\|_p\,[a,b] = O(\frac{1}{n})$ $(n\to\infty) \Longrightarrow f\in S_p$ <u>mit</u> $h \neq o$,

(ii) $f\in S_p$ <u>mit</u> $h \neq o \Longrightarrow \|f-\hat{M}_n f\|_p\,[a_1,b_1] = O(\frac{1}{n})$ $(n\to\infty)$,

(iii) $\|f-\hat{M}_n f\|_p\,[a,b] = o(\frac{1}{n})$ $(n\to\infty) \Longrightarrow f\in S_p$ <u>mit</u> $h = o$,

(iv) $f\in S_p$ <u>mit</u> $h = o \Longrightarrow \|f-\hat{M}_n f\|_p\,[a_1,b_1] = o(\frac{1}{n})$ $(n\to\infty)$.

Beweis. Um (i) zu beweisen gehen wir aus von dem bilinearen Funktional (vergleiche [3])

(3.1) $$A_n(f,g) := 2n \int_a^b [\hat{M}_n f(x) - f(x)]\, g(x)dx,$$

$$f\in L_p(I),\ g\in L_q[a,b]\ (g = 0 \text{ auf } I\setminus[a,b]),\quad p^{-1} + q^{-1} = 1,$$

halten zunächst ein $g\in C_o^2(I) := \{g\in C^2(I) \mid \operatorname{supp} g \subset (a,b)\}$ fest und zeigen: Jedes der linearen Funktionale $A_n(\cdot,g)$ auf $L_p(I)$ ist beschränkt, und die Folge der Normen $\sup\{|A_n(f,g)| : \|f\|_p \leq 1\}$ ist gleichmäßig in $n$ beschränkt. Für ein beliebiges $\xi_k\in I_k$ $(k\in\mathbb{N}_o)$ folgt wegen $\int_I \hat{m}_{nk}(x)dx = 1$ nach einfachen Umformungen

$$\begin{aligned} A_n(f,g) &= 2n \int_I [\hat{M}_n f(x) - f(x)]g(x)dx \\ &= 2n \sum_{k=o}^{\infty} \int_{I_k} f(t)dt \int_I [g(x) - g(\xi_k) - g'(\xi_k)(x-\xi_k)]\, \hat{m}_{nk}(x)dx + \\ &\quad + 2n \sum_{k=o}^{\infty} \int_{I_k} f(t)dt \int_I g'(\xi_k)(x-\xi_k)\, \hat{m}_{nk}(x)dx + \\ &\quad + 2n \sum_{k=o}^{\infty} \int_{I_k} [g(\xi_k) - g(x)]\, f(x)dx. \end{aligned}$$

Verwenden wir die Abschätzungen

$$|g(x) - g(\xi_k)| \leq \|g'\|_\infty \, |x-\xi_k| ,$$

$$|g(x) - g(\xi_k) - g'(\xi_k)(x-\xi_k)| \leq \frac{1}{2} \|g''\|_\infty (x-\xi_k)^2$$

und setzen wir

$$\xi_k := \frac{k}{k+n} \in I_k \quad (k \in \mathbb{N}_o) ,$$

so folgt

$$|A_n(f,g)| \leq n \|g''\|_\infty \sum_{k=o}^{\infty} \int_{I_k} |f(t)| dt \int_I (x - \frac{k}{k+n})^2 \hat{m}_{nk}(x)\, dx +$$

$$+ 2n \|g'\|_\infty \sum_{k=o}^{\infty} \int_{I_k} |f(t)| dt \left| \int_I (x - \frac{k}{k+n}) \hat{m}_{nk}(x) dx \right| +$$

$$+ 2n \|g'\|_\infty \sum_{k=o}^{\infty} \int_{I_k} |f(x)| \left|x - \frac{k}{k+n}\right| dx. \tag{3.2}$$

Durch direktes Ausrechnen findet man

$$\int_I (x - \frac{k}{k+n}) \hat{m}_{nk}(x) dx \leq \frac{1}{n}$$

und

$$\int_I (x - \frac{k}{k+n})^2 \hat{m}_{nk}(x) dx \leq \frac{5}{4n} \quad .$$

Da außerdem $|x - \frac{k}{k+n}| \leq \frac{1}{n}$ ist für $x \in I_k$, folgt aus (3.2) insgesamt

$$|A_n(f,g)| \leq 2 \left(\|g''\|_\infty + 2\|g'\|_\infty\right) \|f\|_p$$

für alle $f \in L_p(I)$ bei festem $g \in C_o^2(I)$. Somit ist

$$\sup \{|A_n(f,g)| : \|f\|_p \leq 1\} \leq 2(\|g''\|_\infty + 2\|g'\|_\infty) < \infty, \forall n \in \mathbb{N} .$$

Aufgrund des Satzes von Banach-Steinhaus ist die Folge $(A_n(\cdot,g))_{n\in\mathbb{N}}$ genau dann schwach* - konvergent gegen ein beschränktes lineares Grenzfunktional $A(\cdot,g)$, falls gilt $A_n(f,g) \to A(f,g)$ $(n \to \infty)$ für alle Elemente aus dem in $L_p(I)$ (bezüglich $\|\cdot\|_p$) dichten Teilraum $C^2(I)$. Sei also $f \in C^2(I)$ und $F$ das unbestimmte Integral von $f$.

Bei festem $g \in C_o^2(I)$ folgt aus (3.1) durch partielle Integration unter

Beachtung von (1.3) und supp $g\subset(a,b)$ die Gleichung

(3.3) $$A_n(f,g) = -\int_a^b 2n\,[M_nF(x) - F(x)]\,g'(x)dx,\ n\in\mathbb{N}.$$

Aufgrund von
$2n\,[M_nF(x) - F(x)] = x(1-x)^2F''(x) + o(1)\ (n\to\infty)$ gleichmäßig auf $[a,b]$ (vgl. [2], (2.4)) folgt aus (3.3) durch Vertauschung von Integration und Limesbildung

$$\lim_{n\to\infty} A_n(f,g) = -\int_a^b x(1-x)^2\,F''(x)\,g'(x)dx = \int_a^b f(x)[x(1-x)^2\,g'(x)]'dx$$

(letzteres durch erneute partielle Integration). Da $g\varepsilon C_o^2(I)$ beliebig war, gilt

(3.4) $$A(f,g) = \int_a^b f(x)[x(1-x)^2\,g'(x)]'dx,\quad \forall f\varepsilon L_p(I),\ g\varepsilon C_o^2(I).$$

Im folgenden halten wir in (3.1) $f\varepsilon L_p(I)$ fest und stellen zunächst fest, daß jedes der linearen Funktionale $A_n(f,\cdot)$ auf $L_q[a,b]$ beschränkt ist und die Folge der Normen sup $\{|A_n(f,g)| : \|g\|_q\,[a,b] \leq 1\}$ gleichmäßig in $n$ beschränkt ist. Letzteres ist erfüllt wegen

(3.5) $$|A_n(f,g)| \leq 2n\|f-\hat{M}_nf\|_p\,[a,b]\,\|g\|_q\,[a,b]$$

und der Voraussetzung in (i).

Wegen der schwachen* - Kompaktheit jeder Kugel des $L_q^*\,[a,b]$ läßt sich also eine Teilfolge $A_{n_p}(f,\cdot)$ auswählen, die schwach* - konvergent ist gegen ein Grenzfunktional $B(f,\cdot)$ auf $L_q[a,b]$. Nach dem Darstellungssatz für beschränkte lineare Funktionale auf $L_q[a,b]$ existiert ein $h\,\varepsilon\,L_p[a,b]$ derart, daß gilt

(3.6) $$B(f,g) = \int_a^b h(x)g(x)dx.$$

Da $f\varepsilon L_p(I)$ beliebig war, gilt (3.6) für alle $f\varepsilon L_p(I)$ und alle $g\varepsilon L_q[a,b]$. Für $f\varepsilon L_p(I)$ und $g\varepsilon C_o^2(I)$ folgt wegen der Eindeutigkeit des Grenzwertes $A(f,g) = B(f,g)$ und somit aus (3.4) und (3.6)

(3.7) $$\int_a^b f(x)[x(1-x)^2g'(x)]'dx = \int_a^b h(x)g(x)dx,\quad \forall f\varepsilon L_p(I),\ g\varepsilon C_o^2(I).$$

Formt man die rechte Seite von (3.7) durch zweimalige partielle Integration um, so erhält man wegen supp $g\subset(a,b)$ und mit $H(x) := c_1 + \int_a^x h(u)du$,

$c_1 \varepsilon \mathbb{R}$,

$$\int_a^b h(x)g(x)dx = - \int_a^b \frac{H(x)}{x(1-x)^2} [x(1-x)^2 g'(x)]dx$$

$$= \int_a^b (c_2 + \int_a^x \frac{H(t)}{t(1-t)^2} dt)[x(1-x)^2 g'(x)]'dx,$$

$c_2 \varepsilon \mathbb{R}$, und hieraus durch Vergleich mit (3.7)(da $g \varepsilon C_o^2(I)$ beliebig ist) als Darstellung von $f$ auf $[a,b]$

$$f(x) = c_2 + \int_a^x \frac{H(t)}{t(1-t)^2} dt, \quad c_2 \varepsilon \mathbb{R}, \quad x \varepsilon [a,b]. \tag{3.8}$$

Aus dieser Darstellung läßt sich unmittelbar ablesen, daß $f \varepsilon S_p$ ist mit $h \neq o$.

Die Aussage (ii) ist wegen $S_p \subset L_p^2[a,b]$ eine unmittelbare Folge von Satz 2.3.

Zu (iii): Sei $f \varepsilon L_p(I)$ und $\| f - \hat{M}_n f \|_p [a,b] = o(\frac{1}{n})$ $(n \to \infty)$.

Aufgrund der bereits bewiesenen Aussage (i) gilt dann auf jeden Fall (3.7) mit der Lösung (3.8). Anderseits ist aber hier $A(f,g) = 0$, $\forall g \varepsilon C_o^2(I)$, wegen

$$|A_n(f,g)| \leq 2n \| f - \hat{M}_n f \|_p [a,b] \| g \|_\infty = o(1) \quad (n \to \infty) .$$

(3.7) impliziert somit $h = o$ und damit $H = c, c \varepsilon \mathbb{R}$, und aus (3.8) folgt durch Differentiation nach der oberen Grenze die behauptete Gleichung

$$x(1-x)^2 f'(x) = c, \quad x \varepsilon [a,b].$$

Zu (iv): Sei $f \varepsilon S_p$ mit $h = o$, d.h. $x(1-x)^2 f'(x) = c, c \varepsilon [a,b]$, **womit** insbesondere $f \varepsilon C^2[a,b]$ ist. Wir wählen eine Funktion $g_o \varepsilon C_o^2(I)$ mit supp $g_o \subset [a+\eta, b-\eta]$ und $g_o(x) = 1$ auf $[a_1-\eta, b_1+\eta]$, $\eta = \frac{1}{3}\min(a_1-a, b-b_1) > o$ vgl. [1]).

Wegen $fg_o = f$ auf $[a_1, b_1]$ ist dort

$$\hat{M}_n f - f = \hat{M}_n f - \hat{M}_n fg_o + \hat{M}_n fg_o - fg_o ,$$

und hieraus folgt wegen

$$1 - g_o(t) \leq \lambda_{[a_1-\eta, b_1+\eta]}(t), \quad t \varepsilon I$$

und mit Hilfe der Dreiecksungleichung

$$\| f-\hat{M}_n f \|_p [a_1,b_1] \leq \| \hat{M}_n \lambda_{[a_1-\eta,\ b_1+\eta]} f \|_p [a_1,b_1] + \| \hat{M}_n fg_0 - fg_0 \|_p [a_1,b_1].$$

Aufgrund von Lemma 2.2 (etwa für $r = 2$) gilt für den ersten Summanden auf der rechten Seite

$$\| \hat{M}_n \lambda_{[a_1-\eta,b_1+\eta]} f \|_p [a_1,b_1] = o(\tfrac{1}{n}) \quad (n \to \infty).$$

Um den zweiten Summanden abzuschätzen, beachten wir zunächst, daß $fg_0 \varepsilon C_0^2(I)$ ist. Sei $G$ das unbestimmte Integral von $fg_0$. Nach [2], Gleichung (2.4), gilt dann

$$2n[M_n G(x) - G(x)] = x(1-x)^2 G''(x) + o(1), \quad (n \to \infty)$$

gleichmäßig auf $[a_1,b_1]$. $G''(x) = (fg_0)'(x) = f'(x)$ und $x(1-x)^2 f'(x) = c, c \varepsilon \mathbb{R}$, auf $[a_1,b_1]$ implizieren $2n[M_n G(x) - G(x)] = c + o(1), (n \to \infty)$ gleichmäßig auf $[a_1,b_1]$. Wenden wir auf diese letzte asymptotische Gleichung den Differentiationsoperator $D$ an, so folgt wegen (1.3)
$2n[\hat{M}_n fg_o - fg_o] = o(1), (n \to \infty)$ gleichmäßig auf $[a_1,b_1]$ und somit

$$\| \hat{M}_n fg_0 - fg_0 \|_p [a_1,b_1] \leq \| \hat{M}_n fg_0 - fg_0 \|_\infty [a_1,b_1] = o(\tfrac{1}{n}) \quad (n \to \infty).$$

Damit ist Satz 3.1 vollständig bewiesen.

## LITERATUR

[1] Ditzian, Z. - May, C.P., $L_p$-saturation and inverse theorems for modified Bernstein polynomials. Indiana Univ. Math. J. 25 (1976), 733 - 751.

[2] Lupaş, A. - Müller, M.W., Approximation properties of the $M_n$ - operators. Aequationes Math. 5 (1970), 19 - 37.

[3] Maier, V., Güte- und Saturationsaussagen für die $L_1$-Approximation durch spezielle Folgen linearer positiver Operatoren. Dissertation, Universität Dortmund 1976, 65 S.

[4] Müller, M.W., $L_p$ -approximation by the method of integral Meyer-König and Zeller operators (Universität Dortmund, Forschungsbericht Nr. 8 der Lehrstühle Mathematik III und VIII (Angewandte Mathematik).) To appear in Studia Math., vol. 63.

[5] Zygmund, A., Trigonometric Series I and II. Cambridge University Press, London - New York 1968.

# Global Approximation Theorems for the Szász-Mirakjan Operators in Exponential Weight Spaces

M. Becker, D. Kucharski, and R.J. Nessel
Lehrstuhl A für Mathematik
Rheinisch-Westfälische Technische Hochschule
Aachen

In this note we continue our previous investigations on the global approximation by Szász-Mirakjan operators. This time the functions to be approximated are in fact allowed to have exponential growth at infinity. The main point will be the derivation of the inverse theorem for the nonsaturated cases $0<\alpha<2$.

## 1. Introduction

In 1972, Berens-Lorentz [9] established the inverse theorem for the Bernstein polynomials in the nonsaturated cases $0<\alpha<2$ (for the saturation case $\alpha=2$ see [15]). In fact, they offered two proofs, one using intermediate space methods covering the whole range $0<\alpha<2$, the other one proceeding more elementarily but only for $0<\alpha<1$. Recently (cf. [2]), the elementary approach was extended to all values $0<\alpha<2$, the main point being an appropriate smoothing via suitable regularization processes (e.g. integral means). Indeed, this approach to (global) inverse results may be applied in other and more general situations (see [1], [3], [7], [8] for the details). In particular, global approximation theorems are given in [3] for the Szász-Mirakjan operators in polynomial weight spaces. It is the purpose of the present note to extend the latter results to functions which are allowed to have exponential growth at infinity.

To be specific, we are concerned with the approximation by the Szász-Mirakjan operators

$$(1.1)\qquad S_n(f(t);x) := S_nf(x) := \sum_{k=0}^{\infty} f(\tfrac{k}{n})p_{k,n}(x), \quad p_{k,n}(x) := \frac{(nx)^k}{k!}\, e^{-nx}$$

in connection with spaces ($\beta>0$)

$$C_\beta := \{f \in C[0,\infty);\ w_\beta f \text{ uniformly continuous and bounded on } [0,\infty)\},$$

(1.2)

$$w_\beta(x) := e^{-\beta x}, \qquad \|f\|_\beta := \sup_{x\geq 0} w_\beta(x)|f(x)|,$$

$C[0,\infty)$ being the set of continuous functions on $[0,\infty)$. Obviously, the operators $S_n$ are well-defined for each $f \in C_\beta$, however (cf. (2.9 - 11)), they do not map the (individual) Banach space $C_\beta$ into itself but only into $C_\gamma$ for any $\gamma>\beta$, provided n is large enough. Therefore it seems to be appropriate to consider the approximation of the operators (1.1) on the locally convex (in fact a countably normed) space (but see also (6.1), Cor. 2)

(1.3)
$$C := \bigcap_{\beta>0} C_\beta .$$

Compare also the remarks already given in [1], [3], [14] as well as [13] for the treatment of the Weierstrass integral on spaces with weights $\exp\{-\beta x^2\}$.

To this end, let $\mathbb{N}$ be the set of natural numbers and set for $h>0$, $\delta>0$, $0<\alpha\leq 2$

(1.4)
$$\begin{aligned}
\Delta_h^2 f(x) &:= f(x+2h) - 2f(x+h) + f(x),\\
\omega_2(C_\beta,f,\delta) &:= \sup_{0<h\leq\delta} \|\Delta_h^2 f\|_\beta ,\\
\mathrm{Lip}_2(C_\beta,\alpha) &:= \{f \in C_\beta;\ \omega_2(C_\beta,f,\delta) = \mathcal{O}(\delta^\alpha),\ \delta\to 0+\},\\
\mathrm{Lip}_2(C,\alpha) &:= \bigcap_{\beta>0} \mathrm{Lip}_2(C_\beta,\alpha).
\end{aligned}$$

In these terms the results of the present note may be summarized by the following equivalence theorem (see also Cor. 2).

THEOREM 1: _For_ $f \in C$, $0<\alpha\leq 2$, _the following assertions are equivalent:_

(i) $f \in \mathrm{Lip}_2(C,\alpha)$,

(ii) _for each_ $\beta>0$ _there exists a constant_ $M_\beta$ _such that_

(1.5)
$$w_\beta(x)|S_n f(x) - f(x)| \leq M_\beta [x/n]^{\alpha/2} \qquad (n \in \mathbb{N},\ x\geq 0).$$

For the corresponding assertions in polynomial weight spaces $C_N$ with weight $w_N(x) := (1+x^N)^{-1}$ see [3] (also [1] in connection with intermediate space methods). In fact, for each $N \in \mathbb{N}$ the operators (1.1) then map the Banach space $C_N$ into itself so that a Banach space frame is sufficient for the formulation of the results. All the other results known so far for the approximation by the Szász-Mirakjan operators (apart from saturation results, cf. Sec. 5) are essentially only of a local character dealing with compact subintervals of $[0,\infty)$. For instance, Ditzian [11] proves local direct theorems using polynomial and exponential weights. May [17] proves local equivalence theorems on shrinking intervals for more general operators of exponential type of which $S_n$ is a special example.

The plan of this note is as follows: In Sec. 2 some preliminary results are delivered whereas in Sec. 3 we prove the direct theorem (Thm. 1, (i) $\Rightarrow$ (ii)) following standard procedures. Sec. 4 is devoted to the proof of the inverse theorem (Thm. 1, (ii) $\Rightarrow$ (i)) for the nonsaturated cases $0<\alpha<2$, the main point of this note. Sec. 5 deals with the saturation case $\alpha=2$. Finally, Sec. 6 gives some outline of related problems.

## 2. Preliminaries

Obviously, one has for any $h>0$, $\beta>0$

$$(2.1) \qquad \| e^{-\beta x} f(x+h)\|_C := \sup_{x\geq 0} |e^{-\beta x} f(x+h)| \leq e^{\beta h} \|f\|_\beta$$

so that translation by a positive increment maps $C_\beta$ into itself. Furthermore, for any $f \in C_\beta$

$$(2.2) \qquad \lim_{\delta\to 0+} \omega_2(C_\beta, f, \delta) = 0$$

in view of the uniform continuity of $e^{-\beta x} f(x)$ on $[0,\infty)$.

In the course of the proofs we make use of some elementary properties of the (modified, cf. [10, p. 317]) Steklov means $(h>0)$

$$f_h(x) := (2/h)^2 \int_0^{h/2} \int_0^{h/2} [\,2f(x+s+t) - f(x+2(s+t))]\, ds\, dt. \tag{2.3}$$

One has (cf. (1.4))

$$\begin{aligned} f(x)-f_h(x) &= (2/h)^2 \iint_0^{h/2} \Delta_{s+t}^2 f(x)\, ds\, dt, \\ f_h''(x) &= h^{-2}[\,8\,\Delta_{h/2}^2 f(x) - \Delta_h^2 f(x)]\,. \end{aligned} \tag{2.4}$$

Therefore for any $\beta>0$, $f \in C_\beta$, $h>0$

$$\|f-f_h\|_\beta \leqslant \omega_2(C_\beta,f,h), \quad \|f_h''\|_\beta \leqslant 9\,h^{-2}\omega_2(C_\beta,f,h). \tag{2.5}$$

Let us continue with some well-known properties of the operators (1.1) (cf. [19], [20]). First we recall that $(j=0,1)$

$$S_n(t^j;x) = x^j, \quad S_n((t-x)^2;x) = x/n. \tag{2.6}$$

Setting for any $\beta>0$, $n \in \mathbb{N}$

$$\beta_n := n(e^{\beta/n} - 1), \tag{2.7}$$

one obviously has

$$\beta < \beta_n \leqslant \beta e^{\beta/n} \leqslant \beta e^{\beta}, \quad \beta_n - \beta \leqslant \beta^2 e^{\beta} n^{-1}. \tag{2.8}$$

Further elementary calculations yield (cf. [11])

$$\begin{aligned} S_n(e^{\beta t};x) &= \exp\{\beta_n x\}, \\ S_n(te^{\beta t};x) &= x\,e^{\beta/n}\exp\{\beta_n x\}, \\ S_n(t^2 e^{\beta t};x) &= [\,x^2 e^{\beta/n} + (x/n)]\,e^{\beta/n}\exp\{\beta_n x\}, \\ S_n((t-x)^2 e^{\beta t};x) &= [\,(\beta_n x/n)^2 + (x/n)e^{\beta/n}]\exp\{\beta_n x\}. \end{aligned} \tag{2.9}$$

In view of the first relation it immediately follows that $f \in C_\beta$ for some

$\beta>0$ does by no means imply $S_n f \in C_\beta$. In fact, given $0<\beta<\gamma$, one has that for any $f \in C_\beta$

$$\|S_n f\|_\gamma \leqslant \|f\|_\beta, \tag{2.10}$$

provided $\gamma \geqslant \beta_n$, thus $n \geqslant n_o(\beta,\gamma)$ with (cf. (2.8))

$$n_o > \beta/\log(\gamma/\beta). \tag{2.11}$$

Therefore, to consider the approximation by Szász-Mirakjan operators on exponential weight spaces, it seems to be appropriate to treat the matter within the framework of the locally convex spaces C (cf. (1.3)) or $C(\eta)$ (cf. (6.1)) rather than within the individual Banach space $C_\beta$, particularly if one is interested in the formulation of an equivalence approximation theorem (like Thm. 1 or Cor. 2). Thus the situation is quite different to the one of polynomial weights, discussed in [1], [3].

As an immediate consequence of (2.2), (2.6), (2.9) it follows by the standard arguments (cf. [20]) that for any $\beta>0$ and $f \in C_\beta$ one has for each $x \geqslant 0$

$$\lim_{n\to\infty} S_n f(x) = f(x), \tag{2.12}$$

the convergence being uniform on any compact subinterval of $[0,\infty)$ (see also Cor. 1). A further classical result is the Voronovskaja-type relation

$$\lim_{n\to\infty} n[S_n f(x) - f(x)] = (x/2)f''(x), \tag{2.13}$$

valid for any $x \geqslant 0$ at which $f \in C_\beta$ is twice continuously differentiable. Moreover, we also employ the identities (cf. [16, p. 475])

$$\begin{aligned}(S_n f)''(y) &= \left(\frac{n}{y}\right)^2 \sum_{k=0}^{\infty} \left[\left(\frac{k}{n} - y\right)^2 - \frac{k}{n^2}\right] f\left(\frac{k}{n}\right) p_{k,n}(y) \qquad (y>0),\\ &= n^2 \sum_{k=0}^{\infty} \Delta_{1/n}^2 f(k/n) p_{k,n}(y) \qquad (y \geqslant 0).\end{aligned} \tag{2.14}$$

Finally, to prove inverse results in the nonsaturated cases $0<\alpha<2$, we shall use the following lemma (cf. [8], see also [7], [9]).

LEMMA 1. Let $\Omega$ be monotonely increasing on some interval $[0,d]$, $0<d\leq 1$. If for some $0<\alpha<r$, $\lambda>0$ one has that for all $h,\delta\in[0,d]$, $h<\delta<\sqrt{\lambda h}$

$$\Omega(h) \leq M[\delta^{\alpha} + (h/\delta)^{r}\Omega(\delta)],$$

then $\Omega(\delta)=\mathcal{O}(\delta^{\alpha})$, $\delta\to 0+$.

## 3. Direct Theorems

In order to prove Thm. 1, (i) $\Rightarrow$ (ii), let us introduce

$$C_{\beta}^{2} := \{f\in C_{\beta};\ f''\in C_{\beta}\}$$

and establish a Jackson-type inequality.

LEMMA 2. Let $g\in C_{\beta}^{2}$ for some $\beta>0$. Then for $\gamma>\beta$ there exists a constant $M_{\beta,\gamma}$ such that for all $x\geq 0$ and $n\geq n_{0}$ (cf. (2.11))

$$w_{\gamma}(x)\,|S_{n}g(x)-g(x)| \leq M_{\beta,\gamma}\|g''\|_{\beta}\,(x/n). \tag{3.1}$$

PROOF. In view of

$$g(t)-g(x) = (t-x)g'(x) + \int_{x}^{t}\int_{x}^{s} g''(u)\,du\,ds \qquad (x,t\geq 0)$$

and the estimate

$$\Big|\int_{x}^{t}\int_{x}^{s} |g''(u)|\,du\,ds\Big| \leq \|g''\|_{\beta}\Big|\int_{x}^{t}\int_{x}^{s}\frac{du\,ds}{w_{\beta}(u)}\Big|$$

$$\leq (1/2)\|g''\|_{\beta}\,(t-x)^{2}[w_{\beta}^{-1}(x)+w_{\beta}^{-1}(t)],$$

one has by (2.6), (2.9) for $\gamma>\beta$

$$w_\gamma(x)|S_n g(x)-g(x)| \leqslant w_\gamma(x)\|g''\|_\beta[e^{\beta x}S_n((t-x)^2;x) + S_n((t-x)^2 e^{\beta t};x)]$$

$$\leqslant (x/n)\|g''\|_\beta[1+((\beta_n^2 x/n)+e^{\beta/n})\exp\{(\beta_n-\gamma)x\}] .$$

Therefore, if $n_0$ is such that $\gamma>\beta_{n_0}$, then there exists a constant $M_{\beta,\gamma}$ such that (3.1) holds true.

THEOREM 2. *Let* $f \in C_\beta$ *for some* $\beta>0$, *and let* $n_0$ *be given via* (2.11) *for some* $\gamma>\beta$. *Then there exists a constant* $M_{\beta,\gamma}$ *such that for all* $x\geqslant 0$, $n\geqslant n_o$

$$w_\gamma(x)|S_n f(x) - f(x)| \leqslant M_{\beta,\gamma}\,\omega_2(C_\beta,f,\sqrt{x/n}). \tag{3.2}$$

*In particular, if* $f\in \mathrm{Lip}_2(C_\beta,\alpha)$ *for some* $0<\alpha\leqslant 2$, *then*

$$w_\gamma(x)|S_n f(x) - f(x)| \leqslant M_{\beta,\gamma}(x/n)^{\alpha/2} \qquad (x\geqslant 0,\ n\geqslant n_o). \tag{3.3}$$

PROOF. Note that the assertion is trivial for $x=0$. For $f\in C_\beta$, $h>0$ one has by (2.5), (2.9), and La. 2 that for $x\geqslant 0$, $n\geqslant n_0$

$$w_\gamma(x)|S_n f(x)-f(x)| \leqslant w_\gamma(x)|S_n[f-f_h](x)| + w_\gamma(x)|S_n f_h(x)-f_h(x)| + w_\gamma(x)|f_h(x)-f(x)|$$

$$\leqslant \|f-f_h\|_\beta w_\gamma(x)[S_n(e^{\beta t};x)+e^{\beta x}] + M_{\beta,\gamma}\|f_h''\|_\beta (x/n)$$

$$\leqslant M_{\beta,\gamma}\omega_2(C_\beta,f,h)[\exp\{(\beta_n-\gamma)x\}+1+9(x/nh^2)]$$

$$\leqslant M_{\beta,\gamma}\omega_2(C_\beta,f,h)[2+9(x/nh^2)] .$$

Thus the result follows upon setting $h = \sqrt{x/n}$.

Obviously, the direct part of Thm. 1 now follows as an immediate consequence of the definitions and the previous result. In particular, one has (cf. (2.12))

COROLLARY 1. *Let* $f\in C_\beta$ *for some* $\beta>0$. *Then for any* $\gamma>\beta$

$$\lim_{n\to\infty} \|S_n f - f\|_\gamma = 0.$$

## 4. Inverse Results for $0<\alpha<2$

The main tool for the proof of the inverse theorem in the nonsaturated cases $0<\alpha<2$ is an appropriate Bernstein-type inequality. This is given by

LEMMA 3. *Let* $f \in C_\beta$ *for some* $\beta>0$. *Then for* $y>0$, $\delta>0$

$$(4.1)\qquad |(S_n f)''(y)| \leq [\beta^2 + 2(n/y) + (9/\delta^2)]\, e^{2\beta/n} e^{\beta_n y}\, \omega_2(C_\beta, f, \delta).$$

PROOF. For any $y>0$, $\delta>0$ one has (cf. (2.3))

$$|(S_n f)''(y)| \leq |(S_n[f-f_\delta])''(y)| + |(S_n f_\delta)''(y)| =: I_1 + I_2 ,$$

say. In view of the first representation (2.14) as well as of (2.5), (2.9) it follows that

$$\begin{aligned} I_1 &\leq (\tfrac{n}{y})^2 \sum_{k=0}^{\infty} |(\tfrac{k}{n} - y)^2 - \tfrac{k}{n^2}|\,|f(\tfrac{k}{n}) - f_\delta(\tfrac{k}{n})|\,p_{k,n}(y) \\ &\leq \omega_2(C_\beta, f, \delta)(\tfrac{n}{y})^2 [S_n((t-y)^2 e^{\beta t}; y) + S_n(t e^{\beta t}; y)/n] \\ &\leq \omega_2(C_\beta, f, \delta)[\beta_n^2 + 2(n/y)e^{\beta/n}]\exp\{\beta_n y\}. \end{aligned}$$

Concerning $I_2$ we make use of the second representation (2.14). Then again by (2.5), (2.9)

$$\begin{aligned} I_2 &\leq n^2 \sum_{k=0}^{\infty} |\Delta^2_{1/n} f_\delta(k/n)|\,p_{k,n}(y) \\ &\leq \| f''_\delta \|_\beta\, n^2 \sum_{k=0}^{\infty} \Big(\iint_0^{1/n} \exp\{\beta(\tfrac{k}{n} + s + t)\}ds\, dt\Big)\, p_{k,n}(y) \\ &\leq \| f''_\delta \|_\beta\, e^{2\beta/n} S_n(e^{\beta t}; y) \leq (9/\delta^2)\omega_2(C_\beta, f, \delta) e^{2\beta/n} e^{\beta_n y}. \end{aligned}$$

In view of (2.8) this establishes (4.1).

LEMMA 4. For any $x \geq 0$, $0<h \leq 1$ one has

$$\iint_0^h \frac{ds\,dt}{x+s+t} \leq M h^2/(x+2h), \tag{4.2}$$

$$\iint_0^h \exp\{\beta_n(x+s+t)\}ds\,dt \leq h^2 \exp\{\beta_n(x+2h)\}, \tag{4.3}$$

$$\iint_0^h \frac{\exp\{\beta_n(x+s+t)\}}{x+s+t}\,ds\,dt \leq \frac{Mh^2}{x+2h} \exp\{\beta_n(x+2h)\}. \tag{4.4}$$

Concerning the proof, see [3] for (4.2). Moreover, (4.3) being obvious, (4.4) is an immediate consequence of (4.2 - 3).

THEOREM 3. Let $\beta>0$ be arbitrary. If $f \in C_\beta$ satisfies for some $0<\alpha<2$ and for all $x \geq 0$, $n \in \mathbb{N}$

$$w_\beta(x)\,|S_n f(x) - f(x)| \leq M(x/n)^{\alpha/2}, \tag{4.5}$$

then $f \in \mathrm{Lip}_2(C_\beta,\alpha)$.

PROOF. For some fixed $0<h$, $\delta \leq 1$, $\delta<\sqrt{2h}$, $x \geq 0$ it follows by (4.5) and La. 3 - 4 that for all $n \in \mathbb{N}$

$$|\Delta_h^2 f(x)| \leq |f(x+2h) - S_n f(x+2h)| + 2|f(x+h) - S_n f(x+h)| + |f(x) - S_n f(x)| + |\Delta_h^2[S_n f](x)|$$

$$\leq M n^{-\alpha/2}\left[\frac{(x+2h)^{\alpha/2}}{w_\beta(x+2h)} + 2\frac{(x+h)^{\alpha/2}}{w_\beta(x+h)} + \frac{x^{\alpha/2}}{w_\beta(x)}\right] + \iint_0^h |(S_n f)''(x+s+t)|\,ds\,dt$$

$$\leq \frac{M}{w_\beta(x)}\left(\frac{x+2h}{n}\right)^{\alpha/2} + \omega_2(C_\beta,f,\delta)e^{2\beta/n}\iint_0^h \left[\beta^2 + \frac{2n}{x+s+t} + \frac{9}{\delta^2}\right]\exp\{\beta_n(x+s+t)\}ds\,dt$$

$$\leq \frac{M}{w_\beta(x)}\left(\frac{x+2h}{n}\right)^{\alpha/2} + \omega_2(C_\beta,f,\delta)e^{2\beta/n}h^2\left[\beta^2 + \frac{2Mn}{x+2h} + \frac{9}{\delta^2}\right]\exp\{\beta_n(x+2h)\},$$

and therefore in view of (2.8)

$$w_\beta(x)\,|\Delta_h^2 f(x)| \leqslant M\left[\left(\frac{x+2h}{n}\right)^{\alpha/2} + \left(\frac{1}{\delta^2}+\frac{n}{x+2h}\right)h^2\omega_2(C_\beta,f,\delta)\exp\{\beta^2 e^\beta\,\frac{x+2h}{n}\}\right]$$

(constants M may have different values at each occurrence). For the case $x=0$ let us only note that the estimate holds true in view of the existence of the integrals for $x=0$ and the continuity of the expressions involved. Now choose n such that

$$\sqrt{(x+2h)/n} \leqslant \delta < \sqrt{(x+2h)/(n-1)} \leqslant \sqrt{2}\sqrt{(x+2h)/n}$$

(thus necessarily $\delta < \sqrt{2h}$, cf. La. 1). Then

$$w_\beta(x)\,|\Delta_h^2 f(x)| \leqslant M[\,\delta^\alpha + (h/\delta)^2\omega_2(C_\beta,f,\delta)\exp\{\beta^2 e^\beta \delta^2\}]\,.$$

Since the right-hand side is independent of x, it follows that

$$\omega_2(C_\beta,f,h) \leqslant M[\,\delta^\alpha + (h/\delta)^2\omega_2(C_\beta,f,\delta)]\,.$$

Therefore an application of La. 1 with $\Omega(t) := \omega_2(C_\beta,f,t)$ delivers $f\in \mathrm{Lip}_2(C_\beta,\alpha)$.

Obviously, Thm. 3 establishes the inverse assertion of Thm. 1, namely (ii) $\Rightarrow$ (i), for $0<\alpha<2$ (even within the individual Banach space $C_\beta$).

## 5. Inverse Results for $\alpha=2$

Concerning the saturation case $\alpha=2$ let us, just for the sake of completeness, mention a short proof of the inverse theorem, using an idea of Grundmann [12] (who gave the proof for the Bernstein polynomials). It is based upon the fact that for any $f\in C_\beta$ one has

(5.1) $\quad$ f convex on $[0,\infty)$ $\Leftrightarrow$ $S_n f(x) \geqslant f(x)$ for all $n\in\mathbb{N}$, $x\geqslant 0$

(cf. [18, p. 75] for this (local) property).

THEOREM 4. *If* $f \in C_\beta$ *satisfies for all* $x \geq 0$, $n \in \mathbb{N}$

$$w_\beta(x)|S_n f(x) - f(x)| \leq M_\beta x/n, \tag{5.2}$$

*then* $f \in Lip_2(C_\gamma, 2)$ *for any* $\gamma > \beta$.

PROOF. By (2.6) the assumption (5.2) in fact states that

$$|S_n(f(t);x) - f(x)| \leq M_\beta w_\beta^{-1}(x)[S_n(t^2;x) - x^2],$$

and therefore

$$\pm f(x) \leq M_\beta w_\beta^{-1}(x)[S_n(t^2;x) - x^2] + S_n(\pm f(t);x).$$

Since by (2.6), (2.9)

$$w_\beta^{-1}(x) S_n(t^2;x) = (x^2 + \frac{x}{n})e^{\beta x} \leq S_n(t^2 e^{\beta t};x),$$

we may conclude

$$\begin{aligned} M_\beta w_\beta^{-1}(x)x^2 \pm f(x) &\leq M_\beta w_\beta^{-1}(x) S_n(t^2;x) + S_n(\pm f(t);x) \\ &\leq S_n([M_\beta w_\beta^{-1}(t)t^2 \pm f(t)];x). \end{aligned}$$

In view of (5.1) this implies that $M_\beta w_\beta^{-1}(t)t^2 \pm f(t)$ is a convex function on $[0,\infty)$, i.e.

$$\Delta_h^2[M_\beta w_\beta^{-1}(t)t^2 \pm f(t)](x) \geq 0 \qquad (x \geq 0).$$

Now it follows that for any $\gamma > \beta$

$$w_\gamma(x)|\Delta_h^2 f(x)| \leq M_\beta w_\gamma(x)\Delta_h^2[t^2 e^{\beta t}](x) \leq M_{\beta,\gamma} h^2,$$

the constant $M_{\beta,\gamma}$ being independent of $x \geq 0$. This proves that $f \in Lip_2(C_\gamma, 2)$ for any $\gamma > \beta$.

For various global saturation results concerning the Szász-Mirakjan operators in polynomial weight spaces see in particular [6], [18] and the literature cited there.

## 6. Concluding Remarks

Since the results of Sec. 3 - 5 are in fact given in terms of the individual Banach spaces $C_\beta$, $C_\gamma$, one immediately may formulate a locally convex summary slightly more general than Thm. 1. Indeed, in view of the definition (1.3) of C, any of the functions $e^{\eta x}$, $\eta>0$, seems to be excluded. Setting, however, for any $\eta>0$

(6.1) $$C(\eta) := \bigcap_{\beta>\eta} C_\beta,$$

the results of the previous sections also establish

COROLLARY 2. *Let* $\eta>0$, $0<\alpha\leq 2$ *be arbitrary. For* $f\in C(\eta)$ *the following assertions are equivalent:*

(i) $$f\in \bigcap_{\beta>\eta} \mathrm{Lip}_2(C_\beta,\alpha),$$

(ii) *for any* $\beta>\eta$ *one has* $\| x^{-\alpha/2}[S_n f(x)-f(x)]\|_\beta = O_\beta(n^{-\alpha/2}) \quad (n\to\infty)$.

In polynomial weight spaces $C_N$ with weight $w_N(x) := (1+x^N)^{-1}$ it is possible to derive corresponding global approximation theorems not only for the Szász-Mirakjan operators (1.1) but also for the Baskakov operators

(6.2) $$V_n(f(t);x) := \sum_{k=0}^{\infty} f(\tfrac{k}{n})b_{k,n}(x),\ b_{k,n}(x) := \binom{n+k-1}{k}x^k(1+x)^{-n-k}.$$

For the details see [3] (also [1]). Since for each $n\in\mathbb{N}$, $N\in\mathbb{N}$ the operator $V_n$ is a bounded linear mapping from $C_N$ into itself, the structure of arguments involved is confined to the theory of Banach spaces. Concerning a treatment of the Baskakov operators on the exponential weight spaces $C_\beta$, however, we observe that $V_n(w_\beta^{-1}(t);x)$ only exists for $x<(e^{\beta/n}-1)^{-1}$, in which case one has

$$(6.3) \qquad V_n(e^{\beta t};x) = (1+x-xe^{\beta/n})^{-n} \qquad (x<(e^{\beta/n}-1)^{-1}).$$

For all other values of x the expression $V_n(e^{\beta t};x)$ does not exist as a real number. Thus one has to restrict oneself to compact subintervals of $[0,\infty)$ so that one may regard polynomial growth as a frame best suited for global (i.e. on the whole interval $[0,\infty)$) approximation results for the Baskakov operators.

Finally, let us mention that in [1] global approximation theorems were also given for the Favard operators (in fact a discrete analog of the familiar Weierstrass integral)

$$(6.4) \qquad F_n f(x) := (\pi n)^{-1/2} \sum_{k=-\infty}^{\infty} f(\tfrac{k}{n}) \exp\{-n(\tfrac{k}{n}-x)^2\} \qquad (x \in (-\infty,\infty))$$

in polynomial weight spaces $C_{2N}(-\infty,\infty)$ with weight $(1+x^{2N})^{-1}$ (concerning saturation see also [5]). Corresponding results, however, may also be obtained in exponential weight spaces $C_{2,\beta}(-\infty,\infty)$ with weight $w_{2,\beta}(x) := \exp\{-\beta x^2\}$ (see the comments given in [5]). In fact, $F_n$ then maps $C_{2,\beta}$ into $C_{2,\gamma}$ for any $\gamma>\beta$, provided n is sufficiently large, so that one is again led to consider the approximation on the locally convex space $C_2 := \cap_{\beta>0} C_{2,\beta}$. For all the details, however, we refer to [4] (see also [13] for a treatment of the Weierstrass integral on $C_2$).

## REFERENCES

[1] Becker, M., Umkehrsätze für positive lineare Operatoren. Dissertation, RWTH Aachen 1977.

[2] Becker, M., An elementary proof of the inverse theorem for Bernstein polynomials. Aequationes Math. (in print).

[ 3] Becker, M., Global approximation theorems for Szász-Mirakjan and Baskakov operators in polynomial weight spaces. Indiana Univ. Math. J. (in print).

[ 4] Becker, M., Inverse theorems for Favard operators in weighted spaces. (to appear).

[ 5] Becker, M. - Butzer, P.L. - Nessel, R.J., Saturation for Favard operators in weighted function spaces. Studia Math. 59 (1976), 33 - 47.

[ 6] Becker, M. - Nessel, R.J., Iteration von Operatoren und Saturation in lokal konvexen Räumen. Forschungsberichte des Landes Nordrhein-Westfalen Nr. 2470, Westdeutscher Verlag Opladen, 1975, 27 - 49.

[ 7] Becker, M. - Nessel, R.J., An elementary approach to inverse approximation theorems. J. Approximation Theory (in print).

[ 8] Becker, M. - Nessel, R.J., Inverse results via smoothing. Proceedings International Conference on Constructive Function Theory, Blagoevgrad, 30.5. - 5.6.1977, Sofia 1978 (in print).

[ 9] Berens, H. - Lorentz, G.G., Inverse theorems for Bernstein polynomials. Indiana Univ. Math. J. 21 (1972), 693 - 708.

[10] Butzer, P.L. - Scherer, K., Jackson and Bernstein-type inequalities for families of commutative operators in Banach spaces. J. Approximation Theory 5 (1972), 308 - 342.

[11] Ditzian, Z., Convergence of sequences of linear positive operators: Remarks and applications. J. Approximation Theory 14 (1975), 296 - 301.

[12] Grundmann, A., Personal communication to Dr. E. Stark. July 1975.

[13] Kemper, J. - Nessel, R.J., Gewichtete Approximation durch variationsvermindernde Operatoren vom Faltungstyp. Forschungsberichte des Landes Nordrhein-Westfalen Nr. 2311, Westdeutscher Verlag Opladen, 1973, 1 - 49.

[14] Kucharski, D., Approximationssätze für Szász-Mirakjan, Baskakov - und Favard-Operatoren in gewichteten Räumen. Diplomarbeit, RWTH Aachen 1977.

[15] Lorentz, G.G., Inequalities and the saturation classes of Bernstein polynomials. in: On Approximation Theory, ed. P.L. Butzer - J. Korevaar, Proc. Oberwolfach, ISNM 5, Birkhäuser Verlag, Basel 1964, 200 - 207.

[16] Martini, R., On the approximation of functions together with their derivatives by certain linear positive operators. Indag. Math. 31 (1969), 473 - 481.

[17] May, C.P., Saturation and inverse theorems for combinations of a class of exponential-type operators. Canad. J. Math. 28 (1976), 1224-1250.

[18] Micchelli, C.A., Saturation classes and iterates of operators. Dissertation, Stanford 1969.

[19] Mirakjan, G.M., Approximation of continuous functions with the aid of polynomials .... Dokl. Akad. Nauk SSSR 31 (1941), 201 - 205.

[20] Szász, O., Generalization of S. Bernstein's polynomials to the infinite interval. J. Res. Nat. Bur. Standards Sect. B. 45 (1950), 239 - 245.

# APPROXIMATION WITH MONOTONIC OPERATORS IN $A$-DISTANCE

Bl. Sendov
Sofia University, Sofia, Bulgaria

## 1. $A$-DISTANCE AND $A$-CONTINUITY

Let $\Omega$ be a metric space, $\Delta\subset\Omega$ and $B_\Omega$ a linear space of real functions defined on $\Omega$. The distance $r_A(f,g)$, $f$, $g\in B_\Omega$ is an $A$-distance in $B_\Omega$ on $\Delta$ if:

1) $r_A(f,g)=r_A(g,f)\geqq 0$;
2) $r_A(f,g)\leqq r_A(f,h)+r_A(h,g)$;
3) if for every $x\in\Delta$
   $\varphi(x)\leqq f(x)\leqq\psi(x)$ and $\varphi(x)-C\leqq g(x)\leqq\psi(x)+C$, where $C$ is a constant, then
   $r_A(f,g)\leqq r_A(\varphi,\psi)+|C|$;
4) if $C$ is a constant, then
   $r_A(f,f+C)=0 \Longleftrightarrow C=0$.

The concept of an $A$-distance is given by P.P.KOROVKIN [1]. Our definition 1) - 4) [2] is slightly different from the Korovkin's definition [1] but in essence they are equivalent.

$A$-distances for example are: the uniform distance, all $L_p$ distances for $p\geqq 1$, the Hausdorff distance [3] and others.

Let $\rho(x,t)$ be the distance between two points $x$, $t\in\Omega$. For every function $f\in B_\Omega$ and every $\delta>0$ we determine

$$S(\delta,f;x)=\sup\{f(t):\rho(x,t)\leqq\delta, x,t\in\Omega\}\ , \tag{1}$$

$$I(\delta,f;x)=\inf\{f(t):\rho(x,t)\leqq\delta, x,t\in\Omega\}\ . \tag{2}$$

Modulus of $A$-continuity of the function $f\in B_\Omega$ on $\Delta$ is called

$$\tau_A(f;\delta)=r_A(I(\delta/2,f),S(\delta/2,f)).$$

Obviously $\tau_A(f;\delta)$ is a monotonically increasing function of $\delta$ and

(3) $\tau_A(f;\delta)\geq r_A(I(f),S(f))$,

where

$$I(f;x)=\lim_{\delta\to+0} I(\delta,f;x), \qquad S(f;x)=\lim_{\delta\to+0} S(\delta,f;x)$$

are the corresponding lower and upper functions of Baire for the function $f$.

The function $f\varepsilon B_\Omega$ is called $A$-continuous [1] on $\Delta$ if

(4) $\lim_{\delta\to+0} \tau_A(f;\delta)=0.$

It is seen from (3) that a necessary condition for $f\varepsilon B_\Omega$ to be $A$-continuous on $\Delta$ is: $r_A(I(f),S(f))=0$. It is possible to prove that this condition is also sufficient.

From condition (3) follows that $\tau_A(f,\delta)$ is always smaller than the modulus of continuity $\omega(f,\delta)$;i.e.

(5) $\tau_A(f;\delta)\leq\omega(f;\delta)=\sup\{|f(x')-f(x'')|:\rho(x',x'')\leq\delta,x',x''\varepsilon\Delta\}.$

## 2. CONVERGENCE OF SEQUENCES OF MONOTONIC OPERATORS

Let $\psi(\delta)$ be a non decreasing, continuous function, $\psi(0)=0$, $0<\psi(\delta)\leq 1$ for $\delta>0$, and let $\varphi\varepsilon B_\Omega$ be a positive continuous function, $\varphi(x)\geq 1$ for every $x\varepsilon\Omega$. We shall examine sequences of monotonic operators $\{L_n\}_1^\infty$, satisfying the condition

(6) $\lim_{n\to\infty} r_A(L_n(C+D\psi(\rho(x,t))\varphi(t);x),C)=0$

for the arbitrary constants $C$ and $D$.

If $\{L_n\}_1^\infty$ is a sequence of linear and positive operators, the condition (6) is equivalent to

(7) $\lim_{n\to\infty} r_A(L_n(1),1)=0, \quad \lim_{n\to\infty} r_A(L_n(\psi(\rho(x,t))\varphi),0)=0.$

THEOREM 1. *Let* $f\varepsilon B_\Omega$ . *A necessary and sufficient condition* $\lim_{n\to\infty} r_A(L_n(t),f)=0$ *to be valid for every sequence of monotonic (or linear and positive) operators* $\{L_n\}_1^\infty$ *satisfying* (6) *respec-*

*tively (7)), is the following: the function* $f$ *to be A-continuous on* $\Delta$ *and*

(8) $$\sup\{|f(x)|/\varphi(x): x\in\Omega\}=M_f<\infty.$$

Proof. Sufficient part. Let $f\in B_\Omega$, $f$ is $A$-continuous on $\Delta$ and $M_f<\infty$. For all $x,t\in\Omega$ and $\rho(x,t)\leqq\delta$ we have

$$I(\delta,f;x)\leqq f(t)\leqq S(\delta,f;x).$$

On the other hand, for $x,t\in\Omega$ and $\rho(x,t)>\delta$

$$-M_f\varphi(t)\psi(\rho(x,t))/\psi(\delta)\leqq f(t)\leqq M_f\varphi(t)\psi(\rho(x,t))/\psi(\delta)$$

because $\psi$ is monotonic nondecreasing function and $|f(x)|\leqq M_f\varphi(x)$ for all $x\in\Omega$. Then, for all $x,t\in\Omega$

(9) $$f(t)\leqq S(\delta,f;x)+M_f\varphi(t)\psi(\rho(x,t))/\psi(\delta)=h_1(t),$$

(10) $$f(t)\geqq I(\delta,f;x)-M_f\varphi(t)\psi(\rho(x,t))/\psi(\delta)=h_2(t).$$

From the monotonicity of the operators $L_n$, (9) and (10), it follows that

(11) $$L_n(h_2;x)\leqq L_n(f;x)\leqq L_n(h_1,x).$$

From (6), (9) and (10) we have that for every $\varepsilon>0$ exists $n(\varepsilon)$ such that for $n>n(\varepsilon)$

(12) $$r_A(L_n(h_1),S(\delta,f))<\varepsilon,\qquad r_A(L_n(h_2),I(\delta,f))<\varepsilon,$$

for fixed $\delta>0$.

Using the properties of the $A$-distance $r_A$ 1) - 4) and (11), (12) we have

$$r_A(L_n(f),f)\leqq r_A(L_n(f),L_n(h_1))+r_A(L_n(h_1),S(\delta,f))$$
$$+r_A(S(\delta,f),f)\leqq r_A(L_n(h_2),L_n(h_1))+\varepsilon+r_A(S(\delta,f),I(\delta,f))$$
$$\leqq r_A(L_n(h_2),I(\delta,f))+r_A(S(\delta,f),L_n(h_1))+\varepsilon+2r_A(S(\delta,f),I(\delta,f))$$

or

(13) $$r_A(L_n(f),f)\leqq 3\varepsilon+\tau_A(f;2\delta).$$

That concludes the proof of the sufficient part, as $f$ is $A$-continuous and $\varepsilon>0$ is chosen arbitrarily.

Necessary part. We shall start with the condition of $A$-continuity. Let $f_1 \varepsilon B_\Omega$ and $f_1$ is not $A$-continuous ($f_1$ may satisfy condition (8)), i.e.

(14) $$\tau_A(f_1;\delta) \geqq r_A(I(f_1),S(f_1))=d>0.$$

We shall construct a sequence $\{L_n^*\}_1^\infty$ of linear and positive operators (that means also monotonic), satisfying (7) but not converging in the $A$-distance for the function $f_1$, i.e. $\lim_{n\to\infty} r_A(L_n^*(f_1),f_1)$ does not exist or is not equal to $0$.

Let $\delta>0$ and $x\varepsilon\Omega$. Define $\delta(x)\varepsilon(0,\delta)$ in such a way that

(15) $$\psi(\delta(x))S(\delta(x),\varphi;x) \leqq \delta.$$

This is possible because $\lim_{\delta\to+0}\psi(\delta)=0$ and $\varphi$ is continuous in $\Omega$.

For every $x\varepsilon\Omega$ we define a $x(\delta)\varepsilon\Omega$, such that $|x-x(\delta)|\leqq\delta(x)$ and

$$f_1(x(\delta))+\delta \geqq \sup\{f_1(t):\rho(x,t)\leqq\delta(x),\ t\varepsilon\Omega\}.$$

We define the operator $L_\delta'(f)$ as

(16) $$L_\delta'(f;x)=f(x(\delta)).$$

From the definition of $L_\delta'$ it follows that

(17) $$L_\delta'(f_1;x)\geqq S(f_1;x)-\delta$$

for every $x\varepsilon\Omega$.

Obviously $L_\delta'$ is monotonic and, even more, a linear and positive operator. If we take $\delta=1,1/2,1/3,\ldots$ we shall have the sequence of linear and positive operators $\{L_n'\}_1^\infty$. We shall show that $\{L_n'\}_1^\infty$ also satisfies condition (6).

Let $x(\delta)=x_n$ for $\delta=1/n$, then

$$L_n'(C+D\psi(\rho(x,t))\varphi(t);x)=C+D\psi(\rho(x,x_n))\varphi(x_n),$$

but according to (15) and the definition of $x_n$

$$|L_n'(C+D\psi(\rho(x,t))\varphi(t);x)-C|\leqq|D|/n$$

and even more

$$r_A(L_n'(C+D\psi(\rho(x,t))\varphi),C)\leqq|D|/n.$$

That means that $\{L_n'\}_1^\infty$ satisfies condition (6).

Analogically we construct a sequence of linear and positive operators $\{L_n\}_1^\infty$ satisfying condition (6), such that

(18) $$L''_n(f_1;x) \leqq I(f_1;x)+1/n.$$

Let us take the sequence of linear and positive operators $\{L_n^*\}_1^\infty$ for which $L^*_{2n-1}=L'_n$, $L^*_{2n}=L''_n$. Obviously $\{L_n^*\}_1^\infty$ satisfies condition (6), but from (14),(17) and (18) follows:

$$r_A(L^*_{2n-1}(f_1),L^*_{2n}(f_1)) \geqq r_A(S(f_1)-n^{-1},I(f_1)+n^{-1})$$
$$\geqq r_A(S(f_1),I(f_1))-2n^{-1} \geqq d-2n^{-1},$$

i.e. the sequence $\{L_n^*(f_1)\}_1^\infty$ is not convergent. The necessity of the $A$-continuity is proved.

The necessity of the condition (8) can be proved easily. Let $f_1 \varepsilon B_\Omega$ and

$$\sup\{|f_1(x)|/\varphi(x):x\varepsilon\Omega\}=\infty .$$

Then for every natural $n$ exists $x_n\varepsilon\Omega$ with

(19) $$|f_1(x_n)|>n^2\varphi(x_n).$$

We define the sequence of operators $\{L_n^*\}_1^\infty$ as follows:

(20) $$L_n^*(f;x)=f(x)+f(x_n)/n\varphi(x_n).$$

The operators (20) are linear and positive. We shall show that $\{L_n^*\}_1^\infty$ satisfies the condition (6). From (20) we have

$$L_n^*(C+D\psi(\rho(x,t))\varphi(t);x)=C+(C+D\psi(\rho(x,x_n))\varphi(x_n))/n\varphi(x_n)$$

and having in mind that $0 \leqq \psi(\delta) \leqq 1$ and $\varphi(x) \geqq 1$, we obtain

$$|L_n^*(C+D\psi(\rho(x,t))\varphi(t);x)-C| \leqq (|C|+|D|)n^{-1}$$

and

$$r_A(L_n(C+D\psi(\rho(x,t))\varphi),C) \leqq (|C|+|D|)n^{-1},$$

i.e. condition (6) is satisfied.

We may consider that all $f_n(x_n)$ have the same sign. Let $f_1(x_n) \geqq 0$ for all natural $n$. Then, from (19) and (20) it follows that $L_n^*(f_1;x) \geqq f_1(x)+n$ and

$$r_A(L_n(f_1),f_1) \geqq r_A(f_1+n,f_1) \geqq n,$$

i.e. the sequence $\{L_n^*\}_1^\infty$ is not convergent. The theorem is proved.

If $\Delta=\Omega$ and $\Omega$ is compact, then all $A$-continuous functions on $\Omega$ are bounded. In this case, in theorem 1, we can take $\varphi(x)\equiv 1$ and shall have

COROLLARY 1. *Let $\psi(\delta)$ be a non decreasing, continuous function, $\psi(0)=0$, $\psi(\delta)>0$, $\delta>0$ and $\Omega$ is compact. Let $\{L_n\}_1^\infty$ be a sequence of monotonic operators, satisfying the condition*

$$\lim_{n\to\infty} r_A(L_n(C+D\psi(\rho(x,t)),C)=0, \tag{21}$$

*for the arbitrary constants $C$ and $D$. A necessary and sufficient condition $\lim r_A(L_n(f),f)=0$ to be valid for every sequence of monotonic (or linear and positive) operators $\{L_n\}_1^\infty$ satisfying (21) is the $A$-continuity of $f$ on $\Omega$.*

This corollary 1 is, in fact, the Korovkin's theorem for convergence of sequences of monotonic operators in $A$-distance [1]. Many theorems for convergence of sequences of linear and positive operators about different metrics follow as corollaries from theorem 1. The theorems of V.M.VESSELINOV[4], L.S.HSU[5] and many others can be shown as examples.

The first extension of the Korovkin theorem in $A$-distance [1] for unbounded functions was given by M.W.MÜLLER[6]. See also G.SCHMID[7].

The results in this paper are announced without proofs in [2], where the next theorem is also formulated.

THEOREM 2. *Let $L$ be a linear and positive operator defined in $B_\Omega$ and $f\in B_\Omega$. Then for every $\delta>0$*

$$r_A(L(f),f)\leq\tau_A(f;2\delta)+\sup_{x\in\Delta}L(\omega(x,\delta,f);x)+M\sup_{x\in\Delta}|1-L(1;x)|,$$

*where* $M=\sup_{x\in\Delta}|f(x)|$ *and*

$$\omega(x,\delta,f;t)=\begin{cases}0 & \text{for } \rho(x,t)\leq\delta,\ t\in\Omega,\\ \omega(f;\rho(x,t)-\delta) & \text{for } \rho(x,t)>\delta,\ t\in\Omega.\end{cases}$$

As a corollary of theorem 2 follows a series of well known estimations for the degree of convergence of concrete sequences of linear and positive operators.

## REFERENCES

[1] Korovkin, P.P., Axiomatic approach to some problems in approximation theory. (Russian). In: Constructive function theory (Proceedings of the Int.Conf. on Constructive Function Theory, Golden Sands (Varna), May 19 - 25, 1970.) Sofia, 1972, 55 - 63.

[2] Sendov, Bl., Convergence of sequences of monotonic operators in A-distance. C.R.Acad.Bulgare Sci., 30 (1977), No 5, 657 - 660.

[3] Sendov, Bl., Some problems in the theory of approximation of functions and sets in the Hausdorff metric. (Russian). Uspehi Mat. Nauk. 24 (1969), 143 - 180.

[4] Vesselinov, V.M., Approximation of non-bounded functions with linear positive operators in Hausdorff distance. (Russian). C.R.Acad.Bulgare Sci., 22 (1969), No 5, 499 - 502.

[5] Hsu, L.S., Approximation of non-bounded continuous functions by certain sequences of linear positive operators or polynomials. Studia Math., 21 (1961), 37 - 43.

[6] Müller, M.W., Approximation unbeschränkter Funktionen bezüglich einer Korovkin-Metrik. Theory of approximation of functions. Moskva, 1977, 269 - 272.

[7] Schmid, G., Approximation unbeschränkter Funktionen. Diss., Stuttgart, 1972.

# JACKSON'S THEOREM FOR POLYNOMIALS AND EXPONENTIAL SUMS WITH RESTRICTED COEFFICIENTS

MANFRED v. GOLITSCHEK
Institut für Angewandte Mathematik und Statistik
Universität Würzburg
Würzburg, BRD

This paper is concerned with the rate of approximation of functions $f \in C[a,b]$ and $f \in L^p[a,b]$, $1 \leq p < \infty$, $0 < a < b$, by means of generalized polynomials and of functions $F \in C[A,B]$ and $F \in L^p[A,B]$, $-\infty < A < B < \infty$, by means of exponential sums with prescribed exponents and suitably restricted coefficients.

## 1. Introduction

Let $\{A_k\}_{k=1}^{\infty}$ be a sequence of positive real numbers and set

$$P_{\{A_k\}} := \{p(x) = \sum_{k=1}^{n} a_k x^k, \ |a_k| \leq (A_k)^k, \ 1 \leq k \leq n, \ n = 1,2,\ldots\}.$$

Recently, necessary and sufficient conditions on $\{A_k\}$ have been obtained in order that $P_{\{A_k\}}$ be dense in $C_o[a,b] := \{f \in C[a,b] : f(a) = 0\}$. The following Theorem A has been proved by Stafney [8], Roulier [7], v. Golitschek [3] and Theorem B by v. Golitschek [3] (see also [6, Theorem 2]).

THEOREM A. The class of polynomials $P_{\{A_k\}}$ is dense in $C_o[0,1]$ if and only if there exists a subset $\{k_i\}_{i=1}^{\infty}$ of positive integers such that

$$\sum_{i=1}^{\infty} 1/k_i = \infty \quad \text{and} \quad \lim_{i \to \infty} A_{k_i} = \infty .$$

THEOREM B. Let $0 < a < b$. The class of polynomials $P_{\{A_k\}}$ is dense in $\{f \in C_o[a,b] : \max_{a \leq x \leq b} |f(x)| \leq 1\}$ if there exists a subset $\{k_i\}_{i=1}^{\infty}$ of positive integers such that

$$\sum_{i=1}^{\infty} 1/k_i = \infty \quad \text{and} \quad A_{k_i} \geq 1/a \text{ for all } 1 \leq i < \infty.$$

More general density theorems have been obtained by v. Golitschek and Leviatan [6] (see also [3])for classes of generalized polynomials with prescribed real and complex exponents and suitably restricted coefficients. In a paper of Bak, v. Golitschek and Leviatan [2] first direct and inverse results on the rate of approximation of functions $f \in C_o[0,1]$ by means of classes of ordinary algebraic polynomials with restricted coefficients have been proved. Finally, the author [5] has published some new results on the rate of approximation of functions $f \in C_o[0,1]$ and $f \in C_o[a,b]$, $0<a<b$, by means of generalized polynomials with restricted coefficients. These results in [5] are not best possible in the case of complex exponents $\{\lambda_k\}_{k=1}^{\infty}$ and function classes $C_o[a,b]$, $0<a<b$.

The purpose of this paper is to provide (almost) best possible theorems on the rate of approximation of functions $f \in C[a,b]$ and $f \in L^p[a,b]$, $1 \leq p < \infty$, $0<a<b$, by means of generalized polynomials

$$\text{(1.1)} \qquad \{p_s(x) = \sum_{k=1}^{s} c_k x^{\lambda_k} \; : \; c_k \text{ complex}\}$$

and of functions $F \in C[A,B]$ and $F \in L^p[A,B]$, $-\infty<A<B<+\infty$, by means of exponential sums

$$\text{(1.2)} \qquad \{e_s(t) = \sum_{k=1}^{s} C_k e^{\lambda_k t} \; : \; C_k \text{ complex}\}$$

where $\Lambda = \{\lambda_k\}_{k=1}^{\infty}$ is a given sequence of distinct complex numbers and the growth of the coefficients $c_k$ and $C_k$ is suitably restricted.

This paper is closely related to the author's paper [4] where Jackson-type theorems have been obtained for generalized polynomials (1.1) and exponential sums (1.2) without restrictions on the coefficients.

Throughout this paper we use the following notations.

Let $[a,b]$ be a finite real interval, $1 \leq p < \infty$, $r \in N_0 := \{0,1,2,\ldots\}$,
$X_\infty^0[a,b] := C[a,b] := \{f:[a,b] \to \mathbb{C} \ :\ f$ continous in $[a,b]\}$,
$X_\infty^r[a,b] := \{f:[a,b] \to \mathbb{C} \ :\ f^{(r)} \in C[a,b]\}$,
$\|f\|_{\infty,a,b} := \max_{a \leq x \leq b} |f(x)|$ if $f \in X_\infty^0[a,b]$,
$X_p^0[a,b] := L^p[a,b]$ denotes the space of the measureable complex-valued functions f for which

$$\|f\|_{p,a,b} := \{\int_a^b |f(x)|^p dx\}^{1/p} < +\infty ,$$

$X_p^r[a,b] := \{f: f^{(r-1)}$ absolutely continous in $[a,b], f^{(r)} \in L^p[a,b]\}$.
Finally, if $1 \leq p \leq \infty$ and $g \in X_p^0[a,b]$, the $L^p$ modulus of continuity $w_p$ of g is defined by

$$w_p(g;h) := \sup_{|t| \leq h} \|g(x+t) - g(x)\|_{p,a,b} , \quad 0 \leq h \leq b-a ,$$

where we continue the function g outside of $[a,b]$ by

$$g(x) := \begin{cases} g(2a-x) , & 2a-b \leq x < a \\ g(2b-x) , & b < x \leq 2b-a \end{cases} .$$

## 2. Statement of Main Results

Throughout this paper $\Lambda = \{\lambda_k\}_{k=1}^\infty$ is a sequence of distinct complex numbers with positive real parts and the following properties. There exists a positive number M and a positive integer $k_0$ such that

$$(2.1) \qquad 0 < |\lambda_k| \leq |\lambda_{k+1}| , \quad |\lambda_i - \lambda_k| \geq M(i-k) \text{ for } k_0 \leq k < i$$

and

$$(2.2) \qquad \sum_{k=1}^\infty \operatorname{Re} \lambda_k / |\lambda_k|^2 = \infty$$

where $\operatorname{Re} \lambda_k$ denotes the real part of $\lambda_k$.
The following definitions play an important role.

DEFINITION 1. <u>For positive integers</u> j <u>and</u> s, $j \leq s$, <u>we set</u>

$$(2.3) \qquad \varphi(j,s) := \exp(\sum_{k=j}^s \operatorname{Re} \lambda_k / |\lambda_k|^2) .$$

DEFINITION 2. *For* $\varepsilon>0$ *and* $0<a<1$ *and any sufficiently large integer* $s$ *the number* $\Psi=\Psi_s(\varepsilon,a,\Lambda)$ *is the largest integer such that*

$$(2.4)\qquad \sum_{k=\Psi}^{s} \operatorname{Re}\lambda_k/|\lambda_k|^2 \geq \varepsilon - \frac{1}{2}\log a$$

*or, equivalently, such that*

$$(2.5)\qquad e^{\varepsilon}\, a^{-1/2} \leq \varphi(\Psi,s) < e^{\varepsilon+\operatorname{Re}\lambda_\Psi/|\lambda_\Psi|^2}\, a^{-1/2} .$$

Theorem 1 below is valid under very general assumptions. Its long and complete proof is the content of Sections 4 and 5. Theorems 2-5 are immediate corollaries of Theorem 1. We emphasize that the factor $e^{29|\lambda_k|/M}$ in (2.7) is not supposed to be best possible but sufficient for the applications in Theorems 2-5.

THEOREM 1. *Let* $\Lambda$ *satisfy* (2.1) *and* (2.2). *Let* $r\in N_o$, $1\leq p\leq\infty$, $0<a<1$, *and* $0<\varepsilon\leq \min\{1;1/M\}$. *There exist positive numbers* $K_1$ *(only depending on* $r,p,a$*) and* $K_1^*$ *(only depending on* $r,p,a,f$*) such that for any function* $f\in X_p^r[a,1]$ *and any sufficiently large integer* $s$ *we can find coefficients* $c_{ks}$, $\Psi_s\leq k\leq s$, *for which*

$$(2.6)\qquad \|f(x)-\sum_{k=\Psi_s}^{s} c_{ks}\, x^{\lambda_k}\|_{p,a,1}$$

$$\leq K_1\varkappa^r(1+\varkappa)\,\Psi_s^{-r} w_p(f^{(r)};\Psi_s^{-1}) + O(e^{-\Psi_s/\varkappa})$$

*and*

$$(2.7)\qquad |c_{ks}| \leq K_1^*\, |\lambda_k|^{1/2}\, e^{29|\lambda_k|/M}\, a^{-\operatorname{Re}\lambda_k} ,$$

$\Psi_s\leq k\leq s$, *where* $\varkappa := 8(\varepsilon+2)^2(\varepsilon M)^{-2}$ .

THEOREM 2. *Let* $\Lambda$ *satisfy* (2.1), (2.2), *and*

$$(2.8)\qquad \operatorname{Re}\lambda_k \geq N|\lambda_k| \;,\quad |\lambda_k| \leq M^* k \quad \textit{for } k\geq k_o$$

*where* $0<N\leq 1$ *and* $M^*>0$ *are constants. For any function* $f\in X_p^r[a,1]$, $0<a<1$, *any number* $\eta>0$ *and any sufficiently large* _integer_ s _there exist coefficients_ $c_{ks}$ _such that_

$$(2.9)\quad \|f(x)-\sum_{k=1}^{s} c_{ks}x^{\lambda_k}\|_{p,a,1} \leq K_2\, s^{-r}\, w_p(f^{(r)};s^{-1}) + O(e^{-\alpha s})$$

_and_

$$(2.10)\qquad |c_{ks}| \leq K_2^* \, e^{\eta|\lambda_k|} a^{-\mathrm{Re}\,\lambda_k}, \quad 1\leq k\leq s\ .$$

_where_ $K_2$ _and_ $\alpha$ _are positive numbers independent of_ s _and_ f _and_ $K_2^*$ _is positive and independent of_ s.

PROOF. Set $\gamma:=1+[30/(M\eta)]$ where $[x]$ denotes the largest integer less or equal to x. Obviously, the sequence $\Lambda^*=\{\mu_k\}_{k=1}^{\infty}$, $\mu_k:=\lambda_{\gamma k}$, has the properties (2.2) and

$$(2.1)^*\quad 0<|\mu_k|\leq|\mu_{k+1}|,\ |\mu_i-\mu_k|\geq M\gamma(i-k) \text{ for } k_o^*\leq k<i$$

(where $k_o^*:=1+k_o/\gamma$) and

$$(2.8)^*\qquad \mathrm{Re}\,\mu_k \geq N|\mu_k|\ ,\quad |\mu_k|\leq M^*\gamma\, k \quad \text{for } k\geq k_o^*\ .$$

For any s* and j, $k_o^*\leq j<s^*$, the inequality

$$\sum_{k=j}^{s^*} \mathrm{Re}\,\mu_k/|\mu_k|^2 \geq \frac{N}{M^*\gamma}\log(s^*/j)$$

holds and thus there exists a positive number $\beta$ (depending on $N,M^*,M,\eta,\varepsilon,a$) such that

$$(2.11)\qquad \exp\Big(\sum_{\beta s^*\leq k\leq s^*} \mathrm{Re}\,\mu_k/|\mu_k|^2\Big) \geq e^{\varepsilon}\, a^{-1/2}\ .$$

We now apply Theorem 1 for the sequence $\Lambda^*$ and $\varepsilon:=\min\{1;1/(M\gamma)\}$. Let s* be a sufficiently large integer. Then $\Psi_{s^*}^*$ is the largest integer for which

$$\exp\Big(\sum_{k=\Psi}^{s^*} \mathrm{Re}\,\mu_k/|\mu_k|^2\Big) \geq e^{\varepsilon} a^{-1/2}\ ,$$

and by (2.11) we realize that $\Psi_{s^*}^*\geq\beta s^*$. Therefore there exist coefficients $d_{ks^*}$ such that

$$\|f(x)-\sum_{k=1}^{s} d_{ks*}x^{\mu_k}\|_{p,a,1}$$

$$\leq K_1 \varkappa^r (1+\varkappa)(\beta s*)^{-r} w_p(f^{(r)};(\beta s*)^{-1}) + O(e^{-\beta s*/\varkappa})$$

and

$$|d_{ks*}| \leq K_1^* |\mu_k|^{1/2} e^{29|\mu_k|/(M\gamma)} a^{-\operatorname{Re}\mu_k}, \Psi^*_{s*} \leq k \leq s^* ,$$

where $d_{ks*}:=0$ for $1\leq k<\Psi^*_{s*}$ and $\varkappa:=8(\varepsilon+2)^2(\varepsilon\gamma M)^{-2}$ .

Setting $s:=\gamma s*$ and

$$c_{ks}:=\begin{cases} d_{k*s*} & \text{if } k^* = k/\gamma \text{ is integral and } k^* \geq \Psi^*_{s*} \\ 0 & \text{otherwise} \end{cases}$$

we obtain (2.9) with $K_2 = K_1\cdot(\varkappa\gamma/\beta)^r(1+\varkappa)(1+\frac{\gamma}{\beta})$ and $\alpha = \beta/(\varkappa\gamma)$ and for $k=\gamma k^*$

$$|c_{ks}|=|d_{k*s*}|\leq K_1^*|\lambda_k|^{1/2} e^{29\eta|\lambda_k|/30} a^{-\operatorname{Re}\lambda_k}$$

and hence (2.10).

THEOREM 3. _Let_ $\Lambda$ _satisfy_ (2.1), (2.2), _and_

$$\lim_{k_0\to\infty} \sup_{k_0\leq k<i} \frac{|\lambda_i-\lambda_k|}{i-k} = \infty \quad . \tag{2.12}$$

_For any function_ $f\in X_p^r[a,1], 0<a<1$, _any number_ $\eta$, $0<\eta\leq 1$, _and any sufficiently large integer_ $s$ _there exist coefficients_ $c_{ks}$ _such that_

$$\|f(x)-\sum_{k=1}^{s} c_{ks}x^{\lambda_k}\|_{p,a,1} \leq K_3\Psi_s^{-r}w_p(f^{(r)};\Psi_s^{-1}) + O(e^{-\alpha\Psi_s}) \tag{2.13}$$

_and_

$$|c_{ks}|\leq K_3^* \, e^{\eta|\lambda_k|} a^{-\operatorname{Re}\lambda_k} , \quad 1\leq k\leq s \tag{2.14}$$

_where_ $c_{ks} = 0$ _for_ $1\leq k<\Psi_s$. _The integer_ $\Psi_s$ _is defined by_ (2.5) _with_ $\varepsilon:=\eta/30$, $\alpha$ _is a positive constant_, $K_3$ _depends on_ $r,p,a$

<u>and</u> $K_3^*$ <u>on</u> r,p,a, <u>and</u> f.

PROOF. Let s be so large that

$$\sup_{\Psi_s \leq k<i} \frac{|\lambda_i-\lambda_k|}{i-k} \geq 30/\eta .$$

We apply Theorem 1 for $M:=30/\eta$ and $\varepsilon:=\eta/30$. Hence, $\varkappa=8(2+\eta/30)$. There exist coefficients $c_{ks}$ such that (2.13) holds with $K_3:=K_1\varkappa^r(1+\varkappa)$ and $\alpha:=1/\varkappa$. The inequalities (2.14) hold with $K_3^*:=K_1^*$ if s is so large that $|\lambda_k|^{1/2} \leq e^{\eta|\lambda_k|/30}$ for $k \geq \Psi_s$ .

In the last part of Section 2 we obtain Theorems 4-5 from Theorems 2-3 by the substitution

$$(2.15) \qquad x = e^{t-B} , \quad t \in [A,B] , \quad x \in [a,1] , \quad a:= e^{A-B}$$

where $-\infty<A<B<\infty$ and $0<a<1$.
By (2.15) functions $F \in X_p^r[A,B]$ are transformed to functions $f \in X_p^r[a,1]$, $f(x):=F(B+\log x)$. Any modulus of continuity has the property that if $w(h)/h \to 0$ for $h \to 0$, then $w(h)=0$ for all $h \geq 0$. Therefore it is evident that for any function $F \in X_p^r[A,B]$ for which $w_p(F^{(r)};\cdot) \not\equiv 0$ there exists a positive number c (independent of h) such that

$$(2.16) \qquad w_p(f^{(r)};h) \leq c\, w_p(F^{(r)};h) \quad , \quad h \geq 0 .$$

It is easy to see that for any coefficients $C_k$ and $c_k:=C_k e^{B\lambda_k}$, $1 \leq k \leq s$, the inequality

$$(2.17) \qquad \|F(t)-\sum_{k=1}^{s} C_k e^{\lambda_k t}\|_{p,A,B}$$

$$\leq a^{-1/p}\|f(x)-\sum_{k=1}^{s} c_k\, x^{\lambda_k}\|_{p,a,1}$$

is valid. Combining Theorem 2, (2.16), (2.17) leads to the following

THEOREM 4. *Let* $\Lambda$ *satisfy* (2.1), (2.2), *and* (2.8). *For any function* $F \in X_p^r[A,B]$, $w_p(F^{(r)};\cdot)\not\equiv 0$, *and any number* $\eta>0$ *there exists a sequence of exponential sums*

$$(2.18)\qquad e_s(t) = \sum_{k=1}^{s} c_{ks}\, e^{\lambda_k t}\,, \qquad s=1,2,\ldots,$$

*for which*

$$(2.19)\qquad \|F - e_s\|_{p,A,B} = O(s^{-r}\, w_p(F^{(r)};\, s^{-1}))$$

*and*

$$(2.20)\qquad |c_{ks}| \le K_4^* \, e^{\eta|\lambda_k| - A\,\mathrm{Re}\,\lambda_k}\,, \quad 1\le k\le s\,,$$

*holds, where* $K_4^*$ *is independent of* s.

Combining Theorem 3, (2.16), (2.17) leads to the following

THEOREM 5. *Let* $\Lambda$ *satisfy* (2.1), (2.2), *and* (2.12). *For any function* $F \in X_p^r[A,B]$, $w_p(F^{(r)};\cdot)\not\equiv 0$, *and any number* $\eta>0$ *there exists a sequence of exponential sums* (2.18) *for which* (2.20) *and*

$$(2.21)\qquad \|F - e_s\|_{p,A,B} = O(\Psi_s^{-r}\, w_p(F^{(r)};\Psi_s^{-1}))$$

*holds, where* $\Psi_s$ *is the largest integer such that*

$$(2.22)\qquad \varphi(\Psi,s) \ge e^{\eta/30+(B-A)/2}\,.$$

## 3. An Inverse Theorem

In this section we shall prove that the results in Theorems 2-5 are in a certain sense (almost) best possible.

THEOREM 6. *Let* $\Lambda = \{\lambda_k\}_{k=1}^{\infty}$ *be a sequence of distinct complex numbers with positive real parts for which the series*

$$(3.1)\qquad \sum_{k=1}^{\infty} \alpha^{\mathrm{Re}\,\lambda_k} < +\infty$$

*converges for each* $\alpha$, $0<\alpha<1$. *Let* $f \in X_p^0[a,1]$, $0<a<1$, $1\le p\le\infty$, *be given. If there exist a positive constant* K, *a constant* $\delta$,

$0<\delta<1$, *and a sequence of* $\Lambda$-*polynomials* $\{p_s\}_{s=1}^{\infty}$, $p_s(x)=\sum_{k=1}^{s} c_{ks}x^{\lambda_k}$, *such that*

$$\lim_{s\to\infty} \|f-p_s\|_{p,a,1} = 0 \tag{3.2}$$

*and*

$$|c_{ks}| \leq K(\delta/a)^{\operatorname{Re}\lambda_k}, \quad 1\leq k\leq s,\ s=1,2,\ldots\ , \tag{3.3}$$

*then there exist coefficients* $c_k$, $1\leq k<\infty$, *such that the series*

$$g(x)=\sum_{k=1}^{\infty} c_k x^{\lambda_k}, \quad a\leq x<b:=\min\{1;a/\delta\} \tag{3.4}$$

*converges uniformly in any compact subinterval of* $[a,b)$. *The function* $g$ *is analytic in* $[a,b)$ *and* $f(x)=g(x)$ *almost everywhere in* $[a,b)$.

PROOF. We construct a decreasing sequence $\{S_m\}_{m=1}^{\infty}$ of subsets of natural numbers such that

$$\lim_{s\to\infty,\, s\in S_m} c_{ks} = c_k \quad \text{for all } 1\leq k\leq m,\ m=1,2,\ldots\ .$$

Let $m\geq 1$ be fixed. For any $x_0$, $a<x_0<b$, and any sufficiently large $s\in S_m$, $s\to\infty$

$$\|f(x)-\sum_{k=1}^{m} c_k x^{\lambda_k}\|_{p,a,x_0}$$

$$\leq \|f-p_s\|_{p,a,1}+\sum_{k=1}^{m}|c_{ks}-c_k|x_0^{\operatorname{Re}\lambda_k}+\sum_{k=m+1}^{s}|c_{ks}|x_0^{\operatorname{Re}\lambda_k}$$

$$\leq K\sum_{k=m+1}^{\infty}(\delta x_0/a)^{\operatorname{Re}\lambda_k}.$$

Since $\delta x_0/a<1$ it follows from (3.1) that

$$\lim_{m\to\infty} \|f(x)-\sum_{k=1}^{m} c_k x^{\lambda_k}\|_{p,a,x_o} = 0\ . \tag{3.5}$$

Obviously, the coefficients $c_k$ $(1\leq k<\infty)$ satisfy (3.3). Therefore, the series $\sum_{k=1}^{\infty} c_k x^{\lambda_k}$ convergences uniformly in any compact subinterval of [a,b) to a function g which is analytic in [a,b). Because of (3.5) f(x)=g(x) a.e. in [a,b).

## 4. Auxiliary Results

For the proof of Theorem 1 we use a method similar to that in [4-6] and thus need a few lemmas.

LEMMA 1. *Let* $\Lambda$ *satisfy* (2.1). *Let* $j_o$ *be the integer defined by*

$$(4.1) \qquad j_o - 1 < 2(1+k_o+|\lambda_{k_o}|/M) \leq j_o \ .$$

*For any integers* q,n,j,k,s *and any nonnegative real number* m *such that*

$$(4.2) \qquad j_o \leq j \leq k \leq s \ , \quad 0 \leq q \leq n \ , \quad 0 \leq 1+n+m \leq |\lambda_j|/2$$

*the following inequalities are valid.*

$$(4.3) \qquad \prod_{\substack{i=j \\ i \neq k}}^{s} \frac{|1+m+\bar{\lambda}_k+\lambda_i|}{|\lambda_i-\lambda_k|} \leq e^{23|\lambda_k|/M} \varphi(j,s)^{1+m+2\mathrm{Re}\,\lambda_k} ,$$

$$(4.4) \qquad \Pi_{qjs} := \prod_{i=j}^{s} \frac{|q-\lambda_i|}{|q+\lambda_i+m|} \leq e^{8(q+m)^2/(M^2 j)} \varphi(j,s)^{-2q-m}$$

*where the first equality in* (4.4) *serves to define* $\Pi_{qjs}$.

PROOF. From (2.1) and (4.1) we obtain for $i \geq j_o$

$$|\lambda_i| \geq |\lambda_i-\lambda_{k_o}| - |\lambda_{k_o}| \geq M(i-k_o) - |\lambda_{k_o}| \geq M(i+2)/2$$

and thus

$$(4.5) \qquad \sum_{i=j}^{s} 1/|\lambda_i|^2 \leq 4/(M^2 j) \ .$$

Since $(1+q+m)/|\lambda_i| \leq 1/2$ for $i \geq j$,

$$\Pi_{qjs}=|\exp\{\sum_{i=j}^{s}(\log(1-q/\lambda_i)-\log(1+(q+m)/\lambda_i))\}|$$

$$=|\exp\{-\sum_{p=1}^{\infty}\frac{1}{p}(\sum_{i=j}^{s}\frac{q^p+(-1)^{p+1}(q+m)^p}{(\lambda_i)^p})\}|$$

$$\leq \exp\{-(2q+m)\mathrm{Re}\sum_{i=j}^{s}1/\lambda_i\}\ \exp\{\sum_{p=2}^{\infty}\frac{2}{p}(\sum_{i=j}^{s}\frac{(q+m)^p}{|\lambda_i|^p})\}$$

$$\leq \varphi(j,s)^{-2q-m}\exp\{8(q+m)^2\sum_{p=2}^{\infty}\frac{1}{p\cdot 2^p}(\sum_{i=j}^{s}1/|\lambda_i|^2)\}.$$

Now, (4.4) follows by (4.5).

We now deal with the proof of inequality (4.3). We define the integers $k_1$ and $k_2$ by

$$|\lambda_{k_1}|\leq 2|\lambda_k|<|\lambda_{1+k_1}|\ ,\quad k_2\leq k+|\lambda_k|/M<1+k_2\ .$$

It is obvious that

$$(4.6)\quad \prod_{\substack{i=j\\ i\neq k}}^{k_1}\frac{|1+m+\bar{\lambda}_k+\lambda_i|}{|\lambda_i-\lambda_k|}$$

$$\leq \frac{M^{j-k_1}}{(k-j)!(k_1-k)!}\ (1+m+2|\lambda_k|)^{k-j}(1+m+3|\lambda_k|)^{k_1-k}$$

$$\leq e^{(2+2m+5|\lambda_k|)/M}\leq e^{6|\lambda_k|/M}\ .$$

For $i\geq 1+k_1$ it follows from $1+m\leq|\lambda_k|/2$ and $(1+m+|\lambda_k|)/|\lambda_i|\leq 3/4$ that

$$\sum_{p=2}^{\infty}\frac{1}{p}\frac{(1+m+|\lambda_k|)^p+|\lambda_k|^p}{|\lambda_i|^p}<4|\lambda_k|^2/|\lambda_i|^2$$

and therefore

$$\prod_{i=1+k_1}^{s}\frac{|1+m+\bar{\lambda}_k+\lambda_i|}{|\lambda_i-\lambda_k|}=|\exp\{\sum_{p=1}^{\infty}\frac{1}{p}(\sum_{i=1+k_1}^{s}\frac{(-1)^{p+1}(1+m+\bar{\lambda}_k)^p+(\lambda_k)^p}{(\lambda_i)^p})\}|$$

$$(4.7)\qquad \leq \varphi(j,s)^{1+m+2\mathrm{Re}\,\lambda_k}\exp(4|\lambda_k|^2\sum_{i=1+k_1}^{s}1/|\lambda_i|^2)\ .$$

Finally, analogous to (4.5) we have

$$\sum_{i=1+k_2}^{s} 1/|\lambda_i|^2 \leq 4\ M^{-2}/(1+k_2)$$

and, since (by definition) $k_1 \geq k$, $k_2 - k \leq |\lambda_k|/M$ and $1+k_2 \geq |\lambda_k|/M$ it follows that

$$(4.8)\quad \sum_{i=1+k_1}^{s} 1/|\lambda_i|^2 \leq \frac{k_2-k}{4|\lambda_k|^2} + \frac{4}{M^2(1+k_2)} \leq \frac{17}{4M|\lambda_k|} \quad .$$

Combining (4.6) through (4.8) leads to inequality (4.3).

LEMMA 2. *Let* $\Lambda$ *satisfy* (2.1) *and* $j_o$ *be defined by* (4.1). *Suppose that the integers* q,n,j,s *and the real numbers* m,a, *and* p *satisfy the ineqaulities* (4.2) *and* $1 \leq p \leq \infty$, $0<a<1$, $m \geq 4/p$. *Then there exist complex numbers* $b_{kq}$, $j \leq k \leq s$, *such that*

$$(4.9)\qquad B_{qjs} := \| x^q - \sum_{k=j}^{s} b_{kq} x^{\lambda_k} \|_{p,a,1} \leq (4a/m)^{1/p} a^{-m/2} \Pi_{qjs}$$

*and*

$$(4.10)\qquad |b_{kq}| \leq 5|\lambda_k|^{1/2} e^{23|\lambda_k|/M} \varphi(j,s)^{1+m+2\mathrm{Re}\,\lambda_k} \Pi_{qjs} \ ,$$

$j \leq k \leq s$, *where the first equality in* (4.9) *serves to define* $B_{qjs}$ *and* $\Pi_{qjs}$ *is defined in* (4.4).

PROOF. From [4, Lemma 3] it follows that there exist complex numbers $b_{kq}$, $j \leq k \leq s$, such that (4.9) holds. By [4, formula (24)],

$$\| x^{q+m/2} - \sum_{k=j}^{s} b_{kq} x^{\lambda_k + m/2} \|_{\infty,o,1} \leq \Pi_{qjs}$$

and thus for any k, $j \leq k \leq s$,

$$|b_{kq}| \leq \Pi_{qjs} \Big( \inf_{d_i} \| x^{\lambda_k + m/2} - d_o x^{q+m/2} - \sum_{\substack{i=j \\ i \neq k}}^{s} d_i x^{\lambda_i + m/2} \|_{2,o,1} \Big)^{-1}$$

$$= \Pi_{qjs} (1+m+2\mathrm{Re}\,\lambda_k)^{1/2} \frac{|1+m+\bar{\lambda}_k + q|}{|q-\lambda_k|} \prod_{\substack{i=j \\ i \neq k}}^{s} \frac{|1+m+\bar{\lambda}_k + \lambda_i|}{|\lambda_i - \lambda_k|}$$

where the first inequality follows from $\|\cdot\|_{2,0,1} \leq \|\cdot\|_{\infty,0,1}$ and the last equality from Achieser [1, Section 14]. The application of Lemma 1 completes the proof of Lemma 2.

Finally we need a Lemma which has been proved by the author in [4, Lemma 2].

LEMMA 3. _Let_ $r \in N_o$, $1 \leq p \leq \infty$, $0<a<1$. _For any function_ $f \in X_p^r[a,1]$ _and any positive integer_ $n$, $n \geq r+1$, _there exists a polynomial_ $P_n(x) = \sum_{q=o}^{n} a_{qn} x^q$ _such that_

$$(4.11) \qquad \|f-P_n\|_{p,a,1} \leq C\, n^{-r}\, w_p(f^{(r)}; n^{-1}) \; ,$$

$$(4.12) \qquad |a_{qn}| \leq K_f\, n^{1/p} \quad , \quad 0 \leq q \leq r \quad ,$$

$$(4.13) \qquad |a_{qn}| \leq D\, n^{q+1/p-r} w_p(f^{(r)}; n^{-1})/q! \quad , \quad r+1 \leq q \leq n \; .$$

_The positive numbers_ C _and_ D _depend only on_ r,p,a, _and the positive number_ $K_f$ _depends only on_ r,p,a, _and_ f.

## 5. Proof of Theorem 1

Let $\varepsilon$ be any fixed real number such that $0<\varepsilon \leq \min\{1;1/M\}$. For any sufficiently large s the positive integer $\Psi=\Psi_s$ is defined by (2.5). We choose the integers $j=j_s$, $n=n_s$, and the real number $m=m_s$ as follows.

$$(5.1) \qquad j:=\Psi_s \quad , \quad m:= \frac{\varepsilon M^2 j}{4(\varepsilon+2)^2} \quad , \quad n \leq \varepsilon m/2 < n+1 \; .$$

Let s be so large that

$$(5.2) \quad \Psi_s \geq j_o \;,\; |\lambda_{\Psi_s}| \geq \max\{3;1/\varepsilon\} \;,\; m_s \geq 4/p,\; n_s \geq r+1$$

where $j_o$ is defined in (4.1). Then it can easily be verified that for j,n,m (defined in (5.1)) the inequalities

$$(5.3) \qquad 1+n+m \leq 1+Mj/16 \leq |\lambda_j|/2$$

and

$$(5.4)\qquad 8(n+m)^2/(M^2 j) \le \varepsilon m/2$$

hold. Hence, Lemma 1 and Lemma 2 lead to

$$(5.5)\qquad B_{qjs} \le (4a/m)^{1/p}\, a^q\, e^{-\varepsilon m/2} \quad , \quad 0 \le q \le n \quad ,$$

and (since $|\lambda_j| \ge 1/\varepsilon$ and $\varphi(j,s) \le e^{\varepsilon + 1/|\lambda_j|} a^{-1/2} \le e^{2\varepsilon} a^{-1/2}$)

$$(5.6)\qquad |b_{kq}| \le 5|\lambda_k|^{1/2} e^{23|\lambda_k|/M + \varepsilon m/2}\, \varphi(j,s)^{1+2\mathrm{Re}\,\lambda_k - 2q}$$

$$\le 5|\lambda_k|^{1/2} e^{28|\lambda_k|/M}\, a^{q-1/2-\mathrm{Re}\,\lambda_k}$$

for $j \le k \le s$, $0 \le q \le n$.

In the last part of this proof we shall show that the inequalities (2.6) and (2.7) of Theorem 1 are satisfied for the coefficients

$$(5.7)\qquad c_{ks} := \sum_{q=o}^{n} a_{qn}\, b_{kq} \quad , \quad j \le k \le s \ ,$$

where j,m, and n are defined in (5.1), $a_{qn}$ are the coefficients of Lemma 3, $b_{kq}$ are the coefficients of Lemma 2. We set

$$(5.8)\qquad w_n := n^{-r}\, w_p(f^{(r)}; n^{-1}) \ .$$

Obviously, it follows from (5.7), (5.6), and Lemma 3 that

$$|c_{ks}| \le 5|\lambda_k|^{1/2}\, e^{28|\lambda_k|/M}\, a^{-1/2-\mathrm{Re}\,\lambda_k}\, n^{1/p} \,\cdot$$

$$\cdot\ \{K_f \sum_{q=o}^{r} a^q + D\, w_n \sum_{q=r+1}^{n} n^q/q!\}$$

which leads to (2.7) if we apply the inequalities

$$n^{1/p} \le e^n,\ \sum_{q=r+1}^{n} n^q/q! \le e^n \ ,\ n \le \varepsilon m/2 \le |\lambda_k|/(4M) \text{ for } j \le k \le s \ .$$

It follows from (5.5), (5.1), and Lemma 3 that

$$\sum_{q=o}^{n} |a_{qn}| B_{qjs} \le (4a\,n/m)^{1/p}\, e^{-\varepsilon m/2} \cdot$$

$$\cdot \{K_f \sum_{q=o}^{r} a^q + D\,w_n \sum_{q=r+1}^{n} n^q/q!\}$$

$$\le (2a\varepsilon)^{1/p}\{K_f(1-a)^{-1}\, e^{-\varepsilon m/2} + D\,w_n\} .$$

Hence, by the definition of the coefficients $c_{ks}$,

$$\|f-\sum_{k=j}^{s} c_{ks} x^{\lambda_k}\|_{p,a,1} \le \|f-P_n\|_{p,a,1} + \sum_{q=o}^{n} |a_{qn}| B_{qjs}$$

$$\le (C+(2a\varepsilon)^{1/p}D)w_n + O(e^{-n}) .$$

Since

$$j = \Psi_s = 4(\varepsilon+2)^2 m/(\varepsilon M^2) \le \varkappa(n+1) \quad ,$$

$\varkappa := 8(\varepsilon+2)^2/(\varepsilon M)^2$, we finally obtain inequality (2.6) if we apply the property

$$w_p(f^{(r)};\rho h) \le (1+\rho) w_p(f^{(r)};h) \quad , \ h\ge 0, \ \rho \text{ real} \ ,$$

of the modulus of continuity.

## REFERENCES

[1] Achieser, N.I., Vorlesung über Approximationstheorie. Akademie Verlag, Berlin 1953

[2] Bak, J., v. Golitschek, M., and Leviatan, D., The rate of approximation by means of polynomials with restricted coefficients. Israel J., to appear.

[3] v. Golitschek, M., Permissible bounds on the coefficients of generalized polynomials. In "Approximation Theory, Proceedings of a Conference on Approximation Theory, Austin, Texas, 1973" (G.G. Lorentz, Ed.), Academic Press, New York, 1973.

[4] v.Golitschek, M., Lineare Approximation durch komplexe Exponentialsummen. Math. Z. 146 (1976), 17-32.

[5] v. Golitschek, M., Approximation durch komplexe Exponentialsummen und zulässige Koeffizientenrestriktionen. In "Theory of Approximation of Functions, Proceedings of a Conference on Approximation Theory, Kalouga, USSR, 1975".

[6] v. Golitschek, M., and Leviatan, D., Permissible bounds on the coefficients of approximating polynomials with real or complex exponents. J. of Math. Analysis and Applic. 60 (1977), 123-138.

[7] Roulier, J.A., Restrictions on the coefficients of approximating polynomials. J. Approx. Theory 6 (1972), 276-282.

[8] Stafney, J.D., A permissible restriction on the coefficients in uniform polynomial approximation to C[0,1]. Duke Math. J. 34 (1967), 393-396.

# BIRKHOFF QUADRATURE MATRICES

G.G. Lorentz
Department of Mathematics
The University of Texas
Austin, Texas

and

S.D. Riemenschneider
Department of Mathematics
University of Alberta
Edmonton, Alberta

We investigate quadrature schemes based on $m \times (n+1)$ incidence matrices and which are exact for polynomials of degree $n$. The relationship to regularity and singularity of the corresponding Birkhoff interpolation problem is studied, as well as conditions on the matrices which are implied by the existence of quadrature formulae.

## 1. Introduction

Let $E = (e_{ij})_{i=1,j=0}^{m\ \ n}$ be an $m \times (n+1)$ incidence matrix with entries consisting of zeros and ones and having precisely $N+1$ ones. We are interested in quadrature schemes based on the incidence matrix $E$. Specifically, we investigate the following problem.

(1.1) Given the $m \times (n+1)$ incidence matrix $E$ and a set of nodes $X = \{x_1 < \cdots < x_m\}$, when does there exist a quadrature formula of the form

$$\int_a^b f(x)\,dg = \sum_{e_{ik}=1} c_{ik} f^{(k)}(x_i)$$

which is exact for polynomials of degree $n$?

Usually the set of nodes will be restricted to the interval of integration, $X \subset [a,b]$, although the reader will note that in some cases this is unnecessary. The fixed bounded measure $dg$ will also be suitably restricted in the sequel.

The problem (1.1) is related to the Birkhoff interpolation problem: For an $m \times (n+1)$ incidence matrix $E$ with $n+1$ ones and a set of nodes $X = \{x_1 < \cdots < x_m\}$, does there exist a polynomial of degree $n$ satisfying

$$P^{(k)}(x_i) = \gamma_{ik}, \quad (e_{ik} = 1)? \tag{1.2}$$

The pair $(E,X)$ is called *regular* if the equations (1.2) have a unique solution for each set of data $\gamma_{ik}$. The incidence matrix $E$ is *regular* if the pair $(E,X)$ is regular for each selection of nodes $X$. Equations (1.2) generate the coefficient matrix

$$A(E,X) = \left(\frac{x_i^{n-k}}{(n-k)!}, \cdots, \frac{x_i^{-k}}{(-k)!}\right), \quad e_{ik} = 1 \tag{1.3}$$

where $1/r! = 0$ if $r < 0$ and the rows of the matrix are ordered according to the lexicographic ordering of $(i,k)$, $e_{ik} = 1$. If $D_E(X)$ represents the determinant of $A(E,X)$, then $(E,X)$ being regular is equivalent to $D_E(X) \neq 0$.

We say that a pair $(E,X)$ is *regular for quadrature*, or *q-regular*, with respect to $dg$ on $[a,b]$ if problem (1.1) has a solution. In section 2 we consider the relationship between regular and q-regular pairs and formulate a concept of q-regular matrices which properly includes the regular matrices.

An important condition on an incidence matrix is that it satisfies the Pólya condition. Let $M_r$ denote the number of ones in columns 0 to $r$. The incidence matrix $E$ satisfies the *Pólya condition* provided that $M_r \geq r+1$, $r = 0,1,\cdots,n$. If $M_r \geq r+2$, $r = 0,1,\cdots,n-1$, then $E$ is called a *Birkhoff matrix*. Independently, B. Németh [13] and D. Ferguson [5] have shown that $D_E(X)$ is not identically zero if and only if $E$ satisfies the Pólya condition. It is well-known (e.g. Gaussian quadrature) that (1.1) may be solvable for matrices with $N < n$. Consequently, the Pólya condition is not a necessary condition for the q-regularity of a pair $(E,X)$. However, in section 3 we show that the Pólya condition is necessary for our concept of a q-regular matrix with respect to most positive measures.

Another important idea is the concept of an *odd supported sequence*. A sequence (of ones) is a maximal group of elements from a row $e_{ik+1} = e_{ik+2} = \cdots = e_{ik+p} = 1$. The sequence is odd if $p$ is odd, and is supported if there exist ones in positions $(i_1,k_1)$, $(i_2,k_2)$ with $i_1 < i < i_2$, $k_1 < k$, $k_2 < k$. The well-known theorem of Atkinson-Sharma [1] states that a matrix is regular if it contains no odd supported sequences and satisfies the Pólya conditions. Unfortunately, no additional useful sufficient conditions are known for the q-regularity of a matrix. On the other hand, in section 5 we show that there are matrices which cannot be q-regular for any reasonable measure dg.

Finally, we observe that by a linear change of variable $x^* = \tau(x)$, we can transfer the question of the q-regularity for the pair (E,X) with respect to the measure dg on [a,b] to the q-regularity of $(E,X^*)$, $X^* = \{x_1^* < \cdots < x_m^*\}$, with respect to $dg^* = d(g \circ \tau)$ on [0,1]. Since this transformation preserves the properties of measures important to our discussion, we shall assume [a,b] = [0,1] in the sequel.

## 2. Regular Quadrature Matrices

The matrix A(E,X) of equation (1.3) enters into our discussion of the quadrature problem (1.1) in a natural way. Substituting the powers $x^j/j!$, $j = 0,1,\cdots,n$, into the quadrature formula gives a system of $n+1$ equations in $N+1$ unknowns $c_{ik}$. The transposed coefficient matrix of this system is A(E,X). Setting

$$B(E,X,dg) = \begin{pmatrix} A(E,X) \\ \mu_n, \mu_{n-1}, \cdots, \mu_0 \end{pmatrix}$$

where $\mu_j = \int_0^1 x^j/j!\,dg$, we see that (E,X) *is* q-*regular if and only if*

$$\text{rank } A(E,X) = \text{rank } B(E,X,dg). \tag{2.1}$$

The following remarks are immediate consequences of the definitions and (2.1).

REMARK 1. *If (E,X) is regular, then $N=n$, (E,X) is q-regular and the quadrature formula is unique.*

REMARK 2. *Let $E^r$ denote the first $r+1$ columns of E. If (E,X) is q-regular, then $(E^r,X)$ is q-regular in the sense that (1.1) is solvable with exactness for polynomials of degree r.*

A standard way of obtaining a quadrature formula is by integrating the corresponding interpolation formula. Let (E,X) be a regular pair. Then for arbitrary $\gamma_{ik}$ $(e_{ik}=1)$ there is a unique polynomial of degree n which satisfies (1.2) and has the form

$$P(x) = \sum_{e_{ik}=1} \gamma_{ik}\, Q_{ik}(x) \tag{2.2}$$

where $Q_{ik}$ are some polynomials independent of the choice of $\gamma_{ik}$. Integrating (2.2), we obtain

$$\int_0^1 P(x)dg = \sum_{e_{ik}=1} c_{ik}\gamma_{ik}. \tag{2.3}$$

The $c_{ik}$ so obtained solve the problem (1.1). Indeed, if $\gamma_{ik}$ are selected to be $\gamma_{ik} = Q^{(k)}(x_i)$ for some polynomial $Q$ of degree $\le n$, then $P \equiv Q$ and (2.3) gives that the quadrature formula is exact.

The fact that there may be quadrature formula which cannot be derived by interpolation is of importance to us. This was also studied by Epstein and Hamming [4].

It seems natural to call a matrix $E$ q-regular if all pairs $(E,X)$, with $X \subset [0,1]$, are q-regular. The theorem below shows that this would not lead to a new concept.

THEOREM 1. *Suppose that the first* $n+1$ *moments of* $dg$ *on* $[0,1]$ *do not vanish*, i.e. $\mu_\nu \ne 0$, $\nu = 0,1,\cdots,n$. *Then* $(E,X)$ *is* q-*regular with respect to* $dg$ *for all* $X \subset [0,1]$ *if and only if rank* $A(E,X) = n+1$ *for all* $X$. *In particular*, *if* $N=n$, *then* $E$ *is regular*.

The role of the non-vanishing moments is seen in the following lemma.

LEMMA 1. *For distinct real numbers* $y_j$, *the set of* $n+1$ *vectors*

$$(\mu_n y_j^n, \mu_{n-1}y_j^{n-1},\cdots,\mu_0), \quad j = 1,\cdots,n+1 \tag{2.4}$$

*spans* $\mathbb{R}^{n+1}$.

Indeed, the determinant of the matrix with rows (2.4) is the product of $\mu_n\mu_{n-1}\cdots\mu_0$ with the Vandermonde determinant of $y_1,\cdots,y_{n+1}$.

PROOF OF THEOREM. Obviously if rank $A(E,X) = n+1$, then (2.1) holds and $(E,X)$ is q-regular. On the other hand, let $X$ be a node set such that $(E,X)$ is q-regular but rank $A(E,X) \le n$. Since $(E,X)$ is q-regular for all $X \subset [0,1]$, we may assume that $X$ satisfies $0 = x_1 < \cdots < x_m < 1$. Let $X' = \alpha X$, i.e. $x_i' = \alpha x_i$ $(i = 1,\cdots,m)$, $0 < \alpha < 1$. The pair $(E,X')$ is q-regular, hence the vector $(\mu_n,\mu_{n-1},\cdots,\mu_0)$ is a linear combination of the rows

$$\left(\frac{x_i'^{\,n-k}}{(n-k)!},\cdots,\frac{x_i'^{\,-k}}{(-k)!}\right) = \alpha^{-k}\left(\frac{\alpha^n x_i^{n-k}}{(n-k)!},\cdots,\frac{x_i^{-k}}{(-k)!}\right), \quad e_{ik}=1.$$

Thus, the row $(\alpha^{-n}\mu_n,\alpha^{-n+1}\mu_{n-1},\cdots,\mu_0)$ is a linear combination of rows

$$\left(\frac{x_i^{n-k}}{(n-k)!},\cdots,\frac{x_i^{-k}}{(-k)!}\right), \quad e_{ik}=1. \tag{2.5}$$

By taking $n+1$ distinct $\alpha$, we see that (2.5) spans $\mathbb{R}^{n+1}$ by Lemma 1. □

Observe that the above proof could be carried out if we would restrict $X$ to satisfy $X \subset (0,1)$ or $0 < x_1 < \cdots < x_m = 1$ $(0 = x_1 < \cdots < x_m < 1$ as well), but would fail if we considered only $X$ for which $x_1 = 0$, $x_m = 1$. The following examples show that the theorem does not hold in the last case.

EXAMPLE 1. Consider the matrices

$$E = \begin{pmatrix} 0 & 1 & 0 & 0 \\ 1 & 0 & 1 & 0 \\ 0 & 1 & 0 & 0 \end{pmatrix}, \quad E' = \begin{pmatrix} 1 & 0 & 1 & 0 & 0 & 0 \\ 1 & 0 & 1 & 0 & 0 & 0 \\ 1 & 0 & 1 & 0 & 0 & 0 \end{pmatrix}$$

and the node set $X = \{0,x,1\}$, $0 < x < 1$. Simple calculations show that both of these matrices are singular only for the node set $X_0 = \{0,\frac{1}{2},1\}$, and that (2.1) holds in both cases for this node set and $dg = dx$. Thus, $(E,X)$ and $(E',X)$ are q-regular for all node sets of the form $X = \{0,x,1\}$, $0 < x < 1$.

DEFINITION. An $m \times (n+1)$ incidence matrix $E$ is regular for quadrature, or q-regular, with respect to $dg$ if each pair $(E,X)$ is q-regular with respect to $dg$ for $X = \{0 = x_1 < \cdots < x_m = 1\}$.

We emphasize that while for the q-regularity of a matrix $E$ we restrict ourselves to node sets $X$ with $x_1 = 0$ and $x_m = 1$, when we talk about the q-regularity of individual pairs $(E,X)$ no such restriction on the set is implied unless specifically given.

The above examples can be expanded to yield such matrices of arbitrary size with the aid of the following decomposition result. We write $E = E' \oplus E''$ when $E$ is split vertically into two matrices.

PROPOSITION 1. Suppose that the $m \times (n+1)$ incidence matrix $E$ with $N+1$ ones is decomposable as $E = E' \oplus E''$ where $E''$ is a regular matrix. Then *the pair* $(E,X)$ *is q-regular for* $dg$ *if and only if* $(E',X)$ *is q-regular for* $dg$. *Thus,* $E$ *is q-regular if and only if* $E'$ *is q-regular.*

PROOF. Suppose that $E'$ consists of the first $r+1$ columns of $E$, and $E''$ consists of the remaining $n-r$ columns. Since $E''$ is regular, it contains precisely $n-r$ ones and rank $A(E'',X) = n-r$ for any $X$. The following matrix equations are true modulo rearrangement of rows:

$$A(E,X) = \left(\begin{array}{c|c} * & A(E',X) \\ \hline A(E'',X) & 0 \end{array}\right)$$

$$B(E,X,dg) = \left(\begin{array}{c|c} * & A(E',X) \\ \hline A(E'',X) & 0 \\ \mu_n,\cdots,\mu_{r+1} & \mu_r,\cdots,\mu_0 \end{array}\right) = \left(\begin{array}{c|c} * & B(E',X,dg) \\ \hline A(E'',X) & 0 \end{array}\right).$$

Therefore, if $(E',X)$ is q-regular, then

$$\begin{aligned} \text{rank } A(E,X) &= \text{rank } A(E'',X) + \text{rank } A(E',X) \\ &= \text{rank } A(E'',X) + \text{rank } B(E',X,dg) = \text{rank } B(E,X,dg). \end{aligned}$$

Thus, $(E,X)$ is q-regular. The other implication is Remark 2. □

By adjoining the column $(0,1,0)^T$ to the front of either matrix in Example 1, we obtain a matrix $E = E' \oplus E''$ with $E''$ q-regular and $E'$ regular and which is not q-regular (compare Theorem 4).

The next proposition shows that the concept of a q-regular matrix is dependent on the measure $dg$ unless $E$ is already regular (see also Stieglitz [15]).

PROPOSITION 2. *Let* $E$ *be an incidence matrix with* $N = n$ *ones, and let* $X \subset [0,1]$. *If* $(E,X)$ *is q-regular for every non-zero measure* $dg \geq 0$, *then* $(E,X)$ *is regular.*

PROOF. We take $g = g_t$, $0 < t < 1$, to be point mass at $t$. Then $\mu_k = t^k/k!$, $k = 0,\cdots,n$, and we obtain that $(t^n/n!,\cdots,1)$ is a linear combination of rows (2.5). By Lemma 1, we obtain that the rows (1.3) span $\mathbb{R}^{n+1}$, that is $D_E(X) \neq 0$. □

This proposition remains true if we restrict the measures $dg$ in some way; for example, we can allow $dg = \omega(x)dx$ where $\omega(x) > 0$ belongs to

$L^1[0,1]$. Actually, we can restrict ourselves to any $n+1$ measures whose moment sets $\{\mu_n,\cdots,\mu_0\}$ are linearly independent. For example, $\omega_j(x) = x^j$, $j = 1,\cdots,n+1$, has moments $\mu_k^{(j)} = 1/k!(j+k)$, $k = 0,1,\cdots,n$. The determinant formed by the $(j+k)^{-1}$, $k = 0,\cdots,n$, $j = 1,\cdots,n+1$ is the well-known Hankel determinant which is different from zero.

## 3. The Necessity of the Pólya Condition

The aim of this section is to establish that a matrix which is q-regular with respect to some reasonable measure must satisfy the Pólya condition. For the measure $dg = dx$, this was first observed by Stieglitz [14] (see also section 6).

The moment space $M_{n+1}$ for the system $\{t^n/n!,\cdots,1\}$ is the collection of all $n+1^{st}$ moment sets, $(\mu_n,\mu_{n-1},\cdots,\mu_0)$, generated by positive bounded measures on $[0,1]$. It is clear that the concept of q-regularity for an $m \times (n+1)$ matrix $E$ depends only on the $(n+1)^{st}$ moment set of the measure. Every moment set in $M_{n+1}$ admits the representation

$$(3.1) \qquad \mu_i = \sum_{j=1}^{n+2} \alpha_j \, t_j^i/i!, \quad i = 0,1,\cdots,n,$$

where $\alpha_j \geq 0$ and the $t_j$ are distinct points in $[0,1]$ (see [7, p. 39]). For our purposes, we must restrict ourselves to measures not essentially supported at the endpoints. Specifically, let $M^\circ_{n+1}$ be the collection of moment sets in $M_{n+1}$ admitting the representation (3.1) with $\alpha_j > 0$ for some $t_j \in (0,1)$. The set $M^\circ_{n+1}$ contains the interior of $M_{n+1}$ and most of the boundary.

Important for us is the following easily verified remark. If $n \geq 2$, then a measure $dg \geq 0$ does not belong to $M^\circ_{n+1}$ if and only if it is concentrated solely on $\{0,1\}$.

We shall say that a measure $dg$ b e l o n g s  t o  t h e  c l a s s $(P_2)$ if any $2 \times (r+1)$ matrix, $r = 0,\cdots,n$, which is q-regular with respect to $dg$, satisfies the Pólya condition.

LEMMA 2. *A measure* $dg$ *on* $[0,1]$ *belongs to the class* $(P_2)$ *if and only if each* $m \times (n+1)$ *matrix* $E$ *which is* q-*regular with respect to* $dg$ *satisfies the Pólya condition.*

PROOF. The "if" statement is trivial. On the other hand, let $\{\mu_n,\cdots,\mu_0\}$ be the $n+1^{st}$ moment set of the measure dg of class $(P_2)$. Suppose that the $m\times(n+1)$ matrix E is q-regular with respect to dg on [0,1], but does not satisfy the Pólya condition. Let $E^r$ be the first $r+1$ columns of E such that the Pólya condition fails for $E^r$ but holds for $E^{r-1}$. By Remark 2, $E^r$ is q-regular with respect to dg on [0,1]. Let X be an arbitrary set of knots with $0=x_1<\cdots<x_m=1$. Since $A(E^r,X)$ is an $r\times(r+1)$ matrix, relation (2.1) implies

$$\det\begin{pmatrix} A(E^r,X) \\ \mu_r,\cdots,\mu_0 \end{pmatrix} \equiv 0. \tag{3.2}$$

However, we can apply row coalescence to collapse the interior rows of $E^r$ to the first (or last) row. In this way, we obtain a new $2\times(r+1)$ matrix $E^*$ which does not satisfy the Pólya condition, and therefore, $E^*$ cannot be q-regular with respect to dg on [0,1]. Thus,

$$\det\begin{pmatrix} A(E^*,X^*) \\ \mu_r,\cdots,\mu_0 \end{pmatrix} \not\equiv 0 \tag{3.3}$$

for $X^*=\{0,1\}$. But by the Taylor expansion for $D_E(X)$ near $x_{i+1}$ for coalescense of row i to row i+1 (see Karlin and Karon [8] or Lorentz [11]) which applies equally well if one row of the matrix consists of constants, the determinant in (3.2) cannot be identically zero if (3.3) holds for the coalesced matrix. The lemma follows. □

PROPOSITION 3. <u>The following statements are equivalent for a non-zero bounded measure</u> $dg\ge 0$ <u>and</u> $n\ge 2$:

(a) $dg\in(P_2)$

(b) <u>the moment set of</u> dg <u>belongs to</u> $M^\circ_{n+1}$

(c) dg <u>is not solely supported on the two point set</u> $\{0,1\}$.

PROOF. (b) implies (a). Assume that the moment set $\{\mu_i\}$ of dg belongs to $M^\circ_{n+1}$. Since $dg\not\equiv 0$, $\mu_0>0$. Consequently, the condition of property $(P_2)$ holds for dg and $r=0$. Let r be the first integer $\le n$ for which the condition in $(P_2)$ fails for dg. There exists a $2\times(r+1)$ matrix E which is q-regular with respect to dg but does not satisfy the Pólya condition. By our choice of r and Remark 2, $E^{r-1}$ must contain precisely $r$ ones. With $X = \{0,1\}$, $A(E,X)$ is an $r \times (r+1)$ matrix, hence by the q-regularity of $E$,

$$\det \begin{pmatrix} A(E,X) \\ \mu_r, \cdots, \mu_0 \end{pmatrix} = 0. \tag{3.4}$$

Let $X_t = \{0,t,1\}$ and let $E'$ be formed from $E$ by adding an interior row $\{1,0,\cdots,0\}$. Since $E'$ satisfies the Pólya condition and has no odd supported sequences

$$\det \begin{pmatrix} A(E,X) \\ t^r/r!, \cdots, 1 \end{pmatrix} = (-1)^\sigma \det A(E',X_t) \neq 0, \quad 0 < t < 1, \tag{3.5}$$

where $\sigma$ is the number of ones in the second row of $E$. The right hand side of (3.5) is a continuous function $\phi(t)$, defined for $0 \le t \le 1$, hence it is of a constant sign.

Using the representation (3.1) of the $\mu_i$, we obtain

$$\det \begin{pmatrix} A(E,X) \\ \mu_r, \cdots, \mu_0 \end{pmatrix} = (-1)^\sigma \sum_{j=1}^{n+2} \alpha_j \, \phi(t_j), \tag{3.6}$$

with at least one $j$ for which $\alpha_j > 0$, $0 < t_j < 1$. Thus, the determinant (3.6) is not zero, and $E$ is not q-regular. Therefore, the conditions of class $(P_2)$ are valid for $dg$.

Not (c) implies not (a). Since in this case the measure $dg$ is solely supported on $\{0,1\}$, it is sufficient to note that the $2 \times (n+1)$ matrix, $n \ge 2$,

$$\begin{bmatrix} 1,0,\cdots,0 \\ 1,0,\cdots,0 \end{bmatrix}$$

does not satisfy the Pólya condition but is q-regular with respect to $dg$. □

THEOREM 2. *If $dg \not\equiv 0$ is a positive measure on $[0,1]$ which is not solely supported on the two point set $\{0,1\}$, then any matrix $E$ which is q-regular with respect to $dg$ on $[0,1]$ must satisfy the Pólya condition.*

## 4. Matrices of Gaussian Type

The classical Gaussian quadrature formula shows that $(E,X)$ can be q-regular for some $X$ while having $N+1$ ones with $N < n$. Such a matrix will be called of *G a u s s i a n t y p e*. We shall show that any matrix of Gaussian type must have a certain minimal number of ones (the minimum number, $(n+1)/2$, being achieved by the classical formula). Because of the relationship between quadrature formulae and monosplines, the following results are partially contained in a theorem of Ferguson [6, Theorem 2.4]. We present a simple direct argument.

THEOREM 3. *Let* $E$ *be an* $m \times (n+1)$ *incidence matrix with* $N+1$ *ones. Let* $(E,X)$ *be q-regular for some positive measure* $dg$ $(\neq 0)$ *which is not solely supported on the set* $Z = \{0, x_i, 1 : e_{i0} = 1\}$. *If* $E$ *has no odd sequences in the rows corresponding to nodes* $0 < x_i < 1$, *then* $E$ *satisfies the Pólya condition (in particular,* $N \geq n$).

PROOF. If $E$ does not satisfy the Pólya condition, then there is a first $r$ such that $E^r$ does not satisfy the Pólya condition ($r > 0$ since (1.1) is exact for constants). Hence, rank $A(E^r,X)$ = rank $A(E^{r-1},X) \leq r$. There exists a polynomial, $P(x) \neq 0$, of degree $r$ which satisfies $P^{(k)}(x_i) = 0$ for $e_{ik} = 1$, $k \leq r$ ($P$ annihilates $(E^r,X)$). Since $(E^r,X)$ is q-regular with respect to $dg$, we have $\int_0^1 P(x)dg = 0$. This implies that $P(x)$ has a zero at a point $y$ distinct from the set $Z$, or changes sign at some $x_i$ with $e_{i0} = 1$ (A priori we do not know that $P$ changes sign at $y$ since $dg$ could be point evaluation at a zero of $P$). We construct an extended pair $(E',X')$ as follows. If $y$ is not one of the $x_i$, we take $X' = X \cup \{y\}$; then $E'$ is obtained from $E^r$ by adding a new row corresponding to the node $y$ with a single one in column 0. If $y = x_i$, then for some even $\ell$ (which may be zero) we have $e_{i0} = \cdots = e_{i\ell-1} = 1$, $e_{i\ell} = 0$. Then $E'$ is obtained from $E^r$ by adding a one in position $(i,\ell)$. Since $P$ changes sign at $y = x_i$ if $e_{i0} = 1$, we have $P^{(\ell)}(y) = 0$ always.

In all cases the new matrix $E'$ has no odd supported sequences, satisfies the Pólya condition, and, hence, is regular. But this contradicts the fact that $P \neq 0$ annihilates $(E',X')$. □

Theorem 3 can be applied to estimate the number $N+1$ of terms in quadrature formulae (1.1), valid for all polynomials of degree $\leq n$.

COROLLARY 1. *Let* $E$ *be an* $m \times (n+1)$ *matrix with* $N+1$ *ones* $(N \leq n)$. *Let* $(E,X)$ *be q-regular for some positive measure* $dg$ $(\neq 0)$ *which is not solely supported on* $Z = \{0, x_i, 1: e_{i0} = 1\}$. *Let* $p$ *be the minimal number of ones which must be added to* $E$ *to obtain a matrix without odd sequences in rows corresponding to* $0 < x_i < 1$. *Then*

$$N \geq n - p. \tag{4.1}$$

REMARK 3. *We have* $p \leq q$, *where* $q$ *is the number of odd sequences in rows* $i$, $0 < x_i < 1$. *Obviously*, $q \leq N + 1$. *Therefore*, (4.1) *implies*

$$N + 1 \geq (n+1)/2. \tag{4.2}$$

We note the interesting papers of Micchelli and Rivlin [12] and Karlin and Pinkus [9] (see also Barrow [2]), which discuss the problem of existence and uniqueness of the set $X$ of nodes for some Gaussian type formulas.

## 5. q-Singular Matrices

Even though the concept of q-regularity depends on the measure $dg$, there are some matrices which are not q-regular for any reasonable positive measure. Roughly speaking, the matrices which are badly singular for interpolation will be q-singular as well. Here the singularity of $E$ will be measured by rank $A(E,X)$. *We have the inequality*

$$\operatorname{rank} A(E,X) \geq n + 1 - \left[\frac{p+1}{2}\right] \tag{5.1}$$

*where* $p$ *is the number of essential odd supported sequences in* $E$ *and* $[x]$ *is the greatest integer* $\leq x$. An odd supported sequence is essential if it is an odd supported sequence for one of the components of the canonical decomposition of $E$ into Birkhoff matrices. Formula (5.1) appears in [3] with $p$ being the number of odd sequences in $E$, but the proof given there extends to the present case.

THEOREM 4. *Let* $E$ *be a Pólya matrix with* $N = n$, *let* $X \subset [0,1]$, *and let* $p$ *be an odd integer. Assume that the number of odd sequences in the rows of* $E$ *corresponding to* $x_i$, $0 < x_i < 1$, *does not exceed* $p$, *and that none of them begins in column* $0$. *If there exists an* $X$ *such that*

$$\operatorname{rank} A(E,X) = n + 1 - \left[\frac{p+1}{2}\right], \tag{5.2}$$

*then* $(E,X)$ *is* q-*singular with respect to any positive measure* $dg$ $(\neq 0)$

_which is not solely supported on_ $Z = \{0, x_i, 1: e_{i0} = 1\}$.

PROOF. We first consider the case $p = 1$. In this situation, (5.2) takes the form

(5.3) $$\text{rank } A(E,X) = n, \quad X \subset [0,1].$$

(An $X$ of this type exists if and only if $E$ is singular). For any such $X$, there exists a non-trivial polynomial $P(x)$ of degree $\le n$ satisfying $P^{(k)}(x_i) = 0$ for $e_{ik} = 1$. If $E$ is q-regular with respect to $dg$, then $\int_0^1 P(x)dg = 0$ implies that either $P$ has a zero $y$, $0 < y < 1$, distinct from the set $Z$, or $P$ changes sign at an $x_i$ with $e_{i0} = 1$, $0 < x_i < 1$. As in the proof of Theorem 3, $P$ is annihilated by another matrix $E'$, obtained from $E$ by omitting the last one in the odd supported sequence and incorporating $y$. Since $E'$ is regular, $P \equiv 0$; a contradiction. Thus, $(E,X)$ is q-singular.

When $p = 1$, and (5.3) holds, we must have

(5.4) $$\text{rank } B(E,X,dg) = n + 1.$$

The same is true if $\text{rank } A(E,X) = n + 1$, and also for $p = 0$. We have proved (5.4) for $p = 0,1$ and any $X$.

Now let $p > 1$ be odd and suppose that $X$ satisfies (5.2), $X \subset [0,1]$. For a positive measure, we consider the rank of $B(E,X,dg)$. For two given odd sequences, we move the last 1 from one of the sequences to the position immediately behind the other sequence. The choice is made so that the movement is always to the left (or only one column to the right if the sequences end in the same column). It is easy to see that the new matrix will be Pólya and have at most $p - 2$ odd sequences in rows corresponding to $x_i$, $0 < x_i < 1$.

In this way, after at most $(p-1)/2$ steps, we arrive at a Pólya matrix $E'$ with one or no odd sequences in its interior rows. Also, $e'_{i0} = 1$ if and only if $e_{i0} = 1$. By (5.4), $\text{rank } B(E',X,dg) = n + 1$. But the matrix $B(E',X,dg)$ differs from $B(E,X,dg)$ by at most $(p-1)/2$ rows. Hence,

$$\text{rank } B(E,X,dg) \ge n + 1 - (p-1)/2 = \text{rank } A(E,X) + 1.$$

Therefore, $(E,X)$ is q-singular. □

The theorem is certainly true for any positive measure with a non-trivial absolutely continuous part. Further, in the case $p=1$, Lorentz [10,11] has shown that an $X$ satisfying (5.2) always exists if the odd sequence is supported. Thus, we have

COROLLARY 3. *Let* $E$ *be a Pólya matrix with exactly one essential odd supported sequence. If all other sequences in the interior rows of* $E$ *are even, then* $E$ *is q-singular with respect to any* $\omega(x)dx$, $\omega \in L^1[0,1]$, $\omega(x) \geq 0$ *and* $\omega(x) \not\equiv 0$. *In fact,* $(E,X)$ *is q-regular for such a measure if and only if* $(E,X)$ *is regular.*

The matrices in Example 1 show that the condition "all other sequences in the interior rows of $E$ are even" cannot be relaxed.

Other examples of matrices for which (5.2) holds for some $X$ were given in [3], and these satisfy the other conditions of Theorem 4 as well. We also remark that measuring the singularity of $E$ by rank $A(E,X)$ is different than the question of whether $D_E(X)$ changes sign. Indeed, the matrix

$$E = \begin{pmatrix} 1 & 1 & 0 & 0 & 0 & 0 & 0 \\ 0 & 1 & 0 & 1 & 0 & 1 & 0 \\ 1 & 1 & 0 & 0 & 0 & 0 & 0 \end{pmatrix}$$

is q-singular by Theorem 4, but $D_E(X)$ does not change sign.

## 6. Quadrature for dx

For the measure $dg = dx$, there is a convenient way of describing the q-regularity of $E$ in terms of the regularity of certain related matrices. For a pair $(E,X)$, we consider the $m' \times (n+2)$ incidence matrix $E_2$ and node set $X_2$ determined as follows: $X_2$ is the set $X \cup \{0,1\}$ of $m'$ points, $m' = m$, $m+1$, or $m+2$, numbered in increasing order so that $0 = x_0 \leq x_1 < x_2 < \cdots < x_m \leq x_{m+1} = 1$ with repetitions avoided. The matrix $E_2$ will be an $m' \times (n+2)$ matrix with rows corresponding to the node set $X_2$. The first column of $E_2$ has ones only in the first and last row, and the remaining entries of $E_2$ are governed by the rule; $(e_2)_{ij} = 1$ if and only if $e_{i,j-1} = 1$, $j = 1,\cdots,n+1$.

The matrix $A(E_2,X_2)$ (modulo rearrangements) can be formed by taking the rows of $A(E,X)$ with additional zeros for the $(n+2)^{nd}$ column, and adding new first and last rows corresponding to $x_0 = 0$, $x_{m'} = 1$, $k = 0$ respectively; $\{0,\cdots,0,1\}$ and $\{1/(n+1)!,\cdots,1\}$. These latter two rows are independent of each other and of the rows formed from $A(E,X)$, but one of them may be a linear combination of all other rows. Thus,

$$\text{rank } A(E,X) + 1 \le \text{rank } A(E_2,X_2) \le \text{rank } A(E,X) + 2. \tag{6.1}$$

If we subtract the first row of $A(E_2,X_2)$ from the last row, we obtain the matrix

$$\begin{pmatrix} 0,\cdots,0 & 1 \\ & 0 \\ B(E,X) & \vdots \\ & 0 \end{pmatrix}.$$

In particular,

$$\text{rank } A(E_2,X_2) = \text{rank } B(E,X) + 1. \tag{6.2}$$

As a corollary, we have: <u>the pair</u> $(E,X)$ <u>is q-regular if and only if</u>

$$\text{rank } A(E_2,X_2) = \text{rank } A(E,X) + 1. \tag{6.3}$$

Theorem 2 follows quite easily in this setting for $dx$. Now $X_2 = X$ for $X$ with $x_1 = 0$, $x_m = 1$. Hence the form of $E_2$ is the same for all such $X$, and is found by adjoining the column $(1,0,\cdots,0,1)^T$ to $E$. If $E$ is q-regular (for $dx$), then let $r$ be the smallest integer for which the Pólya condition fails ($r \ge 1$ since the quadrature is exact for constants). Then $E^r$ has precisely $r$ ones so rank $A(E^r,X) \le r$ for all $X$. On the other hand, $(E^r)_2$ satisfies the Pólya condition. By the theorem of Ferguson and Németh, rank $A\big((E^r)_2,X\big) = r+2$ for some $X$, and we can assume that $x_1 = 0$, $x_m = 1$. By (6.3), $E^r$ and, consequently, $E$ are not q-regular. (This is essentially the argument of Stieglitz [14]).

LEMMA 3. <u>Let</u> $(E,X)$ <u>be given with</u> rank $A(E,X) = r$. <u>Then</u> $(E,X)$ <u>is q-regular if and only if</u>

$$\text{rank } A\big((\overline{E})_2,X_2\big) \le r+1 \tag{6.4}$$

<u>for all submatrices</u> $\overline{E} \subset E$ <u>with</u> $r$ <u>ones</u>.

PROOF. Among the rows of $A(E_2,X_2)$ formed from $A(E,X)$, there are exactly $r$ rows which are linearly independent. Therefore,

$$\operatorname{rank} A(E_2,X_2) = \max_{\overline{E} \subset E} \operatorname{rank} A\big((\overline{E})_2,X_2\big).$$

Our statement follows from this and the criterion (6.3) for q-regularity. □

The importance of Lemma 3 is that q-regularity can be related to regularity.

COROLLARY 4. *Let* $E = E' \oplus E''$ *and* $N = n$. *If* $E''$ *is regular and* $E'$ *is singular, then a singular pair* $(E,X)$ *is* q-*regular only if the pair* $\big((\overline{E}')_2,X_2\big)$ *is singular for each submatrix* $\overline{E}' \subset E'$ *obtained from* $E'$ *by omitting a single one.*

PROOF. By Proposition 1, we may assume $E = E'$. If the pair $\big((\overline{E}')_2,X_2\big)$ is regular for some $\overline{E}'$, then $\operatorname{rank} A\big((\overline{E}')_2,X_2\big) = n+2$. But $\operatorname{rank} A(E,X) \le n$ for a singular pair and the result follows from Lemma 3. □

Finally, we note that Corollary 3 follows easily for the measure $dx$ from Corollary 4. Indeed, by omitting the last one of the odd supported sequence in the $E$ of Corollary 3, we obtain a matrix $(\overline{E}')_2$ satisfying the Pólya condition and having no odd supported sequences. Therefore, $\big((\overline{E}')_2,X_2\big)$ is regular for any singular node set $X$.

The research of the authors has been supported by the National Science Foundation and the Canadian National Research Council.

## REFERENCES

[1] Atkinson, K. - Sharma, A., A partial characterization of poised Hermite-Birkhoff interpolation problems. SIAM J. Numer. Anal. 6 (1969), 230-235.

[2] Barrow, D., On multiple node Gaussian quadrature formulae. Preprint.

[3] Chalmers, B. - Johnson, D.J. - Metcalf, F.T. - Taylor, G.D., Remarks on the rank of Hermite-Birkhoff interpolation. SIAM J. Numer. Anal. 11 (1974), 254-259.

[4] Epstein, M.P. - Hamming, R.W., Noninterpolatory quadrature formulas. SIAM J. Numer. Anal. 9 (1972), 464-475.

[5] Ferguson, D., The question of uniqueness for G.D. Birkhoff interpolation problems. J. Approximation Theory 2 (1969), 1-28.

[6] Ferguson, D., Sign changes and minimal support properties of Hermite-Birkhoff splines with compact support. SIAM J. Numer. Anal. 11 (1974), 769-779.

[7] Karlin, S. - Studden, W.J., Tchebycheff Systems: With Applications in Analysis and Statistics. Interscience Publishers, New York 1966.

[8] Karlin, S. - Karon, J.M., Poised and non-poised Hermite-Birkhoff interpolations. Indiana Univ. Math. J. 21 (1972), 1131-1170.

[9] Karlin, S. - Pinkus, A., Gaussian quadrature formulae with multiple nodes. In Studies in Spline Functions and Approximation Theory. Academic Press, New York 1976, 113-141.

[10] Lorentz, G.G., Birkhoff interpolation and the problem of free matrices. J. Approximation Theory 6 (1972), 283-290.

[11] Lorentz, G.G., Birkhoff interpolation problem. CNA report, University of Texas in Austin, 1975.

[12] Micchelli, C.A. - Rivlin, T.J., Quadrature formulae and Hermite-Birkhoff interpolation. Advances in Math. 11 (1973), 93-112.

[13] Németh, A.B., Transformations of the Chebyshev systems. Mathematica (Cluj) 8 (31) (1966), 315-333.

[14] Stieglitz, M., Beste Quadraturformeln für Inzidenzmatrizen ohne ungerade gestütze Seguenzen. To appear in J. of Approximation Theory.

[15] Stieglitz, M., Beste Quadraturformeln für Integrale mit einer Gewichtsfunktion. Monatsh. Math. (in print).

# ON SOME PROBLEMS IN INTERPOLATION THEORY

József Szabados
Mathematical Institute
of the Hungarian Academy of Sciences
Budapest

Some problems connected with the fundamental polynomials of interpolation are considered. Also an attempt is made to carry over interpolating-type linear procedures to $L_p$-spaces.

This is a short survey on some recent results in interpolation theory, stated mostly without proofs. Detailed proofs will appear elsewhere (see [3] and [5]).

At first we deal with some extremum problems connected with the fundamental polynomials of interpolation. In [7], p. 92, A. H. Tureckii mentioned the following unsolved problem. Let

$$0 \leq x_0 < x_1 < \dots < x_{2n} < 2\pi, \tag{1}$$

and $t_k(x)$, $k=0,1,\dots,2n$, be that uniquely determined trigonometric polynomial of degree n for which $t_k(x_j) = \delta_{k,j}$ $(k,j = 0,1,\dots,2n)$. For what system of nodes (1) will

$$I_p = I_p(x_0,\dots,x_{2n}) = \int_0^{2\pi} \sum_{k=0}^{2n} |t_k(x)|^p dx \quad (0<p<\infty) \tag{2}$$

be minimal? By a lengthy calculation, Tureckii showed that in case p=1 or 2, the necessary conditions $\partial I_p/\partial x_k=0$ $(k=0,\dots,2n)$ of the minimum hold for the equidistant nodes

$$t_k = t_{k,n} = \frac{2k\pi}{2n+1} \quad (k=0,\dots,2n). \tag{3}$$

However, the problem itself remained unsettled. Recently, R. Schumacher [4] gave a solution in case p=1, as a corollary of a much more general theorem. His method does not seem to be applicable to the class p = 1, because an essential use is made of the fact that $I_1$ is the integral of the Lebesgue function of the trigonometric interpolation.

Now using simple and elementary arguments, we can prove the following

THEOREM 1. Let $p \geq 1$ be an arbitrary real number. The integral (2) is minimal if and only if the nodes (1) are identical with the equidistant nodes (3), or with their translation.

The basic idea of the proof is using the following identity of Marcinkiewicz, Zygmund and Berman (see e.g. [6], pp. 481--482): Let $L_n$ be an arbitrary linear trigonometric polynomial operator which reproduces trigonometric polynomials of degree at most n. Then

$$\frac{1}{2\pi}\int_0^{2\pi} L_n(f(t-h),x+h)\,dh = s_n(f,x) \qquad (-\infty<x<\infty)$$

for all $2\pi$-periodic Lebesgue-integrable function f(x), where $s_n(f,x)$ is the $n^{th}$ partial sum of the Fourier series of f(x).

The problem remains open for $0<p<1$.

The corresponding problem for the Lagrange interpolation in case p=1 has been raised by P. Erdős [2]; but so far the determination of the minimum of

$$\int_{-1}^{1} \lambda_n(x)\,dx \qquad \left(\lambda_n(x) = \sum_{k=0}^{n} f_k(x)\right)$$

is unsettled and seems to be quite hopeless. (Here $f_k(x)$ are the fundamental polynomials of the Lagrange interpolation corresponding to the nodes

$$(4) \qquad (-1\leq)x_0 < x_1 < \dots < x_n(\leq 1).$$

In the same paper Erdős stated (without proof) that with a suitable positive constant c,

$$\int_{-1}^{1} \lambda_n(x)dx \geq c \log n$$

holds for all system of nodes (4). In a recent paper with P. Erdős [3] we could prove this conjecture, even in the following, slightly more general form:

THEOREM 2. <u>For an arbitrary system of nodes</u> (4) <u>and subinterval</u> $[a,b] \subset (-1,1)$ <u>we have</u>

$$\int_{a}^{b} \lambda_n(x)dx \geq c_1(b-a)\log n \qquad (n \geq n_0 = n_0(a,b))$$

<u>with an absolute positive constant</u> $c_1$.

The crucial part of the proof is the following inequality:

$$\max_{a \leq x_k < x_{k+1} \leq b} (x_{k+1}-x_k) \leq 25 \frac{\log \max\limits_{a \leq x \leq b} \lambda_n(x)}{n} \qquad (n \geq n_1(a,b))$$

which may be of independent interest. It would be interesting to deduce another conjecture of Erdős [1, Theorem 2] from our Theorem 2: Given an arbitrary $\varepsilon$, $0 < \varepsilon < b-a$, there exists an $\eta = \eta(\varepsilon)$ such that the measure of the set of $x \in [a,b]$ for which $\lambda_n(x) < \eta \log n$ holds, is less than $\varepsilon$.

Finally, I would like to show that there is a possibility of developping interpolation theory in $L_p$-spaces $(1 \leq p < \infty)$. There are several ways of avoiding the difficulties arising from the fact that, generally, individual values of a function $f(x) \in L_p$ do not determine well-converging linear operators (in $L_p$-metric). Among them perhaps the most suitable is the following:

Using the previous notations, let $f(x) \in L_p[-1,1]$, $h > 0$ a small real number to be determined later, and consider the operator

(5) $$L_n(f,x) = \frac{1}{2h}\sum_{k=0}^{n}\int_{-h}^{h} f(x_k+t)dt\, f_k(x).$$

(Here we assume that f(x) is extended periodically to the whole real line.) This is a polynomial of degree at most n which interpolates the Stekloff-transform

(6) $$F_h(x) = \frac{1}{2h}\int_{-h}^{h} f(x+t)dt$$

of f(x) at the nodes (4). Investigating the convergence-divergence behaviour of the operator (5), the quantity

(7) $$\Lambda_{n,p} = \max_{|\varepsilon_k|\le 1}\left\|\sum_{k=0}^{n}\varepsilon_k f_k(x)\right\|_p$$

plays an important role. (Here $\|\cdot\|_p$ denotes the usual norm in $L_p$-spaces.)

THEOREM 3. <u>For any system of nodes</u> (4) <u>and</u> $f(x)\in L_p[-1,1]$ <u>we have</u>

$$\|f(x) - L_n(f,x)\|_p = O(\omega(f,h)_p)$$

<u>where</u> $\omega(f,h)_p$ <u>is the</u> $L_p$<u>-modulus of continuity of</u> f(x) <u>and</u> h <u>is (uniquely) defined by the relation</u>

(8) $$h^{1/p}\omega(f,h)_p = \omega(f,1/n)_p\Lambda_{n,p}.$$

PROOF. It is well-known that for the Stekloff-transform (6) we have

(9) $$\|f(x) - F_h(x)\|_p \le \omega(f,h)_p.$$

Now the uniform modulus of continuity of $F_h(x)$ is easily estimated by $\omega(f,t)_p$ as follows:

$$|F_h(x+t) - F_h(x)| = \frac{1}{2h}\left|\int_{-h}^{h}[f(x+t+u) - f(x+u)]\,du\right| \leq$$

$$\leq \frac{1}{2h}\int_{x-h}^{x+h}|f(t+u) - f(u)|\,du \leq \frac{1}{2h}(2h)^{1-1/p}\omega(f,t)_p \leq$$

$$\leq (2h)^{-1/p}\omega(f,t)_p$$

using Hölder's inequality. Thus by the classical Jackson theorem, there exist polynomials $p_n(x)$ of degree at most n such that

$$\|F_h(x) - p_n(x)\|_p \leq 2^{1/p}\|F_h(x) - p_n(x)\|_C = O(h^{-1/p})\omega(f,1/n)_p$$

where $\|\cdot\|_C$ denotes the supremum norm in $[-1,1]$. Hence, if we express $p_n(x)$ as a Lagrange interpolating polynomial and use (7), (8) and (9), we get

$$\|f(x) - L_n(f,x)\|_p \leq \|f(x) - F_h(x)\|_p + \|F_h(x) - p_n(x)\|_p +$$

$$+ \left\|\sum_{k=0}^{n}[p_n(x_k) - F_h(x_k)]f_k(x)\right\|_p \leq \omega(f,h)_p +$$

$$+ O(h^{-1/p})\omega(f,1/n)_p(1 + \Lambda_{n,p}) = O(\omega(f,h)_p).$$

Q.E.D.

COROLLARY. *If*

(10) $$\lim_{n\to\infty} \omega(f,1/n)_p\Lambda_{n,p} = 0$$

*then*

$$\lim_{n\to\infty} \|f(x) - L_n(f,x)\|_p = 0.$$

Condition (10) is easily satisfied, even $\Lambda_{n,p}=O(1)$ is possible. Let e.g. (4) be the roots of the $n^{th}$ Legendre polynomial and p=2; then by orthogonality

$$\Lambda_{n,2} = \left(\int_{-1}^{1} \sum_{k=0}^{n} f_k^2(x)dx\right)^{1/2} = \sqrt{2}$$

(cf. [7], p. 91).

The necessity of the condition (10) for the convergence is an open question.

## REFERENCES


[1] Erdős, P., Problems and results on the theory of interpolation I. Acta Math. Acad. Sci. Hungar. 9 (1958), 381-388.

[2] Erdős, P., Problems and results on the theory of interpolation II. Acta Math. Acad. Sci. Hungar. 12 (1961), 235-244.

[3] Erdős, P. - Szabados, J., On the integral of the Lebesgue function of interpolation. Acta Math. Acad. Sci. Hungar. (to appear).

[4] Schumacher, R., Zur Minimalität trigonometrischer Polynomoperatoren. Manuscripta Math. 19 (1976), 133-142.

[5] Szabados, J., On an interpolation theoretic extremum problem. Periodica Math. Hungar. (to appear).

[6] Timan, A. F., Theory of approximation of functions of one real variable. Moscow 1960 (in Russian).

[7] Tureckii, A. H., Theory of interpolation through problems. Minsk 1968 (in Russian).

# BIVARIATE AND MULTIVARIATE INTERPOLATION WITH NONCOMMUTATIVE PROJECTORS

W. J. Gordon
Office of Naval Research
223 Old Marylebone Road
London, England

and

E. W. Cheney
Department of Mathematics
University of Texas at Austin
Austin, Texas 78712

A number of papers appearing in the last decade have been concerned with developing the algebraic and lattice-theoretic aspects of "blending-approximation" operators. This theory has proved most useful in the task of synthesizing multivariate interpolation operators for various special purposes. Often, the fact that the component operators commute with each other is helpful in predicting the properties of the operators constructed from them. In several important situations, however, the basic approximation operators do not commute with each other. A general theory to encompass this case has been lacking, and we offer here the beginnings of such a theory. A full report on this subject is in preparation and will appear among the publications of the Center for Numerical Analysis, University of Texas.

1. Introduction. As a prototype of the noncommutative case in blending approximation, we consider the bivariate interpolation process on triangles as proposed in [2]. Suppose that a function $f$ is defined on the triangle whose vertices are $(0,0)$, $(1,0)$, and $(1,1)$. Simple linear interpolation along lines parallel to the sides of the triangle produces three projectors defined as follows:

$$(P_1f)(x,y) = f(1,y)(x-y)/(1-y) + f(y,y)(1-x)/(1-y)$$
$$(P_2f)(x,y) = f(x,0)(x-y)/x + f(x,x)y/x$$
$$(P_3f)(x,y) = f(1,1-x+y)y/(1-x+y) + f(x-y,0)(1-x)/(1-x+y) .$$

These are "interpolation" operators. Thus $P_if$ interpolates $f$ on a set of points. For example, $(P_1f)(x,y) = f(x,y)$ for all points of the form $(1,y)$ or $(x,x)$. In accordance with definitions given below, we say that the evaluation functionals corresponding to $(1,y)$ and $(x,x)$ lie in the "precision set" of $P_1$. The functions left invariant by $P_i$ we call the "invariance set" of $P_i$. For example, $P_1$ leaves invariant all functions of the form $a(y)(x-y)/(1-y) + b(y)(1-x)/(1-y)$ with arbitrary functions $a(y)$ and $b(y)$. One can verify that in this example $P_iP_j \neq P_jP_i$ if $i \neq j$.

However, a cancellation law $P_iP_jP_i = P_iP_j$ is valid, and this has important consequences.

Proceeding now to formal definitions, let us consider a linear operator L defined on a Banach space E. We define

$$\text{invariance set of } L = i(L) = \{f \in E: Lf = f\}$$

$$\text{precision set of } L = p(L) = \{\phi \in E^*: L^*\phi = \phi\}.$$

Here $E^*$ is the conjugate space of E and $L^*$ is the adjoint of L, defined by $L^*\phi = \phi \circ L$ for all $\phi \in E^*$. Obviously $p(L) = i(L^*)$. An operator L on E is termed a "projector" if $L^2 = L$. For a projector, the invariance set and the precision set are its range and the range of its adjoint, respectively. For two operators $L_1$ and $L_2$, the Boolean sum is defined to be

$$L_1 \oplus L_2 = L_1 + L_2 - L_1L_2 .$$

This operation is associative but not commutative, nor distributive with respect to addition.

2. <u>The Algebra of Approximation Operators</u>. In this section we state a number of propositions which are useful in calculating precision sets and invariance sets. Few proofs are given since these are elementary and use nothing deeper than the Hahn-Banach Theorem.

THEOREM 1. *If* $P$ *and* $Q$ *are projectors such that* $i(P) = i(Q)$ *and* $p(P) = p(Q)$ *then* $P = Q$.

THEOREM 2. *For two linear operators* $L$ *and* $M$ *we have:*

(a) $i(L) \cap i(M) \subset i(LM) \cap i(ML)$

(b) $p(L) \cap p(M) \subset p(LM) \cap p(ML)$

(c) $i(M) \subset i(L \oplus M)$

(d) $p(L) \subset p(L \oplus M)$.

THEOREM 3. <u>For two projectors</u> P <u>and</u> Q <u>we have</u>

(a) $i(P) \cap i(Q) = i(PQ) \cap i(QP)$

(b) $p(P) \cap p(Q) = p(PQ) \cap p(QP)$

(c) $i(P) + i(Q) = i(P \oplus Q) + i(Q \oplus P)$

(d) $p(P) + p(Q) = p(P \oplus Q) + p(Q \oplus P)$.

THEOREM 4. (<u>Duality With Left Absorption</u>) <u>If</u> P <u>and</u> Q <u>are projectors such that</u> $QPQ = PQ$, <u>then</u>

(a) $PQ$ <u>and</u> $Q \oplus P$ <u>are projectors</u>

(b) $i(PQ) = i(P) \cap i(Q)$

(c) $i(Q \oplus P) = i(P) + i(Q)$.

THEOREM 5. (<u>Duality With Right Absorption</u>) <u>If</u> P <u>and</u> Q <u>are projectors such that</u> $QPQ = QP$ <u>then</u>

(a) $QP$ <u>and</u> $P \oplus Q$ <u>are projectors</u>

(b) $p(QP) = p(Q) \cap p(P)$

(c) $p(P \oplus Q) = p(P) + p(Q)$.

THEOREM 6. (<u>Duality With Commutativity</u>) <u>If</u> P <u>and</u> Q <u>are projectors such that</u> $PQ = QP$ <u>then</u>

(a) $PQ$, $QP$, $P \oplus Q$, $Q \oplus P$ <u>are projectors</u>; <u>also</u> $PQ = QP$ <u>and</u> $P \oplus Q = Q \oplus P$.

(b) $i(PQ) = i(QP) = i(P) \cap i(Q)$

(c) $p(PQ) = p(QP) = p(P) \cap p(Q)$

(d) $i(P \oplus Q) = i(Q \oplus P) = i(P) + i(Q)$

(e) $p(P \oplus Q) = p(Q \oplus P) = p(P) + p(Q)$.

A collection $\mathscr{C}$ of projectors on a space E is said to satisfy the "right absorption law" if $PQP = PQ$ for all P and Q in $\mathscr{C}$. There is of course a similar left absorption law, $PQP = QP$.

THEOREM 7. Let $\mathcal{E}$ be a collection of projectors satisfying the right absorption law. Let $\mathcal{E}^+$ be the algebra generated from $\mathcal{E}$ by the operations $\cdot$ and $\oplus$. Then $\mathcal{E}^+$ satisfies the right absorption law, and all members of $\mathcal{E}^+$ are projectors.

PROOF. Let $\mathcal{C}_0 = \mathcal{C}$, and for $n = 0,1,\ldots$ let $\mathcal{C}_{n+1}$ be the set of all operators of the form $PQ$ or $P \oplus Q$ with $P$ and $Q$ taken from $\mathcal{C}_n$. We shall show inductively that $\mathcal{C}_{n+1}$ is right-absorptive and that all its elements are projectors. Let $R$ and $S$ be any two members of $\mathcal{C}_{n+1}$. We shall prove that $RSR = RS$. (Theorem 5 shows that $R$ and $S$ are projectors.) Using $P_1, P_2$, etc. to denote generic elements of $\mathcal{C}_n$, we distinguish four cases.

In Case 1, $R = P_1P_2$ and $S = P_3P_4$. By right-absorption, $RSR = P_1P_2P_3P_4P_1P_2 = P_1P_2P_1P_3P_1P_4P_1P_2 = P_1P_2P_3P_4P_2 = P_1P_2P_3P_2P_4P_2 = P_1P_2P_3P_4 = RS$.

In Case 2, $R = P_1P_2$ and $S = P_3 \oplus P_4$. By Case 1, $RSR = P_1P_2(P_3 \oplus P_4)P_1P_2 = P_1P_2P_3P_1P_2 + P_1P_2P_4P_1P_2 - P_1P_2P_3P_4P_1P_2 = P_1P_2P_3 + P_1P_2P_4 - P_1P_2P_3P_4 = P_1P_2(P_3 \oplus P_4) = RS$.

In Case 3, $R = P_1 \oplus P_2$ and $S = P_3P_4$. By the method of Case 1, $RSR = (P_1 \oplus P_2)S(P_1 \oplus P_2) = (P_1 + P_2 - P_1P_2)S(P_1 + P_2 - P_1P_2) = P_1SP_1 + P_1SP_2 - P_1SP_1P_2 + P_2SP_1 + P_2SP_2 - P_2SP_1P_2 - P_1P_2SP_1 - P_1P_2SP_2 + P_1P_2SP_1P_2 = P_1S + P_1SP_2 - P_1SP_2 + P_2SP_1 + P_2S - P_2SP_1 - P_1P_2S - P_1P_2S + P_1P_2S = P_1S + P_2S - P_1P_2S = RS$. The last case, $R = P_1 \oplus P_2$ and $S = P_3 \oplus P_4$ is similar.

Since all elements of $\mathcal{C}_n$ are projectors, $\mathcal{C}_n \subset \mathcal{C}_{n+1}$. It is easily proved that $\bigcup_{n=0}^{\infty} \mathcal{C}_n$ is algebraically closed. By induction, one proves that any set which is algebraically closed and contains $\mathcal{C}_0$ must contain each $\mathcal{C}_n$. Thus $\mathcal{C}^+ = \bigcup_{n=0}^{\infty} \mathcal{C}_n$. ∎

The duality theorems show that it is important to have convenient tests for right or left absorption. Because of its greater usefulness we concentrate on right absorption.

THEOREM 8. Either of the following suffices for $PQP = PQ$:

(1) $\phi \circ (Q - QP) = 0$ for all $\phi \in p(P) \setminus p(Q)$

(2) The range of $Q^*P^*$ is contained in $p(P)$.

PROOF. In both cases it is enough to prove that $\phi PQ = \phi PQP$ for an arbitrary $\phi \in E^*$. If (2) is true then $\phi PQ$, being in the range of $Q^*P^*$, must be in $p(P)$, and thus $\phi PQP = \phi PQ$. If (1) is true, observe that since $\phi P \in p(P)$, either $\phi P \in p(P) \setminus p(Q)$ or $\phi P \in p(Q)$. In the former case, $\phi P(Q-QP) = 0$ by hypothesis. In the latter case, $\phi PQ = \phi P = \phi PQP$. ∎

3. The Commutativity of Parametric Extensions. As a sample of what can be proved about commutativity, we give a theorem which concerns a common method of constructing operators. This method is called "parametric extension" and can be illustrated by the univariate Lagrange operator. If nodes $t_1, \ldots, t_n$ are prescribed, the Lagrange interpolation operator is defined by

$$(Lf)(x) = \sum_{i=1}^{n} f(t_i)\ell_i(x)$$

where $\ell_i$ are polynomials of degree $< n$ such that $\ell_i(t_j) = \delta_{ij}$. The parameteric extension of $L$ to bivariate functions is then given by

$$(\bar{L}f)(x,y) = \sum f(t_i,y)\ell_i(x).$$

For the general theory, define $\hat{x}: C(X) \to \mathbb{R}$ by $\hat{x}(f) = f(x)$, and define $\hat{x}: C(X \times Y) \to C(Y)$ by $(\hat{x}f)(y) = f(x,y)$. Similarly $\hat{y}: C(Y) \to \mathbb{R}$ is defined by $\hat{y}(f) = f(y)$ and $\hat{y}: C(X \times Y) \to C(X)$ is defined by $(\hat{y}f)(x) = f(x,y)$. If $L_1: C(X) \to C(X)$ then $\bar{L}_1: C(X \times Y) \to C(X \times Y)$ and is defined by

$$(\bar{L}_1 f)(x,y) = \hat{x}L_1\hat{y}f.$$

If $L_2: C(Y) \to C(Y)$, then $\bar{L}_2$ is defined by

$$(\bar{L}_2 f)(x,y) = \hat{y}L_2\hat{x}f.$$

THEOREM 9. The parametric extensions of two operators commute with each other.

PROOF. For each $x \in X$, $\hat{x}L_1 \in C(X)^*$. By the Riesz Representation Theorem, [12, p. 265], there is a measure $\mu$ such that $\hat{x}L_1 f = \int f(t)d\mu(t)$ for all $f \in C(X)$. Likewise, if $y \in Y$, there is a measure $\nu$ such that

$\hat{y}L_2f = \int f(s)d\nu(s)$ for all $f \in C(Y)$. If $f \in C(X \times Y)$ we have then

$$(\bar{L}_1 f)(x,y) = \int f(t,y)d\mu(t)$$

$$(\bar{L}_2 f)(x,y) = \int f(x,s)d\nu(s)$$

$$(\bar{L}_1\bar{L}_2 f)(x,y) = \int (\bar{L}_2 f)(t,y)d\mu(t) = \int\int f(t,s)d\nu(s)d\mu(t)$$

$$(\bar{L}_2\bar{L}_1 f)(x,y) = \int (\bar{L}_1 f)(x,s)d\nu(s) = \int\int f(t,s)d\mu(t)d\nu(s).$$

An application of the Fubini Theorem, [12, p. 193], completes the proof. ∎

## REFERENCES

[ 1 ] Barnhill, R.E., Smooth interpolation over triangles. in Computer Aided Geometric Design. R.E. Barnhill and R.F. Riesenfeld, eds. Academic Press, New York. 1974.

[ 2 ] Barnhill, R.E., Birkhoff, G., Gordon, W.J., Smooth interpolation in triangles. J. Approximation Theory. 8 (1973), 114-128.

[ 3 ] Barnhill, R.E. and Gregory, J.A., Compatible smooth interpolation in triangles. J. Approximation Theory. 8 (1973), 214-225.

[ 4 ] Barnhill R.E. and Gregory, J.A., Polynomial interpolation to boundary data on triangles. Math. Comput. 29 (1975), 726-735.

[ 5 ] Birkhoff, G., Interpolation to boundary data in triangles. J. Math. Anal. Appl. 42 (1973), 474-484.

[ 6 ] Birkhoff, G. and Gordon, W.J., The draftsman's and related equations. J. Approximation Theory. 1 (1968), 199-208.

[ 7 ] Böhmer K. and Coman, Gh., Smooth interpolation schemes in triangles with error bounds. Mathematica (Cluj).

[ 8 ] Böhmer, K. and Coman, Gh., Blending interpolation schemes on triangles with error bounds. pp. 14-37 in Constructive Theory of Functions of Several Variables. Lecture Notes in Mathematics, No 571, Springer-Verlag, 1976.

[ 9 ] Coman, Gh., Multivariate approximation schemes and the approximation of linear functionals. Math. Research Center Report 1254, University of Wisconsin 1974.

[10] Delvos, F.J. and Posdorf, H., On optimal tensor product approximation. J. Approximation Theory.

[11] Delvos, F.H. and Posdorf, H., N-th order blending. pp. 53-64 in Constructive Theory of Functions of Several Variables. Lecture Notes in Mathematics, No. 571, Springer-Verlag, 1976.

[12] Dunford, N. and Schwartz, J.T., Linear Operators, Part I. Interscience Publishers, New York 1958.

[13] Gordon, W.J., Distributive lattices and the approximation of multivariate functions. pp. 223-277 in Approximations with Special Emphasis on Spline Functions. Ed. by I.J. Schoenberg, Academic Press, New York 1969.

[14] Gordon, W.J., Spline-blended surface interpolation through curve networks. J. Math. Mech. 18 (1969), 931-952.

[15] Gordon, W.J., Blending-function methods of bivariate and multivariate interpolation and approximation. SIAM J. Numer. Anal. 8 (1971), 158-177.

[16] Gordon, W.J. and Hall, C.A., Transfinite element methods: blending function interpolation over arbitrary curved domains. Numer. Math. 21 (1973), 109-129.

[17] Gordon, W.J. and Hall, C.A., Construction of curvilinear co-ordinate systems and applications to mesh generation. Internat. J. Numer. Methods in Engrg. 7 (1973), 461-477.

[18] Gordon, W.J. and Wixom, J.A., Pseudo-harmonic interpolation on convex domains. SIAM J. Numer. Anal. 11 (1974), 909-933.

[19] Gregory, J.A., Piecewise Interpolation Theory for Functions of Two Variables. Ph.D. Dissertation, Department of Mathematics, Brunel University, Uxbridge, England, 1975.

# ÜBER EINE HYPOTHESE VON P.P. KOROVKIN

Viktor A. Baskakov
Auto- und Eisenbahninstitut
Moskau

Für die linearen Summierungsmethoden der Fourierreihen wird die Abschätzung der Normen durch die Annäherungsordnung erhalten, aus der unter anderem folgt, daß wenn die Annäherungsordnung der besten gleich ist, dann sind die Normen gleichmäßig beschränkt. Darin bestand die Hypothese von P.P. Korovkin.

In der Approximationstheorie der Funktionen sind zahlreiche Abschätzungen für die Annäherungsordnung der Funktionen durch die linearen Operatoren bekannt, in denen als Regel die Normen von diesen Operatoren benutzt werden.

P.P. Korovkin hat mehrmals den Gedanken geäußert, daß eine umgekehrte Beziehung zwischen der Annäherungsordnung der Funktionen durch die linearen Operatoren und ihren Normen existiert.

Wenn der Extremfall betrachtet wird, bei dem die Annäherungsordnung mit der besten zusammenfällt, so besteht die Hypothese von Korovkin darin, daß, wenn die Reihenfolge der linearen polynomialen Operatoren $\{L_n(f;x)\}$ die recht breite Klasse der Funktionen (z.B. die Klasse Lip $\alpha$ bei irgendwelcher fixierten Zahl $\alpha$) mit der Ordnung gleich der besten annähert, dann sind die Normen dieser Operatoren $\{\|L_n\|\}$ gleichmäßig beschränkt.

In diesem Artikel werden lineare Summierungsmethoden der Fourier-Reihen betrachtet und es wird für sie die Richtigkeit der Hypothese von Korovkin bewiesen.

Es sei also

$$L_n(f;x) = \frac{1}{\pi}\int_{-\pi}^{\pi} f(x+t)U_n(t)dt, \ n = 1,2,\ldots ,$$

wo

$$U_n(t) = \frac{\rho_{o,n}}{2} + \sum_{k=1}^{n} \rho_{k,n} \cos kt.$$

Die Normen von diesen Operatoren werden folgendermaßen bestimmt:

$$\|L_n\| = \frac{2}{\pi} \int_{-\pi}^{\pi} |U_n(t)| dt, \quad n = 1,2,\ldots .$$

Um das Hauptresultat zu beweisen, brauchen wir zwei Lemmata. Das erste Lemma ist eine der Varianten des Lemmas von P.P. Korovkin (siehe [1], S. 13).

LEMMA 1. *Es sei* $\varepsilon$ *eine beliebige positive Zahl und die Menge* $A_n \subset [0,\pi]$ *sei so, daß*

$$\frac{2}{\pi} \int_{A_n} |U_n(t)| dt \geqslant \varepsilon \|L_n\| ;$$

*dann ist das Maß dieser Menge* $mA_n \geqslant \varepsilon/n$ *für alle* $n \geqslant 1$.

BEWEIS. Da

$$\rho_{k,n} = \frac{2}{\pi} \int_{o}^{\pi} \cos kt \; U_n(t) dt, \quad k = 0,1,\ldots,n,$$

so gilt

$$|\rho_{k,n}| \leqslant \|L_n\|, \quad k = 0,1,\ldots,n$$

und folglich

$$\|L_n\| \leqslant \frac{2}{\varepsilon\pi} \int_{A_n} |U_n(t)| dt \leqslant \frac{2}{\varepsilon\pi} \left( \frac{|\rho_{o,n}|}{2} + \sum_{k=1}^{n} |\rho_{k,n}| \right) mA_n$$

$$\leqslant \frac{2n+1}{\varepsilon\pi} \|L_n\| \, mA_n .$$

Aus diesen Ungleichungen ergibt sich das Lemma 1.

Es sei

$$T_n(t) = \frac{a_o}{2} + \sum_{k=1}^{n} (a_k \cos kt + b_k \sin kt)$$

ein beliebiges trigonometrisches Polynom vom Grade n; $\{t_{i,n}\}$, $i = 1,2,\ldots,m_n$, seien alle Nullstellen des Polynoms $T_n(t)$ auf dem halboffenen Intervall $[0,2\pi)$; $\varepsilon$ sei eine beliebige positive Zahl;

$$\delta_n = \frac{\varepsilon}{n}; \; B_n = \bigcup_{j=1}^{m_n} [t_{j,n} - \delta_n ; t_{j,n} + \delta_n] \cap [0,2\pi] .$$

LEMMA 2.

$$\int_{B_n} |T_n(t)|dt \leqslant 2\varepsilon \int_0^{2\pi} |T_n(t)|dt.$$

BEWEIS. Die Menge $B_n$ besteht aus der Vereinigung der Intervalle, die durch die Nullstellen des Polynoms $T_n(t)$ in Teile aufgeteilt werden, deren Längen $\varepsilon/n$ nicht übertreffen.

Es sei $\Delta = [t_0, t_1]$ ein solcher Teil und es sei z.B. der Punkt $t_0$ eine Nullstelle von $T_n(t)$, d.h. $T_n(t_0) = 0$.

Durch partielles Integrieren erhalten wir

$$\int_\Delta |T_n(t)|dt = \left|\int_\Delta T_n(t)d(t-t_1)\right| = \left|T_n(t)(t-t_1)\Big|_{t_0}^{t_1}\right.$$

$$\left.-\int_\Delta T_n'(t)(t-t_1)dt\right| \leqslant \frac{\varepsilon}{n}\int_\Delta |T_n'(t)|dt.$$

Durch Summieren dieser Ungleichungen für alle Segmente $\Delta$, in die die Menge $B_n$ aufgeteilt ist, erhält man, daß

$$\int_{B_n} |T_n(t)|dt \leqslant \frac{\varepsilon}{n}\int_{B_n} |T_n'(t)|dt \leqslant \frac{\varepsilon}{n}\int_0^{2\pi} |T_n'(t)|dt.$$

Durch Anwenden der Bernstein-Ungleichung für die Abschätzung des Integrals vom Betrag der Ableitung des trigonometrischen Polynoms im Raum $L_1$ (siehe, z.B. [2], S. 426) bekommen wir das Lemma 2.

Es seien: $\omega(\delta)$ - ein beliebiger Stetigkeitsmodul und $H_\omega$ - die Klasse der $2\pi$-periodischen Funktionen, für die $\omega(f;\delta) \leqslant \omega(\delta)$ gilt.

Es sei

$$\Delta_n(\omega) = \sup_{f \in H} \|f(x) - L_n(f;x)\|_C.$$

THEOREM. <u>Wenn</u>

$$\Delta_n(\omega) \leqslant C(n)\omega(\tfrac{1}{n}),\ n \geqslant 1,$$

<u>erfüllt wird, so gilt</u>

$$\|L_n\| \leqslant 27\pi C(n).$$

BEWEIS. Es seien $\{t_{j,n}\}$, $j=1,\dots,l_n$ - alle Nullstellen des ungeraden Vielfachen des Polynoms $U_n(t)$ auf dem Intervall $(0,\pi)$ und

$$t_{o,n}=0;\ t_{l_n+1,n}=\pi;\ t^*_{k,n}=\frac{1}{2}(t_{k,n}+t_{k+1,n}),\ k=0,1,\dots,l_n.$$

Wir konstruieren auf dem Segment $[0,\pi]$ die Funktion $f_n(t)$, indem wir sie auf jedem Segment $[t_{j,n}, t_{j+1,n}]$, $j=0,1,\dots,l_n$ folgendermaßen bestimmen

$$f_n(t)=\begin{cases}\frac{1}{3}\,\omega(2(t-t_{j,n})), & t_{j,n}\leqslant t\leqslant t^*_{j,n}\\[2ex] \frac{1}{3}\,\omega(2(t_{j+1,n}-t)), & t^*_{j,n}\leqslant t\leqslant t_{j+1,n}.\end{cases}$$

Nach dem Lemma von A.W. Efimov ([3], S. 11) gehört die $2\pi$-periodische Funktion $f^*_n(t)$, die auf dem Segment $[0,\pi]$ der Funktion $f(t)=(\operatorname{sign} U_n(t))f_n(t)$ gleich ist, der Klasse $H_\omega$ an.

Aufgrund des Lemmas 1 haben wir

$$\frac{2}{\pi}\int_o^{\frac{1}{12n}}|U_n(t)|dt\leqslant\frac{1}{3}\|L_n\|,\ n\geqslant 1.$$

Indem wir in Lemma 2 $\varepsilon=1/12$ annehmen, erhalten wir

$$\frac{2}{\pi}\int_{B_n}|U_n(t)|dt\leqslant\frac{1}{3}\|L_n\|,\ n\geqslant 1.$$

Wenn man jetzt in Lemma 2 $\varepsilon=1/12$ fixiert und bezeichnet

$$F_n=[0,\pi]\setminus([0,\frac{1}{12n}]\cup B_n),$$

so erhält man

(1) $$\frac{2}{\pi}\int_{F_n}|U_n(t)|dt\geqslant\frac{1}{3}\|L_n\|,\ n\geqslant 1.$$

Da $f^*_n(t)\in H_\omega$, so ist

$$\Delta_n(\omega) \geq |L_n(f_n^*;0) - f_n^*(0)| = |L_n(f_n^*;0)|$$

$$= \frac{2}{\pi} \int_0^\pi |f_n^*(t)|\ |U_n(t)|dt \geq \frac{2}{\pi} \int_{F_n} |f_n^*(t)|\ |U_n(t)|dt.$$

Auf der Menge $F_n$ haben wir $|f_n^*(t)| \geq \frac{1}{3}\,\omega(1/6n)$.
Also, zieht man (1) in Betracht, hat man

$$\Delta_n(\omega) \geq \frac{2}{3\pi}\,\omega(\frac{1}{6n}) \int_{F_n} |U_n(t)|dt \geq \frac{2}{9\pi}\,\omega(\frac{1}{6n})\| L_n\|.$$

Aus diesen Ungleichungen und aus der Bedingung des Theorems folgt

$$\| L_n\| \leq \frac{9\pi\Delta_n(\omega)}{2\omega(\frac{1}{6n})} \leq 27\pi C(n).$$

Das Theorem ist bewiesen.

KOROLLAR. Wenn in der Bedingung des Theorems $C(n) = C$ eine absolute Konstante ist (d.h. wenn die Annäherungsordnung der besten gleich ist), so sind die Normen der linearen Summierungsmethoden $\{\| L_n\|\}$ gleichmäßig beschränkt.

BEMERKUNG. Das Theorem gilt, wenn die Klasse $H_\omega$ durch $W^{(r)}H_\omega$ ersetzt wird. Es wird nur etwas die Konstruktion der Funktion $f_n^*(t)$ verändert.

LITERATUR


[1] Baskakov, V.A. Die Annäherungsordnung der stetigen Funktionen durch die linearen Summierungsmethoden der Fourier-Reihen. Proc. of the Intern. Conf. on Constructive Function Theory, Varna, 1970. Publ. House of the Bulg. Acad. of Sciences, Sofia, 1972, (russisch).

[2] Zygmund, A. Trigonometrische Reihen. V.I.Mir, Moskwa, 1965 (russisch).

[3] Efimov, A.V. Lineare Methoden der Annäherung einiger Klassen der stetigen periodischen Funktionen. Trudi Mat. Inst. Steklov 62 (1961), 3-47 (russisch).

# VI
# Best Approximation and Splines

# $L_p[-1,1]$ APPROXIMATION BY ALGEBRAIC POLYNOMIALS

R. DeVore[1)]

Department of Mathematics and Computer Science

University of South Carolina

Columbia, South Carolina 29208

A characterization of the classical Lipschitz spaces in $L_p[-1,1]$ through approximation by algebraic polynomials is still not known for $1 \le p < \infty$. We show by examples that the characterization suggested from the $L_\infty$ case is not valid for $p < \infty$. We also state some results of a more positive nature which give estimates for weighted approximation by algebraic polynomials in $L_p[-1,1]$ $1 \le p < \infty$.

## 1. Introduction

The problem is to characterize the Lipschitz spaces in $L_p[-1,1]$, $1 \le p < \infty$, through algebraic polynomial approximation. This is one of the more intriguing questions still unanswered in one variable constructive function theory. The case $p = \infty$ is of course settled through the work of A. F. Timan [6], V. Dzadyk [3], G. Freud [4], and Yu. Brudnyi [2]. Namely, if we let Lip $(\alpha,p,r)$, $r = 1,2,\ldots$ $0 < \alpha \le r$, $1 \le p \le \infty$, be the set of functions f for which $\omega_r(f,t)_p = 0(t^\alpha)$, then $f \in$ Lip $(\alpha,\infty,r)$, $0 < \alpha < r$ if and only if there are polynomials $p_n \in P_n$, $n = 1,2,\ldots$ so that

$$||\Delta_n^{-\alpha}(f-p_n)||_\infty = 0(1) \qquad (n \to \infty) \tag{1}$$

with $\Delta_n(x) \equiv \sqrt{(1-x^2)n^{-1} + n^{-2}}$. Here, the key ingredient is the weight $\Delta_n$ which indicates improved approximation near the endpoints of the interval.

It might be expected that the condition (1.1) for the $L_p$ norm instead of $L_\infty$ norm would characterize Lip $(\alpha,p,r)$ for $1 \le p < \infty$ as well. This

1) This research was supported by a National Science Foundation Grant MCS76-05847 and Sonderforschungsbereich 72 der Universität Bonn.

fails to be the case, although just barely, as we will show in this paper. Indeed, if $0 < \alpha < 1$, $1 \le p < \infty$, then for each n there is a function $f_n \in \mathrm{Lip}\,(\alpha,p,1)$ so that

(1.2) $$\inf_{p_n \in P_n} ||\Delta_n^{-\alpha}(f_n - p_n)||_p \ge \text{const } ||f_n||_{\alpha,p} \log n$$

with $||\ ||_{\alpha,p}$ the Lip $(\alpha,p,1)$ norm

(1.3) $$||g||_{\alpha,p} \equiv \sup_{t>0} t^{-\alpha}||g(\cdot+t)-g(\cdot)||_p + ||g||_p$$

and the constant independent of n.

These functions can be used to show the existence of a function $f \in \mathrm{Lip}\,(\alpha,p,1)$ with

$$\inf_{p_n \in P_n} ||\Delta_n^{-\alpha}(f-p_n)||_p \ne O(1)$$

Actually (1.2) is a tight estimate in that it can be shown that if $f \in \mathrm{Lip}\,(\alpha,p,1)$ then there are polynomials $p_n \in P_n$ with

(1.4) $$||\Delta_n^{-\alpha}(f-p_n)||_p \le \text{const } ||f||_{\alpha,p} \log n, \quad n = 1,2,\ldots$$

We give estimates of this type in Section 3, without proof. Details will appear elsewhere. Another interesting estimate of this type is that when $f \in B_p^{\alpha,p}$, $0 < \alpha < 1$, $1 \le p \le \infty$, then there are $p_n \in P_n$ with

(1.5) $$||\Delta_n^{-\alpha}(f-p_n)||_p \le \text{const } ||f||_{B_p^{\alpha,p}}$$

where the $B_p^{\alpha,q}$ are the usual Besov spaces. This last result indicates better the scaling with p since the space $B^{\alpha,\infty}$ is Lip $(\alpha,\infty,1)$. The estimates (1.4) and (1.5) are derived using interpolation theory. In fact, they are both contained in inequality (3.3) which gives an estimate for weighted $L_p$ approximation by algebraic polynomials through K functionals. This latter inequality may actually characterize the spaces Lip $(\alpha,p,1)$. Such a characterization would require an inverse theorem to (3.3).

## 2. The Counterexample

We want to construct functions in Lip $(\alpha,p)$ which cannot be approximated well by algebraic polynomials in the $L_p(\Delta_n^{-\alpha})$ norm. We will carry this out only for the case $p = 1$ since the case $p > 1$ is considerably more technical.

Let n be a positive integer which is a multiple of 4, $n = 4m$. Define $x_s = \cos s\pi(3n)^{-1}$ for any real number $0 \le s \le 3n/2$, set $J_j = [x_{2j}, x_{2j-1}]$, $I_j = [x_{2j-1}, x_{2j-2}]$ $j = 1,\ldots,3n$. The intervals $I_j$ and $J_j$ with $0 \le j \le 3m$ are all contained in $[0,1]$ and they get smaller as they get closer to 1.

In fact, there are constants $A_1$, $A_2$, $B_1$, $B_2 > 0$ such that

(2.1) $$A_1 n^{-2} j \le |I_j| \le |J_j| \le A_2 n^{-2} j \qquad j = 1,2,\ldots,3m$$

(2.2) $$B_1 \Delta_n(x) \le |I_j| \le |J_j| \le B_2 \Delta_n(x),\ x \in I_j \cup J_j,\ j = 1,\ldots,3m.$$

We will now define for each n a function $f_n$ which can not be approximated well by polynomials in the $L_1(\Delta_n^{-\alpha})$ norm. Later we can take an appropriate combination of these $f_n$ to get one function which is not approximated well for all n. Through the remainder of this section $0 < \alpha < 1$ is fixed and we do not indicate dependence of constants on $\alpha$.

Define

(2.3) $$f_n(x) = \begin{cases} j^{\alpha-2}\, n^{-2\alpha+2} = \gamma_j, & x \in I_j,\ j = 1,\ldots,3m \\ 0 & \text{otherwise.} \end{cases}$$

In particular $f_n(x) = 0$ for $-\pi \le x \le 0$. For any function $g \in$ Lip $(\alpha,1,1)$ let

$$||g||_{\alpha,1} \equiv ||g||_1 + \sup_{t>0} t^{-\alpha}||g(\cdot+t)-g(\cdot)||_1[-1,1-t].$$

LEMMA 1. <u>There is a constant</u> c > 0 <u>so that</u>

(2.4) $$||f_n||_{\alpha,1} \le c$$

(2.5) $$||f_n(\cdot+t) - f_n(\cdot)||_1 \le c\, n^{-\alpha},\ 0 < t$$

(2.6) $$||f_n(\cdot+t) - f_n(\cdot)||_1 \le c\ t\ n^{-2\alpha+2}, \qquad t \le n^{-2}.$$

PROOF. The function $\phi_n(x) = |f_n(x+t) - f_n(x)|$ can assume only the values 0, $\gamma_j$ or $\gamma_j - \gamma_k$ for some j and k. Each $\gamma_j$ will appear at most four times and each time for an interval of length at most min $(|I_j|, t)$ because when x, x+t are both in $I_j$, $\phi_n(x) = 0$. Hence,

(2.7) $$\int_{-1}^{1-t} |\phi_n(x)| dx \le 4 \sum_{j=1}^{3m} \gamma_j \min(|I_j|, t) \le \text{const} \sum_{j=1}^{3m} \gamma_j \min(t, jn^{-2})$$

because of (2.1). So if $in^{-1} < t \le (i+1)n^{-1}$ with $0 \le i \le 3m-1$ we get

(2.8) $$\int_{-1}^{1-t} |\phi_n(x)| dx \le \text{const}\ \{(\frac{i}{n^2})^{\alpha} + t\ (\frac{i+1}{n^2})^{\alpha-1}\}$$

this together with the fact that

$$\int_{-1}^{1-t} |\phi_n(x)| dx \le 2\ ||f_n||_1 \le \text{const}\ n^{-\alpha}$$

gives (2.4) and (2.5). The inequality (2.6) follows from (2.8) when i = 0.

We turn now to showing that a polynomial $p_n$ of degree n can not approximate $f_n$ well in the weighted $L_1(\Delta_n^{-\alpha})$ space. The reason for this is that the polynomial would have to be close to the value $\gamma_j$ on the interval $I_j$ (at least for many j's) and close to 0 on the intervals $J_j$, a very ambitious polynomial!

Let $J = \bigcup_{k=1}^{6m} J_k$ and $I = \bigcup_{k=1}^{6m} I_k$. We want to show that the integral of a polynomial over I can be estimated by its integral over J.

LEMMA 2. <u>There is a constant</u> $c > 0$ <u>so that for each polynomial</u> p <u>of degree</u> $\le n$

$$\int_I \Delta_n^{-\alpha}(x)|p(x)| dx \le c \int_J \Delta_n^{-\alpha}(x)|p(x)| dx.$$

PROOF. This is proved by establishing similar inequalities for trigonometric polynomials. Let $\theta_k = 2\pi k(3n)^{-1}$, $k = 0,1,\dots,3n-1$ and $-\infty < s < \infty$. If T is any trigonometric polynomial of degree $\le n$, we have (see [7, p.33])

$$(2.9) \qquad T(\theta) = \frac{2}{3n} \sum_{k=0}^{3n-1} T(\theta_k+s)\, V_n(\theta-\theta_k-s)$$

where

$$V_n(t) = \frac{\sin(3nt/2)\sin(nt/2)}{2n\sin^2(t/2)} .$$

When $0 \le s \le \pi/n$, then $|V_n(\theta-\theta_k-s)| \le \text{const. } n^{-1}[|\theta-\theta_k|+n^{-1}]^{-2}$. So, averaging with respect to s over $[0,\pi n^{-1}]$ in (2.9) gives

$$(2.10) \qquad |T(\theta)| \le \text{const. } n^{-2} \sum_{k=0}^{3n-1} (n\int_{J_k'} T(u)du)\, [|\theta-\theta_k|+n^{-1}]^{-2}$$

where $J_k' = [\theta_k, \theta_k+\pi n^{-1}]$.

Now for our algebraic polynomial p, let $T(\theta) = p(\cos\theta)$. Then (2.10) and the fact that $|\sin u| \ge \frac{k}{n}$ on $J_k'$ gives

$$|P(x)| \le \text{const. } n^{-2} \sum_{k=0}^{3n-1} (\frac{n^2}{k} \int_{J_k} |p(t)|dt)\, [|\theta-\theta_k|+n^{-1}]^{-2}.$$

Now multiply by $\Delta_n^{-\alpha}$ and integrate this last inequality over $I_j$, use (2.1), (2.2) and the fact that $[|\theta-\theta_k|+n^{-1}] \ge \text{const } (|j-k|+1)n^{-1}$ for $\cos\theta = x \in I_j$ to find

$$\int_{I_j} |P(x)|\Delta_n^{-\alpha}(x)dx \le \text{const. } \sum_{k=0}^{3n-1} (\frac{n^2}{k} \int_{J_k} |p(t)|dt)(\frac{j}{n^2})^{1-\alpha}(|k-j|+1)^{-2}.$$

Summing over j gives

$$\begin{aligned}
\int_I |P(x)|\Delta_n^{-\alpha}(x)dx &\le \text{const. } \sum_{k=0}^{3n-1} (\int_{J_k} |p(t)|dt)[\frac{n^2}{k} \sum (\frac{j}{n^2})^{1-\alpha}(|k-j|+1)^{-2}] \\
&\le \text{const. } \sum_{k=0}^{3n-1} (\frac{k}{n^2})^{-\alpha} \int_{J_k} |p(t)|dt \\
&\le \text{const. } \sum_{k=0}^{3n-1} \int_{J_k} |p(t)|\Delta_n^{-\alpha}(t)dt \\
&= \text{const. } \int_J |p(t)|\Delta_n^{-\alpha}(t)dt
\end{aligned}$$

as desired.

It is a simple matter to use Lemma 2 and show that $f_n$ can not be approximated well by polynomials of degree n in the weighted $L_1(\Delta_n^{-\alpha})$ norm.

THEOREM 1. For each n, the function $f_n$ defined by (2.3) has

$$||f_n||_{\alpha,1} \leq c \tag{2.11}$$

$$\inf_{p\in P_n} ||\Delta_n^{-\alpha}(f_n-p)||_1 \geq c \log n \tag{2.12}$$

PROOF. The estimate (2.11) was already given in Lemma 1. If p is any polynomial of degree $\leq$ n and $\delta_n = ||\Delta_n^{-\alpha}(f_n-p)||_1$, then

$$\int_J |p(x)|\Delta_n^{-\alpha}(x)dx \leq \int_J |f_n(x)-p(x)|\Delta_n^{-\alpha}(x)dx \leq \delta_n$$

where J is defined as in Lemma 2. Note that $f_n(x) = 0$, $x \in J$. Using Lemma 2, we have

$$\int_I |p(x)|\Delta_n^{-\alpha}(x)dx \leq \text{const.} \int_J |p(x)|\Delta_n^{-\alpha}(x)dx \leq \text{const.}\ \delta_n.$$

Hence

$$||(f_n-p)\Delta_n^{-\alpha}||_1 \geq ||f_n\Delta_n^{-\alpha}||_1 - ||p\Delta_n^{-\alpha}||_1 \geq ||f_n\Delta_n^{-\alpha}||_1 - \text{const.}\ \delta_n \tag{2.13}$$

On each interval $I_j$, we have from (2.1) and (2.2) that $\Delta_n^{-\alpha}(x) \geq \text{const}\ n^{2\alpha}j^{-\alpha}$. Hence

$$\begin{aligned} ||f_n\Delta_n^{-\alpha}||_1 &\geq \text{const.} \sum_{j=1}^{6m} j^{\alpha-2}(n^2)^{-\alpha+1}n^{2\alpha}j^{-\alpha} \cdot |I_j| \\ &\geq \text{const.} \sum_{j=1}^{6m} j^{-2}n^2\ j\ n^{-2} \geq \text{const.} \sum_{j=1}^{6m} j^{-1} \\ &\geq \text{const.}\ \log 6m \geq \text{const.}\ \log n \end{aligned}$$

this combined with (2.13) and the definition of $\delta_n$ shows that

$$||\Delta_n^{-\alpha}(f_n-p)||_1 \geq \text{const.}\ \log n$$

as desired.

As we have mentioned, we would like to construct one function f which cannot be approximated well by polynomials of degree n for all n. This is easy to accomplish. We need only define $f = \sum_1^\infty f_{\phi_k}$ where $\phi_k = 2^{2^k}$. Since $||f_{\phi_k}|| \le \text{const.}\ \phi_k^{-\alpha}$ for each k, the series converges in $L_1$ to a function in $L^1[-1,1]$. Also, given any $0 < t < 1$, we can write

$$f(x) = \sum_{\phi_k \ge t^{-1}} f_{\phi_k}(x) + \sum_{\phi_k \le t^{-1/2}} f_{\phi_k}(x) + \sum_{t^{-1/2} < \phi_k < t^{-1}} f_{\phi_k}(x)$$

$$= s_1(x) + s_2(x) + s_3(x)$$

where $s_3$ has at most one term in it. Using (2.5) on $s_1$, (2.6) and (2.4) on the one term in $s_3$ we have

$$(2.14) \qquad ||f(\cdot+t)-f(\cdot)||_1 \le \text{const.}\ \{ \sum_{\phi_k > t^{-1}} \phi_k^{-\alpha} + t \sum_{\phi_k < t^{-1/2}} \phi_k^{-2\alpha+2} + t^{\alpha} \}$$
$$\le \text{const.}\ t^{\alpha}$$

so that f is in Lip $(\alpha,1,1)$.

From Lemma 1, it follows that each function $f_{\phi_k}$ is in Lip (1,1,1) and in fact $||f_{\phi_k}||_{1,1} \le \phi_k^{2-2\alpha}$. Hence, as we prove in Section 3 (Lemma 3), there is a polynomial $p_k$ of degree n so that

$$||\Delta_n^{-1}(f_{\phi_k} - p_k)||_1 \le \text{const.}\ \phi_k^{2-2\alpha}.$$

Hence,

$$||\Delta_n^{-\alpha}(f_{\phi_k} - p_k)||_1 \le \text{const.}\ (\phi_k^2 n^{-1})^{1-\alpha}.$$

In particular for each $N = \phi_n$, there is a polynomial p of degree $\le N$ with

$$(2.15) \qquad ||\Delta_N^{-\alpha}(\sum_1^{n-1} f_{\phi_k} - p)||_1 \le \text{const.}\ \sum_1^{n-1} \phi_k^2 \phi_n^{-1} \le \text{const.}$$

On the other hand

$$||\Delta_N^{-\alpha}(\sum_{n+1}^{\infty} f_{\phi_k})||_1 \le \text{const.} N^{2\alpha} \sum_{n+1}^{\infty} \phi_k^{-\alpha} \le \text{const.}\ N^{2\alpha} \phi_{n+1}^{-\alpha} \le \text{const.}$$

Here, we used the fact that $\Delta_N \geq N^{-2}$ and $||f_j|| \leq$ const. $j^{-\alpha}$ for each j.

For the function $f_N$, we know that for any polynomial p of degree $\leq N$, we have

$$||\Delta_N^{-\alpha}(f_N - p)||_1 \geq \text{const. } \log N$$

because of Theorem 1. Thus we have proved the following theorem.

THEOREM 2. *There is a function* f *in* Lip $(\alpha,1,1)$ *for which*

$$\inf_{p\in P_n} ||\Delta_n^{-\alpha}(f-p)||_1 \geq c \log n$$

*for infinitely many* n, *in particular any* n *of the form* $2^{2^k}$.

## 3. Direct Theorems

Let us give some results of a more positive nature which estimate the degree of approximation by algebraic polynomials. Proof of these results are for the most part ommitted and will be given elsewhere. Recall that Lip $(1,p,1)$ is the set of functions f with $f' \in L_p$ if $1 < p \leq \infty$ and $f \in BV$, $p = 1$. Let $||\cdot||_{1,p}$ denote the corresponding norm on Lip $(1,p,1)$.

LEMMA 3. *If* $f \in$ Lip $(1,p,1)$ *and* $n \geq 1$, *then there is a bounded linear operator* $L_n$ *from* $L_p$ *into* $L_p(\Delta_n^{-1})$ *such that for each* n, $L_n(f) = p \in P_n$ *and*

$$||\Delta_n^{-1}(f-p)||_p \leq c\ ||f||_{1,p} \tag{3.1}$$

*where* c *is an absolute constant*.

The proof of this lemma is simple when $p = 1$. Indeed if $g(\theta) = f(\cos\theta)$, then g is also of bounded variation on $[-\pi,\pi]$ and $\int_{-\pi}^{\pi} |dg(\theta)| = 2\int_{-1}^{1}|df(x)|$. Hence, if $\overline{L}_n$ is the classical Jackson operator [5, p. 55] then $T = \overline{L}_n(g)$ is a trigonometric polynomial of degree $\leq n$ with

$$||g-T||_1\ [-\pi,\pi] \leq \text{const. } ||g||_{1,1}\ n^{-1}.$$

Defining $L_n(f) = p(x) = T(\cos\theta)$, when $x = \cos\theta$ and changing to $[-1,1]$ gives

$$||(1-x^2)^{-1}(f(x)-p(x))||_1 = \tfrac{1}{2}||g-T||_1\,[-\pi,\pi]$$

$$\le \text{const. } ||g||_{1,1}\, n^{-1} \le \text{const. } ||f||_{1,1} n^{-1}$$

which is stronger than (3.1) for $p = 1$.

In order to extend (3.1) to general $\alpha$, we use interpolation theory. If we interpolate between $L_p$ and Lip $(1,p,1)$ we have with the K method (see [1]);

$$(L_p, \text{Lip } (1,p,1))_{\theta,\infty} = \text{Lip } (\theta,p,1) \quad 0 < \theta < 1.$$

We need also to check interpolation between $L_p$ and $L_p(\Delta_n^{-1})$. It is an easy estimate to show that there are constants $c_1$, $c_2 > 0$ such that

$$(3.2) \qquad c_1\, K(f,t,L_p,L_p(\Delta_n^{-1})) \le \{\int_{-1}^{1} \min(1,t\Delta_n^{-1}(x))|f(x)|^p dx\}^{1/p}$$

$$c_2\, K\,(f,t,L_p,L_p(\Delta_n^{-1})).$$

Hence Lemma 3 gives the following theorem

THEOREM 3. *If* $f \in$ Lip $(\alpha,p,1)$, $n \ge 1$ *and* $L_n$ *is the operator from* Lemma 3, *then* $p = L_n(f)$ *satisfies*

$$(3.3) \qquad ||\min\,(1,t\Delta_n^{-1}(\cdot))(f(\cdot)-p(\cdot))||_p\,[-1,1] \le \text{const. } t^{\alpha}||f||_{\alpha,p}$$

*for all* $t > 0$.

It is very important in this theorem that (3.3) holds for all $t > 0$. By varying $t$ one obtains sharper inequalities. In fact, the inequalities (3.3) falls just short of giving

$$||\Delta_n^{-\alpha}(f-p)||_p\,[-1,1] \le \text{const. } ||f||_{\alpha,p}[-1,1].$$

Let us mention two corollaries of Theorem 3.

COROLLARY 1. *If* $0 < \alpha < 1$, $f \in$ Lip $(\alpha,p,1)$ *and* $n \ge 1$, *then there is a polynomial* $p \in P_n$ *such that*

$$(3.4) \qquad ||\Delta_n^{-\alpha}(f-p)||_p\,[-1,1] \le c\,\log n$$

*with* c *depending only on* p.

This result can not be improved in the sense that Theorem 2 shows the existence of a function for which the opposite inequality in (3.4) holds for infinitely many n.

COROLLARY 2. *If* $0 < \alpha < 1$, $1 \le p \le \infty$, $n \ge 1$ *and* f *is in the Besov space* $B_p^{\alpha,p}$, *then there is a polynomial* $p \in P_n$ *such that*

$$||\Delta_n^{-\alpha}(f-p)||_p \le \text{const.}\ ||f||_{B_p^{\alpha,p}}. \tag{3.5}$$

This last result gives a natural seating of spaces, namely $B_p^{\alpha,p}$, $1 \le p \le \infty$, for which the case $p = \infty$ gives the classical result (1.1).

## REFERENCES

1 Butzer, P. L. - Berens, H., *Semi-Groups of Operations and Approximation*. Springer Verlag, Berlin, 1967.

2 Brudnyi, Yu., *Generalizations of a theorem of A. F. Timan*. Soviet Math. Dokl. *4* (1963), 244-247.

3 Dzadyk, V. K., *A further strengthening of Jackson's theorem on the approximation of continuous functions by ordinary polynomials*. Doklady, *121* (1959), 641-643.

4 Freud G., *Über die Approximation reeler stetiger Funktionen durch gewöhnliche Polynome*. Math. Anal., *137* (1959).

5 Lorentz, G. G., *Approximation of Functions*, Holt, N.Y., 1966.

6 Timan, A. F., *Strengthening of Jackson's theorem on the best approximation of continuous functions on a finite segment of the real axis*. Doklady *78* (1951), 17-20.

7 Zygmund, A., *Trigonometric Series*. vol. II, Cambridge V. Press, N.Y., 1959.

# GEWICHTETE BESTE APPROXIMATION STETIGER FUNKTIONEN DURCH ALGEBRAISCHE POLYNOME

R.L. Stens
Lehrstuhl A für Mathematik
Rheinisch-Westfälische Technische Hochschule
Aachen

A result of Teljakovskiĭ (1966) and Gopengauz (1967) shows that in Timan's (1951) and Dzjadyk's (1956/58) theorems on best approximation of continuous functions by algebraic polynomials the weight function $\Delta_n(x) = \sqrt{1-x^2}/n+n^{-2}$ can be replaced by $\delta_n(x) = \sqrt{1-x^2}/n$. The matter is similar for Trigub's (1962) theorem on simultaneous approximation. The associated Zamansky-type assertion and its converse for $\Delta_n(x)$ were shown by Scherer and Wagner (1972). The purpose of this paper is to establish the counterpart of the latter result for the weight $\delta_n(x)$, so that the assertions of the theorems of Teljakovskiĭ, Trigub, Scherer - Wagner, and their converses are equivalent with respect to $\delta_n(x)$.

## 1. Einleitung

Wie üblich sei $C[-1,1]$ der Raum aller auf dem Intervall $[-1,1]$ definierten, stetigen Funktionen f mit der Norm $\|f\|_C := \sup_{x\in[-1,1]} |f(x)|$ und

$$\mathrm{Lip}_\rho\, \alpha := \{f \in C[-1,1]\,;\ \omega_\rho(f;t) = \mathcal{O}(t^\alpha),\ t\to 0+\}$$

die Lipschitzklasse der Ordnung $\alpha > 0$ bezüglich des $\rho$-ten Stetigkeitsmoduls $\rho$ $\rho \in \mathbb{N}=\{1,2,3,\dots\}$, (vgl. [7, S. 47]). Damit läßt sich die beste Approximation durch algebraische Polynome wie folgt charakterisieren.

SATZ 1.1. Seien $j,k,r \in \mathbb{P} = \{0,1,2,\dots\}$, $0 < \alpha \leq 1$ mit $0 \leq j < r+\alpha < k$, $\Delta_n(x) = \sqrt{1-x^2}/n+n^{-2}$, dann sind für $f \in C[-1,1]$ folgende Aussagen äquivalent:

(i) es existiert eine Folge $\{p_{1,n}\}_{n=1}^\infty$, $p_{1,n} \in \mathcal{P}_n = \mathrm{span}\,\{1,x,x^2,\dots,x^n\}$, mit

(1.1) $$\left\| \frac{f(\cdot) - p_{1,n}(\cdot)}{[n\Delta_n(\cdot)]^{r+\alpha}} \right\|_C = \mathcal{O}(n^{-(r+\alpha)}) \qquad (n\to\infty),$$

(ii) $f^{(j)} \in C[-1,1]$, <u>und es existiert eine Folge</u> $\{p_{2,n}\}_{n=1}^{\infty}$, $p_{2,n} \in \mathcal{P}_n$, <u>mit</u>

$$\left\| \frac{f^{(j)}(\cdot) - p_{2,n}^{(j)}(\cdot)}{[n\Delta_n(\cdot)]^{r+\alpha-j}} \right\|_C = \mathcal{O}(n^{-(r+\alpha-j)}) \qquad (n\to\infty),$$

(iii) $$f^{(r)} \in \begin{cases} \mathrm{Lip}_1\,\alpha\ , & 0<\alpha<1 \\ \mathrm{Lip}_2\,1\ , & \alpha=1 \end{cases},$$

(iv) <u>für die Polynome bester Approximation</u> $\overline{p}_n(r+\alpha,f;x)$, <u>definiert durch</u>

(1.2) $$\hat{E}_n(f;\lambda) \equiv \inf_{p_n\in\mathcal{P}_n} \left\| \frac{f(\cdot) - p_n(\cdot)}{[n\Delta_n(\cdot)]^{r+\alpha}} \right\|_C = \left\| \frac{f(\cdot) - \overline{p}_n(r+\alpha,f;\cdot)}{[n\Delta_n(\cdot)]^{r+\alpha}} \right\|_C$$

<u>gilt</u>

$$\begin{cases} \lim_{n\to\infty} \left\| \dfrac{f(\cdot) - \overline{p}_n(r+\alpha,f;\cdot)}{[n\Delta_n(\cdot)]^{r+\alpha}} \right\|_C = 0 \\ \left\| \dfrac{\overline{p}_n^{(k)}(r+\alpha,f;\cdot)}{[n\Delta_n(\cdot)]^{r+\alpha-k}} \right\|_C = \mathcal{O}(n^{-(r+\alpha-k)}) \qquad (n\to\infty). \end{cases}$$

Die Implikationen (iii) ⇒ (i) dieses Satzes für $0<\alpha<1$ ist das bekannte Ergebnis von Timan [12], während der Fall $\alpha=1$ sowie (i) ⇒ (iii) für $0<\alpha\leqslant 1$ von Dzjadyk [3,2] und (iii) ⇒ (ii) von Trigub [13] stammen. Die Aussage vom Zamansky-Typ (i) ⇒ (iv) und deren Umkehrung stammen von Scherer-Wagner [9], von denen auch der Satz in der vorliegenden Form angegeben wurde.

G.G. Lorentz [8] stellte auf der Oberwolfacher Tagung von 1963 die Frage, ob man in der Aussage (iii) ⇒ (i) die Gewichtsfunktion $n\Delta_n(x) \equiv \sqrt{1-x^2} + n^{-1}$ nicht durch die von n unabhängige Funktion $n\delta_n(x) \equiv \sqrt{1-x^2}$ ersetzen kann. Diese wurde von Teljakovskiĭ [11] und Gopengauz [5,6] positiv beantwortet, letzterer bewies sogar (iii) ⇒ (ii) für dieses Gewicht. Die Umkehrungen (i) ⇒ (iii), (ii) ⇒ (iii) gelten trivialerweise für $\delta_n(x)$, da in diesen Fällen die Voraussetzungen stärker sind als bei $\Delta_n(x)$. Das Ziel dieser Arbeit ist es zu zeigen, daß auch die Äquivalenz von (i) - (iii) zu (iv) richtig bleibt, wenn man $\Delta_n(x)$ durch $\delta_n(x)$ ersetzt. Wir werden sogar beweisen, daß für beliebige $\lambda \in \mathbb{R}$ (=Menge der reellen Zahlen), positive $\beta$ und ganze Zahlen $k > \max\{\lambda,\beta\}$ die Aussagen

$$\left\| \frac{f(\cdot) - p_n(\cdot)}{[n\delta_n(\cdot)]^\lambda} \right\|_C = \mathcal{O}(n^{-\beta}) \qquad (n \to \infty),$$

für eine geeignete Folge von Polynomen $p_n$, und

$$\begin{cases} \lim\limits_{n\to\infty} \left\| \dfrac{f(\cdot) - p_n^*(\cdot)}{[n\delta_n(\cdot)]^\lambda} \right\|_C = 0 \\ \left\| \dfrac{(p_n^*)^{(k)}(\cdot)}{[n\delta_n(\cdot)]^{\lambda-k}} \right\|_C = \mathcal{O}(n^{-(\beta-k)}) \qquad (n \to \infty) \end{cases}$$

äquivalent sind. Hierin sind die $p_n^*(x) \equiv p_n^*(\lambda,f;x)$ wiederum Polynome bester Approximation, die durch eine Gleichung vom Typ (1.2) mit Gewicht $[n\delta_n(x)]^\lambda$ definiert werden. Die entsprechende Verallgemeinerung der Scherer-Wagner Aussage von $r+\alpha$ zu $\lambda \in \mathbb{R}$ auf der linken Seite in (1.1) und von $r+\alpha$ zu $\beta > 0$ auf der rechten Seite in (1.1) wurde von v. Golitscheck [4] bewiesen.

Der Autor möchte sich bei Herrn Professor P.L. Butzer und Herrn Dr. J.J. Junggeburth für zahlreiche Hinweise und die Durchsicht des Manuskriptes bedanken.

## 2. Die Polynome bester Approximation

Wie üblich sei die beste Approximation zu $f \in C[-1,1]$ bezüglich Gewicht $[n\delta_n(x)]^\lambda \equiv \sqrt{1-x^2}^{\,\lambda}$, $\lambda \in \mathbb{R}$, definiert durch

$$E_n(f;\lambda) := \inf_{p_n \in \mathcal{P}_n} \sup_{x \in (-1,1)} \left| \frac{f(x) - p_n(x)}{\sqrt{1-x^2}^{\,\lambda}} \right| \equiv \inf_{p_n \in \mathcal{P}_n} \|f - p_n\|_\lambda ,$$

mit $\|g\|_\lambda := \sup_{x \in (-1,1)} |g(x)\sqrt{1-x^2}^{\,-\lambda}|$.

Für $\lambda \leqslant 0$ ist $\|\cdot\|_\lambda$ eine Norm auf $C[-1,1]$, und somit existiert zu jedem $n \in \mathbb{N}$ und $f \in C[-1,1]$ ein $p_n^*(x) \equiv p_n^*(\lambda,f;x) \in \mathcal{P}_n$ mit

$$(2.1) \qquad E_n(f;\lambda) = \|f - p_n^*\|_\lambda .$$

Ist $\lambda > 0$, dann ist $\|\cdot\|_\lambda$ keine Norm mehr, aber es gilt dennoch:

SATZ 2.1. Zu jedem $f \in C[-1,1]$, $\lambda \in \mathbb{R}$ und $n \in \mathbb{N}$ existiert (mindestens) ein Polynom $p_n^* \in P_n$, das (2.1) erfüllt.

BEWEIS. Nach den Vorbemerkungen genügt es, $\lambda > 0$ zu untersuchen. Ebenso können wir $E_n(f;\lambda) < \infty$ annehmen, da sonst jedes Polynom (2.1) erfüllt. Zunächst fordern wir außerdem $\|f\|_\lambda < \infty$ und setzen

$$\tilde{P}_n = \{\tilde{p}_n \in P_n;\ \|f - \tilde{p}_n\|_\lambda < \infty\}.$$

Das Paar $\tilde{P}_n$, $\|\cdot\|_\lambda$ bildet einen endlichdimensionalen, linearen, normierten Raum; es gilt

$$E_n(f;\lambda) = \inf_{\tilde{p}_n \in \tilde{P}_n} \|f - \tilde{p}_n\|_\lambda .$$

Analog zu den bekannten Beweisen über die Existenz von Elementen bester Approximation (vgl. [1,S.20]) betrachten wir jetzt die Abbildung $T : \tilde{P}_n \to \mathbb{R}$, definiert durch

$$T\tilde{p}_n = \|f - \tilde{p}_n\|_\lambda \qquad (\tilde{p}_n \in \tilde{P}_n).$$

Da die Abbildung T stetig auf $\tilde{P}_n$ ist, nimmt sie auf der kompakten Menge

$$B := \{\tilde{p}_n \in \tilde{P}_n;\ \|f - \tilde{p}_n\|_\lambda \leq \|f\|_\lambda\}$$

ihr Minimum in einem Punkt $p_n^*$ an. Damit gilt

$$\|f - p_n^*\|_\lambda = \inf_{\tilde{p}_n \in B} \|f - \tilde{p}_n\|_\lambda = \inf_{\tilde{p}_n \in \tilde{P}_n} \|f - \tilde{p}_n\|_\lambda = E_n(f;\lambda),$$

womit der Satz für $\|f\|_\lambda < \infty$ bewiesen ist.

Im allgemeinen Fall existiert wegen $E_n(f;\lambda) < \infty$ ein $\hat{q}_n \in P_n$ mit $\|f - \hat{q}_n\|_\lambda < \infty$. Wie gerade bewiesen, gibt es dann ein $q_n^*$ mit

$$E_n(f - \hat{q}_n;\lambda) = \|(f - \hat{q}_n) - q_n^*\|_\lambda ,$$

und die Behauptung des Satzes folgt wegen $E_n(f-\hat{q}_n;\lambda) = E_n(f;\lambda)$.

## 3. Die Zamansky-Typ-Aussage

Zum Beweis der folgenden Sätze benötigen wir eine Bernstein-Typ-Ungleichung, die in dieser speziellen Form von Dzjadyk [2] bewiesen wurde.

LEMMA 3.1. *Sei* $P_n \in \mathcal{P}_n$ *mit*

$$|P_n(x)| \leq (\Delta_n(x))^{\sigma} \qquad (x \in [-1,1])$$

*für ein* $\sigma \in \mathbb{R}$, *dann gilt für alle* $\nu \in \mathbb{N}$

$$|P_n^{(\nu)}(x)| \leq M(\Delta_n(x))^{\sigma-\nu} \qquad (x \in [-1,1])$$ [1],

*wobei* M *eine von* n *und* $P_n$ *unabhängige Konstante ist.*

Unser erstes Ziel ist der Beweis einer Aussage vom Typ (i) ⇒ (iv) in Satz 1.1, die im Falle der besten trigonometrischen Approximation von Zamansky [14] bewiesen wurde.

SATZ 3.2. *Sei* $f \in C[-1,1]$, $\lambda \in \mathbb{R}$, $\beta > 0$ *und* $k \in \mathbb{N}$ *mit* $k > \max\{\beta,\lambda\}$. *Falls eine Folge von Polynomen* $\{p_n\}_{n=1}^{\infty}$, $p_n \in \mathcal{P}_n$, *die Bedingung*

$$(3.1) \qquad \|f - p_n\|_{\lambda} = \mathcal{O}(n^{-\beta}) \qquad (n \to \infty)$$

*erfüllt, dann folgt*

$$(3.2) \qquad \|p_n^{(k)}\|_{\lambda-k} = \mathcal{O}(n^{-(\beta-k)}) \qquad (n \to \infty).$$

BEWEIS. Wir gehen vor wie in [4] (vgl. [9]). Wegen (3.1) existiert eine von n und x unabhängige Konstante $M > 0$ und ein $s_0 \in \mathbb{N}$ mit

1) Im folgenden bezeichne M stets eine Konstante, deren Wert von Fall zu Fall verschieden sein kann. Die Abhängigkeit oder Unabhängigkeit von irgendwelchen Parametern geben wir nur in der Formulierung einer Aussage, beziehungsweise beim ersten Auftreten innerhalb eines Beweises an.

$$|f(x) - p_n(x)| \leqslant M\sqrt{1-x^2}^{\lambda} n^{-\beta} \qquad (x \in [-1,1],\ n \geqslant 2^{s_0}),$$

woraus für beliebige $n_1, n_2 \in \mathbb{N}$ mit $2^{s_0} \leqslant n_1 < n_2 \leqslant 2n_1$ folgt

$$|n_2^{\beta-\lambda}(p_{n_1}(x) - p_{n_2}(x))| \leqslant M(\delta_{n_2}(x))^{\lambda} \leqslant M(\Delta_{n_2}(x))^{\lambda} \qquad (x \in [-1,1]).$$

Hierauf wenden wir La. 3.1. an und erhalten

$$|n_2^{\beta-\lambda}(p_{n_1}^{(k)}(x) - p_{n_2}^{(k)}(x))| \leqslant M(\Delta_{n_2}(x))^{\lambda-k} \leqslant M(\delta_{n_2}(x))^{\lambda-k} \quad (x \in [-1,1]),$$

was wir auch in der Form

$$(3.3) \qquad \| p_{n_1}^{(k)} - p_{n_2}^{(k)} \|_{\lambda-k} \leqslant M n_2^{k-\beta}$$

schreiben können.

Sei nun zu $n \geqslant 2^{s_0}$ ein $s \in \mathbb{N}$ so gewählt, daß $2^s < n \leqslant 2^{s+1}$, dann erhält man mit (3.3)

$$\| p_n^{(k)} \| \leqslant \| p_n^{(k)} - p_{2^s}^{(k)} \|_{\lambda-k} + \| p_{2^{s_0}}^{(k)} \|_{\lambda-k} + \sum_{i=s_0+1}^{s} \| p_{2^i}^{(k)} - p_{2^{i-1}}^{(k)} \|_{\lambda-k}$$

$$\leqslant M n^{k-\beta} + \| p_{2^{s_0}}^{(k)} \|_{\lambda-k} + \sum_{i=s_0+1}^{s} 2^{i(k-\beta)} = \mathcal{O}(n^{k-\beta}).$$

Dabei haben wir noch benutzt, daß $\| p_{2^{s_0}}^{(k)} \|_{\lambda-k} < \infty$, da $\lambda - k < 0$.

## 4. Die Umkehrung der Zamansky-Aussage

Während der Beweis von Satz 3.2 dieselben Methoden benutzte wie der Beweis der entsprechenden Aussage in Satz 1.1, benötigen wir für die Umkehrung eine Reihe weiterer Hilfsmittel. Zunächst eine Verschärfung einer Aussage von Gopengauz [5]:

LEMMA 4.1. <u>Sei</u> $P_n \in \mathcal{P}_n$ <u>mit</u>

$$(4.1) \qquad |P_n(x)| \leqslant (\Delta_n(x))^{\mu+\sigma} \qquad (x \in [-1,1]),$$

für ein $\mu \in \mathbb{P}$ und ein $0 < \sigma \leqslant 1$, sowie $P_n^{(\nu)}(\pm 1) = 0$ für $0 \leqslant \nu \leqslant s$.

a) Ist $s = [\mu/2]$ ($= \max \{i \in \mathbb{P};\ i \leqslant \mu/2\}$), dann existiert eine Konstante $M$, die nur von $\mu$ und $\sigma$ abhängig ist, mit

$$|P_n(x)| \leqslant M(\delta_n(x))^{\mu+\sigma} \qquad (x \in [-1,1]).$$

b) Ist $s = \mu$, und $0 < \varepsilon < 2(\mu+\sigma)$, dann gilt mit einer nur von $\mu$ und $\sigma$ abhängenden Konstanten $M$

$$|P_n(x)| \leqslant Mn^{-\varepsilon}\sqrt{1-x^2}^{\,2(\mu+\sigma)-\varepsilon} \qquad (x \in [-1,1]).$$

BEWEIS. Für $\sqrt{1-x^2} \geqslant 1/n$ gilt

$$(\Delta_n(x))^{\mu+\sigma} \leqslant (2\delta_n(x))^{\mu+\sigma} \leqslant 2^{\mu+\sigma} n^{-\varepsilon}\sqrt{1-x^2}^{\,2(\mu+\sigma)-\varepsilon},$$

womit a) und b) für diese $x \in [-1,1]$ bewiesen sind.

Sei jetzt $\sqrt{1-x^2} \leqslant 1/n$ und $x \geqslant 0$. Mittels Taylorentwicklung um $x_0 = 1$ erhalten wir wegen $P_n^{(\nu)}(1) = 0$, $0 \leqslant \nu \leqslant s$, für ein $\xi \in (x,1)$

$$(4.2) \qquad P_n(x) = \frac{(x-1)^{s+1}}{(s+1)!} P_n^{(s+1)}(\xi).$$

Aus (4.1) und $n^{-2} \leqslant \Delta_n(\xi) \leqslant 2n^{-2}$ folgt jetzt mit La. 3.1

$$|P_n(x)| \leqslant M(1-x^2)^{s+1}(\Delta_n(\xi))^{\mu+\sigma-s-1} \leqslant M(1-x^2)^{s+1} n^{-2(\mu+\sigma-s-1)}$$

Da $n\sqrt{1-x^2} \leqslant 1$ und $2s+2-\mu-\sigma \geqslant 0$, gilt

$$(1-x^2)^{s+1} n^{-2(\mu+\sigma-s-1)} \leqslant (\delta_n(x))^{\mu+\sigma}(n\sqrt{1-x^2})^{2s+2-\mu-\sigma} \leqslant (\delta_n(x))^{\mu+\sigma},$$

womit Teil a) bewiesen ist. Teil b) folgt mit $2-2\sigma+\varepsilon \geqslant 0$ aus

$$(1-x^2)^{s+1} n^{-2(\mu+\sigma-s-1)} = n^{-\varepsilon}\sqrt{1-x^2}^{\,2(\mu+\sigma)-\varepsilon}(n\sqrt{1-x^2})^{2-2\sigma+\varepsilon}$$

$$\leqslant n^{-\varepsilon}\sqrt{1-x^2}^{\,2(\mu+\sigma)-\varepsilon}.$$

Den letzten Fall $\sqrt{1-x^2} \leqslant 1/n$, $x < 0$ erhält man schließlich noch analog zu

$x \geqslant 0$ mit Taylorentwicklung um $x_o = -1$.

LEMMA 4.2. Sei $\mu \in \mathbb{P}$, $0 < \sigma \leqslant 1$, $n \in \mathbb{N}$ mit $n \geqslant \mu + 1$ und $P_{2n} \in \mathcal{P}_{2n}$ mit

$$(4.3) \qquad |P_{2n}(x)| \leqslant (\Delta_n(x))^{\mu+\sigma} \qquad (x \in [-1,1]),$$

dann existiert eine Konstante M, die nur von $\mu$ und $\sigma$ abhängt, und ein $R_n \in \mathcal{P}_n$, so daß

$$|P_{2n}(x) - R_n(x)| \leqslant M(\delta_n(x))^{\mu+\sigma} \qquad (x \in [-1,1]).$$

BEWEIS. Wir benutzen eine Methode von Teljakovskiĭ [11] und Gopengauz [5]. Sei $s = [\mu/2]$ und

$$R_n(x) := \sum_{i=0}^{s} (x^2-1)^i \{P_{2n}^{(i)}(1) A_{i,s}(x) + P_{2n}^{(i)}(-1) B_{i,s}(x)\}$$

$$(4.4) \qquad \begin{aligned} A_{i,s}(x) &:= \sum_{\kappa=0}^{s-i} \frac{1}{i!\kappa!} \left[\frac{1}{(x+1)^{s+1}}\right]^{(\kappa)}_{x=1} (x-1)^{\kappa}(x+1)^{s+1-i} \\ B_{i,s}(x) &:= \sum_{\kappa=0}^{s-i} \frac{1}{i!\kappa!} \left[\frac{1}{(x-1)^{s+1}}\right]^{(\kappa)}_{x=-1} (x+1)^{\kappa}(x-1)^{s+1-i} \end{aligned}$$

Die $R_n$ sind Hermite-Interpolationspolynome höchstens vom Grade $2s+1 \leqslant n$, die den Bedingungen

$$(4.5) \qquad R_n^{(\nu)}(\pm 1) = P_{2n}^{(\nu)}(\pm 1) \qquad (0 \leqslant \nu \leqslant s)$$

genügen. Weiter folgt mit La. 3.1 aus (4.3)

$$|P_{2n}^{(\nu)}(\pm 1)| \leqslant M n^{-2(\mu+\sigma-\nu)} \qquad (0 \leqslant \nu \leqslant s),$$

wobei M nur von $\mu$ und $\sigma$ abhängt. Für die $R_n$ ergibt sich daraus

$$(4.6) \qquad |R_n(x)| \leqslant M \max_{0 \leqslant i \leqslant s} \{\|A_{i,s}\|_C + \|B_{i,s}\|_C\} \sum_{i=0}^{s} (1-x^2)^i n^{-2(\mu+\sigma-i)} \cdot \qquad (x \in [-1,1]).$$

Wegen $\sum_{i=0}^{s} (1-x^2)^i n^{-2(\mu+\sigma-i)} \leqslant (s+1)(\Delta_n(x))^{\mu+\sigma}$ erhalten wir aus (4.6)

$$|R_n(x)| \leqslant M(\Delta_n(x))^{\mu+\sigma} \qquad (x\in[-1,1])$$

und schließlich mit (4.3)

$$|P_{2n}(x) - R_n(x)| \leqslant M(\Delta_n(x))^{\mu+\sigma} \qquad (x\in[-1,1]).$$

Zusammen mit den Interpolationsbedingungen (4.5) folgt daraus die Behauptung mit La. 4.1.

Wir zitieren jetzt noch eine Aussage aus [9].

LEMMA 4.3. <u>Sei</u> $g \in C^{(\nu)}[-1,1]$ <u>mit</u>

$$|g^{(\nu)}(x)| \leqslant (\Delta_n(x))^{\tau} \qquad (x\in[-1,1])$$

<u>für ein</u> $\tau \in \mathbb{R}$ <u>und ein</u> $n \geqslant 2\nu$, <u>dann existiert ein</u> $P_n \in \mathcal{P}_n$ <u>mit</u>

$$|g(x) - P_n(x)| \leqslant M(\Delta_n(x))^{\tau+\nu} \qquad (x\in[-1,1]),$$

<u>wobei</u> M <u>nur von</u> $\tau$ <u>und</u> $\nu$ <u>abhängt</u>.

Damit sind wir in der Lage, die Umkehrung zu Satz 3.2 zu beweisen.

SATZ 4.4. <u>Sei</u> $f \in C[-1,1]$ <u>mit</u> $\lim_{n\to\infty} E_n(f;\lambda) = 0$ <u>für ein</u> $\lambda \in \mathbb{R}$. <u>Weiter sei für ein</u> $k \in \mathbb{N}$, $\beta > 0$ <u>mit</u> $k > \max\{\lambda,\beta\}$

$$(4.7) \qquad \|p_n^{(k)}(\lambda,f;\cdot)\|_{\lambda-k} = \mathcal{O}(n^{(k-\beta)}) \qquad (n\to\infty);$$

<u>dann gilt</u>

$$E_n(f;\lambda) = \mathcal{O}(n^{-\beta}) \qquad (n\to\infty).$$

BEWEIS. Wegen $\lim E_n(f;\lambda) = 0$ existiert ein $n_o \in \mathbb{N}$, so daß $E_{n_o}(f;\lambda) < \infty$ und

$$(4.8)\qquad E_n(f;\lambda) = \sum_{i=0}^{\infty} \{E_{n2^i}(f;\lambda) - E_{n2^{i+1}}(f;\lambda)\} \qquad (n \geq n_0).$$

Wegen

$$E_m(f;\lambda) \leq E_m(f - p^*_{2m};\lambda) + E_m(p^*_{2m};\lambda) \leq E_{2m}(f;\lambda) + E_m(p^*_{2m};\lambda)$$

für $m \in \mathbb{N}$ erhalten wir aus (4.8)

$$(4.9)\qquad E_n(f;\lambda) \leq \sum_{i=0}^{\infty} E_{n2^i}(p^*_{n2^{i+1}};\lambda) \qquad (n \geq n_0).$$

Voraussetzung (4.7) liefert zunächst

$$(4.10)\qquad |m^{\lambda+\beta-2k}(p^*_m)^{(k)}(x)| \leq M \qquad (|x| \leq 1 - m^2,\ m \in \mathbb{N}),$$

wobei M unabhängig von m und x ist. Da die linke Seite in (4.10) ein Polynom ist, gilt diese Ungleichung mit einer anderen von m und x unabhängigen Konstanten sogar für alle $x \in [-1,1]$ (vgl. [7,S.43]), so daß zusammen mit (4.7) für $m \in \mathbb{N}$, $x \in [-1,1]$ folgt

$$(4.11)\qquad |m^{\beta-\lambda}(p^*_m)^{(k)}(x)| \leq M \min\{(\delta_m(x))^{\lambda-k}, m^{-2(\lambda-k)}\} \leq M(\Delta_m(x))^{\lambda-k}.$$

Speziell für die Polynome $p^*_{n2^{i+1}}$ lautet (4.11) für $x \in [-1,1]$, $n \in \mathbb{N}$, $i \in \mathbb{P}$

$$|(n2^{i+1})^{\beta-\lambda}(p^*_{n2^{i+1}})^{(k)}(x)| \leq M(\Delta_{n2^{i+1}}(x))^{\lambda-k} \leq M(\Delta_{n2^i}(x))^{\lambda-k}.$$

Nach La. 4.3 existiert nun eine Folge von Polynomen $P_{n2^i} \in \mathcal{P}_{n2^i}$ mit

$$|(n2^{i+1})^{\beta-\lambda}(p^*_{n2^{i+1}})(x) - P_{n2^i}(x)| \leq M(\Delta_{n2^i}(x))^{\lambda}$$

$$(x \in [-1,1],\ n \geq n_0',\ i \in \mathbb{P}).$$

Wendet man darauf La. 4.2 an, dann kann man sogar eine Folge von Polynomen $Q_{n2^i} \in \mathcal{P}_{n2^i}$ finden, für die

$$|(n2^{i+1})^{\beta-\lambda}(p^*_{n2^{i+1}})(x) - Q_{n2^i}(x)| \leq M(\delta_{n2^i}(x))^{\lambda} \quad (x \in [-1,1], n \geq n_0', i \in \mathbb{P})$$

gilt. Daraus folgt unmittelbar

$$E_n(p^*_{n2^{i+1}};\lambda) \leqslant \| p^*_{n2^{i+1}}(\cdot) - (n2^{i+1})^{\lambda-\beta} Q_{n2^i}(\cdot)\|_\lambda \leqslant M(n2^i)^{-\beta} \qquad (n \geqslant n_o',\ i \in \mathbb{P}),$$

und aus (4.9) erhalten wir

$$E_n(f;\lambda) \leqslant M \sum_{i=0}^{\infty} (n2^i)^{-\beta} = \mathcal{O}(n^{-\beta}) \qquad (n \to \infty),$$

womit der Satz bewiesen ist.

Kombiniert man jetzt Satz 3.2 und Satz 4.4 und wählt speziell $\lambda = \beta = r + \alpha$, dann erhält man die zu Satz 1.1 (i) $\Longleftrightarrow$ (iv) analoge Aussage für $\delta_n(x)$.

KOROLLAR 4.5. <u>Seien</u> $k, r \in \mathbb{P}$, $0 < \alpha \leqslant 1$ <u>mit</u> $r + \alpha < k$, <u>dann sind folgende Aussagen für</u> $f \in C[-1,1]$ <u>äquivalent</u>:

(i) <u>es existiert eine Folge</u> $\{p_n\}_{n=1}^{\infty}$, $p_n \in P_n$, <u>mit</u>

$$\left\| \frac{f(\cdot) - p_n(\cdot)}{[n\delta_n(\cdot)]^{r+\alpha}} \right\|_C = \mathcal{O}(n^{-(r+\alpha)}) \qquad (n \to \infty),$$

(ii) $E_n(f; r+\alpha) = o(1)$, $n \to \infty$, <u>und</u>

$$\left\| \frac{(p_n^*)^{(k)}(r+\alpha, f; \cdot)}{[n\delta_n(\cdot)]^{r+\alpha-k}} \right\|_C = \mathcal{O}(n^{-(r+\alpha-k)}) \qquad (n \to \infty).$$

Wählt man dagegen $\lambda = 0$, dann erhält man eine Aussage über die beste Approximation in der gleichmäßigen Norm ohne Gewicht.

KOROLLAR 4.6. <u>Sei</u> $f \in C[-1,1]$, $\beta > 0$, $k \in \mathbb{N}$ <u>mit</u> $k > \beta$, <u>dann sind äquivalent</u>:

(i) $$E_n(f) \equiv \inf_{p_n \in P_n} \| f - p_n\|_C = \mathcal{O}(n^{-\beta}) \qquad (n \to \infty),$$

(ii) <u>für die Polynome bester Approximation</u> $p_n^*(x) = p_n^*(0, f; x)$ <u>gilt</u>

$$|(p_n^*)^{(k)}(x)\sqrt{1-x^2}^{\,k}| = \mathcal{O}(n^{-(\beta-k)}) \qquad (x \in [-1,1],\ n \to \infty).$$

Dieses Ergebnis ist die in [10, Satz 3] fehlende Aussage vom Zamansky-Typ.

## 5. Eine hinreichende Bedingung für $E_n(f;\lambda) = o(1)$

In Satz 1.1 (iv) kann man die Bedingung $\hat{E}_n(f;r+\alpha) = o(1)$ durch eine Lipschitzbedingung an f ersetzen, so etwa durch $f \in \mathrm{Lip}_k\,\gamma$ für ein $\gamma > (r+\alpha)/2$ (vgl. [9]). Diese Bedingung läßt sich noch abschwächen, man kann jedoch zeigen, daß

$$\left\| \frac{\bar{P}_n^{(k)}(r+\alpha;f;\cdot)}{[n\Delta_n(\cdot)]^{r+\alpha}} \right\|_C = O(n^{-(r+\alpha-k)}) \qquad (n \to \infty)$$

ohne Zusatzbedingung zumindest für bestimmte Werte von $r+\alpha$ nicht äquivalent zu den übrigen Aussagen in Satz 1.1 ist (vgl. [4]). Wir wollen jetzt noch zeigen, daß man $E_n(f;\lambda) = o(1)$ auch in Satz 4.4 durch eine Lipschitzbedingung ersetzen kann. Hierbei ist natürlich nur der Fall $\lambda > 0$ interessant, da für $\lambda \leqslant 0$ nach dem Satz von Weierstraß zu jedem $f \in C[-1,1]$ immer eine Folge von Polynomen $\{p_n\}$ existiert mit $\lim \|f - p_n\|_C = 0$.

SATZ 5.1. <u>Sei</u> $\lambda > 0$ <u>und</u> $f \in \mathrm{Lip}_k\,\gamma$ <u>für ein</u> $k \in \mathbb{N}$, <u>und</u> $\lambda/2 < \gamma$, <u>dann existiert eine Folge von Polynomen</u> $\{p_n\}_{n=n_0}^{\infty}$, $p_n \in P_n$, <u>so daß für ein</u> $\varepsilon > 0$ <u>gilt</u>

$$|f(x) - p_n(x)| \leqslant M n^{-\varepsilon} \sqrt{1-x^2}^{\,\lambda} \qquad (x \in [-1,1],\ n \geqslant n_0),$$

<u>wobei</u> M <u>unabhängig von</u> x <u>und</u> n <u>ist. Insbesondere gilt also</u> $E_n(f;\lambda) = o(1), n \to \infty$.

BEWEIS. Zu $f \in \mathrm{Lip}_k\,\gamma$ existiert eine Folge von Polynomen $q_n \in P_n$ mit

$$(5.1) \qquad |f(x) - q_n(x)| \leqslant M(\Delta_n(x))^{\gamma} \qquad (x \in [-1,1],\ n \in \mathbb{N}).$$

Wählt man $\mu \in \mathbb{P}$, $0 < \sigma \leqslant 1$ und $\varepsilon > 0$, so daß $\gamma = \lambda/2 + \varepsilon = \mu + \sigma$, dann folgt nach [9, Thm. 4] $f^{(\mu)} \in C[-1,1]$ und

$$(5.2) \qquad |f^{(j)}(x) - q_n^{(j)}(x)| \leqslant M(\Delta_n(x))^{\mu-j+\sigma} \qquad (x \in [-1,1],\ n \in \mathbb{N},\ 0 \leqslant j \leqslant \mu)$$

mit M unabhängig von x und n.

Wir definieren jetzt $r_n \in \mathcal{P}_{2\mu+1}$ durch

$$r_n(x) := \sum_{i=0}^{\mu} (x^2-1)^i \{(f^{(i)}(1) - q_n^{(i)}(1))A_{i,\mu}(x) + (f^{(i)}(-1) - q_n^{(i)}(-1))B_{i,\mu}(x)\},$$

wobei die Funktionen $A_{i,\mu}$, $B_{i,\mu}$ wie in (4.5) gegeben sind. Analog zu der Abschätzung der $R_n$ im Beweis von La. 4.2 erhalten wir dann aus (5.2)

$$(5.3) \qquad |r_n(x)| \leqslant M \sum_{i=0}^{\mu} (x^2-1)^i n^{-2(\mu-i+\sigma)} \leqslant M(\Delta_n(x))^{\mu+\sigma} \qquad (x \in [-1,1],\ n \in \mathbb{N}).$$

Außerdem erfüllen die $r_n$ die Interpolationsbedingung

$$(5.4) \qquad r_n^{(j)}(\pm 1) = f^{(j)}(\pm 1) - q_n^{(j)}(\pm 1) \qquad (0 \leqslant j \leqslant \mu).$$

Setzt man jetzt $p_n(x) := q_n(x) + r_n(x)$ für $n \geqslant 2\mu+1$, dann gilt $p_n \in \mathcal{P}_n$, und aus (5.1), (5.3), (5.4) folgt

$$|f(x) - p_n(x)| \leqslant M(\Delta_n(x))^{\mu+\sigma}, \quad p_n^{(j)}(\pm 1) = f^{(j)}(\pm 1) \qquad (0 \leqslant j \leqslant \mu).$$

Daraus erhält man

$$|p_{n2^i}(x) - p_{n2^{i+1}}(x)| \leqslant M(\Delta_{n2^i}(x))^{\mu+\sigma}$$

$$p_{n2^i}^{(j)}(\pm 1) - p_{n2^{i+1}}^{(j)}(\pm 1) = 0 \qquad (0 \leqslant j \leqslant \mu),$$

so daß nach La. 4.1 b) für $x \in [-1,1]$, $n \geqslant 2\mu+1$, $i \in \mathbb{P}$ gilt

$$|p_{n2^i}(x) - p_{n2^{i+1}}(x)| \leqslant Mn^{-\varepsilon} 2^{-i\varepsilon} \sqrt{1-x^2}^{\lambda+\varepsilon}.$$

Die Behauptung des Satzes folgt jetzt sofort wegen

$$|f(x) - p_n(x)| \leqslant \sum_{i=0}^{\infty} |p_{n2^i}(x) - p_{n2^{i+1}}(x)| \leqslant n^{-\varepsilon} \sqrt{1-x^2}^{\lambda+\varepsilon} \sum_{i=0}^{\infty} 2^{-i\varepsilon}.$$

KOROLLAR 5.2. Seien $\beta, \lambda > 0$, $k \in \mathbb{N}$ mit $k > \max\{\lambda\ \beta\}$ und $f \in \mathrm{Lip}_k\, \gamma$ für ein $\gamma > \lambda/2$. Falls

$$\| p_n^{*(k)}(\lambda, f; \cdot) \|_{\lambda-k} = \mathcal{O}(n^{(k-\lambda)}) \qquad (n \to \infty),$$

dann gilt

$$E_n(f;\lambda) = \mathcal{O}(n^{-\beta}) \qquad (n \to \infty).$$

LITERATUR

[ 1] Cheney, E.W., Introduction to Approximation Theory. Mc Graw-Hill Book Co., New York/Toronto/London 1966.

[ 2] Dzjadyk, V.K., Constructive characterization of functions satisfying the condition Lip $\alpha$ $(0 < \alpha < 1)$ on a finite segment of the real axis (Russ.) Ivz. Akad. Nauk SSSR Ser. Mat. 20 (1956), 623-642.

[ 3] Dzjadyk, V.K., Approximation of functions by ordinary polynomials on a finite interval of the real axis. (Russ.) Ivz. Akad. Nauk SSSR Ser. Mat. 22 (1958), 337-354.

[ 4] v. Golitschek, M., Die Ableitungen der algebraischen Polynome bester Approximation. In: Approximation Theory (Proc. Conf., Poznań, 1972), S. 71-86. D. Reidel Publishing Co. Dodrecht/Boston; PWN-Polish Scientific Publishers, Warszawa 1975.

[ 5] Gopengauz, I.E., On a theorem of A.F. Timan on the approximation of functions on a finite interval. (Russ.) Mat. Zametki 1 (1967), 163-172.

[ 6] Gopengauz, I.E., A question concerning the approximation of functions on a segment and in a region with corners. (Russ.) Teor. Funkcii Funkcional. Anal. i Prilozen. 4 (1967), 204-210.

[ 7] Lorentz, G.G., Approximation of Functions. Holt, Rinehart and Winston, New York/Chicago/Toronto 1966.

[ 8] Lorentz, G.G., Unsolved Problem. In: On Approximation Theory (Proc. Conf. Oberwolfach, 1963) S. 185. Birkhäuser Verlag, Basel/Stuttgart 1964.

[ 9] Scherer, K. - Wagner, H.J., An equivalence theorem on best approximation of continuous functions by algebraic polynomials. Applicable Anal. 1 (1972), 343-354.

[ 10] Stens, R.L., Charakterisierung der besten algebraischen Approximation durch lokale Lipschitzbedingungen. In: Approximation Theory (Proc. Conf., Bonn, 1976), Lecture Notes in Math. No. 556, S. 403-415. Springer Verlag, Berlin/Heidelberg/New York 1976.

[ 11] Teljakovskiĭ, S.A., Two theorems on approximation of functions by algebraic polynomials. (Russ.) Math. Sb. 70 (1966), 252-265; Amer. Math. Soc. Transl. 77 (1968), 163-178.

[ 12] Timan, A.F., A strengthening of Jackson's theorem on the best approximation of continuous functions by polynomials on a finite segment of the real axis. (Russ.) Dokl. Akad. Nauk SSSR 78 (1951), 17-20.

[ 13] Trigub, R.M., Approximation of functions by polynomials with integer coefficients. (Russ.) Ivz. Akad. Nauk SSSR Ser. Mat. 26 (1962), 261-280.

[ 14] Zamansky, M., Classes de saturation de certains procédés d' approximation des séries de Fourier des fonctions continues et applications à quelques problèmes d' approximation. Ann. Sci. École Norm. Sup. (3) 66 (1949), 19-93.

# ERWEITERUNG DES SATZES VON MARKOFF

Franz Peherstorfer[1)]
vorgetragen von Paul Otto Runck
Mathematisches Institut
Johannes Kepler Universität
Linz

Markoff proved the following theorem:
Let $f \in L^1[-1,+1]$, $q \in P_{n-1}$, $\lambda(Z(f-q)) = 0$ (Z the zero set). If f-q changes sign exactly at the zeros of the Tschebyscheffpolynomial $U_n$ of $2^{nd}$ type, then q is the best approximation for f on [-1,+1] with respect to $P_{n-1}$ in the $L^1$-norm.

Corresponding results are deduced for the case when f-q changes sign more than n times on (-1,+1), using properties of generalised Tschebyscheff-polynomials of the $2^{nd}$ type. In addition, applications to 1) the Solotareff-problem, 2) the uniqueness of the best approximation of piecewise continuous functions with jumps are given.

$L^1[-1,+1]$ sei der Raum der auf [-1,+1] Lebesgue-integrierbaren Funktionen. $P_n$, $n \in N_o$, sei die Menge der reellen Polynome vom Grad $\leq n$. $q \in P_n$ heißt beste Approximation (b.A.) für $f \in L^1[-1,+1]$ bezüglich $P_n$ auf [-1,+1] genau dann, wenn

$$E_n(f) := \int_{[-1,+1]} |f-q|\,d\lambda = \inf_{p \in P_n} \int_{[-1,+1]} |f-p|\,d\lambda,$$

wobei $\lambda$ das Lebesgue-Maß bezeichne. $E_n(f)$ heißt Minimalabweichung von f bezüglich $P_n$ auf [-1,+1].
Weiter sei $Z(f) := \{x \in [-1,+1] \mid f(x) = 0\}$ für $f \in L^1[-1,+1]$.

---

1) Diese Arbeit wurde aus Mitteln des österreichischen Fonds zur Förderung der wissenschaftlichen Forschung unterstützt.

Eine b.A. läßt sich durch folgende bekannte Orthogonalitätsaussage charakterisieren.

SATZ 1 (siehe KRIPKE und RIVLIN [5]). Sei $f \in L^1[-1,+1]$ und $\lambda(Z(f-q)) = 0$. $q \in P_{n-1}$ ist b.A. für f bezüglich $P_{n-1}$ auf $[-1,+1]$ genau dann, wenn

$$\int_{[-1,+1]} x^k \operatorname{sgn}(f-q)\,d\lambda = 0 \qquad \text{für } k \in \{0,\ldots,n-1\}.$$

In bestimmten Fällen kann eine b.A. für eine vorgegebene Funktion $f \in L^1[-1,+1]$ bezüglich $P_{n-1}$ auf $[-1,+1]$ exakt angegeben werden. Es gilt nämlich folgender auf Markoff zurückgehender Satz.
$U_k$, $k \in \mathbb{Z}$, bezeichne das Tschebyscheffpolynom 2. Art. Zur Definition von $U_k$ für $k \in \mathbb{Z} \setminus \mathbb{N}_0$ siehe MEINARDUS [6], S. 39.

SATZ 2 (MARKOFF). Sei $f \in L^1[-1,+1]$ und $\lambda(Z(f-q)) = 0$.

a) Wechselt $f-q$, $q \in P_{n-1}$, genau in den Nullstellen von $U_n$ das Vorzeichen, dann ist q b.A. für f bezüglich $P_{n-1}$ auf $[-1,+1]$.

b) Ist q b.A. für f bezüglich $P_{n-1}$ auf $[-1,+1]$ und wechselt $f-q$ genau n mal das Vorzeichen auf $(-1,+1)$, dann wechselt $f-q$ in den Nullstellen von $U_n$ das Vorzeichen.

Ähnliche Charakterisierungsaussagen sollen nun für jene Fälle gezeigt werden, wo die Fehlerfunktion öfter als n mal das Vorzeichen wechselt. Hierzu betrachten wir die sogenannten verallgemeinerten Tschebyscheffpolynome 2. Art.

DEFINITION 1. $\prod_{\nu=1}^{m} (x-d_\nu)$, $m \in \mathbb{N}_0$, sei reelles Polynom mit $d_\nu \in \{z \in \mathbb{C} \mid |z| < 1\}$, wobei $\prod_{\nu=1}^{0} (x-d_\nu) := 1$. $a_\mu \in \mathbb{R}$, $\mu \in \{0,\ldots,2m\}$ seien die Koeffizienten des Polynoms

$$\prod_{\nu=1}^{m} (x-d_\nu)^2 = \sum_{\mu=0}^{2m} a_\mu x^\mu.$$

Dann definieren wir

$$\mathcal{U}_n\Big(x, \prod_{\nu=1}^{m} (x-d_\nu)\Big) := 2^{-n} \sum_{\mu=0}^{2m} a_\mu U_{n-2m+\mu}(x), \quad x \in [-1,+1],\ n \in \mathbb{N}_0.$$

(x Funktionswert, $x$ Funktion)

Einige Eigenschaften der Polynome aus Definition 1.

1. $\mathcal{U}_n(\cdot, x^j \prod_{\nu=1}^{m} (x-d_\nu)) = \mathcal{U}_n(\cdot, \prod_{\nu=1}^{m} (x-d_\nu))$ für $j,m \in \mathbb{N}_o$.

2. Sei $d_\nu \neq 0$ für $\nu \in \{1,\dots,m\}$, $\alpha_\nu := \frac{1}{2}(d_\nu + \frac{1}{d_\nu})$, $\nu \in \{1,\dots,m\}$, dann gilt:

$$\mathcal{U}_n(\cdot, \prod_{\nu=1}^{m} (x-d_\nu)) = KU_n(\cdot, \prod_{\nu=1}^{m} (1-\frac{x}{\alpha_\nu})) \quad \text{mit } K \in \mathbb{R} \setminus \{0\},$$

wobei $U_n(\cdot, \prod_{\nu=1}^{m} (1-\frac{x}{\alpha_\nu}))$ das von Bernstein eingeführte verallgemeinerte Tschebyscheffpolynom 2. Art ist (siehe MEINARDUS [6], S.36 und ACHIESER [1], S.251).

3. Ist $n \geq m$, dann besitzt $\mathcal{U}_n(\cdot, \prod_{\nu=1}^{m} (x-d_\nu))$ genau n Nullstellen auf $(-1,+1)$.

SATZ 3. $n,m \in \mathbb{N}_o$, $n \geq m+1$.

a) $\int_{-1}^{+1} x^k \operatorname{sgn} \mathcal{U}_n(x, \prod_{\nu=1}^{m} (x-d_\nu))dx = 0$ <u>für</u> $k \in \{0,\dots,n-m-1\}$.

b) <u>Ist</u> $m \leq [\frac{2n+1}{3}]$, <u>dann gilt</u>

$$\int_{-1}^{+1} |\mathcal{U}_n(x, \prod_{\nu=1}^{m} (x-d_\nu))|dx = 2^{-n+1} \sum_{k=0}^{m} b_k^2 \text{, \underline{wobei} } \prod_{\nu=1}^{m} (x-d_\nu) = \sum_{k=0}^{m} b_k x^k.$$

Wegen Satz 3 b) lassen sich die verallgemeinerten Tschebyscheffpolynome zweiter Art wie folgt abschätzen.

KOROLLAR 4. $n,m \in \mathbb{N}_o$, $m \leq [\frac{2n+1}{3}]$, <u>dann gilt</u>

$$2^{-n+1} \leq \int_{-1}^{+1} |\mathcal{U}_n(x, \prod_{\nu=1}^{m} (x-d_\nu))|dx \leq 2^{-n+1} \sum_{k=0}^{m} (\binom{m}{k})^2 .$$

Aus Satz 3 a) erhalten wir nun eine zu Satz 2 a) analoge Aussage.

KOROLLAR 5. $f \in L^1[-1,+1]$, $\ell \in \mathbb{N}_o$, $\lambda(Z(f-q)) = 0$.
<u>Wechselt</u> $f-q$, $q \in P_{n-1}$, <u>genau in den</u> $(n+\ell)$ <u>Nullstellen eines Polynoms</u> $\mathcal{U}_{n+\ell}(\cdot, \prod_{\nu=1}^{\ell} (x-d_\nu))$ <u>das Vorzeichen, dann ist</u> q <u>b.A. für</u> f <u>bezüglich</u> $P_{n-1}$ <u>auf</u> $[-1,+1]$.

Es stellt sich folgende Frage:
Sei q b.A. für f bezüglich $P_{n-1}$ auf [-1,+1] und f-q wechsle genau $(n+\ell)$ mal das Vorzeichen auf (-1,+1). Wechselt dann f-q in den Nullstellen eines Polynoms $\mathcal{U}_{n+\ell}(\cdot, \prod_{\nu=1}^{\ell}(x-d_\nu))$ das Vorzeichen?

Wie wir sehen werden, muß dies tatsächlich unter gewissen Voraussetzungen gelten. Zunächst betrachten wir

SATZ 6. $n,m \in \mathbb{N}_0$, $m \le [\frac{2n+1}{3}]$, p sei Polynom vom Grad n mit Hauptkoeffizient 1. p wechsle n mal das Vorzeichen auf (-1,+1) und es gelte

$$\int_{-1}^{+1} x^k \operatorname{sgn} p(x)dx = 0 \quad \text{für } k \in \{0,\ldots,n-m-1\};$$

dann existiert ein reelles Polynom $\prod_{\nu=1}^{m}(x-d_\nu)$ mit $d_\nu \in \{z \in \mathbb{C} \mid |z| < 1\}$, sodaß

$$p(x) = \mathcal{U}_n(x, \prod_{\nu=1}^{m}(x-d_\nu)), \quad x \in [-1,+1] .$$

Gilt zusätzlich $\int_{-1}^{+1} x^{n-m} \operatorname{sgn} p(x)dx \neq 0$, so folgt $d_\nu \in \{z \in \mathbb{C} \mid 0 < |z| < 1\}$, $\nu \in \{1,\ldots,m\}$.

Die zu Satz 2 b) analoge Aussage erhält man aus Satz 6.

SATZ 7. $f \in L^1[-1,+1]$, $n,\ell \in \mathbb{N}_0$, $\ell \le 2n+1$, q b.A. für f bezüglich $P_{n-1}$ auf [-1,+1], $\lambda(Z(f-q)) = 0$. Wechselt f-q genau $(n+\ell)$ mal das Vorzeichen auf (-1,+1), dann existiert ein reelles Polynom $\prod_{\nu=1}^{\ell}(x-d_\nu)$, $d_\nu \in \{z \in \mathbb{C} \mid |z| < 1\}$, sodaß f-q genau in den $(n+\ell)$ Nullstellen von $\mathcal{U}_{n+\ell}(x, \prod_{\nu=1}^{\ell}(x-d_\nu))$ das Vorzeichen wechselt.

BEMERKUNG. Für die (n+1) Nullstellen $x_1(d),\ldots,x_{n+1}(d)$ des Polynoms $\mathcal{U}_{n+1}(\cdot,x-d)$ gilt $\cos\frac{k\pi}{n+1} < x_k(d) < \cos\frac{(k-1)\pi}{n+1}$, $k \in \{1,\ldots,n+1\}$.

Mit Satz 7 folgt hieraus

KOROLLAR 8. $f \in L^1[-1,+1]$, q b.A. für f bezüglich $P_{n-1}$ auf [-1,+1]. $\lambda(Z(f-q)) = 0$. Wechselt f-q in den (n+1) Punkten $(1>)\xi_1 > \ldots > \xi_{n+1}(>-1)$ das

Vorzeichen, dann gilt

$$\cos\frac{k\pi}{n+1} < \xi_k < \cos\frac{(k-1)\pi}{n+1}, \quad k \in \{1,\dots,n+1\}.$$

**Mit Hilfe** von Korollar 4 erhält man auch eine Abschätzung der Minimalabweichung für jene Fälle wo f-q, q b.A., öfter als n-mal das Vorzeichen wechselt.

KOROLLAR 9. $f \in C^{n+\ell}[-1,+1]$, $n,\ell \in \mathbb{N}_0$, $\ell \leq 2n+1$, q b.A. für f bezüglich $P_{n-1}$ auf $[-1,+1]$, $\lambda(Z(f-q)) = 0$.
Wechselt f-q genau $(n+\ell)$ mal das Vorzeichen auf $(-1,+1)$, dann gilt

$$\frac{2^{-n-\ell+1}}{(n+\ell)!}\min_{x\in[-1,1]}|f^{(n+\ell)}(x)| \leq E_{n-1}(f) \leq \frac{2^{-n+1}}{(n+\ell)!}\sum_{k=0}^{\ell}\left(\binom{\ell}{k}\right)^2 \max_{x\in[-1,1]}|f^{(n+\ell)}(x)|.$$

Approximiert man ein fix vorgegebenes Polynom durch Polynome niedrigeren Grades, so läßt sich mit Satz 6 eine allgemeine Darstellung der Fehlerfunktion angeben.

SATZ 10. $n,m \in \mathbb{N}_0$, $m \leq [\frac{2n+1}{3}]$, p Polynom vom Grad n, q b.A. für p bezüglich $P_{n-m-1}$ auf $[-1,+1]$.
Wechselt p-q genau $n-\ell$ mal das Vorzeichen auf $(-1,+1)$, $\ell \in \{0,\dots,m\}$, dann existiert ein reelles Polynom $\prod_{\nu=1}^{m-\ell}(x-d_\nu)$, $d_\nu \in \{z \in \mathbb{C} \mid |z| < 1\}$ und ein Polynom $r \in P_\ell$ mit $r(x) > 0$ für $x \in (-1,+1)$, sodaß

$$p(x) - q(x) = \pm\,\mathcal{U}_{n-\ell}\Big(x, \prod_{\nu=1}^{m-\ell}(x-d_\nu)\Big)r(x), \quad x \in [-1,+1].$$

Aus obigem Satz ergibt sich sofort die Lösung des Solotareff-Problems.

BEZEICHNUNG. Für $n \in \mathbb{N}$, $\sigma \in \mathbb{R}$ bezeichne $p_n(\sigma,.)$ jenes Polynom der Form

$$x^n - \sigma x^{n-1} + \sum_{j=0}^{n-2} b_j x^j, \quad (b_0,\dots,b_{n-2}) \in \mathbb{R}^{n-1},$$

das auf $[-1,+1]$ am wenigsten von der Nullfunktion abweicht.

Weiter sei $\hat{U}_k := 2^{-k}U_k$.

KOROLLAR 11. $\sigma \in \mathbb{R}$, $n \in \mathbb{N}$, $n \geq 2$.

a) $$p_n(\sigma,.) = \begin{cases} (x-\sigma)\hat{U}_{n-1} & \underline{\text{für}}\ |\sigma| \geq 1 \\ \mathcal{U}_n(.,x-\sigma) = \hat{U}_n - \sigma\hat{U}_{n-1} + \frac{\sigma^2}{4}\hat{U}_{n-2} & \underline{\text{für}}\ |\sigma| < 1 \end{cases};$$

b) $$\int_{-1}^{+1} |p_n(\sigma,x)|\,dx = \begin{cases} \frac{|\sigma|}{2^{n-2}} & \underline{\text{für}}\ |\sigma| \geq 1 \\ \frac{(1+\sigma^2)}{2^{n-1}} & \underline{\text{für}}\ |\sigma| < 1 \end{cases}.$$

Dieses Problem wurde kürzlich auf andere Weise von GAALEEV [4] gelöst. Mittels einiger elementarer Rechnungen erhält man aus Satz 10 auch die Lösung des erweiterten Solotareff-Problems, wobei zwei Parameter $\sigma,\tau \in \mathbb{R}$ fix vorgegeben werden.

BEZEICHNUNG. Für $n \in \mathbb{N}$, $n \geq 3$ sei $p_n(\sigma,\tau,.)$ jenes Polynom der Form

$$x^n - \sigma x^{n-1} + (\tau - \tfrac{n-1}{4})x^{n-2} + \sum_{j=0}^{n-3} b_j x^j \qquad (b_0,\dots,b_{n-3}) \in \mathbb{R}^{n-2},$$

das auf $[-1,+1]$ am wenigsten von der Nullfunktion abweicht.

KOROLLAR 12. $\sigma,\tau \in \mathbb{R}$, $0 < \sigma < 2$, $n \in \mathbb{N}$, $n \geq 3$.

$$p_n(\sigma,\tau,.) = \begin{cases} (x^2 - \sigma x + \tau - 1/2)\hat{U}_{n-2} & \underline{\text{für}}\ \frac{\sigma^2}{4} - \tau \leq -\frac{1}{2} \\ \mathcal{U}_n(.,x^2 - \sigma x - \frac{\sigma^2}{2} + 2\tau) & \underline{\text{für}}\ -1/2 < \frac{\sigma^2}{4} - \tau < -\frac{\sigma}{2} + \frac{1}{2} \\ (x - \sigma + c)\,\mathcal{U}_{n-1}(.,x-c) & \underline{\text{für}}\ -\frac{\sigma}{2} + \frac{1}{2} \leq \frac{\sigma^2}{4} - \tau < \frac{\sigma^2}{4} + \sigma + \frac{1}{2} \\ (x^2 - \sigma x + \tau - 1/2)\hat{U}_{n-2} & \underline{\text{für}}\ \frac{\sigma^2}{4} + \sigma + \frac{1}{2} \leq \frac{\sigma^2}{4} - \tau, \end{cases}$$

<u>wobei</u> c <u>durch</u> $-\frac{3}{4}c^2 + 6c + \frac{1}{4} = \tau$ <u>und</u> $c \in (-1,\frac{\sigma}{2}-1)$ <u>eindeutig bestimmt ist</u>.

Für $\sigma > 2$ siehe [7].

Mit ähnlichen Beweismethoden lassen sich auch jene Polynome der Form ($\sigma,\tau \in \mathbb{R}$ fix vorgegeben)

$$\hat{U}_n - \sigma\hat{U}_{n-k} + \sum_{j=0}^{n-k-1} b_j x^j, \quad (b_0,\dots,b_{n-k-1}) \in \mathbb{R}^{n-k}$$

bzw.

$$\hat{U}_n - \sigma\hat{U}_{n-k} + \tau\hat{U}_{n-2k} + \sum_{j=0}^{n-2k-1} b_j x^j, \quad (b_0,\dots,b_{n-2k-1}) \in \mathbb{R}^{n-2k}$$

bestimmen, die auf [-1,+1] am wenigsten von Null abweichen.
Hier bedient man sich am besten der folgenden verallgemeinerten Tschebyscheff-polynome zweiter Art (siehe auch [3]).

DEFINITION 2. $\prod_{\nu=1}^{m} (x-d_\nu)$, $m \in \mathbb{N}_0$, sei reelles Polynom mit $d_\nu \in \{z \in \mathbb{C} \mid |z| < 1\}$, wobei $\prod_{\nu=1}^{0} (x-d_\nu) := 1$. $a_\mu \in \mathbb{R}$, $\mu \in \{0,1,\ldots,2m\}$ seien die Koeffizienten des Polynoms

$$\prod_{\nu=1}^{m} (x-d_\nu)^2 = \sum_{\mu=0}^{2m} a_\mu x^\mu .$$

Dann definieren wir

$$\mathcal{U}_{n,k}(x, \prod_{\nu=1}^{m} (x-d_\nu)) := 2^{-n} \sum_{\mu=0}^{2m} a_\mu U_{n-2mk+\mu k}(x), \quad x \in [-1,+1], \; n,k \in \mathbb{N}_0.$$

SATZ 13. $n,m \in \mathbb{N}_0$, $k \in \mathbb{N}$, $n \geq mk + 1$

a) $\int_{-1}^{+1} x^j \operatorname{sgn} \mathcal{U}_{n,k}(x, \prod_{\nu=1}^{m} (x-d_\nu))dx = 0$ für $j \in \{0,\ldots,n-mk-1\}$.

b) Ist $mk \leq [\frac{2n+1}{3}]$, dann gilt

$$\int_{-1}^{+1} |\mathcal{U}_{n,k}(x, \prod_{\nu=1}^{m} (x-d_\nu))| dx = 2^{-n+1} \sum_{i=0}^{m} b_i^2 , \text{ wobei } \prod_{\nu=1}^{m} (x-d_\nu) = \sum_{i=0}^{m} b_i x^i .$$

Zur Eindeutigkeit bei der Approximation von stückweise stetigen Funktionen mit Sprungstellen.

Ist f stetig, so ist bekanntlich die b.A. bezüglich $P_n$ auf [-1,+1] eindeutig bestimmt. Bei der Approximation von stückweise stetigen Funktionen braucht die Eindeutigkeit im allgemeinen nicht mehr gegeben zu sein (siehe [2]). Es gilt hier

SATZ 14. $j,k,n \in \mathbb{N}_0$, $k \leq n+1$, f stückweise stetig auf [-1,+1] mit k voneinander verschiedenen Sprungstellen $\xi_1,\ldots,\xi_k \in (-1,+1)$, $\lambda(Z(f-q)) = 0$. q b.A. für f bezüglich $P_n$ auf [-1,+1] und f-q wechsle (n+1+j) mal das Vorzeichen auf (-1,+1).

a) Ist $j \geq k$, dann ist q eindeutig bestimmte b.A. für f.

b) $0 \leq j \leq k-1$. Gilt für jedes reelle Polynom $\prod_{\nu=1}^{j} (x-d_\nu)$, $d_\nu \in \{z \in \mathbb{C} \mid |z| < 1\}$: Höchstens j Sprungstellen von f sind Nullstellen des Polynoms $\mathcal{U}_{n+1+j}(\cdot, \prod_{\nu=1}^{j} (x-d_\nu))$, dann ist q eindeutig bestimmte b.A. für f.

Spezialfälle: f habe eine bzw. zwei Sprungstellen.

i) f stückweise stetig auf $[-1,+1]$ mit Sprungstelle $\xi_1 \in (-1,+1)$, q b.A. für f bezüglich $P_n$.
Ist $\xi_1 \neq \cos \frac{k\pi}{n+2}$ für $k \in \{1,\ldots,n+1\}$, dann ist q eindeutig bestimmte b.A.

ii) f stückweise stetig auf $[-1,+1]$ mit zwei voneinander verschiedenen Sprungstellen $\xi_1, \xi_2 \in (-1,+1)$, q b.A. für f bezüglich $P_n$.
Ist $\xi_1, \xi_2 \neq \cos \frac{k\pi}{n+2}$ für $k \in \{1,\ldots,n+1\}$ und existiert kein $d \in (-1,+1)$, sodaß $U_{n+2}(\xi_i) - 2dU_{n+1}(\xi_i) + d^2 U_n(\xi_i) = \mathcal{U}_{n+2}(\xi_i, x-d) = 0$ für $i = 1,2$, dann ist q eindeutig bestimmte b.A.

Zum Abschluß sei noch darauf hingewiesen, daß die von Bernstein eingeführten verallgemeinerten Tschebyscheffpolynome zweiter Art auch in der rationalen Approximation eine wichtige Rolle spielen.
Sei $R_{\ell,r}[-1,+1] := \{\frac{p}{q} \mid p \in P_\ell,\ q \in P_r,\ q(x) > 0 \text{ für } x \in [-1,+1],\ \ell, r \in \mathbb{N}_0\}$.

SATZ 15. $\ell \geq r-1$, $f \in L^1[-1,+1]$, $\{\mathbb{1}, x, \ldots, x^\ell, f, xf, \ldots, x^r f\}$ Haarsches System auf $[-1,+1]$.
Ist $\dfrac{p^*}{\prod_{\nu=1}^{k} (1 - \frac{x}{\alpha_\nu})}$ b.A. für f bezüglich $R_{\ell,r}[-1,+1]$, dann wechselt
$f \cdot \prod_{\nu=1}^{k} (1 - \frac{x}{\alpha_\nu}) - p^*$ genau in den $(\ell+r+1)$ Nullstellen des Polynoms
$U_{\ell+r+1}(\cdot, \prod_{\nu=1}^{k} (1 - \frac{x}{\alpha_\nu})^2)$ das Vorzeichen.

Aufgrund dieser Aussage können dann die zwei b.A. des Polynoms $x^n$ bezüglich $R_{n-1,1}[-1,+1]$ explizit bestimmt werden.

Die Beweise der angeführten Sätze und Korollare sowie weitere Fragestellungen der linearen und nichtlinearen $L^1$-Approximation findet man bei PEHERSTORFER [7].

## LITERATUR


[1] Achieser, N.I., Vorlesungen über Approximationstheorie. Akademie-Verlag, Berlin 1953.

[2] Carroll, M.P. - Laughlin, H.W., On $L_1$-Approximation of Discontinuous Functions. J. Approximation Theory 8 (1973), 129-132.

[3] Freilich, J.H., Best and Partial Best $L_1$-Approximations by Polynomials to Certain Rational Functions. J. Approximation Theory 15 (1975), 41-49.

[4] Gaaleev, E.M., Solotarev Problem in the Metric of $L_1$. Math. Notes 17 (1975), 9-13.

[5] Kripke, B.R. - Rivlin, T.J., Approximation in the Metric of $L^1(\mathfrak{X},\mu)$. Trans. Amer. Math. Soc. 119 (1965), 101-122.

[6] Meinardus, G., Approximation von Funktionen und ihre numerische Behandlung. Springer-Verlag, Berlin 1964.

[7] Peherstorfer, F., Lineare und nichtlineare $L^1$-Approximation. Dissertation, erscheint demnächst in der Reihe der Dissertationen der VWGÖ (Wien).

# CONVERGENCE OF SPLINE EXPANSIONS

Zbigniew Ciesielski
Mathematical Institute
Polish Academy of Sciences
Sopot

The aim of this lecture is to give a survey on spline expansions and their applications to function spaces. It concerns the questions for spline systems of being bases, unconditional bases, equivalent bases, bases with shift property, interpolating bases and the a.e. convergence of the spline expansions. These properties of the spline systems are discussed in various classical function spaces on the unit interval, one-dimensional torus, disc, cube, multi-dimensional torus and polydisc. The lecture covers mainly the works related to the author's own investigations.

## 1. Introduction

Long before the theory of splines has been established the spline systems were considered. In 1909 Haar [22] constructed an orthonormal (o.n.) system of step functions (of splines of order 1) closed in $L_1(I)$, $I = \langle 0,1 \rangle$, with the nice property that the Fourier-Haar series are uniformly convergent for all continuous functions. It has been proved by Schauder [29] in 1928 that the Haar system is a basis for $L_p$, $1 \leqslant p < \infty$. The first spline system of order 2 of polygonals was obtained by Faber [20] in 1910 by integration of the Haar functions. Faber established that the new set of functions completed by a constant is a basis in $C(I)$, and this was rediscovered by Schauder [28] in 1927, and the set is called now the S c h a u d e r basis. Applying the Schmidt orthonormalization procedure to the Schauder basis we obtain the Franklin orthonormal set of polygonals discovered in 1928 [21], which is a basis in $C(I)$ and $L_p(I)$, $1 \leqslant p < \infty$, [6]. The Haar and Franklin systems normalized in $L_2$ are not uniformly bounded. Bounded o.n. system of step functions was constructed by Walsh [38] in 1923 and on different way by Paley [24] in

1932. We are interested in the last one, which is known as the Walsh-Paley system. Orthonormal uniformly bounded set of polygonals was introducted by the author in 1968 [8]. These bounded systems do form bases in $L_p$, $1 < p < \infty$, and this was proved for the Walsh-Paley system in 1932 [24], and for the bounded polygonals in 1975 by Ropela [27]. The Franklin set plays essential role in Bockariev's work [2], where he constructs a basis in the disc algebra A.

The question of unconditionality of Haar, Franklin, Walsh-Paley and of the o.n. polygonals systems were considered by Marcinkiewicz [23], Bockariev [3], Paley [24] and Ciesielski-Simon-Sjölin [14], respectively.

Another interesting problem, i.e. the equivalence of the Haar and Franklin systems in $L_p$, $1 \leq p < \infty$, has been resolved recently in [14] and [34]. The equivalence of Walsh-Paley and the bounded o.n. polygonals in $L_p$, $1 < p < \infty$, was established in [15]. Investigation of this problem led the authors of [15] to the shift property for the four bases in question. Namely, the o.n. sets of Haar, Franklin, Walsh-Paley and the bounded polygonals have the shift property in $L_p$, $1 < p < \infty$. Moreover, the Haar and the two bounded systems do not have the shift property in $L_1$. The same question for the Franklin set remains open.

The convergence a.e. of the Fourier series w.r.t the four o.n. systems mentioned above has been investigated by various authors. It is easy to see that the Haar-Fourier series converge a.e. for the $L_1$ functions. Similar result was proved for the Franklin set in [7]. Billard [1] has proved that the Walsh-Paley set is a system of convergence a.e. in $L_2$, and Sjölin [33] proved the same statement for $L_p$, $1 < p < \infty$. For the bounded polygonals the analogue of the $L_2$ case was proved by Schipp [30], and for $L_p$, $1 < p < \infty$, by Ciesielski-Simon-Sjölin [14].

The Schauder basis obtained by integration of the Haar functions is an interpolating basis in C(I) and in the Sobolev space $W_p^1(I)$, $1 \leq p < \infty$. Integrating twice the Franklin functions we are led to cubic interpolating spline basis (c.f.[10]). Using the convergence properties of Haar and Franklin sets one obtains theorems on convergence of interpolating splines of orders 2 and 4.

The o.n. unbounded systems are suitable for characterising some of the function spaces e.g. a function given by the Fourier-Franklin series is of the class Lip $\alpha$, $0<\alpha<1$, iff the n-th coefficient is $O(n^{-\alpha-\frac{1}{2}})$.

All the types of results mentioned here have their analogues for spline o.n. systems of arbitrary order and they are discussed below.

We do not intend to discuss many constructive theory aspects of spline expansions considered e.g. in [10].

## 2. Preliminary results

In the interval $I = \langle 0,1\rangle$ we consider a sequence of dyadic partitions $\pi_n = (s_{n,i},\ i = 0,\ldots,n)$ defined as follows: for $n = 1$, $s_{n,0} = 0$, $s_{n,1} = 1$ and for $n > 1$, $n = 2^k + 1$, $k \geq 0$, $1 \leq 1 \leq 2^k$,

$$(2.1)\qquad s_{n,i} = \begin{cases} \dfrac{i}{2^{k+1}}, & i = 0,\ldots,21; \\[2ex] \dfrac{i-1}{2^k}, & i = 21+1,\ldots n. \end{cases}$$

For each n $\pi_n$ is being extended to a partition of $R = (-\infty,\infty)$ by the formula $s_{n,i+jn} = s_{n,i} + j$ for $i = 0,\ldots,n-1$, and for integer j. To each integer $r > 0$ and to the knots $\pi_n$ there corresponds the space of splines $S^r_n = S^r_n(R)$ of order r (of degree r-1) with multiplicity 1 at each knot. The set of all restrictions to I of f from $S^r_n$ is denoted by $S^r_n(I)$. It is well known that $\dim S^r_n(I) = n+r-1$. We consider two bases in $S^r_n(I)$. The first one form the B-splines $(i = 1-r,\ldots,n-1)$ $N^{(r)}_{n,i}(t) = (s_{n,i+r} - s_{n,i})[s_{n,i},\ldots,s_{n,i+r}; (s-t)^{r-1}_+]$ and the second one an o.n. set $(f^{(r)}_j,\ j = 2-r,\ldots,n)$ defined essentially by the following conditions: $f^{(r)}_{2-r},\ldots,f^{(r)}_1$, are the first r o.n. Lengendre polynomials, $f^{(r)}_j$ is orthogonal to $S^r_{j-1}(I)$ for $j = 2,\ldots,n$. This o.n. basis is completely defined if we impose the condition $\operatorname{sgn} f^{(r)}_n(s_{n,21-1}) = 1$ whenever $n = 2^k+1$, $1 \leq 1 \leq 2^k$. For $r = 1$ we assume that the elements of $S^1_n(I)$ are left continuous and continuous at 0. The o.n. set $(f^{(r)}_j,\ j > 1-r)$ is closed in $L_1$. The particular sets $(f^{(1)}_j)$ and $(f^{(2)}_j)$ are the Haar and Franklin systems correspondingly.

Our main objects of investigations are the orthogonal projections $P^{(r)}_n$ of $L_p(I)$ and $C(I)$ onto $S^r_n(I)$, for which we have

$$P_n^{(r)} f(t) = \int_I K_n^{(r)}(t,s) f(s) ds,$$

$$K_n^{(r)}(t,s) = \sum_{i=2-r}^{n} f_i^{(r)}(t) f_i^{(r)}(s)$$

$$= \sum_{i,j=1-r}^{n} a_{n;j,i}^{(r)} N_{n,j}^{(r)}(t) N_{n,i}^{(r)}(s).$$

Here and later on $(a_{n;i,j}^{(r)})$ denotes the inverse to the Gram matrix of the basic B-splines in $S_n^r(I)$. The local estimates for the entries $a_{n;i,j}^{(r)}$ are essential and in this direction we have the fundamental result

THEOREM 2.1. (Domsta [17]). For each $r > 0$ there are two constants $C_r$ and $q_r$, $0 < q_r < 1$, such that

$$|a_{n;i,j}^{(r)}| < C_r \, n \, q_r^{|i-j|}, \quad i,j = 1-r,\dots,n-1, \qquad n > 0 . \tag{2.2}$$

Similar result holds in the periodic case (Domsta [19]). Many of the results discussed below depend essentially on these Domsta's estimates.

THEOREM 2.2. (Ciesielski and Domsta [13]). Let $(N_{n,i}^{(r)}, \underline{N}_{n,j}^{(r)}, i,j = 1-r,\dots, n-1)$ be in $S_n^r(I)$ the biorthogonal system w.r.t. the scalar product in $L_2$. Moreover, let

$$M_{n,r}^{(p)}(a) = \left(\frac{1}{n+r-1} \sum_{j=1-r}^{n-1} |a_j|^p\right)^{1/p} .$$

Then there is $C_r > 0$ such that

$$C_r^{-1} M_{n,r}^{(p)}(a) \leqslant \Big\| \sum_{j=1-r}^{n-1} a_j N_{n,j}^{(r)} \Big\|_p \leqslant C_r M_{n,r}^{(p)}(a),$$

$$C_r^{-1} n \, M_{n,r}^{(p)}(a) \leqslant \Big\| \sum_{j=1-r}^{n-1} a_j \underline{N}_{n,j}^{(r)} \Big\|_p \leqslant C_r \, n \, M_{n,r}^{(p)}(a),$$

*hold for all* a *and* $1 \leqslant p \leqslant \infty$.

In view of the recent result of Demko [16](see also [5]) Theorems 2.1 and 2.2 are apparently equivalent.

For the approximation of smooth functions it is necessary to consider for each n a family of projections related to $P_n^{(r)}$. The new projections are indexed by integers k, $|k| < r$, and denoted $P_n^{(r,k)}$ whenever $n > |k|+1-r$. For $k=0$ let $P_n^{(r,0)} = P_n^{(r)}$, and for $0<k<r$ $P_n^{(r,k)}$ can be defined by the formula

$$P_n^{(r,k)} D^k f = D^k P_n^{(r)} f, \qquad f \in C^k(I),$$

where D stands for differentiation. Consequently, $P_n^{(r,k)}$, $n > |k|+1-r$ project $L_p(I)$ or $C(I)$ onto $S_n^{(r-k)}(I)$. The conjugate operator to $P_n^{(r,k)}: L_p(I) \to L_p(I)$ is $P_n^{(r,-k)}: L_q(I) \to L_q(I)$, $q = p/(p-1)$. More explicitely, if

$$Hf(t) = \int_t^1 f(s)ds,$$

$$f_n^{(r,k)} = \begin{cases} D^k f_n^{(r)}, & 0 \leqslant k < r \quad, \\ H^{-k} f_n^{(r)}, & 0 \leqslant -k < r \quad; \end{cases}$$

then $P_n^{(r,k)}$ is an integral operator with kernel

$$K_n^{(r,k)}(t,s) = \sum_{j=|k|+2-r}^{n} f_j^{(r,k)}(t)\, f_j^{(r,-k)}(s).$$

THEOREM 2.3, (Ciesielski and Domsta [13], [10]). *There are constants* $C_r$ *and* $q_r$, $0 < q_r < 1$, *such that*

$$|K_n^{(r,k)}(t,s)| \leqslant C_r\, n\, q_r^{n|t-s|}$$

*holds for* $t,s \in I$, $n > 0$, $|k| < r$.

Using the notation of (2.1) we define $s_n = s_{n,\,2l-1}$ and $t_n$ by the formula $|f_n^{(r,k)}(t_n)| = \| f_n^{(r,k)} \|_\infty$ .

THEOREM 2.4, (see [10]). *There are constants* $C_r$ *and* $q_r$, $0 < q_r < 1$, *such that*

$$|f_n^{(r,k)}(t)| \leq C_r\, n^{\frac{1}{2}+k}\, q_r^{n|t-u|}$$

*holds for* $t \in I$ *and* $u$ *equal either* $s_n$ *or* $t_n$.

THEOREM 2.5, (c.f. [10]). *For* $|k| < r$, $1 \leq p \leq \infty$ *and* $m \geq 0$ *we have uniformly in these parameters*

$$\Big\| \sum_{j=2^m+1}^{2^{m+1}} a_j\, f_j^{(r,k)} \Big\|_p \sim \Big\| \sum_{j=2^m+1}^{2^{m+1}} |a_j\, f_j^{(r,k)}| \Big\|_p \sim$$

$$\sim 2^{(k+\frac{1}{2})m} \Big(2^{-m} \sum_{j=2^m+1}^{2^{m+1}} |a_j|^p\Big)^{1/p}.$$

COROLLARY. *For* $|k| < r$, $1 \leq p \leq \infty$ *and* $n > 0$ *we have uniformly in these parameters*

$$\| f_n^{(r,k)} \|_p \sim n^{\frac{1}{2}+k-1/p} .$$

In the periodic case results corresponding to Theorems 2.2.-2.5 follow. The most essential and difficult is the periodic analogue of Theorem 2.3 and it has been established in [11].

We know that $(f_j^{(1)},\ j > 0)$ is the Haar system and let us denote by $(w_j^{(1)},\ j > 0)$ the Walsh-Paley o.n. set. Notice that $w_1^{(1)} = f_1^{(1)} = 1$ and for $2^m < i \leq 2^{m+1}$, $m \geq 0$)

$$w_{2^m+i}^{(1)} = \sum_{j=1}^{2^m} A_{i,j}^{(m)}\, f_{2^m+j}^{(1)} ,$$

where $A_{i,j}^{(m)} = (w_{2^m+i}^{(1)},\ f_{2^m+j}^{(1)})$ are the entries of the $2^m$ by $2^m$ Walsh-Paley orthogonal matrix. Define $w_j^{(r,k)} = f_j^{(r,k)}$ for $|k| + 1-r < j \leq 1$, and for $1 \leq i \leq 2^m$, $m \geq 0$,

$$w_{2^m+i}^{(r,k)} = \sum_{j=1}^{2^m} A_{i,j}^{(m)}\, f_{2^m+j}^{(r,k)} .$$

Moreover, let $w_j^{(r,0)} = w_j^{(r)}$. It is a consequence of Theorem 2.5 that the o.n. set $(w_j^{(r)}, j > 1-r)$ is uniformly bounded.

## 3. Bases

In the $L_p$ case Theorem 2.3 implies (c.f. [10])

THEOREM 3.1. *If $1 \leq p < \infty$ and $|k| < r$, then $(f_j^{(r,k)}, j > |k| + 1-r)$ is a basis in $L_p(I)$, and for f in $L_p$ we have*

$$f = \sum_{j=|k|+2-r}^{\infty} (f, f_j^{(r,-k)}) f_j^{(r,k)} .$$

THEOREM 3.2. *If $0 \leq k < r-1$, then $(f_j^{(r,k)}, j > k+1-r)$ is a basis in C(I) and for f from this space the same formula as in Theorem 3.1 holds.*

COROLLARY. *The system $(f_j^{(r,-r+1)}, j > 0)$ is a simultaneous basis in $W_p^{2r-2}(I)$, $1 \leq p < \infty$. Moreover, $f_j^{(r)}, j > 1-r$ is a simultaneous basis in $C^{r-2}(I)$.*

Using the same technique as in [13] we can prove:

THEOREM 3.3. *Let $1 \leq p \leq \infty$ and the integers $m \geq 0$ and $d > 0$ be given. Then for $|k| < r$ such that $m < r-k$ the set $(f_{i_1}^{(r,k)} \ldots f_{i_d}^{(r,k)}, i_j > 1 - r+k_+, j = 1,\ldots,d)$ ordered properly is a basis in $W_p^m(I^d)$.*

THEOREM 3.4. *Let $m \geq 0$, $d > 0$ and k, $0 \leq k < r-1$, be given. Then the sequence of functions from the previous theorem is a basis in $C^m(I^d)$ whenever $m < r-k-1$.*

The domain of k in Theorem 3.4 can be extended as follows: $-1 \leq k < r-1$. The construction for $k = -1$ is the same if we use $(1, t, f_j^{(r,-1)}, j > 1-r)$ as the original sequence. Since the functionals f(0) and f(1) are continuous this sequence is a basis in C(I). The case of $r = 2$ and $k = -1$ is precisely the Schonefeld's [31] and the author's [9] original construction of a basis in $C^1(I^d)$.

In the case of uniformly bounded o.n. spline systems we have

THEOREM 3.5, (Ropela [27]). *If $|k| < r$ and $1 < p < \infty$, then $(w_j^{(r,k)}, j > |k| + 1-r)$*

*is a basis in* $L_p(I)$.

It follows from an unpublished result of J. Szarek that for each k, $|k| < r$, $(w_j^{(r,k)}, j > |k| + 1-r)$ is not a basis in $L_1(I)$.

By means of the system $(f_j^{(r)}, j > 1-r)$, $r > 1$, one can construct a simultaneous basis in the complex Banach space $A^m(\Delta)$ of analytic functions in $\Delta = \{z: |z| < 1\}$ and m times continuously differentiable on the boundary, and this is described below.

The periodic analogue on the torus $T = \langle -\pi,\pi)$ of $(f_j^{(r)})$ is denoted by $(F_j^{(r)}, j = 1,2,\dots)$. The system $(F_j^{(r)})$ is o.n. w.r.t. the scalar product

$$(f,g) = \int_T f\,\overline{g}\,,$$

and most results established for $(f_j^{(r)})$ can be proved for $(F_j^{(r)})$ as well. For each k, $0 \leq k < r-1$, we define a set of complex functions as follows: $G_1^{(\pm k)} = (2\pi)^{-\frac{1}{2}}$, $G_j^{(k)} = D^k G_j$, $G_j^{(-k)} = H^k G_j$ for $j > 1$ where $G_j = (F_j^{(r)})_+ + i((F_j^{(r)})_+)^{\sim}$,

$$Hf(t) = \int_t^{\pi} f(s)ds - \frac{1}{2\pi}\int_{-\pi}^{\pi}\Big(\int_s^{\pi} f(u)du\Big)ds,$$

$f_+$ is the even part of f and $f^{\sim}$ its trigonometric conjugate. Moreover, let $A(T) = \{f \in C(T): f^{\sim} \in C(T)\}$.

THEOREM 3.6, (c.f. [11]). *For each* k, $0 \leq k < r-1$, $(G_j^{(k)}, j > 0)$ *is a basis in* $A(T)$ *and for* $f \in A(T)$

$$f = \sum_{j=1}^{\infty} (f, \mathrm{Re}\,G_j^{(-k)})G_j^{(k)}\ .$$

COROLLARY. *The set* $(G_j, j > 0)$ *is a simultaneous basis in* $A^{r-2}(T) = \{f \in C^{r-2}(T): D^k f \in A(T),\ 0 \leq k < r-1\}$, *and therefore there is a basis in* $A^m(\Delta^d)$, $m = r-2$.

For related results we refer to [37].

## 4. Unconditional bases

It is convenient to introduce

$$h_j^{(r,k)} = \begin{cases} f_j^{(r,k)}/\|f_j^{(r,k)}\|_2, & 0 \leq k < r; \\ f_j^{(r,k)}\|f_j^{(r,-k)}\|_2, & -r < k \leq 0. \end{cases}$$

The first result on unconditionality in $L_2$ is

THEOREM 4.1, (Ropela [25]). *For given* k *and* r, $|k| < r$, *the set* $(h_j^{(r,k)}$, $j > |k| + 1-r)$ *is an unconditional basis in* $L_2(I)$.

Then we have

THEOREM 4.2, (c.f. [12] and [26]). *Let be given* r, r', k *and* k' *such that* $|k| < r$, $|k'| < r'$, *and let* $\varepsilon_j = +1$ *or* $-1$ *be a fixed sequence. Moreover, let*

$$Tf = \sum_{j=s}^{\infty} \varepsilon_j (f, h_j^{(r',k')}) h_j^{(r,k)},$$

*with* $s = \max(|k| + 2-r, |k'| + 2-r')$. *Then the operator* T *is of weak type* (1,1).

THEOREM 4.3, (c.f. [12] and [26]). *For each* k, $|k| < r$, *the set* $(f_j^{(r,k)}$, $j > |k| + 1-r)$ *is an unconditional basis in* $L_p(I)$, $1 < p < \infty$.

From this result follows Paley's unconditional decomposition into dyadic blocks of the expansions w.r.t. $(w_j^{(r,k)})$ in $L_p(I)$, $1 < p < \infty$.

## 5. Equivalence of bases

Two bases in a Banach space are said to be equivalent if they have the same coefficient spaces.

THEOREM 5.1, (c.f. [12]). *For given pairs* (r,k) *and* (r',k') *for which* $|k| < r$, $|k'| < r'$, *the bases* $(h_j^{(r,k)}$, $j > |k| + 1-r)$ *and* $(h_j^{(r',k')}$,

$j > |k'| + 1 - r'$) *are equivalent in* $L_p(I)$, $1 < p < \infty$.

It has been shown by Sjölin [34] that the Haar and Franklin bases i.e. $(f_j^{(1,0)})$ and $(f_j^{(2,0)})$ are not equivalent bases in $L_1$.

THEOREM 5.2 *Let* $v_j^{(r,k)} = w_j^{(r,k)} / 2^{[\log_2(n-1)]}$ *and let* $(r,k)$, $(r',k')$ *and* $p$ *be given as in the previous theorem. Then* $(v_j^{(r,k)}$, $j > |k| + 1 - r)$ *and* $(v_j^{(r',k')}$, $j > |k'| + 1 - r')$ *are equivalent bases in* $L_p(I)$.

This result depends on the shift property of the Walsh-Paley system (c.f. [15]) and on Theorems 4.1 and 4.2.

## 6. The shift property

The equivalence of spline bases is related to the shift property of these systems.

THEOREM 6.1. *For given* $r$ *and* $k$, $|k| < r$, *the bases* $(h_j^{(r,k)})$ *and* $(v_j^{(r,k)})$ *have the shift property i.e. the operators* $T\colon h_j^{(r,k)} \to h_{j+1}^{(r,k)}$ *and* $S\colon v_j^{(r,k)} \to v_{j+1}^{(r,k)}$ *are bounded in* $L_p(I)$, $1 < p < \infty$.

It has been shown in [15] that $(h_j^{(1,0)})$ does not have bounded shift in $L_1$. Moreover it follows from Bockariev's inequality (c.f. [4], p. 440) that $S$ is unbounded in $L_1$ for all pairs $(r,k)$ satisfying the inequality $|k| < r$.

## 7. Convergence a.e.

The spline bases appear to be systems of convergence a.e. for functions in $L_p$.

THEOREM 7.1. *Let* $|k| < r$ *and let* $1 \leq p < \infty$. *Then for each* $f \in L_p(I)$ *the series*

$$\sum_{j=|k|+2-r}^{\infty} (f, f_j^{(r,-k)}) f_j^{(r,k)}(t)$$

*converges to* $f(t)$ *whenever*

$$f(t) = \lim_{h\to 0} \frac{1}{h} \int_t^{t+h} f(s)ds, \qquad 0 < t < 1.$$

The proof consists of two parts. The first case $0 \leqslant k < r$ was established in [10], Theorem 3.2. If $-r < k < 0$, then it sufficies to check that

$$\int_0^1 K_n^{(r,k)}(t,s)ds \to 1 \quad \text{as} \quad n \to \infty, \; 0 < t < 1,$$

and this follows from the first part.

THEOREM 7.2, (c.f. [12]). *Let* $|k| < r$ *and* $1 < p < \infty$. *Then for* $f \in L_p(I)$

(8.1) $$\sum_{j=|k|+2-r}^{\infty} (f, w_j^{(r,-k)}) \; w_j^{(r,k)}(t)$$

*converges a.e. in* $t \in I$.

For $p = 1$ and $k = 0$ according to a general result of Bockariev [4] there is $f \in L_1$ such that (8.1) diverges on a set of positive Lebesgue measure. The same question remains open for general indices $r$ and $k$ with $|k| < r$.

## 8. Interpolating bases

There are some results in this direction due to Schonefeld [32], Domsta [18] and Subbotin [35], [36]. We are going to state here results on convergence of interpolating spline bases appearing in natural way in our approach.

Let us define a new set of splines of order $2r$ as follows

$$g_0^{(2r)} = 1, \; g_j^{(2r)}(t) = \int_0^t f_j^{(r,-r+1)}(s)ds \qquad \text{for } j = 1,2,\ldots,$$

and put

$$Q_n^{(2r)}f(t) = f(1)g_0^{(2r)}(t) + \sum_{j=1}^{n} \int_I f_j^{(r,-r+1)}df \; g_j^{(2r)}(t) \quad .$$

THEOREM 8.1, [10]. *Let* $r > 0$. *Then the set* $(g_j^{(2r)}, j \geq 0)$ *is an interpolating basis in* $C(I)$ *i.e.* $Q_n^{(2r)} f$ *converges uniformly to* $f \in C(I)$ *and for all* $n$

$$Q_n^{(2r)} f(s_{n,i}) = f(s_{n,i}), \qquad i = 0,1,\ldots,n ,$$

*where* $s_{n,i}$ *is defined as in* (2.1).

Now, let $H^{(2r)} f$ denote the solution of the following two-point Hermite interpolation problem: $D^j H^{(2r)} f(t) = D^j f(t)$ for $t = 0,1$, and $j = 1,\ldots, r-1$, $H^{(2r)} f(0) = H^{(2r)} f(1) = 0$.

THEOREM 8.2. *Let* $p$, $r$, $m$ *be given such that* $1 \leq p < \infty$, $r \leq m < 2r$ *and let* $f \in W_p^m(I)$. *Then in the Sobolev space* $W_p^m(I)$ *we have*

$$f = H^{(2r)} f + \lim_{n\to\infty} Q_n^{(2r)} f.$$

*Moreover, the limit of the* $m$-th *derivative of* $Q_n^{(2r)} f$ *exists a.e.*

In the periodic case we start with $(F_j^{(r)}, j > 0)$ as defined in Section 3, and put $F_j^{(r,k)} = (2\pi)^{-1/2}$

$$F_j^{(r,k)} = \begin{cases} D^k F_j^{(r)}, & 0 \leq k < r, \\ (-1)^k F_j^{(r)} * B_k, & -r < k < 0; \end{cases}$$

where $B_k$ is the periodic Bernoulli polynomial of degree $k$ i.e.

$$B_{2k-1}(t) \sim \frac{(-1)^{k-1}}{\pi} \sum_{n=1}^{\infty} \frac{\sin nt}{n^k} , \qquad k = 1,2,\ldots$$

$$B_{2k}(t) \sim \frac{(-1)^k}{\pi} \sum_{n=1}^{\infty} \frac{\cos nt}{n^k} , \qquad k = 1,2,\ldots .$$

Like in the non-periodic case $(F_i^{(r,-k)}, F_j^{(r,k)}) = \delta_{ij}$ for $|k| < r$ and $i,j = 1,2,\ldots$

Now, a new set of periodic splines of order $(2r)$ is defined as follows

$$H_1^{(2r)}(t) = 1, \quad H_j^{(2r)} = \int_{-\pi}^{t} F_j^{(r,-r+1)}(s)ds, \qquad j = 2,3,\dots .$$

For the corresponding partial sums we introduce the following notation

$$S_n^{(2r)}f = \sum_{j=1}^{n} a_j(f)\, H_j^{(2r)} ,$$

where $a_1(f) = f(0)$, $a_j(f) = \int_T F_j^{(r,-r+1)}df$.

THEOREM 8.3. _If_ $f \in C^m(T)$ _for some_ $m \geqslant 0$, $m < 2r-1$, _then in the space_ $C^m(T)$

$$f = \lim_{n\to\infty} S_n^{(2r)}f,$$

_and_ $S_n^{(2r)}f(s_{n,i}) = f(s_{n,i})$ _for_ $i = 1,\dots,n$, _and_ $s_{n,i}$ _defined as in_ (2.1).

THEOREM 8.4. _Let_ $0 < m < 2r$ _and_ $1 \leqslant p < \infty$. _Moreover let_ $f \in W_p^m(T)$. _Then_ $S_n^{(2r)}f$ _converges to_ $f$ _in_ $W_p^m(T)$ _and_ $D^mS_n^{(2r)}$ _converges to_ $D^mf$ _a.e. on_ $T$.

## 9. Lipschitz classes and Besov spaces

The spline bases appear to be suitable for characterization of Lipschitz classes and Besov spaces by means of sequence spaces.

THEOREM 9.1, [10]. _Let_ $0 < \alpha < r-1$. _Moreover let_ $f \in L_p(I)$ _if_ $1 \leqslant p < \infty$, _and_ $f \in C(I)$ _if_ $p = \infty$, _and let_

$$f = \sum_{j=2-r}^{\infty} a_j\, f_j^{(r)} . \tag{9.1}$$

_Then_ $\omega_{r-1}^{(p)}(f;\delta) = O(\delta^\alpha)$ _if and only if_

$$2^{m(\frac{1}{2}-1/p)} \Big( \sum_{2^m+1}^{2^{m+1}} |a_n|^p \Big)^{1/p} = O(2^{-\alpha m}) \qquad \text{as} \qquad m \to \infty. \tag{9.2}$$

THEOREM 9.2, [10]. *Let* $f \in L_p(I)$ *for* $1 \leqslant p < \infty$, *and* $f \in C(I)$ *for* $p = \infty$. *Moreover let* $0 < \alpha < r-1+1/p$ *and* $r > 0$. *Then* f *given by* (9.1) *satisfies* (9.2) *if and only if* $\omega_r^{(p)}(f;\delta) = \mathcal{O}(\delta^\alpha)$ *for small* $\delta > 0$.

In these theorems and later on $\omega_r^{(p)}$ denotes the modulus of smootheness of order r w.r.t. to the metric in $L_p$.

REMARK. It is interesting that the Zygmund class i.e. the class of functions f such that $\omega_2^{(\infty)}(f;\delta) = \mathcal{O}(\delta)$ can be characterized by the series

$$\sum_{n=2-r}^{\infty} a_n f_n^{(r)}$$

where $a_n = \mathcal{O}(n^{-3/2})$ only if $r > 2$, and in the case of $r = 2$ this cannot be done.

For the Besov spaces we have the following result.

THEOREM 9.3, (Ropela [25]). *Let* $p,r,\alpha$ *and* $\theta$ *be fixed and such that* $1 \leqslant p \leqslant \infty$, $1 \leqslant \theta \leqslant \infty$, $r > 0$ *and* $0 < \alpha < r-1+1/p$. *Moreover let*

$$f = \sum_{n=2-r}^{\infty} a_n f_n^{(r)} .$$

*Then*,

$$\left[\int_0^1 \left(\frac{\omega_r^{(p)}(f;t)}{t^\alpha}\right)^\theta \frac{dt}{t}\right]^{\frac{1}{\theta}} < \infty$$

*if and only if*

$$\left[\sum_{n=0}^{\infty} \left(2^{n(\frac{1}{2}+\alpha-1/p)} \left(\sum_{j=2^n+1}^{2^{n+1}} |a_j|^p\right)^{1/p}\right)^\theta\right]^{\frac{1}{\theta}} < \infty.$$

COROLLARY. The system $(f_j^{(r)})$ is an unconditional basis in the Besov space corresponding to the parameters $p,\alpha,\theta$ and r satisfying the following inequalities: $1 \leqslant p \leqslant \infty$, $1 \leqslant \theta \leqslant \infty$, $r > 0$ and $0 < \alpha < r-1+1/p$.

## REFERENCES


[1] Billard, P., Sur la convergence presque partout des séries de Fourier-Walsh de fonctions de l'espace $L^2(0,1)$. Studia Math. 28(1967), 363 - 388.

[2] Bockariev, S.V., Existence of basis in the space of analytic functions in the disc and some properties of the Franklin system. Mat. Sbornik 95(137), (1974), 3 - 18 (in Russian).

[3] -, Some inequalities for the Franklin series. Analysis Mathematica 1 (1975), 249 - 257.

[4] -, Divergent on a set of positive measure Fourier series for arbitrary bounded orthonormal set. Mat. Sbornik 98(140), (1975), 436 - 449 (in Russian).

[5] De Boor, C., Odd-degree spline interpolation at a biinfinite knot sequence. Approximation Theory. Lecture Notes in Mathematics 556, Springer-Verlag, Berlin 1976, 30 - 53.

[6] Ciesielski, Z., Properties of the orthonormal Franklin system. Studia Math. 23(1963), 141 - 157.

[7] -, Properties of the orthonormal Franklin system, II. ibidem 27(1966), 289 - 323.

[8] -, A bounded orthonormal system of polygonals. ibidem 31(1968), 339 - 346.

[9] -, A construction of basis in $C^{(1)}(I^2)$. ibidem 33(1969), 243 - 247.

[10] -, Constructive function theory and spline systems. ibidem 53(1975), 277 - 302.

[11] -, Bases and approximation by splines. Proc. Intern. Congr. of Mathematicians, Vancouver, 1974, 47 - 51.

[12] -, Equivalence, unconditionality and convergence a.e. of spline bases in $L_p$ spaces. Approximation Theory, Banach Center Publications vol. 4 (to appear).

[13] - and Domsta, J., Construction of an orthonormal basis in $C^m(I^d)$ and $W_p^m(I^d)$. Studia Math. 41(1972), 211 - 224.

[14] -, Simon, P. and Sjölin, P., Equivalence of Haar and Franklin bases in $L_p$ spaces. Studia Math. 60(1977), 195 - 210.

[15] - and Kwapień, S., Some properties of the Haar, Walsh-Paley, Franklin and the bounded polygonal orthonormal bases in $L_p$ spaces. Commentationes Mathematicae (to appear).

[16] Demko, S., Inverses of band matrices and local convergence of spline projections. SIAM J. Numer. Anal.(to appear).

[17] Domsta, J., A Theorem on B-splines. Studia Math. 41(1972), 291 - 314.

[18] -, Approximation by spline interpolating bases. ibidem 58(1976), 223 - 237.

[19] -, A Theorem on B-splines.II. The periodic case. Bull. Acad. Polon. Sci., Série math. astr. 24(1976), 1077 - 1084.

[20] Faber, G., Über die Orthogonalfunktionen des Herrn Haar. Jahresber. Deutsch. Math. Verein. 19(1910), 104 - 112.

[21] Franklin, Ph., A set of continuous orthogonal functions. Math. Ann. 100(1928), 522 - 529.

[22] Haar, A., Zur Theorie der orthogonalen Funktionensysteme. Math. Ann. 69(1910), 331 - 371.

[23] Marcinkiewicz, J., Quelques théorèmes sur les séries orthogonales. Ann. Soc. Polon. Math. 16(1937), 107 - 115.

[24] Paley, R.E.A.C., A remarkable series of orthogonal functions. Proc. London Math. Soc. 34(1932), 241 - 279.

[25] Ropela, S., Spline bases in Besov spaces. Bull. Acad. Polon. Sci., Serie math. astr. 24(1976), 319 - 325.

[26] -, Decomposition lemma and unconditional spline bases. ibidem 467 - 470.

[27] -, Properties of bounded orthonormal spline bases. Approximation Theory. Banach Center Publications, vol. 4 (to appear).

[28] Schauder, J., Zur Theorie stetiger Abbildungen in Funktionalräumen. Math. Z. 26(1927), 47 - 65.

[29] -, Eine Eigenschaft des Haarschen Orthogonalsystems. ibidem 28(1928), 317 - 320.

[30] Schipp, F., On a.e. convergence of expansions with respect to a bounded orthonormal system of polygonals. Studia Math. 58(1976), 287 - 290.

[31] Schonefeld, S., Schauder bases in spaces of differentiable functions. Bull. Amer. Math. Soc. 75(1969), 586 - 590.

[32] -, Schauder bases in the Banach spaces $C^k(T^q)$. Trans. Amer. Math. Soc. 165(1971), 309 - 318.

[33] Sjölin, P., An inequality of Paley and convergence a.e. of Walsh-Fourier series. Arkiv Math. 7(1968), 551 - 570.

[34] -, The Haar and Franklin systems are not equivalent in $L^1$. Bull. Acad. Polon. Sci., Serie math. astr. (to appear).

[35] Subbotin, Yu. N., Spline approximation and smooth bases in $C(0,2\pi)$. Mat. Zametki 12(1972), 43 - 51 (in Russian).

[36] -, Applications of splines in approximation theory. In: Linear Operators and Approximation. ISNM, vol.20, Birkhäuser Verlag, Basel 1972, 405 - 418 (in Russian).

[37] -, Approximation properties of splines. Approximation Theory. Lecture Notes in Math. 556, Springer-Verlag, Berlin 1976, 416 - 427.

[38] Walsh, J.L., A closed set of normal orthogonal functions. Amer. J. Math. 45(1923), 5 - 24.

# DIRECT AND CONVERSE THEOREMS FOR ONESIDE APPROXIMATION

V. A. Popov
Math. Institute of the Bulgarian Academy of Sciences
Sofia, Bulgaria

## 0. Introduction

In this paper we shall consider the socalled onesided approximation of functions. The problem of onesided approximation of functions goes back to A.A. Markov. He has considered the onesided approximation of the step-function. More recently G. Freud [1] was the first to give an estimation of one-sided approximation of functions with derivatives with bounded variation by means of algebraical polynomials, and T. Ganelius [2] obtained the corresponding estimations of the trigonometrical case (with exact constant). Since then many papers [3]-[13] have been published where some other cases of one-sided approximation were considered. In this work we shall present Jackson type and Bernstein type theorems for onesided trigonometrical approximation and a Jackson type theorem for onesided spline approximation. The paper consists of 4 parts. The first contains the necessary notations and some lemmas. In the second we make a brief survey of the achievements in onesided approximation of functions. In part 3 we give the analogues of Jackson's and Bernstein's theorems. These analogues are obtained by introducing one new modulus. Some of the properties of this modulus are also given in part 1. In part 4 we applied the new moduli for estimation of the error of the Newton-Cotes composite quadrature formulas.

## 1. Notations and Lemmas

By $H_n$ we shall denote the set of all algebraic polynomials of $n^{th}$

degree, by $T_n$ the set of all trigonometrical polynomials of $n^{th}$ order, and by $S_{k,\Sigma_n}$ the set of all splines in the interval $[0,1]$ of $k^{th}$ degree with knots $\Sigma_n=\{x_i,\ i=0,\dots,n,\ 0=x_0\leqslant x_1\leqslant\dots\leqslant x_n=1\}$, i.e. s is in $S_{k,\Sigma_n}$ if s is in $C^{k-1}[0,1]$ and in each interval $[x_{i-1},x_i]$, $i=1,\dots,n$, s is an algebraical polynomial of $k^{th}$ degree. As usual we set:

$$\|f\|_{L_p[a,b]} = \left(\int_a^b |f(x)|^p dx\right)^{1/p}, \qquad 1\leqslant p\leqslant\infty.$$

The best approximation in $L_p$ of the function $f\in L_p[a,b]$ by means of trigonometrical polynomials or splines are defined by

$$E_n^T(f)_{L_p[0,2\pi]} = \inf \|f-t\|_{L_p[0,2\pi]}, \quad t\in T_n,$$

$$E_{k,\Sigma_n}(f)_{L_p[0,1]} = \inf \|f-s\|_{L_p[0,1]}, \quad s\in S_{k,\Sigma_n}.$$

In most cases we shall omit the interval $[a,b]$, for example we shall write $E_n^T(f)_{L_p}$.

The best onesided $L_p$-approximation of the bounded function f by means of trigonometrical polynomials or splines are defined by

$$\tilde{E}_n^T(f)_{L_p[0,2\pi]} = \inf \|P-Q\|_{L_p[0,2\pi]},$$

$P,Q\in T_n$, $Q(x)\leqslant f(x)\leqslant P(x)$ for every x,

$$\tilde{E}_{k,\Sigma_n}(f)_{L_p[0,1]} = \inf \|S-s\|_{L_p[0,1]},$$

$s,S\in S_{k,\Sigma_n}$, $s(x)\leqslant f(x)\leqslant S(x)$ for $x\in[0,1]$.

The usual $k^{th}$ modulus of continuity of a function $f\in L_p[0,2\pi]$ is defined by

$$\omega_k(f;\delta)_{L_p} = \sup_{0<h\leqslant\delta} \left(\int_0^{2\pi} |\Delta_h^k f(x)|^p\, dx\right)^{1/p},$$

where

$$\Delta_h^k f(x) = \sum_{m=0}^{k} (-1)^{k+m}\binom{k}{m} f(x+mh).$$

Let the function f be defined on the interval [a,b]. We set:

$$\omega_k(f,x;\delta) = \sup\{|\Delta_h^k f(t)|,\ t,t+kh \in [x-k\delta/2, x+k\delta/2] \cap [a,b]\}.$$

We shall use the following new modulus:

(1) $$\tau_k(f;\delta)_{L_p[a,b]} = \|\omega_k(f,x;\delta)\|_{L_p[a,b]}.$$

A modulus of the type (1) for k=1 was considered, as we know, by Bl. Sendov [15] and P.P. Korovkin [16] first. The case k=1, p=1 is considered by Dolgenko and Sevastianov [17], where many properties of $\tau_1(f;\delta)_{L_1}$ are given. In [18] Bl. Sendov uses the modulus $\tau_1(f;\delta)_{L_p}$ for the study of the convergence of sequences of linear positive operators. For the case k>1 see [20], [21].

The moduli $\tau_k(f;\delta)_{L_p}$ have the following properties:

LEMMA 1. Let f and g be $2\pi$-periodical functions and $f,g \in L_p[0,2\pi]$. Then: $(1 \leq p \leq \infty)$

1) $\tau_k(f;\delta)_{L_p} \leq \tau_k(f;\delta')_{L_p}, \quad \delta \leq \delta'$

2) $\omega_k(f;\delta)_{L_p} \leq \tau_k(f;\delta)_{L_p}$

3) $\omega_k(f;\delta)_{L_\infty} = \tau_k(f;\delta)_{L_\infty}$

4) $\tau_k(f+g;\delta)_{L_p} \leq \tau_k(f;\delta)_{L_p} + \tau_k(g;\delta)_{L_p}$

5) $\tau_k(f;\delta)_{L_p} \leq \delta\, \tau_{k-1}(f';\delta)_{L_p}$

6) $\tau_1(f;\delta)_{L_p} \leq \delta \|f'\|_{L_p}$

7) $$\tau_k(f;\lambda\delta)_{L_p} \leqslant (1+c_1\lambda)^{c_2 k}\tau_k(f;\delta)_{L_p},$$

where $c_1$ and $c_2$ are constants.

The following lemma is useful in the onesided approximations:

LEMMA 2. Let $f,g$ and $\psi$ be $2\pi$-periodical functions and $f,g,\psi \in L_p[0,2\pi]$. If for every $x$ we have

$$|f(x) - g(x)| \leqslant \psi(x)$$

then

$$\tilde{E}_n^T(f)_{L_p} \leqslant \tilde{E}_n^T(g)_{L_p} + \tilde{E}_n^T(\psi)_{L_p} + 2\|\psi\|_{L_p}, \qquad 1\leqslant p\leqslant\infty.$$

## 2. Previous Results on Onesided Approximation

The above-mentioned result of G. Freud [1] is the following: let $f$ be a bounded function in the interval $[-1,1]$, with a derivative $f^{(k)}$ of bounded variation. Then there exists an absolute constant $c(k)$, depending only on $k$, and two polynomials $P\in H_n$, $Q\in H_n$, $Q(x)\leqslant f(x)\leqslant P(x)$ for $x\in[-1,1]$, such that

$$\int_{-1}^{1} \frac{P(x)-Q(x)}{\sqrt{1-x^2}}\,dx \leqslant c(k)\frac{V_{-1}^{1} f^{(k)}}{n^{k+1}}$$

where $V_a^b g$ denotes the variation of function $g$ in the interval $[a,b]$.

The corresponding result of T. Ganelius [2] for the trigonometrical case is as follows:

(2) $$\tilde{E}_n^T(f)_{L_1[0,2\pi]} \leqslant c'(k)\,\frac{V_0^{2} f^{(k)}}{n^{k+1}}.$$

Later on A. Meir and A. Sharma [3] have considered onesided $L_1$ approximation by splines of first and third degree. G. Freud and V.A. Popov in [4] generalized their results for splines of arbitrary degree. The result was the following:

(3) $$\tilde{E}_{k,\Sigma_n}(f)_{L_1[0,1]} \leq c''(k)\Delta_n^{k+1} V_0^1 f^{(k)},$$

where the constant c"(k) depends only on k and

$$\Delta_n = \max |x_i - x_{i-1}|, \quad i=1,\ldots,n.$$

V.F. Babenko, A.A. Ligun, V.G. Doronin [5] - [9] consider onesided approximation in $L_p$, $1 \leq p < \infty$, for some classes of functions. Their main result [5] for the class $W^r L_p$ ($f \in W^r L_p$ if $f^{(r-1)}$ is absolutely continuous and $\|f^{(r)}\|_{L_p} \leq 1$) is the following:

For every p, $1 \leq p < \infty$, we have:

(4) $$\sup_{f \in W^r L_p} \tilde{E}_n^T(f)_{L_p} = \mathcal{O}(n^{-r}), \quad r=1,2,\ldots$$

(5) $$\sup_{f \in W^r L_p} \tilde{E}_{r-1,\Delta_n}(f)_{L_p} = \mathcal{O}(\Delta_n^r), \quad r=1,2,\ldots$$

(for p=1 (4) and (5) follow from (2) and (3)).

Let us mention also the results of G. Freud, J. Szabados [10], G. Freud, P. Nevai [11], P. Nevai [12], G. Freud [13], in which onesided approximation with weight and also on infinite interval is considered.

## 3. Jackson and Bernstein Theorems

We shall give now an analogue of the well-known Jackson theorem and Bernstein theorem for the onesided approximation of functions.

The Jackson theorem states that

$$E_n^T(f)_{L_p} = \mathcal{O}(\omega_1(f;n^{-1})_{L_p}),$$

and its generalization, given by S.B. Steckin [14] states that

(6) $$E_n^T(f)_{L_p} = O(\omega_k(f;n^{-1})_{L_p}).$$

We give the converse approximation theorem of Bernstein in the form, presented by Salem-Steckin (see [14]):

(7) $$\omega_k(f;n^{-1})_{L_p} \leq \frac{c(k)}{n^k} \sum_{s=0}^{n} s^{k-1} E_s^T(f)_{L_p}.$$

It is easy to see that it is not possible to obtain direct theorems for onesided approximation using the moduli $\omega_k(f;\delta)_{L_p}$, $1 \leq p < \infty$. But it is so, if we use the modulus $\tau_k(f;\delta)_{L_p}$, defined in section 1. We shall see that it is possible also to obtain a converse theorem for onesided trigonometrical approximation by means of $\tau_k(f;\delta)_{L_p}$.

The first analogue of Jackson's theorem is given in [19] and is the following:

THEOREM 1. *Let* f *be a* $2\pi$*-periodical function with k-th derivative* $f^{(k)} \in L_p[0,2\pi]$. *Then for* $1 \leq p \leq \infty$ *we have*

$$\tilde{E}_n^T(f)_{L_p} = O(n^{-k}\tau_1(f^{(k)};n^{-1})_{L_p}).$$

*If the function* f *is defined on the interval* $[0,1]$ *and has in this interval a derivative* $f^{(k)} \in L_p[0,1]$ *then for* $1 \leq p \leq \infty$ *we have*

$$\tilde{E}_{k,\Delta_n}(f)_{L_p} = O(\Delta_n^k \tau_1(f^{(k)};\Delta_n)_{L_p}).$$

This theorem was generalized in [20] as follows:

THEOREM 2. *Let* f *be a bounded* $2\pi$*-periodical function or a bounded function in the interval* $[0,1]$. *Then for* $1 \leq p \leq \infty$ *we have*

$$\tilde{E}_n^T(f)_{L_p} \leq C(k)\tau_k(f;n^{-1})_{L_p}$$

$$\tilde{E}_{k,\Delta_n}(f)_{L_p} \leq C'(k)\tau_k(f;\Delta_n)_{L_p}$$

*where* C(k) *and* C'(k) *are constants, depending only on* k.

REMARK. Obviously for $p=\infty$ theorems 1 and 2 are the classical case of uniform approximation of functions. Moreover, evidently from Lemma 1 and Theorem 2 follows Theorem 1.

The analogue of the Salem-Steckin theorem for the best trigonometrical onesided approximation is given in [21]:

THEOREM 3. *We have*

$$\tau_k(f;n^{-1})_{L_p} \leq \frac{c(k)}{n^k} \sum_{s=0}^{n} s^{k-1}\tilde{E}_s^T(f)_{L_p}$$

*where* c(k) *is a constant, depending only on* k.

REMARK. Obviously for $p=\infty$ theorem 3 goes to (7).

## 4. Application of the Moduli $\tau_k(f;\delta)_{L_1}$ to the Quadrature Formulas

Let us consider the composite quadrature formula of Newton-Cotes type of (k,n) order:

$$\int_0^1 f(x)\,dx = \sum_{i=0}^{m} A_i f(x_i) + R_m(f) \tag{8}$$

(for example the rectangular rule, trapezoidal rule, Simpson's rule).

The formula (8) is composed in this manner: we divide the interval $[0,1]$ in n equal parts $\Delta_s = [s/n,(s+1)/n]$, $s=0,\dots,n-1$, and in each part $\Delta_s$ we interpolate the function f in the points $y_{s,i}$, $i=0,\dots,k$ (equidistant in $\Delta_s$) by means of polynomials $p_s$ of $k^{th}$ degree. After this we put

$$\sum_{s=0}^{n-1} \int_{s/n}^{(s+1)/n} p_s(x)\,dx = \sum_{i=0}^{m} A_i f(x_i).$$

It is well-known that it is possible to estimate $R_m(f)$ by means of $\|f^{(k+1)}\|_C$ or $\|f^{(k+2)}\|_C$, $\|g\| = \max_{x\in[0,1]}|g(x)|$. But using the modulus $\tau_k(f;\delta)_{L_1}$ one can obtain an estimation without the assumption that f has derivatives. For example, we have the following

THEOREM 4. *The following estimations are true:*

a) *for the rectangular rule:*

$$\left|\int_0^1 f(x)\,dx - \frac{1}{n}\sum_{i=1}^{n} f((2i-1)/2n)\right| \leq c_1\tau_2(f;n^{-1})_{L_1}$$

b) *for the trapezoidal rule:*

$$\left|\int_0^1 f(x)\,dx - \frac{1}{2n}\left(f(0)+2\sum_{i=1}^{n-1} f(i/n) + f(1)\right)\right| \leq c_2\tau_2(f;n^{-1})_{L_1}$$

c) *for the Simpson rule:*

$$\left|\int_0^1 f(x)\,dx - \frac{1}{6n}\left(f(0) + 2\sum_{i=1}^{n-1} f(i/n) + 4\sum_{i=1}^{n-1} f((2i-1)/2n) + f(1)\right)\right|$$
$$\leq c_3\tau_4(f;n^{-1})_{L_1}.$$

Estimations of this type are true for the general cocomposite quadrature formulas (8) of Newton-Cotes type of (k,n) order. For even k the error $R_m(f)$ is $\mathcal{O}(\tau_{k+2}(f;n^{-1})_{L_1})$ and for odd k the error is $\mathcal{O}(\tau_{k+1}(f;n^{-1})_{L_1})$.

## REFERENCES

[1] Freud, G., Über einseitige Approximation durch Polynome I. Acta Sci. Math. (Szeged). 16 (1955), 12 - 18.

[2] Ganelius, T., On onesided approximation by trigonometrical polynomials. Math. Scand. 4 (1956), 247 - 258.

[ 3] Meir, A. - Sharma, A., Onesided spline approximation. Studia Sci. Math. Hungar. 3 (1968), 211 - 218.

[ 4] Freud, G. - Popov, V.A., Some questions connected with approximation by means of spline functions and polynomials. Studia Sci. Math. Hungar. 5 (1970), 161 - 171. (russian)

[ 5] Babenko, V.F. - Ligun, A.A., The order of the best onesided approximation by means of polynomials and splines in the metric $L_p$. Math. Notes. 19 (1976), 323 - 329. (russian)

[ 6] Doronin, V.G. - Ligun, A.A., The best onesided approximation of some classes of differentiable periodical functions. Dokl. Akad. Nauk SSSR. 230 (1976), 19 - 21. (russian)

[ 7] Doronin, V.G. - Ligun, A.A., Upper bounds of the best onesided approximation by splines of the classes $W^rL_1$. Math. Notes. 19 (1976), 11 - 17. (russian)

[ 8] Doronin, V.G. - Ligun, A.A., On the best onesided approximation of one classe of functions by means of other. Math. Notes. 14 (1973), 627 - 632. (russian)

[ 9] Doronin, V.G., The best onesided approximation of some classes of functions. Math. Notes. 10 (1971), 615 - 626. (russian)

[10] Freud, G. - Szabados, J., Über einseitige Approximation durch Polynome II. Acta Sci. Math. (Szeged). 31 (1970), 59 - 67.

[11] Freud, G. - Nevai, P., Über einseitige Approximation durch Polynome III. Acta Sci. Math. (Szeged). 35 (1973), 65 - 72.

[12] Nevai, P., Einseitige Approximation durch Polynome mit Anwendungen. Acta Math. Acad. Sci. Hungar. 23 (1972), 495 - 506.

[13] Freud, G., On the theory of onesided weighted $L_1$-approximation by polynomials. Linear Operators and Approximation II. (ISNM 25) Birkhäuser Verlag Basel/Stuttgart (1974), 285 - 303.

[14] Steckin, S.B., On the order of the best approximation of continuous functions. Izv. Akad. Nauk SSSR Ser. Mat. 15 (1951), 219 - 242.

[15] Sendov, Bl., Doctoral dissertation. Math. Inst. Akad. Nauk SSSR. 1968.

[16] Korovkin, P.P., Axiomatic construction of some questions of the theory of approximation. Ućen. Zap. Kalinin. Inst. 69 (1969), 91 - 109.

[17] Dolgenko, E.P. - Sevastianov, E.A., Math. Sbornik, 101/143 (1976), 508 - 531.

[18] Sendov, Bl., Convergence of sequences of monotonic operators in A-distance. C.R. Acad. Bulgare Sci. 30 (1977).

[19] Andreev, A.S. - Popov, V.A. - Sendov, Bl., Jackson's type theorems for onesided polynomials and spline approximation. C.R. Acad. Bulgare Sci. 30 (1977).

[20] Popov, V.A. - Andreev, A., Steckin's type theorems for onesided trigonometrical and spline approximation. C.R. Acad. Bulgare Sci. 31 (1978).

[21] Popov, V.A., Converse theorems for onesided trigonometrical approximation. C.R. Acad. Bulgare Sci. 30 (1977).

# VII
# Complex Function Theory and Approximation

# APPROXIMATION VON EBENEN HARMONISCHEN FUNKTIONEN DURCH SOLCHE MIT WACHSTUMSBESCHRÄNKUNG

W.K. Hayman
Dept. of Mathematics
Imperial College
London

Wir betrachten folgende Probleme. Es sei gegeben eine reelle Funktion $\psi(t)$, $t \geq t_o$.

a) Wann existiert für jede nicht konstante ebene harmonische Funktion $u(z)$ ein gegen unendlich strebender Weg $\Gamma$ auf dem

(1) $$u(z) > \psi(|z|), \qquad z \in \Gamma$$

gilt ? Wir sagen in diesem Fall $\psi \in B$.

b) Wir betrachten die Klasse $L_\psi$, definiert wie folgt. Eine Funktion $v(z)$ gehört zu $L_\psi$, wenn $v$ in einem JORDAN Gebiet $D$ definiert und harmonisch ist, $v$ auf dem Rande $F$ von $D$ stetig bleibt und dort der Ungleichung

(2) $$v(z) \leq \psi(|z|), \qquad z \in F$$

genügt.

Wir sagen $\psi \in A$, wenn sich jede ebene harmonische Funktion durch $L_\psi$ approximieren läßt, d.h. wenn für gegebenes positives $\varepsilon$, Kompaktum $E$ und harmonisches Polynom $P(z)$ eine Funktion $v \in L_\psi$ existiert, deren Definitionsbereich $E$ enthält und für welche gilt

(3) $$|P(z) - v(z)| < \varepsilon, \qquad z \in E.$$

Die Resultate, über die ich sprechen möchte, stammen aus einer gemeinsamen Arbeit mit D.A. BRANNAN und K.F. BARTH [2]. Wir kamen zu dem Problem b) durch a) [3, Problem 3.1]. Es scheint mir aber, daß auch b) ein gewisses Interesse hat, obwohl die Klasse $L_\psi$ dadurch, daß jede Funktion in $L_\psi$ ihren eigenen Definitionsbereich besitzt, weit davon entfernt ist, einen linearen Raum zu bilden.

Ich fange mit einigen elementaren Bemerkungen an.

Gehört $\psi$ zu A oder B, so gilt dasselbe für $\psi_1 = a\psi + b$, wenn $a > 0$ und b reell ist. Denn es gilt

$$u(z) > \psi(|z|) \Leftrightarrow au + b > a\psi + b.$$

Also, wenn u, $\psi$ der Ungleichung (1) genügen, so genügen $u_1 = au + b$ und $\psi_1$ der entsprechenden Ungleichung. Da u, $u_1$ zusammen alle ebenen harmonischen Funktionen durchlaufen, folgt die Äquivalenz für a). Die Äquivalenz für b) beweist man ähnlich.

Wir beweisen nun

SATZ 1. $A \cap B = \emptyset$.

Wir nehmen an $\psi \in A$. Wir konstruieren dann eine harmonische Funktion u(z) wie folgt. Wir setzen $\varepsilon_n = 2^{-n-1}$ und definieren Folgen $R_n$ von wachsenden positiven Zahlen, von Funktionen $v_n \in L_\psi$ und von harmonischen Polynomen $P_n(z)$ wie folgt. Es sei $R_1 = 2$,

$$(4) \qquad |v_1(z) - x| < \varepsilon_1, \quad |z| \leq R_1, \quad z = x + iy.$$

Dann folgt, daß der Definitionsbereich $\overline{D}_1$ von $v_1$ die Kreisfläche $|z| \leq R_1$ enthalten muß. Nun folgt aus einem klassischen Approximationssatz die Existenz eines harmonischen Polynoms $P_1(z)$ mit

$$(5) \qquad |v_1(z) - P_1(z)| < \varepsilon_1, \qquad z \in \overline{D}_1.$$

Wir nehmen an, $v_n(z)$ mit Existenzbereich $D_n$ und dessen Begrenzung $\Gamma_n$ seien schon definiert, ebenso das Polynom $P_n(z)$ und der Radius $R_n$. Wir definieren dann $R_{n+1} \geq 2R_n$ und $R_{n+1}$ so groß, daß $D_n$ in der Kreisscheibe $|z| \leq R_{n+1}$ enthalten ist, definieren $v_{n+1} \in L_\psi$ mit Definitionsbereich $D_{n+1}$ und $v_{n+1} \in L_\psi$, so daß

$$(6) \qquad |v_{n+1}(z) - P_n(z)| < \varepsilon_{n+1}, \quad |z| \leqslant R_{n+1},$$

und konstruieren ein Polynom $P_{n+1}$, das der Ungleichung

$$(7) \qquad |v_{n+1} - P_{n+1}| < \varepsilon_{n+1}, \qquad z \in \overline{D}_{n+1}$$

genügt. Wir behaupten nun, daß die Folge $P_n$ lokal gleichmäßig in der Ebene konvergiert gegen eine Grenzfunktion $P(z)$, die bestimmt harmonisch ist.

Tatsächlich schließen wir aus (6) und (7)

$$|P_{n+1} - P_n| \leqslant 2\varepsilon_{n+1} = \varepsilon_n, \quad |z| \leqslant R_{n+1},$$

und dies ergibt schon die gleichmäßige Konvergenz. Für $z \in \overline{D}_n$ folgt ferner

$$\begin{aligned} |P(z) - v_n(z)| &\leqslant |v_n - P_n| + |P - P_n| \\ &\leqslant |v_n - P_n| + \sum_{m=n}^{\infty} |P_{m+1} - P_m| \\ (8) \qquad &\leqslant \varepsilon_n + \sum_{m=n}^{\infty} \varepsilon_m = 3\varepsilon_n < 1. \end{aligned}$$

Da $v_n \in L_\psi$, erhalten wir insbesondere auf der Berandung $\Gamma_n$ von $D_n$,

$$(9) \qquad P(z) < v_n(z) + 1 \leqslant \psi(|z|) + 1, \qquad z \in \Gamma_n.$$

Ferner ist $P(z)$ nicht konstant, denn wir schließen aus (4) und (8) für $|z| \leqslant 2$,

$$|P(z) - x| \leqslant |P(z) - v_1| + |v_1 - x| < 4\varepsilon_1 = 2,$$

also $P(-2) < 0 < P(2)$.

Also ist $P(z)$ eine in der ganzen Ebene harmonische, nicht konstante Funktion, die der Ungleichung (9) genügt. Es sei nun $\Gamma$ ein beliebiger nach unendlich strebender Weg. Dann trifft $\Gamma$ für genügend große $n$ die JORDAN Kurven $\Gamma_n$, also enthält $\Gamma$ bestimmt Punkte, in denen

$$P(z) - 1 \leqslant \psi(|z|)$$

gilt. Also genügt die Funktion $u(z) = P(z) - 1$ auf keinem Weg $\Gamma$ der Ungleichung (1), also $\psi \notin B$, und der Satz 1 ist bewiesen.

Es liegt nun nahe zu fragen, ob es Funktionen gibt, die weder in A noch in B liegen. Es ist dies tatsächlich der Fall. Man setze $\psi(2^n) = 2^n$, $\psi(t) = -C2^n$, $2^{n-1} < t < 2^n$, für $n \geq 1$, wo C eine genügend große, absolute Konstante ist. Dann ist es klar, daß $u(z) = x$ der Bedingung (1) nicht genügen kann, also $\psi(t) \notin B$. Mit etwas mehr Schwierigkeit zeigt man, daß man Polynome vom Grade größer als eins durch $L_\psi$ nicht approximieren kann, also $\psi(t) \notin B$. Für monotone $\psi(t)$ können wir aber beweisen, daß $\psi(t)$ tatsächlich zu A oder B gehören muß.

SATZ 2. <u>Es sei</u> $\psi(t)$ <u>eine wachsende Funktion für</u> $t \geq t_o > 0$. <u>Dann sind folgende drei Bedingungen äquivalent</u>

$$\text{(i)}\quad \psi \in A, \qquad \text{(ii)}\quad \psi \notin B, \qquad \text{(iii)}\quad \int_{t_o}^{\infty} t^{-3/2}\, \psi(t)\,dt = \infty.$$

Volle Beweise würden uns zu weit führen. Nach Satz 1 genügt es zu zeigen, daß $\psi \in A$, wenn das Integral divergiert, und daß $\psi \in B$, wenn das Integral konvergiert. Diese Resultate werden in [2] erscheinen. Hier möchte ich nur die Beweisideen andeuten.

Wir bemerken zuerst, daß wir ohne Einschränkung der Allgemeinheit annehmen dürfen, daß $\psi(t)$ stetig und positiv ist. Denn die Funktion $\psi_o(t) = \psi(t) - \psi(t_o) + 1$ ist offenbar positiv und genügt den Bedingungen (i) bis (iii) genau dann, wenn $\psi(t)$ es tut. Wir nehmen nun an, der Satz 2 sei für positive, stetige, wachsende Funktionen bewiesen, und $\psi_o(t)$ sei jetzt positiv und wachsend. Wir nehmen erst an, daß (iii) erfüllt ist und setzen

$$\psi_1(t) = \int_{t-1}^{t} \psi_o(\tau)\,d\tau, \qquad t \geq t_o + 1.$$

Offenbar ist $\psi_1(t)$ stetig und erfüllt die Bedingung (iii), da $\psi_1(t) \geq \psi_o(t-1)$ gilt. Daher gilt $\psi_1(t) \in A$. Andererseits ist $\psi_1(t) \leq \psi_o(t)$, und so gilt auch $\psi_o(t) \in A$.

Andererseits sei (iii) falsch. Wir setzen dann

$$\psi_1(t) = \int_t^{t+1} \psi_0(\tau)d\tau$$

und sehen, daß $\psi_1(t)$ stetig ist und die Bedingung (iii) nicht erfüllt. Daher gilt $\psi_1(t) \in B$. Da $\psi_0(t) \leqslant \psi_1(t)$ gilt, schließen wir, daß auch $\psi_0(t) \in B$. Also, wenn der Satz 2 für positive, stetige, wachsende Funktionen gilt, so gilt er für allgemeine wachsende Funktionen.

Wir nehmen nun an, $\psi(t)$ sei positiv, wachsend und stetig und

$$\int_{t_0}^{\infty} \frac{\psi(t)dt}{t^{3/2}} = \infty . \tag{10}$$

Wir wollen beweisen, daß dann $\psi(t) \in A$. Zu diesem Zweck brauchen wir einen allgemeinen Approximationssatz, der besagt, daß man unter gewissen Umständen eine harmonische Funktion $u_1(z)$ in einem Gebiet $D_1$ durch eine harmonische Funktion $u_2(z)$ in einem Erweiterungsgebiet $D_2$ approximieren kann. Wir nehmen an, daß $D_2$ aus $D_1$ entsteht, indem man gewisse kleine Randkurven $J_\nu^{(1)}$ durch Randkurven $J_\nu^{(2)}$ ersetzt, für $\nu = 1,2,\ldots,N$. Die Bedingungen an $D_1$ für festes N, nehmen die Form an, daß die $J_\nu^{(1)}$ genügend klein und genügend weit voneinander entfernt sind (von $\varepsilon$, M, N abhängig). Von $u_1(z)$ müssen wir annehmen, daß $u_1(z) \geqslant -M$ in $D_1$ gilt und $u_1(z_0) \leqslant 1/2\, M$ für einen festen Punkt $z_0$ in $D_1$, ferner $u_1(z) \geqslant 0$ auf den $J_\nu^{(1)}$ und $u_1(z) = 0$ auf gewissen Nachbarrandbögen der $J_\nu^{(1)}$. Dann kann man immer $u_2(z)$ finden, so daß

$$|u_1(z) - u_2(z)| < \varepsilon \ .$$

Ferner hat $u_2(z)$, außer auf den $J_\nu^{(2)}$, dieselben Randwerte wie $u_1(z)$, und auf $J_\nu^{(2)}$ kann man beliebige Randwerte $f_\nu(\xi)$ angeben, die nicht negativ und nicht identisch null sind. Dann nimmt $u_2(z)$ die Werte $\alpha_\nu f_\nu(\xi)$ auf $J_\nu^{(2)}$ an, wo $\alpha_\nu \geqslant 0$. Also können wir $u_2(z)$ so schreiben

(11) $$u_2(z) = v_o(z) + \sum_{\nu=1}^{N} \alpha_\nu v_\nu(z),$$

wo $v_o(z)$ auf dem gemeinsamen Rand von $D_1$ und $D_2$ die Randwerte von $u_1$ annimmt und sonst auf dem Rand von $D_2$ verschwindet, und $v_\nu(z)$ auf $J_\nu^{(2)}$ die Randwerte $f_\nu(z)$ annimmt und sonst auf dem Rande von $D_2$ verschwindet.
Die Grundidee von diesem Hilfssatz ist folgende: Wenn die Randbögen $J_\nu^{(1)}$ klein sind, so hängt die Funktion $u_1(z)$ in $D_1$ außerhalb der Umgebung dieser $J_\nu^{(1)}$ nur von der "Gesamtgröße" der Randwerte, aber nicht von ihrer genauen Form ab. Die Konstanten $\alpha_\nu$ können so gewählt werden, daß $u_1(z)$, $u_2(z)$ ungefähr dieselbe Gesamtgröße auf all den Randbögen $J_\nu^{(1)}$ haben.

Nun sei $P(z)$ ein harmonisches Polynom, $\varepsilon$, $R$ positive Zahlen. Wir wünschen $P(z)$ in $|z| < R$ durch $v(z) \in L_\psi$ zu approximieren. Die Zahl $M$ ist durch $P(0) < 1/2\ M$, $P(z) > -M$ in $|z| < R$ fixiert, $N$ ist der Grad von $P(z)$. Das Gebiet $D_1$ wird wie folgt definiert. Wir nehmen an, daß $R$ so groß ist, daß der Ort $P(z) > 0$ für $|z| > R$ aus Gebieten $z = re^{i\theta}$, $r > R$,

(12) $$\theta_{2\nu}(r) < \theta < \theta_{2\nu+1}(r), \qquad \nu = 1,2,\ldots,N$$

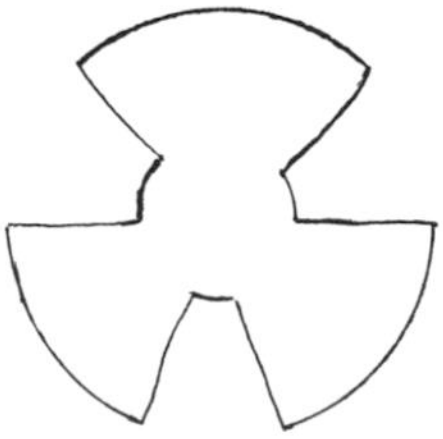

besteht. Dann bilden wir $D_1$, indem wir die Gebiete (12) für $R < r < R_1$ zu $|z| < R$ adjungieren. Die $J_\nu^{(1)}$ sind dann die Grenzstrecken (12) mit $r = R_1$. Es stellt sich heraus, daß die Bedingungen für $P = u_1$, mit $z = 0$ erfüllt sind, wenn $R_1$ genügend groß ist (von $R, \varepsilon, M$ und $N$ abhängig).

Die $J_\nu^{(2)}$ werden nun durch Induktion nach $\nu$ konstruiert. Wir nehmen an für $\nu < \mu \leqslant N$ hätte die Konstruktion schon stattgefunden und das entsprechende JORDAN Gebiet $D^{(\mu)}$ läge in $|z| < r_\mu$. Dann definieren wir ein genügend großes $r_{\mu+1}$ und $r'_\mu = r_\mu + 1$, schreiben $Q_{2\mu} = -r'_\mu i$, $Q_{2\mu+1} = r'_\mu i$ und verbinden $Q_{2\mu}$ und

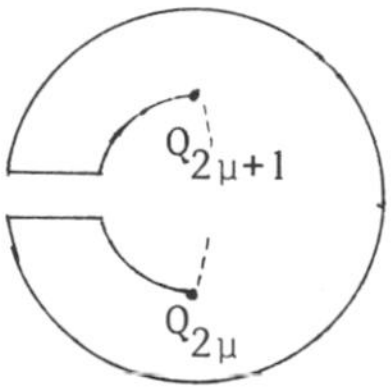


$Q_{2\mu+1}$ mit den Endpunkten von $J_\mu^{(1)}$ durch Kurven, die in $|z| < r'_\mu$, aber außerhalb von $D^{(\mu)}$ liegen. Das Gebiet $D^{(\mu+1)}$ wird

fertig gemacht, indem wir den Sektor

(13) $$r'_\mu < |z| < r_{\mu+1}, |\arg z| < \pi - \eta_\mu$$

adjungieren, wo $\eta$ eine kleine positive Zahl ist. Hierdurch ist auch $J_\mu^{(2)}$ definiert. Die Grenzwerte auf $J_\mu^{(2)}$ definieren wir gleich Null, außer auf $z = re^{\mp i\theta_\mu}$, wo wir $f_\mu(z) = \psi(r)$ für $9r'_\mu \leqslant r \leqslant 1/9\, r_{\mu+1}$ setzen, mit $0 \leqslant f_\mu(r) \leqslant \psi(r)$, für $r'_\mu \leqslant r \leqslant 9r'_\mu$ und $1/9\, r_{\mu+1} \leqslant r \leqslant r_{\mu+1}$, so daß $f_\mu(r)$ stetig bleibt und $f_\mu(r'_\mu) = f_\mu(r_{\mu+1}) = 0$.

Um mit unserem Beweis zu Ende zu kommen, genügt es zu zeigen, daß wenn $r_{\mu+1}$ genügend groß und $\eta_\mu$ genügend klein sind, in (11) die Konstanten $\alpha_\nu$ alle kleiner als eins sein müssen. Denn in diesem Fall gehört $u_2$ sicher zu $L_\psi$.

Nun bemerken wir, daß $\alpha_\mu v_\mu(z)$ eine positive harmonische Funktion in $D_\mu$ ist, die im Nullpunkt und deshalb nach HARNACK auch in $z_\mu = 9r'_\mu$ eine von $r_{\mu+1}$ unabhängige obere Schranke $C_\mu$ hat, sobald $\eta_\mu < \pi/2$ und $r_{\mu+1} > 3^6 r'_\mu$ gilt. Andererseits erhält man aber durch die POISSON-Formel auf dem Sektor (13) eine untere Abschätzung

$$C_\mu \geqslant \alpha_\mu v_\mu(z_\mu) \geqslant K\, r'^{1/2}_\mu \int_{9r_\mu}^{1/9 r_{\mu+1}} \frac{\alpha_\mu \psi(t)\,dt}{t^{3/2}}$$

sobald $r_{\mu+1}$ genügend groß und $\eta_{\mu+1}$ genügend klein genommen werden. Dann folgt aus der Divergenz in (10), daß $\alpha_\mu < 1$ gilt, und damit ist die Approximation bewiesen, also $\psi(t) \in B$.

Wir bemerken, daß dieser Beweis keinen Gebrauch davon macht, daß $\psi(t)$ wächst. Es genügt, daß $\psi(t)$ positiv und stetig ist und daß das Integral (10) divergiert.

Ich möchte nun annehmen, daß

(14) $$\int_{t_o}^{\infty} \frac{\psi(t)\,dt}{t^{3/2}} < \infty$$

und schließe daraus $\psi(t) \in A$. Wir dürfen annehmen, daß $\psi(t)$ nicht nur positiv, stetig und wachsend ist, sondern auch konvex in $\log t$ für $t \geqslant 0$. Im entgegengesetzten Falle setzen wir

$$\psi_1(t) = \int_{t_o}^{et} \frac{\psi(\tau)d\tau}{\tau}, \qquad t \geq t_o$$

$$\psi_1(t) = \psi_1(t_o), \qquad t < t_o.$$

Man sieht dann leicht, daß $\psi_1(t)$ noch immer der Bedingung (14) genügt, und $\psi_1(t)$ konvex in log t, $\psi_1(t) \geq \psi(t)$ ist. Wenn unser Satz also für die Funktion $\psi_1(t)$ bewiesen ist, so folgt er auch für $\psi(t)$.

Nun sei u(z) eine nicht konstante harmonische Funktion und D eine Komponente der Menge $u(z) > 0$. Es folgt aus dem Maximumprinzip, daß D einfach zusammenhängend und unbegrenzt ist. Wir konstruieren nun die Funktion $v_R(z)$, die in $D_R = D \cap \{|z|<R\}$ harmonisch ist und auf dem Rande von $D_R$ die Randwerte $\psi(t)$ annimmt. Da $\psi(t)$ eine konvexe Funktion von log t ist, ist $\psi(|z|)$ eine subharmonische Funktion von z. Hieraus folgt nach dem Maximumprinzip für $R_1 < R_2$ und $z \in D_{R_1}$

$$\psi(|z|) < v_{R_1}(z) < v_{R_2}(z).$$

Hieraus folgt, daß $v_R(z)$ mit wachsendem R gegen eine Grenzfunktion v(z) strebt, und aus der MILLOUX-SCHMIDT Ungleichung[1)] und der Konvergenz (14) folgt, daß v(z) endlich und daher harmonisch ist. Also

$$0 < \psi(|z|) < v(z) \quad \text{in D.} \tag{15}$$

Es sei nun $z_o$ ein Punkt in D. Wir wählen die positive Konstante $\alpha$ so klein, daß $u(z_o) > \alpha v(z_o)$ gilt. Wir setzen

$$u_1(z) = \max\{u(z)-\alpha v(z), 0\} \qquad z \in D$$

$$u_1(z) = 0, \qquad z \notin D.$$

Offenbar ist $u_1(z)$ in der ganzen Ebene subharmonisch und nicht konstant. Denn laut (15) verschwindet $u_1(z)$ in der Umgebung der Grenze von D.

1) BEURLING [1]. Die Methode baut auf Ideen von BEURLING auf.

Hieraus folgt nach einem Satz von TALPUR [4], daß $u_1(z)$ auf einem Weg $\Gamma$ gegen $+\infty$ strebt. Also auf jeden Fall

$$u_1(z) > 0, \quad u(z) > \alpha v(z) > \alpha\psi(|z|)$$

auf einer Teilstrecke von $\Gamma$. Um das volle Resultat zu erreichen, konstruieren wir eine Funktion $\psi_1(t)$, die positiv und wachsend ist und

$$\int_{t_0}^{\infty} \frac{\psi_1(t)dt}{t} < \infty, \quad \frac{\psi_1(t)}{\psi(t)} \to +\infty, \quad \text{wenn } t \to +\infty .$$

Der obige Beweis führt dann zu

$$u(z) > \alpha v(z) > \psi(|z|)$$

auf einer genügend entfernten Teilstrecke des Weges $\Gamma$. Also $\psi \in A$, und der Beweis von Satz 2 ist beendet.

## LITERATUR


[1] Barth, K.F. - Brannan, D.A. and Hayman, W.K. The growth of plane harmonic functions along an asymptotic path. Proc. London Math. Soc. (1978).

[2] Beurling, A., Études sur un problème de majoration. Thèse de Upsal (1933).

[3] Hayman, W.K., Research Problems in Function Theory. Athlone Press, London 1967.

[4] Talpur, M.N.M., On the growth of subharmonic functions on asymptotic paths. Proc. London Math. Soc. (3) 32 (1976), 193 - 198.

# EXTREME POINTS OF SPACES OF UNIVALENT FUNCTIONS

Peter L. Duren
Department of Mathematics
University of Michigan
Ann Arbor, Michigan 48109; U.S.A.

This paper describes the recent venture of functional analysis into an unlikely field: the theory of univalent functions. Our discussion will focus upon the class S of functions

$$f(z) = z + a_2z^2 + a_3z^3 + \ldots, \qquad |z| < 1,$$

analytic and univalent to the unit disk, normalized so that $f(0) = 0$ and $f'(0) = 1$. Univalent means that $f(z_1) \neq f(z_2)$ if $z_1 \neq z_2$.

The leading example, aside from the identity, of a function in S is the Koebe function

$$k(z) = z(1-z)^{-2} = z + 2z^2 + 3z^3 + \ldots,$$

which maps the disk onto the whole plane minus the part of the negative real axis from $-1/4$ to $\infty$. The Koebe function and its rotations $e^{-i\theta}k(e^{i\theta}z)$ are known to maximize various functionals over S, such as $|f(z_o)|$ and $|f'(z_o)|$ at a fixed point $z_o$. This evidence led Bieberbach in 1916 to conjecture that $|a_n| \leqslant n$ for all $f \in S$, $n=2,3,\ldots$, with strict inequality for all n unless f is a rotation of the Koebe function. Despite the efforts of many mathematicians, the conjecture remains unsettled. (See [3] for a survey of recent progress on the Bieberbach conjecture and related problems.)

Because S is invariant under rotations, Bieberbach's problem is equivalent to the linear problem of maximizing $\mathrm{Re}\{a_n\}$ over S. This naturally suggests the general problem of maximizing $\mathrm{Re}\{L(f)\}$ over S, where L is an arbitrary complex-valued linear functional, continuous with respect to the topology of uniform convergence on compact subsets of the disk. The solutions to such a linear extremal problem, where L is not constant on S, are called support points of S.

The space S is far from linear. The sum of two functions in S need not be univalent, and may even have infinite valence. Nevertheless, S may be viewed as a compact subset of the linear space of all analytic functions in the disk, endowed with the topology of local uniform convergence. This being a locally convex space, the Kreĭn-Milman theorem applies, so S is contained in the closed convex hull of its extreme points. Consequently, the maximum over S of each continuous linear (or convex) functional is attained at an extreme point. In other words, there is an extreme point among the support points of every linear functional.

Thus it is important to identify the extreme points of S. This problem has not been solved, but Brickman [ 1] recently obtained the following result.

THEOREM 1. *Each extreme point of* S *maps the disk onto the complement of an arc extending to* $\infty$ *with increasing modulus.*

Brickman's proof is entirely elementary. The argument gives a stronger result, as Brickman and Wilken [ 2] essentially observed:

THEOREM 2. *If a function* $f \in S$ *omits two values of equal modulus, then* f *has the form*

$$f = tf_1 + (1-t)f_2 , \qquad 0 < t < 1,$$

*where* $f_1$ *and* $f_2$ *are distinct functions in* S *which omit open sets.*

The proof is so simple and elegant that we cannot resist giving it here.

PROOF OF THEOREM 2. Let D be the range of f, and let $\alpha$ and $\beta$ be the two omitted values ($|\alpha| = |\beta|$, $\alpha \neq \beta$). Then some branch of

$$\psi(w) = \{(w-\alpha)(w-\beta)\}^{1/2}$$

is analytic in D. We claim:

(a) $\psi(w) \pm w$ are univalent in D;

(b) $\pm\psi(w) - w$ have disjoint ranges.

To prove (a), suppose that

$$\psi(w_1) - \psi(w_2) = \pm(w_1 - w_2).$$

Square both sides, isolate the term in $\psi(w_1)\psi(w_2)$, and square again to obtain (after a calculation)

$$(\alpha - \beta)^2 (w_1 - w_2)^2 = 0.$$

Since $\alpha \neq \beta$, this implies $w_1 = w_2$, which proves (a). To prove (b), suppose that

$$\psi(w_1) + \psi(w_2) = w_1 - w_2,$$

and follow the same calculation to conclude that $w_1 = w_2$, or $\psi(w_1) = 0$, which is clearly impossible. Therefore, the two functions $w \pm \psi(w)$ are univalent in D and omit open sets. Normalize them by defining

$$\psi_1(w) = \frac{w + \psi(w) - \psi(0)}{1 + \psi'(0)} ; \qquad \psi_2(w) = \frac{w - \psi(w) + \psi(0)}{1 - \psi'(0)} .$$

Let $f_1 = \psi_1 \circ f$ and $f_2 = \psi_2 \circ f$. Then $f_1$ and $f_2$ are distinct functions in S which omit open sets, and

$$f = tf_1 + (1-t)f_2 , \qquad t = \tfrac{1}{2}[1 + \psi'(0)] .$$

The assumption that $|\alpha| = |\beta|$ is now used (for the first time) to conclude that $0 < t < 1$.

Hengartner and Schober [6] deduced from Brickman's result that for each extreme point f, log $\{f(z)/z\}$ is univalent and has a range which meets each vertical line in a segment (possibly empty) of length less than $2\pi$. Thus $f(z)/z$ is also univalent.

The Koebe function and its rotations are extreme points of S, but there are others as well. In fact, there are linear functionals which admit no rotation of the Koebe function as support points. An example is $L(f) = f(z_0)$ for suitable choice of $z_0$; see [13, p. 84]. It is not known whether each extreme point of S is a support point, or whether each support point is an extreme point. Although it seems intuitively "obvious" that in a general setting an extreme point must always be a support point, Klee [7] gave a simple counterexample in Hilbert space.

Somewhat more is known about the support points of S. An elementary argument due to Marty [8] (given originally only for $L(f) = a_n$) shows that each support point has dense range; it cannot omit any open set. The following deeper theorem can be established through Schiffer's method of boundary variation (see [4] or [13]).

THEOREM 3. *Let* L *be a continuous linear functional, not of the form* $L(f) = \alpha f(0) + \beta f'(0)$. *Let* $f \in S$ *be a function at which* $\mathrm{Re}\{L\}$ *achieves its maximum over* S, *and let* $\Gamma$ *be the set omitted by* f. *Then* $\Gamma$ *is a single analytic arc satisfying the differential equation*

$$w^{-2} L(f^2/(f-w))\,dw^2 > 0.$$

$\Gamma$ *tends to* $\infty$ *with increasing modulus, and at each point of* $\Gamma$ *the angle between the tangent vector and the radius vector is less than* $\pi/4$. *Furthermore,* $\Gamma$ *is tangent to a line at* $\infty$.

This theorem has been essentially known for some time. All but the single-arc assertion can be proved by standard variational techniques, together with the theory of the local structure of the trajectories of a quadratic differential. The original proof [11, 12, 9] that $\Gamma$ cannot branch at $\infty$, however, involved a difficult argument to show that the quadratic differential in question has a simple pole at $\infty$. As Brickman and Wilken observed, Theorem 2 reduces the single-arc question to a triviality. That $\Gamma$ consists of a single monotonic arc can be proved *a priori*, without resort to variational methods.

Indeed, suppose the extremal function f were to omit two values of equal modulus. Then $f = tf_1 + (1-t)f_2$, where $f_1$ and $f_2$ omit open sets and so (by Marty's result) cannot be support points. Hence $\mathrm{Re}\{L(f_i)\} < \mathrm{Re}\{L(f)\}$, i=1,2, and it follows that

$$\mathrm{Re}\{L(f)\} = t\,\mathrm{Re}\{L(f_1)\} + (1-t)\mathrm{Re}\{L(f_2)\} < \mathrm{Re}\{L(f)\}.$$

This contradiction shows that $\Gamma$ is a monotonic arc.

It is now easy to deduce the $\pi/4$-result from the differential equation. Choose a point $w \in \Gamma$, not the endpoint $w_o$, and let $g = wf/(w-f)$. Clearly, g belongs to S and maps the disk onto the complement of two disjoint arcs extending to $\infty$. Thus g is not a support point: $\mathrm{Re}\{L(g)\} < \mathrm{Re}\{L(f)\}$. Since L is linear, this is equivalent to

$$\mathrm{Re}\{L(f^2/(f-w))\} > 0, \qquad w \in \Gamma,\ w \neq w_o.$$

This last inequality has two consequences. First, the fact that $L(f^2/(f-w)) \neq 0$ assures that the differential equation has no singularities on the interior of $\Gamma$, so that $\Gamma$ has no corners. Second, the inequality may be combined with the differential equation to show that $\mathrm{Re}\{(dw/w)^2\} > 0$ on $\Gamma$, which is equivalent to the $\pi/4$-property.

The same basic argument is readily adapted to other classes of univalent functions [13]. Consider, for example, the class $S_o$ of functions $f$ analytic and univalent in the unit disk, with $f(z) \neq 0$ and $f(0) = 1$. Similar reasoning [5] yields the following information about the extreme points and support points of $S_o$.

THEOREM 4. *Each extreme point of $S_o$ maps the disk onto the complement of an arc from 0 to $\infty$ which is monotonic with respect to the family of ellipses with foci 0 and 1.*

THEOREM 5. *Each support point of $S_o$ maps the disk onto the complement of an analytic arc extending from 0 to $\infty$ monotonically with respect to the family of ellipses with foci 0 and 1, intersecting no hyperbola with foci 0 and 1 at an angle greater than $\pi/4$, and tangent to a line at $\infty$.*

On the other hand, relatively little can be said about the extreme points of the class $\Sigma_o$ of functions

$$g(z) = z + b_1 z^{-1} + b_2 z^{-2} + \dots, \qquad |z| > 1,$$

analytic and univalent in the exterior of the disk except for a simple pole at $\infty$ with residue 1. (Without a normalization such as $b_o = 0$, there would be no extreme points at all.) Some years ago, Springer [14] observed that if the complement of the range of a function $g \in \Sigma_o$ has measure zero, then $g$ is an extreme point of $\Sigma_o$. Whether the converse is true remains an open question. In any event, however, $\Sigma_o$ has too many extreme points.

The extreme points of certain subclasses of S, such as the starlike or close-to-convex functions, can be described explicitly, providing an effective method for the solution of extremal problems within these subclasses. (See recent papers of Brickman, MacGregor, Wilken, and others.) This approach has succeeded in some instances where more direct methods have failed.

## REFERENCES

[ 1] Brickman, L., Extreme points of the set of univalent functions. Bull. Amer. Math. Soc. 76 (1970), 372-374.

[ 2] Brickman, L. - Wilken, D., Support points of the set of univalent functions. Proc. Amer. Math. Soc. 42 (1974), 523-528.

[ 3] Duren, P.L., Coefficients of univalent functions. Bull. Amer. Math. Soc. 83 (1977), 891-911.

[ 4] Duren, P.L., Univalent Functions. Springer-Verlag, Heidelberg/New York, to appear.

[ 5] Duren, P. - Schober, G., Nonvanishing univalent functions. To appear.

[ 6] Hengartner, W. - Schober, G., Extreme points for some classes of univalent functions. Trans. Amer. Math. Soc. 185 (1973), 265-270.

[ 7] Klee, V.L., Extremal structure of convex sets, II. Math. Z. 69 (1958), 90-104.

[ 8] Marty, F., Sur le module des coefficients de Mac Laurin d'une fonction univalente. C.R. Acad. Sci. Paris 198 (1934), 1569-1571.

[ 9] Pfluger, A., Lineare Extremalprobleme bei schlichten Funktionen. Ann. Acad. Sci. Fenn. Ser. A I, No. 489 (1971), 32 pp.

[ 10] Pommerenke, Ch., Univalent Functions. Vandenhoeck & Ruprecht, Göttingen 1975.

[ 11] Schaeffer, A.C. - Spencer, D.C., Coefficient Regions for Schlicht Functions. Amer. Math. Soc. Colloq. Publ., vol. 35, 1950.

[ 12] Schiffer, M., On the coefficient problem for univalent functions. Trans. Amer. Math. Soc. 134 (1968), 95-101.

[13] Schober, G., Univalent Functions - Selected Topics. Lecture Notes in Mathematics, No. 478, Springer-Verlag, 1975.

[14] Springer, G., Extreme Punkte der konvexen Hülle schlichter Funktionen. Math. Ann. 129 (1955), 230-232.

# LACUNARY POLYNOMIAL APPROXIMATION

Jacob Korevaar and Michael Dixon*
Mathematisch Instituut, Universiteit van Amsterdam
Department of Mathematics, California State University, Chico

Approximation theorems of Walsh imply that the nonnegative integral powers $z^n$, or the integral powers, form a spanning set for certain spaces of functions on compacta in $\mathbb{C}$. One may ask how many powers may be omitted in various problems of uniform approximation. The present paper surveys "lacunary" approximation theorems for the following kinds of sets: 1. Closed Jordan regions, 2. Jordan arcs, 3. Jordan curves around the origin. At present the most active area is Müntz-type approximation on arcs, in part because of its relation to the Macintyre conjecture for entire functions with gap power series.

## 1. Approximation on Jordan Regions

The results in this section represent recent joint work of the authors [3].

1.1 Walsh's Jordan Region Theorem. Let $\gamma$ be an arbitrary Jordan curve in the plane, D its interior, $C_H(\bar{D})$ the subspace of the usual normed space $C(\bar{D})$ consisting of those continuous functions on $\bar{D}$ which are holomorphic on D. By Walsh's theorem [21], every function in $C_H(\bar{D})$ is a uniform limit of polynomials on $\bar{D}$. Thus, the *closed span* of the powers $z^n$, $n = 0,1,\dots$ in $C(\bar{D})$, $sp\{z^n\}$, is *precisely* the subspace $C_H(\bar{D})$.

Suppose now that $0 \in D$ and that we have at our disposal only a sequence of integral powers

* Work begun with support from NSF grant MPS 73-08733 at the University of California, San Diego. Second author supported by a grant from the Netherlands research organization ZWO.

(1.1) $$z^{p_n}, \quad 0 \le p_0 < p_1 < \dots .$$

With linear combinations of the powers (1.1) we can at best hope to approximate those functions f in $C_H(\bar{D})$ which, near 0, have an expansion of the form

(1.2) $$f(z) = \sum_0^\infty a_n z^{p_n}.$$

QUESTION 1. Can we approximate all such functions on $\bar{D}$ using only linear combinations of the powers (1.1)?

1.2 Case of Starlike D. The answer to QUESTION 1 is *yes* when D is (strongly) *starlike* relative to 0, that is, every ray from 0 intersects the boundary $\gamma$ exactly once. In this case, the compact set $\bar{D}$ is a subset of the open set $\rho D$ for every $\rho > 1$; an f in $C_H(\bar{D})$ can be approximated on $\bar{D}$ by $f(z/\rho)$ for $\rho$ close to 1. Now $f(z/\rho)$ is holomorphic on $\rho D$, and thus, by Runge's theorem, uniformly approximable by polynomials on $\bar{D}$. Assuming that (1.2) holds near 0, we can use Mittag-Leffler summability of the power series for $f(z/\rho)$ on the starlike set $\rho D$ to assure approximation by linear combinations of powers (1.1).

1.3 Non-Starlike D: Counterexamples. The answer to QUESTION 1 is *no in general*. More precisely, for every number $\delta \in (0,1)$, there exists a sequence $\{p_n\}$ of density $\lim n/p_n = \delta$, a Jordan domain D as close to starlike as one wishes, and a function f in $C_H(\bar{D})$ with a local expansion (1.2) which is not in $sp\{z^{p_n}\}$. We give here a simple example for the case $\delta = 1/2$:

$$f(z) = \frac{1}{1-z^2} = \sum_0^\infty z^{2n},$$

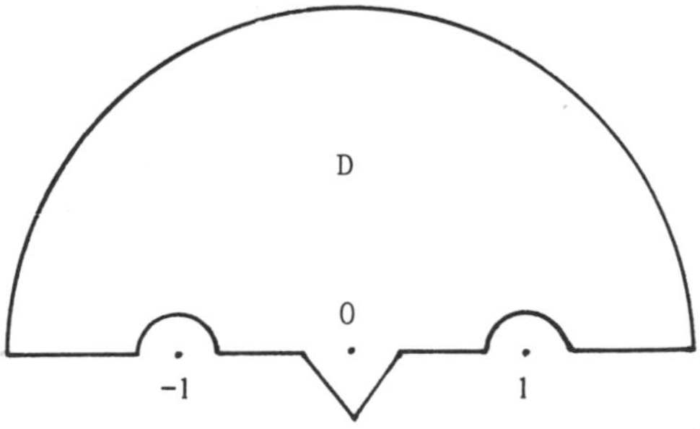


D as in the figure. This f is not a uniform limit of even polynomials on $\bar{D}$. Indeed, if it were, the approximating polynomials would converge uniformly on $\{|z| = 2\}$, hence on $\{|z| < 2\}$. The limit function, an analytic extension of f, would be holomorphic on $\{|z| < 2\}$. However, f can have no such extension!

Appropriate rational functions provide counterexamples for the other rational $\delta \in (0,1)$. For every $\delta \in (0,1)$, our set D is close to a sector of the disc $\{|z| < 2\}$ with opening $2\pi\delta$. In the case of irrational $\delta$ an $L^2$-inequality of Ingham (cf. Hayman [7]) is crucial in showing the non-approximability of our f by linear combinations of the powers (1.1).

1.4 The Cases $\delta = 0,1$. When the sequence $\{p_n\}$ has density 0 or 1, the answer to QUESTION 1 is *yes* whenever $\gamma$ is *smooth*. In the case $\delta = 0$ the proof is quite simple. Let f in $C_H(\bar{D})$ have local expansion (1.2). Then by Fabry's gap theorem, f has a holomorphic extension (also called f) throughout the smallest disc $\{|z| < R\}$ containing D. Using the smoothness of $\gamma$ it can be shown that f is of class $C_H(\bar{D}_1)$ for some strongly starlike domain $D_1 \subset \{|z| < R\}$ which contains D.

In the case $\delta = 1$ the proof is much more complicated. We must show that $\int_\gamma f d\mu = 0$ when f in $C_H(\bar{D})$ has the form (1.2) near 0 (with $n/p_n \to 1$), and $\mu$ is an arbitrary complex Borel measure on $\gamma$ orthogonal to the powers (1.1). The proof makes use of the Cauchy transform of $\mu$, the Fabry gap theorem (applied to the Cauchy transform exterior to $\gamma$), Plemelj's formula for the jump of the Cauchy transform across $\gamma$, and a local version of the F. and M. Riesz theorem.

1.5 The Closed Span of (1.1) in General. In the example associated with the figure above, every function in $sp\{z^{2n}\}$ has an analytic continuation to the disc $\{|z| < 2\}$, and a similar remark applies to our other examples. However, we don't know much about the general case:

QUESTION 1'. What is $sp\{z^{p_n}\}$ in $C(\bar{D})$ when $\{p_n\}$ does not have density 0 or 1, and D is not strongly starlike relative to 0?

## 2. Approximation on Jordan Arcs

2.1 Theorems of Walsh and Müntz. Let $\gamma$ be an arbitrary Jordan arc in $\mathbb{C}$. Then by Walsh's theorem [22], the powers $z^n$, $n = 0,1,\ldots$ span $C(\gamma)$.

In the special case where $\gamma = [a,b]$, $0 < a < b$, the integral powers

$$z^{p_n}, \quad 0 < p_1 < p_2 < \ldots \tag{2.1}$$

span C[a,b] if (Müntz [18]) and only if (Clarkson-Erdös [2], Schwartz [20])

(2.2) $$\Sigma\ 1/p_n = \infty.$$

More precisely, the latter authors proved that if $\Sigma\,1/p_n < \infty$ and f belongs to $sp\{z^{p_n}\}$ in C[a,b], then f has an analytic extension to the disc $\{|z| < b\}$, with power series $\Sigma\, a_n z^{p_n}$.

QUESTION 2. Are there corresponding results for (other) Jordan arcs?

It will be convenient to consider the related problem of uniform approximation by linear combinations of exponentials

(2.3) $$e^{p_n\zeta}, \quad 0 < p_1 < p_2 < \ldots$$

on Jordan arcs $\Gamma$.

2.2 Arcs for which (2.2) guarantees that (2.3) is a spanning set. When $\Gamma$ (is smooth and) meets some vertical line more than once, it must contain two points $\zeta_0$ and $\zeta_0 + 2\pi i/q$ where q is a positive integer. In that case, the exponentials $e^{nq\zeta}$ can not span $C(\Gamma)$, hence (2.2) is not sufficient for a spanning set. However, for (rectifiable) arcs $\Gamma$ of bounded slope,

$$\Gamma: \zeta = t + i\psi(t), \quad a_1 \le t \le b_1, \quad |\psi'(t)| \le M < \infty,$$

condition (2.2) does assure that (2.3) spans $C(\Gamma)$, at least when the $p_n$ are suitably separated. This was proved by the first author in lectures at Imperial College, London (spring 1971). If $M \le 1$, no separation condition is needed [8]; for related results, cf. Leont'ev [14] and Malliavin-Siddiqi [17].

2.3 Arcs for which (2.2) is necessary. Malliavin-Siddiqi [16] and the first author (Imperial College lectures, cf. [8]) found independently that the condition

(2.4) $$\Sigma\ 1/p_n < \infty$$

guarantees that (2.3) fails to span $C(\Gamma)$ whenever $\Gamma$ is *analytic*. It seems plausible that the analyticity condition can be relaxed to simple smoothness, but this has not yet been proved for exponents satisfying no other condition than (2.4). For more restricted exponents, see 2.5.

2.4 Method of quasianalytic classes. The results of 2.2, 2.3 were obtained with the aid of a theory of quasianalyticity for functions on arcs. Let $\{M_n\}$ be a positive, increasing, logarithmically convex sequence of constants. We say that $\phi$ on $\Gamma$ is of class $C\{M_n\}$ if $\phi$ is infinitely differentiable along $\Gamma$ and for certain constants $A, B$,

$$\sup_\Gamma |D^n\phi| \leq A B^n M_n, \quad n = 0, 1 \ldots .$$

For rectifiable $\Gamma$ the condition

$$\Sigma\, M_{n-1}/M_n = \infty$$

assures quasianalyticity of $C\{M_n\}$, that is, $\phi$ in $C\{M_n\}$ and $D^\nu\phi(\zeta_0) = 0$ for some point $\zeta_0 \in \Gamma$ and all $\nu \geq 0$ implies $\phi = 0$ [1]. When $\Gamma$ is analytic, the same condition is also necessary for $C\{M_n\}$ to be quasianalytic.

For the applications of this theory the following observations are of interest. Let $\{q_n\}$ be an increasing sequence of positive numbers such that $q_{n+1} \leq 2q_n$.

(i) Suppose the set $\{\exp(\pm q_n\zeta)\}$ *fails to span* $C(\Gamma)$ where $\Gamma$ is an arc whose slopes are bounded in absolute value by 1. Then there is a *nonzero function* $\phi$ on $\Gamma$ *of class* $C\{M_n\}$, where $M_{2n} = q_1^2 \ldots q_n^2$, *such that* $D^\nu\phi = 0$, $\nu = 0, 1 \ldots$ *at the end-points* $a$ and $b$ of $\Gamma$ (cf. Korevaar [8]). In terms of a nonzero measure $\mu$ on $\Gamma$ orthogonal to our exponentials, $\phi = \lim \phi_k$, where $\phi_0 = d\mu$ and

$$(1 - D^2/q_k^2)\phi_k = \phi_{k-1}, \quad \phi_k = D\phi_k = 0 \quad \text{at } a, b.$$

(ii) Suppose there is a *nonzero function* $\phi$ *of class* $C\{M_n\}$ on a rectifiable arc $\Gamma$ *such that* $D^\nu\phi = 0$ at $a, b$, where $M_{2n} = q_1^2 \ldots q_n^2$. Then *for* $p_n/q_n \to \infty$ and, say, $q_{n+1} \leq 2q_n < q_{3n}$ the set

$\{\exp(\pm p_n \zeta)\}$ f a i l s t o s p a n $C(\Gamma)$. A measure orthogonal to these exponentials can be obtained from $\phi$ by applying the operator $\Pi(1-D^2/p_n^2)$ (cf. [8], [16]).

<u>2.5 Exponents restricted by more than (2.4)</u>. Except on analytic arcs, it is difficult to construct interesting non-quasianalytic classes $C\{M_n\}$ directly. The best that has been achieved by combining such constructions with 2.4 (ii) is Erkama's result [5]: the condition

$$p_n \geq cn\,(\log n)^2, \quad c > 0$$

guarantees that (2.3) fails to span $C(\Gamma)$ whenever $\Gamma$ is of a class related to $C^1$.

The present authors have recently obtained better results by combining (i) and (ii) above with methods that have been used in connection with the (still unproven)

MACINTYRE CONJECTURE [15]. <u>A nonconstant entire function $\Sigma\, a_n z^{p_n}$, with exponents subject to (2.4), can not be bounded on a curve going out to infinity.</u>

Kövari has shown ([12], [13]; cf. also related work of Gaier [6]) that the Macintyre conjecture holds (in a strong form) for all sets of exponents satisfying

$$p_n \geq cn \log n\,(\log\log n)^{2+\varepsilon}, \quad c, \varepsilon > 0.$$

Pavlov has proved [19] that a regularized version of (2.4), namely,

$$\Sigma\, 1/p_n < \infty, \quad p_n/n \uparrow \tag{2.5}$$

also suffices.

We have found that for Pavlov or Kövari (integral) exponents $q_n$, the set $\{\exp(\pm q_n \zeta)\}$ i s n o n s p a n n i n g i n a s t r o n g s e n s e: for fixed $\rho > 1$ the distance of the constant 1 to the closed span of the exponentials has a positive lower bound for the class of all curves $\Gamma$ extending from $\{|z| = 1\}$ to $\{|z| = \rho\}$.

Using suitable Pavlov exponents $q_n$ in part (i) of 2.4, part (ii) gives us the following

THEOREM. Let $L(t)$ be positive for $t \geq 0$, increasing, slowly increasing (that is, $L(ct)/L(t) \to 1$ as $t \to \infty$ for every $c > 0$) and such that $\int_0^\infty dt/t\,L(t) < \infty$. Suppose $\{p_n\}$ is an increasing sequence of positive numbers such that $p_n \geq n\,L(n)$, $n = 1,2,\ldots$ . Then the set $\{\exp(\pm p_n \zeta)\}$ fails to span $C(\Gamma)$ for every $C^1$ arc $\Gamma$.

For example, when

$$p_n \geq n \log n \log\log n \,(\log\log\log n)^{1+\varepsilon},$$

the set $\{\exp(\pm p_n\zeta)\}$ is nonspanning on every smooth arc.

2.6 Analyticity theorem. We have obtained the following extension [4] of the analyticity result of Clarkson-Erdös-Schwartz:

THEOREM. Let $\gamma$ be a piecewise smooth arc, $\{|z| \leq \rho\}$ the smallest disc about 0 which contains $\gamma$, and assume that $\gamma$ is not part of the circle $\{|z| = \rho\}$. Suppose $\{z^{p_n}\}$ fails to span $C(\gamma')$ for every subarc $\gamma'$ of $\gamma$. Then every f which belongs to $sp\{z^{p_n}\}$ in $C(\gamma)$ has an analytic extension to the disc $\{|z| < \rho\}$, with power series $\Sigma\, a_n z^{p_n}$.

The principal tool is the Laplace transform along smooth arcs of bounded slope. Entire functions given by such transforms are of very regular growth in an angle about the positive real axis.

## 3. Approximation on Jordan Curves

3.1 Walsh's Jordan Curve Theorem. Let $\gamma$ be an arbitrary Jordan curve around 0. Then by Walsh's theorem [22], the integral powers $z^n$, $n = 0,\pm 1,\ldots$ span $C(\gamma)$.

QUESTION 3. Are all integral powers needed for a spanning set, or can some be omitted?

3.2 Curves of Finite Length. For the case of the unit circle, the orthogonality of the functions $e^{int}$ on $(-\pi,\pi)$ implies that no power can be omitted. The same is true for any curve $\gamma$ around 0 of finite length L. Indeed,

$$2\pi = \left|\int_\gamma (1/z - \Sigma' c_n z^n)dz\right| \leq \|1/z - \Sigma' c_n z^n\| \cdot L,$$

where $\Sigma'$ denotes an arbitrary finite sum over $n \neq 0$. Thus if $S' = \mathrm{sp}\{z^n\}$, $n \neq 0$,

$$d(z^{-1},S') = \inf_c \|z^{-1} - \Sigma' c_n z^n\| \geq 2\pi/L.$$

It follows that $z^{-1}$ cannot be omitted, and neither can any other power.

The precise value of d may be determined from a standard formula for the distance to a subspace. If the measure $\mu$ on $\gamma$ represents a continuous linear functional on $C(\gamma)$ orthogonal to S', then there is a constant $\alpha$ such that $\mu - \alpha dz$ is orthogonal to all powers of z, hence equal to 0. Thus

(3.1) $$d(z^{-1},S') = \max_{\mu \perp S'} \left|\int_\gamma z^{-1} d\mu\right| / \mathrm{Var}\,\mu = 2\pi/L.$$

This is a *remarkable result*: using combinations of other powers one can approximate $z^{-1}$ better on a very wiggly curve around 0 than on a short smooth one [11]!

3.3 Curves of Infinite Length. It can be shown that (3.1) *holds also when* $L = \infty$: for a curve around 0 of infinite length, not all powers are needed for a spanning set; an arbitrary power may be omitted (Wermer [23], cf. [11]).

QUESTION 3'. How many powers $z^n$ can be omitted in the case of suitably "wild" curves around 0? How sparse can spanning sets be?

3.4 Wild Curves. Pia Pfluger and the first author [11] have shown that for every $p \geq 1$, there is a Jordan curve $\gamma_p$ around 0 for which p *powers can be omitted but not more than* p. More precisely, for each choice of distinct integers $n_1,\ldots,n_p$, the set

$$\{z^n,\ n \neq n_1,\dots,n_p\}$$

is a minimal spanning set for $C(\gamma_p)$. The curve $\gamma_p$ was obtained from the unit circle $z = e^{it}$ by superposition of the "wiggle"

$$e^{it}\, t \sin(t^{-p}), \quad 0 \le t \le \pi^{-1/p}.$$

If the wiggle is made exponential $(t^{-p} \to e^{1/t})$, infinitely many powers may be omitted [9].

Starting with the cardioid-type curve $z = (1+4 \sin \frac{1}{2}t)e^{it}$ and superimposing an exponential wiggle, Alexander and the first author [10] have obtained a curve $\gamma^*$ for which there are spanning sets of the form

$$\{z^n,\ n = 0,1\dots;\ z^{-p_k},\ k/p_k \to 0\}. \tag{3.2}$$

The proof depends on the F. and M. Riesz theorem and the Fabry-Pólya gap theorem.

In any spanning set of powers, infinitely many negative (and positive) ones must occur, but it is not known how thin the sequence of negative exponents can be.

In the case of $\gamma^*$, one may additionally omit a thin sequence of positive powers from (3.2). It is not known if it is possible to have spanning sets in which both the positive and the negative exponents have density zero.

## REFERENCES


[1] Bang, T., On quasi-analytiske Funktioner. Thesis, Univ. of Copenhagen, 1946.

[2] Clarkson, J.A. - Erdös, P., Approximation by polynomials. Duke Math. J. 10 (1943), 5-11.

[3] Dixon, M. - Korevaar, J., Approximation by lacunary polynomials. Nederl. Akad. Wetensch. Proc. Ser. A 80 (1977), 176-194.

[4] Dixon, M. - Korevaar, J., Nonspanning sets of powers on curves: analyticity theorem. Submitted for publication.

[5] Erkama, T., Classes non quasi-analytiques et le théorème d'approximation de Müntz. C.R. Acad. Sci. Paris Sér. A 283 (1976), 595-597.

[6] Gaier, D., Der allgemeine Lückenumkehrsatz für das Borel-Verfahren. Math. Z. 88 (1965), 410-417.

[7] Hayman, W.K., A mini-gap theorem for Fourier series. Proc. Cambridge Philos. Soc. 64 (1968), 61-66.

[8] Korevaar, J., Approximation on curves by linear combinations of exponentials. In: Approximation Theory (editor G.G. Lorentz). Acad. Press, New York 1973, pp. 387-393.

[9] Korevaar, J., Lacunary forms of Walsh' approximation theorems. In: Proc. Internat. Conf. on Approx. of Functions (Kaluga 1975). Soviet Acad. of Sci., Moscow 1977, pp. 229-237.

[10] Korevaar, J. - Alexander, H., Approximation on wild Jordan curves. J. London Math. Soc. (2) 13 (1976), 317-322.

[11] Korevaar, J. - Pfluger, P., Spanning sets of powers on wild Jordan curves. Nederl. Akad. Wetensch. Proc. Ser. A 77 (1974), 293-305.

[12] Kövari, T., On the asymptotic paths of entire functions with gap power series. J. Analyse Math. 15 (1965), 281-286.

[13] Kövari, T., A gap theorem for entire functions of infinite order. Michigan Math. J. 12 (1965), 133-140.

[14] Leont'ev, A.F., On the completeness of a system of exponentials on a curve. (Russian). Sibirsk. Mat. Z. 15 (1974), 1103-1114.

[15] Macintyre, A.J., Asymptotic paths of integral functions with gap power series. Proc. London Math. Soc. (3) 2 (1952), 286-296.

[16] Malliavin, P. - Siddiqi, J.A., Approximation polynomiale sur un arc analytique dans le plan complexe. C.R. Acad. Sci. Paris Sér. A 273 (1971), 105-108.

[17] Malliavin, P., - Siddiqi, J.A., Classes de fonctions monogènes et approximation par des sommes d'exponentielles sur un arc rectifiable de $\mathbb{C}$. C.R. Acad. Sci. Paris Sér. A 282 (1976), 1091-1094.

[18] Müntz, C.H., Über den Approximationssatz von Weierstrass. In: H.A. Schwarz Festschrift, Berlin 1914, pp. 303-312.

[19] Pavlov, A.I., Growth along curves of entire functions specified by gap power series (Russian). Sibirsk. Mat. Z. 13 (1972), 1169-1181.

[20] Schwartz, L., Étude des sommes d'exponentielles reélles. Actualités Sci. Indust. 959, Hermann, Paris 1943.

[21] Walsh, J.L., Über die Entwicklung einer analytischen Funktion nach Polynomen. Math. Ann. 96 (1927), 430-436.

[22] Walsh, J.L., Über die Entwicklung einer Funktion einer komplexen Veränderlichen nach Polynomen. Math. Ann. 96 (1927), 437-450.

[23] Wermer, J., Nonrectifiable simple closed curve. Advanced problems and solutions, no. 4687. Amer. Math. Monthly 64 (1957), 372.

# MÜNTZ-SZASZ THEOREMS AND LACUNARY ENTIRE FUNCTIONS

J.M. Anderson
Mathematics Department,
University College,
London, W.C.1

This lecture discusses the case of non-completeness for the Müntz-Szasz theorem and Malliavin's theorem. Various applications to entire functions with gaps are presented.

## 1. Introduction

For a given set

$$\Lambda = \{\lambda_0, \lambda_1, \lambda_2, \cdots \lambda_n, \cdots\}$$

of positive integers, with $0 = \lambda_0 < \lambda_1 < \lambda_2 < \dots$ , we denote by $V(\Lambda)$ the set of all polynomials with exponents in $\Lambda$. The famous theorem of Müntz and Szasz (see e.g. [26], [27]) is as follows.

THEOREM 1. <u>In order that the set of functions</u> $\{t^\lambda\}$, $\lambda \in \Lambda$, <u>be complete in</u> $C[0,1]$ <u>it is necessary and sufficient that</u>

$$\sum_{n=1}^{\infty} \lambda_n^{-1} = \infty. \tag{1}$$

Here, as usual, $C[0,1]$ denotes the space of functions $f(t)$, continuous for $0 \leq t \leq 1$ with the topology of uniform convergence, and a set of elements is said to be complete in a space X if the linear manifold spanned by the elements is dense in X. With the above notation, Theorem 1 states that $\overline{V(\Lambda)} = C[0,1]$ if and only if (1) holds. The theorem also holds with $C[0,1]$ replaced by $L_2[0,1]$, though the "Hilbert space case" is not essentially different (see e.g. [8] p.272).

From the point of view of entire functions with gaps the more interesting question concerns what happens when (1) fails to hold. In this case $\overline{V(\Lambda)} \neq C[0,1]$. What is it? The answer was provided by Clarkson, Erdös, L. Schwartz and Korevaar, [7], [28], [15], as

THEOREM 2. *If*

(2) $$\sum_{n=1}^{\infty} \lambda_n^{-1} < \infty$$

*then* $\overline{V(\Lambda)}$ *consists of the restriction to the interval* $0 \leq x < 1$ *of functions* $f(z) = \sum_0^\infty a_n z^n$ *analytic for* $|z| < 1$ *with* $a_n = 0$ *for* $n \notin \Lambda$.

Thus $\overline{V(\Lambda)}$ turns out, in this case, to be a surprisingly small subspace of $C[0,1]$.

## 2. Macintyre's Theorem

The connection between Theorem 2 and results for entire functions seems to have been noticed first by Erdős (see [22] p.287). We denote by $E(\Lambda)$ the set of all entire functions $f(z) = \sum_0^\infty a_n z^n$ with $a_n = 0$ for $n \notin \Lambda$. From Theorem 2 we may deduce the following theorem of Macintyre ([22]).

THEOREM 3. *Suppose* $f \in E(\Lambda)$ *where the sequence* $\Lambda$ *satisfies* (2). *If* $f$ *is bounded on the positive real axis,* $|f(z)| < K_1$ *for* $z = x > 0$, *say, then* $f(z) \equiv 0$.

Thus a non-constant entire function in $E(\Lambda)$, where (2) is satisfied, must be unbounded on the positive real axis, and so, by rotation, on any ray $\arg z = \theta$. The gap condition is best-possible (see [22] again).

THEOREM 4. *If* $\Lambda$ *satisfies* (1), *there exists an* $f \in E(\Lambda)$, $f \not\equiv 0$, *such that* $f(x) \to 0$ *as* $z = x \to +\infty$.

It is perhaps instructive to sketch the proof of Theorem 3 given Theorem 2. If (2) holds then the system $\{t^\lambda\}$ $(\lambda \in \Lambda)$ is not complete and so is free in $C[0,1]$; i.e. no $t^{\lambda_n}$ is in the closure of the linear manifold spanned by $\{t^{\lambda_j}\}(j \neq n)$. More precisely,

$$\inf_{a_j} \left\| t^{\lambda_n} - \sum_{\substack{j=1 \\ j \neq n}}^{s} a_j t^{\lambda_j} \right\| > 0, \quad n = 1, 2, 3, \ldots .$$

This is discussed in [28], where it is shown that if $\{t^{\lambda_n}\}$ is not complete then each $f$ in $\overline{V(\Lambda)}$ has an "expansion" of the form

(3) $$f(t) \sim \sum_{n=0}^{\infty} A_n t^{\lambda_n}.$$

Moreover, the coordinate functionals are continuous i.e. there exists a $K = K(\lambda_n, \Lambda)$ such that

(4) $$|A_n| \leq K(\lambda_n, \Lambda)\, \|f\| \quad , n = 0,1,2,\ldots \quad .$$

Indeed, the burden of the proof of Theorem 2 consists in showing that

(5) $$K(\lambda_n, \Lambda) = O(\exp \varepsilon \lambda_n) \quad , \quad n \to \infty,$$

for each $\varepsilon > 0$, so that the formal series (3) actually converges pointwise for $0 \leqslant t < 1$.

To prove Theorem 3 we do not even need estimates like (5). It suffices to fix $R \geq 0$ and consider $f(Rz)$ where $f \in E(\Lambda)$ with (2) satisfied. Then $f(Rz) = \sum_0^\infty a_n R^{\lambda_n} z^{\lambda_n}$ clearly belongs to $\overline{V(\Lambda)}$ and so, from (4),

(6) $$|a_n R^{\lambda_n}| \leq K(\lambda_n, \Lambda)\, \|f(Rz)\| \quad , \quad n = 0,1,2,\ldots \quad .$$

The point is that $K(\lambda_n, \Lambda)$ does not depend on $R$ and $\|f(Rz)\| < K_1$ for all $R > 0$. Let $R \to \infty$ in (6) to obtain $a_n = 0$ for $n = 1,2,3, \ldots$, and so $f(z) \equiv f(0) = 0$.

## 3. A Basis Problem

We digress for a moment to consider a basis problem. The sequence $\{t^{\lambda_n}\}$ of elements of $C[0,1]$ is said to be a basis for the closed linear manifold $\overline{V(\Lambda)} \subset C[0,1]$ which it spans if, for every $f \in \overline{V(\Lambda)}$, there exists a sequence $\{a_k\}$ such that

(7) $$\lim_{n\to\infty} \left\| f(t) - \sum_{k=0}^{n} a_k t^{\lambda_k} \right\| = 0 .$$

It is more convenient in this section to consider the $L_2$ case, so we suppose the norm in (7) to be the $L_2$ norm. If (7) holds then, clearly, the series $\sum_0^\infty a_k t^{\lambda_k}$ must converge for almost all $t \in [0,1]$ and so $f(t)$ must be the restriction to $[0,1)$ of a function $f(z) = \sum_0^\infty a_k z^{\lambda_k}$ analytic for $|z| < 1$. Thus, if (1) holds, then Theorem 1 shows that $\{t^{\lambda_n}\}$ is not a basis for $V(\Lambda) = C[0,1]$. However the interesting possibility arises that perhaps $\{t^{\lambda_n}\}$ is a basis for $\overline{V(\Lambda)}$ if (1) fails to hold. This is not so in general as was shown, for the $L_2$ case, by Gurarii and Macaev [14].

THEOREM 5. *In order that* $\{t^{\lambda_n}\}$ *be a basis for the closed linear sub-manifold* $\overline{V(\Lambda)}$ *of* $L_2[0,1]$ *which it spans it is necessary and sufficient that*

(8) $$\frac{\lambda_{n+1}}{\lambda_n} > q > 1, \qquad n = 1,2,3,\ldots, \; q \text{ independent of } n.$$

Note that (8) is much stronger than (2).

Perhaps it is appropriate to remark here that much of the Müntz-Szasz theory does not depend on the $\lambda_n$'s being integers. Indeed this observation was originally made by Szasz [27]. If we make the change of variable $t = \exp(-s)$ then we may consider the completeness of the system in $L_2(0,\infty)$ with weight $\frac{1}{t}$, or in $C_0[0,\infty)$. Here the $\lambda_n$'s can be any complex numbers with $\operatorname{Re}\lambda_n > 0$, and condition (1) is replaced by $\sum_1^\infty \operatorname{Re}\lambda_n(1+|\lambda_n|^2)^{-1} = \infty$. It is frequently advantageous to work in this slightly more general setting, e.g. in [5] it is shown that Theorem 5 is a straight-forward consequence of an interpolation theorem for $H^2$ due to Shapiro and Shields [29]. For further developments in this direction we refer to [1].

## 4. Some Weighted Banach Spaces

Theorem 3 can also be generalised as follows

THEOREM 6. *If* $f \in E(\Lambda)$ *and* (2) *is satisfied, and if*

$$f(x) = O(H(x)), \qquad x \to +\infty$$

*for some function* $H(x)$ *monotonic increasing on* $[0,\infty)$, *then*

$$M(r,f) = O(H(\sigma r)), \qquad r \to \infty,$$

*for each* $\sigma > 1$. *Here* $M(r,f) = \max |f(z)|$, $|z| = r$.

Thus, in particular if (2) is satisfied and f has order $\rho$ mean type $\kappa$ for $x > 0$ i.e. $f(x) = O(\exp(\kappa+\varepsilon)x^\rho)$ $x \to +\infty$ for each $\varepsilon > 0$, then f is in fact an entire function of order $\rho$ mean type $\kappa$ in the whole plane.

Results of this type appear to have been given first by Gaier [13] and

Kövari [18], [19]. In this generality Theorem 5 appears in [4]. The presence of $H(\sigma r)$ instead of $H(r)$ in the conclusion is a bit of a nuisance, especially when the function $H(x)$ grows very rapidly, but it is not known whether this is necessary.

We now consider some weighted Banach spaces considered by Malliavin [23]. Let $H(r)$ be a positive increasing function of $r$, defined for $0 \leq r < \infty$, and suppose that the function

$$h(s) = \log H(e^s) \tag{9}$$

is a convex function of s. We exclude the case of polynomial growth by insisting that for each integer n

$$r^{-n} H(r) \to \infty \ , \quad r \to \infty .$$

In fact, it is advantageous to think of $H(x)$ as growing very rapidly indeed.

Let $S_H$ denote the Banach space of all functions $f(x)$, continuous on $[0,\infty)$ with $f(0)$ and $\lim_{x\to\infty} |f(x)/H(x)| = 0$. As norm we use

$$\|f\|_H = \max_{x \geq 0} \left| f(x)/H(x) \right| .$$

From the point of view of our considerations we might just as well have considered the weighted $L_2[0,\infty)$ norm instead of the sup norm - the change matters little. In the case $H(x) = e^x$ these spaces were considered by Fuchs, who discussed the relationship between them, as far as completeness theorems are concerned. For our sequence $\Lambda = \{\lambda_n\}_1^\infty$ we define a "logarithmic" counting function

$$\lambda(r) = \sum_{\lambda_n < r} \lambda_n^{-1} . \tag{10}$$

The following basic theorem is due to Malliavin [23].

THEOREM 7. <u>A necessary and sufficient condition that</u> $\overline{V(\Lambda)} = S_H$ <u>is that</u>, <u>for each real constant</u> a,

$$\int^\infty h(2\lambda(r) - a) \frac{dr}{r^2} = \infty . \tag{11}$$

Here $h(s)$ and $\lambda(r)$ are defined by (9) and (10) respectively.

In the case when $H(x) = \exp(x^{\rho})$, which is essentially the Fuchs case, condition (11) becomes independent of a as

$$\int^{\infty} \exp\left(2\rho\,\lambda(r)\right) \frac{dr}{r^2} = \infty .$$

If $\frac{\lambda n}{n} \to \alpha \geq 1$ $(n \to \infty)$ then $\exp 2\rho\lambda(r) \sim r^{2\rho/\alpha}$ $(r \to \infty)$. From (11) we deduce that in this case we have completeness if and only if $\alpha \leq 2\rho$.

For the study of entire functions with gaps, it comes as no surprise to find out that it is the case when (11) fails that is of interest. The case of non-completeness for the Fuchs result was first studied by Leont'ev [21]. He showed, under a somewhat restrictive hypothesis, that functions in $\overline{V(\Lambda)}$ would have to be entire functions satisfying certain growth conditions.

It seems very difficult to identify $\overline{V(\Lambda)}$ in the case when (11) fails to hold. For a given function $H(x)$ we denote by $E_{\sigma}(\Lambda)$ the set of all $f \in E(\Lambda)$ for which $M(r,f) = O(H(\sigma r))$ $(r \to \infty)$. If (2) is satisfied, so that (11) fails and we have non-completeness, it is easy to see, from Theorem 6 that

$$\bigcup_{\alpha<1} E_{\alpha}(\Lambda) \subset \overline{V(\Lambda)} \subset \bigcap_{\beta>1} E_{\beta}(\Lambda).$$

Even in this case, however, a precise characterisation of $V(\Lambda)$ is lacking.

When (1) holds then $V(\Lambda)$ will always consist of entire functions, and, indeed, one can say something about their growth. This follows from [3] Lemma 2.

THEOREM 8. _Suppose that_ $\overline{V(\Lambda)} \neq S_H$. _Then, given any_ $f \in \overline{V(\Lambda)}$ _with_ $f(x) \sim \sum_1^{\infty} a_n x^{\lambda_n}$ _we have the estimate_

$$|a_n| \leq C^{\lambda_n} \exp\left\{-2\lambda_n \sum_{k=1}^{n} \lambda_k^{-1}\right\} . \|f\|_H ,$$

_where_ C _is a constant depending only on the set_ $\Lambda$ _and on_ $H(s)$.

## 5. Densities

In the general case when (11) fails to hold the only result I know is [3] Theorem 3. However, there are various interesting special cases when non-completeness occurs. We examine the entire functions which arise.

Suppose that log h(s), as defined by (9) is a monotonic, convex function of s. For a set $\Lambda$ of positive integers we introduce the counting function

$$L_h(x) = \sum_{\lambda_n < h(x)} \lambda_n^{-1} ,$$

and define the upper and lower h-densities of $\Lambda$ by

$$\overline{D}_h = \limsup_{x\to\infty} x^{-1} L_h(x) , \quad \underline{D}_h = \liminf_{x\to\infty} x^{-1} L_h(x).$$

The maximum h-density of the set $\Lambda$, $D_h^*(\Lambda)$, is defined by

$$D_h^*(\Lambda) = \inf D_h(\mu) ,$$

where the infimum is taken over all sets $\mu$ containing $\Lambda$ and such that $D_h(\mu) = \underline{D}_h(\mu) = \overline{D}_h(\mu)$. When $h(x) = e^x$ these definitions reduce to the well-known concepts of "logarithmic" density as considered, for example, by Edrei [10] and Malliavin [23]. In this case

$$D^*_{exp} = \lim_{\alpha\to 1-} \limsup_{x\to +\infty} \left\{ \frac{\lambda(x) - \lambda(x^\alpha)}{(1-\alpha)\log x} \right\} ,$$

where $\lambda(r)$ is given by (10).

If f(z) is an entire function, the h-order of f is defined by

$$\rho_h(f) = \limsup_{s\to\infty} s^{-1} h^{-1}(\log M(e^s)).$$

We then have ([3] Theorem 2).

THEOREM 9. *Suppose that* $f \in E(\Lambda)$ *with* h-*order at most* $\rho$, *and suppose that* $D_h^*(\Lambda) < \frac{1}{2\rho}$. *Then the hypothesis that* f(z) *has* h-*order* $\sigma < \rho$ *along some ray implies that* f(z) *has, in fact,* h-*order* $\sigma$ *in the whole plane.*

THEOREM 10. *Let* $f \in E(\Lambda)$ *have* h-*order* $\rho < \infty$ *and suppose that* $\underline{D}_h(\Lambda) < \frac{1}{2\rho}$. *If* f *is bounded along some ray* arg z = $\theta$, *then* $f \equiv 0$. *Conversely if* $\Lambda$ *is such that* $\underline{D}_h(\Lambda) \geq \frac{1}{2\rho}$ *then there exists an* $f \in E(\Lambda)$ *with* h-*order at most* $\rho$ *but such that* $f(x) \to 0$ $(x \to \infty)$.

In the case $h(x) = e^x$ Theorem 10 is due to Edrei ([10] Theorem 2). Edrei's proof of his theorem is direct, using Carleman's formula, but it is interesting to note that he also comments on the lack of precision in the result compared with the Müntz-Szasz case.

A somewhat more precise result, which we quote only in the case $h(x) = e^x$ is [4] Corollary 2.

THEOREM 11. <u>If</u> $f \in E(\Lambda)$ <u>and has finite order</u> $\rho$ <u>and finite type</u>, <u>and if</u>

$$\liminf_{r\to\infty} \left\{ \lambda(r) - \frac{1}{2\rho}\log r \right\} = -\infty ,$$

<u>then</u> $f \equiv 0$.

By finite type we mean that the quantity $\limsup_{r\to\infty} \frac{\log M(r)}{r^\rho}$ is finite. The function $f(z) = z^{-\rho}\sin(z^\rho)$, with $2\rho$ an integer is an example of an entire function not identically zero with $f(x) \to 0$ $(x \to \infty)$ and

$$\lambda(r) - \frac{1}{2\rho}\log r = O(1) \quad , \quad r\to\infty.$$

Theorem 11 can be thought of as a limiting case of a theorem of Dzhrbashyan [9], concerning functions bounded along two rays. For similar results see Leont'ev [20].

THEOREM 12. <u>Suppose that the function</u> $f \in E(\Lambda)$ <u>has order</u> $\rho > \frac{1}{2}$ <u>and finite type</u>. <u>Suppose further that</u>

$$\left| f\left(t e^{\pm \frac{i\pi}{2\alpha}}\right) \right| < K ,$$

<u>where</u> $K$ <u>is some constant and</u> $\alpha > \max\left(\rho, \frac{\rho}{2\rho-1}\right)$. <u>If</u>

$$\liminf_{r\to\infty} \left\{ \lambda(r) - \frac{\alpha+\rho}{2\alpha\rho}\log r \right\} = -\infty ,$$

<u>then</u> $f \equiv 0$.

Theorem 11 can be thought of as the case $\alpha = \infty$ of Theorem 12. It is interesting to point out that the theorem is only valid for $\alpha$ sufficiently large. Considerations of a Phragmén-Lindelöf nature, or alternatively an examination of the function $f(z) = z^{-\rho}\sin(z^\rho)$ mentioned above, lead one to expect this.

## 6. Open Problems

There are many interesting problems still remaining. There is the question of determining $\overline{V(\Lambda)}$ precisely whenever the set $\Lambda$ is not complete in $S_H$ (§4 above). It is also not known if Theorem 9 remains valid with the condition $D_h^*(\Lambda) < \frac{1}{2\rho}$ replaced by $\underline{D}_h(\Lambda) < \frac{1}{2\rho}$. Equally, although such conditions are best-possible of their kind perhaps some finer density condition is the "right" one.

However, more far-reaching questions remain:- I mention only two of them. The first concerns the completeness of the system $\{z^{\lambda}\}$ on $C(\Gamma)$ where $\Gamma$ is some curve in the complex plane . To the best of my knowledge, this problem was first discussed by Chen [6] . For $\Gamma$ an analytic arc and (2) satisfied it was shown by Malliavin and Siddiqi [24] that $\{\exp \lambda_n z\}$ is not complete on $C(\Gamma)$. More comprehensive results with various smoothness conditions on $\Gamma$ have been given by Korevaar ( [16] and [17] ); see also [25] . This question still requires a lot of investigation.

The second question concerns the Macintyre conjecture. In [22] Macintyre conjectured that if $f \in E(\Lambda)$ with (2) holding then not only is f unbounded along every ray, but f is unbounded along every Jordan path tending to $\infty$; in particular f can have no finite asymptotic values. This question is obviously related to the previous one, but it is also unsolved. The conjecture has been shown to be true, under a weaker gap condition, if f has finite order, by Fuchs [12]. In the general case the conjecture is known to be true if (2) is replaced by either of the conditions

$$\lambda_n > n(\log n)^{1+\varepsilon}, \ \varepsilon > 0, \quad \text{or} \quad \sum_1^{\infty} \lambda_n^{-1}(\log \lambda_n)^{1+\varepsilon} < \infty,$$

(see [19] Theorem 1 and [2] Theorem 4). Thus the conjecture remains open only in the case when the convergence in (2) is very slow.

## REFERENCES


[1] Amar, D. and E., Bases d'exponentielles dans $L^2(\mathbb{R}^+)$. to appear in J. London Math. Soc.

[2] Anderson, J.M., - Binmore, K.G., Coefficient estimates for lacunary power series and Dirichlet series. Proc. London Math. Soc., (3), 18 (1968), 36-48.

[3] Anderson, J.M., - Binmore, K.G., Closure theorems with applications to entire functions with gaps. Trans. Amer. Math. Soc., 161 (1971), 381-400.

[4] Anderson, J.M., - Binmore, K.G., On entire functions with gap power series. Glasgow Math. J., 12 (1971), 89-97.

[5] Anderson, J.M., A note on a basis problem. Proc. Amer. Math. Soc., 51 (1975), 330-334.

[6] Sen-chan Chen, On the completeness of the system of functions $\{z^{t_n}\}$ on curves in the complex plane. (in Russian), Izv. Akad. Nauk SSSR Ser. Mat., 25 (1961), 253-276.

[7] Clarkson, J.A. - Erdös, P., Approximation by polynomials. Duke Math. J., 10 (1943), 5-11.

[8] Davis, P.J., Interpolation and Approximation. Waltham, Mass., 1963.

[9] Dzhrbashyan, M.M., Investigations in the theory of generalised integral transforms and in the theory of entire functions. Trudy, 3. Vse. Matem. S'yezda 1956, Izdat. Akad. Nauk. SSSR, 3 (1958), 182-189.

[10] Edrei, A., Gap and density theorems for entire functions. Scripta Math., 23 (1957), 1-25.

[11] Fuchs, W.H.J., On the closure of $\{e^{-t}t^{\alpha_\nu}\}$. Proc. Cambridge Philos. Soc., 42 (1946), 91-105.

[12] Fuchs, W.H.J., Proof of a conjecture of Polya concerning gap series. Illinois J. Math., 7 (1963), 661-667.

[13] Gaier, D., On the coefficients and the growth of gap power series. SIAM J. Numer. Anal., 3 (1966), 248-265.

[14] Gurarii, V.J., - Macaev, V.J., Lacunary power sequences in the spaces C and L. (in Russian) Izv. Akad. Nauk. SSSR. Ser. Mat., 30 (1966), 3-14.

[15] Korevaar, J., A characterisation of the sub-manifold of C[a,b] spanned by the sequence $\{x^{n_k}\}$. Nederl. Akad. Wetensch. Proc. Ser. A., 50 (1947) - Indag. Math., 9 (1947), 360-368.

[16] Korevaar, J., Approximation on curves by linear combinations of exponentials. Approximation Theory (Proc. Intern. Sympos., Univ. Texas, Austin, Texas, 1973), 387-393, Academic Press, New York, 1973.

[17] Korevaar, J., Approximation on curves by linear combinations of exponentials. Sympos. on Complex Analysis, Canterbury 1973, London Math. Soc. Lecture Note Series, 12 (1974), 97-99.

[18] Kövari, J., A gap-theorem for entire functions of infinite order. Michigan Math. J., 12 (1965), 133-140.

[19] Kövari, J., On the asymptotic paths of entire functions with gap power series. J. d'Analyse Math., 15 (1965), 281-286.

[20] Leont'ev, An extension of the properties of entire functions of order less than $\frac{1}{2}$ to some other functions. (in Russian), Trudy Mat. Inst. Steklova Akad. Nauk SSSR., 64 (1961), 126-146.

[21] Leont'ev, A.F., On the question of completeness of systems of powers on semi-axis (in Russian). Izv. Akad. Nauk SSSR. Ser. Mat., 26 (1962) 781-792.

[22] Macintyre, A.J., Asymptotic paths of integral functions with gap power series. Proc. London Math. Soc. (3), 2 (1952), 286-296.

[23] Malliavin, P., Sur quelques procédés d'extrapolation. Acta Math., 93 (1955), 179-255.

[24] Malliavin, P. - Siddiqi, J.A., Approximation polynomiale sur un arc analytique dans le plan complexe. C.R. Acad. Sci. Paris, 273 (1971), 105-108.

[25] Malliavin, P. - Siddiqi, J.A., Classes de fonctions monogènes et approximation par des sommes d'exponentielles sur un arc rectifiable de $\mathbb{C}$. C.R. Acad. Sci. Paris, Sci. Paris, 282 (1976), 1091-1094.

[26] Müntz, Ch., Über den Approximation satz von Weierstrass. Festschrift H.A. Schwarz, Berlin 1914.

[27] Szasz, O., Über die Approximation stetiger Funktionen durch lineare Aggregate von Potenzen. Math. Ann., 77 (1916), 482-496.

[28] Schwartz, L., Etude des sommes d'exponentielles. 2ième éd. Publ. Inst. Math. Univ. Strasbourg, V, Actualités Sci. Indust., no. 959, Paris, 1959.

[29] Shapiro, H.S. - Shields, A.L., On some interpolation problems for analytic functions. Amer. J. Math., 83 (1961), 513-532.

# STRUCTURAL AND APPROXIMATIONAL PROPERTIES OF FUNCTIONS IN THE COMPLEX DOMAIN

P.M. Tamrazov

Mathematical Institute of Academy of Sciences

Ukrainian SSR

Kiev

The paper contains an account of some recent results concerning complex finite-difference moduli of smoothness of functions on sets of the complex plane and their applications to polynomial approximation problems and conformal mapping theory. There are given: the general normality result for the moduli of smoothness for a class of sets including all those appearing in the well known direct theorems of polynomial approximation with exact order of approximation; results on moduli of smoothness of function superpositions and applications to conformal mapping; and also strongly local theorems of polynomial approximation, local and global versions of such theorems with mixed majorants.

In [11] there are introduced moduli of smoothness of arbitrary natural order k, well-defined for any set in the complex plane C (see also [12]). These moduli being of purely finite-difference nature are defined axiomatically, and there is given their classification in some respects in [11], [12]. These moduli enabled one to solve a number of the main problems of the theory of finite-difference smoothnesses of order k = 2,3,... (and of approximations connected with them) under very general assumptions upon sets, functions and majorants.

An account and a survey of a part of the results established in terms of these moduli are given in [11] - [13]. During the last two years new results in this field have been obtained.

Among moduli of smoothness introduced in [11], several concrete kinds of them are mostly used in practice, some of them being monotone in the variable $\delta$, and others being almost monotone (i.e. in order of magnitudes equivalent to monotone functions). For instance, let a finite positive number N, a natural k, a point set $E \subset C$ be fixed, and a finite function f(z) be given on E. One of the concrete local moduli of smoothness for $z \in E$ and $\delta > 0$ has been defined through the complex finite differences $[z_o,\ldots,z_k;f,z_o]$ of the function f(z) (see [11], [12]) by means of the formula

$$\omega_{k,N,E,z}(f,\delta) = \sup_{z_o,\ldots,z_k} |[z_o,\ldots,z_k;f,z_o]| ,$$

where the least upper bound is taken with respect to all point collections $z_o,\ldots,z_k \in E \cap \{\zeta : |\zeta - z| \leqslant \delta\}$ satisfying the condition

(1) $$\frac{\delta}{|z_p - z_q|} \leqslant N \qquad \forall p \neq q.$$

If a rectifiable Jordan arc or curve $\Gamma$ is taken as E, and $\rho_\Gamma(\zeta,z)$ is a curvelinear (with respect to $\Gamma$) distance between points $\zeta,\ z \in \Gamma$, then for a function f(z) given on $\Gamma$ there is defined (see [11], [12]) also a local modulus of smoothness

$$\tilde{\omega}_{k,N,\Gamma,z}(f,\delta) = \sup_{z_o,\ldots,z_k} |[z_o,\ldots,z_k;f,z_o]| ,$$

where the least upper bound is taken with respect to all on $\Gamma$ linearly ordered point collections $z_o,\ldots,z_k \in \Gamma \cap \{\zeta : \rho_\Gamma(\zeta,z) \leqslant \delta\}$ satisfying the condition

$$\rho_\Gamma(z_i,z_{i+1})/\rho_\Gamma(z_j,z_{j+1}) \leqslant N \qquad \forall i,\ j = 0,\ldots,k-1 .$$

The global moduli of smoothness $\omega_{k,N,E}(f,\delta)$ and $\tilde{\omega}_{k,N,\Gamma}(f,\delta)$ are defined as the least upper bounds with respect to $z \in E$ or $z \in \Gamma$ of the corresponding local moduli of smoothness. Let us note that the mentioned moduli of the form $\omega_k$ defined by means of the condition (1) are almost monotone, and moduli of the form $\tilde{\omega}_k$ are monotone in $\delta$.

Other concrete kinds of moduli of smoothness have been also defined and used in [11], [12]. For example, the condition (1) can be replaced by the condition

$$|z_i - z_j|/|z_p - z_q| \leqslant N \qquad \forall\, i,j,p,q \mid p > q$$

(see [11], [12]), and the resulting moduli are monotone in $\delta$.

Among properties of moduli of smoothness, the normality property plays an important role in applications (see [11]). Unfortunately this property is valid only for some classes of sets and has been established with difficulties.

Let $H_\lambda$ $(\lambda \geqslant 1)$ be the class of all rectifiable Jordan arcs in C such that the length of each of them does not exceed $\lambda$ times its chord.

Let $H^\lambda$ denote the class of all continua in C such that on each of them every two points can be connected by an arc of the class $H_\lambda$ lying in the continuum.

In [11] there was considered the class $S_\lambda$ of all Jordan lines in C such that on each of them every two points can be connected by an arc of the class $H_\lambda$ lying in the line. Besides there was considered also the class $S^\lambda$ of all continua in C such that on each of them every two points can be connected by an arc of the class $S_\lambda$ belonging to the continuum [12].

One can prove that $H^\lambda = S^\lambda$.

The following normality theorem holds.

THEOREM 1. For any $E \in H^\lambda$, $k = 1,2,\dots$ and $N \in [1,\infty]$, the modulus of smoothness $\omega_{k,N,E}(f,\delta)$ of any function $f(z)$, defined on E, satisfies the estimate

$$\omega_{k,N,E}(f,t\delta) \leqslant c(\lambda,k)t^k\omega_{k,N,E}(f,\delta) \qquad \forall t \geqslant 1,\ \forall \delta > 0,$$

in which $c(\lambda,k)$ depends only on $\lambda$ and k (and does not depend on $t,\delta,N,E,f$).

This theorem complements the normality results given in [11], [12] for functions on lines of the class $S_\lambda$ and on closed sets of the class $S^\lambda$. A proof of theorem 1 is a development of the method of [11], Chapter 5, Sections 3 - 4, based on investigation of properties of complex finite differences.

Normality results for moduli of smoothness have a number of applications in the theory of Cauchy-type integral and singular integrals, in contour-and-solid properties of holomorphic functions, in approximation theorems, etc. (see [11], [12]). For instance the importance of the results for direct theorems of polynomial approximation in the complex domain with exact order of approximation is determined by the fact that all well known approximation theorems of the mentioned kind concern subclasses of the class $H^{\lambda}$ and essentially lean upon the normality property. Therefore either this property is postulated in the form of an additional assumption of normality of a majorant appearing in formulations of the theorems, or normality of the modulus of smoothness is proved (and in this case a direct theorem of approximation is formulated in terms of the modulus of smoothness itself being its own normal majorant).

Investigating a problem concerning finite-difference smoothnesses of conformal mappings, E.W. Karupu has come to posing the problem of finite-difference smoothnesses of any natural order k for superpositions $f \circ g$ of functions f and g in connection with analogous smoothnesses of the functions f and g. In the particular case when $k = 2$ and classical (arithmetical - in terminology of [11]) moduli of smoothness for concrete functions of real variables concerning conformal mapping of a disk onto a smooth domain under a Hölder condition were considered, this problem was formerly treated by S.E. Warschawski [15](in another formulation), R.N. Koval'čuk [9] and L.I. Kolesnik [8], and there it was solved by means of the method due to S.E. Warschawski [15] based on the introduction of additional points. This method was generalized by E.W. Karupu [6] for the case $k > 2$. But the mentioned method contains a roughening step in the replacement of finite differences (and moduli of smoothness) of order k by finite differences (and moduli of smoothness) of order 2, and as a result the less sharp inequalities obtained by means of it do not possess any property important for applications, and have essentially a restricted range of applications.

The mentioned problem of finite-difference smoothnesses of function superpositions has been solved in the paper [13]: there are given estimates for moduli of smoothness of the superposition $f \circ g$ via moduli of smoothness of f and g (the direct estimates) and estimates for moduli of smoothness of the function f via moduli of smoothness of $f \circ g$ and g (the inverse estimates). The main difficulties of derivation of these estimates are concentrated in the establishment of finite-difference identities giving an expression of the complex divided differences of the superposition $f \circ g$ via complex divided differences of f and g and divided differences of f via divided differences of $f \circ g$ and g. A property of these identities and estimates important for applications is named *ordinal homogeneity*. The results of the work [13] are obtained by a method not involving any additional points and attendent roughenings.

For example we formulate some results from [13].

Suppose on a set $G \subset C$ consisting of more than k points there is given a finite function $g(z)$ mapping it onto a set $F \subset C$ in such a way that under some constants a and b the conditions

$$0 < \frac{1}{b} \leqslant \left|\frac{g(z')-g(z'')}{z'-z''}\right| \leqslant a < \infty \qquad \forall z',z'' \in G$$

are fulfilled. Let a finite function $f(w)$ be given on F. Then there holds the following

THEOREM 2. <u>For any</u> $\delta > 0$ <u>there are valid the estimates</u>

$$\omega_{k,N,G}(f\circ g,\delta) - \omega_{k,Nab,F}(f,a\delta) \tag{2}$$

$$\leqslant c \sum_{j=1}^{k-1} \omega_{j,Nab,F}(f,a\delta)\delta^{-j} \sum_{\substack{r_1,\dots,r_j \geqslant 1 \\ r_1+\dots+r_j=k}} \prod_{q=1}^{j} \omega_{r_q,N,G}(g,\delta),$$

$$\omega_{k,N,F}(f,\delta) - \omega_{k,Nab,G}(f\circ g,b\delta) \tag{3}$$

$$\leqslant c\delta^{-k(k-1)/2} \sum_{j=1}^{k-1} \omega_{j,Nab,G}(f\circ g,b\delta)$$

$$\times \sum_{\substack{r_1,\dots,r_{k(k-1)/2} \geqslant 1 \\ r_1+\dots+r_{k(k-1)/2}=k(k+1)/2-j}} \left\{ \prod_{q=1}^{k(k-1)/2} \omega_{r_q,Nab,G}(g,b\delta) \right\},$$

<u>and also their analogs for local moduli of smoothness, the constant</u> c <u>depending only on</u> N,k <u>in</u> (2) <u>and only on</u> N,k,a,b <u>in</u> (3).

Suppose that a Jordan curve or arc $\Gamma$ is defined on an interval I of the real axis R by the natural equation $z = z(\sigma)$, and a finite function $\varphi(\sigma)$ is given on I. If $\Gamma$ is a closed curve, let us suppose that I = R and the functions $z(\sigma)$ and $\varphi(\sigma)$ are periodic with a period $T_z$ corresponding to a single passing of $\Gamma$.

Let $\omega_{k,I}(\varphi,\delta)$ be the usual (arithmetic and strongly centered - in terminology of [11]) modulus of smoothness of the function $\varphi(\sigma)$ of the real variable $\sigma$ (not variable z).

If $\Gamma$ is a closed curve, then for convenience' sake this modulus will be considered only for values $\delta \leqslant (1/2)T_z$.

If $\Gamma$ is rectifiable and $z = z(\sigma)$ is the natural equation of $\Gamma$ ($\sigma$ is the length of an arc on $\Gamma$, $\sigma = \sigma(z)$), then $\omega_{k,I}(\varphi,\delta)$ turns out to be a quantity which is traditionally, by definition, assumed as a modulus $\omega_k(f,t)$ of smoothness of order k for the function $f(z) = (\varphi\circ\sigma)(z)$ on the line $\Gamma$ (under the value $t = \delta/k$). If, furthermore, $\Gamma$ is a closed curve, then $T_z$ is the length of $\Gamma$.

Let $\Gamma$ be a line of the class $S_\lambda$, $1 \leqslant \lambda < \infty$. If $z = z(\sigma)$ is the natural equation of the line $\Gamma$, then there holds

THEOREM 3. <u>There are valid the estimates</u>

$$|\tilde{\omega}_{k,1,\Gamma}(\varphi\circ\sigma,\delta) - \omega_{k,I}(\varphi,\delta)|$$

$$\leqslant c \sum_{j=1}^{k-1} \omega_{j,I}(\varphi,\delta)\delta^{-j} \sum_{\substack{r_1,\ldots,r_j \geqslant 1 \\ r_1+\ldots+r_j=k}} \prod_{q=1}^{j} \tilde{\omega}_{r_q,1,\Gamma}(\sigma,\delta),$$

$$|\omega_{k,I}(\varphi,\delta) - \tilde{\omega}_{k,1,\Gamma}(\varphi\circ\sigma,\delta)| \leqslant c\delta^{-k(k-1)/2} \sum_{j=1}^{k-1} \tilde{\omega}_{j,1,\Gamma}(\varphi\circ\sigma,\delta)$$

$$\times \sum_{\substack{r_1,\ldots,r_{k(k-1)/2} \geqslant 1 \\ r_1+\ldots+r_{k(k-1)/2}=k(k+1)/2-j}} \prod_{q=1}^{k(k-1)/2} \tilde{\omega}_{r_q,1,\Gamma}(\sigma,\delta),$$

<u>in which the constant</u> c <u>depends only on</u> k <u>and</u> $\lambda$.

The given theorem as well as other results of [13] have been essentially used in papers due to E.W. Karupu [6], [7] for the full solution of the problem of finite-difference smoothnesses of conformal homeomorphisms.

Suppose G is a simply connected domain bounded by a rectifiable smooth Jordan curve $\Gamma$, s is an arc length on $\Gamma$, $\tau = \tau(s)$ is the angle between the tangent to $\Gamma$ and the positive real axis; $\zeta = \varphi(z)$ is a homeomorphism of the closed unit disk $\overline{D} = \{z : |z| \leqslant 1\}$ onto the closure $\overline{G}$ of a domain G, conformal in the open unit disk $D = \{z : |z| < 1\}$. Let $\omega_k(\tau, t) = \omega_{k,I}(\tau, tk)$ be the usual modulus of smoothness for $\tau(s)$, and $\omega_k(\varphi'(e^{iv}), \delta)_v$ be the usual modulus of smoothness of the function $\varphi'(e^{iv})$ of the real variable v.

E.W. Karupu has established [7] that, with any natural k and $\alpha \in (0,k)$, the condition

$$\omega_k(\tau, \delta) = \mathcal{O}(\delta^\alpha) \qquad (\delta \to 0) \tag{4}$$

implies the estimates

$$\omega_k(\varphi'(e^{iv}), \delta)_v = \mathcal{O}(\delta^\alpha) \qquad (\delta \to 0), \tag{5}$$

$$\tilde{\omega}_{k,1,\partial D}(\varphi', \delta) = \mathcal{O}(\delta^\alpha) \qquad (\delta \to 0), \tag{6}$$

$$\omega_{k,N,\overline{D}}(\varphi', \delta) = \mathcal{O}(\delta^\alpha) \qquad (\delta \to 0). \tag{7}$$

More generally, if (4) is replaced by the weaker condition

$$\int_0 \omega_k(\tau, t) t^{-1} dt < \infty,$$

then the derivative $\varphi'(z)$ exists and is continuous on $\overline{D}$, does not vanish anywhere on $\overline{D}$, and there hold certain generalizations of the estimates (5) - (7) with proper majorants being some integral transformations of the modulus of smoothness $\omega_k(\tau, \delta)$. E.W. Karupu also obtained inversions of these statements and some other results in the problem considered.

Now we proceed to the treatment of the problem of polynomial approximation of a function f(z) in the closure $\overline{G}$ of a complex domain G. We make use of notions and notations from [11], [12] (see also below), where one can find the history of topics touched upon and a survey of the preceeding results. Among recent achievements in this field let us mention a result due to V.I. Belyi [3] on the direct problem of polynomial approximation for moduli of continuity in a domain G with quasiconformal boundary. V.I. Belyi and the author of the present paper jointly have generalized this result to moduli of smoothness $\omega_{k,N,\overline{G}}$ with arbitrary natural k:

THEOREM 4. *Let* G *be a bounded Jordan domain with quasiconformal boundary. Then for any function* f, *holomorphic in* G *and continuous on* $\overline{G}$ *together with its derivatives of the orders* 0,...,r (r *is a nonnegative integer*), *there exists a sequence* $\{P_n\}_{n=1}^{\infty}$ *of polynomials such that*

$$|f^{(\nu)}(z) - P_n^{(\nu)}(z)| \leq c d(\tfrac{1}{n},z)^{r-\nu} \omega_{k,N,\overline{G}}(f^{(r)}, d(\tfrac{1}{n},z))$$

$$\forall n = 1,2,\dots; \quad \forall z \in \partial G; \quad \forall \nu = 0,\dots,r,$$

*where the constant* c *does not depend on* n, z.

The given result was announced at the All-Union School "Modern Problems of Function Theory" in Baku in May 1977. Here the rate of approximation is estimated directly via the modulus of smoothness thanks to the fact that this modulus is normal. In its turn the normality property follows from the above given Theorem 1 on the basis that a domain with quasiconformal boundary as shown in [3], belongs to the class $H^{\lambda}$ under suitable $\lambda > 1$.

In the work [14] direct and inverse problems of polynomial approximation were solved in strongly local formulation, and also with mixed majorants (in local and global formulations). Notice that the results of [14] are new even for $k = 1$. We give some of their simplest particular cases. For simplicity suppose that F is an arbitrary connected compactum in C with connected complement. Suppose 1 is the diameter of F, d(u,z) is the distance from a point $z \in \partial F$ to the u-th level line of the outer Green function; u(t,z) is the value of $u \in (0,\infty)$ such that $d(u,z) = t$ (see [11], p. 140).

Let f be a function continuous on F and holomorphic in the interior of F. Let $P_n(z)$ denote polynomials of orders not exceeding n.

Suppose a positive function $\mu_z(w,y,x)$ is given for $z \in \partial F$, $w > 0$, $y > 0$, $x > 0$, is nondecreasing in w, y, x, satisfies the condition

$$\mu_z(tw,ty,tx) \leq a t^b \mu_z(w,y,x) \qquad \forall t \geq 1, \ \forall w,y,x > 0, \ \forall z \in \partial F$$

with constants a and b not depending on w, y, x, z, t, and $\mu_z(1,1,1)$ is bounded uniformly with respect to $z \in \partial F$.

Provided $\mu_z(w,y,x)$ does not depend on w, y or z, then let us omit the corresponding parameter and write $\mu(y,x)$, $\mu(x)$ (these notations are used also in the case when $z = z_o$ is fixed).

In the sequel $z_o$ denotes an arbitrary fixed point on $\partial F$.

First we formulate inverse theorems of approximation.

THEOREM 5. _If the sequence_ $\{P_n\}_{n=1}^{\infty}$ _of polynomials is such that_

$$|f(z) - P_n(z)| \leqslant \mu(d(\tfrac{1}{n}, z_o) + |z-z_o|) \qquad \forall z \in \partial F, \quad \forall n = 1,2,\dots, \tag{8}$$

_then_

$$\omega_{k,N,F,z_o}(f,\delta) \leqslant c\delta^k \int_\delta^{21} \frac{\mu(t)}{t^{k+1}}\, dt \qquad \forall \delta \in (0,1], \tag{9}$$

_where_ c _is a constant not depending on_ $\delta$, $z_o$.

There holds also the more general result which arises from this theorem provided the majorant $\mu(.)$ is replaced by a mixed majorant $\mu(1/n,.)$ in (8) and by $\mu(u(t,z_o),.)$ in (9).

In the direct problem of approximation there were obtained the following results in which F was assumed to be a set satisfying the condition (L,S) (see [11], pp. 248 - 249).

THEOREM 6. _If_

$$\omega_{k,N,F,z_o}(f,\delta) \leqslant \mu(\delta) \qquad \forall \delta \in (0,1],$$

_then there exists a sequence_ $\{P_n\}_{n=1}^{\infty}$ _of polynomials such that_

$$|f(z) - P_n(z)| \leqslant c\mu(d(\tfrac{1}{n}, z_o) + |z-z_o|) \qquad \forall z \in \partial F, \ \forall n = 1,2,\dots,$$

_where_ c _does not depend on_ $z_o$, z, n.

THEOREM 7. *If* $v(z)$ *is an arbitrary real bounded function of the variable* $z \in \partial F$ *and*

$$\omega_{k,N,F,z}(f,\delta) \leqslant \mu_z((\delta/u(\delta,z))^{v(z)}, u(\delta,z),\delta) \qquad \forall\delta \in (0,1],$$

*then there exists a sequence* $\{P_n\}_{n=1}^{\infty}$ *of polynomials such that*

$$|f(z) - P_n(z)| \leqslant c\mu_z((nd(\tfrac{1}{n},z))^{v(z)}, \tfrac{1}{n}, d(\tfrac{1}{n},z)) \qquad \forall z \in \partial F,\ n = 1,2,\ldots,$$

*where the constant* $c$ *does not depend on* $z$, $n$.

From these direct and inverse approximation theorems it is easy to derive statements about strongly local and global constructive characterizations of function classes defined by normal and mixed majorants. For instance, let us give the following strongly local results in which the sign "$\preccurlyeq$" denotes the ordinal inequality.

THEOREM 8. *Let*

$$\delta^k \int_\delta^{21} \mu(t)t^{-k-1}dt \preccurlyeq \mu(\delta) \qquad (\delta \to 0).$$

*Then the estimate*

$$\omega_{k,N,F,z_o}(f,\delta) \preccurlyeq \mu(\delta) \qquad (\delta \to 0)$$

*is equivalent to the existence of a sequence* $\{P_n\}_{n=1}^{\infty}$ *of polynomials such that*

$$|f(z) - P_n(z)| \preccurlyeq \mu(d(\tfrac{1}{n}, z_o) + |z-z_o|) \qquad \forall n = 1,2,\ldots; \forall z \in \partial F.$$

In [14] there are obtained also generalizations of these results for derivatives of the function f. As it is noticed in [14], the given results in the direct approximation problem hold also for some other classes of sets including those satisfying the condition (BM)(see [11] pp. 248 - 249).

Analogous results are valid also for domains with more general boundary.

V.V. Bardzinskij [1] has transfered the strongly local approximation theorems to the real case where they also turned out to be new (even in the case k = 1).

We have not considered applications of complex finite-difference moduli of smoothness to other problems, particularly to Cauchy-type integrals and singular integrals, to conjugate functions, to contour-and-solid properties of holomorphic functions (see [11], [12]). Recently the young participants of the seminar in complex analysis at the Mathematical Institute of the Ukrainian Academy of Sciences V.V. Bardzinskij, O.F. Herus, E.W. Karupu, A.J. Ščehorskij have obtained a number of new results in topics touched upon in this paper, and it concerns both the one-dimensional and higher-dimensional cases (see [1], [2], [4] - [7], [10]). Unfortunately we have here no possibility to mention some works due to other authors.

## REFERENCES

[1] Bardzinskij, V.V., Local approximation theorems for periodical functions. Finite-difference smoothnesses in problems of function theory. Preprint IM-77-10 (Collect. of preprints) (Russian), pp. 3 - 8. Inst. Mat. Akad. Nauk Ukrain. SSR, Kiev, 1977.

[2] Bardzinskij, V.V., On polynomial-approximational properties of functions and their derivatives on complex sets. (Russian). Ukrain. Mat. Ž., 28 (1976), 368 - 373.

[3] Belyi, V.I., Conformal mappings and approximation of analytic functions in domains with quasiconformal boundary. (Russian). Mat. Sb. (N.S.), 102 (144), (1977), 331 - 361.

[4] Herus, O.F., Finite-difference smoothnesses of Cauchy-type integrals. (Russian). Ukrain. Mat. Ž., 29 (1977), 642 - 646.

[5] Herus, O.F., Some estimates of moduli of smoothness of Cauchy-type integrals. Finite-difference smoothnesses in problems of function theory, Preprint IM-77-10 (Collect. of preprints) (Russian), pp. 9 - 22. Inst. Mat. Akad. Nauk Ukrain. SSR, Kiev, 1977.

[6] Karupu, E.W., On finite-difference smoothnesses of conformal mappings. Preprint IM-77-6. (Russian). Inst. Mat. Akad. Nauk Ukrain. SSR, Kiev, 1977.

[7] Karupu, E.W., Moduli of smoothness of conformal homeomorphisms. Preprint 77-10, (Russian). Inst. Mat. Akad. Nauk Ukrain. SSR, Kiev, 1977.

[8] Kolesnik, L.I., Inversion of theorem of Kellogg type. (Russian). Ukrain. Mat. Ž., 21 (1969), 104 - 108.

[9] Koval'čuk, R.N., On one generalization of Kellogg's theorem. (Russian). Ukrain. Mat. Ž., 17 (1965), 104 - 108.

[10] Ščehorskij, A.J., Contour-and-solid theorems for holomorphic functions in $C^n$. Finite-difference smoothnesses in problems of function theory. Preprint IM-77-10 (Collect. of preprints) (Russian), pp. 23 - 27. Inst. Mat. Akad. Nauk Ukrain. SSR, Kiev, 1977.

[11] Tamrazov, P.M., Smoothnesses and Polynomial Approximations. (Russian). Izdat. "Naukova Dumka", Kiev, 1975.

[12] Tamrazov, P.M., Finite-difference smoothnesses and polynomial approximations. Preprint IM-75-10. (Russian). Inst. Mat. Akad. Nauk Ukrain. SSR, Kiev, 1975.

[13] Tamrazov, P.M., Finite-difference identities and estimates of moduli of smoothness of function superpositions. Preprint 77-5. (Russian,. Inst. Mat. Akad. Nauk Ukrain. SSR, Kiev, 1977.

[14] Tamrazov, P.M. - Bardzinskij, V.V., On complex finite-difference smoothnesses and polynomial approximations. Preprint IM-76-7. (Russian). Inst. Mat. Akad. Nauk Ukrain. SSR, Kiev, 1976.

[15] Warschawski, S.E., Über einen Satz von O.D. Kellogg. Nachr. Ges. Wiss., Göttingen (1932), 73 - 86.

# VIII
# Differential Operators and Equations

# A GENERALIZATION OF THE CAUCHY-KOWALEVSKY THEOREM AND BOUNDARY VALUES OF SOLUTIONS OF ELLIPTIC EQUATIONS

Hikosaburo Komatsu
Department of Mathematics, Faculty of Science
University of Tokyo
Tokyo

An analogue of the Cauchy-Kowalevsky theorem is given for ultradifferentiable functions, and its dual is used to characterize those solutions of a homogeneous elliptic equation on one side of a hyperplane that have boundary values in a class of ultradistributions.

## 1. Introduction

One of the origins of modern analysis seems to be in Hardy's paper [2] where he gave a new proof of the non-differentiability of Weierstrass' non-differentiable function

$$f(x) = \sum_{n=0}^{\infty} a^{-\rho n} e^{ia^n x}, \qquad 0 < \rho < 1, \quad a > 1.$$

He represents $f(x)$ as the boundary value $F(x+i0)$ of the holomorphic function

$$F(z) = \sum_{n=0}^{\infty} a^{-\rho n} e^{ia^n z}$$

defined on the upper half plane $\operatorname{Im} z > 0$. Then he establishes the fact that the boundary value $f(x)$ is Hölder continuous of exponent $0 < \alpha < 1$ at $x$ if and only if

$$F'(x+iy) = O(y^{\alpha-1}) \quad \text{as } y \to 0 \tag{1.1}$$

at $x$. Since $F(x+iy)$ does not satisfy (1.1) for any $\alpha > \rho$, $f(x)$ cannot be Hölder continuous of exponent $\alpha$ and therefore cannot be differentiable at $x$.

Hardy and Littlewood developed this idea further in [3] and [4] and proved many theorems of the following type.

$X$ and $Y$ are Banach spaces of functions $f$ on $\mathbb{R}$ (or on $\mathbb{T}$) which are represented as boundary values of holomorphic or harmonic functions $F$ on the upper half plane (or on the unit disk). $Y$ is continuously imbedded in $X$. There are two function spaces $\mathcal{Y}_1$ and $\mathcal{Y}_2$ with variable $y$ and an integer $m_0$ such that the following conditions are equivalent for $f \in X$:

(a) $f \in Y$;

(b) $\|y^m F^{(m)}(x+iy)\|_X \in \mathcal{Y}_1$;

(c) $\|\sum_{p=0}^{m} \binom{m}{p} (-1)^p F(x+ipy)\|_X \in \mathcal{Y}_2$,

where $m$ is any integer $\geqq m_0$. Then usually $F(x+iy)$ converges to $f(x)$ in the topology of $Y$.

It is remarkable that they introduced Besov spaces and proved the Sobolev imbedding theorem as well as Sobolev's inequality for functions of one variable.

The results of Hardy-Littlewood have been generalized to the case of several variables by Taibleson [13] and then by Butzer-Berens [1] and Komatsu [5], [6], [7] from the viewpoint of semi-groups of operators.

As condition (b) shows, the above theorem characterizes actually the distributions $f^{(m)}$ obtained as the m-th derivatives of elements in $Y$.

More generally we can prove that the boundary values $F(x',+0), \ldots, \partial^{m-1}F(x',+0)/\partial x_n^{m-1}$ of a solution $F(x',x_n)$ on the upper half part $\Omega_+ = \{x \in \Omega;\ x_n > 0\}$ of an open set $\Omega$ in $\mathbb{R}^n$ of an elliptic homogeneous equation

$$Q(x,\partial)F(x) = 0 \tag{1.2}$$

of order $m$ are distributions on $\Omega' = \{x \in \Omega;\ x_n = 0\}$ if and only if for each compact set $K'$ in $\Omega'$ there are constants $L$ and $C$ such that

(1.3) $$\sup_{x'\in K'} |F(x',x_n)| \leqq C\, x_n^{-L}.$$

On the other hand, Komatsu-Kawai [11] have shown that all solutions $F$ of (1.2) on $\Omega_+$ without any restrictions have boundary values $F(x',+0)$, $\ldots$, $\partial^{m-1}F(x',+0)/\partial x_n^{m-1}$ in the sense of hyperfunction of Sato [12]. In this paper we are concerned with the case where $F$ behaves more wildly than (1.3) but has some growth order as $x_n \to 0$.

## 2. A Generalization of the Cauchy-Kowalevsky Theorem

The classical Cauchy-Kowalevsky theorem asserts the following. Let

(2.1) $$P(x,\partial) = \sum_{|\alpha|\leqq m} a_\alpha(x)\partial^\alpha$$

be a partial differential operator defined on an open set $\Omega$ in $\mathbb{R}^n$, which we assume to be linear for the sake of simplicity. Here we write for a multi-index $\alpha = (\alpha_1, \ldots, \alpha_n)$ with $\alpha_i = 0,1,2,\ldots$ ,

(2.2) $$\partial^\alpha = \partial_1^{\alpha_1} \cdots \partial_n^{\alpha_n} = \left(\frac{\partial}{\partial x_1}\right)^{\alpha_1} \cdots \left(\frac{\partial}{\partial x_n}\right)^{\alpha_n}$$

and

(2.3) $$|\alpha| = |\alpha_1| + \cdots + |\alpha_n|.$$

We assume:

(i) The hypersurface

(2.4) $$\Omega' = \{x \in \Omega;\ \ x_n = 0\}$$

is non-characteristic, i.e.,

(2.5) $$a_{(0,\ldots,0,m)}(x',0) = 0, \quad x' \in \Omega' ,$$

where $\Omega'$ is identified with an open set in $\mathbb{R}^{n-1}$;

(ii) The coefficients

$$a_\alpha(x) \in \mathcal{A}(\Omega) , \tag{2.6}$$

where $\mathcal{A}(\Omega)$ denotes the space of all real analytic functions on $\Omega$ .

Then we conclude:

For each Cauchy data

$$g_1(x'), \ldots, g_m(x') \in \mathcal{A}(\Omega') \tag{2.7}$$

and

$$g(x) \in \mathcal{A}(\Omega) \tag{2.8}$$

there exists a unique solution

$$u(x) \in \mathcal{A}(\Omega_1) \tag{2.9}$$

of

$$\partial_n^{j-1} u(x',0) = g_j(x'), \quad j = 1,\ldots,m , \tag{2.10}$$

and

$$P(x,\partial)u(x) = f(x) \tag{2.11}$$

on an open neighborhood $\Omega_1$ of $\Omega'$ in $\Omega$.

We want to generalize the theorem for wider classes of functions than the real analytic functions.

Let $M_p$, $p = 0,1,2,\ldots,$ be a sequence of positive numbers. An infinitely differentiable function $f(x)$ on $\Omega$ is said to be an ultradifferentiable function of class $(M_p)$ (resp. of class $\{M_p\}$) if for each compact set $K$ in $\Omega$ and $h > 0$ there exists a constant $C$ (resp. there exist constants $h$ and $C$) such that

(2.12) $$\sup_{x\in K}|\partial^\alpha f(x)| \leqq Ch^{|\alpha|}M_{|\alpha|}, \quad |\alpha| = 0,1,2,\dots .$$

We denote by $*$ either $(M_p)$ or $\{M_p\}$ and by $\mathcal{E}^*(\Omega)$ and $\mathcal{D}^*(\Omega)$ the space of all ultradifferentiable functions of class $*$ on $\Omega$ and its linear subspace of all elements with compact support.

It is well known that $\mathcal{E}^{\{p!\}}(\Omega)$ is $\mathcal{A}(\Omega)$ and that $\mathcal{E}^{(p!)}(\Omega)$ is the set of restrictions to $\Omega$ of all entire functions provided that $\Omega$ is connected. We want, however, to mean by ultradifferentiable something between differentiable and real analytic. To be more precise we impose the following conditions on $M_p$:

(M.0) $$M_0 = M_1 = 1;$$

(M.1) $$M_p^2 \leqq M_{p-1}M_{p+1};$$

(M.2) $$M_p \leqq AH^p \min_{0\leqq q\leqq p} M_q M_{p-q};$$

(M.3) $$\sum_{q=p}^{\infty} \frac{M_q}{M_{q+1}} \leqq Ap\frac{M_p}{M_{p+1}};$$

(M.4) $$\left(\frac{M_p}{p!}\right)^2 \leqq \left(\frac{M_{p-1}}{(p-1)!}\right)\left(\frac{M_{p+1}}{(p+1)!}\right)$$

and $pM_p/M_{p+1} \longrightarrow 0$ as $p \longrightarrow \infty$. Here $A$ and $H$ are constants.

Typical examples are the sequences

(2.13) $$M_p = (p!)^s \qquad \text{for } s > 1.$$

In this case we denote $(M_p)$ and $\{M_p\}$ by $(s)$ and $\{s\}$ respectively for short. The corresponding classes of ultradifferentiable functions are called Gevrey classes of functions.

We cannot simply replace $\mathcal{A}$ in (2.6), (2.7), (2.8) and (2.9) by $\mathcal{E}^*$. For, suppose that $P(x, \partial)$ is an elliptic operator for example and that $f(x)$ is real analytic. Then every solution $u(x)$ of (2.11) is real analytic and therefore the Cauchy data $g_j(x')$ must be real analytic.

An operator $P(x,\partial)$ is called *-hyperbolic if the conclusion of the theorem holds with $\mathcal{A}$ replaced by $\mathcal{E}^*$. An almost necessary and sufficient condition for (s)- and {s}-hyperbolicity is known (see e.g. Komatsu [10]) and it shows that those operators are very special.

We have, however, the following generalization of the theorem independent of the type of operators.

THEOREM 1. *Let $*$ be either $(M_p)$ or $\{M_p\}$ for a sequence satisfying (M.0) - (M.4). If $P(x,\partial)$ is a linear partial differential operator with coefficients $a_\alpha(x) \in \mathcal{E}^*(\Omega)$ such that $\Omega'$ is non-characteristic, then for each Cauchy data $g_j(x') \in \mathcal{E}^*(\Omega')$, $j = 1,\ldots,m$, and $f(x) \in \mathcal{E}^*(\Omega)$ there exists an $u(x) \in \mathcal{E}^*(\Omega)$ satisfying (2.10) and*

$$\partial^\gamma(P(x,\partial)u(x)-f(x)) = 0 \quad \text{on } \Omega' \text{ for all } \gamma. \tag{2.14}$$

We note that (2.14) is equivalent to (2.11) in the real analytic case. The proof is also similar. We construct a formal solution and then estimate the coefficients. For this purpose we introduce the following space of formal power series in $x_n$ with coefficients in $\mathcal{E}^*(\Omega')$.

DEFINITION 1. *We define $\mathcal{E}_\Omega^{(M_p)}(\Omega')$ (resp. $\mathcal{E}_\Omega^{\{M_p\}}(\Omega')$) to be the space of all formal power series*

$$f(x', \langle\!\langle x_n \rangle\!\rangle) = \sum_{j=0}^{\infty} f_j(x')x_n^j/j! \tag{2.15}$$

*with coefficients $f_j(x')$ such that for each compact set $K'$ in $\Omega'$ and $h > 0$ there is a constant $C$ (resp. there exist constants $h$ and $C$) satisfying*

$$\sup_{x'\in K'} |\partial^{\alpha'} f_j(x')| \leqq Ch^{|\alpha'|+j} M_{|\alpha'|+j} \tag{2.16}$$

*for all multi-indices $\alpha' = (\alpha_1, \ldots, \alpha_{n-1})$.*

If an $f$ is given by (2.15), its *support* is defined by

(2.17)
$$\operatorname{supp} f = \overline{\bigcup_j \operatorname{supp} f_j}.$$

We denote by $\mathcal{D}^*_\Omega(\Omega')$ the linear subspace of $\mathcal{E}^*_\Omega(\Omega')$ composed of all elements with compact support.

The spaces $\mathcal{E}^*(\Omega)$, $\mathcal{D}^*(\Omega)$, $\mathcal{E}^*_\Omega(\Omega')$ and $\mathcal{D}^*_\Omega(\Omega')$ have natural locally convex topologies, under which the mapping $\rho$ sending each $f \in \mathcal{E}^*(\Omega)$ (resp. $\mathcal{D}^*(\Omega)$) to

(2.18)
$$\rho(f) = \sum_{j=0}^{\infty} \partial_n^j f(x',0) x_n^j / j!$$

in $\mathcal{E}^*_\Omega(\Omega')$ (resp. $\mathcal{D}^*_\Omega(\Omega')$) is a continuous algebraic homomorphism. The following lemma is a special case of the Whitney type extension theorem with bounds proved in [9].

LEMMA 1. *If* $M_p$ *satisfies* (M.0) - (M.3), *then*

(2.19)
$$\rho : \mathcal{E}^*(\Omega) \longrightarrow \mathcal{E}^*_\Omega(\Omega')$$

*and*

(2.20)
$$\rho : \mathcal{D}^*(\Omega) \longrightarrow \mathcal{D}^*_\Omega(\Omega')$$

*are surjective topological homomorphisms.*

In view of this lemma Theorem 1 is reduced to the following Cauchy-Kowalevsky theorem for $\mathcal{E}^*_\Omega(\Omega')$.

THEOREM 2. *If* $M_p$ *satisfies* (M.4), *then*

(2.21)
$$\begin{array}{ccccccccc} 0 & \longrightarrow & \mathcal{E}^*_\Omega(\Omega')^P & \longrightarrow & \mathcal{E}^*_\Omega(\Omega') & \xrightarrow{P(x,\partial)} & \mathcal{E}^*_\Omega(\Omega') & \longrightarrow & 0 \\ & & \wr\| & \swarrow_{\Gamma_m} & & & & & \\ & & \mathcal{E}^*(\Omega')^m & & & & & & \end{array}$$

*is a splitting topologically exact sequence of locally convex spaces, where*

$\mathcal{E}^*_\Omega(\Omega')^P$ is the space of all solutions $u \in \mathcal{E}^*_\Omega(\Omega')$ of $Pu = 0$ and $\Gamma_m$ is the mapping $\sum u_j(x')x_n^j/j! \mapsto (u_{j-1}(x'))_{j=1,\dots,m}$ of taking the initial values.

The sequence (2.21) remains to be a splitting topologically exact sequence of locally convex spaces if we replace all $\mathcal{E}^*$ by $\mathcal{D}^*$.

In other words, given $g_1(x'), \dots, g_m(x') \in \mathcal{E}^*(\Omega')$ and $f(x', \langle\!\langle x_n \rangle\!\rangle) \in \mathcal{E}^*(\Omega')$ there is a unique $u(x', \langle\!\langle x_n \rangle\!\rangle) = \sum u_j(x')x_n^j/j! \in \mathcal{E}^*_\Omega(\Omega')$ such that

(2.22) $$u_j(x') = g_{j-1}(x'), \quad j = 0,\dots,m-1,$$

and

(2.23) $$P(x,\partial)u(x', \langle\!\langle x_n \rangle\!\rangle) = f(x', \langle\!\langle x_n \rangle\!\rangle) \ ,$$

and the correspondence $u \longleftrightarrow (g_1, \dots, g_m; f)$ is topological and support-preserving.

Since $\Omega'$ is non-characteristic, (2.23) is equivalent to

(2.24) $$\partial_n^m u(x', \langle\!\langle x_n \rangle\!\rangle) = \sum_{\substack{|\alpha| \le m \\ \alpha_n < m}} b_\alpha(x, \langle\!\langle x_n \rangle\!\rangle)\partial^\alpha u(x', \langle\!\langle x_n \rangle\!\rangle) + g(x', \langle\!\langle x_n \rangle\!\rangle),$$

where $b_\alpha = \rho(-a_\alpha/a_{(0,\dots,0,m)})$ and $g = \rho(f/a_{(0,\dots,0,m)})$.

The first $m$ coefficients $u_j(x')$ of $u$ are given by (2.22). The other coefficients are uniquely determined by induction on $j$ from (2.24) and its formal derivatives in $x_n$.

We have $\operatorname{supp} u \subset \operatorname{supp} g_1 \cup \cdots \cup \operatorname{supp} g_m \cup \operatorname{supp} f$ because we need only differentiation and multiplication by functions to obtain $u_j(x')$. The other inclusion is trivial.

Lastly the order of $|\partial^{\alpha'} u_j(x')|$ is estimated by the method of majorants as in the classical case.

## 3. A Division Theorem of Ultradistributions with Support in a Hyperplane

DEFINITION 2. *A continuous linear functional on the space $\mathcal{D}^*(\Omega)$ is called an ultradistribution of class $*$ on $\Omega$.*

The space $\mathcal{D}^{*\prime}(\Omega)$ of all ultradistributions of class $*$ on $\Omega$ is endowed with the strong topology as the dual of the locally convex space $\mathcal{D}^*(\Omega)$.

If $\Omega_1$ is an open subset of $\Omega$, the restriction mapping $\mathcal{D}^{*\prime}(\Omega) \to \mathcal{D}^{*\prime}(\Omega_1)$ is defined to be the dual of the continuous imbedding $\mathcal{D}^*(\Omega_1) \to \mathcal{D}^*(\Omega)$. Since we can construct a partition of unity on $\Omega$ by functions in $\mathcal{D}^*(\Omega)$, the notion of support of an ultradistribution is defined similarly to the case of distribution.

The dual $\mathcal{E}^{*\prime}(\Omega)$ of $\mathcal{E}^*(\Omega)$ is canonically identified with the subspace of $\mathcal{D}^{*\prime}(\Omega)$ of all elements with compact support.

We write

$$\mathcal{D}^{*\prime}_{\Omega'}(\Omega) = \{f \in \mathcal{D}^{*\prime}(\Omega);\quad \operatorname{supp} f \subset \Omega'\} \tag{3.1}$$

and $\mathcal{E}^{*\prime}_{\Omega'}(\Omega) = \mathcal{D}^{*\prime}_{\Omega'}(\Omega) \cap \mathcal{E}^{*\prime}(\Omega)$. Then we have the following lemma as a special case of the structure theorem of ultradistributions with support in a submanifold [9].

LEMMA 2. *If $M_p$ satisfies (M.0) - (M.3), then the closed linear subspace $\mathcal{D}^{*\prime}_{\Omega'}(\Omega)$ (resp. $\mathcal{E}^{*\prime}_{\Omega'}(\Omega)$) of $\mathcal{D}^{*\prime}(\Omega)$ (resp. $\mathcal{E}^{*\prime}(\Omega)$) is canonically isomorphic to the strong dual of $\mathcal{D}^*_{\Omega}(\Omega')$ (resp. $\mathcal{E}^*_{\Omega}(\Omega')$).*

Similarly to the case of distribution the operation in $\mathcal{D}^{*\prime}(\Omega)$ of a linear differential operator

$$Q(x,\partial) = \sum_{|\alpha|\leq m} b_\alpha(x)\partial^\alpha \tag{3.2}$$

with coefficients $b_\alpha(x) \in \mathcal{E}^*(\Omega)$ is defined to be the dual of the formal dual $Q'(x,\partial)\colon \mathcal{D}^*(\Omega) \to \mathcal{D}^*(\Omega)$, where

$$(3.3)\qquad Q'(x,\partial)\varphi(x) = \sum_{|\alpha|\leq m} (-1)^{|\alpha|}\partial^{\alpha}(b_{\alpha}(x)\varphi(x)).$$

Suppose that $P(x,\partial)$ and $Q(x,\partial)$ are formal duals to each other. Then taking the dual of Theorem 2, we obtain the following.

THEOREM 3. *If* $M_p$ *satisfies* (M.0) - (M.4), *then*

$$(3.4)\qquad \begin{array}{ccccccc} 0 \longleftarrow & (\mathcal{D}^*(\Omega)^P)' & \longleftarrow & \mathcal{D}^{*\prime}_{\Omega'}(\Omega') & \xleftarrow{Q(x,\partial)} & \mathcal{D}^{*\prime}_{\Omega'}(\Omega') & \longleftarrow 0 \\ & \wr\| & \nearrow \Gamma'_m & & & & \\ & \mathcal{D}^{*\prime}(\Omega')^m & & & & & \end{array}$$

*is a splitting topologically exact sequence of locally convex spaces, where* $(\mathcal{D}^*(\Omega)^P)'$ *is the strong dual of* $\mathcal{D}^*(\Omega)^P$ *and* $\Gamma'_m$ *is the mapping*

$$(v_j(x'))_{j=0,\ldots,m-1} \longmapsto \sum_{j=0}^{m-1} (-1)^j v_j(x') \otimes \delta^{(j)}(x_n).$$

(3.4) *is also a splitting topologically exact sequence if we replace* $\mathcal{D}^*$ *by* $\mathcal{E}^*$.

Namely for each $u \in \mathcal{D}^{*\prime}_{\Omega'}(\Omega)$ (resp. $\mathcal{E}^{*\prime}_{\Omega'}(\Omega)$) there are unique $v_0(x'), \ldots, v_{m-1}(x') \in \mathcal{D}^{*\prime}(\Omega')$ (resp. $\mathcal{E}^{*\prime}(\Omega')$) and $w(x) \in \mathcal{D}^{*\prime}_{\Omega'}(\Omega)$ (resp. $\mathcal{E}^{*\prime}_{\Omega'}(\Omega)$) such that

$$(3.5)\qquad u(x) = P(x,\partial)w(x') + v_0(x')\otimes\delta(x_n) + \cdots + v_{m-1}(x')\otimes\delta^{(m-1)}(x_n).$$

## 4. Boundary Values of Homogeneous Ultradistribution Solutions

Suppose that $v \in \mathcal{D}^{*\prime}(\Omega_+)$ is a solution of the homogeneous equation

$$(4.1)\qquad Q(x,\partial)v(x) = 0$$

on the upper half part $\Omega_+ = \{x \in \Omega;\ x_n > 0\}$ of $\Omega$. We assume that $v$ can be continued to an ultradistribution $\tilde{v} \in \mathcal{D}^{*\prime}(\Omega)$. Then $v$ has a continuation $\tilde{v}$ which vanishes on the lower half part $\Omega_- = \{x \in \Omega;\ x_n < 0\}$ by the structure theorem of ultradistribution [9]. Since $Q(x,\partial)\tilde{v}(x) \in \mathcal{D}^{*\prime}_{\Omega'}(\Omega)$, there are unique $v_0(x'), \ldots, v_{m-1}(x') \in \mathcal{D}^{*\prime}(\Omega')$ and $w(x) \in \mathcal{D}^{*\prime}_{\Omega'}(\Omega)$ such that

$$(4.2)\qquad Q(x,\partial)(\tilde{v}(x)-w(x)) = v_0(x')\otimes\delta(x_n)+\cdots+v_{m-1}(x')\otimes\delta^{(m-1)}(x_n).$$

The coefficients $v_0(x'), \ldots, v_{m-1}(x')$ depend only on the solution $v(x)$ and have the meaning of boundary values of $v(x)$. In fact, the local Green formula

$$(4.3)\qquad Q(x,\partial)(\theta(x_n)v(x)) = \theta(x_n)Q(x,\partial)v(x) + \sum_{i=0}^{m-1} B_i(x,\partial)v(x)|_{x_n=0}\otimes\delta^{(i)}(x_n)$$

shows that

$$(4.4)\qquad v_i(x') = B_i(x,\partial)v(x)|_{x_n=0}$$

if $v$ is smooth in $x_n$ so that the product with the Heaviside function $\theta(x_n)$ makes sense. Since $\Omega'$ is non-characteristic, we can find differential operators $A_{ji}(x,\partial')$ in $x'$ defined on a neighborhood of $\Omega'$ such that

$$(4.5)\qquad \partial_n^j v(x',0) = \sum_{i=0}^{m-1} A_{ji}(x,\partial')B_i(x,\partial)v(x)|_{x_n=0} .$$

Therefore we can define the boundary values $\partial_n^j v(x',+0)$, $j = 0,\ldots,m-1$, by

$$(4.6)\qquad \partial_n^j v(x',+0) = \sum_{i=0}^{m-1} A_{ji}(x,\partial')v_j(x') .$$

As for the extendability of $v(x)$ we have the following criterion.

LEMMA 3. *A measurable function* $v(x)$ *on* $\Omega_+$ *can be continued to an ultradistribution* $\tilde{v}(x) \in \mathcal{D}^{(M_p)\prime}(\Omega)$ *(resp.* $\mathcal{D}^{\{M_p\}\prime}(\Omega)$*) if for each compact set* $K'$ *in* $\Omega'$ *there are constants* $L$ *and* $C$ *(resp. and* $L > 0$ *there is a constant* $C$*) such that*

$$(4.7)\qquad \sup_{x'\in K'} |v(x',x_n)| \le C \exp M^*(L/x_n) ,$$

where

$$M^*(\rho) = \sup_p \log(\rho^p p!/M_p) . \tag{4.8}$$

If $M_p = p!^s$, then $M^*(\rho)$ is equivalent to $(s-1)\rho^{1/(s-1)}$.

THEOREM 4. *Suppose that* $Q(x,\partial)$ *is an elliptic linear differential operator of order* $m$ *with coefficients in* $\mathcal{Q}(\Omega)$. *Then a solution* $v(x)$ *on* $\Omega_+$ *of* (4.1) *has boundary values* $\partial_n^j v(x',+0)$, $j = 0,\ldots,m-1$, *in* $\mathcal{D}^{*\prime}(\Omega')$ *if and only if* $v(x)$ *satisfies the criterion of Lemma* 3. *Then* $\partial_n^j v(x',x_n)$ *converge to* $\partial_n^j v(x',+0)$ *in the topology of* $\mathcal{D}^{*\prime}(\Omega')$ *as* $x_n \to 0$.

The sufficiency is clear from the above discussion. The necessity is proved by constructing a fundamental solution of $Q(x,\partial)$. The details will be discussed elsewhere. When $Q(x,\partial)$ is the Cauchy-Riemann operator $(\partial_1+i\partial_2)/2$, a proof is given in [9].

## REFERENCES

[1] Butzer, P.L. - Berens, H., *Semi-groups of Operators and Approximation*. Springer-Verlag, Berlin/Heidelberg/New York 1967.

[2] Hardy, G.H., *Weierstrass's non-differentiable functions*. Trans. Amer. Math. Soc. *17* (1916), 301-325.

[3] Hardy, G.H. - Littlewood, J.E., *Some properties of fractional integrals*. Math. Z. *27* (1928), 565-606, and *34* (1932), 403-439.

[4] Hardy, G.H. - Littlewood, J.E., *Theorems concerning mean values of analytic and harmonic functions*. Quart. J. Math. Oxford Ser. *12* (1941), 221-256.

[5] Komatsu, H., *Fractional powers of operators, II: Interpolation spaces*. Pacific J. Math. *21* (1967), 89-111.

[6] Komatsu, H., Fractional powers of operators, VI: Interpolation of non-negative operators and imbedding theorems. J. Fac. Sci. Univ. Tokyo Sect. IA Math. 19 (1972), 1-63.

[7] Komatsu, H., Generalized Poisson integrals and regularity of functions. Fractional Calculus and its Applications, Lecture Notes in Math. 457 (1975), 232-248.

[8] Komatsu, H., Ultradistributions, I: Structure theorems and a characterization. J. Fac. Sci. Univ. Tokyo Sect. IA Math. 20 (1973), 25-105.

[9] Komatsu, H., Ultradistributions, II: The kernel theorem and ultradistributions with support in a submanifold. Ibid. to appear.

[10] Komatsu, H., Irregularity of characteristic elements and hyperbolicity. Publ. Res. Inst. Math. Sci. Kyoto University 12 (1977), 233-245.

[11] Komatsu, H. - Kawai, T., Boundary values of hyperfunction solutions of linear partial differential equations. Ibid. 7 (1971), 95-104.

[12] Sato, M., Theory of hyperfunctions. J. Fac. Sci. Univ. Tokyo Sect. IA Math. 8 (1959-1960), 139-193 and 387-437.

[13] Taibleson, M.H., On the theory of Lipschitz spaces of distributions on euclidean n-space. J. Math. Mech. 13 (1964), 407-479, 14 (1965), 821-839, and 15 (1966), 973-981.

# LAX-TYPE THEOREMS WITH ORDERS IN CONNECTION WITH INHOMOGENEOUS EVOLUTION EQUATIONS IN BANACH SPACES

P.L. Butzer, W. Dickmeis, and R.J. Nessel

Lehrstuhl A für Mathematik
Rheinisch-Westfälische Technische Hochschule
Aachen

In this note we continue our previous investigations on Lax-type theorems with orders in the abstract setting of Banach spaces. Whereas the latter exclusively treat homogeneous problems in connection with time-independent operators A, we are now concerned with the numerical approximation of the solution of the more general intitial-value problem du(t)/dt=A(t)u(t) + g(t), u(0) = f. On the basis of the Sobolevski - Tanabe theory, Lax equivalence theorems with orders in the sense that stability, consistency, and convergence are considered with orders are derived, structural properties of the elements being measured via K - functionals.

## 1. Introduction

The classical Lax equivalence theorem (cf.[ 14] , [ 16, p. 39 ff] ) on the approximation of the exact solution of a given properly posed initial-value problem by some finite difference scheme states that if the scheme is consistent, then stability is necessary and sufficient for convergence. This fundamental result of numerical analysis being a pure convergence theorem, the question arose whether one can equip it with orders in the sense that consistency, stability, and convergence are considered with orders. Theorems of the type that consistency with order plus ordinary stability implies convergence with order were first given by Peetre - Thomée [ 15] in the frame of specific (e.g. Sobolev) spaces; here structural properties are expressed in terms of classical moduli of continuity. This was continued by a number of authors (see [ 4] and the literature cited there). Lax-type theorems with orders in the abstract setting of Banach spaces in the sense that stability is not only sufficient but also necessary for convergence provided the scheme is consistent, all concepts taken with orders, were only considered rather recently, structural properties of the elements being measured via K-functionals (see [8]). An alternative version of the Lax theorem with orders in the sense that consistency plus stability of the difference scheme are necessary and sufficient for convergence, all concepts taken with orders, was regarded in [6]. Apart from being of interest in its own, the essential feature of the abstract approach is that it enables one to treat various applications in different fields from a unified point of view. When considering, for example, different difference schemes for the equation $\partial u(x,t)/\partial t = \partial u(x,t)/\partial x$, the general theory reproduces pointwise direct theorems for the Bernstein polynomials, the Szász-Mirakjan and the Baskakov operators. As a further application we may mention that certain classical limit theorems of probability theory such as the central limit theorem or the weak law of large numbers (with orders) may be derived from Lax-type theorems (with orders). See [7,10] for the details.

This note is concerned with the numerical approximation of solutions of initial-value problems of the form

$$(1.1) \qquad \frac{du(t)}{dt} = A(t)u(t) + g(t) \qquad (t \geq \sigma \geq 0),$$

$$(1.2) \qquad u(\sigma) = f \in X.$$

Here X is an arbitrary Banach space (with norm $\|\circ\|_X$), $A(t)$ are closed linear operators in X with domain $D(A(t)) = D \subset X$, independent of $t \geq 0$, whereas g is an X-valued function on the non-negative real axis $\mathbb{R}^+ := [0,\infty)$ and f is an element of X describing the initial state. Let us mention that problem (1.1 - 2) extends our previous studies inasmuch as the latter only deal with situations which correspond to $g(t) = 0$ (i.e. homogeneous problems) and to $A(t) = A$, independent of t.

Under some regularity conditions upon $A(t)$ and $g(t)$ one may describe the solution of the homogeneous problem, i.e. (1.1 - 2) with $g(t) \equiv 0$, via

$$(1.3) \qquad u(t) := u(t,\sigma;f) = E(t,\sigma)f \qquad (t \geq \sigma \geq 0)$$

and the solution of the general problem (1.1 - 2) via

$$(1.4) \qquad u(t) := u(t,\sigma;g,f) := L(t,\sigma;g)f = E(t,\sigma)f + \int_\sigma^t E(t,s)g(s)ds \qquad (t \geq \sigma \geq 0).$$

Here the family of operators $\{E(t,s);\ 0\leq s\leq t<\infty\}\subset[X]$ (:= set of bounded linear operators of X into itself) satisfies

$$(1.5)\qquad E(t,s)E(s,r) = E(t,r) \qquad (0\leq r\leq s\leq t<\infty),$$

$$E(t,t) = I, \text{ the identity} \qquad (t\geq 0),$$

and is called a family of evolution operators (or propagators). For this so-called Sobolevski - Tanabe theory see e.g. [9, p. 103], [13, p. 55] [20, p. 431] (for approximation theorems in this respect see Köhnen [12]). Note that (1.5) is just a generalization of the semigroup properties which the solution operators $E(t,s) := E(t-s)$ possess if $A(t) = A$, independent of t (cf. [14], [16], also [6]).

The numerical approximation of the solution (1.3 - 4), thus the approximation of the evolution operators $E(t,s)$ by certain finite difference schemes, has already been studied by many authors, including Stetter [17], Thompson [18,19], Ansorge [1], Hass [11]. In these papers, even more general situations are considered, for example, semilinear problems for which $g(t)$ in (1.1) is replaced by some Hölder continuous operator $G(t;u(t))$. Apart from (pure) convergence assertions, Ansorge - Geiger (-Hass) [2,3] also studied rates of convergence, but in a somewhat different, more concrete way.

The difference schemes used so far reduce in case of problems of type (1.1 - 2) to

$$(1.6)\qquad C(t+\tau,t;g)f := D(t+\tau,t)f + d(t+\tau,t)g.$$

Here the family

$$\{D(t+\tau,t);\ t\geq 0,\ 0\leq\tau\leq \delta\} \subset [X]$$

describes the approximation of the homogeneous part of (1.4), thus of the evolution operators $E(t+\tau,t)$ (cf. (1.3)), whereas $d(t+\tau,t)$ is a linear mapping on some Banach space of X-valued functions on $\mathbb{R}^+$ describing the approximation of the inhomogeneity in (1.4). In these terms one is interested in estimates of the approximation error

$$(1.7)\qquad \Big\| \prod_{j=0}^{n-1} C(t_{j+1},t_j;g)f - L(t_n,t_0;g)f\Big\|_X$$

$$0\leq\tau\leq\delta,\ 0\leq\sigma\leq t_0,\ t_j := t_0 + j\tau,\ j\in\mathbb{N},$$

$\mathbb{N}$ being the set of natural numbers. In case $A(t) = A$, independent of $t$, Thompson [18,19] proved that for piecewise continuous $g$ the difference scheme (1.6) with $d(t+\tau,t) := \tau g(t)$ is convergent, i.e. for fixed $t = n\tau$ the error (1.7) tends to zero as $\tau \to 0+$ (thus $n \to \infty$), provided the difference scheme $\{D(t+\tau,t)\}$ for the homogeneous problem is convergent.

Following the latter procedure, our aim will be to derive error bounds for (1.7) in dependence upon $t_o, n, \tau$ and smoothness properties of the initial value $f$ and the inhomogeneity $g$. This will be carried out in terms of K-functionals, which are defined for Banach spaces $X$ and subspaces $U \subset X$ with seminorm $|\circ|_U$ by

$$K(t,f;X,U) := \inf_{h \in U} [\|f-h\|_X + t|h|_U] .$$

They have the properties that for each $t \geq 0$

$$(1.8) \qquad K(t,f;X,U) \leq \begin{cases} \|f\|_X , & f \in X \\ t|f|_U , & f \in U \end{cases}$$

and that $\lim_{t\to 0+} K(t,f;X,U) = 0$ for each $f \in X$, provided $U$ is dense in $X$ (see [5, p. 167 ff], also for further properties).

With the concepts of stability, consistency, and convergence with orders we first prove Lax-type theorems with orders in connection with the homogeneous problem (cf. Thm. 1 - 2 of Sec. 2). On the basis of these estimates Sec. 3 then considers the influence of the inhomogeneity $g$. Finally, Sec. 4 treats a first example.

The contribution of W. Dickmeis was supported by a DFG research grant (Bu 166/30) which is gratefully acknowledged.

## 2. The Homogeneous Problem

In this section we assume that $g(t) = 0$ for all $t \geq 0$, i.e., we only consider the approximation of the evolution operators $E(t,s)$ (cf. (1.3)) by some difference scheme $\{D(t+\tau,t)\}$ (cf. (1.6)). In order to treat the error (1.7), the most important properties of the difference scheme are stability and consistency; for these the following definitions (with orders) are used (cf. [4;6;10] for the case $A(t) = A$, independent of $t$, and the literature cited there).

DEFINITION 1. *A difference scheme*

(2.1) $$\{D(t+\tau,t);0\leq t<\infty,\ 0\leq\tau\leq\delta\}\subset[X]$$

*is said to be stable of order* $\mathcal{O}(1/\psi(\tau,t_o,t_n))$ *if*

(2.2) $$\|\prod_{j=0}^{n-1} D(t_{j+1},t_j)\|_{[X]}\leq S/\psi(\tau,t_o,t_n),$$

*the constant* $S\geq 1$ *being independent of*

(2.3) $$t_o\geq 0,\ 0\leq\tau\leq\delta,\ t_j:=t_o+j\tau,\ 0\leq j\leq n,\ n\in\mathbb{N}.$$

*Hereby the function* $\psi$ *is assumed to satisfy*

(2.4) $$1\leq 1/\psi(\tau;t_j,t_n)\leq 1/\psi(\tau,t_o,t_n)$$

*for each* $\tau$, $t_j$ *subject to* (2.3).

DEFINITION 2. *A difference scheme* (2.1) *is said to be consistent of order* $\mathcal{O}(\varphi(\tau))$ *on* $U\subset X$ *(with respect to the evolution operators* (1.5)) *if there exists a constant* C, *independent of* $0\leq\sigma\leq t<\infty$, $0\leq\tau\leq\delta$, *such that*

(2.5) $$\|[D(t+\tau,t)-E(t+\tau,t)]E(t,\sigma)f\|_X\leq C\tau\varphi(\tau)\alpha_\tau(t)|f|_U.$$

*Here* $|\circ|_U$ *denotes a seminorm on the subspace* $U\subset X$, *and* $\varphi,\alpha_\tau$ *are non-negative functions on* $[0,\delta]$, $[0,\infty)$, *respectively*.

Let us observe that if $E(t,\sigma)f\in U$ for all $f\in U$ and

(2.6) $$|E(t,\sigma)f|_U\leq C|f|_U \qquad (f\in U)$$

for $0\leq\sigma\leq t<\infty$, then it would be sufficient to assume the consistency condition (2.5) only for $\sigma=t$ (cf. (1.5)).

With these definitions one may formulate the following Lax-type theorem together with its alternative version, both with built-in orders:

THEOREM 1. *If the evolution operators* (1.5) *are uniformly bounded, i.e.*

(2.7) $$\|E(t,\sigma)\|_{[X]} \leq M \qquad (0 \leq \sigma \leq t < \infty),$$

<u>and if the difference scheme</u> (2.1) <u>is consistent with order</u> $\mathcal{O}(\varphi(\tau))$ <u>on</u> $U \subset X$, <u>the following assertions are equivalent</u>:

a) $$\|\prod_{j=0}^{n-1} D(t_{j+1},t_j)f - E(t_n,t_o)f\|_X \leq \frac{C_1}{\psi(\tau,t_o,t_n)} K(C_2\varphi(\tau)\beta_\tau(t_o,t_n),f;X,U)$$

<u>for all</u> $f \in X$ <u>and</u> $\tau$, $t_j$ <u>subject to</u> (2.3), <u>where</u>

(2.8) $$\beta_\tau(t_o,t_n) := \tau \sum_{k=0}^{n-1} \alpha_\tau(t_k)$$

<u>and</u> $C_1$, $C_2$ <u>are some non-negative constants</u>.

b) $$\|\prod_{j=0}^{n-1} D(t_{j+1},t_j)f - E(t_n,t_o)f\|_X \leq \begin{cases} M_f/\psi(\tau,t_o,t_n) & (f \in X), \\ \dfrac{C\varphi(\tau)\beta_\tau(t_o,t_n)}{\psi(\tau,t_o,t_n)} |f|_U & (f \in U), \end{cases}$$

<u>for all</u> $\tau$, $t_j$ <u>subject to</u> (2.3), <u>where</u> C <u>denotes some non-negative constant</u>.

c) <u>The difference scheme</u> (2.1) <u>is stable of order</u> $\mathcal{O}(1/\psi(\tau,t_o,t_n))$.

THEOREM 2. <u>If the evolution operators</u> (1.5) <u>satisfy</u> (2.6 -7), <u>and if</u>

(2.9) $$1/\psi(\tau,t,t+\tau) \leq S_o < \infty \qquad (0 \leq t < \infty, 0 \leq \tau \leq \delta),$$

<u>then the following assertion is equivalent to</u> (a) <u>and</u> (b) <u>of Thm. 1</u>:

(c') <u>The difference scheme</u> (2.1) <u>is stable of order</u> $\mathcal{O}(1/\psi(\tau,t_o,t_n))$ <u>plus consistent of order</u> $\mathcal{O}(\varphi(\tau))$ <u>on</u> U.

PROOFS. (a) ⇒ (b): This follows by (1.8) with $M_f := C_1\|f\|_X$.
(b) ⇒ (c): This follows by an application of the uniform boundedness principle to the bounded linear operators

$$[\prod_{j=0}^{n-1} D(t_{j+1},t_j) - E(t_n,t_o)]\,\psi(\tau,t_o,t_n),$$

using (2.4) and (2.7).

(b) ⇒ (c'): To show in addition the consistency, let $t_o=t$, $n=1$, thus $t_n=t_1=t+\tau$. In view of (2.6) one may take (b) with f replaced by $E(t,\sigma)f$, giving for any $f\in U$

$$\|[D(t+\tau,t)-E(t+\tau,t)]E(t,\sigma)f\|_X \leqslant \frac{C\varphi(\tau)\beta_\tau(t,t+\tau)}{\psi(\tau,t,t+\tau)}\,|E(t,\sigma)f|_U.$$

Since $\beta_\tau(t,t+\tau)=\tau\alpha_\tau(t)$ (cf. (2.8)), the consistency condition (2.5) follows by (2.6), (2.9).

(c') ⇒ (a): Setting $\Pi_{j=n}^{n-1} D(t_{j+1},t_j):=I$, one has for any $h\in U$ (cf. (1.5)

$$\|\prod_{j=0}^{n-1} D(t_{j+1},t_j)h-E(t_n,t_o)h\|_X$$

$$=\|\sum_{k=0}^{n-1}\Big(\prod_{j=k+1}^{n-1} D(t_{j+1},t_j)\Big)[D(t_{k+1},t_k)-E(t_{k+1},t_k)]E(t_k,t_o)h\|_X$$

$$\leqslant \sum_{k=0}^{n-1}\frac{S}{\psi(\tau,t_{k+1},t_n)}\,C\tau\varphi(\tau)\alpha_\tau(t_k)\,|h|_U \leqslant \frac{CS\varphi(\tau)}{\psi(\tau,t_o,t_n)}\,\beta_\tau(t_o,t_n)\,|h|_U,$$

using consistency (2.5) for $t=t_k$, $\sigma=t_o$, stability (2.1) for $t_o=t_{k+1}$ as well as (2.2), (2.8). Therefore for any $f\in X$, $h\in U$

$$\|\prod_{j=0}^{n-1} D(t_{j+1},t_j)f-E(t_n,t_o)f\|_X$$

$$\leqslant [\|\prod_{j=0}^{n-1} D(t_{j+1},t_j)\|_{[X]}+\|E(t_n,t_o)\|_{[X]}]\,\|f-h\|_X$$

$$+\|\prod_{j=0}^{n-1} D(t_{j+1},t_j)h-E(t_n,t_o)h\|_X$$

$$\leqslant \Big[\frac{S}{\psi(\tau,t_o,t_n)}+M\Big]\|f-h\|_X+\frac{CS\varphi(\tau)\beta_\tau(t_o,t_n)}{\psi(\tau,t_o,t_n)}\,|h|_U.$$

Thus, taking the infimum over $h\in U$ yields

$$\|\prod_{j=0}^{n-1} D(t_{j+1},t_j)f - E(t_n,t_o)f\|_X \leq \frac{C_1}{\psi(\tau,t_o,t_n)} K(C_2\varphi(\tau)\beta_\tau(t_o,t_n),f;X,U),$$

which completes the proof.

## 3. The Inhomogeneous Problem

For the difference scheme (1.6) it follows by induction that

$$(3.1)\qquad \prod_{j=0}^{n-1} C(t_{j+1},t_j;g)f = \prod_{j=0}^{n-1} D(t_{j+1},t_j)f + \sum_{k=1}^{n}\prod_{j=k}^{n-1} D(t_{j+1},t_j)d(t_k,t_{k-1})g.$$

Therefore the error (1.7) may be estimated by (cf. (1.4 - 5))

$$(3.2)\qquad \|\prod_{j=0}^{n-1} C(t_{j+1},t_j;g)f - L(t_n,t_o;g)f\|_X \leq \|\prod_{j=0}^{n-1} D(t_{j+1},t_j)f - E(t_n,t_o)f\|_X$$

$$+ \sum_{k=1}^{n} \|\prod_{j=k}^{n-1} D(t_{j+1},t_j)[d(t_k,t_{k-1})g - \int_{t_{k-1}}^{t_k} E(t_k,s)g(s)ds]\|_X$$

$$+ \sum_{k=1}^{n} \|[\prod_{j=k}^{n-1} D(t_{j+1},t_j) - E(t_n,t_k)]\int_{t_{k-1}}^{t_k} E(t_k,s)g(s)ds\|_X.$$

Let us now assume that for the homogeneous problem there is a convergence assertion of the type given in Thm. 1 (a). Thus we suppose that for all $f \in X$ and all $\tau,t_j$ subject to (2.3)

$$(3.3)\qquad \|\prod_{j=0}^{n-1} D(t_{j+1},t_j)f - E(t_n,t_o)f\|_X \leq \frac{C}{\psi(\tau,t_o,t_n)} K(\eta(\tau,t_o,t_n),f;X,U)$$

with some function $\eta$ satisfying

$$\eta(\tau,t_j,t_n) \leq \eta(\tau,t_o,t_n) \qquad (0 \leq j \leq n).$$

Then (3.2) together with (2.2) yields

$$(3.4)\qquad \|\prod_{j=0}^{n-1} C(t_{j+1},t_j;g)f - L(t_n,t_o;g)f\|_X \leq \frac{C}{\psi(\tau,t_o,t_n)} K(\eta(\tau,t_o,t_n),f;X,U) +$$

$$+ \sum_{k=1}^{n} \frac{S}{\psi(\tau,t_k,t_n)} \| d(t_k,t_{k-1})g - \int_{t_{k-1}}^{t_k} E(t_k,s)g(s)ds \|_X$$

$$+ \sum_{k=1}^{n} \frac{C}{\psi(\tau,t_k,t_n)} K(\eta(\tau,t_k,t_n), \int_{t_{k-1}}^{t_k} E(t_k,s)g(s)ds;X,U)$$

$$\leq \frac{C}{\psi(\tau,t_o,t_n)} \Big\{ K(\eta(\tau,t_o,t_n),f;X,U)$$

$$+ \sum_{k=1}^{n} K(\eta(\tau,t_o,t_n), \int_{t_{k-1}}^{t_k} E(t_k,s)g(s)ds;X,U)$$

$$+ \sum_{k=1}^{n} \| d(t_k,t_{k-1})g - \int_{t_{k-1}}^{t_k} E(t_k,s)g(s)ds \|_X \Big\}.$$

In order to treat the last term we have to specify the operators $d(v,y)$ (cf. (1.6)) in more detail. Since they have to approximate an integral, we commence with a usual quadrature formula. The integrand being the (unknown) function $E(t_k,s)g(s)$, however, one has to introduce an additional difference scheme $\{\tilde{D}(t+\tau,t)\} \subset [X]$ to approximate the integrand. These considerations lead to operators $d(v,y)$ of the form

$$\text{(3.5)} \qquad d(v,y)g := (v-y) \sum_{j=0}^{N} b_j \tilde{D}(v,y+\tau_j)g(y+\tau_j)$$

where $\tau_j$, $b_j \in \mathbb{R}$, $0 \leq \tau_j \leq v-y$, $0 \leq j \leq N$, $N \in \mathbb{N}$. Here, however, we do not treat the general case (3.5) but confine ourselves to the following particular one

$$\text{(3.6)} \qquad d(t+\tau,t)g = \tau g(t+\tau_o) \qquad (0 \leq t < \infty, 0 \leq \tau \leq \delta, 0 \leq \tau_o \leq \tau),$$

i.e., we only consider in (3.5) the case

$$\tilde{D}(t+\tau,t+\tau_o) = I, \quad v-y = \tau, \quad N = 0, \quad b_o = 1.$$

In this instance one has for sufficiently smooth $g$ (cf. second property of (1.5))

$$(3.7)\qquad \| d(t_k,t_{k-1})g - \int_{t_{k-1}}^{t_k} E(t_k,s)g(s)ds\|_X$$

$$\leqslant \| \tau[E(t_k,t_{k-1}+\tau_o)-I]g(t_{k-1}+\tau_o)\|_X$$

$$+ \| \tau E(t_k,t_{k-1}+\tau_o)g(t_{k-1}+\tau_o) - \int_{t_{k-1}}^{t_k} E(t_k,s)g(s)ds\|_X$$

$$\leqslant \tau(\tau-\tau_o) \sup_{t_{k-1}+\tau_o\leqslant y\leqslant t_k} \|\frac{d}{dy}[E(y,t_{k-1}+\tau_o)]g(t_{k-1}+\tau_o)\|_X$$

$$+ \tau^2 \sup_{t_{k-1}\leqslant y\leqslant t_k} \|\frac{d}{dy}[E(t_k,y)g(y)]\|_X.$$

To describe these smoothness conditions upon g more explicitly, one may define the following function spaces ($0\leqslant y\leqslant v<\infty$)

$$\widetilde{X}[y,v] := \{g\in C([y,v],X); \|g\|_{\widetilde{X}[y,v]} := \sup_{y\leqslant s\leqslant v} \|g(s)\|_X < \infty\},$$

$$\widetilde{W}[y,v] := \{g\in \widetilde{X}[y,v]; |g|_{\widetilde{W}[y,v]} < \infty\},$$

$$|g|_{\widetilde{W}[y,v]} := \sup_{y\leqslant s\leqslant t\leqslant v} \{\|\frac{d}{dt} E(t,s)g(s)\|_X; \frac{d}{ds} E(t,s)g(s)\|_X\},$$

$C([y,v],X)$ being the space of X-valued functions defined and continuous on $[y,v]$. Then in view of (2.7), (3.6 - 7) one has

$$\| d(t_k,t_{k-1})g - \int_{t_{k-1}}^{t_k} E(t_k,s)g(s)ds\|_X \leqslant \begin{cases} C\,\tau\,\|g\|_{\widetilde{X}[t_{k-1},t_k]} & (g\in\widetilde{X}),\\ C\,\tau^2|g|_{\widetilde{W}[t_{k-1},t_k]} & (g\in\widetilde{W}).\end{cases}$$

Proceeding as in the proof of Thm. 2, (c') ⇒ (a), this gives

$$\sum_{k=1}^{n} \| d(t_k,t_{k-1})g - \int_{t_{k-1}}^{t_k} E(t_k,s)g(s)ds\|_X \leqslant (t_n-t_o)CK(\tau,g;\widetilde{X}[t_o,t_n],\widetilde{W}[t_o,t_n]).$$

Analogously, one may discuss the second term of the error (3.4). Indeed, let

$$\widetilde{U}[y,v] := \{g: C[y,v], U); \ |g|_{\widetilde{U}[y,v]} := \sup_{y\leq s\leq v} |g(s)|_U < \infty\}$$

with the additional assumption that U is complete under the norm $\|\circ\|_U := \|\circ\|_X + |\circ|_U$. In view of (2.6) one then has for $g\in\widetilde{U}[y,v]$ that $\int_y^v E(v,s)g(s)ds \in U$ and

$$|\int_y^v E(v,s)g(s)ds|_U \leq \int_y^v |E(v,s)g(s)|_U ds \leq C \int_y^v |g(s)|_U ds$$

$$\leq (v-y)C|g|_{\widetilde{U}[y,v]}.$$

By (1.8), (2.7) this yields

$$K(\eta(\tau,t_o,t_n), \int_{t_{k-1}}^{t_k} E(t_k,s)g(s)ds;X,U) \leq \begin{cases} M\tau\|g\|_{\widetilde{X}[t_{k-1},t_k]}, \\ M\tau\eta(\tau,t_o,t_n)|g|_{\widetilde{U}[t_{k-1},t_k]}, \end{cases}$$

and therefore

$$\sum_{k=1}^{n} K(\eta(\tau,t_o,t_n), \int_{t_{k-1}}^{t_k} E(t_k,s)g(s)ds;X,U) \leq \begin{cases} (t_n-t_o)M\|g\|_{\widetilde{X}[t_o,t_n]}, \\ (t_n-t_o)M\eta(\tau,t_o,t_n)|g|_{\widetilde{U}[t_o,t_n]}, \end{cases}$$

for $g\in\widetilde{X}[t_o,t_n]$, $g\in\widetilde{U}[t_o,t_n]$, respectively. As above this implies for $g\in\widetilde{X}[t_o,t_n]$ that

$$\sum_{k=1}^{n} K(\eta(\tau,t_o,t_n), \int_{t_{k-1}}^{t_k} E(t_k,s)g(s)ds;X,U)$$

$$\leq (t_n-t_o)MK(\eta(\tau,t_o,t_n),g;\widetilde{X}[t_o,t_n],\widetilde{U}[t_o,t_n]).$$

Summarizing, we may state the following convergence assertion with orders.

THEOREM 3. *If the difference scheme* (2.1) *and the evolution operators* (1.5) *satisfy* (2.2), (2.6 - 7) *as well as* (3.3), *then one has for the step operator* (1.6), (3.6):

$$(3.8) \quad \|\prod_{j=0}^{n-1} C(t_{j+1},t_j;g)f - L(t_n,t_o;g)f\|_X \leq \frac{C}{\psi(\tau,t_o,t_n)}\Big\{K(\eta(\tau,t_o,t_n),f;X,U) +$$

$$+ (t_n - t_o) K(\eta(\tau,t_o,t_n), g; \tilde{X}[t_o,t_n], \tilde{U}[t_o,t_n])$$

$$+ (t_n - t_o) K(\tau, g; \tilde{X}[t_o,t_n], \tilde{W}[t_o,t_n])] \Big\}$$

<u>for all</u> $f \in X$, $g \in \tilde{X}[t_o,t_n]$, <u>and</u> $\tau$, $t_j$ <u>subject to</u> (2.3).

## 4. An Example

Let us conclude with a first, very simple example, namely with the initial-value problem

$$(4.1) \qquad \begin{aligned} \frac{d}{dt} u(x,t) &= a(t) \frac{d^2}{dx^2} u(x,t) + g(x,t) \\ u(x,0) &= f(x) \end{aligned} \qquad (x \in \mathbb{R}, t \geq 0)$$

in the space $X := C_B(\mathbb{R})$ (:= space of bounded, uniformly continuous functions on $\mathbb{R}$) with norm $\|f\|_C := \sup_{x\in\mathbb{R}} |f(x)|$. The function $a(t)$ is assumed to be positive and continuously differentiable with

$$\sup_{0\leq t} a(t) := B < \infty, \qquad \sup_{0\leq t} |a'(t)| := B' < \infty,$$

whereas $g(x,t)$ be strongly continuous with respect to $t \geq 0$. Then the solution of (4.1) is given by (cf. (1.4))

$$(4.2) \qquad L(t,\sigma;g)f = W(b(t,\sigma))f + \int_\sigma^t W(b(t,s))g(\cdot,s)ds,$$

where $b(t,s) := \int_s^t a(v)dv$ for $0 \leq s \leq t < \infty$ and

$$(4.3) \qquad [W(r)f](x) := \frac{1}{\sqrt{4\pi r}} \int_{\mathbb{R}} f(y) \exp(-\frac{(x-y)^2}{4r}) dy$$

describes the solution of the classical heat conduction problem (with $a(t) \equiv 1$, see e.g. [5, p. 59 ff]). Thus the evolution operators (1.5) are given by

$$(4.4) \qquad E(t,\sigma) = W(b(t,\sigma)).$$

In view of the well-known properties of the operators (4.3), one immediately has (2.6 - 7), the first with respect to every subspace

$$U := C_B^r := \{f; f^{(j)} \in C_B,\ 0 \leqslant j \leqslant r \in \mathbb{N}\}, \quad |f|_U := \sum_{j=0}^{r} \|f^{(j)}\|_C .$$

To approximate the solution of the homogeneous problem, let us consider the explicit difference scheme (cf. (1.6))

$$(4.5)\qquad D(t+\tau,t) := (1-2\lambda a(t))I + \lambda a(t)(T_{-h}+T_h), \quad \lambda := \tau/h^2,$$

where $[T_h f](x) := f(x+h)$ for $x,h \in \mathbb{R}$. This scheme is (ordinarily) stable, i.e. satisfies (2.2) with $\psi \equiv 1$, if $\lambda \leqslant 1/2B$. To establish consistency (2.5) with $U := C_B^4$, in view of (2.6) it suffices to show (via a Taylor expansion) that

$$\|D(t+\tau,t)f - E(t+\tau,t)f\|_C \leqslant \tau\varphi(\tau)\alpha_\tau(t)|f|_U,$$

$$\varphi(\tau) := \tau\left(\frac{1}{2}+\frac{1}{12\lambda}\right), \quad \alpha_\tau(t) := \sup_{0\leqslant s\leqslant\tau} \{a(t)+a^2(t+s)+a'(t+s)\} \leqslant B + B^2 + B'.$$

COROLLARY 1. <u>For the evolution operators</u> (4.4) <u>and the difference scheme</u> (4.5) <u>one has that</u> $f \in Lip_4(\alpha, C_B(\mathbb{R}))$ <u>for some</u> $0<\alpha\leqslant 4$ <u>implies</u>

$$(4.6)\qquad \left\|\prod_{j=0}^{n-1} D(t_{j+1},t_j)f - E(t_n,t_0)f\right\|_C = \mathcal{O}(\min\{1;[(t_n-t_0)\tau/\lambda]^{\alpha/4}\})$$

<u>for all</u> $\tau$, $t_j$ <u>subject to</u> (2.3).

PROOF. An application of Thm. 2, (c') $\Rightarrow$ (a), gives the error (4.6) in a form including the K-functional with argument $(t_n-t_0)C(B+B^2+B')\varphi(\tau)$. Therefore with (cf. [5, p. 191 ff])

$$(4.7)\qquad K(t^r,f,C_B,C_B^r) \leqslant C[\min(1,t^r)\|f\|_C + \sup_{0\leqslant h\leqslant\delta} \|(I-T_h)^r f\|_C],$$

$$(4.8)\qquad Lip_r(\alpha,C_B(\mathbb{R})) := \{f \in C_B(\mathbb{R});\ \sup_{0\leqslant h\leqslant\delta} \|(I-T_h)^r f\|_C = \mathcal{O}(\delta^\alpha), \delta\to 0+\}$$

the convergence assertion (4.6) follows.

Concerning the general (inhomogeneous) problem (4.1), let us only consider the particular case of functions $g(x,t) := g_1(x)g_2(t)$ with $g_1 \in C_B(\mathbb{R})$, $g_2 \in C_B(\mathbb{R}^+)$. Then an application of Thm. 3 yields

COROLLARY 2. *Let the problem* (4.1) *be given with* $g(x,t) := g_1(x)g_2(t)$. *For the evolution operators* (4.4) *and the difference scheme* (4.5), (3.6) (cf. (1.6)) *one has that* $f \in Lip_4(\alpha, C_B(\mathbb{R}))$, $g_1 \in Lip_4(\beta, C_B(\mathbb{R}))$, $g_2 \in Lip_1(\gamma, C_B(\mathbb{R}^+))$ *for some* $0<\alpha\leqslant 4$, $0<\beta\leqslant 2$, $0<\gamma\leqslant 1$ *implies* $(\tau/\lambda := h^2)$

$$\Big\| \prod_{j=0}^{n-1} C(t_{j+1},t_j;g)f - L(t_n,t_o;g)f \Big\|_C$$

$$= \mathcal{O}\big(\max\{(t_n-t_o);(t_n-t_o)^{\alpha/4}\}(\tau/\lambda)^{\min\{\alpha/4;\beta/2;\gamma\}}\big)$$

*for all* $\tau$, $t_j$ *subject to* (2.3).

PROOF. On account of Thm. 2, (c') ⇒ (a), one has (3.3) with $\psi(\tau,t_o,t_n) \equiv 1$, $\eta(\tau,t_o,t_n) = (t_n-t_o)\tau/\lambda$. Since the subspace $U := C_B^4(\mathbb{R})$ is complete, an application of Thm. 3 gives an estimate of type (3.8). Here the first K-functional is already treated in the proof of Cor. 1, so that we only have to regard the remaining two. For $g(x,t) := g_1(x)g_2(t)$, however, one has

$$K(s,g;\tilde{X}[t_o,t_n],\tilde{U}[t_o,t_n]) \leqslant \|g_2\|_{C(\mathbb{R}^+)} K(s,g_1;C_B(\mathbb{R}),C_B^4(\mathbb{R})),$$

$$K(s,g;\tilde{X}[t_o,t_n],\tilde{W}[t_o,t_n]) \leqslant$$

$$\leqslant \inf_{\substack{h(x,t):=h_1(x)h_2(t)\\ h_1\in C_B^2(\mathbb{R}),\, h_2\in C_B^1(\mathbb{R}^+)}} \{\|g_1g_2-h_1h_2\|_{\tilde{X}[t_o,t_n]} + s(2B\|h_1^{(2)}h_2\|_{\tilde{X}[t_o,t_n]} + \|h_1h_2'\|_{\tilde{X}[t_o,t_n]})\}$$

$$\leqslant \inf_{\substack{\|h_1\|_C\leqslant 3\|g_1\|_C\\ \|h_2\|_C\leqslant 3\|g_2\|_C}} \{\|g_2\|_C(\|g_1-h_1\|_C + 6Ms\|h_1^{(2)}\|_C) + 3\|g_1\|_C(\|g_2-h_2\|_C + s\|h_2'\|_C)\}$$

$$\leqslant \|g_2\|_C K(6Ms,g_1;C_B(\mathbb{R}),C_B^2(\mathbb{R})) + 3\|g_1\|_C K(s,g_2;C_B(\mathbb{R}^+),C_B^1(\mathbb{R}^+)),$$

which already establishes the assertion, noting (4.7 - 8).

REFERENCES

[1] Ansorge, R., Der Äquivalenzsatz von Lax für halblineare Probleme. Z. Angew. Math. Mech. 46 (1966), T35 - T37.

[2] Ansorge, R. - Geiger, C., Approximationstheoretische Abschätzung des Diskretisationsfehlers bei verallgemeinerten Lösungen gewisser Anfangswertaufgaben. Abh. Math. Sem. Univ. Hamburg 36 (1971), 99 - 110.

[3] Ansorge, R. - Geiger, C. - Hass, R., Existenz und numerische Erfaßbarkeit verallgemeinerter Lösungen halblinearer Anfangswertaufgaben. Z. Angew. Math. Mech. 52 (1972), 597 - 605.

[4] Brenner, P. - Thomée, V. - Wahlbin, L., Besov Spaces and Applications to Difference Methods for Initial Value Problems. (Lecture Notes in Mathematics 434), Springer Verlag, Berlin/Heidelberg/New York 1975.

[5] Butzer, P.L. - Berens, H., Semi-Groups of Operators and Approximation. Springer Verlag, Berlin/Heidelberg/New York 1967.

[6] Butzer, P.L. - Dickmeis, W. - Jansen, Hu. - Nessel, R.J., Alternative forms with orders of the Lax equivalence theorem in Banach spaces. Computing (Arch. Elektron. Rechnen) 17 (1977), 335-342.

[7] Butzer, P.L. - Dickmeis, W. - Hahn, L. - Nessel, R.J., Lax-type theorems and a unified approach to some limit theorems in probability theory with rates. (to appear).

[8] Butzer, P.L. - Weis, R., On the Lax equivalence theorem equipped with orders. J. Approximation Theory 19 (1977), 239-252.

[9] Carroll, R.W., Abstract Methods in Partial Differential Equations. Harper & Row, New York/Evanston/London 1969.

[10] Dickmeis, W. - Nessel, R.J., Classical approximation processes in connection with Lax equivalence theorems with orders. Acta Sci.

Math. (Szeged) (to appear).

[11] Hass, R., Stabilität und Konvergenz von Differenzenverfahren für halblineare Probleme. Dissertation, Universität Hamburg 1971.

[12] Köhnen, W., Das Anfangswertverhalten von Evolutionsgleichungen in Banachräumen. Teil I: Approximationseigenschaften von Evolutionsoperatoren. Tôhoku Math. J. 22 (1970), 566-596. Teil II: Anwendungen. Tôhoku Math. J. 23 (1971), 621-639.

[13] Ladas, G.E. - Lakshmikantham, V., Differential Equations in Abstract Spaces. Academic Press, New York/London 1972.

[14] Lax, P.D. - Richtmyer, R.D., Survey of the stability of linear finite difference equations. Comm. Pure Appl. Math. 9 (1956), 267-293.

[15] Peetre, J. - Thomée, V., On the rate of convergence for discrete initial-value problems. Math. Scand. 21 (1967), 159-176.

[16] Richtmyer, R.D. - Morton, K.W., Difference Methods for Initial-Value Problems. Interscience, New York/London/Sydney 1967.

[17] Stetter, H.J., Anwendung des Äquivalenzsatzes von P. Lax auf inhomogene Probleme. Z. Angew. Math. Mech. 39 (1959), 396-397.

[18] Thompson, R.J., Difference approximation for inhomogeneous and quasilinear equations. SIAM J. Appl. Math. 12 (1964), 189-199.

[19] Thompson, R.J., Difference approximation for some functional differential equations. In: Numerische, insbesondere approximationstheoretische Behandlung von Funktionalgleichungen (Ansorge, R., Törnig, W., eds., Lecture Notes in Mathematics 333), pp. 263-273; Springer Verlag, Berlin/Heidelberg/New York 1973.

[20] Yosida, K., Functional Analysis. Springer Verlag, Berlin/Heidelberg/New York 1968.

# EVOLUTION EQUATIONS IN SUP-NORM CONTEXT AND IN $L^2$ VARIATIONAL CONTEXT

G. Lumer
Faculté des Sciences
Université de l'Etat
Mons, Belgium

We consider evolution equations in sup-norm context for arbitrary open subsets of some locally compact space $\Omega$ (with 0 boundary values, and initial values in an appropriate domain), associated to a local operator A, as treated in [5]. We compare these evolution problems with the corresponding $L^2$ variational problems for "the same" operator, (at least when the open sets are relatively compact), showing that under rather general assumptions the "variational operator" $\mathcal{A}_V$ associated to a given relatively compact open set V, indeed extends the "sup-norm operator" $A_V$ associated to the same set V, (both operators corresponding of course to the same underlying local operator A on $\Omega$). This relies on maximum principle considerations through the use of approximation techniques and results as given in [6], as well as on the extension of a variational argument given by R. Beals for the case of the ordinary laplacian (1).

Moreover, the fact that $A_V \subset \mathcal{A}_V$, implies that when a sup-norm evolution equation such as mentioned above is solvable for a given V, the solution coincides a.e. with the solution of the $L^2$ variational problem. In particular in the "selfadjoint case" under quite general assumptions, the solution of the sup-norm problem can be computed by a spectral (eigenfunction) series of the type $\sum_{n=1}^{\infty} \exp\{\lambda_n t\} c_n \varphi_n$ (where the initial value is $f = \sum_{n=1}^{\infty} c_n \varphi_n$). We show that these results apply in particular to quite general second order elliptic operators in arbitrary bounded open subsets of $R^n$.

## 0. Notations, General Hypotheses, Previous Results

We take up below the context, terminology, and notations concerning local operators on a locally compact Hausdorff space $\Omega$, as developed in [5]; moreover we assume here for the sake of simplicity that $\Omega$ is connected non-compact, with countable basis for its topology. Let A be such a local opera-

(1) Unpublished; communicated to us during the Nato Advanced Study Institute on Boundary value problems for evolution partial differential equations, Liège, September 1976.

tor on $\Omega$. We shall always assume below, unless otherwise mentioned, that A is real, locally dissipative, locally closed, and that indeed all the hypotheses of the basic Theorem 5.4 of [5] are satisfied. We denote as in [7],[8], by $\mathcal{O} = \mathcal{O}(\Omega)$ the set of all nonempty open subsets of $\Omega$, and by $\mathcal{O}_c = \mathcal{O}_c(\Omega)$ the set of relatively compact nonempty open sets in $\Omega$. In accordance with what was said above, we shall use freely the notations introduced in [5]. This gives us the context for our sup-norm problem (to be precise, the Cauchy problem as described in Section 3 of [5]). The context and assumptions for the $L^2$ variational problem will be described in the next section.

We recall now some sup-norm extension results which we shall need, from the statement and proof of Theorem 2.2 of [6], (in stating these results, like elsewhere below unless otherwise mentioned, A is a local operator on $\Omega$ satisfying the hypotheses described above).

THEOREM 0.1. *Let* $V \in \mathcal{O}_c(\Omega)$. *Then there exists a negative operator* B *(in the sense "*$0 \leqslant g$ *real* $\Rightarrow Bg \leqslant 0$"*), bounded, from* $C_0(V)$ *into* $L^\infty(V)$ *(the space of all bounded Borel-measurable complex-valued functions on* V*, provided with the sup-norm), such that*

(1) $$A_V^{-1} \subset B.$$

*Let* $G_n \in \mathcal{R}$ *(exhaustive family of regular open sets, see 5.4 of* [5]*),* $n=1,2,3,\dots$, $G_n \subset V$, $G_n \nearrow V$, *then for all* $g \in C_{00}(V)$ *(i.e. for all* $g \in C_0(V)$ *with compact support in* V*), we have*

(2) $$Bg = \lim_n A_{C_n}^{-1}(g|G_n),$$

*the sequence on the right hand side of* (2) *converging pointwise boundedly,* n *being large enough so that* supp $g \subset G_n$.

## 1. Sup-norm Problems and $L^2$ Variational Problems

Given the context defined in the previous section, we now add the structures needed to set up the corresponding variational problems. An example will help understand what we must do in the general context.

EXAMPLE 1.1. Consider the simple case in which $\Omega = R^n$, say n=3, and A is the ordinary laplacian (in the distributional sense). For $V \in \mathcal{O} = \mathcal{O}(R^3)$, we have according to the general sup-norm scheme (see [5]):

$$(3)\qquad \begin{aligned} D(A_V) &= \{f \in C_o(V)\colon \Delta f \text{ (distributional)} \in C_o(V), \text{ in } V\} \\ A_V f &= \Delta f \quad \text{for } f \subset D(A_V). \end{aligned}$$

The sup-norm problem (Cauchy problem) which we consider, is then formulated as the following Banach space Cauchy problem, (posed in the Banach space $C_o(V)$ provided as always with the sup-norm):

$$(4)\qquad \frac{du}{dt} = A_V u, \quad u(o) = f \quad \text{(for given } f \in D(A_V)),$$

(see [5]). Such a problem may or may not have a solution; even for rather "simple" bounded open sets of $R^3$ it may fail to have a solution: for instance if $V = \{\text{open unit ball of } R^3\} \setminus \{0\}$ (see [5], 6.7 p. 439). On the other hand the corresponding $L^2$ variational problem will always have a solution for $V \in \mathcal{O}_c$ (but in a weaker sense). The variational problem is defined as follows (see for instance Lions, [10] Chap. IV)(2): to $V \in \mathcal{O}_c = \mathcal{O}_c(R^3)$ we associate the sesquilinear form $a_V(u,v): H_o^1(V) \times H_o^1(V) \to L^2(V)$ defined by

$$(5)\qquad a_V(u,v) = \sum_{j=1}^{j=3} \int_V \frac{\partial u}{\partial x_j} \frac{\partial \bar{v}}{\partial x_j} dx,$$

for u,v elements of the Sobolev space $H_o^1(V)$. By the Lax-Milgram theorem, and the Poincaré inequality, (see [10] Chap. IV, and 2.1 p. 33; Mizohata [11] p. 169), there exists a uniquely determined operator $A_V$ in $L^2(V)$ (the "variational operator" for the laplacian, associated to V) satisfying:

(2) From the discussion in [10] it is easily seen why and in what sense this problem corresponds to the "operator laplacian" and "boundary values 0" in the special example considered. See also the references indicated in [10] Chap. IV p. 115, and Friedman [3] (in particular sections 12; 13).

$$D(A_V) = \{f \in H_o^1(V) : \exists g \in L^2(V) \text{ with } a_V(f,v) = (g,v)_{L^2(V)} \quad \forall v \in H_o^1(V)\},$$

(6)

$$A_V f = -g \quad \text{for } f \in D(A_V),\ g \text{ as above;}$$

here $( \, , \, )_{L^2(V)} = ( \, , \, )$ denotes of course the usual scalar-product in $L^2(V)$. The corresponding $L^2$ variational problem is then the Banach space Cauchy problem posed in $L^2(V)$ shown below:

(7) $$\frac{du}{dt} = A_V u, \quad u(o) = f \quad (\text{for given } f \in D(A_V)).$$

One can proceed similarly for quite general second order elliptic operators in lieu of the laplacian.

We describe now the set up in the general context. We thus assume given on $\Omega$ a Borel measure $\mu \geq 0$, $0<\mu(V)<\infty$ for $V$ in $\mathcal{O}_c$, and for each $V \in \mathcal{O}$ we denote by $L^2(V) = L^2(V,\mu)$ the $L^2$ space with respect to the Borel measure obtained by restricting $\mu$ to the Borel sets of $V$. $( \, , \, )_{L^2(V)}$, or simply $( \, , \, )$ when no confusion is likely, denotes the corresponding inner-product. Furthermore, we assume that we have a "variational structure defined on $\mathcal{O}_c$" in the following sense:

1) To each $V \in \mathcal{O}_c$ is associated a subspace $H_V$ of $L^2(V)$ dense in $L^2(V)$, $H_V$ being itself a Hilbert space with norm $\| \ \|_{H_V}$, and inner-product $( \, , \, )_{H_V}$, $\| \ \|_{L^2(V)} \leq (\text{constant}) \cdot \| \ \|_{H_V}$ on $H_V$.

2) There is defined for all $V \in \mathcal{O}_c$ a continuous sesquilinear form $a_V$ from $H_V \times H_V$ into $\mathbb{C}$.

If $V_1, V_2 \in \mathcal{O}_c$, $V_1 \subset V_2$, and "$\sim$" denotes "extension to $V_2$ by 0 outside of $V_1$", then for $u,v \in H_{V_1}$, one has $\tilde{u},\tilde{v} \in H_{V_2}$, $(u,v)_{H_{V_1}} = (\tilde{u},\tilde{v})_{H_{V_2}}$, $a_{V_1}(u,v) = a_{V_2}(\tilde{u},\tilde{v})$. We assume furthermore that $\{\tilde{u} : u \in H_W,\ W \in \mathcal{O}_c(V)\}$ is dense in $H_V$.

We shall say that the given structure "satisfies a coerciveness condition" iff:

3) for all $V \in \mathcal{O}_c$ there exist $\lambda_V \geq 0$, $\alpha_V > 0$, such that for all $u \in H_V$,

$$\operatorname{Re} a_V(u,u) + \lambda_V \|u\|^2_{L^2(V)} \geq \alpha_V \|u\|^2_{H_V}.$$

We shall say that the given structure is "compatible with the local operator A" iff:

4) for all $V \in \mathcal{O}_c$ there exists a sequence of $G_n \in \mathcal{R}$, with $\overline{G_n} \subset V$, $G_n \nearrow V$, and one has (for all n)

$$A_{G_n} \subset \mathcal{A}_{G_n}.$$

(Notice that for $V \in \mathcal{O}_c$, "$A_V \subset \mathcal{A}_V$" $\Leftrightarrow$ "$A_{\lambda V} \subset \mathcal{A}_{\lambda V}$", where $A_\lambda = A-\lambda$, $\lambda \geqslant 0$, and $\mathcal{A}_{\lambda V}$ is the variational operator corresponding to $a_{\lambda V}(u,v) = a_V(u,v)+\lambda(u,v)_{L^2(V)}$, $\mathcal{A}_{\lambda V} - \mathcal{A}_V - \lambda$).

Now if conditions 1), 2) and 3) are satisfied, then the usual arguments, as used in [10] loc. cit. show that for all $V \in \mathcal{O}_c$ there exists a uniquely determined operator $\mathcal{A}_V$ in $L^2(V)$ defined by

$$D(\mathcal{A}_V) = \{f \in H_V : \exists g \in L^2(V) \text{ with } a_V(f,v) = (g,v)_{L^2(V)}, \forall v \in H_V\} \tag{8}$$

$$\mathcal{A}_V f = -g \quad \text{for } f \text{ and } g \text{ as above.}$$

In other words, we have $D(\mathcal{A}_V) = \{f \in H_V : v \mapsto a_V(f,v),\ v \in H_V$, is continuous in the topology induced by $L^2(V)$ on $H_V\}$, $(\mathcal{A}_V f, v)_{L^2(V)} = -a_V(f,v)$ for all $v \in H_V$, $f \in D(\mathcal{A}_V)$. Furthermore, (because of condition 3)) by the arguments mentioned (Lax-Milgram theorem), there exists $(\mathcal{A}_V - \lambda)^{-1} = \mathcal{A}_{\lambda V}^{-1} \in \mathcal{B}(L^2(V))$ for $\lambda \geqslant \lambda_V$; in fact $\mathcal{A}_{\lambda V}^{-1} \in \mathcal{B}(L^2(V), H_V)$ i.e. $\mathcal{A}_{\lambda V}^{-1}$ is bounded from $L^2(V)$ into $H_V$.

We now have the following result:

THEOREM 1.2. <u>Assume we have a variational structure defined on $\mathcal{O}_c(\Omega)$, compatible with A, satisfying a coerciveness condition. Then for all $V \in \mathcal{O}_c$ we have</u>

$$A_V \subset \mathcal{A}_V. \tag{9}$$

PROOF. To prove (9) it will suffice to show that $(A_{\lambda_V V})^{-1} \subset (\mathcal{A}_{\lambda_V V})^{-1}$, since this implies $A_V - \lambda_V = A_{\lambda_V V} \subset \mathcal{A}_{\lambda_V V} = \mathcal{A}_V - \lambda_V$, hence $A_V \subset \mathcal{A}_V$.

Let now $g \in C_{oo}(V)$, and set for $\operatorname{supp} g \subset G_n$,

$$f_n = A_{\lambda_V G_n}(g|G_n), \tag{10}$$

where the $G_n$ are those of the "compatible with A" condition 4) above. Then $f_n \in D(A_{\lambda_V G_n})$ and $A_{\lambda_V G_n} f_n = g|G_n$, so

$$(11) \qquad -a_{\lambda_V V}(\tilde{f}_n,\tilde{v}) = -a_{\lambda_V G_n}(f_n,v) = (g|G_n,v)_{L^2(G_n)} = (g,\tilde{v})_{L^2(V)},$$

for all $v \in H_{G_n}$. By the coerciveness condition, and (11) used with $\tilde{v} = \tilde{f}_n$, we have $\alpha_V \|\tilde{f}_n\|^2_{H_V} \leq c_V \|g\|_{L^2(V)} \|\tilde{f}_n\|_{H_V}$, thus

$$(12) \qquad \|\tilde{f}_n\|_{H_V} \leq c_V \|g\|_{L^2(V)},$$

$c_V$ denoting different constants depending on V only. By (12) and the weak compactness of the unit ball of the Hilbert space $H_V$, we may asssume that the $\tilde{f}_n$ converge weakly to $f \in H_V$. By a well-known theorem of Mazur ([13] p. 120) there exist for k=1,2,3,..., convex combinations of the $\tilde{f}_n$ with $n \geq k$, say

$$(13) \qquad f'_k = \sum \alpha_j \tilde{f}_{n_j} \quad \text{(finite sum, all } n_j \geq k,\ \alpha_j \geq 0,\ \sum \alpha_j = 1),$$

such that $\|f'_k - f\|_{H_V} \to 0$ as $k \to \infty$.

Now by (11) and (13) we have for any $v \in H_{G_k}$, $-a_{\lambda_V V}(f'_k,\tilde{v}) = (g,\tilde{v})_{L^2(V)}$, and by the continuity of $a_{\lambda_V V}$ on $H_V \times H_V$ we see that

$$(14) \qquad -a_{\lambda_V V}(f,\tilde{v}) = (g,\tilde{v})_{L^2(V)} \quad \text{for all } v \in \bigcup_{n=1}^{\infty} H_{G_n},$$

and since the latter $\tilde{v}$ are dense in $H_V$ we see that

$$(15) \qquad f \in D(A_{\lambda V}), \quad A_{\lambda V} f = g.$$

Now by Theorem 0.1, the $f_n \to B_\lambda g$ pointwise boundedly ($B_\lambda$ is the operator B of 0.1 corresponding to $A_\lambda$ instead of A). So also $f'_k \to B_\lambda g$ pointwise; but $\|f'_k - f\|_{H_V} \to 0$ implies $\|f'_k - f\|_{L^2(V)} \to 0$, hence (modulo going to a subsequence) $f'_k \to f$ a.e., and therefore (a.e.)

$$(16) \qquad B_\lambda g = f = A^{-1}_{\lambda V} g \quad \text{for all } g \in C_{oo}(V).$$

For any $g \in C_o(V)$, take $g_n \in C_{oo}(V)$ with $\|g-g_n\|_{C_o(V)} \to 0$, then also $g_n \to g$ in $L^2(V)$, and since $B_\lambda$ and $A_{\lambda V}^{-1}$ are bounded operators, in sup-norm and $L^2$ norm respectively, we conclude that $B_\lambda = A_{\lambda V}^{-1}|C_o(V)$. By Theorem 0.1, we have $A_{\lambda V}^{-1} \subset B_\lambda$, hence $A_{\lambda V}^{-1} \subset \mathcal{A}_{\lambda V}^{-1}$, and as observed earlier this yields $A_V \subset \mathcal{A}_V$.□

## 2. Application to Partial Differential Equations. Eigenfunction Expansions of Solutions of Sup-norm Problems.

Let $\Omega$ be a (connected) nonempty open set in $R^n$. Suppose given on $\Omega$ a second order differential operator

$$A(x,D) = \sum_{|\alpha|\leq 2} c_\alpha D^\alpha, \tag{17}$$

written in the usual multi-index notation. All coefficients are real and at least measurable and bounded functions on $\Omega$ (i.e. $\in L^\infty(\Omega)$); for $|\alpha|=2$ they are assumed to be continuous and with distributional partial derivatives in $L^\infty(\Omega)$; we also assume $c_o \leq 0$. Furthermore we assume that $A(x,D)$ is elliptic in $\Omega$, i.e.

$$\sum_{|\alpha|=2} c_\alpha(x)\xi^\alpha > 0 \quad \text{for each } x \in \Omega,\ \xi \in R^n \setminus \{0\}.$$

Writing out $A(x,D)$ in more detail, we have

$$A(x,D) = \sum_{i,j=1}^{n} a_{ij} D_i D_j + \sum_{j=1}^{n} b_j D_j + c, \tag{18}$$

where $D_i = \partial/\partial x_i$.

Now $A(x,D)$ induces on $\Omega$ a local operator $A$ satisfying the assumptions of Section 0, in the way explained in [9] (first defining a nonlocally closed operator and then taking the closure - see [9] Section II). The corresponding variational structure is obtained by taking for $V \in \mathcal{O}_c(\Omega)$, $H_V$ equal to the usual Sobolev space $H_o^1(V)$, and setting

$$a_V(u,v) = \sum_{i,j=1}^{n} \int_V a_{ij} D_j u \overline{D_i v}\, dx - \sum_{j=1}^{n} \int_V b^*(D_j u)\overline{v}\, dx - \int_V c\, u\, \overline{v}\, dx, \tag{19}$$

where $b_j^* = b_j - \sum_{i=1}^{n} D_i a_{ij} \in L^\infty(V)$. Moreover write

$$(18') \qquad A_{var} = A_{var}(x,D) = \sum_{i,j=1}^{n} D_i a_{ij} D_j + \sum_{j=1}^{n} b_j^* D_j + c,$$

which is well defined in the distributional sense on $H_o^1(V)$ (i.e. for $u \in H_o^1(V)$, $D_i a_{ij} D_j u$ is the distribution $D_i(a_{ij} D_j u)$, etc.).

THEOREM 2.1. $H_V$ _and_ $a_V$ _being as described above in this section, for all_ $V \in \mathcal{O}_c(\Omega)$, _they define a variational structure on_ $\Omega$ _compatible with_ A, _satisfying a coerciveness condition. Hence Theorem_ 1.2 _applies and if for_ $V \in \mathcal{O}_c(\Omega)$, $A_V$ _and_ $\mathcal{A}_V$ _are the corresponding sup-norm and variational operators, we have_ $A_V \subset \mathcal{A}_V$.

PROOF. That condition 1) and 2) for a variational structure (Section 1) are satisfied is clear. Condition 3) is Garding's inequality which holds under the present conditions (see [3] Section 12, p. 34). We now prove that condition 4) is also satisfied. There exists a sequence of very regular open sets (in the sense of [10] p. 42, having in particular $C^\infty$ boundary) $G_n \subset V$, $\overline{G_n} \subset V$, $G_n \nearrow V$ (and of course $\mathcal{R}$ may be chosen so that $G_n \in \mathcal{R}$). Let G be any one of these $G_n$; we shall show that for $\lambda \geq \lambda_V$, $A_{\lambda G}^{-1} \subset \mathcal{A}_{\lambda G}^{-1}$. To that end take $\psi \in \mathcal{D}(G) = C^\infty(G) \cap C_{oo}(G)$. By classical results of Agmon et al., [1], (see also Bony [2]), or see [4] 10 Section 3, for fixed $p > n$ ($p \geq 2$), there exists a unique u such that

$$(20) \qquad \begin{aligned} &u \in W^{2,p}(G) \cap W_o^{1,p}(G), \\ &A(x,D)u = \psi \quad \text{a.e.}, \end{aligned}$$

and since G is very regular, $2-n/p > 1$, standard "Sobolev imbedding results" (see [3] p. 30) show that

$$(21) \qquad u \in C^1(\overline{G}).$$

Again by standard results (see for instance [4] p. 237) (20) and (21) imply that

(22) $$u|\partial G = 0.$$

(20), (21), (22), show that

(23) $$u \in D(A_G), \quad A_G u = \psi.$$

On the other hand we have for all $\varphi \in \mathcal{D}(G)$,

(24) $$\begin{aligned} a_G(u,\varphi) &= -\langle A_{var}u,\overline{\varphi}\rangle = -\langle A(x,D)u,\overline{\varphi}\rangle = \langle -\psi,\overline{\varphi}\rangle \\ &= (-\psi,\varphi)_{L^2(G)} = (-\mathcal{A}_G u,\varphi)_{L^2(G)}, \end{aligned}$$

where the fact that $A_{var}u = A(x,D)u$ follows from (18), (18'), $u \in W^{2,p}(G)$, $a_{ij} \in W^{1,\infty}(G)$, (since for any $f \in W^{1,\infty}(G)$, $g \in W^{1,p}(G)$, we have $D_i(fg) = fD_i g + gD_i f$ ). (24) shows that

(25) $$u \in D(\mathcal{A}_G), \quad \mathcal{A}_G u = \psi.$$

The same thing holds of course with $A_\lambda$ in lieu of $A$, $\lambda \geqslant \lambda_V$, so that from (23), (25), for $A_{\lambda G}$, $\mathcal{A}_{\lambda G}$, we conclude that $A_{\lambda G}^{-1}|\mathcal{D}(G) \subset \mathcal{A}_{\lambda G}^{-1}|\mathcal{D}(G)$; but since $A_{\lambda G}^{-1} \in \mathcal{B}(C_o(G))$, $\mathcal{A}_{\lambda G}^{-1} \in \mathcal{B}(L^2(G))$, it follows that $A_{\lambda G}^{-1} \subset \mathcal{A}_{\lambda G}^{-1}$.□

As we have seen in [6], the fact that $A_V \subset \mathcal{A}_V$ will permit to compute, in the selfadjoint case, sup-norm solutions by spectral integrals or expansions. In the present situation we can establish the following result:

THEOREM 2.2. *Let* $\Omega$, $A(x,D)$, $A$, *the variational structure and variational operators* $\mathcal{A}_V$, *be as described above in this section. For* $V \in \mathcal{O}_c(\Omega)$ *assume* $a_V$ *is a selfadjoint form, then the spectrum of* $\mathcal{A}_V$, $sp(\mathcal{A}_V)$, *is a discrete point spectrum* $\Pi_o(\mathcal{A}_V) = \{\lambda_1,\lambda_2,\lambda_3,\ldots\}$, $\lambda_1 \geqslant \lambda_2 \geqslant \ldots \geqslant \lambda_n \to -\infty$, *where the* $\lambda_n$ *are not necessarily all different, but rather each eigenvalue is repeated* r-*times iff its multiplicity is* r. *Correspondingly, there exists a complete orthonormal basis of eigenvectors* $\varphi_n$ *of* $\mathcal{A}_V$, *for* $L^2(V)$, *such that* $\mathcal{A}_V$ *has the spectral representation*

(26) $$\mathcal{A}_V f = \sum_{n=1}^{\infty} \lambda_n c_n \varphi_n, \quad c_n = (f,\varphi_n);$$

*if* $f \in D(A_V)$, *then the solution of the (sup-norm) Cauchy problem corresponding to* $A$, *with initial value* $f$, *say* $u(t,f)$, *is given by*

(27) $$u(t,f) = \sum_{n=1}^{\infty} e^{\lambda_n t} c_n \varphi_n, \quad c_n = (f,\varphi_n),$$

$u(t,f)$ *being regarded as an* $L^2(V)$ *element, the right-hand side converging in* $L^2(V)$.

PROOF. For $\lambda \geqslant \lambda_V$, there exists $(A_V-\lambda)^{-1} \in \mathcal{B}(L^2(V), H_o^1(V))$, and the injection $H_o^1(V) \mapsto L^2(V)$ is compact (3), so that $(A_V-\lambda)^{-1}$ is a compact operator in $L^2(V)$, selfadjoint since $a_V$ is selfadjoint (see [10] Chap. IV). The standard Hilbert-Schmidt theorem gives a spectral eigenfunction representation for $(A_V-\lambda)^{-1}$ from which the representation (26) follows immediately. If T being any generator of a semigroup, we use the notation $\exp\{tT\}$ for that semigroup (rather than $(P_t)_{t\geqslant 0}$, or $\{P_t\}_{t\geqslant 0}$), then it is also a standard consequence of spectral theory (see [12] p. 139) that $\exp\{t(A_V-\lambda)\}$ admits a representation of the type of (27), and hence so does $\exp\{tA_V\}$. But as seen in [6] Theorem 3.1, $A_V \subset \mathcal{A}_V$ implies that $u(t,f)$ is also a solution of the $L^2$ Cauchy problem corresponding to $\mathcal{A}_V$, so that $u(t,f)$ coincides (a.e. as an element of $L^2(V)$) with $\exp\{t\mathcal{A}_V\}f$. This proves (27) (4). □

REMARK. Of course the result analogous to 2.2 holds in the general context of section 1 under the assumptions of 1.2 plus the assumption that the injection of $H_V$ into $L^2(V)$ is compact for all $V \in \mathcal{O}_c$, (and of course the assumption that we are in the selfadjoint case, i.e. that the form $a_V$ is a selfadjoint form).

---

(3) $\overline{V} \subset$ some very regular open set $G \in \mathcal{O}_c$, and for each $u \in H_o^1(V)$, $\tilde{u} \in H_o^1(G)$, so it suffices to use a standard compactness result such as 7.1 of [10] p. 53, or 11.2 of [3] p. 31.

(4) For an eigenfunction $\varphi_n$, $A_V\varphi_n = \lambda_n\varphi_n$ implies if we assume $C^\infty$ coefficients, and say V very regular, that $\varphi_n \in C^\infty(V) \cap C_o(V)$, by iterated use of standard elliptic regularity results (see [3] 17.2, p. 67) and by the fact that $\varphi_n \in H_o^1(V)$. Certainly $\varphi_n \in C^1(V) \cap C_o(V)$ is true under quite weaker assumptions, but further work is needed in this area.

## 3. Concerning the Intrinsic Connection with A, of a Variational Structure Compatible with a Given Local Operator A.

We now return to the general context of Section 1, (where it is understood that the basic measure $\mu$ is fixed once and for all, as well as the local operator A).

THEOREM 3.1. Suppose we have the context and the hypothesis of Theorem 1.2. Then for any variational structure satisfying conditions 1) to 4) of Section 1, compatible with the given local operator A, $a_V(u,v)$ is uniquely determined on $D(A_V)\times D(A_V)$ for every $V \in \mathcal{O}_c$, and $\mathcal{A}_V$ is uniquely determined whenever the sup-norm Cauchy problem is solvable for V, (in particular for all $V \in \mathcal{R}$).

PROOF. Consider $V \in \mathcal{O}_c$, then $A_V \subset \mathcal{A}_V$, and hence

$$a_V(u,v) = -(\mathcal{A}_V u,v) = -(A_V u,v), \tag{28}$$

for $u \in D(A_V) \subset D(\mathcal{A}_V) \subset H_V$, $v \in H_V$. Hence $a_V$ is uniquely determined via (28) on $D(A_V)\times D(A_V)$. Now suppose $A_V$ is the generator of a contraction semigroup in $C_o(V)$; then for large $\lambda>0$, $\mathcal{A}_{\lambda V}$ is dissipative in $L^2(V)$, $A_{\lambda V} \subset \mathcal{A}_{\lambda V}$, and $I(A_{\lambda V}-1)$ is $C_o(V)$-dense, hence $L^2(V)$-dense, so that $A_{\lambda V}$ is a pregenerator in $L^2(V)$, while $\mathcal{A}_{\lambda V}$ is a semigroup generator in $L^2(V)$ extending $A_{\lambda V}$; hence (by maximality of generators) $\mathcal{A}_{\lambda V} = \overline{A_{\lambda V}}$ (closure in $L^2(V)$ norm), so

$$\mathcal{A}_V = \overline{A_V}, \tag{29}$$

and this shows that whenever the (sup-norm) Cauchy problem is solvable, $\mathcal{A}_V$ is uniquely determined, (this holds in particular for $V \in \mathcal{R}$).□

## REFERENCES

[1] Agmon, S. - Douglis, A. - Nirenberg, N., Estimates near the boundary for elliptic partial differential equations satisfying the general boundary condition (1). Comm. Pure Appl. Math. 12 (1959), 623 - 727.

[ 2] Bony, J.M., Principe du maximum dans les espaces de Sobolev. C.R. Acad. Sci. Paris Ser. A. 265 (1967), 333 - 336.

[ 3] Friedman, A., Partial Differential Equations. Holt, New York, 1969.

[ 4] Friedman, A., Stochastic Differential Equations and Applications. Vol. 2, Academic Press, New York, 1976.

[ 5] Lumer, G., Problème de Cauchy pour opérateurs locaux et "changement de temps". Annales Inst. Fourier. 25 (1975) fasc. 3 et 4, 409 - 446.

[ 6] Lumer, G., Principe du maximum et équations d'évolution dans $L^2$. To appear in: Séminaire de Théorie du Potentiel, Paris, No. 3, Lect. Notes in Math., Springer - Verlag.

[ 7] Lumer, G., Problème de Cauchy pour opérateurs locaux. C.R. Acad. Sci. Paris Ser. A. 281 (1975), 763 - 765.

[ 8] Lumer, G., Problème de Cauchy avec valeurs au bord continues. C.R. Acad. Sci. Paris Ser. A. 281 (1975), 805 - 807.

[ 9] Lumer, G., Equations d'évolution en norme uniforme pour opérateurs elliptiques. Régularité des solutions. C.R. Acad. Sci. Paris Ser. A. 284 (1977), 1435 - 1437.

[ 10] Lions, J., Problèmes aux Limites dans les Equations aux Dérivées Partielles. 2 nd ed., Les Presses de l'Univ. de Montréal, 1965.

[ 11] Mizohata, S., The Theory of Partial Differential Equations. Cambridge Univ. Press, 1973.

[ 12] Vilenkin, Ya., et al., Functional Analysis. Wolters-Noordhoff, Groningen (The Netherlands), 1972.

[ 13] Yosida, K., Functional Analysis. Several ed., 1965-1974, Springer - Verlag.

# ZUR DISKRETISIERUNG VON RANDWERTAUFGABEN GEWÖHNLICHER DIFFERENTIALGLEICHUNGEN

Henning Esser
Institut für Geometrie und Praktische Mathematik
Rheinisch-Westfälische Technische Hochschule
Aachen

For higher order discretizations of boundary value problems extra boundary conditions are needed. For stability reasons they must be constructed such that a Gårding's inequality for the highest (discrete) derivative is satisfied. Two possibilities of constructing extra boundary conditions are studied in detail. Under natural conditions it is shown that they lead to stable approximations.

Es sei $n \in \mathbb{N}$ und $C^n \in [a,b]$ der lineare Raum der auf $[a,b]$ n mal stetig differenzierbaren Funktionen. Für $y \in C^n[a,b]$ betrachten wir den linearen Differentialoperator L

$$(1) \qquad (L\,y)(x) = y^{(n)}(x) + \sum_{j=0}^{n-1} A_j(x) y^{(j)}(x) \qquad (x \in [a,b])$$

mit $A_j \in C[a,b]$ $(j = 0,1,\ldots n-1)$. Ferner seien n lineare Randbedingungen der Form

$$(2) \qquad B_l(y) = \sum_{j=0}^{n-1} \left\{ B_{j,l}(a) y^{(j)}(a) + B_{j,l}(b)\, y^{(j)}(b) \right\} \qquad (l=0,1,\ldots n-1)$$

gegeben. Wir untersuchen Diskretisierungen des Randwertproblems

$$(3) \qquad \begin{cases} L\,y = f & (f \in C[a,b]) \\ B_l(y) = \gamma_l & (\gamma_l \in \mathbb{R},\ l = 0,1,\ldots n-1)\ . \end{cases}$$

Hierzu sei $N \in \mathbb{N}$, $h = \frac{b-a}{N}$ und

$T_h = \{ t\ ;\ t = a + ih\ ,\ i = 0,1,\ldots N \}$ ein äquidistantes Gitter über $[a,b]$ mit Schrittweite h. Der lineare Raum der Gitterfunktionen über $T_h$ sei mit $C(T_h)$ bezeichnet, und für $1 \leq p \leq \infty$ sind die diskreten p-Normen üblicherweise definiert durch

$$(4) \qquad \begin{aligned} \| y_h \|_{h,p} &= \{ h \sum_{t \in T_h} |y_h(t)|^p \}^{1/p} && (1 \leq p < \infty) \\ \| y_h \|_{h,\infty} &= \max_{t \in T_h} |y_h(t)| && (p = \infty)\ . \end{aligned}$$

Für $y_h \in C(T_h)$ sind die Verschiebungsoperatoren $E$, $E^{-1}$ definiert durch $(E\, y_h)(t) = y_h(t+h)$ $(t = a,\dots b-h)$ bzw $(E^{-1} y_h)(t) = y_h(t-h)$ $(t = h,\dots b)$ , und wir setzen $E^{-k} = (E^{-1})^k$ $(k = 1,2,\dots)$ . Ferner sind die Differenzenoperatoren $\Delta$, $\Delta_-$, $D$, $D_-$ erklärt durch $\Delta = (E - I)$, $\Delta_- = (I - E^{-1}) = E^{-1}\Delta$, $D = h^{-1}\Delta$ und $D_- = h^{-1}\Delta_- = E^{-1}D$. Für $[c,d] \subset [a,b]$ bezeichnen wir die Menge der Gitterpunkte in $[c,d]$ mit $[c,d]_h$ , so daß insbesondere $[a,b]_h = T_h$ ist. Ist

$$A = \sum_{k=-p}^{q} q_k E^k \qquad (p,\, q \in \mathbb{N})$$ ein linearer Differenzenoperator

$A: C([a,b]_h) \to C([a+ph,\, b-qh]_h)$ , so ist $\| A\, y_h \|_{h,p}$ definiert durch den den entsprechenden Ausdruck in (4), wobei $T_h$ ersetzt ist durch $[a+ph,\, b-qh]_h$. Für Gitterfunktionen $y_h(t)$ benutzen wir auch die Abkürzung $y_h(a + jh) = y_j$ $(j = 0,1,\dots N)$ .

Jede vernünftige Differenzenapproximation von L in (1) ist von der Form

$$(5) \quad (L_h y_h)(t) = h^{-n} \sum_{k=-p}^{q} C_k(t,h)\,(E^k y_h)(t) \quad (t \in [a+ph, b-qh]_h;\ p,q \in \mathbb{N}),$$

wobei die $C_k(t,h)$ $(k = -p,\dots q)$ Polynome in $h$ mit stetigen Koeffizienten sind. Nach H.O. Kreiss ([2]) heißt $w = p + q$ die W e i t e von $L_h$. Aus Konsistenzgründen muß stets $w \geq n$ gelten. Durch (5) sind $N-w+1$ lineare Gleichungen für $y_h(t)$ $(t \in T_h)$ gegeben. Definiert man das Polynom (s. [1])

$$(6) \quad P_w(x;t,h) = \sum_{k=0}^{w} C_{k-p}(t,h)\, x^k \quad (t \in [a+ph,\, b-qh]_h) ,$$

so findet man für (5) die Darstellung $(t_j = a+jh)$

$$(7) \quad L_h y_j = S(t_j,h) D^n y_{j-p} + \sum_{l=0}^{n-1} A_l(t_j,h)\, D^l y_{j-p} \quad (j=p,\dots N-q)$$

mit $A_l(t_j,h) = \frac{h^{l-n}}{l!} P_w^{(l)}(1;\, t_j,h)$ $(l = 0,1\dots n-1)$ und dem linearen Differenzenoperator

$$(8) \quad S(t_j,h) = \sum_{k=0}^{w-n} a_k(t_j,h)\, \Delta^k ,$$

wobei $a_k(t_j,h) = \frac{1}{(n+k)!} P_w^{(n+k)}(1;\, t_j,h)$ $(k = 0,1,\dots w-n)$

ist.

O.E.d.A. wollen wir annehmen, daß $S(t_j, 0)$ (was nur von der Diskretisierung von $y^{(n)}$ abhängt) konstante Koeffizienten besitzt:

$$(8)' \quad S(t_j,0) = S(0) = \sum_{k=0}^{w-n} a_k(0)\, \Delta^k .$$

Diskretisiert man ähnlich die $n$ Randbedingungen in (3), so erhält man zusammen mit (5) bzw. (7) $(N-w+1) + n$ lineare Gleichungen zur Bestimmung der Näherungslösung $y_j$ $(j = 0,1,\ldots N)$. Es fehlen daher $w-n$ lineare Gleichungen. Diese Gleichungen werden als *zusätzliche Randbedingungen* bezeichnet (s. [1], [2]). Aus Stabilitätsgründen wollen wir die zusätzlichen Randbedingungen so wählen, daß für das diskrete Problem eine a-priori Abschätzung für $D^n y_j$ $(j = 0,1,\ldots N-n)$ gilt (s. (12)). Durch (7) erhalten wir nämlich $N-w+1$ Gleichungen für $z_j = D^n y_j$ $(j= 0,1,\ldots N-n)$. Die fehlenden $w-n$ Gleichungen zur Festlegung von $D^n y_j$ $(j=0,1,\ldots N-n)$ müssen daher von den $w-n$ zusätzlichen Randbedingungen geliefert werden (die diskreten Randbedingungen erhalten nur Ableitungen bis zur Ordnung $(n-1)$). Die zusätzlichen Randbedingungen sind daher von der Form

$$(9) \quad B_h^i(y_h) = h^{-\alpha} \sum_{k=0}^{\beta} \{ D_k^i(a,h)(E^k y_h)(a) + D_k^i(b,h)(E^{-k} y_h)(b)\}$$
$$(i=1,2,\ldots w-n),$$

wobei (damit in (9) Bedingungen für $D^n y_j$ enthalten sind) $\beta \geq \alpha \geq n$ $(\alpha,\beta \in \mathbb{N})$ gilt, und die $D_k^i$ Polynome in $h$ mit beschränkten Koeffizienten sind. Wie bei (7) findet man die Darstellung ([1])

$$(10) \quad B_h^i(y_h) = h^{n-\alpha}\{Q_i(a,h)D^n y_h(a) + Q_i(b,h)\, D_-^n\, y_h(b)\} + O\left(\sum_{i=0}^{n-1} \| D^i y_h \|_{h,\infty}\right)$$

mit geeigneten Differenzenoperatoren

$$(11) \quad \begin{aligned} Q_i(a,h) &= \sum_{l=0}^{\beta-n} q_{li}(a,h)\, \Delta^l \\ Q_i(b,h) &= \sum_{l=0}^{\beta-n} q_{li}(b,h)\, \Delta_-^l \quad (i=1,2,\ldots w-n). \end{aligned}$$

Für beliebige Gitterfunktionen soll nun die folgende Gårding'sche Ungleichung erfüllt sein:

$$(12) \quad \|D^n y_h\|_{h,1} \leq c\{ \|L_h y_h\|_{h,1} + h\cdot h^{\alpha-n} \sum_{i=1}^{w-n} | B_h^i(y_h) | + \|y_h\|_{h,1}\}$$
$$(c \neq c(h),\ h \leq h_0).$$

Im Fall $w = n$ ist (12) automatisch gegeben. Gilt nun (12), dann kann man die folgende Stabilitätsungleichung beweisen (s. [1]), die der Schlüssel für die scharfen Konvergenzordnungsaussagen in [1] ist (entscheidend ist die

Abschätzung durch die 1-Norm) :

$$(13)\quad \sum_{i=0}^{n-1} \|D^i y_h\|_{h,\infty} \leq c\{\|L_h y_h\|_{h,1} + h\cdot h^{\alpha-n} \sum_{i=1}^{w-n} |B_h^i(y_h)| + \sum_{l=0}^{n-1} |B_{h,l}(y_h)|\}$$

($B_{h,l}$ bezeichnet die diskretisierten Randbedingungen) .

Die Abschätzung (12) muß sich aus (7) und (10) ergeben bzw. aus einer a-priori Abschätzung für die Differenzenrandwertaufgabe

$$(14)\quad \begin{cases} S(0)z_{j-p} = f_j & (j = p,\dots N-q) \\ Q_i(a,0)z_o + Q_i(b,0)\, z_{N-n} = g_i & (i = 1,2,\dots w-n)\ , \end{cases}$$

die folgendermaßen lautet

$$(15)\quad h \sum_{j=0}^{N-n} |z_j| \leq c\{ h \sum_{j=p}^{N-q} |Sz_{j-p}| + h \sum_{i=1}^{w-n} |Q_i(a,0)z_o + Q_i(b,0)z_{N-n}|\}$$

$$(c \neq c(h))\ .$$

Man sieht leicht, daß aus (15) die Abschätzung (12) folgt ([1]).

Folgende Charakterisierung von (15) ist nützlich ([1]) (vergl. [2] für die Max-Normabschätzung).

L E M M A 1. Es sei $p(x) = \sum_{k=0}^{w-n} a_k\, (x-1)^k$ das charakteristische Polynom des Differenzenoperators S(0) (s.(8)'). Dann gilt für die Differenzenrandwertaufgabe (14) die Abschätzung (15) genau dann, falls

(i) S(0) elliptisch ist, dh. $p(e^{i\xi}) \neq 0$ ($|\xi| \leq \pi$; $i^2=-1$), und

(ii) (15) für jede Lösung $\{z_j\}_{j=0}^{N-n}$ der Differenzengleichung $S(0)z_{j-p} = 0$ ($j=p,\dots N-q$) gilt.

Im folgenden nehmen wir daher an, daß S elliptisch ist und das charakteristische Polynom p(x)M verschiedene Nullstellen $\lambda_k$ ($k = 1,2,\dots M$) der Vielfachheit $m_k$ ($k = 1,2,\dots M$ ; $\sum_{k=1}^{M} m_k = w-n$) besitzt mit

$$(16)\quad |\lambda_i| < 1\ (i=1,2,\dots L)\ ,\quad |\lambda_i| > 1\ (i=L+1,\dots M)\quad .$$

In [1] haben wir (ii) aus Lemma 1 mit Hilfe einer Darstellung der allgemeinen Lösung von $S(0)z_{j-p} = 0$ noch weiter charakterisiert. Wir wollen hier eine geeignetere Darstellung dieser Lösung benutzen, nämlich

$$(17)\quad \begin{aligned} z_j = & \sum_{k=1}^{L} \{ \sigma_{k1}\lambda_k^j + \sum_{\mu=2}^{m_k} \sigma_{k\mu} j(j-1)\ldots(j-\mu+2)\, \lambda_k^{j-\mu+1} \} + \\ & + \sum_{k=L+1}^{M} \{\sigma_{k1}\lambda_k^{j-N+n} + \sum_{\mu=2}^{m_k} \sigma_{k\mu}\, (j-N+n)\ldots(j-N+n-\mu+2)\, \lambda_k^{j-N+n-\mu+1}\} \\ & (j=o,1,\ldots N-n)\ . \end{aligned}$$

Wie Satz 3.6 in [1] beweist man dann

SATZ 1. $S(0)$ sei elliptisch, und es gelte für die Nullstellen des charakteristischen Polynoms $p(x)$ die Aufteilung (16) . Setzt man

$$(18)\quad \begin{cases} a_{ik}^{1} = Q_i(a,0)\ \{\lambda_k^j\}\ \big|_{j=0} & (k=1,2,\ldots L\ ;\ i=1,2,\ldots w-n) \\ a_{ik}^{\mu} = Q_i(a,0)\ \{\ j(j-1)\ldots(j-\mu+2)\ \lambda_k^{j-\mu+1}\}\ \big|_{j=0} & \\ \qquad (k=1,2,\ldots L\ ;\ \mu=2,\ldots m_k\ ;\ i=1,2,\ldots w-n) & \end{cases}$$

$$(19)\quad \begin{cases} b_{ik}^{1} = Q_i(b,0)\{\ \lambda_k^{j-N+n}\}\big|_{j=N-n} & (k=L+1,\ldots M\ ;\ i=1,2,\ldots w-n) \\ b_{ik}^{\mu} = Q_i(b,0)\{\ (j-N+n)\ldots(j-N+n-\mu+2)\lambda_k^{j-N+n-\mu+1}\}\big|_{j=N-n} & \\ \qquad (k=L+1,\ldots M\ ;\ \mu=2,\ldots m_k\ ;\ i=1,2,\ldots w-n)\ , & \end{cases}$$

und definiert die $(w-n)\times(w-n)$ Matrix $H$ durch

$$(20)\qquad H = (\ A\ ,\ B\ )\quad ,$$

wobei $A$, $B$ durch (18) bzw. (19) definiert ist, dann gilt die a-priori Abschätzung (15) genau dann, falls

$$(21)\qquad \det H \neq 0$$

ist .

Nun kann man aber (18) und (19) noch weiter ausrechnen.

L E M M A 2. Es sei $q_i(a,x) = \sum_{l=0}^{\beta-n} q_{li}\ (a,0)\ (x-1)^l$ bzw. $q_i(b,x) = \sum_{l=0}^{\beta-n} q_{li}(b,0)\ (1-x)^l$ das charakteristische Polynom des Differenzenoperators $Q_i(a,0)$ bzw. $Q_i(b,0)$ (s.(11)). Dann gelten für die Koeffizienten $a_{ik}^{\mu}$, $b_{ik}^{\mu}$ aus Satz 1 die Darstellungen

$$(22) \qquad a^{\mu}_{ik} = \frac{d}{dx}^{\mu-1} q_i\ (a;x)\ \Big|_{x=\lambda_k}$$

$(k=1,2,\ldots L\ ;\ \mu=1,\ldots m_k\ ;\ i=1,2,\ldots w-n)$

$$(23) \qquad b^{\mu}_{ik} = \frac{d^{\mu-1}}{dx} q_i\ (a;\tfrac{1}{x})\ \Big|_{x=\lambda_k}$$

$(k = L+1,\ldots M\ ;\ \mu=1,2,\ldots m_k\ ;\ i=1,2,\ldots w-n)$ .

BEWEIS. Ergibt sich unmittelbar aus (18) und (19).

In der Regel werden die zusätzlichen Randbedingungen separiert sein. Dh. man wird in $x = a$ $P$ Bedingungen und in $x = b$ $w-n-P$ Bedingungen stellen. Es gilt dann

$$(24) \qquad \begin{cases} Q_i(a,h) = 0 & (i = P+1,\ldots w-n) \\ Q_i(b,h) = 0 & (i = 1,2,\ldots P)\ , \end{cases}$$

und die Matrix $H$ ist von der Form

$$(25) \qquad H = \begin{pmatrix} A & 0 \\ 0 & B \end{pmatrix} .$$

L E M M A 3. Gegeben seien separierte zusätzliche Randbedingungen. Damit unter der Voraussetzung von Satz 1 $\det H \neq 0$ gilt, muß für die Anzahl $P$ der Randbedingungen in $x = a$

$$(26) \qquad P = \sum_{k=1}^{L} m_k$$

gelten. Dh. die Matrizen $A,B$ in (25) sind notwendigerweise quadratisch.

BEWEIS. Denn für $\sum_{k=1}^{L} m_k \neq P$ ist stets $\det H = 0$.

Lemma 3 gibt also Auskunft darüber, wieviele Randbedingungen man in jedem Randpunkt zu stellen hat. Ferner gilt dann $\det H = \det A \det B$. Wir betrachten jetzt zwei Möglichkeiten von separierten Randbedingungen.

R a n d e x t r a p o l a t i o n . Hier definiert man sich die zusätzlichen Randbedingungen durch

$$(27)\quad \begin{aligned} &B_h^i(y_h) = \Delta^{i-1+l_o} D^n y_h(a) = 0 \qquad (i=1,2,\ldots P\ ;\ l_o \geq 0) \\ &B_h^{P+i}(y_h) = \Delta_-^{i-1+l_o} D_-^n y_h(b) = 0 \quad (i=1,2,\ldots w-n-P;\ l_o \geq 0). \end{aligned}$$

Offenbar ist

$$(28)\quad \begin{aligned} &q_i(a;x) = (x-1)^{i-1+l_o} \quad (i=1,2,\ldots P) \\ &q_{P+i}(b;x) = (1-x)^{i-1+l_o} \quad (i=1,2,\ldots w-n-P)\ , \end{aligned}$$

so daß die Determinanten von A und B wegen (22) und (23) verallgemeinerte Vandermondsche Determinanten sind. Randextrapolation führt also auf eine stabile Approximation.

D i s k r e t i s i e r u n g i n R a n d n ä h e . Hier verwendet man in Randnähe eine Diskretisierung mit einer kleineren Weite $w_1 \geq n$ . Für $x = a$ erhalten wir daher mit einem Differenzenoperator $S_1(h)$(vergl.(7))

$$S_1(h)D^n y_{j-p_o} + \ldots = f_j \quad (j=p_o \ldots (p_o + P-1)\ )\ ,\ \text{oder}$$

$$(29)\quad B_h^i\ (y_h) = S_1(h)\ E^{i-1}\ D^n y_h(a) + \ldots = f_{p_o+i-1} \quad (i=1,2,\ldots P)\ .$$

Also ist

$$(30)\quad Q_i\ (a,0) = S_1(0)\ E^{i-1} \qquad \text{und}$$

$$(31)\quad q_i\ (a,0) = p_1(x)\ x^{i-1} \quad (i=1,2,\ldots P)\ ,$$

wobei $p_1(x)$ das charakteristische Polynom des Operators $S_1(0)$ ist. Nach (22) ist

$$(32)\quad a_{ik}^{\mu} = \left(\frac{d}{dx}\right)^{\mu-1} \{\ x^{i-1} p_1(x)\ \}\ \Big|_{x=\lambda_k}$$

$$(\mu=1,2,\ldots m_k;\ k=1,2,\ldots L\ ;\ i=1,2,\ldots P)$$

bzw.

$$(33)\quad A = (A_1,\ A_2,\ldots\ A_L)\ ,\ A_k = (a_{ik}^{\mu})_{\substack{i=1,2,\ldots P \\ \mu=1,2,\ldots m_k}} \qquad (k = 1,2,\ldots L).$$

Wir betrachten die Matrix $A_1$. Addiert man ein geeignetes Vielfaches der ersten Spalte zu der i-ten Spalte $(2 \leq i \leq m_1)$, so kann man erreichen, daß der erste Summand jedes Elementes der i-ten Spalte verschwindet. Addiert man anschließend ein geeignetes Vielfaches der zweiten Spalte zur i-ten Spalte $(3 \leq i \leq m_1)$, so kann man erreichen, daß der erste Summand jedes Elementes der i-ten Spalte (der vorher erzeugten Matrix) verschwindet. Usw.. Durch diese Spaltenoperationen erreicht man, daß $A_1$ äquivalent ist zu der Matrix

$$(34) \qquad \tilde{A}_1 = \begin{pmatrix} p_1(\lambda_1) & p_1(\lambda_1)\cdot 0 & p_1(\lambda_1)\, 0 \\ p_1(\lambda_1)\lambda_1 & p_1(\lambda_1)\cdot 1 & 0 \\ p_1(\lambda_1)\lambda_1^2 & p_1(\lambda_1) 2\lambda_1 \ddots & \vdots \\ \vdots & \vdots & p_1(\lambda_1)(m_1-1)\,! \\ \vdots & \vdots & \vdots \\ p_1(\lambda_1)\lambda_1^{P-1} & p_1(\lambda_1)(P-1)\lambda_1^{P-2} & p_1(\lambda_1)(P-1)\ldots(P-1-m_1)\lambda_1^{P-m_1} \end{pmatrix}.$$

Dies machen wir mit jeder Matrix $A_k$ aus (33). Dann erhalten wir unter der Voraussetzung (26) schließlich

$$(35) \qquad \det A = \prod_{k=1}^{L} p_1(\lambda_k)^{m_k} \cdot V \quad ,$$

wobei V eine verallgemeinerte Vandermondsche Determinante ist. Für $x = b$ erhält man ein analoges Resultat. Zusammenfassend haben wir daher

S A T Z 2. Unter den Voraussetzungen von Satz 1 seien separierte zusätzliche Randbedingungen entweder durch "Randextrapolation" oder durch "Diskretisierung in Randnähe" gegeben. Ferner sei jeweils die (notwendige) Bedingung (26) erfüllt. Dann gilt für die "Randextrapolation" stets $\det H \neq 0$. Besitzt das charakteristische Polynom $p_1(x)$ der "Diskretisierung in Randnähe" keine gemeinsame Nullstelle mit dem charakteristischen Polynom $p(x)$ der gegebenen Diskretisierung, so ist auch $\det H \neq 0$.

LITERATUR

[1] Esser, H., Stabilitätsungleichungen für Diskretisierungen von Randwertaufgaben gewöhnlicher Differentialgleichungen. Numer. Math. 28 (1977), 69 - 100.

[2] Kreiss, H.O., Difference approximations for boundary- and eigenvalue problems in ordinary differential equations. Math. Comput. 26 (1972), 605 - 624.

# IX
# Probability Theory and Other Applications

# FOURIER SERIES AND MARTINGALE TRANSFORMS

Ferenc Schipp
Department of Numerical Analysis
Eötvös Loránd's University
Budapest

In this paper a theorem of D.L. Burkholder [2], [3] on martingale transforms is generalized for the case when the index set on the martingale is a directed set. Using a generalization of the notion of stopping time and applying an elementary lemma, the proof of the generalized theorem is similar to the original one. From the mentioned theorem there follows without difficulties a generalization of a theorem of P. Billard [1]: The product system of independent complex valued functions with zero expectation and module one is an a.e. convergence system. The results obtained show that Carleson's method [4] is essentially a martingale theoretic method.

## 1. Introduction

Let $(X,A,P)$ be a probability space, $(A_n,\ n\in\mathbb{N})$ ($\mathbb{N}:=\{0,1,2,\dots\}$) a non-decreasing sequence of sub-$\sigma$-fields of $A$. Denote by $\|f\|_p$ $(1\leq p\leq\infty)$ the $L^p(X,A,P)$-norm of the function $f\in L^p(X,A,P)$, $E_n$ the conditional expectation operator relative to $A_n$. By the well known martingale maximal inequality (see e.g. [3], [5], [8]) the maximal operator $E^*f := \sup_n |E_nf|$ $(f\in L^1)$ is of weak type (1,1), more precisely, for every $y>0$

$$yP\{E^*f>y\}\leq \int_{\{E^*f>y\}} |f|\,dP \leq \|f\|_1. \tag{1.1}$$

Doob's inequality

$$\|E^*f\|_p \leq q\|f\|_p \qquad (1<p<\infty,\ p^{-1}+q^{-1}=1) \tag{1.2}$$

follows immediately from (1.1).

If $a_n\in L^1(X,A_{n-1},P)$ and $\|a_n\|_\infty\leq 1$, then the sequence of partial sums $\sum_{k=1}^n a_k(E_kf-E_{k-1}f)$ $(n\in\mathbb{N}^* :=\mathbb{N}\setminus\{0\},\ f\in L^1)$ is a martingale (with respect to $(A_n,\ n\in\mathbb{N})$), which is called the transform of the martingale $(E_nf,\ n\in\mathbb{N})$.

The following generalization of the martingale maximal theorem is due to D.L. Burkholder [2]; see also [5] and [8].

THEOREM A. *Denote by*

$$T_a f := \sup_n \left|\sum_{k=1}^n a_k (E_k f - E_{k-1} f)\right| \quad (a = (a_1, a_2, \ldots),\ f \in L^1)$$

*the maximal operator of the transform of* $E_n$. *Then the operator is of weak type* (1,1), *i.e. for every* $y>0$

$$y\,P\{T_a f > y\} \leqslant 18 \|f\|_1 \qquad (f \in L^1). \tag{1.3}$$

For functions $f \in L^1$ satisfying the inequalities

$$|E_{n+1} f| \leqslant c\,|E_n f| \qquad (n \in \mathbb{N}) \tag{1.4}$$

by using stopping time method and an elementary lemma, (1.3) can easily be proved. Recall that the function $\nu: X \to \overline{\mathbb{N}} := \mathbb{N} \cup \{\infty\}$ is a stopping time, relative to $(A_n,\ n \in \mathbb{N})$, if for all $n \in \mathbb{N}$ $\{\nu=n\} := \{x \in X:\ \nu(x)=n\} \in A_n$.

From the fact that $T_a$ is of strong type (2,2), by the Marcinkiewicz interpolation theorem and usual duality arguments it follows that for every $1<p<\infty$ $T_a$ has (uniformly) strong type (p,p), i.e.

$$\|T_a f\|_p \leqslant K_p \|f\|_p \qquad (f \in L^p) \tag{1.5}$$

with a constant $K_p$ depending only on p (see [5], [8]).

In this paper we generalize the above mentioned theorem for some martingales with directed index set. We will assume that the countable ordered index set $(T, \leqslant)$ has the following properties: a) every non-empty subset of T has a minimal element, b) for every $s,t \in T$ there exists the envelope $s \vee t := \sup\{s,t\} \in T$, c) for every $s \in T$ the set $\{t \in T:\ s \leqslant t\}$ is linearly ordered, d) for all $s \in T$ the set $\{t \in T:\ t \leqslant s\}$ is finite.

Let $(B_t, t \in T)$ be a nondecreasing sequence of sub-$\sigma$-fields of A, and denote $M := \{\min H:\ H \subseteq T\}$. Suppose that $B_s = B_t$ if $s_+ = t_+$, where $\{s_+\} := \min\{t:\ s \leqslant t,\ s \neq t\}$, further let $B_{r-} := B_s$ if $s_+ = r$. We introduce the following generalization of the concept of stopping time: A mapping $\tau: X \to M$ is called a stopping time (relative to $(B_t,\ t \in T)$) if

$$\{t \in \tau\} := \{x \in X:\ t \in \tau(x)\} \in A_t \quad \text{for all } t \in T.$$

If $T$ is a linearly ordered set, then $\tau$ is a stopping time in the usual sense. Let $g_t : X \to [0,+\infty)$ $(t \in T)$ be $B_t$-measurable, i.e. let $(g_t,\ t \in T)$ be an adapted sequence with respect to $(B_t,\ t \in T)$. Then the functions $\tau_y : X \to M$ defined by

$$\tau_y(x) := \min\{t \in T:\ g_t(x) > y\} \quad (x \in X,\ y > 0) \tag{1.6}$$

are stopping times.

Inequality (1.1) is equivalent to

$$y \sum_{n=0}^{\infty} P\{\nu_y = n\} = y\, P\{E^*f > y\} \leqslant \int_{\{\nu_y < \infty\}} |f|\, dP, \tag{1.7}$$

where $\nu_y$ denotes the following stopping time (relative to $(A_n,\ n \in \mathbb{N})$),

$$\nu_y(x) := \min\{n:\ |(E_n f)(x)| > y\} \quad (x \in X,\ y > 0). \tag{1.8}$$

This form of the martingale maximal inequality can be generalized as follows. Let $h_t : X \to \mathbb{C}$ $(t \in T_o := \min I)$ be a system of A-measurable functions for which $|h_t| = 1$ $(t \in T_o)$ and

$$\text{(1.9)} \qquad \begin{aligned} &\text{i)}\ \ h_s \bar{h}_t \in L^1(X, B_{(s \vee t)+}, P), \\ &\text{ii)}\ \ E(h_s \bar{h}_t \mid B_{s \vee t}) = 0 \quad (s,t \in T_o,\ s \neq t). \end{aligned}$$

Here $E(h \mid B_t)$ denotes the conditional expectation of $h \in L^1$ relative to $B_t$.

THEOREM 1. <u>Let</u> $f \in L^2$ <u>and</u>

$$g_t := \sup\{|E(f\bar{h}_s \mid B_t)| :\ s \in T_o,\ s \leqslant t\}. \tag{1.10}$$

*Then for the stopping time* $\tau_y$ *defined in* (1.6) *we have*

$$y^2 \sum_{t\in T} P\{t\in\tau_y\} \leq \int_{\{\tau_y \neq \emptyset\}} |f|^2 \, dP \quad (y>0). \tag{1.11}$$

We give a generalization of Theorem A. Denote $\Delta_t(f) := E(f|B_{t_+}) - E(f|B_t)$ $(t\in T)$, and let $b_t \in L^\infty(X, B_t, P)$ $(t\in T)$ be a function system with $\|b_t\|_\infty \leq 1$ $(t\in T)$. We will consider the following condition analogous to (1.4):

$$|E(f\bar{h}_r|B_{t_+})| \leq c \sup\{|E(f\bar{h}_s|B_t)| : s\in T_o,\ s\leq t\} \quad (r\in T_o,\ r\leq t). \tag{1.12}$$

Note that by (1.9) i)

$$|E(f\bar{h}_r|B_{t_+})| = |E(f\bar{h}_s|B_{t_+})| \quad (r\leq t,\ s\leq t,\ r,s\in T_o,\ t\in T). \tag{1.13}$$

THEOREM 2. *Suppose that* f *satisfies condition* (1.12), *and let*

$$S_b f := \sup\{|\textstyle\sum_{s\leq t\leq r} b_t \Delta_t(f\bar{h}_s)| : s\leq r,\ s\in T_o\}. \tag{1.14}$$

*Then for every* y>0

$$y^2 P\{S_b f > y\} \leq K_c \|f\|_2^2. \tag{1.15}$$

*where* $K_c$ *depends only on the constant* c *in* (1.12).

To prove Theorem A and Theorem 2 we use an elementary lemma. Assume that G is a nonnegative decreasing function on $[0,+\infty)$ satisfying the growth condition $G(y/2) \leq 2^u G(y)$ with some u>0. Suppose that $g_y$ (y>0) are nonnegative measurable functions on the probability space (X,A,P) with $\lim_{y\to 0} g_y = 0$, and that $g_y$ is increasing in y, i.e. $g_y \leq g_t$ if 0<y<t.

LEMMA. *Let* 0<u<v, c>0 *be real numbers such that*

$$P\{g_{2y} - g_y > czy\} \leq z^{-v} G(y) \quad (z>1,\ y>0). \tag{1.16}$$

*Then there exist two constants* C *and* R, *depending only on* u, v *and* c, *such that*

(1.17) $$P\{g_y > Cy\} \leqslant R\,G(y) \quad (y>0).$$

Theorem 2 has some interesting applications. Let $\varphi_n : X \to \mathbb{C}$ $(n \in \mathbb{N}^*)$ be a function system having the following properties:

(1.18) $$\text{i) } |\varphi_n| = 1, \quad \text{ii) } E_{n-1}(\varphi_n) = 0, \quad \text{iii) } \varphi_n \in L^1(X, A_n, P).$$

The system

$$\psi_n := \prod_{k=1}^{\infty} \varphi_k^{n_k} \qquad (n = \textstyle\sum_{k=1}^{\infty} n_k 2^{k-1} \in \mathbb{N})$$

is called the product system of $(\varphi_n,\ n \in \mathbb{N}^*)$. Applying Theorem 2 we obtain

THEOREM 3. The system $(\psi_n,\ n \in \mathbb{N})$ is an a.e. convergence system, i.e. for every sequence $(a_n,\ n \in \mathbb{N})$ with $\sum |a_n|^2 < \infty$ the series $\sum a_n \psi_n$ converges a.e.

Hence it follows that

COROLLARY. The product system of complex valued, independent functions with zero expectation and absolute value 1 is a convergence system.

This is a generalization of Billard's result [1] which asserts that the Walsh-Paley system is a convergence system. Further examples are given in [7].

## 2. Proof of the Theorems

2.1 Stopping Times. We shall use some properties of stopping times. First we introduce a relation in the set $\{A :\ A \subseteq T\}$ denoted by $\leqslant$. For $A, B \subseteq T$ let $A \leqslant B$, if for every $b \in B$ there exists an $a \in A$ such that $a \leqslant b$. It is easy to see that the relation $\leqslant$ is an ordering on the set M; further, for every $A, B \subseteq T$

(2.1) $$\text{i) } \min A \leqslant A, \quad \text{ii) } A \subseteq B \text{ implies } B \leqslant A,$$
$$\text{iii) } A \subseteq B \text{ implies } \min B \leqslant \min A.$$

From this there immediately follows that for every $A,B\in M$ there exist the envelopes $A\vee B := \sup\{A,B\}$, $A\wedge B := \inf\{A,B\}$ and

$$A\vee B = \min\{s\vee t : s\in A,\ t\in B\},\qquad A\wedge B = \min A\cup B; \tag{2.2}$$

thus $(M,\leqslant)$ is a net.

Denote by $\mathcal{T}$ the set of stopping times relative to $(B_t,\ t\in T)$. For $\tau,\sigma\in\mathcal{T}$ let $\tau\leqslant\sigma$, if for every $x\in X$ $\tau(x)\leqslant\sigma(x)$ holds. Further, let $(\tau\vee\sigma)(x) := \tau(x)\vee\sigma(x)$, $(\tau\wedge\sigma)(x) := \tau(x)\wedge\sigma(x)$ $(x\in X)$. In this way an ordering is defined in $\mathcal{T}$ and an easy computation shows that $(\mathcal{T},\leqslant)$ is a net. Further, for every $t\in T$ the stopping time $X\ni x\to\{t\}\subset T$ is denoted by $t$, and for $\tau,\sigma\in\mathcal{T}$ we use the notation $\{\tau\leqslant\sigma\} := \{x\in X :\ \tau(x)\leqslant\sigma(x)\}$.

Note that by the definition of stopping time

$$\text{(2.3)}\qquad \begin{array}{ll} \text{i)} & \{t\in\tau\}\cap\{s\in\tau\} = \emptyset \ \text{ if } \ \tau\in\mathcal{T} \text{ and } s<t\ (s,t\in T),\\ \text{ii)} & \tau\in\mathcal{T} \text{ if and only if } \{\tau\leqslant t\}\in B_t \text{ for all } t\in T. \end{array}$$

From the definition of $\tau_y$ it follows (see (1.6), (2.1), and (2.2)) that

$$\text{(2.4)}\qquad \begin{array}{ll} \text{i)} & s\leqslant t<s\vee\tau_y(x) \quad \text{implies} \quad |g_t(x)|\leqslant y,\\ \text{ii)} & \tau_y\leqslant\tau_z \quad \text{if} \quad 0<y<z\\ \text{iii)} & s\vee r = s\vee\tau_y(x) < s\vee\tau_{2y}(x) \quad (r\in\tau_y(x)) \text{ implies}\\ & \qquad\qquad r\vee\tau_{2y}(x) = s\vee\tau_{2y}(x). \end{array}$$

2.2 Proof of the Lemma. Let $0<q<1$ be a number such that $w:=u-qv<0$. Applying (1.14) for $z=2^{qk}$ and for $y2^{-k}$ $(k\in\mathbb{N})$ instead of $y$, we get

$$P\{g_{y2^{-k+1}} - g_{y2^{-k}} > 2^{-k(1-q)}c\,y\} \leqslant 2^{-vkq}G(y2^{-k}) = 2^{wk}G(y) \quad (y>0,\ k\in\mathbb{N}^*),$$

and this gives

$$P\{g_y > c(2^{1-q}-1)^{-1}y\} \leqslant \sum_{k=1}^{\infty} P\{g_{y2^{-k+1}} - g_{y2^{-k}} > 2^{-k(1-q)}y\}$$

$$\leqslant (2^{-w}-1)^{-1}G(y) \quad (y>0).$$

2.3 Proof of Theorem A under Condition (1.4). Let

$$g_y := \sup\{|\textstyle\sum_{k=1}^{n} a_k(E_k f - E_{k-1} f)| : n \leqslant \nu_y\} \qquad (y>0),$$

where $\nu_y$ denotes the stopping time introduced in (1.8). Let I(A) denote the indicator function of the set $A \subseteq X$. Obviously,

$$g_{2y} - g_y \leqslant \sup\{|\textstyle\sum_{k=1}^{n} I\{\nu_y < k \leqslant \nu_{2y}\}\, a_k\, (E_k - E_{k-1}) f| : n \in \mathbb{N}^*\},$$

and the set $\{\nu_y < k \leqslant \nu_{2y}\}$ is $A_{k-1}$-measurable. This implies that the functions $u_k := I\{\nu_y < k \leqslant \nu_{2y}\} a_k (E_k - E_{k-1}) f$ $(k \in \mathbb{N})$ are orthogonal, and by (1.2) we have

$$P\{g_{2y} - g_y > zy\} \leqslant 4(zy)^{-2} \sup_n \|\textstyle\sum_{k=1}^{n} u_k\|_2^2 = 4(zy)^{-2} \sup_n \|\textstyle\sum_{k=1}^{n} |u_k|^2\|_1 \leqslant$$

$$\leqslant 4(zy)^{-2} \sup_n \|\textstyle\sum_{k=1}^{n} I\{\nu_y < k < \nu_{2y}\}(E_k - E_{k-1}) f\|_2^2$$

$$= 4(zy)^{-2} \sup_n \|(E_{\nu_{2y\wedge n}} f - E_{\nu_y} f)\, I\{\nu_y < \nu_{2y}\}\|_2^2,$$

where $E_{\nu_y} f = E_m f$ on the set $\{\nu_y = m\}$. By the definition of $\nu_y$ and by (1.4), on the set $\{\nu_y < \nu_{2y}\}$ we have $|E_{\nu_y} f| \leqslant 2y$ and $|E_{\nu_{2y\wedge n}} f| \leqslant 2cy$ if $n \geqslant 1$; therefore by (1.7)

$$P\{g_{2y} - g_y > zy\} \leqslant 16(c+1)^2 z^{-2} P\{\nu_y < \infty\} \leqslant 16(c+1)^2 z^{-2} y^{-1} \|f\|_1.$$

Applying the lemma with $G(y) = 16(c+1)^2 y^{-1} \|f\|_1$, u=1 and v=2, we get

$$P\{g_y > Cy\} \leqslant 16R(c+1)^2 y^{-1} \|f\|_1.$$

Since $T_a f = g_y$ on the set $\{\nu_y = \infty\}$ by (1.7), we have

$$P\{T_a f > Cy\} \leqslant P\{g_y > Cy\} + P\{\nu_y < \infty\} \leqslant \tilde{R} y^{-1} \|f\|_1$$

and (1.3) is proved.

2.4 Proof of Theorem 2. Let

$$U_y^s := \sup\{|\sum_{s\leq t\leq \bar{t}} b_t\Delta_t(f\bar{h}_s)| : s\leq\bar{t}<s\vee\tau_y\} \qquad (s\in T_o),$$

$$U_y := \sup\{U_y^s : s\in T_o\}$$

where $\tau_y$ denotes the stopping time defined in Theorem 1. If $s\in T_o$, $s\vee\tau_y(x) < s\vee\tau_{2y}(x)$ and $r\in\tau_y(x)$ is such an element that $s_o:=s\vee r=s\vee\tau_y(x)$, then by (2.4) iii) $r\vee\tau_{2y}(x) = s\vee\tau_{2y}(x)$. Therefore by (1.9) i), (2.4) i) and by the definition of $\tau_y$ for an arbitrary $\bar{r}\leq r$, $\bar{r}\in T_o$ we have

$$U_{2y}^s(x) \leq U_y^s(x) + \sup\{|\sum_{s_o\leq t\leq\bar{t}} b_t(x)\Delta_t(f\bar{h}_s)(x)| : s_o\leq\bar{t}<s\vee\tau_{2y}(x)\}$$

$$\leq U_y^s(x) + |E(f\bar{h}_s|B_{s_o})(x)| + |E(f\bar{h}_{\bar{r}}|B_{s_o})(x)|$$

$$+ \sup\{|\sum_{s_o\leq t<\bar{t}} b_t(x)\Delta_t(f\bar{h}_{\bar{r}})(x)| : s_o\leq\bar{t}<r\vee\tau_{2y}(x)\}$$

$$\leq U_y^s + 4y + 2\,V_y^r(x),$$

where

$$V_y^r := I\{r\in\tau_y\}\sup\{|\sum_{r\leq t\leq\bar{t}} I\{t<r\vee\tau_{2y}\}b_t\Delta_t(f\bar{h}_{\bar{r}})| : r<\bar{t}\}$$

and $\bar{r}\leq r$, $\bar{r}\in T_o$. Thus

$$U_{2y}-U_y \leq 4y + \sup\{2\,V_y^r : r\in T\},$$

and for every $z>1$, $y>0$

$$P\{U_{2y}-U_y > 6zy\} \leq \sum_{r\in T} P\{V_y^r > zy\}.$$

From (1.5), (2.4) i) and by the definition of $\tau_y$ we have

$$P\{V_y^r > zy\} \leq K_6(zy)^{-6} \sup_{r \leq \bar{t}} \| I\{r \in \tau_y\} \sum_{r \leq t \leq \bar{t}} I\{t < r \vee \tau_{2y}\} \Delta_t(f\bar{h}_{\bar{r}}) \|_6^6$$

$$\leq K_6 z^{-6} (2(c+1))^6 \, P\{r \in \tau_y\},$$

and by (1.11)

$$P\{U_{2y} - U_y > 6zy\} \leq \bar{K}(c) z^{-6} y^{-2} \|f\|_2^2.$$

From the definition of $U_y$ by (1.12) it follows that $U_y \leq U_z$ if $0<y<z$ and $\lim_{y \to 0} U_y = 0$. Applying Lemma with c=6, u=2, v=6 and $G(y) = \bar{K}_c y^{-2} \| f \|_2^2$, we get

$$P\{U_y > Cy\} \leq \tilde{K}(c) y^{-2} \| f \|_2^2.$$

Since $S_b f = U_y$ on the set $\{\tau_y = \emptyset\}$ by (1.11), we get

$$P\{S_b > Cy\} \leq P\{\tau_y \neq \emptyset\} + P\{U_y > Cy\} \leq K_c y^{-2} \| f \|_2^2$$

and Theorem 2 is proved.

2.5 Proof of Theorem 1. From the definition of $g_t$ it follows that there exists a system of sets $H_{s,t}$ $(s \leq t,\ s \in T_o,\ t \in T)$ such that $H_{s,t} \in B_t$, $H_{s,t} \cap H_{\bar{s},t} = \emptyset$ if $s \neq \bar{s}$, $|E(f\bar{h}_s | B_t)| \geq |E(f\bar{h}_{\bar{s}} | B_t)|$ on the set $H_{s,t}$ for all $\bar{s} \leq t$, $\bar{s} \in T_o$ and $\bigcup_{s \leq t,\ s \in T_o} H_{s,t} = \{t \in \tau_y\}$. By the definition of $\tau_y$ we have $|E(f\bar{h}_s | B_t)| \geq y$ on the set $H_{s,t}$. Let $u_{s,t} = I(H_{s,t}) h_s$ $(s \leq t,\ s \in T_o,\ t \in T)$. Then by (1.9) ii) and (2.3) i) we have $E(u_{s,t} \bar{u}_{\bar{s},\bar{t}} | B_{s \vee \bar{s}}) = 0$ if $(s,t) \neq (\bar{s},\bar{t})$, thus $(u_{s,t},\ s<t,\ s \in T_o,\ t \in T)$ is a $(B_t,\ t \in T)$ orthonormal system (see [6]). Applying the generalization of Bessel's inequality [6] to the function $I\{\tau_y \neq \emptyset\} f$ we obtain

$$\int_{\{\tau_y \neq \emptyset\}} |f|^2 \, dP \geq \sum_{t \in T} \sum_{\substack{s \leq t \\ s \in T_o}} \int_X I(H_{s,t}) |E(f\bar{h}_s | B_t)|^2 dP \geq y^2 \sum_{t \in T} P\{t \in \tau_y\}.$$

2.6 Proof of Theorem 3. Let f be a $\psi$-polynomial, i.e. a linear combination of the $\psi_k$'s. Then the n-th partial sum of the Fourier series of f with respect to the orthonormal system $(\psi_n, n\in N)$ can be written in the form (see [7])

$$S_n f = \psi_n \sum_{k=1}^{\infty} n_k (E_k - E_{k-1})(f\,\bar{\psi}_n) \qquad (n = \sum_{k=1}^{\infty} n_k 2^{k-1} \in \mathbb{N}).$$

For $n = \sum_{k=1}^{\infty} n_k 2^k \in \mathbb{N}$ set $n^l := \sum_{k=1}^{\infty} n_l 2^{l-1}$ and let

$$T := \{(n^l, l) : n \in \mathbb{N},\ l \in \mathbb{N}\}.$$

We introduce in the set T the following ordering: let $(n^r,r) < (m^s,s)$, if $r<s$ and $m^s = n^s$. Then the relation $\leqslant$ is a (partial) ordering on the set T and T satisfies conditions a)-d). Further, for $t=(n^l,l)\in T$ we set $B_t = A_{l-1}$, $b_t = n_l$ and $h_{\bar{t}} = \psi_n$ if $\bar{t} = (n^l,l)\in T_0$. Then

$$|S_n f| = \Big|\sum_{\bar{t}\leqslant t} b_t \Delta_t (f\psi_{\bar{t}})\Big| \qquad (\bar{t} = (n^l,l)\in T_0),$$

and the condition (1.12) is satisfied with c=2 for every $\psi$-polynomial. Applying Theorem 2 we obtain Theorem 3.

## REFERENCES

[1] Billard, P., Sur la convergence presque partout des series de Fourier-Walsh des fonctions de l'espace $L^2(0,1)$. Studia Math. 28 (1967), 363 - 388.

[2] Burkholder, D.L., Martingale transforms. Ann. Math. Statist. 37 (1966), 1494 - 1504.

[3] Burkholder, D.L., Distribution function inequalities for martingales. Annals of Prob. 1 (1973), 19 - 42.

[4] Carleson, L., On convergence and growth of partial sums of Fourier series. Acta Math. 116 (1966), 135 - 157.

[5] Neveu, I., Discrete-parameter Martingales. North-Holland Math. Library, Amsterdam, Oxford, New-York 1975.

[6] Schipp, F., On a generalization of the concept of orthogonality. Acta Sci. Math. 37 (1975), 275 - 285.

[7] Schipp. F., Pointwise convergence of expansions with respect to certain product systems. Anal. Math. 2 (1976), 65 - 75.

[8] Stein, E.M., Topics in Harmonic Analysis related to the Littlewood-Paley Theory. Ann. of Math. Studies, Princeton 1970.

# INVERSE THEOREMS ON THE RATE OF APPROXIMATION FOR CERTAIN LIMIT THEOREMS IN PROBABILITY THEORY

Lothar Hahn
Lehrstuhl A für Mathematik
Rheinisch-Westfälische Technische Hochschule
Aachen

In this paper it is shown that the results in [5], concerning direct theorems for convergence in distribution with rates of random variables to general limiting random variables, are best possible in the sense that the existence of certain conditions upon the moments of the random variables in question are not only sufficient for a prescribed rate of convergence to zero and a fixed class of functions but also necessary. Different versions of $\mathcal{O}$-inverse theorems as well as $o$-inverse theorems are proved.

## 1. Introduction

In [5], it is mentioned that the results of the general as well as of the concrete direct theorems are best possible. Partial results, i.e. in the particular case of the central limit theorem (CLT) for identically distributed (i.d.) random variables (r.v.), were already presented in [4] and [2] (in the latter one for the weak law of large numbers (WLLN) too). The purpose of this paper is to give rather general results concerning inverse theorems on rate of convergence in distribution of sequences of r.v.

Just as in the paper [5], our goal is again to try to avoid the Fourier analytic machinery, thus the use of the characteristic functions - used in [6] for inverse results -, and instead to employ elementary methods, particularly the calculus of operators and methods of approximation theory as well as the $\varphi$-decomposition of the limiting r.v. in question.

While Sec. 2 is concerned with questions of notations, the K-functional and generalized moduli of continuity and Lipschitz classes, Sec. 3 deals with general inverse theorems for i.d. r.v. and these are applied in Sec. 4 to the stable limit law, the CLT and the WLLN. In the first part of Sec. 5, a general inverse theorem together with its applications for not necessarily i.d. r.v. is presented; it seems to be the first inverse result in the literature for not necessarily i.d. r.v. In the second part of Sec. 5 there follows a brief discussion of the difficulties that occur if one tries to generalize all different versions of the inverse theorems to not necessarily i.d. r.v.

I would like to thank Prof. Dr. P.L. Butzer for his critical reading of the manuscript and for valuable comments as well as Dr. W. Splettstößer for lively discussions.

This work was supported by research grant No II B4 - FA 7107 of "Der Minister für Wissenschaft und Forschung des Landes Nordrhein-Westfalen".

## 2. Notations and Preliminaries

Let $C = C(\mathbb{R})$ denote the vector space of all continuous, real-valued functions defined on the real axis $\mathbb{R}$, $C_b = C_b(\mathbb{R})$ the subset of C consisting of all bounded and uniformly continuous functions on $\mathbb{R}$, endowed with norm $\|f\| := \sup_{x\in\mathbb{R}}|f(x)|$. For $r \in \mathbb{P} := \{0,1,2,\ldots\}$ set

$$C_b^r = \{f \in C;\ \ f', f'', \ldots, f^{(r-1)} \in C,\ f^{(r)} \in C_b\} .$$

A further function class needed below will be $L(F_Z)$, the space of all functions $f(x)$ for which also all of their translations $f(x+y)$ are integrable with respect to $F_Z$, Z being any real r.v.

For any f belonging to the algebraic sum

$$C_b + C_b^r := \{f \in C;\ f = f_1 + f_2,\ \ f_1 \in C_b,\ \ f_2 \in C_b^r\}$$

and any $t \geq 0$, the K-functional is defined by

$$K(t;f;C_b + C_b^r, C_b^r) := \inf_{f=f_1+f_2} \{\|f_1\| + t\|f_2^{(r)}\|\} .$$

It satisfies the inequality

$$(2.1) \qquad K(t;f;C_b + C_b^r, C_b^r) \leqslant \begin{cases} \|f\| , & f \in C_b \\ t\|f^{(r)}\| , & f \in C_b^r \end{cases} ,$$

and is equivalent to the rth modulus of continuity, defined for $f \in C_b + C_b^r$ by

$$\omega_r(t;f;C_b + C_b^r) := \sup_{|h|\leqslant t} \| \sum_{k=0}^{r} (-1)^{r-k} \binom{r}{k} f(u+kh)\| .$$

Indeed, for any $f \in C_b + C_b^r$, $t \geqslant 0$, there are constants $c_{1,r}$, $c_{2,r}$ such that (see [1, pp 192, 258])

$$(2.2) \qquad c_{1,r}\omega_r(t^{1/r};f;C_b + C_b^r) \leqslant K(t;f;C_b + C_b^r, C_b^r) \leqslant c_{2,r}\omega_r(t^{1/r};f;C_b + C_b^r) .$$

Lipschitz classes of order $r \in \mathbb{N}$ are defined as usual for $0 < \alpha \leqslant r$ by

$$(2.3) \qquad \mathrm{Lip}(\alpha;r;C_b + C_b^r) := \{f \in C_b + C_b^r ; \omega_r(t;f;C_b + C_b^r) \leqslant L_f t^{\alpha}\} .$$

If Z is any real r.v., the operator $V_Z$ is defined by

$$(2.4) \qquad V_Z f(y) := \int_{\mathbb{R}} f(x+y)dF_Z(x) \qquad (f \in L(F_Z);\ y \in \mathbb{R}) .$$

Finally, set $f_j(x) := x^j$, $j \in \mathbb{P}$, and for $\alpha \in \mathbb{R}^+$, let $]\alpha[$ be the greatest integer less than or equal to $\alpha$, and $[\alpha]$ the smallest integer greater than or equal to $\alpha$.

## 3. General Inverse Theorems for Identically Distributed Random Variables

3.1 Basic Lemma and First General Theorem. Let $Z_{i,n}$ be the independent components of the $\varphi$-decomposition of the limiting r.v. Z, associated with the given normalizing function $\varphi : \mathbb{N} \to R^+$, i.e.,

$$(3.1) \qquad F_{\varphi(n)\Sigma_{i=n}^{n} Z_{i,n}} = F_Z .$$

For abbrevation set $U_n := \sum_{i=1}^n Z_{i,n}$ and $S_n := \sum_{i=1}^n X_i$, where $(X_i)_{i\in\mathbb{N}}$ is a sequence of real , independent r.v.

In [5], it was stated that for $f \in L(F_{T_n+Z})$

$$(3.2) \qquad \|V_{\varphi(n)S_n} f - V_Z f\| = \|V_{\varphi(n)S_n} f - V_{\varphi(n)U_n} f\| \leqslant \sum_{i=1}^{n} \|V_{\varphi(n)X_i} - V_{\varphi(n)Z_{i,n}}\| .$$

This inequality was essential for the proofs of the direct theorems given in [5]. In order to obtain inverse results, we are forced to look for those functions f that guarantee equality in (3.2). Under some further restrictions, the functions $f_j$ will do so, with (3.2) being taken not in the norm but in the pointwise sense. This is the mathematical background of the following lemma concerning moments. In this instance, we need not restrict ourselves to the special case of i.d. r.v.

LEMMA 1. Let Z, $X_1$, $X_2$,... be real, independent r.v. with $E(X_i^j) < \infty$ and $E(Z_{i,n}^j) < \infty$ for $1 \leqslant i \leqslant n$, $n \in N$ and some $j \in \mathbb{N}$. Suppose further that

$$(3.3) \qquad \mu_{m,i,n} := \int_{\mathbb{R}} x^m d[F_{X_i}(x) - F_{Z_{i,n}}(x)] = 0 \qquad (0 \leqslant m \leqslant j-1;\ 1 \leqslant i \leqslant n,\ n \in \mathbb{N}).$$

Then one has

$$E([\varphi(n)S_n]^j) - E(Z^j) = \sum_{i=1}^{n} \{E([\varphi(n)X_i]^j) - E([\varphi(n)Z_{i,n}]^j)\} .$$

PROOF. From the assumptions follows at once that $E([\varphi(n)S_n]^j)$ as well as $E(Z^j)$ are finite. Because of (3.1) one further has $E(Z^j) = E([\varphi(n)U_n]^j)$, which gives

$$E([\varphi(n)S_n]^j) - E(Z^j) = \varphi(n)^j [E(S_n^j) - E(U_n^j)].$$

Now the multinomial theorem and the independence of the r.v. in question yield

$$(3.4) \qquad E(S_n^j) = \sum \frac{j!}{\nu_1!\dots\nu_n!} \alpha_{\nu_1,1}\, \alpha_{\nu_2,2} \cdots \alpha_{\nu_n,n}$$

$$(3.5) \qquad E(U_n^j) = \frac{j!}{\nu_1!\dots\nu_n!} \eta_{\nu_1,1,n}\, \eta_{\nu_2,2,n} \cdots \eta_{\nu_n,n,n} \qquad ,$$

where $\alpha_{k,i} := E(X_i^k)$, $\eta_{k,i,n} := E(Z_{i,n}^k)$, and both sums are extended over all integers for which $\sum_{k=1}^n \nu_k = j$, $\nu_k \in \mathbb{P}$.

Since $\alpha_{k,i} = \eta_{k,i,n}$ by (3.3), each summand in (3.4) occurs in (3.5) if $\nu_k \leq j-1$, $1 \leq k \leq n$. It follows that for the difference $E(S_n^j) - E(U_n^j)$ those terms vanish for which $(\nu_1,\dots,\nu_n) \in \mathbb{P}^n$ with $\nu_k \leq j-1$, $1 \leq k \leq n$. In other words, the only remaining n terms are those for which one $\nu_k$ is equal to j, $1 \leq k \leq n$, which in turn implies that all other $\nu_i = 0$, $i \neq k$. Altogether, this yields the desired assertion.

As a simple Corollary we obtain

COROLLARY 1. _Under the assumptions of La. 1 it follows that for each_ $y \in \mathbb{R}$, $1 \leq i \leq n$, $n \in \mathbb{N}$,

i) $$V_{\varphi(n)X_i} f_j(y) - V_{\varphi(n)Z_{i,n}} f_j(y) = V_{\varphi(n)X_i} f_j(0) - V_{\varphi(n)Z_{i,n}} f_j(0),$$

ii) $$V_{\varphi(n)S_n} f_j(y) - V_Z f_j(y) = \sum_{i=1}^n [V_{\varphi(n)X_i} f_j(y) - V_{\varphi(n)Z_{i,n}} f_j(y)] .$$

REMARK 1. In [4], La. 1 was proved in the special case that the r.v. $X_i$ are i.d., the limiting r.v. Z as well as the components $Z_{i,n}$ all being (0,1) normally distributed (see Sec. 4,b) and $\varphi(n) = n^{-1/2}$. But the proof presented there, based upon a combinatorial identity, was longer and not so elegant as that given here, although La. 1 is much more general.

Now we are in position to prove inverse results for theorems on $\mathcal{O}$ - as well as $o$ - rates of convergence in distribution for i.d. r.v. $X_i$ and $Z_{i,n}$, $1 \leq i \leq n$, $n \in \mathbb{N}$. It can indeed be shown that conditions upon the existence of the moments $E(X_1^j) - E(Z_{1,1}^j)$ are necessary for the convergence in distribution with rates of the sums $\varphi(n)S_n$ towards Z.

THEOREM 1. _Suppose there exists_ $s \in \mathbb{R}^+$ _such that_ $E(Z^s) < \infty$. _Then_

$$\| (V_{\varphi(n)S_n} - V_Z) f \| \leq M_f n \varphi(n)^\beta \qquad (f \in C_b^{]s[}) \tag{3.6}$$

_for some_ $\beta \in \mathbb{R}^+$ _and constants_ $M_f$ _implies that_

(3.7) i) $E(X_1^{]s[}) < \infty$ ,

(3.8) ii) $E(X_1^j) = E([Z/\varphi(1)]^j)$ $(0 \leq j \leq [\min(s,\beta)] - 1)$.

PROOF. i) Applying (3.6) to the function $f_{]s[}$, which belongs to $C_b^{]s[}$, and setting $y = 0$ in the operator $V_{\varphi(n)S_n} - V_Z$, there exist a constant $\bar{M}$ such that

(3.9) $$|E([\varphi(n)S_n]^{]s[} - Z^{]s[})| \leq \bar{M}n\varphi(n)^\beta \qquad (n \in \mathbb{N}).$$

This proves (3.7) by setting $n = 1$.
ii) Since the r.v. $Z_{i,n}$ are i.d., it follows that

$$E(Z_{i,n}^s) = E(Z_{1,1}^s) = \varphi(1)^{-1}E(Z^s) < \infty.$$

Now suppose that there exists $j_0 \leq [\min(s,\beta)] - 1$ such that

(3.10) $$E(X_1^{j_0}) \neq E(Z_{1,1}^{j_0}).$$

Without loss of generality assume that $j_0 \geq 1$ and that $j_0$ is the first index for which (3.10) holds. Then $E(X_1^m) = E(Z_{1,1}^m)$, $0 \leq m \leq j_0 - 1$, and so La. 1 may be applied. This yields

$$n^{-1}\varphi(n)^{-\beta}|E([\varphi(n)S_n]^{j_0}) - E(Z^{j_0})| = \varphi(n)^{j_0-\beta}|E(X_1^{j_0}) - E(Z_{1,1}^{j_0})| ,$$

which tends to infinity for $n \to \infty$ since $j_0 - \beta < 0$ and $\varphi(n) \to 0$, $n \to \infty$ as well as (3.10). But this contradicts (3.6) in view of (3.9) since $f_{j_0} \in C_b^{]s[}$ .

REMARK 2. Looking at the proof of Thm. 1, it is evident that instead of (3.6) it suffices to assume that

$$|(V_{\varphi(n)S_n} - V_Z)f(0)| = |\int_{\mathbb{R}} f(x)d(F_{\varphi(n)S_n} - F_Z)(x)| \leq M_f n\varphi(n)^\beta .$$

<u>3.2. Alternative Versions.</u> The next theorem presents another version of an inverse theorem.

THEOREM 2. *If there exists* $r \in \mathbb{N}$ *with* $E(Z^r) < \infty$ *and* $\alpha \in (0,r]$ *such that*

(3.11) $$[\varphi(n)]^{\alpha-r+1} = o(n^{(r-\alpha)/r}) \quad ,$$

*then assumption*

(3.12) $$\| (V_{\varphi(n)S_n} - V_Z)f\| \leq M_f n^{\alpha/r}\varphi(n)^{\alpha} \qquad (f \in \mathrm{Lip}(\alpha;r;C_b + C_b^r)\ ,$$

*implies that*

(3.13) i) $$E(X_1^r) < \infty \quad ,$$

(3.14) ii) $$E(X_1^j) = E([Z/\varphi(1)]^j) \qquad (0 \leq j \leq r-1).$$

PROOF. i) Since $f_r \in C_b^r \subset \mathrm{Lip}(\alpha;r;C_b + C_b^r)$ for each $\alpha \in (0,r]$, the proof follows immediately from (3.12) by setting $f = f_r$ and $n = 1$.
ii) Assume there exists a (first) index $j_o \leq r-1$ such that $E(X_1^{j_o}) \neq E(Z_{1,1}^{j_o})$. Then La. 1 leads to

$$n^{-\alpha/r}\varphi(n)^{-\alpha}|E([\varphi(n)S_n]^{j_o}) - E(Z^{j_o})|$$

$$= n^{1-\alpha/r}\varphi(n)^{j_o-\alpha}|E(X_1^{j_o}) - E(Z_{1,1}^{j_o})|$$

$$\geq n^{1-\alpha/r}\varphi(n)^{r-1-\alpha}|E(X_1^{j_o}) - E(Z_{1,1}^{j_o})| \to \infty \qquad (n \to \infty)$$

by (3.11). But this contradicts (3.12) when setting $f = f_{j_o}$ and $y = 0$, noting that $f_{j_o} \in \mathrm{Lip}(\alpha;r;C_b + C_b^r)$ for each $0 < \alpha \leq r$.

If one assumes instead of (3.12) a sharper condition then (3.11) can be dropped and the proof doesn't make use of La. 1.

THEOREM 3. *If* $E(Z^r) < \infty$, *then*

(3.15) $$\|(V_{\varphi(n)S_n} - V_Z)f\| \leqslant M_r \omega_r(n^{1/r}\varphi(n); f; C_b + C_b^r)$$

*implies* (3.13) *and* (3.14).

PROOF. By (2.2) hypothesis (3.15) gives

(3.16) $$\|(V_{\varphi(n)S_n} - V_Z)f\| \leqslant c_{1,r}^{-1} M_r K(n\varphi(n)^r; f; C_b + C_b^r; C_b^r) .$$

Setting $f = f_r \in C_b^r$, this leads by (2.1) to

$$|E([\varphi(n)S_n]^r - Z^r)| \leqslant c_{1,r}^{-1} M_r n\varphi(n)^r r\ !$$

Taking n = 1, (3.13) follows.

Since the K-functional $K(t, f_j, C_b + C_b^r, C_b^r)$ vanishes identically by (2.1) for each $t \geqslant 0$, $j \in \{0, 1, \ldots, r-1\}$, (3.14) follows by (3.16) when setting n = 1.

We finally give an inverse theorem in connection with $\mathcal{O}$-rates of convergence.

THEOREM 4. *If* $E(Z^r) < \infty$ *then*

(3.17) $$\|(V_{\varphi(n)S_n} - V_Z)f\| = \mathcal{O}(n\varphi(n)^r) \qquad (f \in C_b^r)$$

*implies that*

i) $E(X_1^r) < \infty$

ii) $E(X_1^j) = E([Z/\varphi(1)]^j)$. $(0 \leqslant j \leqslant r)$

PROOF. i) This follows from Thm. 1 by setting $s = \beta = r$.
ii) Similarly as in the proof of Thm. 1, we obtain from La. 1 for the first index $j_0$, $0 \leqslant j_0 \leqslant r$, satisfying (3.10),

$$n^{-1}\varphi(n)^{-r}|E([\varphi(n)S_n]^{j_o}) - E(Z^{j_o})| \geqslant |E(X_1^{j_o}) - E(Z_{1,1}^{j_o})| \neq 0 \quad ,$$

which contradicts assumption (3.17) for $f = f_r \in C_b^r$.

## 4. Applications for Identically Distributed Random Variables

4.1 The Stable Limit Law with Index $\gamma \in (1,2)$. The first application of our general inverse theorems lead to results for which the d.f. of the limiting r.v. is the symmetric stable d.f. with index $1 < \gamma < 2$ and corresponding r.v. $Y_\gamma$, the characteristic function of which has the form

$$\exp[-c|t|^\gamma] \qquad (c > 0,\ 1 < \gamma < 2).$$

Here the independent components $Z_{i,n}$ are given by $F_{Z_{i,n}} := F_{Y_\gamma}$ and $\varphi(n) := n^{-1/\gamma}$, leading to $\varphi(1) = 1$. Then the following result is a simple application of Thm.1, recalling that $E(Y_\gamma^s) < \infty$ for $s < \gamma$.

THEOREM 5. Let $(X_i)_{i \in \mathbb{N}}$ be a sequence of real, independent i.d. r.v. and $1 < \gamma < 2$, $\beta > 1$. Then

$$\sup_{y \in \mathbb{R}} \left| \int_{\mathbb{R}} f(x+y)\,dF_{S_n/n^{1/\gamma}}(x) - \int_{\mathbb{R}} f(x+y)\,dF_{Y_\gamma}(x) \right| \leqslant M_f n^{1-\beta/\gamma} \qquad (f \in C_b^1)$$

implies that

(4.1) i) $E(X_1) < \infty$, ii) $E(X_1) = E(N_\gamma) = 0$ .

In this instance, Thms. 2 and 3 are not applicable since one has to assume $r \geqslant 2$ (to obtain the same result as in Thm. 5), which is too strong since $C_b^2 \not\subset L(F_{Y_\gamma})$, $\gamma < 2$.

On the other hand we can use the $0$-inverse theorem to obtain immediately from Thm. 4.

THEOREM 6. *Let* $(X_i)_{i\in N}$ *be a sequence of real, independent i.d. r.v. and* $1<\gamma<2$. *Then*

$$\sup_{y\in\mathbb{R}} \left|\int_{\mathbb{R}} f(x+y)\,dF_{S_n/n^{1/\gamma}}(x) - \int_{\mathbb{R}} f(x+y)\,dF_{Y_\gamma}(x)\right| = o(n^{1-1/\gamma}) \qquad (f\in C_b^1;\ n\to\infty)$$

*implies* (4.1).

*4.2 The Central Limit Theorem.* In this application let us consider the limiting r.v. $X^*$ stably distributed with index $\gamma = 2$ and $c = 1/2$, i.e., (0,1) normally distributed with d.f. $F_{X^*}(x) = (1/\sqrt{2\pi})\int_{-\infty}^{x} e^{-u^2/2}du$, and define the independent components by $F_{Z_{i,n}} = F_{X^*}$, $1\leq i\leq n$, $n\in\mathbb{N}$ with $\varphi(n) = n^{-1/2}$. Contrary to the case of stable distributions (with index $0<\gamma<2$), moments of all orders exist for the normal distribution. So one can detach the matter from the particular values $1<s<\gamma<2$, $r=1$, respectively, and instead consider arbitrary $s\in\mathbb{R}^+$, $r\in\mathbb{N}$. The theorems of Sec. 3 lead at once to

THEOREM 7. *Let* $(X_i)_{i\in\mathbb{N}}$ *be a sequence of real, independent i.d. r.v.*
a) *The assumption*

$$D_n(f) := \sup_{y\in\mathbb{R}} \left|\int_{\mathbb{R}} f(x+y)\,dF_{S_n/\sqrt{n}}(x) - \int_{\mathbb{R}} f(x+y)\,dF_{X^*}(x)\right| \leq M_f n^{1-\beta/2}$$

*for* $f\in C_b^{]\beta[}$ *and some* $\beta\in R^+$ *implies that*

$$\text{i)}\quad E(X_1^{]\beta[}) < \infty\ , \qquad \text{ii)}\quad E(X_1^j) = E(X^{*j}) \qquad (0\leq j\leq[\beta]-1).$$

b) $$D_n(f) \leq M_f n^{\alpha/r-\alpha/2} \qquad (f\in \mathrm{Lip}(\alpha;r;C_b+C_b^r),$$

*for some* $r\in\mathbb{N}$, $r\geq 2$ *and*

$$(4.2) \qquad \alpha > \frac{r(r-3)}{r-2} \qquad \text{if } r\geq 4$$

*implies that*

$$(4.3)\quad \text{i)}\quad E(X_1^r) < \infty, \qquad \text{ii)}\quad E(X_1^j) = E(X^{*j}) \qquad (0\leq j\leq r-1).$$

c) $$D_n(f) \leq M_r \omega_r(n^{1/r-1/2};f;C_b + C_b^r)$$

*implies* (4.3).

For the proof of a) we use Thm. 1 (setting $s = \beta$) and for parts b) and c) Thm. 2 and Thm. 3, resp. Thereby, condition (4.2) corresponds to (3.11).

Together with the direct results of [5] for the limiting r.v. X* we are now in a position to formulate an equivalence theorem with rates for the CLT.

COROLLARY 2. *Let* $(X_i)_{i \in \mathbb{N}}$ *be a sequence of real, independent i.d. r.v.*
a) *Assume that there exists* $\beta \in \mathbb{R}^+ \setminus \mathbb{N}$, $\beta > 2$, *with* $E(X_1^\beta) < \infty$. *Then the following three assertions are equivalent*:

$$\text{i)} \quad E(X_1^j) = E(X^{*j}) \qquad (0 \leq j \leq [\beta]-1),$$

$$\text{(4.4)} \quad \text{ii)} \quad \sup_{y\in\mathbb{R}} \left| \int_{\mathbb{R}} f(x+y)dF_{S_n/\sqrt{n}}(x) - \int_{\mathbb{R}} f(x+y)dF_{X^*}(x) \right| \leq M_f n^{-\frac{(\beta-2)}{2}} \qquad (f \in C^{]\beta[})$$

$$\text{(4.5)} \quad \text{iii)} \quad \left| \int_{\mathbb{R}} f(x)dF_{S_n/\sqrt{n}}(x) - \int_{\mathbb{R}} f(x)dF_{X^*}(x) \right| \leq M_f n^{-\frac{(\beta-2)}{2}} \qquad (f \in C_b^{]\beta[}).$$

b) *If* $\beta = r \in \mathbb{N}$, $r \geq 3$, *then* (4.4), resp. (4.5) *is equivalent to the validity of both*

$$\text{i)} \quad E(X_1^r) < \infty \quad \text{and} \quad \text{ii)} \quad E(X_1^j) = E(X^{*j}) \qquad (0 \leq j \leq r-1).$$

Finally, one can use Thm. 4, to obtain the following $o$-inverse result.

THEOREM 8. *Let* $(X_i)_{i \in \mathbb{N}}$ *be a sequence of real, independent i.d. r.v. Then for some* $r \geq 2$, $r \in \mathbb{N}$,

$$D_n(f) = o(n^{-\frac{(r-2)}{2}}) \qquad (f \in C_b^r)$$

*implies that*

$$\text{i)} \quad E(X_1^r) < \infty, \qquad \text{ii)} \quad E(X_1^j) = E(X^{*j}) \qquad (0 \leq j \leq r).$$

The corresponding $o$-equivalence theorem reads

COROLLARY 3. Let $(X_i)_{i\in\mathbb{N}}$ be a sequence of real, independent i.d. r.v. Then for $r\geq 2$, $r\in\mathbb{N}$, the following are equivalent

i) $E(X_1^r)<\infty;\ E(X_1^j)=E(X^{*j})$ $(0\leq j\leq r)$,

ii) $\sup_{y\in\mathbb{R}}\left|\int_{\mathbb{R}} f(x+y)dF_{S_n/\sqrt{n}}(x)-\int_{\mathbb{R}} f(x+y)dF_{X^*}(x)\right| = o(n^{-\frac{(r-2)}{2}})$ $(f\in C_b^r)$

In [4], it was shown that under the common assumption of the existence of the rth moment the assertions of Cor. 2b are also equivalent to the validity of (4.4) respt. (4.5), not for the class $C_b^r$ but either for the smaller classes $C_B^r := \{f\in C;\ f',f'',\dots f^{(r)}\in C_b\}$ or $\{e^{itx},\ t\in\mathbb{R}\}$. The last one corresponds to the convergence of the characteristic functions. In [4], properties of the characteristic functions were used in the proofs, provided $E(X^r)<\infty$. With the same methods one surely can extend these results to the case $\beta\in\mathbb{R}^+$, $\beta>2$, i.e. the counterparts of Cor. 2a, the function class $C_b^{]\beta[}$ being replaced by $C_B^{]b[}$ or $\{e^{itx},\ t\in\mathbb{R}\}$, are valid.

4.3 The Weak Law of Large Numbers. As a last application of the general theorems of Sec. 3, we shall deduce inverse results for the WLLN. In this instance, the limiting r.v. will be taken to be $X_o$ with d.f.

$$F_{X_o}(x) = \begin{cases} 0 & ;\ x<0 \\ 1 & ;\ x\geq 0\ , \end{cases}$$

while $\varphi(n)$ is arbitrary and the components $Z_{i,n}$ are given by $F_{Z_{i,n}} = F_{X_o}$, $1\leq i\leq n$, $n\in\mathbb{N}$.

THEOREM 9. Let $(X_i)_{i\in\mathbb{N}}$ be a sequence of real, independent r.v.

a)

(4.6) $$\overline{D}_n(f) := \sup_{y\in\mathbb{R}}\left|\int_{\mathbb{R}} f(x+y)dF_{\varphi(n)S_n}(x)-\int_{\mathbb{R}} f(x+y)dF_{X_o}(x)\right| \leq M_f n\varphi(n)^{\beta}$$

*for* $f \in C^{]\beta[}$ *and some* $\beta \in \mathbb{R}^+$, *implies that*

i) $E(X_1^{]\beta[}) < \infty$ ,

(4.7) ii) $E(X_1^j) = E(X_0^j) = 0$ $(0 \leq j \leq [\beta]-1)$.

b)

(4.8) $\overline{D}_n(f) \leq M_f n^{\alpha/r} \varphi(n)^\alpha$ $(f \in \mathrm{Lip}(\alpha;r;C_b + C_b^r))$

*for some* $r \in \mathbb{N}$ *together with* (3.11) *implies that*

(4.9) i) $E(X_1^r) < \infty$ ,

(4.10) ii) $E(X_1^j) = E(X_0^j)$ $(0 \leq j \leq r-1)$.

c) $\overline{D}_n(f) \leq M_r \omega_r(n^{1/r}\varphi(n);f;C_b + C_b^r)$

*implies* (4.9) *and* (4.10).

The proofs again use the corresponding theorems of Section 3.

REMARK 3. From (4.7) resp. (4.10) one easily can see that the assumption of Thm. 9 only makes sense if $\beta \leq 2$ resp. $r \leq 2$, because otherwise $F_{X_1} = F_{X_0}$ , and therefore

$$\int_{\mathbb{R}} f(x+y)\,dF_{\varphi(n)S_n}(x) \equiv \int_{\mathbb{R}} f(x+y)\,dF_{X_0}(x) \qquad (n \in \mathbb{N}).$$

This moreover implies that not only $E(X_1^{]\beta[}) < \infty$ resp. $E(X_1^r) < \infty$, but also $E(X^s) < \infty$, for all $s \in \mathbb{R}^+$. So a reasonable convergence rate in (4.6) resp. (4.8) is at most $n\varphi(n)^2$. If one looks for the "lowest" null-sequence $\varphi(n)$ to yield convergence in (4.6), one of course has to assume that $\varphi(n) = o(n^{-1/2})$; thus $\varphi(n) = n^{-1/2}$ doesn't work. But this must be so since in this case we have convergence not to $X_0$ but to $X^*$, i.e., the CLT holds.

Finally, an application of Thm. 4, the $\mathcal{O}$-theorem, shows that $\mathcal{O}(n\varphi(n)^2)$ is precisely the best possible rate in (4.6), i.e., the rate $o(n\varphi(n)^2)$ in (4.6) yields the trivial solution $F_{X_1} = F_{X_o}$ for the i.d. r.v. $X_i$.

THEOREM 10. Let $(X_i)_{i\in\mathbb{N}}$ be a sequence of real, independent i.d. r.v.

$$\sup_{y\in\mathbb{R}} \left| \int_{\mathbb{R}} f(x+y)dF_{\varphi(n)S_n}(x) - \int_{\mathbb{R}} f(x+y)dF_{X_o}(x) \right| = o(n\varphi(n)^r) \qquad (f\in C_b^r)$$

for some $r\in\mathbb{N}$ implies that

$$\text{i)} \quad E(X_1^r) < \infty \qquad \text{ii)} \quad E(X_1^j) = E(X_o^j) = 0 \qquad (0\leqslant j\leqslant r).$$

## 5. Not Necessarily Identically Distributed Random Variables

5.1 General Theorems. In this section we want to extend the theorems of Sec. 3 to the more general case of not necessarily i.d. r.v. Except Thm. 3, they depend upon La. 1, which leads to some difficulties when extending these theorems to independent not necessarily i.d. r.v. Nevertheless let us recall that La. 1 was formulated for arbitrary independent r.v. We shall now generalize Thm. 3 - and this is somewhat surprising in contrast to the i.d. case - by applying La. 1, but in such a manner that the difficulties mentioned above do not occur. But concerning the limiting r.v. Z, we have to demand that the components $Z_{i,n}$ are not arbitrarily distributed; they have to fulfill the following moment condition ($r\in\mathbb{N}$)

$$(5.1) \qquad E(Z_{i,n}^j) = E(Z_{i,k}^j) \qquad (1\leqslant j\leqslant r-1;\ 1\leqslant i\leqslant n,\ 1\leqslant k\leqslant n,\ n\in\mathbb{N}).$$

This means that the moments up to order r-1 are uniquely determined by the moments of the "diagonal components" of $Z_{i,i}$. A sufficient condition for (5.1) to hold is that $F_{Z_{i,n}} = F_{Z_{i,k}}$.

THEOREM 11. If there exists $r\in\mathbb{N}$ with $E(Z_{i,n}^r) < \infty$, $1\leqslant i\leqslant n$, $n\in\mathbb{N}$, then

$$(5.2)\qquad \|V_{\varphi(n)S_n}f - V_Z f\| \leq M_r\omega_r([\varphi(n)^r \sum_{i=1}^{n} a_{r,i,n}]^{1/r};f;C_b + C_b^r)$$

_for some_ $a_{r,i,n} \in \mathbb{R}^+$, $1 \leq i \leq n$, $n \in \mathbb{N}$, _implies that_

$$(5.3)\qquad i)\quad E(X_i^r) < \infty \qquad (i \in \mathbb{N}),$$

$$(5.4)\qquad ii)\quad E(X_i^j) = E(Z_{i,i}^j) \qquad (0 \leq j \leq r-1;\ i \in \mathbb{N})\ .$$

REMARK 4. The $a_{r,i,n}$ in (5.2) may be taken as
$a_{r,i,n} := \int_{\mathbb{R}} |x|^r d|(F_{X_i} - F_{Z_{i,n}}(x)|$.

PROOF. i) By (2.2) it follows that

$$(5.5)\qquad \|V_{\varphi(n)S_n}f - V_Z f\| \leq c_{1,r}^{-1} M_r K(\varphi(n)^r \sum_{i=1}^{n} a_{r,i,n};f;C_b + C_b^r;C_b).$$

Choosing $f = f_r \in C_b^r$, this leads by (2.1) to

$$|E([\varphi(n)S_n]^r) - E(Z^r)| \leq c_{1,r}^{-1} M_r \varphi(n)^r \sum_{i=1}^{n} a_{r,i,n} r! < \infty \quad (n \in \mathbb{N}),$$

and therefore $E(S_n^r) < \infty$, $n \in \mathbb{N}$, which in turn implies that $E(X_i^r) < \infty$, $i \in \mathbb{N}$.
ii) Since $K(\varphi(n)^r \sum_{i=1}^n a_{r,i,n}, f, C_b + C_b^r, C_b^r) = 0$ for $f = f_j$, $0 \leq j \leq r-1$, $n \in \mathbb{N}$, it follows by (5.5) that

$$(5.6)\qquad E([\varphi(n)S_n]^j) = E(Z^j) \qquad (0 \leq j \leq r-1,\ n \in \mathbb{N}).$$

We will prove (5.4) by induction. It is trivial for $j = 0$, so suppose that (5.4) holds for all $m \leq j-1$ ($\leq r-2$), $i \in \mathbb{N}$. We have to establish (5.4) for $j$ ($\leq r-1$), $i \in \mathbb{N}$. Since $E(X_i^m) = E(Z_{i,n}^m)$, $0 \leq m \leq j-1$, $1 \leq i \leq n$, $n \in \mathbb{N}$ we obtain by La. 1 and (5.6)

$$(5.7)\qquad E([\varphi(n)S_n]^j) - E(Z^j) = \sum_{i=1}^{n} \{E([\varphi(n)X_i]^j) - E([\varphi(n)Z_{i,n}]^j)\}$$
$$= \sum_{i=1}^{n} \{E(X_i^j) - E(Z_{i,n}^j)\} = 0$$

Now applying (5.7) and (5.1) twice,

$$E([\varphi(n)X_n]^j) = \sum_{i=1}^{n} E([\varphi(n)X_i]^j) - \sum_{i=1}^{n-1} E([\varphi(n)X_i]^j)$$

$$= \sum_{i=1}^{n} \{E([\varphi(n)X_i]^j) + E([\varphi(n)Z_{i,n}]^j) - E([\varphi(n)X_i]^j)\} - \sum_{i=1}^{n-1} E([\varphi(n)X_i]^j)$$

$$= \sum_{i=1}^{n-1} \{E([\varphi(n)Z_{i,n}]^j) - E([\varphi(n)X_i]^j)\} + E([\varphi(n)Z_{n,n}]^j)$$

$$= E([\varphi(n)Z_{n,n}]^j) .$$

Remark 4 is justified because of the direct theorem in [5], which is applicable since (5.4) implies that

$$(5.8) \qquad E(X_i^j) = E(Z_{i,n}^j) \qquad (0 \leq j \leq r-1,\ 1 \leq i \leq n,\ n \in \mathbb{N}).$$

Note that concerning the inverse result of Thm. 11 (5.1) is a very reasonable condition because in the direct theorem (5.8) is assumed which in turn implies (5.1).

For the particular instances of the CLT and the WLLN, the last theorem leads immediately to

THEOREM 12. Let $(X_i)_{i\in\mathbb{N}}$ be a sequence of real, independent r.v. with variance $\mathrm{Var}(X_i) := \sigma_i^2 > 0$, $i \in \mathbb{N}$. Then

$$\sup_{y\in\mathbb{R}} \left| \int_{\mathbb{R}} f(x+y)\,dF_{S_n/s_n}(x) - \int_{\mathbb{R}} f(x+y)\,dF_{X^*}(x) \right| \leq M_r\omega_r([s_n^{-r} \sum_{i=1}^{n} a_{r,i}]^{1/r}; f; C_b + C_b^r).$$

with $s_n^2 = \sum_{i=1}^{n} \sigma_i^2$, $a_{r,i} \in \mathbb{R}^+$, $i \in \mathbb{N}$ and some $r \in \mathbb{N}$, implies that

$$\text{i)} \quad E(X_i^r) < \infty \quad (i \in \mathbb{N}), \qquad \text{ii)} \quad E(X_i^j) = \sigma_i^j\, E(X^{*j}) \quad (0 \leq j \leq r-1,\ i \in \mathbb{N}).$$

PROOF. Decompose the limiting r.v. $X^*$ into the components $Z_{i,n}$ defined by $F_{Z_{i,n}} = F_{\sigma_i X^*}$, and let $\varphi(n) = s_n^{-1}$. Here we see that $F_{Z_{i,n}}$ does not depend on $n \in \mathbb{N}$, so that (5.1) holds trivially. Then the proof follows immediately by

Thm. 11.

Considering the limiting r.v. $X_o$, we obtain

THEOREM 13. <u>Let</u> $(X_i)_{i\in\mathbb{N}}$ <u>be a sequence of real, independent r.v. Then</u>

$$\sup_{y\in\mathbb{R}} \left| \int_{\mathbb{R}} f(x+y)\,dF_{\varphi(n)S_n}(x) - \int_{\mathbb{R}} f(x+y)\,dF_{X_o}(x) \right| \leqslant M_r \omega_r\Big([\varphi(n)^r \sum_{i=1}^{n} b_{r,i}]^{1/r}; f; C_b + C_b^r\Big)$$

<u>with</u> $b_{r,i}\in\mathbb{R}^+$, $i\in\mathbb{N}$ <u>and some</u> $r\in\mathbb{N}$, <u>implies</u>

i) $E(X_i^r) < \infty \quad (i\in\mathbb{N})$, ii) $E(X_i^j) = E(X_o^j) = 0 \quad (0\leqslant j\leqslant r-1,\ i\in\mathbb{N})$.

<u>5.2 Further Partial Results.</u> Here we want to outline in short the difficulties that arise when trying to extend the other inverse limit theorems to not necessarily i.d. r.v. Following the proof of such a theorem of Sec. 3 that use La. 1, we see that there is needed the equality

$$(5.9)\quad \left| \sum_{i=1}^{n} \{E([\varphi(n)X_i]^j) - E([\varphi(n)Z_{i,n}]^j)\} \right| \stackrel{!}{=} \sum_{i=1}^{n} \left| E([\varphi(n)X_i]^j) - E([\varphi(n)Z_{i,n}]^j) \right|,$$

which, of course, is valid if $X_i$ and $Z_{i,n}$ are i.d. For the further discussion, it suffices to restrict ourselves to the CLT and the $\mathcal{O}$-case. Without loss of generality assume that $E(X_i) = 0$, $i\in\mathbb{N}$.

Firstly, let us consider the case r = 4. Then we can prove the following

LEMMA 2. <u>Let</u> $(X_i)_{i\in\mathbb{N}}$ <u>be a sequence of real, independent r.v. with</u> $\mathrm{Var}(X_i) > 0$. <u>Then</u>

$$(5.10)\qquad \|V_{S_n/s_n} f - V_{X^*} f\| \leqslant M_f s_n^{-4} \sum_{i=1}^{n} a_{4,i} \qquad (f\in C_b^4)$$

<u>with</u> $a_{4,i}\in\mathbb{R}^+$, $i\in\mathbb{N}$, <u>implies</u>

i) $E(X_i^4) < \infty \qquad (i\in\mathbb{N})$,

$$(5.11)\ \text{ii)}\quad s_n \left| \sum_{i=1}^{n} E(X_i^3) \right| \leqslant C_3 \sum_{i=1}^{n} a_{4,i} .$$

PROOF. Remembering that $s_n^2 := \sum_{i=1}^n \sigma_i^2$ and $F_{Z_{i,n}} := F_{\sigma_i X^*}$. i) follows similarly as the first part of Thm. 11.

ii) Since $E(X_i) = 0 = E(\sigma_i X^*)$, $E(X_i^2) = \sigma_i^2 = E([\sigma_i X^*]^2)$ and $E([\sigma_i X_i]^3) = 0$, La. 1 and (5.10) for $f = f_3$ lead to

$$s_n^{-4}\left(\sum_{i=1}^n a_{4,i}\right)^{-1}|E([S_n/s_n]^3)| = s_n\left(\sum_{i=1}^n a_{4,i}\right)^{-1}\left|\sum_{i=1}^n E(X_i^3)\right| \leqslant C_3 := M_{f_3} .$$

But to obtain an equivalence theorem, instead of (5.11) we would have to have

$$s_n \sum_{i=1}^n |E(X_i^3)| \leqslant C_3 \sum_{i=1}^n a_{4,i} \tag{5.12}$$

which shows the difficulty, already mentioned above concerning (5.9). But the situation is even worse. If one tries to extend La. 2, to the case $r > 4$; say e.g. $r = 5$, then in order to apply La. 1 for $j = 4$, instead of (5.11) or (5.12) we need the sharper condition

$$E(X_i^3) = E([\sigma_i X^*]^3) = 0. \tag{5.13}$$

But it is very easy to construct a sequence of real,independent r.v. that has only two different distributions, i.e. $F_{X_{2i}} = F_1$, $F_{X_{2i-1}} = F_2$, $i \in \mathbb{N}$, such that (5.11) holds but not (5.13). What we need are further restrictive assumptions upon the r.v. $X_i$ which would be so strong that it does not seem worthwhile to formulate in this instance an inverse theorem with rates for not necessarily i.d. r.v.

Let us conclude with the remark that if ones wishes to extend the inverse theorem with $o$-rates to no necessarily i.d. r.v. then in addition to the difficulties for the $O$-case described above, one further difficulty occurs, namely with the generalized Lindeberg condition of order r, which need be posed upon the r.v. $X_i$ in the $o$-direct theorem (compare [3], [5]).

## REFERENCES

[1] Butzer, P.L. - Berens, H., Semi-groups of Operators and Approximation. Springer-Verlag, Berlin 1967.

[2] Butzer, P.L. - Dickmeis, W. - Hahn, L. - Nessel, R.J., Lax-type theorems and a unified approach to some limit theorems in probability theory with rates. (to appear)(1977).

[3] Butzer, P.L. - Hahn, L. - Westphal, U., On the rate of approximation in the central limit theorem. J. Approximation Theory 13 (1976), 327 - 340.

[4] Butzer, P.L. - Hahn, L., On the connections between the rates of norm and weak convergence in the central limit theorem. Math. Nachr. (in print)(1978).

[5] Butzer, P.L. - Hahn, L., General theorems on rates of convergence in distribution of random variables. I. General limit Theorems. II. Applications to the stable limit laws and weak law of large numbers. (to appear)(1978).

[6] Ibragimov, I.A., On the Chebyshev-Cramer asymptotic expansions. Theor. Probability Appl. 12 (1967), 455 - 469.

# MAXIMAL INEQUALITIES AND CONVERGENCE PROPERTIES OF MULTIPLE ORTHOGONAL SERIES AND RANDOM FIELDS

F. Móricz
Bolyai Institute
University of Szeged
Szeged

Let $Z_+^d$ be the set of d-tuples $\underset{\sim}{k} = (k_1,k_2,\ldots,k_d)$ with positive integers for coordinates, where $d \geq 1$ is a fixed integer. Let $(X,A,\mu)$ be a positive measure space and let $\{\zeta_{\underset{\sim}{k}}\} = \{\zeta_{\underset{\sim}{k}} : \underset{\sim}{k} \in Z_+^d\}$ be a set of measurable functions defined on $(X,A,\mu)$. Consider the d-multiple series $\sum_{\underset{\sim}{k}\geq \underset{\sim}{1}} \zeta_{\underset{\sim}{k}} = \sum_{j=1}^{d} \sum_{k_j=1}^{\infty} \zeta_{k_1,k_2,\ldots,k_d}$ with rectangular partial sums $S(\underset{\sim}{m}) = \sum_{\underset{\sim}{1}\leq\underset{\sim}{k}\leq\underset{\sim}{m}} \zeta_{\underset{\sim}{k}}$, where $\underset{\sim}{m} = (m_1,m_2,\ldots,m_d) \in Z_+^d$. Convergence properties of the following types are discussed: (i) $S(\underset{\sim}{m})$ converges a.e. as $\min_{1\leq j\leq d} m_j \to \infty$, which expresses the a.e. convergence of $\sum \zeta_{\underset{\sim}{k}}$; (ii) $S(\underset{\sim}{m})/\Pi_{j=1}^{d} m_j$ converges to 0 a.e. as $\max_{1\leq j\leq d} m_j \to \infty$, which expresses a strong law of large numbers for $\{\zeta_{\underset{\sim}{k}}\}$. The investigations are made separately under moment restrictions of second or or higher orders, using maximal inequalities for $M(\underset{\sim}{m}) = \max_{\underset{\sim}{1}\leq\underset{\sim}{k}\leq\underset{\sim}{m}} |S(\underset{\sim}{k})|$, which are interesting in their own right, too.

## 1. Introduction

Let $Z^d$ be the set of d-tuples $\underset{\sim}{k} = (k_1,k_2,\ldots,k_d)$ with non-negative integers for coordinates, where $d \geq 1$ is a fixed integer. If the coordinates $k_j$ are positive integers, we write $\underset{\sim}{k} \in Z_+^d$. Let $\underset{\sim}{k} = (k_1,k_2,\ldots,k_d)$ and $\underset{\sim}{m} = (m_1,m_2,\ldots,m_d)$ be two tuples. $Z^d$ is p a r t i a l l y o r d e r e d by agreeing that $\underset{\sim}{k} \leq \underset{\sim}{m}$ iff $k_j \leq m_j$ for each j. Consequently, $\underset{\sim}{k} \nleq \underset{\sim}{m}$ means that for at least one j we have $k_j > m_j$. If $\underset{\sim}{k} \leq \underset{\sim}{m}$ and $\underset{\sim}{k} \neq \underset{\sim}{m}$, then we write $\underset{\sim}{k} < \underset{\sim}{m}$.

Let $\underset{\sim}{k}+\underset{\sim}{m}$ and $\underset{\sim}{k}\underset{\sim}{m}$ denote the usual coordinatewise sums and products, respectively. Let $2^{\underset{\sim}{k}} = (2^{k_1},2^{k_2},\ldots,2^{k_d})$ and let $|\underset{\sim}{k}|$ stand for the product $k_1k_2\ldots k_d$. Further, let us write $\underset{\sim}{0}$ and $\underset{\sim}{1}$ for the tuples $(0,0,\ldots,0)$ and $(1,1,\ldots,1)$, respectively.

Let $(X,A,\mu)$ be a (not necessarily finite) positive measure space. Let $\{\zeta_{\underset{\sim}{k}}\} = \{\zeta_{\underset{\sim}{k}} : \underset{\sim}{k} \in Z_+^d\}$ be a set of measurable functions defined on $(X,A,\mu)$, and having finite second or higher moments. Consider the d-multiple series

(1) $$\sum_{\underset{\sim}{k} \geq \underset{\sim}{1}} \zeta_{\underset{\sim}{k}} = \sum_{j=1}^{d} \sum_{k_j=1}^{\infty} \zeta_{k_1,k_2,\ldots,k_d}.$$

For any $\underset{\sim}{b} \in Z^d$ and $\underset{\sim}{m} \in Z_+^d$ set

$$S(\underset{\sim}{b},\underset{\sim}{m}) = \sum_{\underset{\sim}{b}+\underset{\sim}{1} \leq \underset{\sim}{k} \leq \underset{\sim}{b}+\underset{\sim}{m}} \zeta_{\underset{\sim}{k}} = \sum_{j=1}^{d} \sum_{k_j=b_j+1}^{b_j+m_j} \zeta_{k_1,k_2,\ldots,k_d}.$$

In case $\underset{\sim}{b} = \underset{\sim}{0}$ the abbreviated notation $S(\underset{\sim}{m}) = S(\underset{\sim}{0},\underset{\sim}{m})$ is used. If there is not supposed any interrelation among the coordinates $m_1,m_2,\ldots,m_d$ of $\underset{\sim}{m}$, then $S(\underset{\sim}{m})$ is called the *rectangular* partial sum of (1).

Convergence properties of the following types will be discussed:
(i) $S(\underset{\sim}{m})$ converges a.e. as $\underset{\sim}{m} \to \infty$, which expresses the a.e. convergence of the *d-multiple series* (1);

(ii) $S(\underset{\sim}{m})/w(\underset{\sim}{m})$ converges to 0 a.e. as $\underset{\sim}{m} \to \infty$, where $\{w(\underset{\sim}{m}): \underset{\sim}{m} \in Z_+^d\}$ is a d-multiple sequence of numbers, in particular, $w(\underset{\sim}{m}) = |\underset{\sim}{m}|$, and this statement expresses a strong law of large numbers for $\{\zeta_{\underset{\sim}{k}}\}$ (called *random field* in probability theory).

We want to emphasize that the term "$\underset{\sim}{m} \to \infty$" in (i) and (ii) has different meanings. By the limit $\underset{\sim}{m} \to \infty$ in statements of type (i) we mean $\min_{1 \leq j \leq d} m_j \to \infty$, while in statements of type (ii) we mean $\max_{1 \leq j \leq d} m_j \to \infty$. In other words, the neighbourhood of $\infty$ defined by some $\underset{\sim}{m} \in Z^d$ in the first case is $\bigcap_{j=1}^{d} \{\underset{\sim}{k} \in Z_+^d : k_j > m_j\}$, whereas in the second case is $\bigcup_{j=1}^{d} \{\underset{\sim}{k} \in Z_+^d : k_j > m_j\}$.

Beside the rectangular partial sums the asymptotic behaviour of both square and spherical partial sums is often studied in connection with multiple function series. We shall consider them in the following more general setting. Let $Q_1 \subset Q_2 \subset \ldots$ be an arbitrary sequence of finite regions in $Z_+^d$ such that either $\bigcup_{r=1}^{\infty} Q_r = Z_+^d$ in statements of type (i) or $\bigcup_{r=1}^{\infty} Q_r$ contains infinitely many points from $Z_+^d$ in statements of type (ii). For r=1,2,... set

$$T(r) = \sum_{\underset{\sim}{k} \in Q_r} \zeta_{\underset{\sim}{k}}.$$

The choice $Q_r = \{\underset{\sim}{k} \in Z_+^d : k_j \leq r \text{ for each } j\}$ provides the *square* partial sums, while $Q_r = \{\underset{\sim}{k} \in Z_+^d : k_1^2 + k_2^2 + \ldots + k_d^2 \leq r^2\}$ provides the *spherical* partial sums of (1). Thus the sums T(r) can be considered as generalized partial sums of the d-multiple series (1), and they form a set

$\{T(r)\}_{r=1}^{\infty}$ depending only on one parameter.

Since $Z_+^d$ is a partially ordered set, the main difficulties in convergence properties of $S(\underset{\sim}{m})$ arise from the lack of linear ordering when $d \geq 2$. On the other hand, $Z_+^1$ has a linear ordering and this explains the better convergence properties of $T(r)$.

Our results will be obtained by making use of d-multiple maximal inequalities of [6] which state bounds on a certain moment of

$$M(\underset{\sim}{b},\underset{\sim}{m}) = \max_{\underset{\sim}{1} \leq \underset{\sim}{k} \leq \underset{\sim}{m}} |S(\underset{\sim}{b},\underset{\sim}{k})| - \max_{1 \leq j \leq d} \max_{1 \leq k_j \leq m_j} |S(b_1,b_2,\ldots,b_d;k_1,k_2,\ldots,k_d)|$$

in terms of bounds on the same moment of $S(\underset{\sim}{b},\underset{\sim}{m})$, whilst $\underset{\sim}{b}$ and $\underset{\sim}{m}$ run over $Z^d$ and $Z_+^d$, respectively.

## 2. Convergence Properties under Moment Restrictions of Order Two

### 2.1. A Generalization of the Rademacher - Menšov Inequality.

In the theory of multiple orthogonal series it is more convenient to write $\zeta_{\underset{\sim}{k}}$ into the form $\zeta_{\underset{\sim}{k}} = a_{\underset{\sim}{k}}\phi_{\underset{\sim}{k}}$, where $\{a_{\underset{\sim}{k}}: \underset{\sim}{k} \in Z_+^d\}$ is a set of numbers (coefficients) and $\{\phi_{\underset{\sim}{k}}: \underset{\sim}{k} \in Z_+^d\}$ is a set of o r t h o n o r m a l functions:

$$\int \phi_{\underset{\sim}{k}}\phi_{\underset{\sim}{1}}\,d\mu = \begin{cases} 0 & \text{if } \underset{\sim}{k} \neq \underset{\sim}{1} \\ 1 & \text{if } \underset{\sim}{k} = \underset{\sim}{1} \quad (\forall k, \forall 1). \end{cases}$$

Here and in the sequel we write simply $\int .d\mu$ instead of $\int_X .d\mu$. We obviously have

$$\int S^2(\underset{\sim}{b},\underset{\sim}{m})\,d\mu = \sum_{\underset{\sim}{b}+\underset{\sim}{1} \leq \underset{\sim}{k} \leq \underset{\sim}{b}+\underset{\sim}{m}} a_{\underset{\sim}{k}}^2 \qquad (\forall \underset{\sim}{b}, \forall \underset{\sim}{m}). \tag{2}$$

If the functions $\phi_{\underset{\sim}{k}}$ are, in addition, uniformly bounded:

$$|\phi_{\underset{\sim}{k}}(x)| \leq B \qquad \text{a.e.} \qquad (\forall \underset{\sim}{k}),$$

then by the well-known Menšov - Paley inequality (see, e.g., [11, p. 190]) we have, for any $\gamma \geq 2$,

$$\int |S(\underset{\sim}{b},\underset{\sim}{m})|^{\gamma}\,d\mu \leq B^{\gamma-2}|\underset{\sim}{m}|^{\gamma-2} \sum_{\underset{\sim}{b}+\underset{\sim}{1} \leq \underset{\sim}{k} \leq \underset{\sim}{b}+\underset{\sim}{m}} |a_{\underset{\sim}{k}}|^{\gamma} \qquad (\forall \underset{\sim}{b}, \forall \underset{\sim}{m}). \tag{3}$$

Let us denote by $f(\underset{\sim}{b},\underset{\sim}{m})$ either the right-hand side of (2) or the right-hand side of (3), disregarding the factor $|\underset{\sim}{m}|^{\gamma-2}$ in the latter case. The non-negative function $f(\underset{\sim}{b},\underset{\sim}{m})$ is clearly *additive* in each pair $b_j, m_j$ of its variables ($j=1,2,\ldots,d$), i.e. for any values of $\underset{\sim}{b}_j = (b_1,\ldots,b_{j-1},b_{j+1},\ldots,b_d) \in Z^{d-1}$, $\underset{\sim}{m}_j = (m_1,\ldots,m_{j-1},m_{j+1},\ldots,m_d) \in Z_+^{d-1}$, $b_j, m_j$, and $1 \leqslant h_j < m_j$ we have

$$(4) \qquad f(\underset{\sim}{b}_j, b_j; \underset{\sim}{m}_j, h_j) + f(\underset{\sim}{b}_j, b_j+h_j; \underset{\sim}{m}_j, m_j-h_j) = f(\underset{\sim}{b},\underset{\sim}{m}) .$$

In the sequel it will be enough for our purposes that the relation (4) holds true with "$\leqslant$" instead of "=" (with so-called *superadditivity* instead of additivity). This is the case, e.g., when the functions $\phi_{\underset{\sim}{k}}$ are not supposed to be orthogonal (but they are supposed, of course, to have finite second moments). In this case we can assert only the following trivial estimation:

$$(5) \qquad \int S^2(\underset{\sim}{b},\underset{\sim}{m})\,d\mu \leqslant \sum_{\underset{\sim}{b}+\underset{\sim}{1} \leqslant \underset{\sim}{k},\underset{\sim}{l} \leqslant \underset{\sim}{b}+\underset{\sim}{m}} |a_{\underset{\sim}{k}} a_{\underset{\sim}{l}} \int \phi_{\underset{\sim}{k}} \phi_{\underset{\sim}{l}}\, d\mu| \qquad (\forall \underset{\sim}{b},\ \forall \underset{\sim}{m}).$$

The inequalities (2), (3), and (5) can be rewritten into the following common form:

$$(6) \qquad \int |S(\underset{\sim}{b},\underset{\sim}{m})|^{\gamma} d\mu \leqslant \prod_{j=1}^{d} \lambda_j^{\gamma}(m_j) f(\underset{\sim}{b},\underset{\sim}{m}), \qquad (\forall \underset{\sim}{b},\ \forall \underset{\sim}{m}),$$

where each $\{\lambda_j(m)\}_{m=1}^{\infty}$ is a non-decreasing sequence of positive numbers: $\lambda_j(m) \equiv 1$ for cases (2) and (5), while $\lambda_j(m) = m^{(\gamma-2)/\gamma}$ for case (3), $j=1,2,\ldots,d$; furthermore, $f(\underset{\sim}{b},\underset{\sim}{m})$ is a non-negative and superadditive function.

Let us introduce new sequences $\Lambda_j(m)$ by the following recursive definition: for $m=1$ set $\Lambda_j(1) = \lambda_j(1)$, and for $m \geqslant 2$ let $h$ be the integral part of $m/2$, and set

$$\Lambda_j(m) = \lambda_j(h+1) + \Lambda_j(h).$$

It is obvious that the sequences $\Lambda_j(m)$ are also non-decreasing. Further, if $2^p \leqslant m < 2^{p+1}$, $p$ integer, then

$$\Lambda_j(m) \leqslant \Lambda_j(2^{p+1}-1) = \lambda_j(2^p) + \Lambda_j(2^p-1) = \ldots$$

$$\ldots = \lambda_j(2^p) + \lambda_j(2^{p-1}) + \ldots + \lambda(2) + \lambda(1).$$

Now if $\lambda_j(m) \equiv 1$, then

$$\Lambda_j(m) \leqslant p + 1 < \log 2m,$$

the logarithm being of base 2. If $\lambda_j(m) = m^\beta$ with $\beta = (\gamma-2)/\gamma > 0$, then

$$\Lambda_j(m) \leqslant 2^{p\beta} + 2^{(p-1)\beta} + \ldots + 2^\beta + 1 < \frac{(2m)^\beta}{2^\beta - 1} = O\{\lambda_j(m)\},$$

having the same order of magnitude for $\Lambda_j(m)$ and for $\lambda_j(m)$.

After these preliminaries our first maximal inequality can be formulated as follows.

THEOREM 1 ([6]). Let $\gamma \geqslant 1$. Suppose that there exist positive non-decreasing sequences $\{\lambda_j(m)\}_{m=1}^\infty$ for $j=1,2,\ldots,d$, and a non-negative, superadditive function $f(\underset{\sim}{b},\underset{\sim}{m})$ such that (6) holds. Then we have

$$\int M^\gamma(\underset{\sim}{b},\underset{\sim}{m})\,d\mu \leqslant \prod_{j=1}^{d} \Lambda_j^\gamma(m_j) f(\underset{\sim}{b},\underset{\sim}{m}) \qquad (\forall \underset{\sim}{b},\ \forall \underset{\sim}{m}).$$

By Theorem 1 from (2) it follows that

$$\int M^2(\underset{\sim}{b},\underset{\sim}{m})\,d\mu \leqslant \prod_{j=1}^{d} (\log 2m_j)^2 \sum_{\underset{\sim}{b}+\underset{\sim}{1} \leqslant \underset{\sim}{k} \leqslant \underset{\sim}{b}+\underset{\sim}{m}} a_{\underset{\sim}{k}}^2 \qquad (\forall \underset{\sim}{b},\ \forall \underset{\sim}{m}).$$

This is the d-multiple form of the Rademacher-Menšov inequality. In the non-orthogonal case from (5) it follows that

$$\int M^2(\underset{\sim}{b},\underset{\sim}{m})\,d\mu \leqslant \prod_{j=1}^{d} (\log 2m_j)^2 \sum_{\underset{\sim}{b}+\underset{\sim}{1} \leqslant \underset{\sim}{k},\underset{\sim}{l} \leqslant \underset{\sim}{b}+\underset{\sim}{m}} \left|a_{\underset{\sim}{k}} a_{\underset{\sim}{l}} \int \phi_{\underset{\sim}{k}} \phi_{\underset{\sim}{l}}\,d\mu\right|;$$

while from (3), for $\gamma > 2$,

$$\int M^\gamma(\underset{\sim}{b},\underset{\sim}{m})\,d\mu \leqslant C_{d,\gamma} B^{\gamma-2} |\underset{\sim}{m}|^{\gamma-2} \sum_{\underset{\sim}{b}+\underset{\sim}{1} \leqslant \underset{\sim}{k} \leqslant \underset{\sim}{b}+\underset{\sim}{m}} |a_{\underset{\sim}{k}}|^\gamma,$$

where $C_{d,\gamma}$ is a positive constant depending only on d and $\gamma$. The latter inequality is the d-multiple form of the Menšov-Paley inequality.

2.2. A.e. Convergence. On the basis of the above inequalities we can prove the d-multiple form of the classical Rademacher-Menšov theorem.

THEOREM 2 (non-orthogonal version [7]). *If*

$$\sum_{\underset{\sim}{m} \geq \underset{\sim}{0}} |\underset{\sim}{m}+\underset{\sim}{1}|^2 \sum_{2^{\underset{\sim}{m}} \leq \underset{\sim}{k},\underset{\sim}{l} \leq 2^{\underset{\sim}{m}+\underset{\sim}{1}}-\underset{\sim}{1}} |a_{\underset{\sim}{k}} a_{\underset{\sim}{l}} \int \phi_{\underset{\sim}{k}} \phi_{\underset{\sim}{l}} d\mu| < \infty,$$

*then the d-multiple series* (1) *converges a.e. in the sense that the rectangular partial sum* $S(m)$ *converges a.e. as* $m \to \infty$.

This theorem for $d = 1$ was essentially proved by Szép [10] (although it is stated in a slightly weaker form), while Corollary 1 below for $d = 2$ was proved by Agnew [1].

COROLLARY 1 (orthogonal version). *If* $\{\phi_k\}$ *is orthogonal and*

$$\sum_{\underset{\sim}{k} \geq \underset{\sim}{1}} a_{\underset{\sim}{k}}^2 \prod_{j=1}^{d} (\log 2k_j)^2 < \infty,$$

*then* (1) *converges a.e.*

Let us now turn to the question of a.e. convergence of the square or the spherical partial sums of (1). This will be done in the more general setting mentioned in the introduction. Let us consider the generalized partial sums $T(r)$ defined by

$$T(r) = \sum_{\underset{\sim}{k} \in Q_r} a_{\underset{\sim}{k}} \phi_{\underset{\sim}{k}} \qquad (r = 1,2,\ldots),$$

where $Q_1 \subset Q_2 \subset \ldots$ is a given sequence of finite regions in $Z_+^d$ such that $\bigcup_{r=1}^{\infty} Q_r = Z_+^d$. Put $Q_0 = \emptyset$. We can conclude the following results in a simple way.

THEOREM 3 ([7]). *If*

$$\sum_{p=0}^{\infty} (p+1)^2 \sum_{\underset{\sim}{k},\underset{\sim}{l} \in Q_{2^{p+1}-1} \setminus Q_{2^p-1}} |a_{\underset{\sim}{k}} a_{\underset{\sim}{l}} \int \phi_{\underset{\sim}{k}} \phi_{\underset{\sim}{l}} d\mu| < \infty,$$

then $T(r)$ converges a.e. as $r \to \infty$.

COROLLARY 2. If $\{\phi_{\underset{\sim}{k}}\}$ is orthonormal and

$$\sum_{r=1}^{\infty} \Big( \sum_{\underset{\sim}{k} \in Q_r \setminus Q_{r-1}} a_{\underset{\sim}{k}}^2 \Big) \log^2 2r < \infty,$$

then $T(r)$ converges a.e. as $r \to \infty$.

2.3. Strong Laws of Large Numbers. Let us assume that the functions $\zeta_{\underset{\sim}{k}}$ defined on $(X,A,\mu)$ (which can be considered random variables in case $\mu(X) = 1$) have finite second moments:

$$\sigma_{\underset{\sim}{k}}^2 = \int \zeta_{\underset{\sim}{k}}^2 d\mu < \infty \qquad (\forall \underset{\sim}{k} \in Z_+^d).$$

An application of the results of the preceding section to the series $\sum_{\underset{\sim}{k} \geq \underset{\sim}{1}} \zeta_{\underset{\sim}{k}}/|\underset{\sim}{k}|$ yields, via the appropriate d-multiple version of the Kronecker lemma, criteria for the a.e. convergence to 0 of $S(\underset{\sim}{m})/|\underset{\sim}{m}|$ as $\min_{1 \leq j \leq d} m_j \to \infty$. However, as we stressed in the introduction, the a.e. convergence to 0 of $S(\underset{\sim}{m})/|\underset{\sim}{m}|$ is intended to study under the limit relation $\max_{1 \leq j \leq d} m_j \to \infty$. Since the latter convergence notion is somewhat stronger than the former one, we have to follow another way to obtain strong laws of large numbers for $\{\zeta_{\underset{\sim}{k}}\}$.

THEOREM 4 (non-orthogonal version [7]). If

$$\sum_{\underset{\sim}{m} \geq \underset{\sim}{0}} \frac{|\underset{\sim}{m}+\underset{\sim}{1}|^2}{|2^{\underset{\sim}{m}}|^2} \sum_{2^{\underset{\sim}{m}} \leq \underset{\sim}{k},\underset{\sim}{l} \leq 2^{\underset{\sim}{m}+\underset{\sim}{1}}-\underset{\sim}{1}} |\int \zeta_{\underset{\sim}{k}} \zeta_{\underset{\sim}{l}} d\mu| < \infty,$$

then

(7) $$\lim_{\underset{\sim}{m} \to \infty} S(\underset{\sim}{m})/|\underset{\sim}{m}| = 0 \qquad \text{a.e.}$$

COROLLARY 3 (orthogonal version). If the $\zeta_{\underset{\sim}{k}}$ are pairwise orthogonal (called uncorrelated in probability theory) and

$$\sum_{\underset{\sim}{k} \geq \underset{\sim}{1}} \frac{\sigma_{\underset{\sim}{k}}^2}{|\underset{\sim}{k}|^2} \prod_{j=1}^{d} (\log 2k_j)^2 < \infty,$$

then (7) follows.

For $d = 1$ Corollary 3 is well-known, it is an immediate consequence of the Rademacher – Menšov theorem by using the Kronecker lemma.

Given any sequence $Q_1 \subset Q_2 \subset \ldots$ of finite regions in $Z_+^d$ such that $\bigcup_{r=1}^{\infty} Q_r$ contains infinitely many points of $Z_+^d$, we can give sufficient conditions that ensure the fulfillment of the following weaker relation

$$\lim_{r\to\infty} |Q_r|^{-1} \sum_{\underset{\sim}{k} \in Q_r} \zeta_{\underset{\sim}{k}} = 0 \qquad \text{a.e.,} \tag{8}$$

where $|Q_r|$ denotes the number of the points $\underset{\sim}{k}$ from $Z_+^d$ contained in $Q_r$. Put $Q_o = \emptyset$.

THEOREM 5 ([7]). If

$$\sum_{p=0}^{\infty} \frac{(p+1)^2}{|Q_{2^p}|^2} \sum_{\underset{\sim}{k},\underset{\sim}{1} \in Q_{2^{p+1}-1} \setminus Q_{2^p-1}} |\int \zeta_{\underset{\sim}{k}} \zeta_{\underset{\sim}{1}} d\mu| < \infty,$$

then (8) follows.

COROLLARY 4. If the $\zeta_{\underset{\sim}{k}}$ are pairwise orthogonal and

$$\sum_{r=1}^{\infty} \Big( \sum_{\underset{\sim}{k} \in Q_r \setminus Q_{r-1}} \sigma_{\underset{\sim}{k}}^2 \Big) \frac{(\log 2r)^2}{|Q_r|^2} < \infty,$$

then (8) follows.

## 3. Convergence Properties under Moment Restrictions of Order Higher than Two

3.1. An Asymptotically Optimal Maximal Inequality. This result provides a bound for $\int M^{\gamma}(\underset{\sim}{b},\underset{\sim}{m})d\mu$ which is asymptotically optimal (as $\underset{\sim}{m}\to\infty$) in the sense that it is of the same order of magnitude as the bound for $\int |S(\underset{\sim}{b},\underset{\sim}{m})|^{\gamma}d\mu$.

THEOREM 6 ([6]). Let $\alpha > 1$ and $\gamma > 0$. Suppose that there exists a non-negative and superadditive function $f(\underset{\sim}{b},\underset{\sim}{m})$ such that

$$\int |S(\underset{\sim}{b},\underset{\sim}{m})|^{\gamma}d\mu \leqslant f^{\alpha}(\underset{\sim}{b},\underset{\sim}{m}) \qquad (\forall\underset{\sim}{b},\ \forall\underset{\sim}{m}).$$

Then we have

$$\int M^{\gamma}(\underset{\sim}{b},\underset{\sim}{m})d\mu \leqslant C_{d,\alpha,\gamma}\ f^{\alpha}(\underset{\sim}{b},\underset{\sim}{m}) \qquad (\forall\underset{\sim}{b},\ \forall\underset{\sim}{m})$$

where $C_{d,\alpha,\gamma}$ is a positive constant.

Taking the special case, when $\alpha=\gamma/2$ and $f(\underset{\sim}{b},\underset{\sim}{m}) = \sum_{\underset{\sim}{b}+\underset{\sim}{1}\leqslant\underset{\sim}{k}\leqslant\underset{\sim}{b}+\underset{\sim}{m}} a_{\underset{\sim}{k}}^{2}$, where $\{a_{\underset{\sim}{k}}\}$ is a given set of numbers, we come to the multiple version of the Erdős-Stečkin inequality (for $d=1$ see, e.g., Gapoškin [2, pp. 29-31]).

COROLLARY 5. Let $\gamma > 2$. Suppose that there exists a set $\{a_{\underset{\sim}{k}}:\underset{\sim}{k}\in Z_{+}^{d}\}$ of numbers such that

$$\int |S(\underset{\sim}{b},\underset{\sim}{m})|^{\gamma}d\mu \leqslant C_{d,\gamma}\Big(\sum_{\underset{\sim}{b}+\underset{\sim}{1}\leqslant\underset{\sim}{k}\leqslant\underset{\sim}{b}+\underset{\sim}{m}} a_{\underset{\sim}{k}}^{2}\Big)^{\gamma/2} \qquad (\forall\underset{\sim}{b},\ \forall\underset{\sim}{m}), \tag{9}$$

then

$$\int M^{\gamma}(\underset{\sim}{b},\underset{\sim}{m})d\mu \leqslant C^{*}_{d,\gamma}\Big(\sum_{\underset{\sim}{b}+\underset{\sim}{1}\leqslant\underset{\sim}{k}\leqslant\underset{\sim}{b}+\underset{\sim}{m}} a_{\underset{\sim}{k}}^{2}\Big)^{\gamma/2} \qquad (\forall\underset{\sim}{b},\ \forall\underset{\sim}{m}). \tag{10}$$

We note that the maximal inequalities stated in Theorems 1 and 6 were proved in [5] for $d=1$.

3.2. A.e. Convergence. Write again $\zeta_{\underset{\sim}{k}}$ into the form $\zeta_{\underset{\sim}{k}} = a_{\underset{\sim}{k}}\phi_{\underset{\sim}{k}}$, where $\{a_{\underset{\sim}{k}}\}$ is a set of numbers and $\{\phi_{\underset{\sim}{k}}:\underset{\sim}{k}\in Z_{+}^{d}\}$ is a set of measurable functions defined on $(X,A,\mu)$. Let $\gamma$ now be an even integer, $\gamma\geqslant 4$. $\{\phi_{\underset{\sim}{k}}\}$ is said to be *multiplicative of order* $\gamma$ if for all systems of pairwise distinct points $\underset{\sim}{k}_1,\underset{\sim}{k}_2,\ldots,\underset{\sim}{k}_\gamma$ from $Z_{+}^{d}$ we have

(11) $$\int \left(\prod_{i=1}^{\gamma} \phi_{\underset{\sim}{k}_i}\right) d\mu = 0.$$

In addition, suppose that, with a constant C,

(12) $$\int \phi_{\underset{\sim}{k}}^{\gamma} d\mu \leq C \qquad (\forall \underset{\sim}{k}).$$

Following Komlós - Révész [4] and Gapoškin [3] (who proved Theorem 7 below for $d = 1$) it can be easily shown that, for functions $\phi_{\underset{\sim}{k}}$ satisfying (11) and (12), the assumption (9) of Corollary 5 holds true. Hence the conclusion (10) follows. This implies in a routine way the following

THEOREM 7 ([8]). _If_ $\{\phi_{\underset{\sim}{k}}\}$ _is multiplicative of order_ $\gamma$ $(\geq 4)$ _and_ (12) _holds, then the_ d-_multiple series_ (1) _converges unconditionally a.e. for every_ $\{a_{\underset{\sim}{k}}\}$ _satisfying_

$$\sum_{\underset{\sim}{k} \geq \underset{\sim}{1}} a_{\underset{\sim}{k}}^2 < \infty.$$

Any one-to-one mapping $\underset{\sim}{k} = \underset{\sim}{k}(\underset{\sim}{l})$ of $Z_+^d$ onto itself defines a r e a r r a n g e m e n t

$$\sum_{\underset{\sim}{l} \geq \underset{\sim}{1}} a_{\underset{\sim}{k}(\underset{\sim}{l})} \phi_{\underset{\sim}{k}(\underset{\sim}{l})}$$

of the terms of (1). Setting

$$\bar{S}(\underset{\sim}{m}) = \sum_{\underset{\sim}{1} \leq \underset{\sim}{l} \leq \underset{\sim}{m}} a_{\underset{\sim}{k}(\underset{\sim}{l})} \phi_{\underset{\sim}{k}(\underset{\sim}{l})},$$

the series (1) is said to c o n v e r g e u n c o n d i t i o n a l l y a.e. if in every rearrangement of the terms of (1) the partial sum $\bar{S}(\underset{\sim}{m})$ of the rearranged series converges a.e. as $\underset{\sim}{m} \to \infty$.

We remark that the vanishing of the integrals in (11) is of no relevance, only their "relative smallness as $\underset{\sim}{k}_1, \underset{\sim}{k}_2, \ldots, \underset{\sim}{k}_\gamma$ are far from each other" is needed. Without entering into details, we refer to [8].

3.3. Strong Laws of Large Numbers. For simplicity let us assume in this section that $a_{\underset{\sim}{k}} \equiv 1$, i.e. $\zeta_{\underset{\sim}{k}} = \phi_{\underset{\sim}{k}}$. Corollary 5 makes it possible to estimate the growth of the rectangular partial sum $S(\underset{\sim}{m})$ as follows.

THEOREM 8 ([8]). *If* $\{\phi_{\underset{\sim}{k}}\}$ *is multiplicative of order* $\gamma$ $(\geq 4)$ *and* (12) *holds, then we have, for any* $\delta > 0$,

$$\lim_{\underset{\sim}{m}\to\infty} \frac{S(\underset{\sim}{m})}{|\underset{\sim}{m}|^{1/2}\left(\prod_{j=1}^{d} \log 2m_j\right)^{1/\gamma}(\log\log 4|\underset{\sim}{m}|)^{(1+\delta)/\gamma}} = 0 \qquad \text{a.e.}\ .$$

This theorem for $d = 1$ was obtained by Serfling [9]. The conclusion improves as $\gamma$ increases. By letting $\gamma \to \infty$ we find

COROLLARY 6. *Suppose that* $\{\phi_{\underset{\sim}{k}}\}$ *is multiplicative of order* $\gamma$ *and satisfies* (12) *for infinitely many even integers* $\gamma$. *Then, for any* $\delta > 0$,

$$\lim_{\underset{\sim}{m}\to\infty} \frac{S(\underset{\sim}{m})}{|\underset{\sim}{m}|^{1/2}\left(\prod_{j=1}^{d} \log 2m_j\right)^{\delta}} = 0 \qquad \text{a.e.}\ .$$

This result is not far from the "$\leq$" part of the law of the iterated logarithm.

REFERENCES

[1] Agnew, R.P., On double orthogonal series. Proc. London Math. Soc. II. s. 33 (1932), 420-434.

[2] Gapoškin, V.F., Lacunary series and independent functions. (Russian) Uspehi Mat. Nauk 21 (1966), 3-82.

[3] Gapoškin, V.F., The convergence of series in weakly multiplicative systems of functions. (Russian) Mat. Sb. 89 (1972), 355-365.

[ 4] Komlós, J. - Révész, P., Remark to a paper of Gaposhkin. Acta Sci. Math. (Szeged) 33 (1972), 237-241.

[ 5] Móricz, F., Moment inequalities and the strong laws of large numbers. Z. Wahrscheinlichkeitstheorie und Verw. Gebiete 35 (1976), 299-314.

[ 6] Móricz, F., Moment inequalities for the maximum of partial sums of random fields. Acta Sci. Math. (Szeged) 39 (1977) (to appear).

[ 7] Móricz, F., Multiparameter strong laws of large numbers I. (Second order moment restrictions). Acta Sci. Math. (Szeged) 40 (1978) (to appear).

[ 8] Móricz, F., Multiparameter strong laws of large numbers. II. (Higher order moment restrictions). Acta Sci. Math. (Szeged) 40 (1978) (to appear).

[ 9] Serfling, R.J., Convergence properties of $S_n$ under moment restrictions. Ann. Math. Statist. 41 (1970), 1235-1248.

[ 10] Szép, A., The non-orthogonal Menchoff - Rademacher theorem. Acta Sci. Math. (Szeged) 33 (1972), 231-235.

[ 11] Zygmund, A., Trigonometric Series II. University Press, Cambridge 1959.

# SOME EXTENSIONS OF THE SAMPLING THEOREM

Wolfgang Splettstößer
Lehrstuhl A für Mathematik
Rheinisch-Westfälische Technische Hochschule
Aachen

Although the Shannon sampling theorem itself is only valid for bandlimited functions, it does hold for non-bandlimited functions approximately. A review of several generalizations of the classical sampling sums of P.L. Butzer and the author are given, including its analogue in Walsh analysis, sampling approximation of derivates and Hilbert transform, interpolation of Hermite's type, and discrete versions of approximate identities.

## 1. Introduction

Let us begin with stating the Shannon sampling theorem which is fundamental for this paper.

THEOREM 1.1. *Let* $f \in L(\mathbb{R}) \cap C(\mathbb{R})$ *such that* $f^\wedge(v) := (1/\sqrt{2\pi}) \int_{-\infty}^{\infty} f(t) e^{-ivt} dt = 0$ *for all* $|v| > \pi W$ *and some* $W > 0$. *Then for each* $t \in \mathbb{R}$

$$f(t) = \sum_{k=-\infty}^{\infty} f\left(\frac{k}{W}\right) \frac{\sin \pi(Wt-k)}{\pi(Wt-k)} . \tag{1.1}$$

This theorem has found its applications in signal theory as a basis for digital transmission of signal functions. It is connected with the names of C.E. Shannon [24], V.A. Kotel'nikov [16] and H. Raabe [22], all of them electrical engineers. In their language the theorem states that every bandlimited function with cut off frequency $\pi W$ can be reconstituted by its sampling series (1.1). In mathematical papers this series has been dealt with earlier, e.g. by Ch. de La Vallée Poussin [26], E.T. Whittaker [28], and J.M. Whittaker [29]. For a complete historical overview compare e.g. H.D. Lüke [20].

## 2. Sampling Theorem for Non-Bandlimited Functions

Time-limited functions, i.e. functions with bounded support, cannot be bandlimited simultaneously (compare e.g. [9]) unless they are identically zero; therefore Theorem 1.1 cannot be applied. Several authors, compare [2,3, 4,23], have raised the question as to what happens if one misinterprets Theorem 1.1 for time-limited resp. non-bandlimited functions. The result was the following approximate representation.

THEOREM 2.1. *If* $f \in C(\mathbb{R}) \cap L(\mathbb{R})$ *with* $f^\wedge \in L(\mathbb{R})$, *then*

$$f(t) = \lim_{W\to\infty} \sum_{k=-\infty}^{\infty} f\left(\frac{k}{W}\right) \frac{\sin \pi(Wt-k)}{\pi(Wt-k)} \tag{2.1}$$

*uniformly in* $t \in \mathbb{R}$.

Obviously the sums in (2.1) interpolate $f(t)$ at the nodes $t = k/W$, thus they approximate and interpolate the function simultaneously.

The proof of Theorem 2.1 as well as that for Theorem 1.1 is based on a connection between the Fourier transform on the real line and the (periodic) Fourier coefficients. As the method is fundamental for the results stated later on, we would like to give a sketch (see [5,3]) of the

PROOF. The starting point is the Fourier inversion integral of f splitted into two parts

$$f(t) = \frac{1}{\sqrt{2\pi}} \int_{-\pi W}^{\pi W} f^\wedge(v) e^{ivt} dv + \frac{1}{\sqrt{2\pi}} \int_{|v|>\pi W} f^\wedge(v) e^{ivt} dv . \tag{2.2}$$

Then $e^{ivt}$ on the interval $(-\pi W, \pi W)$ is replaced by its boundedly convergent Fourier series

$$e^{ivt} = \sum_{k=-\infty}^{\infty} \frac{\sin \pi(Wt-k)}{\pi(Wt-k)} e^{ivk/W} \qquad (v \in (-\pi W, \pi W))$$

(for the convergence see [12]). Integrating termwise and using the Fourier inversion formula (2.2) for f once more, now at the nodes $k/W$, yields

$$f(t) = \sum_{k=-\infty}^{\infty} \frac{\sin \pi(Wt-k)}{\pi(Wt-k)} \left\{ f\left(\frac{k}{W}\right) - \frac{1}{\sqrt{2\pi}} \int_{|v|>\pi W} f^{\wedge}(v) e^{ivk/W} dv \right\}$$

$$+ \frac{1}{\sqrt{2\pi}} \int_{|v|>\pi W} f^{\wedge}(v) e^{ivt} dv .$$

Therefore the approximation error $R_W(f;t)$ of (2.1) is equal to

$$(2.3) \quad R_W(f;t) = \frac{1}{\sqrt{2\pi}} \int_{|v|>\pi W} f^{\wedge}(v) \left\{ e^{ivt} - \sum_{k=-\infty}^{\infty} \frac{\sin \pi(Wt-k)}{\pi(Wt-k)} e^{ivk/W} \right\} dv .$$

If, now, $f^{\wedge}$ vanishes outside $(-\pi W, \pi W)$, then $R_W(f;t) = 0$ for all t, that is (1.1). If $f^{\wedge} \in L(\mathbb{R})$, then the supremum norm of $R_W(f;t)$ can be estimated from (2.3) by

$$(2.4) \qquad \|R_W(f;\cdot)\| \leqslant \sqrt{\frac{8}{\pi}} \int_{\pi W}^{\infty} |f^{\wedge}(v)| dv = o(1) \qquad (W \to \infty),$$

which proves Theorem 2.1.

Introducing Lipschitz classes by

$$\mathrm{Lip}\, \alpha = \{ f \in C(\mathbb{R});\ \omega(f;\delta) := \sup_{|h|<\delta} \|f(\cdot) - f(\cdot + h)\| = O(\delta^{\alpha}) \}$$

for $\alpha > 0$, it is possible (see [4]) to estimate the remainder integral $\int_{\pi W}^{\infty} |f^{\wedge}(v)| dv$, which yields the following order of approximation for (2.4).

THEOREM 2.2. Let $f(t) = 0$ for all $|t| > T$, some $T > 0$ and $f^{\wedge} \in L(\mathbb{R})$. If $f^{(r)} \in \mathrm{Lip}\, \alpha$, $r \in \mathbb{N}$, $0 < \alpha \leqslant 1$, then

$$(2.5) \qquad \|R_W(f;\cdot)\| = O(W^{-r-\alpha+1}) \qquad (W \to \infty).$$

## 3. Sampling Theorem in Walsh Analysis

Several extensions and generalizations of the classical sampling theorem have been achieved in the last thirty years, compare e.g. the review paper [14] by A.J. Jerri. One method to derive sampling series similar to (1.1) is that of Kramer [17] who generalized the concept of bandlimitation by using other orthonormal sets than that of the Euler functions $e^{ivx}$. He only derives, however, the analogue of Theorem 1.1 and does not deal with the non-bandlimited case similar to that of Theorem 1.2. We would like to restate a sampling theorem from [6], based on the system of the Walsh functions. Although it is trivally simple in the bandlimited (here called sequency-limited) case, it yields an interesting result in the non-sequency-limited case.

The generalized Walsh functions on $\mathbb{R}_+ := \{t \in \mathbb{R},\ t > 0\}$ are given by

$$\psi_v(t) = \exp\{\pi i \sum_{j=-N(t)}^{N(v)+1} v_{1-j} t_j\} \qquad (t, v \in \mathbb{R}_+), \tag{3.1}$$

which coincide with the classical Walsh functions on $[0,1)$ for $v = k \in \mathbb{P} := \{0,1,\ldots\}$ in the Paley-ordering. The integer $N(t)$ (resp. $N(v)$) is given via the dyadic expansion of $t \in \mathbb{R}_+$

$$t = \sum_{j=-N(t)}^{\infty} t_j 2^{-j} \qquad (t_j \in \{0,1\}). \tag{3.2}$$

The dyadic addition $t \oplus u$ of two non-negative numbers $t$ and $u$ is defined by

$$t \oplus u = \sum_{j=-N}^{\infty} |t_j - u_j| 2^{-j}, \tag{3.3}$$

where $N = \max\{j \in \mathbb{Z};\ |t_{-j} - u_{-j}| = 1\}$.

If the Walsh transform $f_W^\wedge$ is given by

$$f_W^\wedge(v) = \int_0^\infty f(t)\psi_v(t)dt \qquad (v \in \mathbb{R}_+), \tag{3.4}$$

then the inversion formula

$$f(t) = \int_0^\infty f_W^\wedge(v)\psi_t(v)dv \tag{3.5}$$

is valid for all $t \in \mathbb{R}_+$, provided $f$ and $f_W^\wedge$ belong to $L(\mathbb{R}_+)$, and $f$ is continuous on $\mathbb{R}_+ \setminus \mathbb{D}_+$ and right-hand continuous on $\mathbb{D}_+ := \{t \in \mathbb{R}_+;\ t = p/2^q,\ p \in \mathbb{P},\ q \in \mathbb{Z}\}$, the set of dyadic rational points. Now, the counterpart of the sampling theorem in Walsh analysis reads

THEOREM 3.1. *Let* $f, f_W^\wedge \in L(\mathbb{R}_+)$ *such that* $f$ *is continuous on* $\mathbb{R}_+ \setminus \mathbb{D}_+$ *and right-hand continuous on* $\mathbb{D}_+$ *with* $f^\wedge(v) = 0$ *for* $v \geq 2^n$, $n \in Z$. *Then*

$$(3.6) \qquad f(t) = \sum_{k=-\infty}^{\infty} f(k/2^n) J(1; 2^n t \oplus k) \qquad (t \in \mathbb{R}_+).$$

Here $J(\omega, t) := \int_0^\omega \psi_v(t)dv$, $t, \omega \in \mathbb{R}_+$, is the Dirichlet kernel introduced by Fine [10] in Walsh-Fourier analysis.

This theorem was first proved by Kak [15] using Kramer's general result. A proof similar to that of Theorem 1.1 sketched above is contained in [6] where the Walsh transform on $\mathbb{R}_+$ and (periodic) Walsh coefficients were connected. On the other hand, the result (3.6) is obvious when substituting

$$(3.7) \qquad J(1; 2^n t \oplus k) = \begin{cases} 1, & t \in [2^{-n}k, 2^{-n}(k+1)] \\ 0, & \text{otherwise} \end{cases}$$

into (3.6) and using the following identy due to Crittenden [8]

$$(3.8) \qquad \int_0^{2^n} f_W^\wedge(v)\psi_t(v)dv = 2^n \int_{2^{-n}k}^{2^{-n}(k+1)} f(u)du \qquad (t \in [2^{-n}k, 2^{-n}(k+1)))$$

valid for functions $f \in L(\mathbb{R}_+)$, as well as the inversion formula (3.5). Thus the assumption of sequency-limitation is too restrictive and yields no new results. But replacing this condition by duration-limitation one gets the following assertion on approximation by step functions.

THEOREM 3.2. *Let* $f$ *be continuous on* $\mathbb{R}_+ \setminus \mathbb{D}_+$ *and right-hand continuous on* $\mathbb{D}_+$ *such that* $f, f_W^\wedge \in L(\mathbb{R}_+)$, *and let* $f(t)$ *vanish outside* $[0,T)$, $T \in \mathbb{R}_+$. *Then for each* $t \in \mathbb{R}_+$

$$(3.9) \qquad f(t) = \lim_{n \to \infty} \sum_{k=0}^{K} f(k/2^n) J(1; 2^n t \oplus k)$$

$K = K(n,T) \in \mathbb{P}$ *being the smallest integer with* $2^{-n}(k+1) \geq T$.

Using the concept of dyadic differentiation (compare [7,37]) it is possible to derive error estimates for the approximation of functions which may even have jumps at each dyadic rational point by special step functions, a new result in spline theory. If $D^{[r]}f$ denotes the r-th dyadic (Walsh-) derivate and $\mathrm{Lip}_W\,\alpha$ the dyadic Lipschitz class (for definitions see [27]), one has

THEOREM 3.3. *If in addition to the assumptions of Theorem* 3.2 $D^{[r]}f$ *exists and* $D^{[r]}f \in \mathrm{Lip}_W\,\alpha$, $r \in \mathbb{N}$, $\alpha > 0$, *then*

$$\sup_{t\in\mathbb{R}_+} |R_n(t)| = \mathcal{O}(2^{-n(r+\alpha-1)}) \qquad (n\to\infty). \tag{3.10}$$

Here $R_n$ is the approximation error of (3.9).

## 4. Derivatives and Hilbert Transform in Sampling Approximation.

In 1955 Fogel [11] investigated a sampling expansion involving sampling points of the derivate of f too. This research was extended later on by several authors (see [13,18,19,21]) by employing higher derivates and using various methods of proof. In all these papers only bandlimited functions were dealt with. Using the approach of Sec. 2 it is possible to approximate functions f, for which $f^\wedge$ need not have bounded support, by sampling f and f' [5].

THEOREM 4.1. *If* $f,f' \in C(\mathbb{R}) \cap L(\mathbb{R})$ *and* $[f']^\wedge \in L(\mathbb{R})$, *then one has uniformly in* $t \in \mathbb{R}$

$$f(t) = \lim_{W\to\infty} \sum_{k=-\infty}^{\infty} \left[\frac{\sin \frac{\pi}{2}(Wt-2k)}{\frac{\pi}{2}(Wt-2k)}\right]^2 \left\{f(\tfrac{2k}{W}) + (t-\tfrac{2k}{W})f'(\tfrac{2k}{W})\right\}. \tag{4.1}$$

The proof begins with the inversion formula (2.1) where $e^{ivt}$ in the first integral is replaced by

$$e^{ivt} = \varepsilon_1(v)e^{ivt} + iv\varepsilon_2(v)e^{ivt} \qquad (v \in (-\pi W,\pi W)) \tag{4.2}$$

with

$$\varepsilon_1(v) = 1 - \frac{|v|}{\pi W}(1 - e^{i\pi Wt\,\mathrm{sgn}\,v})$$

and

$$\varepsilon_2(v) := \frac{i\,\mathrm{sgn}\,v}{\pi W}\, e^{-i\pi Wt\,\mathrm{sgn}\,v} .$$

Since

$$\varepsilon_i(v+\pi W) = \varepsilon_i(v) \qquad (v \in (0,\pi W),\ i=1,2),$$

both functions may be expanded in their $\pi W$-periodic boundedly convergent Fourier series on $(-\pi W,\pi W)\setminus\{0\}$ namely

$$\varepsilon_1(v) = \sum_{k=-\infty}^{\infty} \left\{\frac{\sin \frac{\pi}{2}(Wt-2k)}{\frac{\pi}{2}(Wt-2k)}\right\}^2 e^{iv2k/W} \qquad v \in (-\pi W,\pi W)\setminus\{0\}$$

and

$$\varepsilon_2(v) = \sum_{k=-\infty}^{\infty} \left\{\frac{\sin \frac{\pi}{2}(Wt-2k)}{\frac{\pi}{2}(Wt-2k)}\right\}^2 (t-2k/W)e^{iv2k/W} .$$

After substituting those functions in (4.2) and (2.1) the proof goes along similar lines to that of Theorem 2.1. After some calculations it turns out that the approximation error of (4.1) has the same estimate as that in (2.4) although the nodes are double the distance apart compared to that in (2.1). Note that (4.1) gives an interpolation formula of Hermite type.

In Theorem 4.1 differentiable functions were approximated by sampling the function and its first derivate. On the other hand, the first derivate can be approximated by sampling only the given function.

THEOREM 4.2. <u>If</u> $f,f' \in C(\mathbb{R}) \cap L(\mathbb{R})$ <u>and</u> $[t']' \in L(\mathbb{R})$, <u>then</u>, <u>uniformly</u> <u>in</u> $t \in \mathbb{R}$,

$$(4.3) \qquad f'(t) = \lim_{W\to\infty} \pi W \sum_{k=-\infty}^{\infty} f\left(\frac{k}{W}\right)\left\{\frac{\cos \pi(Wt-k)}{\pi(Wt-k)} - \frac{\sin \pi(Wt-k)}{[\pi(Wt-k)]^2}\right\} .$$

The proof is based on the $2\pi W$-periodic Fourier series expansion of the function $ive^{ivt}$, $v \in (-\pi W,\pi W)$.

Also the Hilbert transform defined by $f(t) = \lim_{\delta\to 0+} \frac{1}{\pi} \int_{|u|\geq\delta} (f(t-u)/u)du$ can be approximated using samples of f. The result is one answer to a question raised by Prof. F. Schipp (Budapest) at the present conference concerning the rôle of the Hilbert transform in sampling theory.

THEOREM 4.3. _If_ $f \in C(\mathbb{R}) \cap L(\mathbb{R})$, $f^{\wedge} \in L(\mathbb{R})$ _and_ $f^{\sim} \in L(\mathbb{R})$, _then_

$$f^{\sim}(t) = \lim_{W\to\infty} \sum_{k=-\infty}^{\infty} f\left(\frac{k}{W}\right) \frac{[\sin \frac{\pi}{2}(Wt-k)]^2}{\frac{\pi}{2}(Wt-k)} \tag{4.4}$$

_uniformly in_ $t \in \mathbb{R}$.

Using a method of proof somewhat similar to that given in the present paper Boas [1] gave the following representation for the first derivate of functions f bandlimited to $(-\pi W, \pi W)$

$$f'(t) = \frac{1}{\pi W} \sum_{k=-\infty}^{\infty} f\left(t + \frac{2k+1}{W}\right) \frac{(-1)^k}{[(2k+1)/(2W)]^2} . \tag{4.5}$$

For non-bandlimited functions it turns out that other approximation formulae with sums of the type (4.5) are valid. In fact, if one substitutes the function $iv$, $v \in (-\pi W, \pi W)$, in the inversion integral of $f'$ by its $2\pi W$-periodic Fourier series (instead of $ive^{ivt}$ as in the proof of (4.3)), it can be shown (see [5])

THEOREM 4.4. _If_ $f, f' \in C(\mathbb{R})$ _and_ $f', [f']^{\wedge} \in L(\mathbb{R})$, _then, uniformly in_ $t \in \mathbb{R}$,

$$f'(t) = \lim_{W\to\infty} \sum_{\substack{k=-\infty \\ k\neq 0}}^{\infty} f\left(t + \frac{k}{W}\right) \frac{(-1)^{k+1}}{(k/W)} \tag{4.6}$$

Under suitable conditions for the second derivative one has

$$f''(t) = \lim_{W\to\infty} 2 \sum_{\substack{k=-\infty \\ k\neq 0}}^{\infty} f\left(t + \frac{k}{W}\right) \frac{(-1)^{k+1}}{(k/W)^2} \qquad (t \in \mathbb{R}). \tag{4.7}$$

Note that the sum for the r-th derivative, $r > 2$, becomes more complicated and cannot be derived by substituting the number 2 by r in (4.7). An approximation formula of type (4.6) for the Hilbert transform also holds. It reads

THEOREM 4.5. _If_ $f \in C(\mathbb{R}) \cap L(\mathbb{R})$, $f^{\wedge} \in L(\mathbb{R})$ _and_ $f^{\sim} \in L(\mathbb{R})$, _then_

$$f^{\sim}(t) = \lim_{W\to\infty} \sum_{k=-\infty}^{\infty} f\left(t + \frac{2k+1}{W}\right) \frac{-2}{(2k+1)\pi} \tag{4.8}$$

_uniformly in_ $t \in \mathbb{R}$.

## 5. Generalized Sampling Sums

The aim of this section is to improve the rate of convergence in (2.5) by constructing new sampling sums. But first of all we show that the order of approximation by the sums of (2.1) itself can be improved by the factor $(\log W)/W$ when using the concept of approximate identities. All the results of this section are treated in detail in [25].

THEOREM 5.1. Let $f \in C(\mathbb{R}) \cap L(\mathbb{R})$ with $f(t) = O(|t|^{-\gamma})$ $(|t| \to \infty)$ for some $\gamma > 0$. If $f^{(r)} \in \mathrm{Lip}\,\alpha$, $0 < \alpha \leq 1$, $r \in \mathbb{P}$, then

$$\|R_W(f;\circ)\| = O(W^{-r-\alpha}\log W) \qquad (W \to \infty). \tag{5.1}$$

The proof makes use of the fact that the Riesz means

$$R_{\kappa,\lambda}(f;t;\rho) := \frac{1}{\sqrt{2\pi}} \int_{-\rho}^{\rho} \left(1 - \left|\frac{v}{\rho}\right|^{\kappa}\right)^{\lambda} f^{\wedge}(v)e^{ivt}dv$$

have Fouriertransform with bounded support $[-\pi W, \pi W]$ if $\rho = \pi W$ and order of approximation

$$\|f(\circ) - R_{\kappa,\lambda}(f;\circ;\rho)\| = O(\rho^{-r-\alpha}) \qquad (\rho \to \infty),$$

if $r+\alpha < \rho$. As Theorem 1.1 is valid for these means we obtain

$$R_W(f;t) = (f(t) - R_{\kappa,\lambda}(f;t;\pi W)) + \sum_{k=-\infty}^{\infty} \left(R_{\kappa,\lambda}(f;\tfrac{k}{W};\pi W) - f(\tfrac{k}{W})\right) \frac{\sin \pi(Wt-k)}{\pi(Wt-k)},$$

where the first term has the order $O(W^{-r-\alpha})$ and the second can be calculated to behave like $W^{-r-\alpha}\log W$ for $W \to \infty$.

Note that we have been able to drop the hypothesis $f^{\wedge} \in L(\mathbb{R})$ and to replace the assumption $f(t) = 0$ for all $|t| > T$ by $f(t) = O(|t|^{-\gamma})$ $(|t| \to \infty)$.

Before we formulate a general new sampling theorem let us explain an obvious connection between the Fourier inversion integral of a bandlimited function

$$f(t) = \frac{1}{\sqrt{2\pi}} \int_{-\pi W}^{\pi W} f^{\wedge}(v)e^{ivt}dv = W \int_{-\infty}^{\infty} f(u) \frac{\sin \pi W(t-u)}{\pi W(t-u)} du \tag{5.2}$$

and the classical sampling series

$$f(t) = \sum_{k=-\infty}^{\infty} f(\tfrac{k}{W}) \frac{\sin \pi W(t - \frac{k}{W})}{\pi W(t - \frac{k}{W})} \quad . \tag{5.3}$$

Indeed, if one takes a Riemann sum of (5.2) with nodes k/W, one obtains the sum in (5.3). In this instance a convolution integral is equal to a convolution sum. A generalization of this fact is the following

LEMMA 5.2. *Let $f,g \in C(\mathbb{R}) \cap L(\mathbb{R})$ with $f^\wedge(v) = g^\wedge(v) = 0$ for all $|v| > \pi W$ and some $W > 0$. If $g^\wedge$ is absolutely continuous on $(-\pi W, \pi W)$, then*

$$\begin{aligned} \sqrt{2\pi}(f * g)(t) &:= \int_{-\infty}^{\infty} f(u)g(t-u)\,du \\ &= \frac{1}{W} \sum_{k=-\infty}^{\infty} f(\tfrac{k}{W}) g(t - \tfrac{k}{W}) \qquad (t \in \mathbb{R}). \end{aligned} \tag{5.4}$$

We are now able to replace the Dirchlet kernel contained in the classical sampling series by certain kernels of convolution integrals.

THEOREM 5.3. *Let $\chi \in C(\mathbb{R}) \cap L(\mathbb{R})$ with $\chi(x) = O(|x|^{-\gamma})$ $(|x| \to \infty)$ for some $\gamma > 0$ and $\int_{-\infty}^{\infty} \chi(u)du = \sqrt{2\pi}$. Further, let $\chi^\wedge(v) = 0$ for all $|v| > V$ and some $V > 0$, and let $\chi^\wedge$ be absolutely continuous on $(-V,V)$. If $f \in C(\mathbb{R}) \cap L(\mathbb{R})$, and if*

$$\| f(\circ) - J(f;\circ;\rho) \| = O(\rho^{-\alpha}) \qquad (\rho \to \infty)$$

*for some $\alpha > 0$, where the convolution integral J is defined by $J(f;t;\rho) = (f * \chi_\rho)(t)$ with $\chi_\rho(t) = \rho\chi(\rho t)$, then*

$$\Big| f(t) - \frac{1}{\sqrt{2\pi} W} \sum_{k=-\infty}^{\infty} f(\tfrac{k}{W}) \chi_{\pi W/V}(t - \tfrac{k}{W}) \Big| = O(W^{-\alpha}) \qquad (W \to \infty) \tag{5.5}$$

*uniformly in $t \in \mathbb{R}$.*

The order of approximation of f by the convolution sums in (5.5) is therefore just the same as that by the convolution integrals $J(f;t;\pi W)$.

With Theorem 5.3 we are in the position to construct a number of new sampling series approximating the given function. Furthermore we are able to give the rate of convergence at once provided that the rate for the associated convolution integrals is known. Let us only state two examples, the first of which is based on Fejer's kernel.

COROLLARY 5.4. *Let* $f \in L(\mathbb{R})$ *with* $f^{(r)} \in \mathrm{Lip}\,\alpha$ *for some* $r \in \mathbb{P}$ *and* $0 < \alpha \leq 1$. *Then for each* $t \in \mathbb{R}$

$$f(t) = \lim_{W\to\infty} \frac{1}{2} \sum_{k=-\infty}^{\infty} f\left(\frac{k}{W}\right)\left\{\frac{\sin \frac{\pi}{2}(Wt-k)}{\frac{\pi}{2}(Wt-k)}\right\}^2 \tag{5.6}$$

*and*

$$\|R_W(f;\sigma;\circ)\| = \begin{cases} O(W^{-\alpha}) & , \alpha < 1,\ r=0 \\ O(W^{-1}\log W) & , \alpha=1,\ r=0 \\ O(W^{-1}) & , r \geq 1, \end{cases} \tag{5.7}$$

*where* $R_W(f;\sigma;t)$ *is the approximation error of* (5.6).

Note that the rate of convergence in (5.7) is better than that in (5.1) only for $0 < \alpha < 1$ and $r = 0$. The second example is connected with the de La Vallée Poussin means. As they are not saturated in $C(\mathbb{R})$ the rate of convergence of (5.1) is, however, improved by the factor $1/W$ for $0 < \alpha \leq 1$ and each $r \in \mathbb{P}$.

COROLLARY 5.5. *Let* $f \in L(\mathbb{R})$ *with* $f^{(r)} \in \mathrm{Lip}\,\alpha$ *for some* $r \in \mathbb{P}$, $0 < \alpha \leq 1$, *then*

$$f(t) = \lim_{W\to\infty} \sum_{k=-\infty}^{\infty} f\left(\frac{k}{W}\right) \frac{\sin \frac{3\pi}{4}(Wt-k)\sin \frac{\pi}{4}(Wt-k)}{[\frac{\pi}{4}(Wt-k)]^2} \qquad (t \in \mathbb{R}) \tag{5.7}$$

*and the order of approximation is*

$$\|R_W(f;\theta;\circ)\| = O(W^{-r-\alpha}) \qquad (W \to \infty).$$

This research was partially supported by Grant II B 4 - FA 7107, Minister für Wissenschaft und Forschung, Nordrhein-Westfalen.

## REFERENCES


[ 1] Boas, R.P., Jr., Entire Functions. Academic Press, New York,1954.

[ 2] Boas, R.P., Jr., Summation formulas and band-limited signals. Tôhoku Math. J. 24 (1972), 121-125.

[ 3] Brown, J.L., Jr., On the error in reconstructing a non-bandlimited function by means of the band pass sampling theorem. J. Math. Anal. Appl. 18 (1967), 75-84.

[ 4] Butzer, P.L. - Splettstößer, W., A sampling theorem for duration limited functions with error estimates. Information and Control 34 (1977), 55-65.

[ 5] Butzer, P.L. - Splettstößer, W., Approximation und Interpolation durch verallgemeinerte Abtastsummen. Forschungsberichte des Landes Nordrhein - Westfalen Nr. 2708: Westdeutscher Verlag, Opladen 1977.

[ 6] Butzer, P.L. - Splettstößer, W., Sampling principle for duration-limited signals and dyadic Walsh analysis. Information Sciences 14 (1978), 14pp.

[ 7] Butzer, P.L. - Wagner, H.J., A calculus for Walsh functions defined on $\mathbb{R}_+$. In: Applications of Walsh functions (Proc. Sympos. Naval Res. Lab., Washington D.C., April 18-20, 1973; Ed. R.W. Zeek - A.E. Showalter) Washington, D.C. 1973, xi + 298pp.; 75-81.

[ 8] Crittenden, R.B., Walsh-Fourier transforms. In: Applications of Walsh functions (Proc. Sympos. Naval Res. Lab. Washington, D.C. March - - April 1970; Ed. C.A. Bass), Washington, D.C. 1970, viii + 274pp.; 170-174.

[ 9] Dym, H. - McKean, H.P., Fourier Series and Integrals. Academic Press, New York and London, 1972.

[10] Fine, N.J., The generalized Walsh functions. Trans. Amer. Math. Soc. 69 (1950), 66-77.

[11] Fogel, L.J., A note on the sampling theorem. IRE Trans. Information Theory 1 (1955), 47-48.

[12] Hardy, G.H. - Rogosinski, W.W., Fourier Series. 3rd ed., University Press, Cambridge, 1956.

[13] Jagerman, D.L. - Fogel, L.J., Some general aspects of the sampling theorem. IRE Trans. Information Theory 2 (1956), 139-156.

[14] Jerri, A.J., The Shannon sampling theorem - its various extensions and applications: a tutorial review. Proc. IEEE 65 (1977), 1565-1596.

[15] Kak, S.C., Sampling theorem in Walsh-Fourier analysis. Electron. Lett. 6 (1970), 447-448.

[16] Kotel'nikov, V.A., Die Übertragungskapazität des "Äthers" und des Drahts bei der elektrischen Nachrichtentechnik. (russ.) Materialien zur 1. Allunionskonferenz über Probleme des technischen Wiederaufbaus des Nachrichtenwesens und der Entwicklung der Schwachstromindustrie, 1933.

[17] Kramer, H.P., A generalized sampling theorem. J. Math. Phys. 38 (1959), 68-72.

[18] Linden, D.A., A discussion of sampling theorems. Proc. IRE 47 (1959), 1219-1226.

[19] Linden, D.A. - Abramson, N.M., A generalization of the sampling theorem. Information and Control 3 (1960), 26-31; Errata. Ibid. 4 (1961), 95-96.

[20] Lüke, H.D., Zur Entwicklung des Abtasttheorems. NTZ (to appear).

[21] Nathan, A., On sampling a function and its derivatives. Information and Control 22 (1973), 172-182.

[22] Raabe, H., Untersuchungen an der wechselseitigen Mehrfachübertragung (Multiplexübertragung). Elektr. Nachrichtentechnik 16 (1939), 213-228.

[23] Schüssler, H.W., Über das Abtasttheorem und seine Anwendung zur Berechnung von Spektralfunktionen aus Zeitfunktionen und umgekehrt. Dissertation, RWTH Aachen 1958.

[24] Shannon, C.E., Communication in the presence of noise. Proc. IRE 37 (1949), 10-21.

[25] Splettstößer, W., Über die Approximation stetiger Funktionen durch die klassischen und durch neue Abtastsummen mit Fehlerabschätzungen. Dissertation, RWTH Aachen 1977.

[26] de La Vallée Poussin, C.J., Sur la convergence des formules d'interpolation entre ordonnées équidistantes. Bull. Acad. Roy. de Belgique (1908), 319-410.

[27] Wagner, H.J., On dyadic calculus for functions defined on $\mathbb{R}_+$. In: Theory and Applications of Walsh Functions (and Other Nonsinusoidal Functions). Sympos. Hatfield, Herts., July 1-3, 1975.

[28] Whittaker, E.T., On the functions which are represented by the expansions of the interpolation theory. Proc. Roy. Soc. Edinburgh 35 (1915), 181-194.

[29] Whittaker, J.M., The Fourier theory of the cardinal functions. Proc. Math. Soc. Edinburgh 1 (1929), 169-176.

# A BIBLIOGRAPHY ON THE APPROXIMATION OF FUNCTIONS BY OPERATORS OF CLASS $S_{2m}$ OR $S_m$ INVOLVING KERNELS OF FINITE OSCILLATIONS

Eberhard L. Stark
Lehrstuhl A für Mathematik
Rheinisch-Westfälische Technische Hochschule
Aachen

## Introduction

Concerning research on the approximation of functions by means of positive linear operators (PLO), great progress has been made, in particular due to the famous test function theorem of H. BOHMAN - P.P. KOROVKIN. On the other hand, all these investigations are limited in their efficiency by a second theorem of P.P. KOROVKIN stating e.g. that for singular convolution integrals with positive polynomial kernel the optimal (critical) order of approximation cannot exceed $O(n^{-2})$, $n \to \infty$. Many ways have been tried to bypass this dilemma, thus e.g. by taking different linear combinations of positive kernels, iterates of kernels, m-singular integrals, etc. The most attractive approach (at least for the author) seems to be by introducing kernels of f i n i t e (l i m i t e d) o s c i l l a t i o n s, this being so since the graphical behaviour and the peaking property of these kernels is, in comparison with positive ones, very clear and intuitive.

Thus e.g. in case of $2\pi$-periodic functions, an even trigonometric polynomial $p_n(x)$ of degree n is said to be of finite oscillation of order 2m, i.e., $p_n \in \mathcal{T}_{2m}$, if there are exactly 2m symmetrical changes of sign (zeroes of simple multiplicity) in the interval $(-\pi,\pi)$ with m being independent of n. Then the corresponding singular integral is of class $S_{2m}$ (or $S_m$ in the analogous algebraic case). The optimal order of approximation of operators of class $S_{2m}$ is characterized by the following theorem: if $p_n \in \mathcal{T}_{2m}$, $p_n(0) > 0$, then the critical order of approximation is given by $O(n^{-2-2m})$, $n \to \infty$. This gives a truly simple relation between the number of sign changes and the optimal order of approximation.

The research in this field was initiated in 1962 by the paper [28] of P.P. KOROVKIN (see also the conference papers [29],[30] of the same year). Independently but later, on the occasion of the Gatlinburg conference on approximation theory of 1963, J.R. RICE brought up the problem to P.L. BUTZER. This led to the papers [47] ([14]) and [25] ([26],[27]); see also the remarks in [14, p.88],[48, p.38/39],[12, p.80]. However it seems that M. GHERMANESCO [22],[23] first considered the problem in 1932/33 implicitly, without recognizing it as formulated above; cf. [51, p.447][12, p.82, footnote 7]. Another contribution to the subject before 1962 is due to V.A. BASKAKOV [2] (written communication); compare also the remarks of this author in [4, p.14],[3, p.474]. Since 1965/66 a series of papers appeared giving various contributions to this theory. Included are five candidate or doctoral dissertations [2],[5],[25],[47],[48]; in two monographs on approximation theory the problem is indicated, however just in the "Notes and Remarks" sections [13, p.93], [16, p.120]. Finally, this method of improved approximation is mentioned in two survey articles [12, p.79-83],[21, p.133].

In the bibliography all papers - known to the author by personal inspection or (in some few cases) only by a review or written communications - which are connected in any way with kernels of finite oscillations are listed. Though completeness is, of course, aspired, there obviously will be gaps. The author would like to thank all readers who will attract his attention to errors and supplements, missing papers (among others especially those marked with an asterisk) and reviews that have been overlooked, and for providing him with preprints and reprints of new papers.

This bibliography has been prepared with the hope that all workers in this field will derive profit from it.

Acknowledgement

A first version of this bibliography (=Arbeitsbericht 56, Lehrstuhl A für Mathematik, RWTH Aachen, August 1975) was forwarded to many of the contributors appearing therein: the additions (e.g. [2],[3],[46]) suggested have been incorporated into this manuscript. The author would like to thank all of those who helped to realize this bibliography by sending reprints, preprints, rare collections of papers, etc. and even their reviewing copies of missing papers, namely V.A. BASKAKOV, B. BOJANOV, Z. DITZIAN, G. FREUD, J.C. HOFF, A. LUPAŞ, S.M. NIKOL'SKIĬ, J.R. RICE, S.D. RIEMENSCHNEIDER, S. ROLEWICZ, Ju.A. ŠAŠKIN, J. SZABADOS.

Thanks are also due to Prof. P.L. BUTZER for a careful reading of the manuscript and for his support in publishing this bibliography.

## Notations

If available the corresponding reviews are added; the abbreviations are as follows

| | |
|---|---|
| MR | Mathematical Reviews; |
| Zbl | Zentralblatt für Mathematik und ihre Grenzgebiete; |
| RZM | Referativnyĭ Žurnal. Matematika; |
| FdM | Jahrbuch über die Fortschritte der Mathematik; |
| DA | Dissertations Abstracts, Ser. B. |

The abbreviations of names of journals etc. are those used in the MR; if not listed, the abbreviations are assimilated (with other pertinent information given when desirably for clarity). The name of a reviewer appears if there are critical remarks, etc. An asterisk indicates that this paper was not at the author's disposal.

## Bibliography

[ 1] ABAKUMOV, Ju.G.
A certain problem of P.P. Korovkin (Russ.).
In: Application of Functional Analysis in Approximation Theory; I. (Russ.)(Ed. A.V. Efimov, A.L. Garkavi, V.N. Nikol'skiĭ) Kalinin Gos. Univ., Kalinin 1973, 178 pp.; pp. 3-5.
RZM 1974, 6B 111.

[ 2]* BASKAKOV, V.A.
On some sequences of linear operators which converge in the space of continuous functions (Russ.).
Cand. Diss., Moscow 1955.

[ 3] BASKAKOV, V.A.
The generalization of some theorems of P.P. Korovkin on positive operators (Russ.).
Mat. Zametki 13 (1973) 785-794 = Transl.: Math. Notes 13 (1973) 471-476.
MR 48 ≠≠ 6776; Zbl 278 ≠≠ 43011, 283 ≠≠ 41009; RZM 1973, 9B 88.

[ 4] BASKAKOV, V.A.
A generalization of theorems of Korovkin on conditions for and the order of convergence of a sequence of positive operators.
In: Approximation Theory (Proc. Conf. Poznán, 22.-26.8.1972; Eds. Z. Ciesielski - J. Musielak). Warszawa - Dordrecht 1975, xii + 289 pp.; pp. 11-19.
Zbl 308≠≠ 41017.

[ 5]* BUĬ, V.P.
The asymptotic properties of linear operators of class $S_m$ (Russ.).
Cand. Diss., Moscow 1967.
(compare Zbl 283≠≠ 41008; RZM 1975, 5B 65).

[ 6]* BUĬ, V.P.
On linear polynomial operators of class $S_{2m}$ realizing the best order of approximation of functions (Russ.).
Trudy Moscov. Vysš. Tehn. Učilišče im. N.È. Baumana, Kalužsk. Fil. 2, no. 2 (1967) 236-244.
RZM 1968, 1B 609.

[ 7]* BUĬ, V.P.
On a construction of linear operators of class $S_m$ (Russ.).
Trudy Moskov. Vysš. Tehn. Učilišče im N.È. Baumana, Kalužsk. Fil. 2, no. 2 (1967) 245-255.
RZM 1968, 1B 610.

[ 8]* BUĬ, V.P.
On asymptotic properties of trigonometric operators of class $S_{2m}$ (Russ.).
Trudy Moskov. Vysš. Tehn. Učilišče im N.È. Baumana, Kalužsk. Fil. 2, no. 2 (1967) 256-260.
RZM 1968, 1B 611 {G. Fomin}.

[ 9] BUĬ, V.P.
Examples of construction of linear operators of class $S_{2m}$ (Russ.).
In: Trudy Moskov. Vysš. Tehn. Učilišče im. N.È. Baumana, Kalužsk. Fil. 139 Mašinostroenie Vyp. 3 (1970) 537-543.
RZM 1971, 11B 129.

[10] BUĬ, V.P.
The order of approximation of continuous functions by certain linear operators (Russ.).
In: Trudy Moskov. Vysš. Tehn. Učilišče im. N.È. Baumana, Kalužsk. Fil. 139 Mašinostroenie Vyp. 3 (1970) 544-550.
RZM 1971, 10B 57.

[11] BUĬ, V.P.
Certain constructions of linear operators (Russ.).
In: Trudy Moskov. Vysš. Tehn. Učilišče im. N.È. Baumana, Kalužsk. Fil. 139 Mašinostroenie Vyp. 3 (1970) 551-561.
RZM 1971, 10B 56.

[12] BUTZER, P.L.
A survey of work on approximation at Aachen, 1968-1972.
In: Approximation Theory (Proc. Internat. Symp. Univ. of Texas, Austin, Nat. Sci. Foundat., 22.-24.1.1973; Ed. G.G. Lorentz) New York 1973; xv + 525 pp.; pp. 31-100.
MR 49 ≠ ≠ 9476; RZM 1975, 2B 507.

[13] BUTZER, P.L. - NESSEL, R.J.
Fourier Analysis and Approximation. Vol. I, One-dimensional Theory.
Birkhäuser Verlag, Basel - Stuttgart, Academic Press, New York 1971, xvi + 553 pp.
Zbl 217, 426-431; RZM 1972, 9B 715.

[14] BUTZER, P.L. - NESSEL, R.J. - SCHERER, K.
Trigonometric convolution operators with kernels having alternating signs and their degree of convergence.
Jber. Deutsch. Math.-Verein 70 (1967) 86-99.
MR 37 ≠≠ 4489; Zbl 177, 312; RZM 1969, 5B 147.

[15] BUTZER, P.L. - STARK, E.L.
On a trigonometric convolution operator with kernel having two zeroes of simple multiplicity.
Acta Math. Acad. Sci. Hungar. 20 (1969) 451-461.
Zbl 189, 350; RZM 1970, 7B 770.

[16] DEVORE, R.A.
The Approximation of Continuous Functions by Positive Linear Operators.
Lecture Notes in Math. 293 (1972) viii + 289 pp.
Zbl 276 ≠≠ 41011; RZM 1973, 2B 919.

[17] DITZIAN, Z.
Saturation classes for a sequence of convolution operators with limited oscillation.
Israel J. Math. 17 (1974) 315-324.
MR 50 ≠≠ 7903; Zbl 298 ≠≠ 44013; RZM 1975, 2B 525.

[18] DITZIAN, Z. - FREUD, G.
Linear approximating processes with limited oscillation.
J. Approximation Theory 12 (1974) 23-31.
MR 50 ≠≠ 10628; Zbl 292 ≠≠ 41013; RZM 1975, 3B 71.

[19] DUDIN, V.I.
On the best approximation of functions of class $H^{(1)}$ by operators of class $S_2$ (Russ.).
In: Theoretical Mechanics, Constructive Mechanics, Higher Mathematics (Russ.)(Collect. Sci. Rep. Candid. etc.) Moskov. Avtomobil'no-dorožniĭ Inst., Moscow 1969, 206 pp.; pp. 191-194.
RZM 1970, 6B 110.

[20] DUDIN, V.I.
On the boundedness of the norm of operators of class $S_2$ (Russ.).
In: Theoretical Mechanics, Constructive Mechanics, Higher Mathematics (Russ.)(Collect. Sci. Rep. Candid. etc.) Moskov. Avtomobil'no-dorožniĭ Inst., Moscow 1969, 206 pp.; pp. 194-200.
RZM 1970, 7B 144.

[21] GARKAVI, A.L.
The theory of best approximation in normed linear spaces.
In: Progress in Mathematics, Vol. 8, Mathematical Analysis; Ed. R.V. Gamkrelidze. New York - London 1970, viii + 215 pp.; pp. 83-150 (Orig. Russ. Ed. Moscow 1967, pp. 75-132).
MR 43 ≠≠ 7843; Zbl 258 ≠≠ 41019; RZM 1969, 7B 584.

[22] GHERMANESCO, M.
Sur l'intégrale de Poisson.
Bull. Sci. École Polytechnique de Timişoara 4, fasc. 3-4 (1932) 159-184.
FdM 58, 1068.

[23] GHERMANESCO, M.
Sur l'intégrale de Poisson.
Bull. Sci. École Polytechnique de Timişoara 5, fasc. 1-2 (1933) 41-74.
FdM 58, 1068.

[24] GÖRLICH, E.
Über optimale Approximationsoperatoren.
In: Constructive Function Theory (Proc. Internat. Conf. Constructive Function Theory, Varna / Bulgaria, 19.-25.5.1970; Ed. B. Penkov - D. Vačov) Sofia 1972, 363 pp.; pp. 187-191.
MR 51# 1224; Zbl 231# 41020; RZM 1973, 12B 828.

[25]* HOFF, C.J.
Approximation with kernels of finite oscillations.
Thesis, Purdue Univ., June 1968, 116 pp.
RZM 1968, 4B 158; DA 29, 2973.

[26] HOFF, C.J.
Approximation with kernels of finite oscillations. Part I, Convergence.
J. Approximation Theory 3 (1970) 213-228.
MR 41# 5850; Zbl 208, 148; RZM 1970, 12B 66.

[27] HOFF, C.J.
Approximation with kernels of finite oscillations. Part II, Degree of approximation.
J. Approximation Theory 12 (1974) 127-145.
MR 50# 14008; Zbl 288# 41010; RZM 1975, 5B 65.

[28] KOROVKIN, P.P.
Convergent sequences of linear operators (Russ.).
Uspehi Mat. Nauk 17, no. 4 (106) (1962) 147-152 = Transl. (German) Univ. Hannover, TIB /Ü-17/23.
MR 25# 4356; Zbl 107, 321; RZM 1963, 4B 82.

[29] KOROVKIN, P.P.
On conditions of convergence of sequences of operators (Russ.).
In: Studies of Contemporary Problems of Constructive Theory of Functions (Russ.). (Proc. Second All-Union Conf., Baku 8.-13.10. 1962; Ed. I.I. Ibragimov) Baku 1965, 638 pp.; pp. 95-97.
MR 33# 3023; Zbl 178, 173; RZM 1966, 8B 437.

[30] KOROVKIN, P.P.
On the order of approximation of functions by linear polynomial operators of class $S_m$ (Russ.).
In: Studies of Contemporary Problems of Constructive Theory of Functions (Russ.). (Proc. Second All-Union Conf., Baku 8.-13.10. 1962; Ed. I.I. Ibragimov) Baku 1965, 638 pp.; pp. 163-166.
MR 34# 1763; Zbl 195, 72; RZM 1966, 8B 438.

[31] KOVALENKO, A.I.
Certain summability methods for Fourier series (Russ.).
Mat. Sb. (N.S.) 71 (113) (1966) 598-616.
MR 34 ≠≠ 8080; Zbl 171, 26; RZM 1967, 6B 108.

[32] KOVALENKO, A.I.
On the extreme value of a certain functional (Russ.).
In: Interuniversity Scientific Conference on the Problem "Application of Functional Analysis in Approximation Theory" (Russ.) (Proc. Conf.; Ed. V.N. Nikol'skiĭ) Kalinin Gos. Ped. Inst., Kalinin 1970, 204 pp.; pp. 66-71.
MR 43 ≠≠ 2400.

[33] LABSKER, L.G.
A certain cone in the space of continuous functions that is connected with the determination of the functionals of class $S_m$ (Russ.).
In: Interuniversity Scientific Conference on the Problem "Application of Functional Analysis in Approximation Theory" (Russ.) (Proc. Conf.; Ed. V.N. Nikol'skiĭ) Kalinin Gos. Ped. Inst., Kalinin 1970, 204 pp., pp. 84-90.
MR 42 ≠≠ 3478 (compare RZM 1971, 5B 955K).

[34] LABSKER, L.G.
Certain sufficient conditions for the approximation of continuous functions by operators of the class $S_m$ (Russ.; Azerbaijani sum.).
Akad. Nauk Azerbaĭdžan. SSR Dokl. 26, no. 9 (1970) 3-7.
MR 44 ≠≠ 1974; Zbl 208, 333; RZM 1971, 7B 889.

[35] LABSKER, L.G. - MARKOVA, L.A.
Constructive determination of the functionals of class $S_m$ (Russ.).
Izv. Vysš. Učebn. Zaved. Matematika 1970,no. 11 (102) (1970) 59-70.
MR 44 ≠≠ 787; Zbl 214, 121; RZM 1971, 3B 539.

[36] LUPAŞ, A.
On the approximation by linear operators of the class $S_m$ (Roum. sum.). An. Şti. Univ. "Al. I. Cuza" Iaşi Secţ I a Mat. 17 (1971) 133-137.
MR 46 ≠≠ 5911; Zbl 252 ≠≠ 41015; RZM 1971, 11B 1012.

[37] LUPAŞ, A.
Die Folge der Betaoperatoren.
Diss., Univ. Stuttgart, April 1972, 75 pp.

[38] MARSDEN, M.J. - RIEMENSCHNEIDER, S.D.
Korovkin theorems for integral operators with kernels of finite oscillation.
Canad. J. Math. 26 (1974) 1390-1404.
MR 50 ≠≠ 7902, Zbl 293 ≠≠ 47017; 269 ≠≠ 47025; RZM 1975, 7B 626.

[39] MIN'KOVA, R.M.
On the convergence of linear operators of class $S_m$ (Russ.).
In: Interuniversity Scientific Conference on the Problem "Application of Functional Analysis in Approximation Theory" (Russ.) (Proc. Conf.; Ed. V.N. Nikol'skiĭ) Kalinin Gos. Ped. Inst., Kalinin 1970, 204 pp.; pp. 99-104.

[40] MIN'KOVA, R.M.
On the convergence of operators of class $S_m$ in the space $C(-\infty,\infty)$ (Russ.).
Ural. Gos. Univ. Mat. Zap. 7, no. 4 (1970) 60-69.
MR 44≠≠ 5670; Zbl 309≠≠ 41017; RZM 1971, 11B 1013.

[41] MIN'KOVA, R.M.
On the convergence of derivatives of linear operators (Russ.).
C.R. Acad. Bulgare Sci. 23 (1970) 627-629.
MR 43≠≠ 7830; Zbl 219≠≠ 41013; RZM 1971, 2B 830.

[42] MIN'KOVA, R.M.
On Korovkin systems for operators of class $S_m$ (Russ.).
Mat. Zametki 13 (1973) 147-158 = Transl. Math. Notes 13 (1973) 87-93.
MR 48≠≠ 767 {B. Bojanov}; Zbl 256≠≠ 41021 {A.L. Brown}, 262≠≠ 41016; RZM 1973, 6B 681.

[43] MIN'KOVA, R.M.
Approximation of continuous functions by certain classes of linear operators (Russ.).
In: Application of Functional Analysis in Approximation Theory, II. (Russ.)(Ed. A.V. Efimov, A.L. Garkavi, V.N. Nikol'skiĭ, A.M. Rubinov) Kalinin Gos. Univ., Kalinin 1974, 160 pp.; pp. 85-100.
MR 51≠≠ 6240; RZM 1974, 8B 97.

[44] MIN'KOVA, R.M. - ŠAŠKIN, Ju. A.
On the convergence of linear operators of class $S_m$ (Russ.).
Mat. Zametki 6 (1969) 591-598 = Transl.: Math. Notes 6 (1969) 816-820.
MR 41≠≠ 4083; Zbl 189, 431; RZM 1970, 4B 795.

[45] RIEMENSCHNEIDER, S.D.
Korovkin theorems for a class of integral operators.
J. Approximation Theory 13 (1975) 316-326.
MR 52≠≠ 1106; Zbl 296≠≠ 41017; RZM 1975, 9B 605.

[46] ŠAŠKIN, Ju.A.
Topological properties of the extremal boundary with applications to a moment problem (Russ.).
In: Some Applications to Measure Theory (Russ.). Sb. Stateĭ, Trudy Inst. Mat. Meh., Ural'sk. Naučn. Zentr Akad. Nauk SSSR, Vol. 13 (Eds. Ju. A. Šaškin, S.T. Zavališčin), Sverdlovsk 1974, 140 pp.; pp. 96-119.
Zbl 313 ≠≠ 42021; RZM 1975, 6B 819.

[47] SCHERER, K.
Die Abhängigkeit der optimalen Approximationsordnung trigonometrischer Faltungsoperatoren von der Anzahl der Vorzeichenwechsel ihrer Kerne.
Diplomarbeit, RWTH Aachen; Juli 1966, iii + 31 pp.(unpublished; compare [11]).

[48] STARK, E.L.
Über trigonometrische singuläre Faltungsintegrale mit Kernen endlicher Oszillation.
Diss., RWTH Aachen; July 1970, iv + 85 pp.

[49] STARK, E.L.
On approximation improvement for trigonometric singular integrals by means of finite oscillation kernels with separated zeros.
In: Constructive Function Theory (Proc. Internat. Conf. Constructive Function Theory, Varna/Bulgaria, 19.-25.5.1970; Ed. B. Penkov - D. Vačov) Sofia 1972, 363 pp.; pp. 337-344.
MR 51 # 3766; Zbl 234 # 42003; RZM 1972, 11B 154.

[50] STARK, E.L.
An extension of a theorem of P.P. Korovkin to singular integrals with not necessarily positive kernels.
Nederl. Akad. Wetensch. Proc. Ser. A 75 = Indag. Math. 34 (1972) 227-235.
MR 46 # 2316; Zbl 238 # 42006; RZM 1972, 11B 107.

[51] STARK, E.L.
On a generalization of Abel - Poisson's singular integral having kernels of finite oscillation.
Studia Sci. Math. Hungar. 7 (1972) 443-455.
MR 48 # 11864; Zbl 273 # 41016; RZM 1974, 5B 715.

[52] SZABADOS, J.
On convolution operators with kernels of finite oscillations.
Acta Math. Acad. Sci. Hungar. 27 (1976) 179-192.
Zbl 329 # 41017; RZM 1977, 7B 87.

[53] TIHOMIROV, N.B.
On the approximation of derivatives of functions by means of linear operators (Russ.).
In: Proceedings of the Central Regional Union of Mathematical Departments, Functional Analysis and Theory of Functions, II. (Russ.)(Ed. V.A. Efimov, A.L. Garkavi, V.N. Nikol'skiĭ) Kalinin Gos. Ped. Inst., Kalinin 1971, 196 pp.; pp. 162-176.
RZM 1971, 11B 1015.

[54] VASIL'EV, R.K.
On the convergence of operators of class $O_m$ in certain normed spaces of functions (Russ.).
In: Theoretical Mechanics, Constructive Mechanics, Higher Mathematics (Russ.)(Collect. Sci. Rep. Cand. etc.) Moskov. Avtomobil' no-dorozniĭ Inst. Moscow 1969, 206 pp.; pp. 183- 191.
RZM 1970, 6B 764.

[55] VASIL'EV, R.K.
Convergent sequences of linear operators in semi-ordered spaces (Russ.).
Mat. Zametki 8 (1970) 475-486 = Transl.: Math. Notes 8 (1970) 736-741.
MR 43 # 2543; Zbl 204, 160; 208, 391; RZM 1973, 2B 832.

[56] VASIL'EV, R.K.
Order of the approximation of functions on sets by polynomial operators of class $S_m$ (Russ.).
Mat. Zametki 20 (1976) 409-416 = Transl.: Math. Notes 20 (1976) 785-789.
RZM 1977, 3B 596.

[57] VÉRTESI, P.
Saturation of certain operator-sequences.
Acta Math. Acad. Sci. Hungar. 27 (1976) 161-177.
Zbl 333≠≠ 41020.

[58] VINOGRADOVA, G.N.
On the transformation of certain positive operators (Russ.).
Volž. Mat. Sb. 3 (1965) 62-68.
MR 34≠≠ 3184 {J.T. Scheick}; Zbl 269≠≠ 41018; RZM 1966, 3B 533.

[59] VINOGRADOVA, G.N.
Asymptotic value of approximation of functions by operators of a certain class (Russ.).
Volž. Mat. Sb. 4 (1966) 24-29.
MR 36≠≠ 584; Zbl 283≠≠ 41008, 249≠≠ 00002; RZM 1967, 4B 103.

[60] VINOGRADOVA, G.N.
The convergence of a sequence of transformed operators (Russ.).
Kaliningrad. Gos. Univ. Učen. Zap. 1 (2)(1968) 109-119 (1969).
MR 43≠≠ 7833; RZM 1969, 10B 111.

[61]* ZYBIN, L.M.
On conditions for the convergence of a sequence of linear operators of class $S_m$ (Russ.).
Novgorod. Golovn. Gos. Ped. Inst. Učen. Zap. 7 (1966) 37-43.
MR 37≠≠ 4473; RZM 1967, 5B 545.

## Appendix

[App] MIN'KOVA, R.M.
The convergence of derivatives of linear operators (Russ.).
Izv. Vysš. Učebn. Zaved. Matematika 1976, no. 8 (1976) 52-59 =
Transl.: Soviet Math. (Iz.VUZ) 20, no. 8 (1976) 41-47.
RZM 1977, 3B 597.

Chronology

| | |
|---|---|
| 1932/33 | M. Ghermanesco [22,23] |
| 1955 | V.A. Baskakov [2] |
| 1962 | P.P. Korovkin [28] |
| 1965 | P.P. Korovkin [29,30]<br>G.N. Vinogradova [58] |
| 1966 | A.I. Kovalenko [31]<br>K. Scherer [47]<br>G.N. Vinogradova [59]<br>L.M. Zybin [61] |
| 1967 | V.P. Buĭ [5-8]<br>P.L. Butzer - R.J. Nessel - K. Scherer [14]<br>A.L. Garkavi [21] |
| 1968 | C.J. Hoff [25]<br>G.N. Vinogradova [60] |
| 1969 | P.L. Butzer - E.L. Stark [15]<br>V.I. Dudin [19,20]<br>R.M. Min'kova - Ju.A. Šaškin [44]<br>R.K. Vasil'ev [54] |
| 1970 | V.P. Buĭ [9-11]<br>C.J. Hoff [26]<br>A.I. Kovalenko [32]<br>L.G. Labsker [33,34]<br>L.G. Labsker - L.A. Markova [35]<br>R.M. Min'kova [39-41]<br>E.L. Stark [48]<br>R.K. Vasil'ev [55] |
| 1971 | P.L. Butzer - R.J. Nessel [13]<br>A. Lupaş [36]<br>N.B. Tihomirov [53] |
| 1972 | R.A. DeVore [16]<br>E. Görlich [24]<br>A. Lupaş [37]<br>E.L. Stark [49-51] |
| 1973 | Ju.G. Abakumov [1]<br>V.A. Baskakov [2]<br>P.L. Butzer [12]<br>R.M. Min'kova [42] |
| 1974 | Z. Ditzian [17]<br>Z. Ditzian - G. Freud [18]<br>C.J. Hoff [27]<br>M.J. Marsden - S.D. Riemenschneider [38]<br>R.M. Min'kova [43]<br>Ju.A. Šaškin [46] |
| 1975 | V.A. Baskakov [3]<br>S.D. Riemenschneider [45] |
| 1976 | J. Szabados [52]<br>R.K. Vasil'ev [56]<br>P. Vértesi [57]<br>R.M. Min'kova [App] |

# A SURVEY OF SOME RESULTS ON INVARIANT SUBSPACES IN OPERATOR THEORY

A. SHIELDS
Department of Mathematics
University of Michigan
Ann Arbor

The subject of invariant subspaces is very broad and the present survey is intended primarily as an introduction to that part of the theory relating to compactness. And even here we are not complete: for example, no mention is made of operators on Hilbert space with compact imaginary part. For an account of the entire subject up to 1973 see the book of Radjavi and Rosenthal [34], where complete proofs are given. For more recent material see the lectures of C. Pearcy [32] (especially Sections 4 - 8).

Let X denote a complex Banach space and let T denote a linear transformation of X into itself. It is known that T is continuous if and only if T is bounded, that is,

$$(1) \qquad \|T\| = \sup\{\|Tf\| : f \in X, \|f\| \leq 1\} < \infty .$$

In this case we call T an <u>operator</u> on X. A <u>subspace</u> of X will always denote a vector subspace that is a closed set in the topology of X. A subspace M is said to be <u>invariant</u> for T if $TM \subset M$. The two improper subspaces, 0 and X, are invariant for every T.

We make contact with the classical notion of eigenvector by noting that $Tf = \lambda f$ if and only if the one-dimensional subspace spanned by f is invariant for T (here $\lambda$ is a complex number, and $f \neq 0$). If X is finite dimensional then it is classical that every operator has an eigenvector. In fact we have the following theorem of Schur.

THEOREM 1. _If_ $\dim X = n$ _and if_ T _is an operator on_ X, _then there exists a chain of invariant subspaces_

$$M_1 \subset M_2 \subset \dots \subset M_n = X,$$

_with_ $\dim X_i = i$ $(i = 1,\dots,n)$.

NOTE. If X is a Hilbert space then we can choose an orthonormal basis $\{e_1,\dots,e_n\}$ such that $E_i = \mathrm{span}\{e_1,\dots,e_i\}$ $(i = 1,\dots,n)$. The matrix of T with respect to this basis will be upper triangular.

Also, if $\dim X < \infty$ we may decompose X into a direct sum of invariant subspaces on each of which T acts in a very simple manner (Jordan canonical form). Thus invariant subspaces can be used to provide a useful representation of the operator. One reason for the interest in invariant subspaces in the infinite-dimensional case is that one hopes to use them to provide concrete representations of operators. But here we run up against the following basic problem.

QUESTION 1. (Invariant subspace problem). Does every operator on a Banach space have a proper invariant subspace?

In this generality the problem has been answered in the negative by Per Enflo [22]. However, the Banach space that he constructs is not reflexive and in fact is quite complicated. Thus the question is still open for the classical Banach spaces and, in particular, for Hilbert space.

One might hope to answer this question as in the finite-dimensional case by showing that every operator has an eigenvector. A moments thought shows, however, that the shift operator on $\ell^2$:

(2) $$(a_o, a_1, a_2, \ldots) \longmapsto (0, a_o, a_1, a_2, \ldots)$$

$(\Sigma |a_n|^2 < \infty)$, has no eigenvectors.

Curiously, invariant subspaces always exist if X is not separable. Indeed, if f is any non-zero vector then the smallest invariant subspace containing f is spanned by the countable set of vectors f, Tf, $T^2f$, ... , and hence is separable.

One approach to the invariant subspace problem is to restrict attention to special classes of operators. Thus on Hilbert space, guided by physical considerations, one considers self-adjoint operators, and normal operators. These operators have many invariant subspaces and in fact there is a concrete representation for all such operators (the spectral theorem). For a separable Hilbert space one form of this theorem states that every normal operator is (unitarily equivalent to) the operator of multiplication by some bounded measurable function on the $L^2$ space of some finite measure space. The self-adjoint operators correspond to multiplications by real-valued functions (see, for example, [27]). If the Hilbert space is not separable we have the same statement except that the measure space need not be finite, but it can always be taken to be a direct sum of finite measure spaces. Multiplication operators have many invariant subspaces, for example, the subspace of $L^2$ functions that vanish on a fixed set of positive measure is invariant.

Another important direction was taken in pioneering work by B. Szőkefalvi-Nagy and C. Foiaş [36] (see Chapter III, Sect. 4 - 7, pp. 122 - 140). They showed how to define $\phi(T)$, where $\phi$ is any bounded analytic function in the unit disc and T is any (completely non-unitary) contraction operator on Hilbert space. In particular they singled out the class $C_o$ of those T for which $\phi(T) = 0$ for some $\phi$ not identically zero. They showed that operators of this class have enough invariant subspaces to develop an analogue of the Jordan canonical form (see [37]).

The class we want to concentrate on is the class of <u>compact</u> operators. An operator T is said to be compact if the image of the unit ball is a pre-compact set (in reflexive spaces the image of the closed unit ball is always closed, and so the prefix "pre" can be deleted). A theorem of F. Riesz ([35], pp. 75 - 79, esp. Hilfssätze 2,5; see also [11], Chap. V, §3) states that the closed unit ball of a Banach space is compact if and only if the space is finite dimensional; hence in an infinite-dimensional space the identity operator is never compact. Thus the set of compact operators coincides with the set of all operators in the finite-dimensional case, but is a proper subset otherwise. So one might hope to generalize theorems that hold for operators on finite-dimensional spaces at least to the class of compact operators. Unlike the finite-dimensional case, however, it is not the case that every compact operator has eigenvectors. For example, consider the integration operator on $L^2$;

$$(Vf)(x) = \int_0^x f(t)dt, \qquad f \in L^2(0,1).$$

This operator is sometimes called the Volterra operator

EXERCISES. 1) Show that V has no eigenvectors. 2) Show that V is compact. [Hint. Use the Arzela theorem that a closed, bounded, uniformly equicontinuous family of functions is compact in C([0,1]).]

Despite this we have the following basic result.

THEOREM 2 (von Neumann; Aronszajn and Smith). *Every compact operator on a Banach space has a proper invariant subspace.*

This theorem was first proved by von Neumann for Hilbert space, but was not published by him. Later it was rediscovered by Aronszajn, with the same proof. Then he and K. T. Smith extended the result to general Banach spaces in 1954 in [8]. (Incidentally, John Wermer told the author that he once asked von Neumann why he had never published the proof of the theorem; von Neumann replied that he thought the proof was too close to Hilbert's original proof of the spectral theorem to be worth publishing.)

This beautiful result stood in isolation for a number of years. Various authors used it to develop analogues of the "triangular form" representation of finite operators (Theorem 1). See, for example, the book of Gohberg and Krein [23]. But one didn't see how to use the method of proof to proceed further. For example, the following question of Smith and Halmos remained unanswered: if p(T) is compact for some polynomial $p \neq 0$, must T have invariant subspaces? In particular if $T^2$ is compact does T have invariant subspaces? These questions were finally answered in 1966 by Bernstein and Robinson [14].

THEOREM 3. *If T is an operator on Hilbert space and if p(T) is compact for some polynomial $p \neq 0$, then T has a proper invariant subspace.*

The proof was very remarkable since it used Robinson's theory of non-standard analysis (although, in essence, it is based on the ideas in the von Neumann, Aronszajn and Smith proof). Halmos [24] succeeded in eliminating the non-standard analysis from the proof. Then began a very active period. We shall not attempt to list all contributions. In 1968 Arveson and Feldman [9] showed that the conclusion of Theorem 3 remains true if instead of assuming that p(T) is compact we assume that there is a sequence of polynomials in T that converge, in the operator norm (1), to a non-zero compact operator, and if we also assume that T is quasi-nilpotent (that is, zero is the only point in the spectrum of T.)

Also in 1968 Halmos [25] invented the notion of _quasi-triangular_ operator. Roughly, the idea is that there is an increasing sequence of finite-dimensional subspaces, whose union is dense in the space, that are "asymptotically invariant" for the operator. On Hilbert space this can be formulated in terms of orthogonal projections. If M is a subspace and P is the projection onto M, then one verifies that M is invariant for T if and only if $TP = PTP$. Even if M is not invariant for T we can consider the _compression_ of T to M, which by definition is the restriction of PT to M. This is an operator on M.

DEFINITION. _An operator T on Hilbert space is said to be quasitriangular if there exists a sequence $P_n$ of finite-rank projections converging strongly to the identity such that_

$$\lim \|P_n T P_n - T P_n\| = 0.$$

In the proof of Theorem 2 one shows, in effect, that compact operators are quasitriangular. Thus there is a sequence, $\{M_n\}$, of finite-dimensional subspaces associated with the operator. In the Hilbert space case one uses Theorem 1 to produce, for each n, a chain of subspaces of $M_n$ invariant under the compression of T to $M_n$. Then one makes a clever choice of one of these subspaces, for each n, and shows that some subsequence of them "converges" to a limiting subspace that is proper, and that is invariant for T (compactness is used again here).

In [25] Halmos showed that every compact operator is quasitriangular, as is every normal operator. He obtained a number of other properties of such operators. In [26] and [21] Halmos, and Douglas and Pearcy, showed that every operator whose spectrum is at most countable is quasitriangular. For every quasitriangular operator there is a method for producing invariant subspaces (possible trivial), based on the method of proof of Theorems 2 and 3 (this is developed by Deckard, Douglas, and

Pearcy in [18]). In particular, in the Arveson-Feldman theorem the hypothesis that T be quasinilpotent can be replaced by the hypothesis that T be quasitriangular. In 1971 Meyer-Nieberg carried these ideas over to general Banach spaces [31].

Earlier Pearcy had conjectured that the adjoint of every non-quasitriangular operator had an eigenvector. This was finally established in a remarkable series of papers by Apostol, Foiaş, Voiculescu, and Zsido [7], [2], [3], and [4]. The proof was then simplified by three of these authors in [5],[6] and by Douglas and Pearcy in [20-A]. (The converse is true and is much easier to establish; see [21]). Thus we have the following remarkable result.

THEOREM 4. _An operator T on Hilbert space is quasitriangular if and only if T* has no eigenvectors._

A related question which was not solved by these developments was the following: if two compact operators commute must they have a common invariant subspace? One might try to prove this using the preceding methods. A variant of Theorem 1 still holds: two commuting operators on a finite-dimensional space have a chain of subspaces invariant under both operators. The basic difficulty is that if $T_1$ and $T_2$ are commuting operators on an infinite-dimensional Hilbert space, their compressions to a finite-dimensional subspace will not, in general, commute (although they will almost commute in the sense that $A_1A_2 - A_2A_1$ will have small norm, if the subspace is large enough, where $A_1$ and $A_2$ denote the two compressions. Something can still be done in this case; see Bernstein [12] and [13]. Sharper results were obtained by Pearcy and Shields, but only under the extra hypothesis that one operator is self-adjoint. They obtained the following result (unpublished).

PROPOSITION. _If A, B are operators on an n-dimensional Hilbert space H, if A is self-adjoint, and if_

$$||AB - BA|| < \frac{2\varepsilon^2}{n-1}$$

*then there exist two commuting operators* A', B' *on* H, *with* A' *self-adjoint, such that* $||A - A'|| < \varepsilon$, $||B - B'|| < \varepsilon$. *Also, if* B *is self-adjoint then* B' *may be chosen to be self-adjoint*.

Related to this is the concept of *hyperinvariant* subspace.

DEFINITION. *A subspace* M *of a Banach space* X *is said to be hyperinvariant for an operator* T *on* X *if it is invariant for every operator commuting with* T.

This concept was first introduced by Sz.-Nagy and Foiaş [39] in 1965 under another name. The term "hyperinvariant" was first used by Douglas and Pearcy [20].

DEFINITION. *An operator will be called a "scalar" if it is a scalar multiple of the identity operator*.

Scalar operators commute with every operator and hence cannot have hyperinvariant subspaces. No other examples are known of Hilbert space operators without hyperinvariant subspaces.

QUESTION 2. Does every non-scalar operator on Hilbert space have a proper hyperinariant subspace?

Even for general Banach spaces the only known example is that of Enflo [22]. Unlike the invariant subspace problem, this question seems to be just as difficult for non-separable spaces as for separable ones. It can be shown that self-adjoint and normal operators have hyperinvariant subspaces (the invariant subspaces described earlier for multiplication operators turn out to be hyperinvariant). Also, if an operator has an eigenvalue then the full eigensubspace corresponding to that eigenvalue is hyperinvariant. From Theorem 4 we see that non-quasitriangular operators have hyperinvariant subspaces. (On Hilbert space one verifies that M is hyperinvariant for T if and only if the orthogonal complement is invariant for T*.) Thus we have the striking fact that if there are any operators on Hilbert space that don't have hyperinvariant subspaces, then these operators must belong to the class of quasitriangular operators, the very class of "good" operators that was introduced to help make the invariant subspace proof work!

In the spring of 1973 a most extraordinary result became known; it was obtained by a young Moscow mathematician named Victor Lomonosov [30].

THEOREM 5. *Let T and K be commuting operators on a Banach space, with $K \neq 0$ and T not a scalar. Then T has a hyperinvariant subspace.*

COROLLARY 1. *Every compact operator has a hyperinvariant subspace.*

COROLLARY 2. *If T,K are as in the theorem, and if A is any operator commuting with T, then A has an invariant subspace.*

The proof of this very general theorem is surprisingly simple, but very original. An even simpler proof for Corollary 1 was found by H.M. Hilden. For details and further discussion see [34] or [33]. In particular it follows from Corollary 1 that any commuting family of operators, at least one of which is compact (and not the zero operator) has a common invariant subspace. Somewhat overshadowed by the Lomonosov result was an important paper (also in 1973) by Voiculescu [40], in which he managed to use the technique based on quasitriangular operators to prove, in particular, that two commuting compact operators have a common invariant subspace. A year later he obtained the following striking result. (An operator T is said to be biquasitriangular if both T and T* are quasitriangular. It is said to be algebraic if p(T) = 0 for some non-zero polynomial p.

THEOREM 6 (Voiculescu [41]). The set of biquasitriangular operators coincides with the norm closure of the set of algebraic operators.

We already know that if there are any operators on Hilbert space with no proper invariant subspaces then they must be biquasitriangular. Voiculescu's theorem tells us that these operators can be approximated arbitrarily closely by operators satisfying polynomial equations.

It is conceivable that Corollary 2 to Theorem 5 already solves the invariant subspace problem for Hilbert space operators.

QUESTION 3. Does there exist an operator A on Hilbert space such that no (non-scalar) operator commuting with A commutes with a (non-zero) compact operator?

The unilateral shift operator (2) has been suggested as a possible counterexample, but despite several very nice results this remains unproved. See, for example [19], [10], [39], [15], [1].

One might ask whether the conclusion to Corollary 2 could be strengthened to the statement that A has a hyperinvariant subspace? Rather surprisingly it turns out that this is as difficult as the whole hyperinvariant subspace problem. This was shown by Alan Lamber (unpublished). We produce his proof here.

THEOREM 7. (A. Lambert). *If it is true that every (non-scalar) operator on Hilbert space that commutes with a non-scalar operator that commutes with a non-zero compact operator has a hyperinvariant subspace, then it is also true that every (non-scalar) operator has a hyperinvariant subspace.*

PROOF. Let $B$ be a non-scalar operator on Hilbert space $H$, and let $A$ be the operator on $H \oplus H$ defined by the operator matrix

$$A = \begin{pmatrix} B & 0 \\ 0 & B \end{pmatrix}$$

Let $I_1 = = \begin{pmatrix} I & 0 \\ 0 & 0 \end{pmatrix}$, $I_2 = \begin{pmatrix} 0 & 0 \\ 0 & I \end{pmatrix}$, where $I$ is the identity operator on $H$, and let $K$ be any non-zero compact operator on $H$. Since $A$ commutes with $I_1$ which commutes with $\begin{pmatrix} K & 0 \\ 0 & 0 \end{pmatrix}$, $A$ has a hyperinvariant subspace $M \subset H \oplus H$. Since this subspace must be invariant under both $I_1$ and $I_2$, one verifies that there are two closed subspaces $M_1$, $M_2$ in $H$ such that $M = M_1 \oplus M_2$. Since $M$ is invariant under $\begin{pmatrix} B & 0 \\ 0 & 0 \end{pmatrix}$ and $\begin{pmatrix} 0 & 0 \\ 0 & B \end{pmatrix}$ we see that $M_1$ and $M_2$ are each separately invariant under $B$. Finally, we must show that at least one of them is a proper subspace. They cannot both be $\{0\}$, or both be $H$, since $M$ is proper. Suppose that $M_1 = \{0\}$ and $M_2 = H$. Since $A$ commutes with $\begin{pmatrix} 0 & B \\ 0 & 0 \end{pmatrix}$, $M$ will be invariant for this operator. A calculation shows that this implies that

$BM_2 \subset M_1$, in other words, that $B = 0$, which is a contradiction. QED.

The following question is not of special significance, but is suggested by Question 3.

QUESTION 4. If $B$ is any operator on Hilbert space can one always find non-scalar operators $T$ and $A$, and a non-zero compact operator $K$, such that $B$ commutes with $T$ which commutes with $A$ which commutes with $K$?

It is easy to see that this is true if $B$ is the unilateral shift operator, since then $B^2$ can be identified with the operator $\begin{pmatrix} B & 0 \\ 0 & B \end{pmatrix}$ on $H \oplus H$.

Interesting progress was made in another direction by J. Daughtry [16] in 1975. In Theorem 5 he replaced the Lomonosov hypothesis that $T$ commute with a compact operator by the weaker hypothesis that $TK - KT$ have rank at most one. (The <u>rank</u> of an operator $T$ is the dimension of the image space $TH$.) With this hypothesis he was able to show that $T$ has an invariant subspace. Subsequently Kim, Pearcy and Shields [28] were able to show that $T$ actually has hyperinvariant subsapces.

THEOREM 8. *If $T$ is a non-scalar operator on a Banach space and if*

$$\mathrm{rank}(TK - KT) \leq 1$$

*for some non-zero compact operator $K$, then $T$ has a hyperinvariant subspace.*

One might hope to prove the theorem under the weaker hypothesis that $\mathrm{rank}(TK - KT) \leq n$ for some compact operator $K$ with $\mathrm{rank}\ K > n/2$. However in [29] it is shown that to every non-scalar operator $T$ and every positive integer $n$

there corresponds a compact operator $K$, with rank $K \geq n$, such that $\text{rank}(TK - KT) \leq 2$. Thus the suggested improvement, if true, is as difficult as showing that every operator has a hyperinvariant subspace (which is false, for general Banach spaces, by Enflo's example).

In [29] it is shown that the Hypotheses of Theorem 8 are satisfied for a large class of operators, including all operators with disconnected spectrum, all operators $T$ such that either $T$ or $T^*$ has an eigenvector, and, on Hilbert space, all normal (and even, n-normal) operators.

QUESTION 5. Does there exist an operator $T$ on Hilbert space with $\text{rank}(TK - KT) \geq 2$ for every non-zero compact operator $K$?

In this connection W. Brown has shown (unpublished) that if $T$ is any operator having a proper hyperinvariant subspace, and if

$$\mathcal{M} = \{TK - KT : K \in C^1\}$$

then the closure of $\mathcal{M}$ in $C^1$ (in the trace norm) contains an operator of rank at most one. (Here $C^1$ denotes the trace class of operators on Hilbert space.) This suggests that, at least on Hilbert space, the property of having a hyperinvariant subspace may be equivalent to the existence of a compact operator $K$ such that $\text{rank}(TK - KT) \leq 1$.

We conclude by mentioning an unpublished result of Jaime Bravo.

THEOREM 9. *If it is true that every non-scalar operator for which there is a compact operator $K \neq 0$ with $\text{rank}(TK + KT) \leq 1$ has a hyperinvariant subspace, then it is also true that every non-scalar operator has a hyperinvariant subspace.*

## BIBLIOGRAPHY

[1] M.B. Abrahamse, Analytic Toeplitz operators with automorphic symbol. Proc. Amer. Math. Soc. 52(1975), 297-302.

[2] C. Apostol, C. Foiaş, and D. Voiculescu, Some results on non-quasitriangular operators II. Rev. Roum. Math. Pures et Appl. 18(1973), 159-181.

[3] __________, Some results on non-quasitriangular operators III. Rev. Roum. Math. Pures et Appl. 18(1973), 309-324.

[4] __________, Some results on non-quasitriangular operators IV. Rev. Roum. Math. Pures et Appl. 18(1973), 487-514.

[5] __________, Some results on non-quasitriangular operators V. Rev. Roum. Math. Pures et Appl. 18(1973), 1133-1149.

[6] __________, Some results on non-quasitriangular operators VI. Rev. Roum. Math. Pures et Appl. 18(1973), 1473-1494.

[7] C. Apostol, C. Foiaş, and L. Zsido, Some results on non-quasitriangular operators. Indiana Univ. Math. J. 22(1973), 1151-1161.

[8] N. Aronszajn and K.T. Smith, Invariant subspaces of completely continuous operators. Annals of Math. 60 (1954), 345-350.

[9] W.B. Arveson and J. Feldman, A note on invariant subspaces. Mich. Math. J. 15(1968), 61-64.

[10] I.N. Baker, J. Deddens, and J. Ullman, A theorem on entire functions with applications to Toeplitz operators. Duke Math. J. 41(1974), 739-745.

[11] S. Banach, Théorie des opérations linéaires. Warszawa-Lwow (1932).

[12] Allen R. Bernstein, Almost eigenvectors for almost commuting matrices. SIAM Journ. Applied Math, 21(1971), 232-235.

[13] __________, Invariant subspaces for certain commuting operators on Hilbert sapce, Annals o. Math. 95(1972), 253-260.

[14] Allen R. Bernstein and A. Robinson, Solution of an invariant subspace problem of K.T. Smith and P.R. Halmos. Pac. J. Math. 16(1966), 421-431.

[15] C.Cowen, The commutant of an analytic Toeplitz operator. Trans. Amer. Math. Soc., to appear.

[16] J. Daughtry, An invariant subspace theorem. Proc. Amer. Math. Soc. 49(1975), 267-8.

[17] L. DeBranges, Some Hilbert spaces of analytic functions II. J. Math. Analysis and Applic. 11(1965), 44-72.

[18] D. Deckard, R.G. Douglas, and C. Pearcy, On invariant subspaces of quasitriangular operators. Amer. J. Math. 9 (1969), 637-647.

[19] J. Deddens and T.K. Wong, The commutant of analytic Toeplitz operators. Trans. Amer. Math. Soc. 184(1973), 261-273.

[20] R.G. Douglas and C. Pearcy, On a topology for invariant subspaces. J. Func. Anal. 2(1968), 323-341.

[20-A] __________, Invariant subspaces of non-quasitriangular operators. Proc. Conf. Op. Theory, Lecture Notes Math. #345 Springer Verlag (1973), 13-57.

[21] __________, A note on quasitriangular operators. Duke Math. J. 37(1970), 177-188.

[22] P. Enflo, On the invariant subspace problem in Banach spaces. preprint.

[23 ] I.C. Gohberg and M.G. Krein, The theory of Volterra operators in Hilbert space and its applications. Translations Math. Monographs, Vol. 24, Amer. Math. Soc., Providence (1970).

[24 ] P.R. Halmos, Invariant subspaces of polynomially compact operators. Pac. J. Math. 16(1966), 433-437.

[25 ] __________, Quasitriangular operators. Acta Sci. Math. (Szeged) 29(1968), 283-293.

[26 ] __________, Capacity in Banach algebras. Indiana Univ. Math. J. 20(1971), 855-863.

[27 ] __________, What does the spectral theorem say? Amer. Math. Monthly 70(1963), 241-247.

[28 ] H.W. Kim, C. Pearcy, A.L. Shields, Rank-one cummutators and hyperinvariant subspaces. Mich. Math. J. 22(1975), 193-4.

[29 ] __________, Sufficient conditions for rank-one commutators and hyperinvariant subspaces. Mich. Math. J. 23(1976), 235-243.

[30 ] V. Lomonosov, On invariant subspaces of families of operators commuting with a completely continuous operator. Funkcion. Anal. i Priloz. 7(1973), 55-56 (Russian).

[31 ] P. Meyer-Nieberg, Quasitriangulierbare Operatoren und invariante Untervektorräume stetiger linearer Operatoren. Arch. Math. 22(1971), 186-199.

[32 ] C. Pearcy, Some recent developments in operator theory. CBMS Regional Conference Series, to appear.

[33 ] C. Pearcy and A.L. Shields, A survey of the Lomonosov technique in the theory of invariant subspaces. Topics in operator theory, Amer. Math. Soc. Surveys #13, Providence (1974), 219-229.

[34] H. Radjavi and P. Rosenthal, Invariant subspaces. Springer Verlag, New York-Heidelberg(1973).

[35] F. Riesz, Über lineare Funktionalgleichungen. Acta Math. 41(1916), 70-98.

[36] B. Szőkefalvi-Nagy and C. Foiaş, Harmonic analysis of operators on Hilbert space. North-Holland, Amsterdam (1970).

[37] ___________, Modèle de Jordan pour une classe d'opérateurs de l'espace de Hilbert. Acta Sci. Math. (Szeged) 31 (1970) 91-115.

[38] ___________, Quasi-similitude des opérateurs et sous-espaces invariantes. C.R. Acad. Sci. Paris, groupe 1, 261(1965), 3938-3940.

[39] J. Thomson, Intersections of commutants of analytic Toeplitz operators. Proc. Amer. Math. Soc. 52(1975), 305-310.

[40] D. Voiculescu, Some extensions of quasitriangularity II. Rev. Roum. Math. Pures et Appl. 18(1973), 1439-1456.

[41] ___________, Norm limits, of algebraic operators. Rev. Roum. Math. Pures et Appl. 19(1974), 371-378.

# NEW AND UNSOLVED PROBLEMS

Most of the 30 problems presented were provided in written form by the responsible authors. The others, specifically 1,2,4,5,10b,11,12,13,15,16 are based on notes taken during the two special sessions devoted to new and unsolved problems; the editors assume responsibility for any possible inaccuracies in formulation.

## 1. J.M. ANDERSON: Banach Subspaces of $H^1$ with the $\mathcal{F}$ Property

A Banach subspace $X \subset H^1$ of analytic functions on the unit disc is said to have the $\mathcal{F}$ property, iff for any $f \in X$ and any inner function I such that $f/I \in H^1$ one has $f/I \in X$. Many spaces have this property, for instance the spaces $X = H^p$, $p > 1$, and the Lipschitz classes $\Lambda_{n,\alpha}$ (= those functions for which the n-th derivative belongs to the Lipschitz class of order $\alpha$). The only example known so far (given by V.J. Gurarii) of a space which does not have the $\mathcal{F}$ property is $l^1$.

Question. Does there exist an $X \subset H^1$ and an $f \in X$ with $f = I \cdot O$ such that the outer factor O of f is not an element of X?

## 2. C. BENNETT: Functions of Bounded Mean Oscillation and Best Approximation by Linear Fractional Functions

a) The space BMO of functions of bounded mean oscillation is essentially the range of the Hilbert transform H on $L^\infty$, in the sense that

$$BMO = L^\infty + H(L^\infty).$$

Question. Is there a similar description for $L^1$ (instead of $L^\infty$)?

b) Let f be a real-valued, even function on $[-1,1]$ with $f(0) = 0$, $f(1) = 1$, $0 \leqslant f(x) \leqslant 1$, and

$$E(f) = \inf_{a,b,c,d \in \mathbb{C}} \{ \sup_{x \in [-1,1]} |\frac{ax+b}{cx+d} - f(x)| \} .$$

Question. Does there exist among the best approximants $u^*(x) = (a^*x + b^*)/(c^*x + d^*)$ (with $a^*$, $b^*$, $c^*$, $d^*$ complex) a symmetric one, i.e. one such that $u^*(-x) = \overline{u^*(x)}$, $x \in [-1,1]$?

The problem is partially solved by K. Rudnick and J. Vaaler. For the matter see also E.B. Saff and R.S. Varga.

3. P.L. BUTZER - R.L. STENS: On the K-Funktional in the Jacobi Frame

Let the modulus of continuity be defined by

$$\omega_r(\delta;f) = \sup_{0\leq h\leq\delta} \| [1-\tau_h]^r f\|_C ,$$

where $\tau_h$ is the generalized translation operator with respect to Jacobi polynomials [see R. Askey - S. Wainger, Amer.Math.Soc. 91 (1969), 463 - 485]. The problem is to establish the equivalence between this modulus and the associated K-functional, i.e.

$$(1) \qquad c_1\omega_r(\delta,f) \leq K(\delta^{2r};f;C[-1,1];\ \mathcal{D}(D^r))$$

$$:= \inf_{g\in\mathcal{D}(D^r)} \{\| f-g\|_C + \delta^{2r}\| D^r g\|_C\} \leq c_2\omega_r(\delta;f),$$

where $\mathcal{D}(D^r)$ is the domain of the differential operator $D^r$ given by

$$D^1 f = \operatorname*{s-lim}_{h\to 0} \frac{f-\tau_h f}{h^2}, \qquad D^r = D^1 D^{r-1} .$$

It is known that (1) is valid for $r = 1$, as well as in the particular case of the Chebyshev polynomials [see P.L. Butzer - R.L. Stens, Abh.Math.Sem.Univ. Hamburg 45 (1976), 165 - 190]. Moreover, assertions of type (1) are known in the case $\tau_h$ is a semigroup of operators and $D^1$ is replaced by the infinitesimal generator $(-A)$ [see P.L. Butzer - H. Berens, Semigroups of Operators and Approximation, Springer Grundlehren, Vol. 145, 1967, p. 258].

The solution of (1) would, for example, be needed in order to characterize the best approximation $E_n(f;C)$ of $f \in C[-1,1]$ by algebraic polynomials in terms of moduli of continuity. Indeed, for $r = 0,1,2,\ldots$, $0 < \alpha < 1$ there holds

$$(2) \qquad E_n(f;C) = \mathcal{O}(n^{-2(r+\alpha)}) \quad (n \to \infty) \Leftrightarrow \omega_1(\delta, D^r f) = \mathcal{O}(\delta^{2\alpha}) \quad (\delta \to 0+),$$

the case $\alpha = 1$ being unsolved [see H. Bavinck, Applicable Anal. 5 (1976), 239 - 312; S. Pawelke, in: Approximation Theory (Proc. Conf. Poznan 1972), Warszawa, Dordrecht, Boston 1975, pp.157 - 173]. If (1) would be valid for $r = 2$, then (2) would hold for $\alpha = 1$ with $\omega_2$ replacing $\omega_1$. In this sense establishing (1) would amount to showing the Jackson-type theorem

$$E_n(f;C) \leqslant c\omega_r(n^{-1};f).$$

4. W. CHENEY: Minimal Projections

Find a projection of least norm from $C[-1,1]$ onto the set $\Pi_n$ of algebraic polynomials of degree at most n $(n \geqslant 2)$. In particular, do there exist projections $P_n : C[-1,1] \to \Pi_n$ such that

$$\|P_n\| = c \log n + \mathcal{O}(1)$$

with $c < 4/\pi^2$? Note that the value $4/\pi^2$ is attained for Fourier-Chebyshev projections. See P.L. Butzer - R.L. Stens, The operational properties of the Chebyshev transform. I. General properties. Funct. Approximativ. Comment. Math. 5 (1977), 129 - 160.

5. Z. CIESIELSKI: Properties of Hermite Polynomials

a) Let $L^2(\mathbb{R})$ be equipped with the measure $d\mu(x) = \exp(-x^2)dx$, and let $H_n$ $(n = 0,1,2,\dots)$ denote the Hermite polynomial. Then the polynomials $\tilde{H}_n(x) := (\sqrt{\pi}\, 2^n n!)^{-1/2} H_n(x)$ are orthonormal with respect to the inner product $(f,g) := \int_{\mathbb{R}} f(x)\overline{g(x)}d\mu(x)$.

Question. Prove the monotonicity of $\|\tilde{H}_n\|_p$ with respect to n for each $p (1 \leqslant p < \infty)$. For $p = 2$ the monotonicity is obvious; for $p = 1$ it was proved by O. Szász (1951), and for $p = 4$ by G. Freud.

b) The following (sharp version of) the Hausdorff-Young inequality $(1/p + 1/q = 1,\ 1 < p \leqslant 2)$ was proved by W. Beckner (1975)

$$\|f^\wedge\|_q \leq \sqrt{p^{1/p}/q^{1/q}}\,\|f\|_p \qquad (f^\wedge(x) := \int_{\mathbb{R}} e^{-i2\pi xy} f(y)dy).$$

Equality holds for $\tilde{H}_o$. Note that this result is closely connected with Heisenberg's inequality. For any $f \in L_2$ with $\|f\|_2 = 1$ the entropy $E(f)$ is defined by

$$E(f) = -\int_{\mathbb{R}} |f|^2 \log|f|^2 - \int_{\mathbb{R}} |f^\wedge|^2 \log|f^\wedge|^2.$$

It is well known that the entropy $E$ assumes its maximum for $H_o$, i.e. $E(f) \leq E(H_o)$.

Question. Prove the monotonicity of $E(H_n)$, i.e. $E(H_{n+1}) \leq E(H_n)$ $(n = 0,1,2,\ldots)$.

6. J.L.B. COOPER: Approximation to Functions with Group Symmetry

The following problem arises from a question concerning antisymmetric wave functions for three particles on a line. Let $(\varphi_r)$, $(\psi_r)$ be any two complete orthonormal sets in $L_2(R^2)$. Let $\xi(x_1,x_2)$ be a function of unit norm in $L^2(R^2)$ with the following symmetry properties: $\xi(-x_1,x_2) = -\xi(x_1,x_2)$ and $\xi(y_1,y_2) = \xi(x_1,x_2)$ if $(y_1,y_2)$ is derived from $(x_1,x_2)$ by a rotation of the plane through $2\pi/3$. Let $\psi(x_1,x_2) = \Sigma\, c_{rs}\varphi_r(x_1)\psi_s(x_2)$. What is the maximum possible value that $|c_{rs}|$ can have, for any r,s and for any choice of the systems $(\varphi_r)$ and $(\psi_r)$?

If $(\varphi_r)$ and $(\psi_r)$ are both the usual Hermite orthonormal system, it can be shown that the maximum possible value of $|c_{rs}|$ is $\sqrt{3}/2$. It seems likely that this is the maximum for any choice of the systems $(\varphi_r)$, $(\psi_r)$. It would be of interest even to know that the maximum in the general case is less than 1.

7. G. GOES: Trigonometric Series on Banach Spaces of Distributions

Characterize those Banach spaces E of distributions on $T = R/2\pi Z$ for which

(1) $\qquad \sup_n \|s_n(f)\|_E < \infty$ does not imply $\|\sigma_n(f)-f\|_E \to 0 \quad (n \to \infty)$.

Here $s_n(f)(t) = \sum_{k=-n}^{n} f^\wedge(k)e^{ikt}$, $\sigma_n(f)(t) = \sum_{k=-n}^{n}(1-\frac{|k|}{n+1})f^\wedge(k)e^{ikt}$, where $f^\wedge$

is the sequence of Fourier coefficients of the distribution f.

REMARKS. a. It was shown by M. Weiss [2] that the non-implication (1) is true if $E = L^1_{2\pi}$.

b. By Y. Katznelson [1] even $s_n(f)(t) \geq 0$ for all $n = 0,1,2,\ldots$ and all $t \in T$ does not imply $f \in L^1_{2\pi}$.

c. The problem is related and for some spaces E equivalent to the following multiplier problem:

Let $\Omega$ be the space of all complex sequences $x = (x_k)$, $A \subset \Omega$ and

$$A^\gamma = \{x \in \Omega:\ \sup_n \Big|\sum_{k=-n}^{n} x_k y_k\Big| < \infty \qquad \text{for all } y \in A\},$$

$$A^\sigma = \{x \in \Omega:\ \lim_{n\to\infty} \sum_{k=-n}^{n} \Big(1 - \frac{|k|}{n+1}\Big) x_k y_k \quad \text{exists for all } y \in A\}.$$

Problem. Characterize those sets $A \subset \Omega$ for which

$$A^\gamma \not\subset A^\sigma. \tag{2}$$

If $A = L^{\wedge\infty}$ is the space of sequences of Fourier coefficients of $f \in L^\infty_{2\pi}$, then (2) is the above result of M. Weiss.

REFERENCES

[1] Katznelson, Y., Trigonometric series with positive partial sums. Bull. Amer. Math. Soc. 71 (1965), 718 - 719.

[2] Weiss, M., On a problem of Littlewood. J. London Math. Soc. 34 (1959), 217 - 221.

## 8. M. DE GUZMÁN: Approximation of the Identity on $\mathbb{R}^n$

Let $k \in L^1(\mathbb{R}^n)$, $k \geq 0$, $\int k = 1$, $k_\varepsilon(x) = \varepsilon^{-n} k(x/\varepsilon)$ for $\varepsilon > 0$. One knows that if k is radial, i.e. $k(x) = k^*(|x|)$, then for each $f \in L^1(\mathbb{R}^n)$, at a.e. $x \in \mathbb{R}^n$, $k_\varepsilon * f(x) \to f(x)$ as $\varepsilon \to 0$.

One can also prove, by means of the rotation method, that if k is not radial but is nonincreasing along rays, i.e. $k(\lambda x)$ is a nonincreasing function of $\lambda > 0$ for each x with $|x| = 1$, then for each $f \in L^p(\mathbb{R}^n)$, with $p > 1$, at a.e. $x \in \mathbb{R}^n$, $k_\varepsilon * f(x) \to f(x)$ as $\varepsilon \to 0$.

Can one say also in this last case that there is a.e. convergence if $f \in L^1(\mathbb{R}^n)$?

9. J. KOREVAAR: Complex Approximation and Macintyre Exponents

a) When $p_n > n \log n (\log\log n)^{1+\varepsilon}$, $\varepsilon > 0$, $n > n_0$, the positive integral powers $z^{p_n}$ fail to span $C(\gamma)$ for every smooth Jordan arc $\gamma$. Are such $p_n$ Macintyre exponents, that is, must a nonconstant entire function $\sum a_n z^{p_n}$ necessarily be unbounded on every curve going out to infinity? By Kövari's work, the answer is yes when $\varepsilon > 1$.

J. Korevaar and M. Dixon, Lacunary polynomial approximation. These Proceedings, pp. 479 - 489. Also, same authors, Interpolation, strongly non-spanning powers and Macintyre exponents. Nederl. Akad. Wetensch. Proc., Ser. A 81 (1978), to appear.

b) Is there a (wild) Jordan arc $\gamma$ such that $C(\gamma)$ admits a spanning set of positive integral powers $\{z^{p_n}\}$ with $\sum 1/p_n < \infty$?

c) Is there a (wild) Jordan curve $\gamma$ around the origin such that $C(\gamma)$ admits a spanning set of integral powers $\{z^{p_1}, z^{-p_2}, z^{p_3}, z^{-p_4}, \ldots\}$ with $0 < p_n/n \to \infty$?

10. G.G. LORENTZ: Approximation by Algebraic Polynomials

a) Let $\theta$, $0 < \theta < 1$, be given. Determine the smallest possible $\delta = \delta(\theta) > 0$ with the following property. If $f(x)$ is continuous on $[\delta, 1]$, then there exists a sequence of polynomials of the form

$$P_n(x) = \sum_{n\theta \leq k \leq n} a_{n,k} x^k$$

which converges uniformly to $f(x)$ on compact subsets of $(\delta, 1]$. It is known that $\theta^2 \leq \delta(\theta) \leq \theta$.

b) Let $f$ denote a continuous function on $[-1,1]$, $P_n$ the set of polynomials $p_n$ of degree at most $n$, and $p_n^* f \in P_n$ the polynomials of best approximation to $f$ with respect to the supremum norm. Then the following theorem holds:

If f is odd, then (i) $p_n^*(0) = 0$ $(n \in \mathbb{P})$;

(ii) $p_{2k+1}^* f = p_{2k+2}^* f$ $(k = 0,1,2,\ldots)$.

What about the converse statement, i.e. prove or disprove:

1. If $p_n^*(0) = 0$ $(n \in \mathbb{P})$, then f is odd.
2. If $p_n^*(a) = 0$ for some $a \in [-1,1]$ and all $n = 0,1,2,\ldots$, then either $a = 0$ or $f \equiv 0$.
3. If $p_{2k+1}^* f = p_{2k+2}^* f$ $(k = 0,1,2,\ldots)$, then f is odd.
4. If $p_{2k}^* f = p_{2k+1}^* f$ $(k = 0,1,2,\ldots)$, then f is even.

11. P. MASANI: On Wiener's Space

a) Define $Q_1(\mathbb{R}) = \{f;\ f \text{ measurable}, |f|_1 < \infty\}$ where

$$|f|_1 = \overline{\lim} \frac{1}{2h} \int_{-\infty}^{\infty} |f(t+h)-f(t-h)|dt.$$

Then $|f|_1$ is a norm on $Q_1(\mathbb{R})$. Show that $Q_1(\mathbb{R})$ is complete (normed linear space) under this norm. (The space $Q_p(\mathbb{R})$, $1 < p < \infty$, is connected with Helix-theory).

b) If $1_0^+(t) = 1/[\sqrt{\pi}(t+i)]$ and $f \in L_2(\mathbb{R},c)$, with

$$c(E) = \frac{1}{\pi} \int_E \frac{dt}{1+t^2},$$

denoting the Cauchy measure on $\mathbb{R}$, then $f \cdot 1_0^+ \in L_2(\mathbb{R})$. Define the operator $\Sigma$ by $\Sigma(f) = (f \cdot 1_0^+)^\sim$, with $\sim$ denoting the Hilbert transform, and the spaces $X$ and $P$ by

$$X = \{f;\ \overline{\lim_{T\to\infty}} \frac{1}{2T} \int_{-T}^{T} |f(t)|^2 dt < \infty\},$$

$$P = \{f;\ \lim_{T\to\infty} \frac{1}{2T} \int_{-T}^{T} |f(t)|^2 dt \ \text{ exists}\}.$$

For any $\alpha \in L_2(\mathbb{R})$, N. Wiener and I proved that

$$|\alpha|_Q^2 = \overline{\lim_{h\to 0}} \frac{1}{2h}|T(-h,h)\alpha|_2^2$$

with

$$T(a,b) = \frac{1}{N^2}\{T_b - T_a - \int_a^b \tau_t dt\}.$$

Conjecture. The restriction T of $\Sigma$ to the space $X$ is a contraction of norm 1.

12. V. POPOV: Rational Approximation

Let X be one of the spaces $C[0,1]$, $L_p[0,1]$ $(1 \leqslant p < \infty)$, $f \in X$, and $R_n(f)$ the best rational approximation of f, i.e.

$$R_n(f)_X = \inf_{r \in \mathcal{R}_n} \|f-r\|_X ,$$

where $\mathcal{R}_n$ denotes the set of all rational functions r of degree at most n, i.e. $r(x) = (a_k x^k + \ldots + a_0)/(b_m x^m + \ldots + b_0)$, $k,m \leqslant n$. Then the following statement holds (Newman's conjecture): If $f \in \mathrm{Lip}(1;C)$, i.e. $\omega_1(f;\delta;C) = \mathcal{O}(\delta)$, then $R_n(f)_C = o(n^{-1})$, see: V. Popov, Acta Math. Acad. Sci. Hungar. 29 (1977), 119 - 129.

Question. Is the same true for the spaces $L_p$ $(1 < p < \infty)$? Note that the answer is "yes" for p = 1 (P.P. Petrushev).

13. J.B. PROLLA: On the Approximation Property

A Banach space E over the complex field $\mathbb{C}$ is said to have the "approximation property", iff the identity map id: $E \to E$ can be approximated, uniformly on every compact set K in E, by continuous linear maps of finite rank. Then $\mathrm{id} \in \overline{E' \otimes E}^K$ for every compact set $K \subset E$.

Question. On which spaces E (over $\mathbb{C}$) is the following true:

$$\mathrm{id} \in \overline{\mathcal{P}_f \otimes E}^K$$

for every compact set K? Here $\mathcal{P}_f(E)$ denotes the algebra of continuous polynomials of finite type on E.

14. J. ROVNYAK: On $\delta$ - Spectral Sets

Let J denote the operator on $L^2(0,1)$ given by

$$J : f(x) \to \int_0^x f(t)dt.$$

We call an open set G in the complex plane a $\delta$ - spectral set for J if there is a homomorphism $\varphi(z) \to \varphi(J)$ from the space $H^\infty(G)$ of bounded analytic functions on G to the space of bounded operators on $L^2(0,1)$ which extends the functional calculus for rational functions and satisfies

$$\|\varphi(J)\| \leq \delta \sup_{z \in G} |\varphi(z)|$$

for all $\varphi \in H^\infty(G)$. It can be shown that every disc $G_\varepsilon = \{z: |z-\varepsilon| < \varepsilon\}$, where $\varepsilon > 0$, is a $\delta$ - spectral set for J for some $\delta = \delta(\varepsilon)$. See R. Frankfurt and J. Rovnyak, Finite Convolution Operators. J. Math. Anal. Appl. 49 (1975), pp. 356 - 357. What are all of the $\delta$ - spectral sets for J, and what is the operator theoretic significance of this concept?

15. BL. SENDOV: Restricted Polynomial Approximation

By $H_n$ we denote the set of all polynomials P of degree at most n on [-1,1], and by $H_n^*$ the set

$$H_n^* = \{P \in H_n;\ P'(x) \geq 0 \text{ for all } x \in [-1,1],\ P(-1) = -1,\ P(1) = 1\}.$$

For a function $f \in C[-1,1]$ let

$$e_{nm}(f) = \inf_{P \in H_n} \inf_{Q \in H_m^*} \max_{x \in [-1,1]} |f(Q(x))-P(x)|;$$

note that m = 1 is the case of best uniform approximation.

Question. What is the order of magnitude of $e_{n,m}(f)$, if

$$f(x) = \begin{cases} f_1(x) & x \in [-1,0] \\ f_2(x) & x \in [0,1] \end{cases}$$

with entire functions $f_1$, $f_2$ such that $f_1(0) = f_2(0)$ (even if $m = n$)? In the special case $f(x) = |x|$, the order is $n^{-1}$ (S.N. Bernstein), even $\exp(-c\sqrt{n^2 \log n})$ (G.L. Iliev).

16. A.L. SHIELDS: On the Bergman Space of Analytic Functions

Consider the Bergman space B, namely the space of analytic functions f on the unit disc $\{z;\ |z| < 1\}$ such that $\iint_{|z|<1} |f|^2 < \infty$. B is a Hilbert space. If $M_z$ denotes the operator of multiplication by z, then a function $f \in B$ is cyclic for $M_z$, iff the set {pf; p polynomial} is dense in B. The problem now is to characterize such functions. As is already known, a necessary condition for f is that $|f(z)| > 0$ ($|z| < 1$), whereas the condition $|f(z)| \geq c > 0$ is sufficient.

1. Conjecture (H.S. Shapiro - A.L. Shields). The condition $|f(z)| \geq c(1-|z|)^k$ for some c,k is sufficient.

2. Conjecture. If f, $1/f \in B$, then f is cyclic.

17. E.L. STARK: On a Sequence of de La Vallée Poussin Factors

The convergence factors (= Fourier coefficients) $v_{k,n}$ of the de La Vallée Poussin kernel $V_n$ are given by

$$v_{k,n} := \frac{(n!)^2}{(n-k)!(n+k)!}, \quad 1 \leq k \leq n \in \mathbb{N}; \qquad V_n(x) := \frac{(n!)^2}{(2n)!}\left(2 \cos \frac{x}{2}\right)^{2n}.$$

Consider the sequence $\{s_n\}_{n \in \mathbb{N}}$ defined by

$$s_n := \sup_{1 \leq k \leq n} \frac{1-v_{k,n}}{k};$$

what is the explicit representation of $\{s_n\}$? This is in connection with the problem of determining Nikol'skiĭ constants for the singular integral of de La Vallée Poussin in $L^2_{2\pi}$-space.

18. J. SZABADOS: Saturation of an Interpolating Operator

Let m be a fixed positive integer, and consider the sequence of positive linear operators (with $x_k = k/n$)

$$L_{n,m}(f,x) = \frac{\sum_{k=0}^{n} f(x_k)\,(x-x_k)^{-2m}}{\sum_{k=0}^{n} (x-x_k)^{-2m}} \qquad (n = 1,2,\ldots)$$

defined for all continuous functions $f(x)$ in $[0,1]$. Solve the saturation problem of this operator. As to the rate of convergence of $L_{n,m}$ and operators of similar type, see J. Szabados, On a problem of R. DeVore. Acta Math. Acad. Sci. Hungar. 27 (1976), 219 - 223.

REMARK. Meanwhile the above problem was partially solved (for $m > 1$), even in a more general form, by G. Somorjai, His solution will appear in the Acta Math. Acad. Sci. Hungar. (1979).

19. O. TAUSSKY - TODD: Common Invariant Subspaces of Operators and Commutativity

a) In the finite dimensional case a pair of simultaneously triangularizable matrices has a common eigen vector. Is there an operator analog, as it is for the case of the invariant subspace of commuting operators?

b) Is the concept of central polynomial (see E. Formanek, Central polynomials for matrix rings. J. Algebra 23 (1972), 129 - 132) meaningful in the operator case?

c) The matrix equation $AX - XB = 0$ arises when studying the commutativity of $\begin{pmatrix} A & 0 \\ 0 & B \end{pmatrix}$ with conformally partitioned matrices $\begin{pmatrix} X_{11} & X_{12} \\ X_{21} & X_{22} \end{pmatrix}$.
In this finite dimensional case,

$$(*) \qquad \sigma(A) \cap \sigma(B) = \emptyset$$

implies $X_{12} = X_{21} = 0$. Pearcey proved that,

$$(^{**}) \qquad AX - XB = 0 \Rightarrow X = 0$$

for operators A, B satisfying (*).

However, Taussky (A generalization of matrix commutativity, Linear Algebra and Appl. 2 (1969), 349 - 353) showed that in the finite dimensional case (*) is not necessary, only sufficient for (**) to hold.

What is the situation for operators?

20. J. TODD: On Mixed Norms

In connection with the theory of norms in finite dimensional spaces as developed by A.M. Ostrowski, V.N. Faddeeva, N. Gastinel, J.L. Maître, F.L. Bauer, H.W. Wielandt, among others, the following problems appear of interest.

a) If V,W are vector spaces (over $\mathbb{R}$, for instance) with norms $\|\cdot\|_V$, $\|\cdot\|_W$ and A is a matrix such that $Av \in W$ for $v \in V$, defining the mixed norm

$$\|A\|_{V,W} = \sup_{v\neq 0} \frac{\|Av\|_W}{\|v\|_V}, \tag{1}$$

determine $\|A\|_{V,W}$ in the classical cases when $V \equiv W$ and the norms are the 1, 2, $\infty$ norms. E.g. $\|A\|_{\infty,1} = \max_{i,j} |a_{i,j}|$.

b) In the case when the p-norm is taken in each space the following results are known:

$$\|A\|_{\infty,\infty} = \text{max absolute row sum of A.}$$

$$\|A\|_{1,1} = \text{max absolute column sum of A.}$$

$$\|A\|_{2,2} = \text{max singular value of A.}$$

Is there any convenient result for $\|A\|_{p,p}$?

c) The mixed norm defined in (1) is in general not sub-multiplicative. However, given any sub-multiplicative norm m(A) there is a (least) multiplier $\mu$ which makes it into a submultiplicative norm

$$\mu m(A\ B) \leqslant (\mu m(A))(\mu m(B)).$$

For instance if A is an $n \times n$ matrix and $m(A) = \max_{i,j} |a_{i,j}|$, then $\mu = n$.

Determine the multipliers in the case of other mixed norms.

For more details and references see e.g., J. Todd, Basic Numerical Mathematics, v.2. Numerical Algebra. ISNM 22, Birkhäuser Verlag, 1977.

# Alphabetical list of papers

# AMS (MOS) subject classification numbers*



*Given by the authors; numbers behind subject indicate first page of respective paper.

# Key words and phrases*



* Given by the authors; numbers indicate first page of respective paper.